TOWARDS THE DEVELOPMENT OF THE INTERNATIONAL PENAL SYSTEM

Based on extensive empirical research, this ground-breaking book describes and analyses existing systems for enforcing sentences of imprisonment imposed by international criminal courts and makes recommendations for the strategic and structural development of the international penal system. In particular, it advocates a resocialisation-focused international penal policy delivered using restorative justice modalities post-conviction and the creation of an accountable international prison system. Singly or combined, these developments will contribute to the institutionalisation of the international penal system and enhance the international nature of the sanction, international control over the way international punishment is enforced and the equal treatment of international prisoners. These developments will also help to ensure that international punishment is principled and progressive and implemented in a humane and effective manner.

RÓISÍN MULGREW is a lecturer in law at the University of Nottingham, where she teaches international human rights law and international criminal law.

TOWARDS THE DEVELOPMENT OF THE INTERNATIONAL PENAL SYSTEM

RÓISÍN MULGREW

CAMBRIDGE UNIVERSITY PRESS

CAMBRIDGE
UNIVERSITY PRESS

University Printing House, Cambridge CB2 8BS, United Kingdom

Published in the United States of America by Cambridge University Press, New York

Cambridge University Press is part of the University of Cambridge.

It furthers the University's mission by disseminating knowledge in the pursuit of education, learning and research at the highest international levels of excellence.

www.cambridge.org
Information on this title: www.cambridge.org/9781107027411

© Róisín Mulgrew 2013

This publication is in copyright. Subject to statutory exception and to the provisions of relevant collective licensing agreements, no reproduction of any part may take place without the written permission of Cambridge University Press.

First published 2013

Printed in the United Kingdom by CPI Group Ltd, Croydon, CR0 4YY

A catalogue record for this publication is available from the British Library

Library of Congress Cataloguing in Publication data
Mulgrew, Roisin, 1980–
Towards the development of the international penal system / Roisin Mulgrew.
   pages   cm
Includes bibliographical references and index.
ISBN 978-1-107-02741-1
1. International criminal law. 2. Criminal justice, Administration of. I. Title.
KZ7235.M85 2013
344.03′5–dc23
                2012050602

ISBN 978-1-107-02741-1 Hardback

Additional resources for this publication at www.cambridge.org/9781107027411

Cambridge University Press has no responsibility for the persistence or accuracy of URLs for external or third-party internet websites referred to in this publication, and does not guarantee that any content on such websites is, or will remain, accurate or appropriate.

This book is dedicated to my husband Eugene.

CONTENTS

Acknowledgments   *page* xii
Abbreviations   xiv

Introduction   1
1 Exploring the international penal system   3
2 Structure of the book   6

PART I   **The international penal system**   9

1   The international penal system   11
   1 International penalties   11
   2 The international criminal justice system   17
   3 The international penal system   19
   4 Reconceptualising the implementation of international punishment   21
   5 Conclusion   29

PART II   **Systems: systems for the enforcement of international punishment**   31

2   Decentralised national enforcement   33
   1 Securing state cooperation   33
   2 Designation of and transfer to enforcing states   39
   3 Division of responsibility   45
      3.1 Welfare of the international prisoner   45
      3.2 Length of the term of imprisonment   56
      3.3 Responsibility for the international prisoner and the international sentence   83
   4 International punishment in national prison systems   84
      4.1 Inequality of treatment among international prisoners   85

vii

4.2 Inequality between international and national prisoners 86
4.3 Rehabilitation and preparation for release 96
5 Conclusion 102

3 Centralised international enforcement 103

1 Imprisonment at an international detention facility 105
2 Contact with the outside world 111
3 Medical care 116
4 Maintaining order 121
   4.1 Regulatory frameworks governing the maintenance of order 122
   4.2 Management and staff approaches to the maintenance of order 125
5 Oversight 131
   5.1 Complaints 131
   5.2 Internal oversight 134
   5.3 External oversight 139
   5.4 Oversight of imprisonment at IDFs 140
6 Standards at IDFs 143
7 Release 151
8 Centralised national enforcement: the ICC's residual facility 153
9 Conclusion 154

4 Localised national enforcement 156

1 Statutory options for localised national enforcement 156
   1.1 The SCSL and Sierra Leone 157
   1.2 The ICTR and Rwanda 159
2 Rule 11*bis* transfers 160
   2.1 The ICTY, Rule 11*bis* and Bosnia-Herzegovina 161
   2.2 The ICTR, Rule 11*bis* and Rwanda 167
   2.3 Rule 11*bis* and its operation post-completion 170
3 Conclusion 173

5 The contemporary international penal system 175

1 The international penal system 175
2 Humane punishment 181
   2.1 Equal treatment 182
   2.2 Oversight of international punishment 185
3 The effectiveness of international punishment 187
4 The evolution of the international penal system 190
5 Conclusion 194

PART III **Strategy: developing and operationalising international penal strategy** 195

6 International penal policy 197
   1 The need for international penal policy 197
      1.1 Preventing the aggravation of international punishment 197
      1.2 International courts' support role 199
      1.3 International penal policy 202
   2 A normative foundation for international penal policy 203
      2.1 Justifications for the establishment of international criminal courts 203
      2.2 Justifications for the imposition of international custodial sanctions 203
      2.3 A justification for the implementation of international custodial sanctions? 207
   3 Rehabilitation 208
      3.1 The normative common denominator of the international penal system 209
      3.2 A theoretical framework for the incorporation of a rehabilitative penal policy within a retributive justice process 211
      3.3 Reconceptualising rehabilitation for the international penal system 213
   4 Conclusion 216

7 International penal practice 218
   1 A restorative approach to resocialisation 218
   2 Restorative justice principles and processes 224
      2.1 Recognition of harm 224
      2.2 Repairing harm 226
      2.3 Reconciliation 226
      2.4 Reintegration 230
      2.5 Restoring and maintaining peace 232
   3 Utilising restorative tools to implement international penal policy 235
      3.1 Individual resocialisation 236
      3.2 Inter-relational resocialisation 238
      3.3 Links with external mechanisms 244
   4 Dealing with conflict, crime and transition 246
      4.1 Context and causes of conflict and crime 247
      4.2 Creating an accepted truth 250
      4.3 Breaking cycles of violence 254

5 Reparative actions   255
6 Ethical issues   260
7 A comprehensive justice system   262
8 Conclusion   264

8 Operationalising international penal strategy   266
1 Operationalising international penal policy and practice   267
2 Centralised support to centralised control   270

PART IV Structure: creating an accountable international prison system   273

9 An international prison system   275
1 Arguments in favour of creating an international prison system   277
2 Establishing an international prison system   279
   2.1 Precedence and practice   280
   2.2 Legal mandate   282
   2.3 Location   283
3 Models for international prisons   286
   3.1 An island   286
   3.2 Host State   286
   3.3 Choosing a suitable model   294
4 Operating an international prison system   296
   4.1 Funding   296
   4.2 Management   300
   4.3 Custodial staff   302
5 Conclusion   305

10 Guarding the guardians   307
1 Oversight of an international prison system   308
2 Responsibility for an international prison system   311
   2.1 The responsibility of international organisations   312
   2.2 The responsibility of states   318
   2.3 Responsibility for seconded staff   323
   2.4 The responsibility of individuals   326
3 An accountable international prison system   329
4 Conclusion   332

PART V The development of the international penal system   333

11 The development of the international penal system   335
1 The legitimacy of the international penal system   336

2 The institutionalisation of the international penal system   340
3 Towards the development of the international penal system   343

Appendix I: Empirical research   345
Appendix II: Enforcing states   354
Bibliography   356
Table of cases   370
Official documents, treaties, resolutions and reports   378
Index   401

ACKNOWLEDGMENTS

This book began as a question that formed at the back of my mind during a post-graduate degree on international criminal justice. After spending the year studying why international courts had been created, the crimes and individuals they had jurisdiction over, the trial process, penalties and sentencing rationales, I was left wondering what happened after the conviction. Where did the international prisoners go, what happened to them, what did an international sentence of imprisonment mean or do? I began a Ph.D. to explore these issues.

I am extremely grateful to the Economic and Social Research Council for funding my Ph.D. and providing me with an additional Overseas Research Grant to cover the costs incurred while conducting empirical research. I also owe the School of Law at the University of Nottingham a huge debt of gratitude for providing me with additional funding to facilitate further fieldwork and study leave to give me the time necessary to finalise the book. I would like to thank all the academic, administrative and support staff at the University of Nottingham who have helped me throughout the years. In particular, I wish to thank Professor Van Zyl Smit for his expert supervision and support. His guidance and encouragement, on both professional and personal levels, have kept me motivated and focused. I will always appreciate the time and effort he has invested in my academic development. I also wish to thank Almut Gadow de Mayor for her research assistance.

Given the nature of the system used to enforce international punishment, the fieldwork undertaken during my doctorate studies and subsequent research has taken me far and wide and involved discussions with many individuals. It is not possible to name everyone here but I am genuinely grateful to each and every person that participated in my research for taking the time to meet or speak with me. I would, however, like to extend my sincere gratitude to Bibiana Becerra-Suarez, Harry

Tjonk and Anne-Li Ferguson for their belief in my research and for making it a joy to do!

I also wish to thank the editorial team at Cambridge University Press and the anonymous reviewers who provided detailed feedback and recommendations on how to improve the book and the arguments therein.

I am indebted to my parents, Bernadette and Damian, for instilling respect for education, inquisitiveness and hard work in me and for their support in all that I do.

Last, but certainly not least, I wish to express my appreciation to my fantastic husband, Eugene, for his patience and love over the years.

ABBREVIATIONS

ACHR	American Convention on Human Rights
ACHPR	African Charter on Human and Peoples' Rights
ACmHPR	African Commission on Human and Peoples' Rights
API	Agreement on Privileges and Immunities
ASO	Agreement on Security and Order
BEA	Bilateral Enforcement Agreement
CPIUN	Convention on the Privileges and Immunities of the United Nations
CPR	Complaints Procedure Regulations
CPT	Committee for the Prevention of Torture
CRC	Convention on the Rights of the Child
DARIO	Draft Articles on the Responsibility of International Organisations
DARS	Draft Articles on the Responsibility of States for Internationally Wrongful Acts
DPR	Disciplinary Procedure Regulations
ECHR	European Convention on Human Rights
ECtHR	European Court of Human Rights
EPR	European Prison Rules 2006
GARes	General Assembly Resolution
HQA	Headquarters Agreement
HRC	Human Rights Committee
ICC	International Criminal Court
ICCDC	ICC Detention Centre
ICCSt	ICC Statute
ICCPR	International Covenant on Civil and Political Rights
ICESR	International Covenant on Economic and Social Rights
ICRC	International Committee of the Red Cross
ICTR	International Criminal Tribunal for Rwanda
ICTRSt	ICTR Statute
ICTY	International Criminal Tribunal for the former Yugoslavia
ICTYSt	ICTY Statute
ILA	International Law Association
IMTFE	International Military Tribunal, Far East
IMTN	International Military Tribunal, Nuremberg
IOM	Independent Oversight Mechanism
MDP	ICTY Manual of Developed Practice

MICT	Mechanism for International Criminal Tribunals
MICTSt	MICT Statute
NRA	Negotiated Relationship Agreement
OPCAT	Optional Protocol to the Convention Against Torture
OSCE	Organisation for Security and Cooperation in Europe
PDD	Practice Direction on Designation
PDER	Practice Direction on Early Release
PSSU	Penal Strategy Support Unit
ROC	Regulations of the Court
ROD	Rules of Detention
ROR	Regulations of the Registry
RPE	Rules of Procedure and Evidence
RSCSL	Residual Special Court for Sierra Leone
RSCSLSt	RSCSL Statute
SCA	Agreement Between the UN and the Government of Sierra Leone on the Establishment of a Special Court for Sierra Leone
SCRes	Security Council Resolution
SCSL	Special Court for Sierra Leone
SCSLDF	SCSL Detention Facility
SCSLSt	SCSL Statute
SLPS	Sierra Leone Prison Service
SPT	Subcommittee for the Prevention of Torture
STL	Special Tribunal for Lebanon
UDHR	Universal Declaration of Human Rights
UN	United Nations
UNBOP	UN Body of Principles for the Protection of all Persons under Any Form of Detention or Imprisonment
UNBP	UN Basic Principles for the Treatment of Prisoners
UNDF	UN Detention Facility (ICTR)
UNDU	UN Detention Unit (ICTY)
UNSC	UN Security Council
UNSMR	UN Standard Minimum Rules on the Treatment of Prisoners
UNTAET	UN Transitional Administration in East Timor
VCR	Visits and Communications Regulation
WMA	World Medical Association

Introduction

2012 was a significant year in the evolution of the international penal system. Ten years after it began operating, the International Criminal Court (ICC) imposed its first sentence of imprisonment.[1] The Special Court for Sierra Leone (SCSL) made history by being the first international court to convict a former head of state.[2] The Mechanism for the International Criminal Tribunals (MICT) became responsible for supervising the sentences imposed by the International Criminal Tribunal for Rwanda (ICTR) and made arrangements to do the same for the International Criminal Tribunal for the former Yugoslavia (ICTY).[3] These international courts form an international criminal justice system and, collectively, they have imposed sentences of imprisonment on over one hundred and fifty individuals. Despite the fact that the first modern international sentence of imprisonment was handed down in 1997, little is known about the systems used to enforce international custodial sanctions or the realities of international punishment.

Beyond the sparse legal provisions governing its enforcement in the statutes and rules of the international criminal courts, it is difficult to find information about the modern phenomenon of international punishment. In contrast to the vast range of academic literature dealing with international criminal justice principles, institutions and processes, there is a notable lack of discussion of the systems used to enforce international sentences of imprisonment. Much of the literature devoted to this topic is limited to technical discussions of legal and regulatory frameworks. This may be attributable to their location in commentaries on the international criminal courts' Statutes or Rules of Procedure and

---

[1] *Lubanga* (Sentence) ICC-01/04-01/06, 10.07.2012.
[2] See *Taylor* (Sentencing Judgment) SCSL-03-01-T, 30.05.2012; SCSL Press Release, "Charles Taylor Sentenced to 50 Years in Prison", 30.05.2012 and SCSL Press Release "Charles Taylor Convicted on all 11 Counts", 26.04.2012.
[3] See para. 1 SCRes 1966(2010); Art. 25(2), 26 MICTSt.

Evidence,[4] or due to the fact that many of the authors are, or were, officials of the international courts.[5] While some publications do provide a broader and more critical analysis of the phenomenon of international detention[6] and imprisonment[7] and the infrastructure of the international penal system,[8] many are outdated and omit recent developments in terms of regulations, mechanisms and bilateral enforcement agreements. Moreover, the vast majority of these works do not provide the insight that can be attained through empirical research. Building on

---

[4] See T. B. Chimiba, "Establishing an Enforcement Regime" in R. S. Lee (ed.), *The ICC: The Making of the Rome Statute* (1999), 345–56; K. Prost, "Enforcement" in R. S. Lee (ed.), *The ICC: Elements of Crimes and Rules of Procedure and Evidence* (2001), 673–702; A. Marchesi, "The Enforcement of Sentences of the International Criminal Court" in F. Lattanzi and W. Schabas (eds.), *Essays on the Rome Statute of the International Criminal Court* (1999), 427–45.

[5] See D. Tolbert, "International Criminal Tribunal for the Former Yugoslavia and the Enforcement of Sentences" (1998) 11 *Leiden Journal of International Law* 655–69; C. De Sampayo Garrido, "Problems and Achievements Seen from the Viewpoint of the Registry" (2004) 2 *Journal of International Criminal Justice* 474–9; D. Tolbert and A. Rydberg "Enforcement of Sentences" in R. May et al. (eds.), *Essays on ICTY Procedure and Evidence in Honour of Gabrielle Kirk McDonald* (2001), 538–43; H. Abathi and S. A. Koh, "The Emerging Enforcement Practice of the International Criminal Court" (2012) 45 *Cornell International Law Journal* 1–23.

[6] D. Abels, *Prisoners of the International Community: The Legal Position of Persons Detained at International Criminal Tribunals* (2012).

[7] D. Van Zyl Smit, "International Imprisonment" (2005) 54 *International and Comparative Law Quarterly* 357–86; C. Kreß and G. Sluiter, "Imprisonment" in A. Cassese et al. (eds.), *The Rome Statute of the International Criminal Court: A Commentary*, Vol. II (2002), 1757–821; A. Klip, "Enforcement of Sanctions Imposed by the International Criminal Tribunals for Rwanda and the Former Yugoslavia" (1997) 5(2) *European Journal of Crime, Criminal Law and Criminal Justice* 144–64; J. C. Nemitz, "Execution of Sanctions Imposed by Supranational Criminal Tribunals" in R. Haveman and O. Olusanya (eds.), *Sentencing and Sanctioning in Supranational Criminal Law* (2006), 125–44; Chapter 6 "The Post-Trial Stage" in C. J. M. Safferling, *Towards an International Criminal Procedure* (2001); K. Hoffmann, "Some Remarks on the Enforcement of International Sentences in the Light of Galić Case at the ICTY" (2011) ZIS 838–42; R. Culp, "Enforcement and Monitoring of Sentences in the Modern War Crimes Process: Equal Treatment before the Law?", 07.04.2011.

[8] See M. Penrose, "Spandau Revisited: The Question of Detention for International War Crimes" (1999) 16 *New York Law School Journal of Human Rights* 553–91; M. Penrose, "No Badges, No Bars: A Conspicuous Oversight in the Development of an International Criminal Court" (2003) 38(3) *Texas International Law Journal* 621–42; M. Penrose, "Lest We Fail: The Importance of Enforcement in International Criminal Law" (2000) 15 *American University International Law Review* 321–94; N. Grosselfinger "The United Nations Detention Unit" in P. J. Van Krieken and D. McKay (eds.), *The Hague: Legal Capital of the World* (2005), 317–22.

previous papers which adopted a comparative[9] and case-study[10] approach, the research underpinning this book was designed to ensure the systemic analysis of the international penal system.

1. Exploring the international penal system

To discover the realities of implementing and serving international sentences of imprisonment, it was considered necessary to conduct empirical research. Fieldwork provides an added dimension to knowledge that cannot be attained through "theorising or reading in an office".[11] Empirical data can fill the gaps in available sources and provide unofficial accounts of a studied social phenomenon. The subject matter and potential sample sizes indicated that a qualitative approach was the most appropriate. Although questionnaires and observation were used at several sites, semi-structured interviews were the primary data collection tool utilised.

As Liebling argues, empirical research requires attention to synthesis, the analysis of the whole and the discovery of different perspectives.[12] As the aim of the research was to understand the social reality of the operation of the international penal system and the impact of international imprisonment, it was important to discover the perspectives of all those involved with or subject to the system. By asking its actors and subjects how a system works, the "institutional practices that shape their reality"[13] can be explored. Research was conducted at both micro-sociological and macro-sociological levels to enable enquiry into "the internal dynamics of an institution which can reveal what the experience of imprisonment is like for the keepers and the kept" as well as "the external function of imprisonment … what punishment is for".[14]

---

[9] R. Mulgrew, "The International Movement of Prisoners: Exploring the Evolution of the Inter-State and International Criminal Justice Systems for the Transfer of Sentenced Persons" (2011) 22(1) *Criminal Law Forum* 103–43.

[10] R. Mulgrew, "Implementing International Sentences of Imprisonment: Challenges Faced by the Special Court for Sierra Leone" (2009) 7(2) *Journal of International Criminal Justice* 373–96.

[11] R. D. King, "Doing Research in Prisons" in R. D. King and E. Wincup (eds.), *Doing Research on Crime and Justice* (2000), 285–312 at 298.

[12] A. Liebling, "Whose Side Are We On? Theory, Practice and Allegiance in Prison Research" (2001) 41 *British Journal of Criminology* 472–84 at 482.

[13] E. Babbie, *The Practice of Social Research*, 9th edn (2001), 287.

[14] Carrabine "Discourse, Governmentality and Translation: Towards a Social Theory of Imprisonment" (2000) 4 *Theoretical Criminology* 309–31 at 310.

Accordingly, the research was designed to ascertain the perspectives of those who work at international courts, international detention facilities, national ministries and prisons systems, inspection bodies, and to discover the experiences of those subject to international detention or imprisonment.

Fieldwork was conducted over two phases. The first phase involved research for a Ph.D. undertaken at the University of Nottingham, which was funded by the Economic and Social Research Council. Over a period of twenty months in 2007 and 2008, research was conducted in seven different countries (Belgium, Bosnia-Herzegovina, The Netherlands, Sierra Leone, Sweden, Tanzania and the UK) at international criminal courts, international and national detention facilities and prisons, international, regional and national governmental and non-governmental entities, with court, government and prison service officials, and with former and current detained persons. The second phase of the research, carried out in the summer of 2012, was funded by the School of Law at the University of Nottingham. This phase was undertaken to update data previously collected and to extend the range of subjects interviewed. Research was completed in Norway, The Hague and Wales with international court and detention facility officials, national government officials and international prisoners. In total, over 115 individuals in ten countries were interviewed or corresponded with. The precise details of the empirical work undertaken can be found in Appendix I.

While access to officials was typically forthcoming at the international criminal courts, it was more difficult to gain access to officials in enforcing states, and even more challenging to gain access to speak with detained or imprisoned persons housed in either international detention facilities or enforcing states. With that being said, the countries that participated in the research represented a good proportion of the states that were enforcing international sentences of imprisonment at the time the project was being designed and implemented. In relation to detained persons, communication was only possible with three international prisoners serving sentences in three enforcing states (Sweden, Norway and the UK) and three former UNDU detained persons who had been acquitted or had their indictments withdrawn. The sample is further limited by the fact that all of these individuals had been deprived of their liberty by the same international court, the ICTY, and housed in facilities in Europe. The sample's limitations are due to limited funds, the denial of access by states and international courts, the conditions placed on access where it was granted and the wishes of approached detained persons or prisoners. With more time, money and cooperation, it may have been possible to interview a wider and more representative range of prisoners. The small size and opportunistic nature of the sample do not, however, detract, from the insights these interviews provided into the deprivation of liberty in the international penal system from the perspective of both detained and released individuals.

Overall, the data gained during the fieldwork provides an important snap-shot of the international penal system at a critical point in its operation. Information was gathered during the height of the operations of the temporary international courts. Research continued until the recent hand-over of enforcement supervision to the MICT and the handing down of the ICC's first sentence of imprisonment. The empirical data gathered contributes to knowledge about the under-documented international penal system at the end of the operation of the temporary international courts and the beginning of the penal system of the world's only permanent international criminal court. This data provides insights into the realities of implementing, and being subject to, international punishment that could not be attained from legal analysis alone and uncovers lessons that must be learned in order to develop an effective and humane penal system.

By grounding theory in data, claims are substantiated by evidence and findings appear more credible as they can be linked to social reality.[15] This analytical process involves "treading the middle road between grand theory and abstracted empiricism".[16] The data obtained from empirical research was contextualised by consulting academic literature on a wide range of related topics such as restorative justice, transitional justice, penology, human rights and international law on the responsibility of international organisations. To move beyond a description of the international penal system, the empirical material was interpretively integrated with these supplementary sources to provide new insights.[17] This cross-fertilisation of normative, legal, political and penological perspectives with the practical realities of implementing international sentences of imprisonment in national and international facilities resulted in a rich body of knowledge. This body of knowledge formed the foundation upon which conclusions were drawn, inferences were made and ultimately formed the basis of this book's findings. The goal was to move beyond a thin, narrow and legalistic description of the

---

[15] See C. Seale, *The Quality of Qualitative Research* (1999), 88.   [16] *Ibid.*
[17] H. Boeije, *Analysis in Qualitative Research* (2010), 153.

systems used to implement international sentences of imprisonment, to provide a rich body of information and legal analysis that could form a foundation for complex, multi-layered and critical scholarship.[18] This book, therefore, provides integrated explanations of the operations and implications of the international penal system and advocates systemic change designed to contribute to its development.

2. Structure of the book

To reconceptualise the way in which international punishment is implemented in the **international penal system**, it is necessary to appraise the **systems** presently being used to enforce international sentences of imprisonment and make recommendations for the future development of the international penal system's **strategy** and **structure**.

Part I highlights some of the problems associated with implementing international punishment in the contemporary **international penal system** that this book seeks to address. Chapter 1 examines the penalties used in the international criminal justice system, defines the international penal system for the purposes of this book and analyses the context in which international punishment is and should be implemented.

Part II describes and analyses the **systems** for the enforcement of international sentences of imprisonment. Chapters 2, 3 and 4 provide in-depth information about the decentralised, centralised and localised systems for implementing international punishment in national and international facilities. Chapter 5 reviews the realities of operating the contemporary international penal system, its impact on those subject to it and challenges for its future.

Part III builds on the findings and analysis of Part II to make recommendations for the development of international penal **strategy**. Penal strategy requires both international penal policy and international penal practice. Chapter 6 highlights the need to devise international penal policy to govern the enforcement of international sentences of imprisonment, outlines key issues it should address and sets out a normative guide for its development. Chapter 7 discusses how international penal policy objectives can be achieved through the post-conviction utilisation of restorative justice tools. The incorporation of restorative dialogue and

---

[18] See K. McEvoy, "Letting go of Legalism: Developing a 'Thicker' Version of Transitional Justice" in K. McEvoy and L. McGregor (eds.), *Transitional Justice from Below* (2008), 17–18.

reparative actions into international penal practice can contribute to the attainment of penological goals of resocialisation and reintegration and international criminal justice goals of reconciliation and the maintenance of peace. Chapter 8 concludes this part of the book by discussing methods for, and possible obstacles to, the operationalisation of international penal strategy.

Part IV of the book focuses on the **structure** of the international penal system. Chapter 9 advocates international control over the implementation of international punishment through the creation of an international prison system. This chapter explores the feasibility of different models that can be used for international prisons and the operational challenges an international prison system would face. Given the need to ensure that an international prison system operates in an accountable and rights-compliant manner, Chapter 10 explores issues relating to the oversight of international prisons and legal liability for an international prison population.

Part V highlights the reasons it is necessary to **develop the international penal system**. Chapter 11 concludes the book by reiterating the need to ensure that the international criminal justice system is a comprehensive justice system and that international punishment is implemented in a humane and effective manner. It argues that the recommendations made in the book would lead to the institutionalisation of the international penal system and, consequently, contribute to the enhancement or protection of the legitimacy of the international criminal justice system as a whole.

PART I

The international penal system

1

The international penal system

Over the last two decades, a variety of international judicial institutions have been created to prosecute persons for crimes committed during conflicts.[1] These courts are the product of a powerful transition from tolerance of almost absolute impunity for crimes committed during conflict, to an increasingly embedded culture of accountability. The creation of international criminal courts symbolises the crystallisation of humanitarian aspirations to uphold the rule of law, vindicate the rights of victims, bring perpetrators to justice and punish those convicted. International criminal justice, for so long a normative construct, has become a social reality: the "grotesque paradox that one is more likely to be punished for killing another person than for helping to annihilate an entire people"[2] is no longer true.

Like domestic criminal prosecutions, international trials may result in the imposition of penalties. The primary penalty imposed by contemporary international criminal courts is imprisonment. International criminal courts now routinely impose custodial sanctions on those convicted of international crimes. International punishment is a social reality and the logical conclusion of the international criminal justice process. This chapter highlights the emergence of imprisonment as the primary international penalty and discusses the system and context in which international custodial sanctions are implemented.

1. International penalties

The previous two decades have witnessed a proliferation of international criminal courts established to prosecute persons accused of international

---

[1] See para. 2 SCRes 827(1993); para. 1 SCRes 955(1994); Art. 1 SCSLSt.; Preamble ICCSt.
[2] A. A. Schvey, "Striving for Accountability in the Former Yugoslavia" in J. E. Stromseth (ed.), *Accountability for Atrocities: National and International Responses* (2003), 40.

crimes, including war crimes, crimes against humanity and genocide. As these represent some of the most serious crimes of international concern, it seems logical that the worst offenders "should be penalised with the ultimate penalty allowed by international law".[3] The nature of punishments considered to be appropriate sanctions for international criminal justice institutions, however, has changed over time.

Although post First World War attempts to bring political and military leaders to justice largely failed,[4] the Allies were determined to impose liability for crimes committed by the Axis during the Second World War.[5] Accordingly, International Military Tribunals were established in Nurnberg (IMTN)[6] and Tokyo (IMTFE)[7]. Although these tribunals have been criticised for being selective and politicised,[8] they established a powerful international legal precedent for the punishment of individuals for crimes committed during conflict.[9] While custodial sanctions were imposed, capital punishment was both a legal, and the likely punishment for persons convicted by these tribunals.[10] Yet less than half a century later, when the UN Security Council (UNSC) was considering the establishment of a new model of *temporary international court*, the UN Secretary-General recommended that it "should not be empowered to impose the death penalty".[11] In 1993, the UNSC invoked Chapter VII of the UN Charter to create the International Criminal Tribunal for the former Yugoslavia (ICTY) to prosecute persons responsible for serious violations of international humanitarian law committed

---

[3] D. Van Zyl Smit, *Taking Life Imprisonment Seriously: In National and International Law* (2002), 167.

[4] See Arts. 227–9 Treaty of Versailles 1919; Arts. 226–7 Treaty of Sevres 1920; J. Maogoto, *War Crimes and Realpolitik: International Justice from World War I to the 21st Century* (2004) 37–64.

[5] See Maogoto, *War Crimes and Realpolitik*, 88–91.

[6] The London Agreement for the Prosecution and Punishment of Major War Criminals of the European Axis and Establishing the Charter of the International Military Tribunal, 08.08.1945.

[7] Special Proclamation, General MacArthur, Supreme Commander of the Allied Powers for the Pacific Theatre, "Establishment of an International Military Tribunal for the Far East", 19.01.1946.

[8] See H. Köchler, *Global Justice or Global Revenge: International Criminal Justice at Crossroads* (2003), 10, 67–8, 150, 155, 160.

[9] See GARes 95(I)(1946).

[10] See Art. 27 IMTN Charter; Art. 16 IMTFE Charter; W. Schabas, *The Abolition of the Death Penalty in International Law*, 3rd edn (2002), 236–7.

[11] Para. 112, Report of the Secretary-General pursuant to para. 2 of Security Council Resolution 808 (1993) S/25704 + Corr.1, 03.05.1993.

in the territory of the former Yugoslavia from 1 January 1991.[12] In contrast to the law and practice of the international military tribunals, the maximum penalty this new international criminal court could impose was life imprisonment.[13]

On the day that the ICTY issued its first indictment, the UNSC established another *temporary international* court, the International Criminal Tribunal for Rwanda (ICTR), to prosecute those responsible for the genocide and other serious violations of international humanitarian law in Rwanda and neighbouring states between 1 January and 31 December 1994.[14] Although the Rwandan Government argued that the exclusion of the death penalty would result in a "fundamental injustice",[15] given that those considered less responsible for the genocide and tried in national courts could face capital punishment, the ICTR Statute implicitly excluded this sanction. The maximum penalty was, again, life imprisonment.[16]

By the time these UN Tribunals were operational, the majority of states had either de facto or de jure abolished capital punishment;[17] a trend undoubtedly influenced by international and regional human rights law.[18] Yet despite the fact that the death penalty had been excluded from the UN Tribunals' Statutes and earlier drafts of the International Law Commission's Code of Crimes Against the Peace and Security of Mankind, the issue threatened to undo consensus on the provisions of, and even the adoption of, a statute for the proposed *permanent international* criminal court at the Rome Diplomatic Conference.[19] A minority of states opposed the exclusion of the death penalty for religious and cultural reasons, and due to fears that such a move would have implications for national law and practice.[20] To achieve consensus, Article 80 was inserted into the proposed statute. This article explicitly states that, in accordance with the principle of complementarity,[21] "nothing in this Part [Penalties] affects the application by States of penalties prescribed

---

[12] SCRes 827(1993). [13] Art. 24(1) ICTYSt. [14] SCRes 955(1994).
[15] See Rwanda's statement, UNSC 3453rd Meeting, 08.11.1994.
[16] Art. 23(1) ICTRSt.
[17] W. Schabas, "War Crimes, Crimes Against Humanity and the Death Penalty" (1996) 60 *Albany Law Review* 733–70 at 733.
[18] See Van Zyl Smit, *Taking Life Imprisonment Seriously*, 170, 179.
[19] See Schabas, *The Abolition of the Death Penalty in International Law*, 246, 251.
[20] *Ibid.*, 253–5.
[21] See para. 53, 9th Plenary Meeting, 17.07.1998, A/CONF.183/SR.9 in Official Records of the UN Diplomatic Conference of Plenipotentiaries on the Establishment of an International Criminal Court, Vol. II, 124–5.

by their national law". While some view the Rome Statute as "an important benchmark in an unquestionable trend towards universal abolition",[22] others feel that Article 80 diminished the "precedential impact"[23] of the exclusion of the death penalty from the range of permissible sanctions.

On 17 July 1998, 120 states adopted the Rome Statute,[24] creating the world's first permanent International Criminal Court (ICC) to prosecute persons accused of the most serious crimes of international concern: genocide, crimes against humanity and war crimes.[25] In spite of the difficult negotiations, the maximum penalty allowed by the world's only permanent international criminal court's statute is life imprisonment. The ICC may only impose a term of life imprisonment, however, if it is considered to be justified by the extreme gravity of the crime and the individual circumstances of the convicted persons.[26] The primary penalty the ICC will impose will be determinate sentences of imprisonment of up to a maximum of thirty years.[27]

The establishment of the ICC, however, did not make other models of international criminal justice institutions obsolete. Indeed, a new *temporary internationalised* model was established in Cambodia, East Timor, Sierra Leone etc. These courts were jointly created and/or operated by the UN and the state in which the relevant conflict occurred.[28] In contrast to the *international* models, they operate in the state affected by the conflict, rely on a mixture of international and national law and have both international and national judges and staff.[29] The founding instruments of these courts all limit legal punishment to imprisonment.[30] Given that the UN Secretary-General had warned that it would require a great deal of persuasion to convince nations that had witnessed such terrible atrocities "that the exclusion of the death penalty and its replacement by imprisonment is not an 'acquittal' of the accused, but an

---

[22] W. Schabas, *An Introduction to the International Criminal Court*, 4th edn (2011), 335.
[23] F. P. King and A. La Rosa, "Penalties under the ICC Statute" in F. Lattanzi and W. Schabas (eds.), *Essays on the Rome Statute of the International Criminal Court*, Vol. I (1999), 311–38 at 320.
[24] Entered into force 01.07.2002. [25] Art. 5(1) ICCSt. [26] Art. 77(1)(b) ICCSt.
[27] Art. 77(1)(a) ICCSt.
[28] See Art. 1(1) SCA; GARes 57/228B (2003); UNTAET Reg. 2000/15.
[29] See for example para. 9, Report of the Secretary General on the Establishment of a Special Court for Sierra Leone, 14.10.2000; Arts. 2–3, 10 SCA; Arts. 2–5, 11, 12(1), 15 (3)–(4) SCSLSt.
[30] See Art. 38 Law on the Establishment of the Extraordinary Chambers, 27.10.2004; Section 10.1(a) UNTAET Reg. 2000/15; Art. 19(1) SCSLSt.

imposition of a more humane punishment",[31] this must be viewed as a highly significant international legal development.

There therefore appears to be a presumption that the death penalty, once "carried out with enthusiasm by international justice"[32] is no longer a legally acceptable penalty for persons convicted of international crimes by international courts.[33] While the inclusion of life imprisonment was viewed as a necessary compromise given the exclusion of the death penalty, this sanction is also viewed by some to be problematic. It remains unclear what a life sentence entails in the international criminal justice system. A life sentence in domestic criminal justice systems can result in the imposition of a variety of terms from fifteen years upwards.[34] The regulatory frameworks of some of the international courts permit the imposition of a term for the remainder of the convicted person's life.[35] Even at the ICC, where the statutory requirement for mandatory review[36] provides a "possibility to moderate the lengthy or perpetual character"[37] of a life sentence, the Rome Statute does not exclude the possibility of a life sentence without parole. In fact, the recent sentencing decision in the *Lubanga* case referred to the possibility of imposing a "whole life sentence".[38] The conflation of the term "life sentence" and "whole life sentence" is unfortunate as this uncertainty may affect enforcement cooperation. Imprisonment without the possibility of parole is illegal or unconstitutional in some states due to its potential to violate fundamental human rights principles.[39] Imprisonment without a "real and tangible prospect of release" may violate an individual's human dignity.[40] A whole life sentence may also be considered to constitute

---

[31] Para. 7 Report of the Secretary-General on the Establishment of a Special Court for Sierra Leone, 14.10.2000.
[32] Schabas, *The Abolition of the Death Penalty in International Law*, 258.
[33] See N. Rodley and M. Pollard, *The Treatment of Prisoners under International Law*, 3rd edn (2009), 289.
[34] K. Hoffmann, "Some Remarks on the Enforcement of International Sentences in the Light of Galić Case at the ICTY" (2011) ZIS 838–42 at 838–9.
[35] See Rule 101(A) ICTY/ICTR RPE; Rule 125 MICT RPE.
[36] Art. 110(3), (5) ICCSt.; Rule 224(3) ICC RPE.
[37] D. Scalia, "Long-term Sentences in International Criminal Law: Do they Meet the Standards set out by the European Court of Human Rights" (2011) 9(3) *Journal of International Criminal Justice* 669–87 at 687.
[38] Para. 16 *Lubanga* (Sentence) ICC-01/04-01/06, 10.07.2012.
[39] King and La Rosa, "Penalties under the ICC Statute", 321; R. Cryer *et al.*, *An Introduction to International Criminal Law and Procedure*, 2nd edn (2010), 496.
[40] Scalia, "Long-term Sentences in International Criminial Law", 670, 686; E. Gumboh, "The Penalty of Life Imprisonment under International Criminal Law" (2011) 11 *African Human Rights Law Journal* 75–92 at 78.

a cruel, inhuman or degrading punishment as it fails to facilitate the rehabilitation or reintegration of the offender and its indeterminate nature may mean it is disproportionate, arbitrary and lacking in legal certainty.[41] Despite these human rights concerns, a sentence of life imprisonment may be imposed for the commission of international crimes. Although some international courts do not permit the imposition of indeterminate sentences,[42] life imprisonment, including a whole life sentence, is currently the maximum penalty that can be imposed by international criminal courts.[43]

International criminal courts can impose other penalties in addition to imprisonment. Taking into account the rights of bona fide third parties,[44] international criminal courts may order the restitution of property, proceeds and assets, acquired directly or indirectly from criminal conduct, to victims.[45] The ICC Statute permits a broader concept of forfeiture as an order may be issued irrespective of whether the rightful owner can be identified, with such property being transferred to the Trust Fund.[46] The ICC also has a broader range of potential sanctions as the Court may impose fines on persons convicted of committing international crimes.[47] At the temporary courts, a fine could only be imposed on persons convicted of contempt of court.[48] International courts often face difficulties in imposing these additional penalties due to the need to rely on the cooperation of states and the frequent indigence of convicted persons.[49] Indeed, the ICC refused to impose a fine in its first sentence due to the financial situation of the convicted person and the lack of any identifiable funds.[50]

The system for the enforcement of fines at the ICC introduces another unique additional penalty. The ICC Presidency, on its own motion or at the request of the Prosecutor, may extend the term of imprisonment imposed

---

[41] Schabas, *An Introduction to the International Criminal Court*, 336; Gumboh, "The Penalty of Life Imprisonment", 77–8; Scalia, "Long-term Sentences in International Criminal Law", 685.
[42] Art. 19(1) SCSLSt; Section 10.1(a) UNTAET Reg. 2000/15.
[43] Van Zyl Smit, *Taking Life Imprisonment Seriously*, 196.
[44] Rule 105(B)–(C) ICTY/ICTR RPE; Rule 104(B) SCSL RPE; Art. 77(2)(b) ICCSt; Rule 147 (2)–(3) ICC RPE.
[45] Art. 24(3) ICTYSt; Rules 98*ter*(B), 105 ICTY RPE; Art. 23(3) ICTRSt; Rule 105 ICTR RPE; Art. 19(3) SCSLSt; Rule 104(C) SCSL RPE; Art. 77(2)(b) ICCSt; Rule 147(4) ICC RPE. See also Art. 22(4) MICTSt; Rule 129 MICT RPE.
[46] King and La Rosa, "Penalties under the ICC Statute", 326.
[47] Art. 77(2)(a) ICCSt; Rule 146 ICC RPE.
[48] See Rule 77(G) ICTY/ICTR RPE; Art. 22(1) MICTSt; Rule 90(G) MICT RPE; Rule 77(G) SCSL RPE.
[49] King and La Rosa, "Penalties under the ICC Statute", 326.
[50] See Rule 146(1) ICC RPE; paras. 105–6 *Lubanga* (Sentence) ICC-01/04-01/06, 10.07.2012.

on an individual in the case of continued wilful non-payment for a period of up to five years or a quarter of the sentence, whichever is less (except in cases of life imprisonment or determinate sentences if this would result in a total sentence exceeding the statutory maximum of thirty years).[51] If the individual pays some, or all, of the fine, the Presidency may reduce or revoke the extended term of imprisonment.[52] This penal measure would seem to violate the principle of *nulla poena sine lege* established in Article 23 of the Rome Statute which states that "a person convicted by the Court may be punished only in accordance with this Statute". The Statute only permits the imposition of a term of imprisonment for crimes listed in Article 5,[53] which does not include non-payment of fines. Moreover, this measure is created by the Rules, not the Statute. This power is a "remarkable occurrence ... as the Presidency's role is normally solely one of enforcement after a person has been sentenced by Chambers ... in this case the Presidency itself has the authority to extend the sentence".[54] The possibility of an increased term may create cooperation problems. At present, the bilateral enforcement agreements only state that the Presidency may ask the enforcing state for observations in relation to the possible extension of a sentence.[55] The lack of an obligation to consult with the enforcing state is surprising given that an increased term may create legal or practical difficulties that could result in the impossibility of continued enforcement. Although the Rules acknowledge that this is a measure of last resort,[56] there seem to be fundamental problems with this additional sanction.

Fines and forfeiture orders may only, however, be imposed in addition to imprisonment. They are not alternative penalties. Moreover, neither additional penalty has been imposed to date.[57] As imprisonment is the sole penalty that has been imposed by international criminal courts, **international punishment**, for the purpose of this book, refers only to imprisonment.

2. The international criminal justice system

As the previous section outlined, the contemporary international criminal justice system is comprised of three models of international criminal

---

[51] Rule 146(5) ICC RPE.   [52] Reg. 118(2) ICC ROC.   [53] Art. 77(1) ICCSt.
[54] H. Abathi and S. A. Koh, "The Emerging Enforcement Practice of the International Criminal Court" (2012) 45 *Cornell International Law Journal* 1–23 at 22.
[55] See Art. 17(4) ICC–Serbia BEA.   [56] Rule 146(5) ICC RPE.
[57] The cut-off point for research was 10 October 2012.

court: temporary international, permanent international and temporary internationalised. Both of the *temporary international* courts, the ICTY and ICTR, will be studied as these courts provide the majority of enforcement practice to date. Furthermore, it was considered important to study the enforcement processes of these temporary institutions as they had completion strategies in place.[58] The supervision of the enforcement of sentences was identified as one of the essential functions that would remain when the temporary international courts were closed.[59] Rather than transferring residual duties to relevant states or the ICC,[60] retaining both Tribunals[61] or creating two stand-alone residual mechanisms,[62] the UNSC decided to adopt the UNSG's proposal[63] to establish one residual body with two branches to carry on the residual functions of the ICTY and the ICTR.[64] The Mechanism for the International Criminal Tribunals (MICT), with a seat in both Arusha and The Hague,[65] commenced functioning on 1 July 2012 for the ICTR and will commence functioning on 1 July 2013 for the ICTY.[66] In addition to its power to prosecute or transfer the cases of those already indicted by the UN Tribunals or those convicted of offences against the administration of justice, the MICT will take over the rights, obligations and essential functions of the ad hoc Tribunals.[67] These functions include the supervision of the enforcement of sentences of imprisonment imposed by the ICTY, the ICTR and the MICT itself.[68]

The ICC's enforcement systems will be examined as it is the only *permanent international* court. Moreover, its Statute provides for an unprecedented method of enforcement in the Host State.

Of the current *temporary internationalised* courts, the SCSL has been selected. The SCSL was jointly established by the UN and the

---

[58] See SCRes 1503(2003); SCRes 1534(2004).
[59] See para. 239 Report of the Secretary-General on the Administrative and Budgetary Aspects of the Options for Possible Locations for the Archives of the ICTY and ICTR and the Seat of the Residual Mechanism(s) for the Tribunals S/2009/258, 21.05.2009, (Residual Mechanism Report).
[60] V. Oosterveld, "The International Criminal Court and the Closure of the Time-Limited International and Hybrid Criminal Tribunals" (2010) 8(1) *Loyola University Chicago International Law Review* 13–31 at 23–4, 27.
[61] R. Frolich, "UN Security Council Resolution 1966: International Residual Mechanism for the ICTY and ICTR" (2011) 50(3) *International Legal Materials* 323–39 at 323.
[62] C. Acquaviva, "Was a Residual Mechanism for International Criminal Tribunals Really Necessary" (2011) 9(4) *Journal of International Criminal Justice* 789–96 at 793–4.
[63] See Residual Mechanism Report.   [64] SCRes 1966(2010).   [65] Art. 3 MICTSt.
[66] Para. 1 SCRes 1966(2010).   [67] Para. 4 SCRes 1966(2010).
[68] See para. 1 SCRes 1966(2010); Arts. 25(2), 26 MICTSt.

Government of Sierra Leone in January 2002 to try those bearing greatest responsibility for war crimes and crimes against humanity committed in Sierra Leone since 30 November 1996.[69] Due to its method of establishment and framework for operations, this internationalised court is considered to be more international and independent than other contemporary models.[70] Perhaps more significantly for the purposes of this book, its enforcement system is directly linked to those of the UN Tribunals. Not only does the SCSL use the ICTR's Rules of Procedure and Evidence,[71] its Statute enables it to rely on the bilateral agreements entered into by states with either the ICTY or ICTR to enforce its sentences of imprisonment.[72] This temporary court's mandate will be complete once final judgment is delivered in the *Charles Taylor* case. From this point, the supervision of enforcement of sentences will be tasked to the Residual Special Court for Sierra Leone (RSCSL)[73] established by an agreement between the UN and the Government of Sierra Leone.[74] The RSCSL will be composed of Chambers, Prosecutor and a Registrar assisted by five to seven staff. The RSCSL will function from its interim seat in The Hague, although a sub-office in Freetown will deal with witness protection matters.[75]

The **international criminal justice system**, for the purposes of this book, is represented by a range of international judicial institutions, ICTY, ICTR, ICC and SCSL (and their respective residual mechanisms where applicable).

3. The international penal system

The establishment and operation of the contemporary international criminal courts has effectively linked the condemnation of international crime with the legal imposition and implementation of international punishment. International punishment, in practice, means imprisonment. To date, the UN Tribunals, SCSL and ICC have convicted and sentenced over 150 persons to terms of imprisonment. Unlike national

---

[69] Art. 1(1) SCA; Art. 1(1) SCSLSt.
[70] See S. Linton, "Cambodia, East Timor and Sierra Leone: Experiments in International Justice" (2001) 12 *Criminal Law Forum* 185–246 at 188, 233; D. Shraga "The Second Generation UN-Based Tribunals: A Diversity of Mixed Jurisdictions" in C. P. R. Romano et al. (eds.), *Internationalized Criminal Courts: Sierra Leone, East Timor, Kosovo, and Cambodia* (2004), 16, 36.
[71] Art. 14(1) SCSLSt.   [72] Art. 22(1) SCSLSt.   [73] Art. 1 RSCSLSt.
[74] See the Residual Special Court for Sierra Leone Agreement (Ratification) Act, 2011.
[75] SCSL Ninth Annual Report, 38.

criminal justice systems, international courts do not have access to an international prison system that can enforce the sentences they impose. In September 2012, nearly sixty international prisoners were serving their sentences in the national prison systems of fourteen European and three African countries. Many convicted persons were also serving their sentences in the international detention facilities attached to the international courts awaiting the outcome of their appeal, transfer to an enforcing state or release. By September 2012, over fifty individuals had been released from national prisons or international detention facilities after serving their sentences. Therefore, while it may not be visible or acknowledged, there is an operational penal system that facilitates the incarceration of international prisoners. The lack of recognition of the system, which has been in operation since the first conviction was handed down by the ICTY in 1997, may be due to the variety of methods that can be used to enforce international punishment.

The various methods for the enforcement of international punishment are governed by a range of international legal instruments. Provisions relating to enforcement can be found in the statutes, rules and regulations of the international criminal courts, in memoranda of understanding or cooperation agreements with courts, countries and prison services, in the headquarters agreements concluded between the international courts and their Host States, in bilateral enforcement agreements concluded with states and agreements entered into with inspecting bodies.

The primary statutory system for the enforcement of international sentences of imprisonment involves transferring international prisoners to the national prison facilities of cooperating states that are not associated with the conflict in question. At present, twenty-four states in three continents have signed enforcement agreements with international criminal courts. This *decentralised national enforcement* system[76] does not always provide the international criminal courts with sufficient penal capacity. As a result, international sentences of imprisonment may have to be, partially or fully, served in the remand centres of the international criminal courts. Each international criminal court has an international detention facility (IDF). The ICTY's Detention Unit (UNDU) is situated within the Scheveningen Penitentiary Complex in The Hague. The ICC's Detention Centre (ICCDC) is in the same building as the UNDU. The ICTR's Detention Facility (UNDF) is outside Arusha within the

---

[76] See Chapter 2.

perimeter of a Tanzanian prison and the SCSL's Detention Facility (SCSLDF) is located within the grounds of the SCSL in Freetown. This *centralised international enforcement* system,[77] however, is not authorised by any statutory provision. The Rome Statute introduces a unique provision that provides access to a modified form of centralised enforcement. The ICC's default system of *centralised national enforcement*[78] enables the ICC to transfer convicted persons to a facility operated by the Host State. The ICTR and SCSL statutes also introduce an alternative method of enforcement. Both statutes explicitly provide for the enforcement of international sentences of imprisonment in the state in which the conflict occurred. However, *localised national enforcement* has not been relied on to date.[79] To understand the realities of the local enforcement of custodial sanctions imposed for war crimes, the Rule 11*bis* procedure will be examined. Although Rule 11*bis* transfers from the ICTY to Bosnia-Herzegovina and the ICTR to Rwanda result in the enforcement of national sentences of imprisonment in national prison facilities, the process provides insights into the difficulties that would be associated with enforcing custodial sanctions imposed by international courts for crimes committed during a local conflict in local prisons.

Just as the ICC, ICTY, ICTR (MICT) and SCSL (RSCSL) are all part of an interlinked network of international criminal justice, the systems used by these courts to enforce their sentences of imprisonment form a network that comprises the **international penal system**. This book analyses the operations, impact and effectiveness of the various systems used to implement international punishment.

4. Reconceptualising the implementation of international punishment

Prior to the Second World War, responsibility for international crime was primarily placed on states and the sanction for its commission was typically financial.[80] In 1946, the IMTN laid down the important precedent, later affirmed by the UNGA,[81] that "crimes against international law are committed by men, not abstract entities, and only by punishing individuals who commit such crimes can the provisions of international

---

[77] See Chapter 3. [78] See Chapter 3, Section 8. [79] See Chapter 4.
[80] F. Hassan, "The Theoretical Basis of Punishment in International Criminal Law" (1983) 15 *Case Western Reserve Journal of International Law* 39–60 at 39, 40, 47 and 54.
[81] GARes. 95(I)(1946).

law be enforced".[82] There is now considered to be an international legal duty not only to investigate and prosecute those accused of perpetrating international crimes, but also to punish those found guilty of their commission. Even international prisoners who protest their innocence accept that individuals responsible for the commission of international crimes should be tried and punished.[83]

International punishment may be defined as "punishment inflicted on individuals under international law through a judicial tribunal".[84] The potential imposition of a punitive custodial sanction differentiates international criminal justice from other forms of transitional justice.[85] While it is clear that imprisonment is the primary penalty used in the international criminal justice system, it is not so clear what purpose this punishment should serve or how it should be implemented.

The focus to date has been on the humanness of permissible penalties and the priority given to various sentencing rationales. In spite of the length of sentences imposed by the international courts, they "rarely consider the role of punishment and its effect".[86] International sentencing judgments do not set out how international punishment should be implemented or what aims it should achieve. International sentences of imprisonment are often discussed as though they are an end in themselves; that the simple pronouncement of guilt and the imposition of a term of years will, by itself, achieve the numerous aims professed for the international criminal justice system. The international courts, however, will be judged not only on the "fairness of ... the sanctions they impose"[87] but also on the manner in which those sanctions are implemented. The time has come to evaluate and develop the system used to implement these sanctions.

International sentences of imprisonment are primarily enforced in the domestic prisons of cooperating states. During their sentence, international prisoners are treated in accordance with domestic penal policy and practices. Drumbl points out that "despite the extraordinary nature of ... [international] criminality, its modality of punishment ... remains

---

[82] IMTN, Judgment and Sentences (1947) 41 AJIL 172 at 223.
[83] Blagojević, Trondheim Prison, 28.06.2012; Krajišnik, Usk Prison, 27.09.2012.
[84] Hassan, "The Theoretical Basis of Punishment", 45.
[85] Schabas, *An Introduction to the International Criminal Court*, 331.
[86] N. J. W. Goda, *Tales from Spandau: Nazi Criminals and the Cold War* (2007), 8.
[87] S. Beresford, "Unshackling the Paper Tiger: the Sentencing Practices of the ad hoc International Criminal Tribunals for the Former Yugoslavia and Rwanda" (2001) 1 *International Criminal Law Review* 33–90 at 89.

disappointingly ordinary".[88] He argues that the classic isolating penitentiary model adopted by international criminal courts is uninspiring and results in the paradox that, despite the normative difference international lawyers have pronounced between ordinary national crimes and extraordinary international crime, "the enemy of mankind is punished no differently from a car thief [or] armed robber".[89] International criminals are sent to national prisons that are not equipped to deal with international criminality.[90] Indeed, practice has shown that international prisoners are not rehabilitated or prepared for release or reintegration back into society. This lack of preparation is particularly problematic given that as the international criminal justice system has no parole system, international prisoners are deported and released without conditions, support or supervision.

The structure of the primary enforcement system also has implications for the equal treatment of international prisoners. If consistency in the imposition of punishment is one of the fundamental elements of a fair criminal justice system,[91] the equality of treatment of persons convicted by the same court during the implementation of those sanctions must be a fundamental element of a fair penal system. The variation in the conditions and regimes in the domestic prison systems of cooperating states inevitably results in persons convicted by the same court being treated differently.

The dispersal of international prisoners throughout a network of national prison systems reduces the visibility of, and dilutes the international nature of, the sanctions being imposed. The delegation of custodial duties to enforcing states results in the nationalisation of international punishment, reducing the international court's ability to exercise control over the sanction and the manner in which it is implemented. International custodial sanctions are presently implemented in a system that has no stated penal policy objectives, practices or prison cells. The international penal system, therefore, seems capable of doing little more than warehousing international prisoners in facilities unsuited to the enforcement of international punishment. Courts that strive to act as models for domestic criminal justice systems punish the individuals they convict in a basic and regressive penal system.

---

[88] M. Drumbl, "Collective Violence and Individual Punishment: The Criminality of Mass Atrocity" (2005) 99(2) *Northwestern University Law Review* 539–610 at 541.
[89] *Ibid.*, 542.
[90] *Ibid.*, 549, 566; M. Drumbl, *Atrocity, Punishment and International Law* (2007), 6, 9, 11.
[91] Para. 526 *Krnojelac* (Judgment) IT-97-25-T, 15.03.2002.

Despite the obvious deficiencies of the contemporary enforcement system, it has been replicated by each new emerging international court. The lack of appraisal or development is perhaps due to the lack of recognition of the existence of the system. It may also be due to the fact that international criminal justice institutions tend to view themselves as self-contained systems validated by the manner of their creation.[92] While this may explain the failure to undertake any meaningful internal evaluation, there is a notable dearth of external critique of the manner in which international punishment is implemented. In contrast to their traditional role as guardians of prisoners' rights, many human rights advocates have actively promoted the punishment of international criminals. The absence of human rights-based evaluation is unfortunate as the manner in which institutions that hold themselves up as guardians of human rights and accountability treat persons they deprive of their liberty will ultimately be a critical factor in perceptions of their legitimacy. Human rights lawyers should not blindly support international institutions out of a "sense of bureaucratic territoriality or loyalty to international governance".[93] The current narrow focus on prosecutions and convictions fails to achieve the stated objectives of the international criminal justice system, meet the expectations of stakeholders or uphold the rights of those punished. Robert Jackson argued back in 1946 that "if punishment is to lead to progress, it must be carried out in a manner which world opinion will regard as progressive and as consistent with fundamental morality".[94] Though interest typically fades after the first few days of a trial,[95] media attention can be sparked by the situation of prisoners decades after the court in question has closed. Even the most reviled international criminals can become viewed as humanitarian causes if they are detained in inhumane regimes or conditions.[96] As Ohlin notes, "nothing else in the system matters if the last step, punishment, is handled inadequately".[97] It is time to move beyond a simple system concerned only with securing sufficient capacity, to create a

---

[92] G. Verdirame, *The UN and Human Rights: Who Guards the Guardians?* (2011), 349.
[93] Drumbl, "Collective Violence and Individual Punishment", 608.
[94] Cited in Beresford, "Unshakling the Paper Tiger", 43, footnote 33.
[95] G. K. McDonald, "The International Criminal Tribunals: Crime & Punishment in the International Arena" (2001) 25 *Nova Law Review* 463–84 at 469.
[96] Goda, *Tales from Spandau* 9, 130.
[97] J. D. Ohlin, "Proportional Sentences at the ICTY" in B. Swart *et al.* (eds.), *The Legacy of the International Criminal Tribunal for the former Yugoslavia* (2011), 322–41 at 323.

humane and effective penal system which can deliver principled and progressive punishment.

The effectiveness of the international penal system is difficult to determine as it has no stated objectives. King and Meernik argue that the lofty aspirations and judicial romanticism of the international criminal justice system need to be replaced by clear and viable benchmarks established following a systematic and objective analysis.[98] The same is true for the international penal system. International punishment must be implemented in a system that operates in accordance with international human rights law and penological standards governing the detention of convicted persons. These standards dictate, *inter alia*, that punishment cannot be inhuman or degrading, that it must be implemented in a way that respects equality, rights to family life and an effective remedy, and ensures the rehabilitation and reintegration of prisoners. Though it is logical that a penal system must aspire to achieve penological objectives of rehabilitation and reintegration, a penal system that operates within the international criminal justice context must also aspire to the attainment of broader goals. As a product and symbol of the international criminal justice system, international punishment must also be implemented in a manner that aligns with the reconciliation and peace maintenance goals professed by the founding bodies of the international courts.

As it is currently implemented, international punishment fails to achieve penological or broader transitional justice goals. If international punishment is deemed to be inhumane or ineffective, and therefore an illegitimate exercise of power, support for the international criminal justice project will be undermined. Legitimacy cannot be borrowed by adopting the sanitising rhetoric of international human rights standards if the reality of punishment fails to accord with these standards. While international criminal justice goals may be aspirational, they create public expectations which are often disappointed with detrimental effects for the perceived legitimacy of the courts.[99] International punishment must also, therefore, be implemented in a manner that accords with the expectations of the stakeholders of the international criminal

---

[98] K. L. King and J. D. Meernik, "Assessing the Impact of the ICTY: Balancing International and Local Interests While Doing Justice" in B. Swart *et al.* (eds.), *The Legacy of the International Criminal Tribunal for the Former Yugoslavia*, 2011, 7–54 at 14, 52.

[99] See R. Haveman, "Supranational Expectations of a Punitive Nature" in R. Haveman and O. Olusanya (eds.), *Sentencing and Sanctioning in Supranational Criminal Law* (2006), 145–60 at 148; Drumbl, *Atrocity, Punishment and International Law*, 9.

justice system. It is recognised that international criminal justice has a complex victimology, that on a basic level can be broken down into the international community on the one hand and actual victims and their communities on the other.[100] Within these two groups there are numerous sub-categories with diverse interests.[101] It has been argued, however, that due to the nature of their creation and operation, international criminal courts tend to focus on fulfilling the professional interests of the international community (maintaining the justice process) rather than the personal wishes of the victim communities (the justice outcome).[102]

The disparity between the social and normative values of the international criminal justice system and the reality of the international penal system represent a threat to the legitimacy of the sanctioning courts. If international courts wish to ensure that their legitimacy is not detrimentally affected by the manner in which international custodial sanctions are enforced, they must reconceptualise the way in which international punishment is implemented. Although the international criminal justice system has witnessed unprecedented institution building in a short period of time,[103] the relative youth of the international criminal justice institutions are often cited as excuses for the lack of development or innovation.[104] Shortcomings can no longer be explained away with rhetoric, resource excuses or reference to the temporary nature of the courts. It is understandable that the temporary courts adopted a pragmatic system that ensured penal capacity for enforcement purposes. With the permanent international criminal court handing down its first sentence, however, the time has come to take stock and seriously address the deficiencies of the system. The international penal system must evolve beyond its practical focus on securing capacity and develop specific goals, means and modalities for the implementation of international punishment.

The international criminal justice system has been accused of adopting a strict legalistic approach that results in amateur policies and its insulation from disciplines such as criminology and sociology that are important for its operation and development.[105] A greater

---

[100] Drumbl, "Collective Violence and Individual Punishment", 578.
[101] King and Meernik, "Assessing the Impact of the ICTY", 7.   [102] Ibid., 8, 12–13.
[103] See McDonald, "The International Criminal Tribunals", 464, 469.
[104] Drumbl, "Collective Violence and Individual Punishment", 608.
[105] See Ohlin, "Proportional Sentences at the ICTY", 322; W. Schabas, "Criminology, Accountability and International Justice" in M. Bosworth and C. Hoyle (eds.), *What*

openness to and engagement with other forms of knowledge will facilitate the development of a specialist and effective penology designed to enhance the system's ability to fulfil broader justice goals. International penology should be drawn from and informed by a range of relevant disciplines. International punishment should be implemented in accordance with a specifically tailored international penal policy that conforms to human rights and penological standards and draws on victimology, transitional justice and restorative justice principles to develop modalities that can address "the realities that produce and sustain conflict and social breakdown".[106] The international penal process should not only punish (retribution) but ensure the attainment of human rights inspired penological objectives (rehabilitation and reintegration) and broader justice goals (reconciliation and peace). To create possibilities to achieve these outcomes, it is necessary to create and adopt methods that facilitate resocialisation and dialogue.

The unique nature of international crime and the unique situation of international prisoners make it necessary to design modalities that enable "intervention going beyond the normal boundaries of conventional" methods.[107] Given that international punishment should contribute to the attainment of transitional justice goals and help reintegrate prisoners back into society, international penal practice should be derived from transitional and restorative justice principles and methodologies. Post-conviction practices informed by these approaches to dealing with crime can help to ensure that punishment is enforced in a more visible, inclusive and culturally relevant manner for affected societies and assist with resocialisation, reintegration, reconciliation and the transition of society towards more peaceful times. The need to address such a wide range of goals necessitates this more comprehensive and holistic approach to the implementation of international punishment.

As international courts are ultimately responsible for international sanctions and international prisoners, international punishment should be implemented in accordance with international policies. The centralised creation and implementation of international penal policy and

---

is *Criminology* (2011), 346–57 at 346–9; K. McEvoy, "Letting go of Legalism: Developing a 'Thicker' Version of Transitional Justice" in K. McEvoy and L. McGregor (eds.), *Transitional Justice from Below: Grassroots Activism and the Struggle for Change (Human Rights Law in Perspective)* (2008), 16, 18, 21.

[106] R. Henham, *Punishment and Process in International Criminal Trial* (2005), 140.

[107] R. Henham, "Theorizing the Penality of Sentencing in International Criminal Trials" (2004) 8 *Theoretical Criminology* 429–63 at 445.

practices will enable the international courts to move beyond the passive oversight of international punishment to more active engagement with and support for the states to which they delegate the task of enforcement and the institutions which implement the international sentences of imprisonment. An international policy would also enhance the equal treatment of persons convicted by the same court and increase international control over the sanctions being implemented. International control would, of course, be much easier to ensure if international punishment was implemented in international prisons. Rather than provide centralised support to national prisons, the international courts could directly implement the sanctions they impose in their own prisons. Although they have no mandate to do so, the temporary international courts have directly enforced international sentences of imprisonment in their detention facilities. International courts have also directly funded the renovation and operation of special facilities established to house international prisoners in cooperating states. This precedence and practice suggests that the international criminal justice system both can and should have an international prison system. In fact, an international prison system seems to be a logical institutional development in an international criminal justice system. The creation of an international prison system would ensure access to capacity conforming to international standards, increase the visibility and international nature of the sanctions imposed, enhance the equal treatment of persons convicted by the same court, reduce the potential for isolation and facilitate the implementation and development of international penal policy and practices.

As international punishment is both a product and a tangible symbol of the international criminal justice system, the enforcement of international sentences of imprisonment is critical to the modern struggle to end impunity for gross violations of human rights. As international courts are rights-enforcing institutions, they must ensure that the processes and outcomes they are responsible for comply with human rights standards. International punishment is a relatively new phenomenon, the law in relation to the responsibility of international organisations is an emerging area of international law and an international prison system is unprecedented. It would, therefore, be necessary to establish clear lines of responsibility for conduct that takes place within an international prison and ensure that there are avenues for international prisoners to seek effective redress from the outset. To ensure there are no remedial gaps, an international organisation responsible for the creation and operation of an international prison system must ensure that international prisoners have access to independent bodies that are capable of adequately dealing with complaints of criminal and tortious activities and human rights violations and are empowered to award remedies where required.

5. Conclusion

The international penal system is no longer a normative construct, but a functioning social reality. This cursory overview reveals that international punishment is implemented in a detached manner, without any ends or means discourse. Without goals, techniques or facilities, the international penal system simply disperses and warehouses international prisoners in the cells of the prison systems of cooperating states. This basic system fails to accord with international standards or to meet the expectations of the systems' stakeholders. Combined, these problems have the potential to detrimentally impact upon the (perceived) legitimacy of the international criminal justice system. International punishment must be considered in a more systemic manner and the international penal system must be developed so that it "rivals a domestic system".[108] In addition to providing insights into the realities of the enforcement of international punishment, this book advocates the reconceptualisation of the way in which international punishment is implemented. To make recommendations for the development of international penal strategy and structure, it is first necessary to analyse the current systems for the enforcement of international punishment in detail.

---

[108] Ohlin, "Proportional Sentences at the ICTY", 341.

PART II

Systems: systems for the enforcement
of international punishment

2

Decentralised national enforcement

The post-Second World War International Military Tribunals relied on a single prison facility located in their Host States to implement their custodial sanctions.[1] In contrast, the modern international courts primarily rely on a system of dispersal that involves sending convicted persons to states that have declared their willingness to enforce the sentences handed down by the international courts.[2] Although there are other statutory and non-statutory options for the enforcement of international sentences of imprisonment, which will be discussed in the following chapters, the primary system used by the current international courts involves sending international prisoners from the state in which the court is located, to states with no connection with the conflict in question. The national prison systems of the cooperating states provide the international criminal courts with access to penal infrastructure, services and regulatory frameworks.

This chapter discusses the challenges faced by the courts in securing state cooperation, the procedures used to designate a state for the enforcement of a particular sentence and the division of responsibility for international prisoners and sentences between the sentencing courts and cooperating states. It also outlines the reality of implementing international punishment in national prisons, focusing on the potential of the system to isolate international prisoners and its failure to rehabilitate or prepare international prisoners for release.

1. Securing state cooperation

Although states must cooperate with the UN Tribunals and ICC in relation to the investigation and prosecution of international crimes,[3]

---

[1] Spandau Prison, Berlin and Sugamo Prison, Tokyo.
[2] Art. 27 ICTYSt; Art. 26 ICTRSt; Art. 22(1) SCSLSt; Art. 103(1)(a) ICCSt.
[3] See para. 4 SCRes 827(1993); para. 2 SCRes 955(1994); Art. 86 ICCSt.

there is no legal obligation on states to enforce international sentences of imprisonment. Proposed statutory provisions that would have resulted in a duty to enforce ICC sentences were dropped during the drafting process.[4] Given the lack of reciprocal benefits for cooperating states, it is perhaps not surprising that there does not appear to be any political will to introduce a compulsory enforcement system.[5] The international courts can only refer to a general duty of states to assist and cooperate.[6] As the international courts have "no prisons, no prison system or coercive powers to enforce its sentences"[7] they must rely on the voluntary assistance of states. However, states rarely declare their willingness to cooperate on their own volition. Cooperation is usually only secured following persistent lobbying by court and other international officials.[8]

Efforts to secure political support for the conclusion of bilateral enforcement agreements are directed at both formal and informal diplomatic channels.[9] Visits and calls are made to government ministries in capitals, embassies in the Host State, state missions to the UN and other international and regional organisations.[10] Initially, the vast amounts of time, money and effort invested proved unproductive. Many states were, and continue to be, reluctant to implement international sentences of imprisonment for a range of reasons.

Although the stigma attached to international crime is a factor in the reluctance of states to cooperate, most decisions appear to be resource-led. The acceptance into custody of notorious war criminals with lengthy sentences involves a long-term financial commitment that domestic taxpayers may not approve of, particularly if the national prison system's

---

[4] A. Marchesi, "The Enforcement of Sentences of the International Criminal Court" in F. Lattanzi and W. Schabas (eds.), *Essays on the Rome Statute of the International Criminal Court* (1999), 427–45 at 427–30.

[5] R. Mulgrew "The International Movement of Prisoners: Explaining the Evolution of the Inter-State and International Criminal Justice Systems for the Transfer of Sentenced Persons" (2011) 22 *Criminal Law Forum* 103–43 at 127–8.

[6] See D. Tolbert, "The International Criminal Tribunal for the Former Yugoslavia and the Enforcement of Sentences" (1998) 11 *Leiden Journal of International Law* 655–99 at 658.

[7] Para. 2 MDP, 151.

[8] See C. De Sampayo Garrido, "Problems and Achievements Seen from the Viewpoint of the Registry" (2004) 2 *Journal of International Criminal Justice* 474–9 at 476; paras. 2, 3, 5 European Parliament Resolution on the Special Court for Sierra Leone B6-0244/2009.

[9] See paras. 156–7 ICTR Third Annual Report. Vincent, SCSL/ICTY, 27.04.2007; Mochochoko, ICC 30.08.2007.

[10] See SCSL Fifth Annual Report, 11, 26, 34, 36. Vicente, ICTY, 16.02.2007; Abathi, ICC, 15.02.2007.

capacity and budget are already strained.[11] If the prisoner is also a protected witness, more expensive and more secure facilities are required.[12] Politicians are keen to avoid public discussions of high profile cases, and potentially costly commitments, in the run up to national elections.[13] Foreign policy objectives and how the court is perceived in a requested state may also affect the outcome of negotiations.[14] Beyond political considerations, states have also expressed humanitarian concerns regarding the potential for the socio-cultural isolation of international prisoners within their national prison systems and the difficulties prisoners may face in maintaining familial relations.[15]

The UN delegates authority to the UN Tribunals' Registrars to enter into enforcement agreements with states on its behalf.[16] The SCSL is empowered to enter into agreements with states "as may be necessary for the exercise of its functions and for the operation of the Court".[17] Under the Rome Statute, there is no legal requirement for the ICC to conclude enforcement agreements, but the Rules indicate that they can be entered into.[18] Bilateral enforcement agreements flesh out the procedures alluded to in the courts' statutes and rules, and provide a more detailed legal framework for the implementation and supervision of international custodial sanctions.[19] The ICTY can sign enforcement agreements with any state bar the countries of the former Yugoslav Republic.[20] The ICTR can sign agreements with any state, as can the SCSL, which has the additional statutory option of relying on agreements signed with the UN Tribunals.[21] While the ICC's goal is to secure agreements worldwide, current efforts are being focused on securing bilateral enforcement agreements with State Parties. Although there is nothing in the Statute or Rules that would bar non-State Parties from enforcing sentences for the ICC, their cooperation is not being actively sought at present.[22] Any request from a non-State Party to enforce sentences or a particular

---

[11] Siller, ICTY, 07.06.2007; Dubuisson, ICC, 06.06.2007; Mochochoko, ICC, 30.08.2007; Mäkelä, Finland, 01.07.2008; Friman, Sweden, 22.09.2008.
[12] Schusterschitz, Austria, 05.02.2008; Fofana, ICTY, 29.08.2007.
[13] See para. A.1(9) MDP, 152.   [14] O'Donnell, ICTR, 25.06.2007.
[15] See para. A.1(9) MDP, 152.   [16] De Witt, ICTY, 07.06.2007.
[17] Article 11(D) SCA.   [18] Rule 200(5) ICC RPE; Reg. 114 ICC ROC.
[19] See C. Kreß and G. Sluiter, "Imprisonment" in A. Cassese *et al.* (eds.), *The Rome Statute of the International Criminal Court: A Commentary*, Vol. II (2002), 1757–821 at 1782.
[20] Para. 121 Report of the Secretary-General pursuant to para. 2 of Security Council Resolution 808 (1993) 03.05.1993.
[21] Art. 22(1) SCSLSt.   [22] Abathi, ICC, 05.07.2012.

sentence would be considered on a case-by-case basis. Agreements with non-State Parties require more detail as they would have to explicitly include obligations already accepted by State Parties under the Statute, Rules, Regulations etc.[23]

Enforcement agreements are negotiated on the basis of a model enforcement agreement. The UN Tribunals' Model Agreement was drafted by the UN Office of Legal Affairs. The SCSL and ICC had the benefit of considering this model as well as concluded bilateral agreements when drafting their own versions. The ICC revised its model enforcement agreement in 2011 to introduce greater clarity and to avoid some interpretation issues that had arisen under the previous agreement.[24] The new template was used to negotiate the Malian and Columbian agreements. Model agreements set out the core conditions that will govern the bilateral relationship, such as the procedures for designation, inspection, release, splitting costs and the termination of enforcement etc. The model agreement is forwarded to the Ministry of Foreign Affairs of states that have declared their willingness to cooperate. The Ministry of Foreign Affairs typically coordinates the domestic discussion of the document, communicating with the Ministry of Justice and Prison Service and relays the decision whether or not to accept the agreement back to the court.[25] If a state accepts the agreement, it may enter into force automatically upon signature,[26] after a certain period of time[27] or after internal formalities (Head of State's signature, parliamentary ratification, legislation or the incorporation of the treaty into national law) have been complied with.[28] The agreement represents a general commitment from the state to consider all requests to enforce international sentences of imprisonment. Only one state, Germany, has chosen not to enter into a general agreement. Due to the federal nature of the German political structure, the Government preferred to enter into a separate agreement with the ICTY upon the acceptance of responsibility to implement a sentence imposed on a particular individual.[29]

---

[23] Abathi, ICC, 15.02.2007.   [24] Abathi, ICC, 05.07.2012.
[25] Mäkelä, Finland, 01.07.2008; Friman, Sweden, 22.09.2008; Schusterschitz, Austria, 05.02.2008.
[26] Art. 12 ICTY–Norway/Belgium/Sweden BEAs; Art. 13 ICTR–Benin BEA.
[27] Art. 12 ICTY–Austria/Finland/UK BEAs; Art. 13 ICTY–Slovakia BEA.
[28] Art. 12 ICTY–France/Italy/Albania/Estonia/Poland/Portugal/Ukraine/Spain BEAs; Art. 13 ICTY–Denmark BEA; Art. 12 ICTR–France/Italy/Sweden BEA; Art. 13 ICTR–Mali/Rwanda/Swaziland BEAs; Art. 21 ICC–Denmark BEA.
[29] The ICTY and Germany have signed four agreements to govern the enforcement of sentences imposed on Tadić, Kunarac, Galić and Tarčulovski.

To date, the ICTY has secured the cooperation of seventeen states, which are all located in Europe.[30] The ICTR has concluded seven bilateral enforcement agreements, three with European countries and four with African countries.[31] The SCSL has concluded four public agreements, three in Europe and one in Africa.[32] The ICC has secured eight agreements with countries located in Europe, Africa and South America.[33]

Although the decentralised enforcement system is operational with the present numbers, all the courts feel that more agreements are necessary to ensure they can effectively fulfill their mandates.[34] The pressure to conclude agreements is intensified for the UN Tribunals nearing completion as their Host States have made it clear that international prisoners may not remain on their territory after their sentences have been served.[35] Moreover, all the courts are competing at the same time for state cooperation.[36] Given these pressures, the UN Security Council has urged states to conclude agreements with the temporary courts for the enforcement of sentences and insisted that the courts intensify their efforts to do so.[37] Due to the problems it experienced, the ICTY has highlighted the need for international courts to establish the level of political support from the Host State and potential enforcing states in relation to enforcement from the outset of operations.[38] Taking this on board, the ICC's ASP has repeatedly made the conclusion of enforcement agreements a priority and called on states to enter into such arrangements.[39] The level of cooperation is not, however, dependent solely on the number of bilateral enforcement agreements concluded. In a bid to increase the pool of potential enforcing states, the courts have accepted conditions relating to cooperation.[40]

---

[30] Italy, Finland, Norway, Sweden, Austria, Germany, France, Spain, Denmark, UK, Belgium, Ukraine, Portugal, Estonia, Slovakia, Poland, Albania. See Appendix II.
[31] Italy, Sweden, France, Swaziland, Benin, Mali, Rwanda.
[32] UK, Sweden, Finland, Rwanda. The SCSL has entered into a fifth agreement but the identity of this state has not been disclosed.
[33] Austria, UK, Denmark, Serbia, Finland, Belgium, Mali and Colombia.
[34] See Comprehensive Report of the SCSL Residual Issues Expert Group Meeting, 57; para. 79 ICTY Eighteenth Annual Report.
[35] See para. 34 R. Amoussago, "The ICTR's Challenges in the Relocation of Acquitted Persons, Released Prisoners and Protected Witnesses", 2008.
[36] Vincent, SCSL/ICTY, 27.04.2007.   [37] See para. 8 SCRes 1534(2004).
[38] Para. C.5(56) MDP, 188.
[39] See paras. 15–16 Cooperation, ICC-ASP/8/Res.2, 26.11.2009; paras. 6, 14 Cooperation, ICC-ASP/10/Res.2, 20.11.2011.
[40] See Art. 103(1)(b) ICCSt; Rule 200(2)–(3) ICC RPE.

These conditions can reduce the scope of cooperation. For example, the UK will not accept female or young offenders as the Prison Service does not have facilities to hold them.[41] Other states limit the number of convicted persons that will be accepted.[42] National legal requirements or political preferences can result in limits being placed on the length or type of sentence that may be accepted.[43] For instance, Finland is only prepared to implement SCSL sentences imposed for the commission of international crimes.[44] Conditions may result in non-cooperation in practice. Negotiations between the ICTY and Switzerland to conclude an enforcement agreement broke down when it became apparent that a rigid insistence on, and a narrow interpretation of, a nationality requirement would result in non-cooperation in practice.[45] To avoid a similar situation occurring, Sweden removed the nationality or residence precondition on the acceptance of ICTY prisoners: it now limits its commitment by stating the number of prisoners it will accept.[46]

Because of the complexity of the enforcement agreements, negotiations can be very time consuming. Model agreements may need to be redrafted to accommodate linguistic and procedural preferences or to align the agreement with national law. It is crucial that international courts and states ensure they are satisfied with the terms of the agreement, as few of the bilateral agreements concluded with the temporary courts allow for subsequent amendments[47] (the ICC BEAs do seem to permit amendment if both parties consent[48]).

To avoid conditions resulting in inconsistency in the enforcement of sentences,[49] the Rome Statute states that conditions must be attached at

---

[41] Daw, Wilkinson, UK, 24.05.2006.

[42] See A. Klip, "Enforcement of Sanctions Imposed by the International Criminal Tribunals for Rwanda and the Former Yugoslavia" (1997) 5(2) *European Journal of Crime, Criminal Law and Criminal Justice* 144–64 at 149–50; ICTY–Norway BEA.

[43] See Art. 3(2) ICTY–Estonia/Portugal/Spain BEAs; Art. 2(2) ICTY–Slovakia BEA; para. A.1(12) MDP, 153; J. C. Nemitz, "Execution of Sanctions Imposed by Supranational Criminal Tribunals" in R. Haveman and O. Olusanya (eds.), *Sentencing and Sanctioning in Supranational Criminal Law* (2006), 125–44 at 128.

[44] The SCSL Statute enabled the court to prosecute domestic crimes and Finland did not wish to enforce sentences imposed for domestic crimes. Mäkelä, Finland, 01.07.2008.

[45] Fofana, ICTY, 29.08.2007.

[46] See Art. 2(2)(d) ICTY–Sweden BEA. Friman, Sweden, 22.09.2008.

[47] Art. 15 ICTR–Rwanda/Swaziland BEAs; Art. 14 SCSL–Sweden BEA; Art. 16 SCSL–Finland BEA; Art. 15 SCSL–Rwanda BEA; Art. 21 ICC–Austria BEA; Art. 19 ICC–UK BEA.

[48] Art. 21 ICC–Belgium/Finland/Serbia BEAs; Art. 14 ICC–Mali BEA; Art. 22 ICC–Denmark BEA.

[49] Marchesi, "The Enforcement of Sentences of the International Criminal Court", 433.

the time of acceptance of general willingness to accept sentenced persons, they must be in accordance with Part 10 of the Statute and they must be agreed to by the Court.[50] Conditions may include the need to establish that the sentenced person has ties with the enforcing state.[51] Fears that the ICC would have to accept any condition proposed by states due to the Court's "relative helplessness" in relation to enforcement have proven unwarranted in practice.[52] The Presidency can choose not to include a state on the list of possible states if it does not agree with the conditions attached to acceptance,[53] and while conditions may be withdrawn after the conclusion of the agreement, conditions may only be amended or added to with the confirmation of the Presidency.[54] If during the enforcement of a sentence, the enforcing state and the Presidency cannot agree to a change or a new condition, the Court can designate another enforcing state.[55]

2. Designation of and transfer to enforcing states

In contrast to the practice of the International Military Tribunals, where it was known beforehand where convicted persons would serve their sentences, modern international criminal courts must designate a country from a list of states that have offered to receive convicted persons. The designation procedure is set out in the courts' statutes, rules, practice directions and enforcement agreements and is very similar for all the courts.[56]

No formal steps in relation to designation can be taken before the final sentence is pronounced.[57] Following sentencing, however, the Registrar makes a preliminary informal inquiry to states on the list of cooperating states, about their readiness to accept a particular prisoner.[58] The conditions

---

[50] Art. 103(1)(b) ICCSt.   [51] Art. 2(1)(e) ICC–Denmark BEA.
[52] H. Abathi and S. A. Koh, "The Emerging Enforcement Practice of the International Criminal Court" (2012) 45 *Cornell International Law Journal* 1–23 at 8.
[53] Rule 200(2) ICC RPE.
[54] Rule 200(3) ICC RPE; Art. 2(3) ICC–Serbia/Mali BEAs; Art. 2(4) ICC–Finland/Denmark BEAs; Art. 2(5) ICC–Belgium BEA.
[55] Art. 8(1) ICC–Belgium BEA; Art. 2(4) ICC–Mali BEA; Art. 6(2) ICC–Finland/Serbia/Denmark BEAs.
[56] Art. 27 ICTYSt; Rule 103(A) ICTY RPE; Art. 26 ICTRSt; Rule 103(A) ICTR RPE; Art. 22 SCSLSt; Rule 19(B) SCSL RPE; Art. 103(1)(a) ICCSt.
[57] Abathi, ICC, 05.07.2012.
[58] Para. 2 ICTY PDD; para. 2(a) ICTR PDD; para. 2 SCSL PDD.

attached to enforcement agreements may limit the states that may be approached.[59] In particular, the Registrar should consider whether the proposed enforcing state's national law relating to pardon and commutation and the length of sentences that can be served are compatible with the international sentence, whether that state can provide a compatible socio-cultural environment for the prisoner and the geographical accessibility of that state for the prisoner's family.[60] The Registrar tends to select one state to avoid the embarrassment of having more than one state agree to enforce a particular sentence.[61] Once a potential state has been selected, a request is transmitted to that state via its embassy in the Host State or the Ministry of Foreign Affairs, which communicates the request to the Ministry of Justice and Prison System.[62] To help it make an informed decision, the court provides the requested state with information relating to the sentenced person, the judgment, the sentence and time left to be served.[63] A positive response to accept a convicted person does not, however, automatically result in a designation. The President/Presidency must first consider a range of factors. The Registrar prepares a file containing the relevant information.

The suitability of a state for the enforcement of a particular sentence is dependent on the state's ability to enforce the sentence effectively.[64] On a practical level, the courts must consider the ability of the state to provide a secure prison and, on a legal level, whether the national legal system can support the nature and length of the sentence imposed.[65] The national prison system is also scrutinised to ensure it can provide the requisite material conditions and has a good record in relation to the treatment of prisoners.[66] The courts use both primary information obtained during visits to the state and secondary data obtained from public documents, such as human rights and inspection reports of international and regional governmental and non-governmental organisations to determine suitability.[67] The court must consider the

---

[59] See Art. 103(2)(a) ICCSt. [60] Para. 3(a) ICTY PDD; para. A.2(16) MDP, 154.
[61] Para. A.2(19) MDP, 155. [62] Vicente, ICTY, 16.02.2007.
[63] Para. 2 ICTY PDD; para. 2(b) ICTR PDD; para. 3 SCSL PDD; Rule 204 ICC RPE.
[64] Art. 103(3)(e) ICCSt.
[65] See M. Penrose, "Spandau Revisited: The Question of Detention for International War Crimes" (1999) 16 *New York Law School Journal of Human Rights* 553–91 at 568–9.
[66] Para. 4(f) ICTY PDD; para. 3(vi) ICTR PDD; para. 4(viii) SCSL PDD; Art. 103(3)(b) ICCSt.
[67] Siller, ICTY, 07.06.2007. See also C. J. M. Safferling, *Towards an International Criminal Procedure* (2001), 350.

prisoner's circumstances, nationality, religion, health and linguistic skills.[68] Moreover, the court should assess the ability of the prisoner's family to pay for visits.[69] Procedural issues, such as the need for the sentenced person to be transferred to stand as a witness or to be relocated as a protected witness, must also be taken into consideration.[70]

The procedure of the temporary courts and the ICC varies slightly in relation to hearing the views of the proposed transferee. The Presidents of the UN Tribunals and SCSL are not obliged to hear prisoners' views, though they may choose to do so.[71] ICC prisoners, in contrast, have a right to express their views on designation and transfer to the Presidency, either orally or in writing.[72] Moreover, they must be given adequate time and facilities to prepare their submissions.[73] IDF occupants appear to have a hierarchy of preferred states due to perceptions relating to security regimes, conditions and release procedures in potential enforcing states.[74] Whether or not the prisoners' views are heard, international prisoners cannot veto the designation decision.[75] In fact, as is made explicit in the ICTY's agreement with Poland, a prisoner can be transferred without his consent.[76] Even with the stronger right at the ICC to voice an opinion, this will rarely be more than a courtesy, for the final decision to accept a prisoner lies with the state, and the Presidency must ensure the equitable geographical distribution of prisoners among potential enforcing states.[77] However, given that placement in a particular state could aggravate the sentence imposed, the prisoner's view should be an integral part of the decision-making process.[78] Indeed, it appears that the rejection of Rwanda as a state of enforcement by ICTR convicted persons, due to the prisoners' anxiety about conditions and their safety, has seriously impeded transfers to this state.[79]

---

[68] Para. 4(a),(d),(e) ICTY PDD; para. 3(i), (iv), (v) ICTR PDD; para. 4(i), (iv)–(vii) SCSL PDD; Art. 103(3)(d)–(e) ICCSt.
[69] Paras. 4(a), 5 ICTY PDD; paras. 3(i), 4 ICTR PDD; paras. 4(i), 5 SCSL PDD.
[70] Para. 4(b)–(c) ICTY PDD; para. 3(ii)–(iii) ICTR PDD; para. 4(ii)–(iii) SCSL PDD.
[71] Para. 5. ICTY PDD; para. 4 ICTR PDD; para. 5 SCSL PDD; para. B.1(22) MDP, 155.
[72] Art. 103(3)(c) ICCSt; Rule 203 ICC RPE.   [73] Rule 203(3) ICC RPE.
[74] Custodial staff, UNDU, 22–27.08.2007; Falke, ICCDC/UNDU, 04.02.2008; Mwuangulu, Wastelain, Endeley, ICTR, 25.06.2007; Delalić, 20.08.2008.
[75] Mulgrew, "The International Movement of Prisoners", 110–11.
[76] Art. 3(2) ICTY–Poland BEA.
[77] See Art. 103(1)(c), 103(3)(a) ICCSt; Rule 201 ICC RPE.
[78] See Kreß and Sluiter, "Imprisonment", 1775–6.
[79] Mwuangulu, Wastelain, Endeley, ICTR, 25.06.2007; O'Donnell, ICTR, 25.06.2007.

It may not be possible to take a prisoner's transfer preferences into consideration due to security concerns. For example, Mr Taylor declared a preference to be transferred to an African state to serve his sentence should his conviction be upheld on appeal. This is highly unlikely to occur due to the perceived threat to regional security his presence in the region was considered to pose, which resulted in the transfer of his trial to The Hague from Freetown.[80] The SCSL may rely on the UK's undertaking to implement any sentence imposed on him, or seek to secure the cooperation of the other European states that have concluded enforcement agreements with the court.

The courts have therefore, in practice, taken the convicted person's view into account during the informal stages of the designation procedure to avoid approaching states in which enforcement may aggravate the sanction. Security concerns, however, may prevent preferred transfers. Moreover, prisoners cannot rely on plea agreements with the Prosecutor which offer the prospect of enforcement in a particular requested state.[81] Overall, expressed preferences will be difficult to fulfil given that the final decision lies with the requested state and the courts have adopted a policy of equitable distribution of the burden of enforcement.[82]

Once sentencing is final, the President/Presidency, following possible consultations with other judges, the Prosecutor, the Registrar, and the prisoner, designates a state for the convicted person to serve his or her sentence.[83] Although Rule 103(A) ICTR RPE states that the Government of Rwanda must be notified prior to a decision on the place of imprisonment, established practice shows that the ICTR President has jurisdiction to make designation decisions.[84] A formal request is sent to the state to accept responsibility for the enforcement of the individual's sentence.[85] The request is usually forwarded to the Ministry of Foreign Affairs, though it may also be sent to a national court,[86] or Attorney General's Office.[87] The requested state retains the right to refuse to accept custody of a particular prisoner.[88] If this happens, the President/Presidency uses the

---

[80] Ras, SCSL Sub-Office, 05.07.2012.
[81] See *Strugar* (Appeal Decision) IT-01-42.Misc.1, 07.06.2007.
[82] See para. 3(b) ICTY PDD; Art. 103(3)(a) ICCSt; Rule 201 ICC RPE.
[83] Para. 5 ICTY PDD; para. 4 ICTR PDD; para. 5 SCSL PDD; Art. 103(1)(a) ICCSt.
[84] Para. 7 *Ruggiu* (President's Decision) ICTR-97-32-A26, 13.02.2008.
[85] Para. 7 ICTY PDD; para. 6 ICTR PDD; para. 7 SCSL PDD.
[86] See Art. 3(5) ICTY–Slovakia BEA.   [87] See Art. 2(3) ICTY–Portugal BEA.
[88] Para. 9 ICTY PDD; para. 8 ICTR PDD; para. 9 SCSL PDD; Art. 103(1)(c) ICCSt.

same procedure to designate another state.[89] In practice, a formal request will only be made after a positive response to the initial informal request. A public refusal of a formal request is unlikely and there is no record of it happening to date. States have, however, responded negatively to informal requests. These refusals have been attributed to a range of reasons including capacity, the nationality, ethnicity or personal circumstances of the prisoner, security and health-care costs, the location of the prisoner's family and the length of the sentence.[90] One of the most frequent reasons for refusing to enforce a particular sentence is the insistence that the burden of enforcement be spread equally among the list of potential states.

Convicted persons should be transferred to an enforcing state as soon as possible after the enforcing state accepts the request to enforce a particular sentence[91] or the time limit for appeal has elapsed.[92] In practice, there are often delays. Many ICTY prisoners spent more than one[93] or two years[94] in the UNDU following the finalisation of their sentence. Several SCSL convicted persons spent more than a year at the SCSLDF before being transferred to Rwanda.[95] The situation was more serious at the UNDF with prisoners spending one,[96] two,[97] three,[98] four,[99] six[100] and even seven[101] years serving sentences in an international remand centre before being moved to a national prison. More recent transfers from the UNDF to Mali and Benin, however, do appear to have occurred within one year of the finalisation of the sentence.[102]

---

[89] Para. 9 ICTY PDD; para. 8 ICTR PDD; para. 9 SCSL PDD; Rule 205 ICC RPE.
[90] Daw, Wilkinson, UK, 24.05.2006; Schusterschitz, Austria, 05.02.2008; Korhonen, Finland, 02.06.2008; Mäkelä, Finland, 01.07.2008; Koeck, Austria, 13.08.2008; Friman, Sweden, 22.09.2008; Isaksson, Sweden, 07.10.2008.
[91] Rule 206(2) ICC RPE. [92] Rule 103(B) ICTY/ICTR RPE; Rule 103(C) SCSL RPE.
[93] See ICTY cases *Jokić* (IT-01-42); *Žigić* (IT-98-30/1); *D. Nikolić* (IT-02-60/1); *M. Nikolić* (IT-94-2); *Kordić* (IT-95-14/2); *Jokić* (IT-02-60); *Jelisić* (IT-95-10); *Češić* (IT-95-10/1).
[94] See *Krnojelac* (IT-97-25), *Naletilić* (IT-98-34), *Martinović* (IT-98-34), *Galić* (IT-98-29).
[95] See *Brima, Kamara, Kanu* (SCSL-04-16), *Fofana, Kondewa* (SCSL-04-14); SCSL Press Release, "Special Court Prisoners Transferred to Rwanda to Serve Their Sentences", 31.10.2009.
[96] *Simba* (ICTR-01-76); *Serushago* (ICTR-98-39); *Seromba* (ICTR-01-66); *Rugambarara* (ICTR-00-59); *Muhimana* (ICTR-95-1); *Kambanda* (ICTR-97-23); *Imanishimwe* (ICTR-97-36); *Gacumbitsi* (ICTR-01-64).
[97] *Nbindabahizi* (ICTR-01-71); *Bisengimana* (ICTR-00-60); *Barayagwiza* (ICTR-97-19).
[98] *Kamuhanda* (ICTR-99-54); *Semanza* (ICTR-97–20).
[99] *Ntakirutimana* (ICTR-96-17); *Niyitegeka* (ICTR-96-14); *Kajelijeli* (ICTR-98-44).
[100] *Rutaganda* (ICTR-96-3). [101] *Ruggiu* (IT-97-32).
[102] See ICTR Press Release, "More ICTR Convicts Transferred to Mali and Benin to Serve their Sentences", 03.07.2012.

While some delays may be attributed to the need for cooperating states to go through internal and exequatur procedures, the real problem lies with a lack of cooperating and suitable states.[103]

The Registrar makes transfer arrangements and informs the convicted person of the contents of the governing enforcement agreement.[104] Due to security concerns, the transfer is not made public and the prisoner is only told about the location of the state (not the receiving prison) and the date of the transfer very close to the time.[105] It is difficult for IDFs to prepare international prisoners for transfer to enforcing states, as staff and managers have little knowledge about the realities of the numerous potential domestic prison systems. In order to prepare international prisoners for transfers to the UK, a prison governor familiar with the operational realities of the domestic prison system travels to the IDF to meet the prisoner and explain the new regime he will be subject to.[106] This measure is considered to be necessary to facilitate transition from detention in a relatively relaxed regime where the international prisoner is surrounded by peers or persons from his state of origin, to imprisonment in a normal domestic prison.[107] Other enforcing states should consider implementing this measure, or, at the very least, sending information about their prisons systems, in a language the prisoner can understand, to the IDF in advance of transfer.

The prisoner is transported from the IDF to an airport by officers from the court's detention and security sections and usually with the help of the Host State's police or security forces.[108] Enforcing state representatives can take over custody of the prisoner in an airport in the Host State and accompany the prisoner to a reception prison in the enforcing state,[109] or take over custody of the international prisoner when he arrives in the enforcing state.[110] Despite the delays, transfers are not always straightforward procedures. For example, on one occasion, the Austrian Ministry of the Interior forgot to book a plane ticket for an

---

[103] See para. A.2(13) MDP, 153.
[104] See para. B.2(31) MDP, 159; para. 8 ICTY PDD; para. 7 ICTR PDD; para. 8 SCSL PDD; Rule 206(3) ICC RPE.
[105] See para. B.2 (32) MDP, 159.   [106] Wilkinson, UK, 10.10.2012.   [107] Ibid.
[108] See ICTR Press Release, "Georges Omar Ruggiu Transferred to Italy", 28.02.2008; SCSL Press Release, "Special Court Prisoners Transferred to Rwanda to Serve Their Sentences", 31.10.2009.
[109] Schusterschitz, Austria, 05.02.2008; Korhonen, Finland, 02.06.2008; Lönnberg, Sweden 07.10.2008.
[110] Wilkinson, UK, 10.10.2012.

ICTY prisoner. The mistake was only noticed when they were trying to check the prisoner onto a flight at the airport. The Austrian officials managed to buy a ticket for the prisoner and get authorisation from the captain to fly with armed marshals on-board, just in time for the departure of the scheduled commercial flight.[111]

3. Division of responsibility

At present, twenty-four ICTY, thirty-three ICTR and eight SCSL prisoners are serving international sentences of imprisonment in national prison systems. How is responsibility for the implementation of international sentences of imprisonment divided between enforcing states and the international courts? According to the courts' statutes, international imprisonment is governed by the enforcing state's national law, but remains subject to the supervision of the international court.[112] This supervisory role relates to two major components of custodial punishment: responsibility for the welfare of the international prisoner and control over the length of the sentence to be served.

3.1 Welfare of the international prisoner

International sentences of imprisonment must be implemented in accordance with international standards governing conditions of detention and the treatment of prisoners.[113] The preamble of the majority of enforcement agreements refer to UN standards: the 1957 Standard Minimum Rules for the Treatment of Prisoners (UNSMR),[114] the 1988 Body of Principles for the Protection of all Persons under any Form of Detention or Imprisonment (UNBOP)[115] and the 1990 Basic Principles for the Treatment of Prisoners (UNBP).[116] Although these are not legally binding instruments, they represent what states have agreed should be minimum practice. More importantly, the international courts and enforcing states have agreed that these standards should govern the implementation of international sentences of imprisonment.[117] Some

---

[111] Schusterschitz, Austria, 05.02.2008.
[112] Art. 27 ICTYSt; Art. 26 ICTRSt; Art. 22(2) SCSLSt; Art. 106(1)–(2) ICCSt.
[113] See para A.1(8) MDP, 152.
[114] ECOSOC Resolutions 663 C (XXIV) 31.07.1957 and 2067 (LXII) 13.05.1977.
[115] GARes 43/173 (1988). [116] GARes 45/111 (1990).
[117] See paras. 8, 10–11 *Ruggiu* (TC Decision) ICTR-97-32-A26, 13.02.2008.

states refer more generally to the human rights standards that they are obliged to respect under international law[118] or to specific rules such as the European Prison Rules.[119]

The Rome Statute states that its sentences should be implemented in accordance with "widely accepted international treaty standards governing the treatment of prisoners".[120] It has been suggested that the word "treaty" was inserted in Article 106 due to reservations about customary international law.[121] This provision appears to limit the regulation of international sentences to standards found in widely ratified international treaty law. Some regret that "the opportunity has been missed to elevate the [UN] recommendations ... to the level of binding rules through the back door of the ICC enforcement regime".[122] However, as this UN soft law is used as a tool to interpret international treaty law provisions relating to imprisonment,[123] it provides a valid and relevant yardstick for oversight.[124] In practice, enforcing states have referred to these UN Standards in their bilateral enforcement agreements.[125] Moreover, the term 'widely accepted' may not necessarily refer to ratification status and may be interpreted to include lesser ratified treaties such as the UN Convention against Torture and regional conventions and standards. Indeed, the UK refers explicitly to the European Convention on Human Rights in its agreement with the ICC.[126] Moreover, while some ICC enforcing states refer to international treaty standards in their bilateral enforcement agreements,[127] others do not. By omitting the treaty reference, states can implicitly include soft law in the standards governing international punishment. Several states have opted for this approach.[128] This should be viewed as a positive development as the European Prison Rules and case law of the European Court for Human Rights provide more contemporary reflections on prison policy

---

[118] Para. 2(5) ICTY–Germany BEA re Tarčulovski.
[119] Preamble SCSL–Finland BEA. [120] Art. 103(3)(b), 106(1)–(2) ICCSt.
[121] Abathi and Koh, "The Emerging Enforcement Practice of the International Criminal Court", 12.
[122] Kreß and Sluiter, "Imprisonment", 1802.
[123] See para. 5 HRC General Comment 21.
[124] D. Van Zyl Smit, "International Imprisonment" (2005) 54 *International and Comparative Law Quarterly* 357–86 at 376.
[125] Preamble ICC–Denmark/Belgium/Finland/Serbia/Mali BEAs.
[126] Preamble, Art. 5 ICC–UK BEA.
[127] Art. 4(1) ICC–Serbia BEA; Art. 4(2), 6(1) ICC–Denmark BEA.
[128] Art. 4(2), 6(1) ICC–Belgium BEA; Art. 4(1), 6(1) ICC–Finland BEA.

and detailed discussions on what constitutes humane treatment than the older and more general UN Standards.[129]

Unlike the majority of European enforcing states, however, enforcing states in Africa have not yet referred to regional standards relating to imprisonment or guidelines for the improvement of conditions (such as Article 5 of the African Charter on Human and People's Rights, the 1996 Kampala Declaration on Prison Conditions in Africa, the 1999 Arusha Declaration on Good Prison Practice, the 2000 Robben Island Guidelines and the 2002 Ouagadougou Declaration and Plan of Action on accelerating prison reform in Africa) in their enforcement agreements, preferring to cite the UN standards outlined in the model agreements of the courts.[130] Although the UN standards are considered by many to be in need of modernisation, and of little practical value as they are viewed by many states as ceilings rather than minimum standards, they do provide a recognised international standard for implementation and therefore a degree of consistency. Not all enforcing states, however, have prison systems that conform to these standards.

Without actual consistency of standards, references to international standards may serve only to "paper over cracks in the legitimacy of imprisonment".[131] It became apparent that although African states were willing to cooperate, many of the domestic prisons systems on the continent did not comply with the requisite international standards.[132] For instance, there were serious concerns relating to overcrowding and medical care in the prisons of Benin and Mali.[133] Consequently, agreements with African states contain modified provisions relating to the costs of enforcement.

The standard provision states that the courts are responsible for expenses arising from supervision and transporting the prisoner while the enforcing state pays for all other costs relating to the implementation

---

[129] See K. Neale, "The European Prison Rules: Contextual, Philosophical and Practical Aspects" in J. Munice and R. Sparks (eds.), *Imprisonment: European Perspectives* (1991), 207, 211.
[130] See Preamble, Art. 3(3) ICTR–Senegal BEA.
[131] Carlen cited in A. Liebling, *Prisons and Their Moral Performance: A Study of Values, Quality and Prison Life* (2004), 49.
[132] Para. 157 ICTR Third Annual Report; R. Culp, "Enforcement and Monitoring of Sentences in the Modern War Crimes Process: Equal Treatment before the Law?" 07.04.2011, 4.
[133] See F. Viljoen, "The Special Rapporteur on Prisons and Conditions of Detention in Africa: Achievements and Possibilities" (2005) 27(1) *Human Rights Quarterly* 125–71 at 164, 166.

of the sentence.[134] Agreements with the ICC also state that the Court will cover the costs of returning an escapee should no state take responsibility for their return.[135]

The first wave of modified conditions saw the ICTR undertake to help Benin, Mali and Swaziland approach potential donors with a view to securing financial assistance for projects to upgrade facilities that would hold international prisoners to international standards and to cover extraordinary costs entailed in the enforcement of international sentences.[136] The UN General Assembly gave US$250,000 for the upgrade of facilities in Mali.[137] This donation was blocked by the UN Office for Legal Affairs for two years[138] until the UNSC affirmed that it was within the powers of the ICTR to fund the renovation of prisons in states that signed agreements with the UN for the purpose of carrying out prison sentences, if this money was being used to bring facilities up to international minimum standards.[139] Fund-raising has also taken place at a regional level. The EU Parliament, for example, urged Member States to provide funds to ensure that international sentences imposed on African nationals can be enforced in Africa.[140] The ICC has followed this approach in its agreement with Mali, pledging to approach potential donors to mobilise financial assistance for projects that will align facilities housing international prisoners to international standards.[141] While the ICC will endeavour to secure the assistance required by enforcing states, an official from the Enforcement Unit has stated that the Court has neither the mandate nor the budget to act as a development agency.[142]

The second wave of modified conditions went beyond assistance with fund-raising to include explicit commitments from both the ICTR and

---

[134] See Art. 11 ICTR–Sweden BEA; Art. 11 SCSL–UK BEA; Art. 17(1) ICC–UK BEA; Rule 208 ICC RPE.
[135] Art. 18(3) ICC–Belgium BEA; Art. 19(3) ICC–Denmark BEA; Art. 11(3) ICC–Mali BEA.
[136] See Art. 11(2)–(4) ICTR–Benin/Mali/Swaziland BEAs; para. 158 ICTR Third Annual Report; para. 121 ICTR Fourth Annual Report.
[137] Para. 134 ICTR Sixth Annual Report.
[138] See Amoussago's Comments in Report of the Proceedings of the Colloquium of Prosecutors of the International Criminal Tribunals on The Challenges of International Criminal Justice, 2004, 22.
[139] Statement by the President of the Security Council on the ICTR, S/PRST/2003/18, 27.10.2003. See also GARes 57/289 (2003).
[140] See European Parliament Resolution on the Special Court for Sierra Leone B6-0244/2009.
[141] Art. 11(4) ICC–Mali BEA.   [142] Abathi, ICC, 05.07.2012.

SCSL to provide Rwanda with funding for not only renovations but also upkeep and maintenance costs relating to meals, communications, incidentals, sanitation and medical care.[143] Under the new cost division, the enforcing state remains liable for the safety and security of the facility, the prison warders' remuneration and utilities.[144] In return for this assistance and substantial investment, the international courts can ensure that international prisoners are placed in a pre-identified facility that provides international standards of imprisonment.[145] For instance, all SCSL prisoners have been transferred to the newly-built, Dutch funded, Mpanga prison in Rwanda.[146] This model was also adopted in the ICTR's agreement with Senegal. The ICTR pays for the individual's transfer, repatriation and return of the body in the event of death,[147] maintenance costs of the convicted person (including food, phone calls, incidental and sundry medical costs) and the refurbishment of a mutually designated block,[148] while Senegal pays for other costs including the protection and security of the block, the salaries of the prison staff and basic services.[149] This agreement, uniquely, adds a further stipulation. It explicitly states that the Tribunal is responsible for paying the costs related to the "inspection, supervision and evaluation of the sentence enforcement".[150]

These provisions result in real costs. The SCSL provides the Rwandan Government with US$802 per month to meet the agreed additional costs.[151] In 2002, it was projected that it would cost the ICTR approximately US$2,500 to transfer international prisoners to enforcing states, US$6,000 to relocate prisoners whose continued imprisonment in a particular state had become impossible, over US$15,000 to inspect conditions, US$14,500 to pay for the upkeep costs per prisoner, US$2,800 to repatriate the body of a prisoner who had died in the enforcing state and

---

[143] Art. 11(1)(a)(iii)–(iv) ICTR–Rwanda BEA; Art. 11(1)(c) SCSL–Rwanda BEA.
[144] Art. 11(1)(b)(i)–(ii) ICTR-Rwanda BEA; Art. 11(2)(a)–(b) SCSL–Rwanda BEA.
[145] See Art. 3(1) ICTR–Rwanda BEA; Arts. 3(1), 11(2)(a) SCSL–Rwanda BEA; para. 83 ICTR Sixth Annual Report.
[146] See SCSL Ninth Annual Report, 24; SCSL Press Release, "Special Court Concludes Enforcement Agreement with Rwanda", 20.03.2009; SCSL Press Release, "Special Court Prisoners Transferred to Rwanda to Serve Their Sentences", 31.10.2009.
[147] Art. 11(1)(a),(b) and (e) ICTR–Senegal BEA.
[148] Art. 11(1)(c) ICTR–Senegal BEA.   [149] Art. 11(2) ICTR–Senegal BEA.
[150] Art. 11(1)(d) ICTR–Senegal BEA.
[151] See footnote 72, para. 56 *Uwinkindi* (Referral Decision) ICTR-2001-75-R11*bis*, 28.06.2011.

the same cost to transfer the prisoner upon completion of sentence.[152] In 2009, the annual upkeep cost per prisoner in an enforcing state was over US$14,500.[153]

Efforts to raise conditions in African prisons housing international prisoners, though intended to ensure equal treatment among international prisoners, can result in double standards emerging between international and national prisoners. For instance, the Mpanga facility in Rwanda, a country with a prison system with serious overcrowding and poor conditions, was described by a former SCSL Registrar as "beyond international standards".[154] This problem is particularly noticeable when international prisoners are housed in special quarters within an overcrowded national prison with deplorable conditions, and they receive the same privileges that they received in IDFs. For example, ICTR prisoners serving in Mali are housed in accommodation and receive medical treatment, food and other privileges that national prisoners "can only dream of".[155] This can create both a financial and security burden on the enforcing state. These high standards can also have a negative impact on victims living in poverty[156] or suffering from health problems without the same level of medical care.[157]

Despite these political difficulties, the international community and developed enforcing states cannot reduce conditions or breach their international obligations to equalise treatment with prisoners in developing states and remain credible. Consequently, standards must be raised in the facilities in developing countries. Rather than view the result as the creation of double standards, it should be viewed as providing a catalyst for penal reform.[158] Different standards may however cause difficulties for the enforcement of ICC sentences of imprisonment, as the Rome Statute states that "in no case shall such conditions be more or less favourable than those available to prisoners convicted of similar offences in the State of enforcement".[159]

---

[152] Para. 180 Residual Mechanism Report.
[153] Paras. 182, 251 Residual Mechanism Report.
[154] SCSL Press Release, "Special Court Concludes Enforcement Agreement with Rwanda", 20.03.2009.
[155] See J. Baxter, "War Criminals Stretch Mali's Hospitality", 21.03.2002.
[156] See SCSL Ninth Annual Report 24.
[157] Ngoga, Crane's Comments in Report of the Proceedings of the Colloquium of Prosecutors of the International Criminal Tribunals on The Challenges of International Criminal Justice 2004, 23.
[158] Diop, ICTR, 27.06.2007.   [159] Art. 106(2) ICCSt.

The need to obtain resources to upgrade facilities and to contribute to the cost of enforcement is not a problem unique to Africa. Less developed countries in Europe have been reluctant to enforce ICTY sentences due to the costs involved.[160] Cost considerations may also result in limited forms of cooperation. For instance, Slovakia has explicitly stated that an unexpected rise in the costs associated with the enforcement of ICTY sentences may make continued enforcement impossible and therefore lead to international prisoners being transferred to other states.[161]

Whether or not financial assistance is provided, the international courts monitor conditions in enforcing states to ensure international standards are respected.[162] All enforcing states agree to allow a designated inspection body to visit international prisoners at any time and on a periodic basis, at a frequency determined by the inspecting body.[163] The vast majority of enforcing states have designated the International Committee of the Red Cross (ICRC) to monitor their implementation of international sentences of imprisonment.[164] The ICRC was selected due to its experience in the field and its reputation as an objective and neutral body. Some states, however, objected to the appointment of the ICRC,[165] and opted instead to use the Council of Europe's Committee for the Prevention of Torture (CPT).[166] The UK preferred to work with the CPT, as it had previous experience of overseeing peace-time prison conditions and monitoring would be based on existing agreements and standards.[167] For the same reasons, Klip feels that the CPT is a more suitable monitoring mechanism than the ICRC.[168] While the two bodies have a slightly different focus and operating procedures, these differences are reduced in practice as the ICRC refers to European and CPT standards when conducting visits in Europe.[169] The designation of a

[160] See para. A.1(9) MDP, 152.　[161] Art. 12 ICTY–Slovakia BEA.
[162] Rule 104 ICTY/ICTR RPE.
[163] See Art. 7 ICTY–Slovakia BEA; Art. 7 SCSL–Finland BEA.
[164] Denmark, Austria, Finland, France, Italy, Norway, Belgium, Estonia, Poland, Slovakia, Sweden, Serbia, Benin, Mali, Swaziland and Rwanda. See Agreement between the ICC and the ICRC on Visits to Persons Deprived of Liberty Pursuant to the Jurisdiction of the ICC, ICC-PRES/02-01-06, 13.04.06 (ICC–ICRC Agreement).
[165] Para. C.1(35) MDP, 159.
[166] Albania, Portugal, Ukraine, UK (ICTY, SCSL, ICC) and ICTY–Germany BEA re Galić. See also Letter from the Registrar of the ICTY to the President of the CPT and the Secretary General of the Council of Europe, 07.11.2000 (ICTY–CPT Agreement).
[167] Daw and Wilkinson, UK, 24.05.2006.
[168] Klip, "Enforcement of Sanctions Imposed by the International Criminal Tribunals for Rwanda and the Former Yugoslavia", 150–1.
[169] Chetwynd, CPT, 08.06.2007.

particular inspection body should not be seen as limiting oversight to the methods of one group but rather as an explicit insurance policy of humanitarian oversight from independent and specialised bodies. Moreover, international prisoners in states that nominate the ICRC will also have the benefit of access to other national and international inspection bodies. For instance, prisoners held in Europe may be visited by the CPT and prisoners in Africa may be visited by the Special Rapporteur on Prisons and Conditions of Detention (SRP).[170] For overseeing international imprisonment, the ICRC may be preferable to the SRP, as the SRP's methodology has been criticised for failing to link observations to relevant standards, making it difficult to track national progress and compare different prison systems.[171] Further, despite the fact that both Benin and Mali have been visited twice by the SRP, an invitation is required from the government of the country in question.[172]

Where the consensual nature of the enforcement system has created problems is in cases where the state has opted to nominate an oversight body comprised of ICTY and national officials. Both Spain[173] and Germany[174] designated special parity commissions to visit ICTY prisoners held on their territory. The ICTY has noted that these arrangements are "far from ideal"[175] and is concerned that their establishment will be viewed as precedent for other potential enforcing states to insist on less independent forms of oversight.[176] Indeed, complaints received by the ICTY President from prisoners serving in these states in relation to both the conditions of detention and their treatment by ICTY officials on these commissions has resulted in the President having to request the relevant government to allow an independent monitoring body to investigate the alleged violations of the prisoner's rights.[177] The lack of independent monitoring can affect not only prisoners' rights[178] but it

---

[170] Established in 1996 by the African Commission on Human and Peoples' Rights to examine the situation of persons deprived of their liberty within the territories of State Parties to the African Charter on Human and Peoples' Rights (ACHPR).
[171] See R. Murray, "The African Commission's Approach to Prisons" in J. Sarkin (ed.), *Human Rights in African Prisons* (2008), 204–23 at 207–8.
[172] See Viljoen, "The Rapporteur on Prisons and Conditions of Detention in Africa", 137, 139 and 164.
[173] Art. 4(1) ICTY–Spain BEA. The commission was comprised of four officials representing the Spanish prison system, the Spanish judiciary, the UNDU and the ICTY Registry. Vicente, ICTY, 16.02.2007.
[174] See para. 5(1) ICTY–Germany BEAs re Tadić/Kunarać/Galić.
[175] Para. C.1(37) MDP, 160.   [176] Fofana, ICTY, 29.08.2007.
[177] Para. C.1(37) MDP, 160.   [178] Para. 54 CPT Second General Report.

may also damage public confidence in the international court's credibility.[179] The problem seemed to have been resolved in Germany. A new provision was inserted in the third agreement with the ICTY, which enables the CPT to inspect conditions of detention and the treatment of this particular prisoner and make a report on findings to the ICTY President.[180] Although the CPT would have had access to international prisoners in both states, this new provision formalises the oversight of international prisoners and ensures that the court receives independent feedback. Surprisingly, the most recent agreement with Germany reverts back to the system of oversight by ICTY representatives.[181] The ICTY has stated that this means "persons under the authority of the ICTY".[182] This provision is perhaps broader than it would first appear and may simply be recognition of the right of the Tribunal to send officials. Indeed, unlike previous agreements, this agreement also acknowledges the right of the ICRC to inspect the conditions of detention[183] in accordance with the terms of the 1997 Exchange of Letters between the ICTY and ICRC.[184] Senegal's agreement with the ICTR also adopts this dual inspection approach.[185]

The German agreements demonstrate the difficulties with a consensual approach to oversight. Not only are different groups responsible for overseeing the punishment of persons convicted by the same court, different oversight bodies are responsible for overseeing the punishment of persons convicted by the same court housed in the same state. The enforcing state's choice of inspection body also has financial consequences for the international courts. Whereas the ICRC pledges to cover the costs of its inspections as a donation,[186] the international courts must bear all reasonable costs and expenses incurred by the CPT[187] and the parity commissions.[188]

Both the ICRC and CPT provide the international court with a report on their findings and any recommendations for change.[189] These reports are not available to the public.[190] This is in line with the ICRC's practice

---

[179] Para. C.1(37) MDP, 160.   [180] Para. 5(2) ICTY–Germany BEA re Galić.
[181] Para. 5(1) ICTY–Germany BEA re Tarčulovski.
[182] Letter from the Ambassador of the Federal Republic of Germany to the Registrar of the ICTY, 16.06.2011.
[183] Para. 5(2) ICTY–Germany BEA re Tarčulovski.
[184] Letter from the Ambassador of the Federal Republic of Germany to the Registrar of the ICTY re Tarčulovski, 16.06.2011.
[185] Art. 6(1) ICTR–Senegal BEA.
[186] Para. 7 Letter from the ICTY President to the ICRC President.
[187] Para. F ICTY–CPT Agreement.   [188] Vicente, ICTY, 16.02.2007.
[189] See Art. 15(2)–(3) ICC–ICRC Agreement; paras. b(1), d(1) ICTY–CPT Agreement.
[190] See Art. 6(1) most ICTY/ICTR BEAs; Art. 15(3) ICC–ICRC Agreement.

of confidentiality (although this is conditional on the quality and impact of dialogue and in cases of serious and repeated abuse, the ICRC reserves the right to make public condemnations[191]). The CPT also operates under a guarantee of confidentiality, with reports only published with the relevant state's permission.[192]

Both the inspection bodies and the international courts can follow up concerns with states.[193] However, the recommendations made by the inspection bodies are not binding on enforcing states. The President/Presidency of the court cannot make a declaration of a violation or demand changes to the national regime. Instead, the court enters into dialogue with the state about the findings of the report, requests information from the state on any changes that have been implemented in light of the recommendations and encourages changes to be made.[194]

In addition to the information received from independent oversight mechanisms, the President/Presidency also monitors enforcement through correspondence from the prisoners themselves, their families, national authorities and other sources.[195] The ICC Presidency may request information from the enforcing state and send a delegated judge or court official to meet with the international prisoner in the enforcing state.[196] International prisoners may write confidentially to the designated monitoring mechanism and the international court that convicted them to make a complaint or request a visit.[197] For example,

---

[191] See ICRC, "Action by the ICRC in the Event of Violations of IHL or of other Fundamental Rules Protecting Persons in Situations of Violence" (2005) 87(858) *International Review of the Red Cross*, 395–8; D. Stillhart, "Confidentiality: Key to the ICRC's Work but not Unconditional", 20.09.2010.

[192] See para. E, ICTY–CPT Agreement; Art. 6(1) ICC–UK BEA; J. Murdoch, "The Work of the Council of Europe's Torture Committee" (1994) 5 *European Journal of International Law* 220–48 at 221, 223–4.

[193] Chetwynd, CPT, 08.06.2007; Mochochoko, ICC, 30.08.2007.

[194] See Art. 6(2) most BEAs except for Art. 4(3) ICTY–Spain BEA; Art. 7(2) ICTY–Slovakia BEA; Art. 5(2) ICTY–Germany BEAs re Tadić/Kunarac/Galić; Art. 7(2) SCSL–Finland BEA; Art. 7(2) ICC–Austria BEA; para. C.1(36) MDP, 160.

[195] See para. C.1(36) MDP, 160; Rules 211(1)(b), 216 ICC RPE; Arts. 6(3), 16(3) ICC–UK BEA; Art. 17(3) ICC–Austria BEA.

[196] Rules 211(a), (c) ICC RPE; Art. 5 ICC–Austria BEA; Art. 6(2) ICC–Belgium BEA; Art. 5 ICC–Finland/Serbia BEAs; Art. 4(1)(a) ICC–Mali BEA; Art. 5(b) ICC–Denmark BEA.

[197] See Art. 106(3) ICCSt; Rule 211(1)(a) ICC RPE; Art. 7 ICC–UK BEA; Art. 8 ICC–Austria/Finland BEAs; Art. 5(1) ICC–Belgium BEA; Art. 8(1)–(2) ICC–Serbia/Denmark BEAs; Art. 4(3) ICC–Mali BEA. Daw and Wilkinson, UK, 24.05.2006; Chetwynd, CPT, 08.06.2007; Fofana, ICTY, 29.08.2007; Hurwitz, ICTY, 10.07.2008; Matinpuro, Finland, 25.06.2008; Friman, Sweden, 22.09.2008.

the SCSL Registrar and Deputy Registrar meet with the SCSL prisoners housed in Rwanda to discuss complaints about treatment and their dissatisfaction with new phone and supply assessment procedures.[198] In addition, the SCSL paid for a delegation comprised of representatives from the Government of Sierra Leone, the Human Rights Commission of Sierra Leone and Prison Watch Sierra Leone to visit Mpanga Prison to meet the prisoners and staff to discuss allegations of mistreatment reported in the Sierra Leonean press.[199] These meetings and the inspection were recorded and broadcasted on television in Sierra Leone, which resulted in the Special Court's Interactive Forum submitting complaints that the conditions of imprisonment provided for SCSL prisoners in Rwanda were too good, particularly in light of the widespread poverty in Sierra Leone.[200]

If the diplomatic follow-up to a complaint or request for change fails to secure the necessary conditions for international imprisonment, the international court has the power to terminate enforcement in a particular state and transfer the prisoner elsewhere.[201] This is the only tool at the disposal of the international courts to protect prisoners from unacceptable conditions, attacks or ill-treatment. For the temporary courts, this is likely to involve transferring the prisoner to another state rather than back to the international court due to their pending closure. This will be problematic given the problems associated with securing state cooperation and the foreseeable reluctance of states to accept a person who has created difficulties in the first state of enforcement. The ICC may transfer such prisoners to the residual facility provided by the Dutch Government, although this will only be available as a last resort and for a short-term period only.[202] Practice has shown that enforcing states are normally open to discussion and willing to implement recommendations made in relation to international sentences of imprisonment.[203] Some situations, for example, where the international prisoner's safety is at risk due to threats from national prisoners, may necessitate transfers to another country.

---

[198] Paras. 78, 83 *Munyagishari* (Referral Decision) ICTR-2005-89-R11*bis*, 06.06.2012.
[199] See SCSL Ninth Annual Report, 24.   [200] Ibid.
[201] See Art. 9(2) ICTY/ICTR BEAs (except Art. 10(2) ICTY–Slovakia BEA; Art. 8(2) ICTY–Germany BEAs re Tadić/Kunarac/Galić); Art. 9(2) SCSL–UK/Sweden/Rwanda BEAs; Art. 10(2) SCSL–Finland BEA; Art. 13(1)–(2) ICC–Austria/Finland/Serbia BEAs; Art. 14(1)–(2) ICC–Belgium/Denmark BEAs; Art. 9 ICC–Mali BEA; Art. 12 ICC–UK BEA; Art. 104 ICCSt; Rules 209–10 ICC RPE.
[202] Art. 103(4) ICCSt; Art. 50(2) ICC HQA. Blom, Moonen, The Netherlands, 24.08.2007.
[203] Siller, ICTY, 07.06.2007; Chetwynd, CPT, 08.06.2007.

3.2 Length of the term of imprisonment

International custodial sanctions are enforced by states who agree to be bound by the duration of international sentences.[204] While enforcing states may make decisions relating to temporary release for work or leisure purposes,[205] decisions relating to permanent release remain within the mandate of the international courts. The legal framework governing release can be found in provisions of the courts' statutes, rules and bilateral enforcement agreements. The UN Tribunals' Presidents rely on a Practice Direction on pardon and commutation of sentence, although only the ICTY's has been published. This section outlines and analyses the procedures for determining eligibility for release, the appropriateness of release and actual release.

3.2.1 Eligibility for commutation of sentence and pardon

For prisoners of the temporary courts, eligibility for commutation of sentence or pardon is determined by the domestic law of enforcing states. When international prisoners become eligible under domestic law, the enforcing state notifies the international court.[206] Enforcing states may forward national judicial orders stating that the international prisoner is eligible for release under domestic law.[207] As the determination of eligibility for commutation is an administrative duty charged to enforcing states, attempts by ICTY sentencing chambers to set minimum terms that must be served before a prisoner can be considered for release have been held to be *ultra vires*.[208]

In practice, this notification system has not always followed the rules. Due to delay[209] or the failure of enforcing states to notify the courts, convicted persons or their counsel have notified the court directly of their eligibility for release when their situation was comparable to other

---

[204] Art. 3(1) ICTY/ICTR/SCSL BEAs (except Art. 2(1) ICTY–Germany BEAs re Tadić/Kunarac/Galić), Art. 4(1) ICC BEAs; Art. 105(1), 110(1)–(2) ICCSt.

[205] See Art. 4(5) ICC–UK BEA; Art. 6(3) ICC–Austria BEA. Enforcing states often consult with the international courts before granting such measures. Wilkinson, UK, 10.10.2012.

[206] Art. 28 ICTYSt; Rule 123 ICTY RPE; para. 1 ICTY PDER; Art. 8(1) ICTY BEAs (except Art. 9(1) ICTY–Slovakia BEA; Art. 2(3), 7(1) ICTY–Germany BEAs re Tadić/Kunarac/Galić); Art. 7(1)(d) ICTY–UK BEA; Art. 27 ICTRSt; Rule 124 ICTR RPE; Art. 8(1) ICTR BEAs; Art. 23 SCSLSt; Rule 123 SCSL RPE; Art. 8(1) SCSL BEAs (see also Art. 7(1)(d) SCSL–UK BEA; Art. 9(1) SCSL–Finland BEA).

[207] Para. 3 *Stakić* (President's Decision) IT-97-24-ES, 15.07.2011; paras. 1–2 *Rajić* (President's Decision) IT-95-12-ES, 22.08.2011.

[208] See paras. 392–3 *Stakić* (Appeal Judgment) IT-97-24-A, 22.03.2006.

[209] See para. 1 *Banović* (President's Decision) IT-02-65/1-ES, 03.09.2008.

ICTY prisoners.[210] Although the Rules do not recognise the right of a convicted person to petition the court directly for release, Presidents have considered and granted such applications.[211] The ICTY Practice Direction on Early Release was therefore revised to reflect this practice and now contains a provision stating that convicted persons may petition the President directly for pardon, commutation of sentence or early release if he believes he is eligible and that the procedures outlined in the Practice Direction apply *mutatis mutandis* to such applications.[212] Upon receipt of a direct petition, the Tribunal asks the enforcing state for its opinion as to the eligibility of the individual for pardon, commutation of sentence or early release according to its domestic law.[213]

A system that places the trigger for release eligibility with enforcing states lacks certainty and creates the potential for discrimination due to the variation between the different domestic laws.[214] In a bid to equalise the treatment of prisoners, ICTY Presidents adopted a rule of thumb whereby prisoners become eligible for release when they have served two thirds of their sentence.[215] The two-thirds point was adopted as this was considered to reflect the domestic law of the majority of enforcing states.[216] However, this is not the case for all enforcing states. Prisoners in Belgium may be eligible for release after serving one-third of their sentence,[217] while prisoners in the UK,[218] Austria[219] and France[220] may be eligible at the half-way point of the sentence. In Spain, prisoners must typically serve three-quarters of their sentence before they are eligible for release.[221] The

---

[210] See paras. 1, 4 *Josipović* (President's Decision) IT-95-16-ES, 30.01.2006; para. 3 *Tadić* (President's Decision) IT-94-1-ES, 17.07.2008; para. 10 *Banović* (President's Decision) IT-02-65/1-ES, 03.09.2008; para. 1 *Šantić* (President's Decision) IT-95-16-ES, 16.02.2009; para. 1 *Krnojelac* (President's Decision) IT-97-25-ES, 09.07.2009; ICTY Press Release, "Stevan Todorovic Case: President of the Tribunal Grants Request for Commutation of Sentence", 29.06.2005; para. D.2(41) MDP, 161.
[211] See paras. D.2(42–3) MDP, 161; para. 1 *Krnojelac* (President's Decision) IT-97–25-ES, 09.07.2009.
[212] Para. 2 ICTY PDER.   [213] Para. 2(b) ICTY PDER.
[214] Para. D.4.4(52) MDP, 163.
[215] See para. 11 *Vuković* (President's Decision) IT-96-23 & 23/1-ES, 11.03.2008.
[216] See para. D.4.4 (52) MDP, 162.
[217] Para. 2 *Zelenović* (President's Decision) IT-96-23/2-ES, 10.06.2010; paras. 1–2 *Zelenović* (President's Decision) IT-96-23/2-ES, 21.10.2011.
[218] See para. 1 *Krajišnik* (President's Decision) IT-00-39-ES, 26.07.2010.
[219] Para. 2 *Kordić* (President's Decision) IT-95-14/2-ES, 13.05.2010.
[220] Para. 2 *Radić* (President's Decision) IT-98-30/1-ES, 23.04.2010.
[221] J. L. De la Cuesta and I. Blanco, "Spain" in D. Van Zyl Smit and F. Dunkel (eds.), *Imprisonment Today and Tomorrow: International Perspectives on Prisoners Rights and Prison Conditions*, 2nd edn (2001), 624.

Spanish penal code only permits early release at the two-thirds stage in exceptional circumstances: where the prisoner had progressed through three grades of prisoner status, behaved well and displayed a high likelihood of successful reintegration into society.[222] In practice, Spain has applied these provisions flexibly, facilitating the release of ICTY prisoners at the two-thirds point.

In accordance with the rules, enforcing states notify the relevant court when an international prisoner is eligible for release under national law. This process appears to be pointless, given the rule of thumb adopted by the court. The ICTY has rejected arguments that the Tribunal is bound by national law on eligibility where it entitles prisoners to release before the two-thirds point, and that the two-thirds rule of thumb is unlawful, on the basis of the statutory stipulation that enforcement is "subject to the supervision" of the Tribunal (Article 27) and the rule that states that the President must take the treatment of similarly situated prisoners into account (Rule 125).[223] The "two-thirds practice has [therefore] been applied consistently ... notwithstanding the domestic law in enforcement states".[224]

The two-thirds rule of thumb has been retained even with the recognition that national remission or sentence advancement systems may be compatible with the terms of the bilateral enforcement agreements. To ensure the equal treatment of international prisoners, however, the President still decides if the proposed remission is appropriate and, even then, it is only provisionally accepted for consideration at the two-thirds point.[225]

While it is called a rule of thumb, ICTY prisoners will be considered for release "only after"[226] or when "at least"[227] two-thirds of the sentence has been served. The two-thirds point marks eligibility for consideration for release, however, and not an entitlement to release.[228] While the

---

[222] See ICTY Press Release, "Stevan Todorovic Case: President of the Tribunal Grants Request for Commutation of Sentence", 29.06.2005; para. 4 *Josipović* (President's Decision) IT-95-16-ES, 30.01.2006; para. 7 *Šantić* (President's Decision) IT-95-16-ES, 16.02.2009.
[223] Paras. 2, 12–15 *Radić* (President's Decision) IT-98-30/1-ES, 23.04.2010.
[224] Para. 20 *Simić* (President's Decision) IT-95-9-ES, 15.02.2011.
[225] Paras. 1–2, 13–16 *Bala* (President's Decision) IT-03-66-ES, 15.10.2010; paras. 19–25, 38 *Stakić* (President's Decision) IT-97-24-ES, 15.07.2011; paras. 11, 14 *Rajić* (President's Decision) IT-95-12-ES, 31.01.2011.
[226] Para. 13 *Zelenović* (President's Decision) IT-96-23/2-ES, 10.06.2010.
[227] Para. 14 *Krajišnik* (President's Decision) IT-00-39-ES, 26.07.2010.
[228] Para. 20 *Simić* (President's Decision) IT-95-9-ES, 15.02.2011.

majority of applicants are granted release at the two-thirds point, some applications have been rejected. When the rule has been applied in a nearly automatic fashion in the vast majority of cases, the rejection of an application for release at the two-thirds point creates frustration and disappointment for prisoners.[229] The lack of certainty and notice in relation to release decisions can also make it difficult for enforcing states to adequately prepare international prisoners for release.[230]

Moreover, the ICTY rule of thumb does not ensure equal treatment for prisoners serving life sentences.[231] This oversight is likely to create problems, particularly as the various enforcing states have different constitutional and legal requirements for considering lifers for parole which may conflict with the "primacy of the international judgment".[232] Under German Law, for example, an international prisoner sentenced to life imprisonment will become eligible for consideration for release under national law before a person convicted to a term over twenty-three years.[233] The ICTY Practice Direction should be amended to include guidance on this issue.

In contrast, neither the SCSL nor ICTR have pre-determined points for release eligibility. This may be problematic as the release triggers for enforcing states may differ. Prior to 2011, only one ICTR convicted person, Mr. Ruggiu, had been released early from an enforcing state. While he was released three months short of his twelve-year sentence,[234] this was due to remission by the Italian authorities rather than early release granted by the ICTR. This mirrored the ICTR practice of releasing prisoners from enforcing states and the UNDF only after they had completed their sentences in full.[235] Until October 2011, the Tribunal rejected all applications for release, stating that the factors submitted had already been considered in mitigation, that the gravity of the crimes was too high, the term remaining to be served did not militate in favour of

---

[229] Blagojević, Trondheim Prison, 28.06.2012.   [230] Wilkinson, UK, 10.10.2012.
[231] See Van Zyl Smit, "International Imprisonment", 371.
[232] K. Hoffmann, "Some Remarks on the Enforcement of International Sentences in the Light of Galić case at the ICTY" (2011) ZIS 838–42 at 839.
[233] *Ibid.* at 841.
[234] He was transferred from Kenya to the UNDF on 23 July 1997 and released from prison in Italy on 21 April 2009.
[235] See ICTR Press Release, "Elizaphan Ntakirutimana Released After Serving Sentence", 06.12.2008; ICTR Press Release, "Vincent Rutaganira Released After Completing his Sentence", 03.03.2008; ICTR Press Release, "More ICTR Convicts Transferred to Mali and Benin to Serve their Sentences", 03.07.2012.

release etc.[236] Mr Bagaragaza was the first ICTR prisoner to be granted early release after serving three-quarters of his sentence.[237] While the President was keen to note that this decision was "not intended to create a precedent for early release at three quarters" and that "future decisions will continue to be determined on a case-by-case basis,"[238] Mr Rugambarara was also granted early release in February 2012 at the three-quarters point.[239] It is significant to note that in both cases, their guilty pleas and significant cooperation with the Prosecutor were strong positive factors in deliberations.[240] Release at the three-quarters point is therefore unlikely to be used as a general rule of thumb.

To avoid the potential for disparity of treatment that arises from reliance on national triggers for release eligibility, and the lack of certainty for persons serving indeterminate sentences, the ICC has introduced a statutory trigger. After prisoners have served two thirds of a determinate sentence or twenty-five years of a life sentence, the Court must review the sentence to determine whether it should be reduced.[241] During the drafting of the Rome Statute, earlier provisions on eligibility for release set the threshold at twenty years.[242] This was altered to twenty-five years, creating a distinction between prisoners serving determinate and indeterminate sentences. The longest determinate sentence that can be imposed is thirty years.[243] Accordingly, prisoners serving the longest determinate sentences will become eligible for a sentence review after twenty years, whereas prisoners serving life sentences will only become eligible after twenty-five years. This distinction reflects the statutory requirement that life sentences must be justified by the extreme gravity of the crime and the individual circumstances of the convicted person.[244] The statutory trigger introduces transparency, predictability and consistency. Release eligibility for ICC prisoners may alter if the Presidency uses Rule 146(5) to increase the length of the sentence. The Presidency may, but is under no obligation to, consult with the enforcing state before doing so.[245]

---

[236] See D. Scalia, "Long-term Sentences in International Criminal Law: Do They Meet the Standards Set out by the European Court of Human Rights" (2011) 9(3) *Journal of International Criminal Justice* 669–87 at 676.
[237] Para. 8 *Bagaragaza* (President's Decision) ICTR-05-86-S, 24.10.2011.
[238] Para. 17 *ibid*.
[239] Para. 17 *Rugambarara* (President's Decision) ICTR-00-59, 08.02.2012.
[240] Paras. 10, 13 *ibid*. [241] Art. 110(3) ICCSt.
[242] See draft Art. 100(1)(a) [option 2] Draft Statute for the ICC in Report of the Preparatory Committee on the Establishment of an International Criminal Court, 1998, 156.
[243] See Art. 77(1)(a) ICCSt. [244] See Art. 77(1)(b) ICCSt.
[245] Art. 6(3) ICC–Mali BEA; Art. 9(4) ICC–Belgium BEA; Art. 17(4) ICC–Finland/Serbia BEAs.

One issue that might prove contentious for the ICC is the start date of the sentence. The ICC Statute states that any time spent in detention in accordance with an order of the Court must be deducted from a sentence of imprisonment.[246] The Court may, however, choose to deduct "any time otherwise spent in detention in connection with conduct underlying the crime".[247] In its first sentencing judgment, however, the Court refused to accept that the three-year period spent in detention and under house arrest in the arresting state qualified as detention for conduct underlying the crime[248] and consequently held that the sentence would run from the date of the convicted person's surrender and transfer to The Hague.[249] Given the Court's reliance on states to arrest individuals, there should be clear guidelines as to what can be considered detention in connection with the conduct underlying the crime, and what factors should influence the Court's decision to take this time into account.

In relation to pardon, its availability for international prisoners also varies between states. In Sweden, for example, the executive prerogative of pardon was considered to be available for international prisoners but an application for such pardon has been refused.[250] The Royal Prerogative of Pardon is only considered to apply to sentences imposed by courts in the UK and therefore not to international sentences.[251] In either case, Klip feels that it is doubtful if there will be impassioned calls for the pardon of international criminals in enforcing states.[252] When the Rome Statute was being drafted, states questioned the appropriateness of the role of pardon in the international criminal justice process, as powers of revision and reduction of sentence seemed sufficient to address the interests of convicted persons.[253] Accordingly, the Rome Statute provides convicted persons with the option to apply for a revision of conviction or sentence[254] or a review concerning the reduction of the sentence,[255] but not pardon. Despite the fact that the "ICC statute does

---

[246] Art. 78(2) ICCSt.   [247] Ibid.
[248] Paras. 101–2 *Lubanga* (Sentence) ICC-01/04-01/06, 10.07.2012.
[249] Paras. 104, 108 *ibid.*
[250] Swedish Ministry of Justice, "Request for Pardoning Mrs Biljana Plasvic has been Rejected", 24.06.2007.
[251] Daw and Wilkinson, UK, 24.05.2006.
[252] Klip, "Enforcement of Sanctions Imposed by the International Criminal Tribunals for Rwanda and the Former Yugoslavia" 161.
[253] Para. 361 Vol. I Report of the Preparatory Committee on the Establishment of an International Criminal Court 1996.
[254] Art. 84 ICCSt.   [255] Art. 110 ICCSt.

not make any provision for the granting of pardon",[256] the bilateral enforcement agreement with Denmark refers to the possibility of pardon eligibility under national law.[257] This agreement, which appears to be the only agreement to do so to date, is discussed in more detail below.[258]

3.2.2 Enforcing states and international release decisions

As eligibility for early release under the legal frameworks of the temporary international courts is determined by the law of enforcing states, and as enforcing institutions in enforcing states implement international sentences of imprisonment, they are involved in the release process. What is not clear is the degree of involvement that enforcing states or prisons have or should have in this process. While national law governs the detention regime, to what extent does it govern or influence the release decision-making procedure?[259] Does it relate only to eligibility for release and the provision of information relevant to making such a decision or should enforcing institutions or states forward recommendations as to whether or not an individual should be released? Eligibility under national law seems irrelevant where an international court relies on a rule of thumb in practice. Even determining when a prisoner is eligible for release under national law can be problematic.[260] Should the prison, national prison system or Ministry of Justice make a recommendation that the President or Review Panel can approve or reject, or should they simply provide a report on a number of pre-determined factors? Some release jurisprudence from the ICTY reveals that some officials, prisons, local or central authorities do make explicit recommendations for release or continued detention.[261]

The individuals responsible for providing reports to the international courts must be provided with clear guidelines to follow in relation to release procedures.[262] At a very basic level, it should be clarified whether they are required to provide a recommendation in relation to release or information only. It is also important that it is clear what information is

---

[256] A. Cassese, *International Criminal Law*, 2nd edn (2008), 432.
[257] Art. 12(3) ICC–Denmark BEA.   [258] See Chapter 2, Section 3.2.4.
[259] Mollan, Trondheim Prison, 27.06.2012.
[260] *Martinović* (President's Decision) IT-98-34-ES, 22.10.2010.
[261] Para. 15 *Jokić* (President's Decision) IT-02-60-ES, 13.01.2010; para. 19 *Radić* (President's Decision) IT-98-30/1-ES, 23.04.2010; para. 21 *Bala* (President's Decision) IT-03-66-ES, 15.10.2010.
[262] Mollan, Trondheim Prison, 27.06.2012.

required, who it should be sent to and when it should be sent. Strict and feasible time-frames must be put in place to ensure that persons are not deprived of their liberty any longer than is necessary due to inefficient communication channels. The current system for transmitting information between enforcing institutions and the international courts in some states appears problematic. Reports compiled in enforcing prisons may have to go through regional or central directors, the Ministry of Justice and the Ministry of Foreign Affairs in the enforcing state before they are sent to the state's Embassy in the Host State of the international court which transmits the necessary paperwork to the Registry of the relevant international court. This timely and tedious process can result in delays in the transmission of information crucial to the release decision-making process. To reduce the time-frame for such communications, reports should be sent directly to the international court with a copy to the relevant Embassy.

3.2.3 The procedure and criteria for determining the appropriateness of early release

Release decisions are not based solely on the amount of time served and eligibility for commutation under the domestic law of the enforcing state,[263] but also on a range of criteria set out in the courts' statutes and rules. The courts formulated criteria for release decisions to avoid repeating the practice of the International Military Tribunals,[264] whose release decisions were primarily political considerations lacking penal analysis and predictability.[265] This section looks at the criteria set out in the statutes and rules of the temporary international criminal courts before discussing the factors that must be demonstrated under the ICC's statute and rules.

3.2.3.1 Temporary international criminal courts
The general rule is that the release of prisoners of the temporary courts should be in the interests of justice and general principles of law.[266] As this direction provides little practical guidance,[267] the criteria are expanded in the

---

[263] See para. 7 *Josipović* (President's Decision) IT-95-16-ES, 30.01.2006; para. 2 *Krnojelac* (President's Decision) IT-97-25-ES, 09.07.2009; para. D.4.5(55) MDP, 163.
[264] See Art. 29 IMTN Charter; Art. 17 IMTFE Charter.
[265] Van Zyl Smit, "International Imprisonment", 358–60; Kreß and Sluiter, "Imprisonment", 1759, 1762.
[266] Art. 28 ICTY St; Art. 27 ICTR St; Art. 23 SCSLSt; Rule 124 SCSL RPE.
[267] Van Zyl Smit, "International Imprisonment", 371.

Rules of the UN Tribunals to include the gravity of the crime for which the prisoner was convicted, the treatment of similarly-situated prisoners, the prisoner's demonstration of rehabilitation and cooperation with the Prosecutor.[268]

Consideration of the gravity of the offence has been described by Van Zyl Smit as "palpably unjust"[269] as this was the most powerful determinant of the sentence imposed. The ICTR has often cited the gravity of the crimes committed as a factor for the denial of an application for release.[270] Despite being an explicit criterion in its rules, the gravity of the offence did not feature as a real factor in many ICTY release considerations, with release being granted "notwithstanding" the gravity of the crime.[271] More recent decisions have discussed gravity at greater length, referring to the crimes committed by the individual, quoting from the sentencing judgment, and stating that gravity is a factor going against release.[272] Yet, release has still been granted in spite of the high gravity of crimes committed[273] and it appears that gravity is most frequently used as a factor militating against release in cases where the individual has not served two-thirds of his sentence.[274]

In ICTY jurisprudence, consideration of the treatment of convicted persons in similar situations has referred solely to the release eligibility at the two-thirds point of the sentence and has not really acted as an additional criterion.[275] The Tribunal rejected submissions that periods of detention should be equated with those of co-accused, particularly if they were convicted of more serious offences, stating that this was not appropriate and that release decisions were made on a case-by-case basis

---

[268] Rule 125 ICTY RPE; Rule 126 ICTR RPE.
[269] Van Zyl Smit, "International Imprisonment", 373.
[270] *Ruggiu* (President's Decision) ICTR-97-32-S, 12.05.2005.
[271] See para. 17 *Tadić* (President's Decision) IT-94-1-ES, 17.07.2008; para. 15 *Banović* (President's Decision) IT-02-65/1-ES, 03.09.2008; para. 10 *Plavšić* (President's Decision) IT-00-39&40/1-ES, 14.09.2009; para. D.4.1(48) MDP, 162.
[272] Paras. 13–16 *Rajić* (President's Decision) IT-95-12-ES, 22.08.2011.
[273] See *Simić* (President's Decision) IT-95-9-ES, 15.02.2011.
[274] Para. 23 *Kordić* (President's Decision) IT-95-14/2-ES, 13.05.2010; paras. 23–4 *Krajišnik* (President's Decision) IT-00-39-ES, 26.07.2010; paras. 12–13 *Žigić* (President's Decision) IT-98-30/1-ES, 08.11.2010; para. 14 *Rajić* (President's Decision) IT-95-12-ES), 31.01.2011; para. 27 *Stakić* (President's Decision) IT-97-24-ES, 15.07.2011; para. 32 *Zelenović* (President's Decision) IT-96-23/2-ES, 21.10.2011.
[275] See para. 17 *Tadić* (President's Decision) IT-94-1-ES, 17.07.2008; para. 15 *Banović* (President's Decision) IT-02-65/1-ES, 03.09.2008; para. 10 *Plavšić* (President's Decision) IT-00-39&40/1-ES, 14.09.2009.

on the facts.[276] The focus has remained on the time that has been served by the individual in question.[277]

The President must, however, form an opinion on the prisoner's demonstration of rehabilitation, which is then submitted for consideration by the other judges.[278] ICTY jurisprudence places a lot of weight on good behaviour in prison, work, education, participation in activities and good relations with staff and other prisoners, particularly in light of the difficulties experienced in serving a sentence in a foreign country.[279] Some decisions, however, conclude that even when numerous positive factors are present, they will only be considered to constitute limited rehabilitation.[280] This may be due to a lack of remorse or acknowledgment of responsibility, or it may be that the requisite time had not been served. In some decisions, 'good behaviour' appears to be used interchangeably with rehabilitation[281] or is advanced as a critical factor in relevant determinations.[282] Good behaviour alone does not demonstrate rehabilitation. Relationships with other prisoners are of course relevant; particularly if the other prisoners have the same nationality, ethnicity or religion as the accused's victims.[283] Conversely, the avoidance of violent altercations with other prisoners by requesting a transfer to a more restrictive regime was also considered to be evidence of rehabilitation.[284]

---

[276] Para. 15 *Krajišnik* (President's Decision) IT-00-39-ES, 26.07.2010.
[277] Para. 16 *ibid.*   [278] Para. 6 ICTY PDER.
[279] See para. 11 *Josipović* (President's Decision) IT-95-16-ES, 30.01.2006; paras. 4, 11 *Vuković* (President's Decision) IT-96-23&23/1-ES, 11.03.08; paras. 6–7 *Landžo* (President's Order) IT-96-21-ES, 13.04.2006; paras. 7, 20 *Delić* (President's Decision) IT-96-21-ES, 24.06.2008; paras. 8, 16 *Tadić* (President's Decision) IT-94-1-ES, 17.07.2008; paras. 6, 13 *Banović* (President's Decision) IT-02-65/1-ES, 03.09.2008; paras. 11–12 *Šantić* (President's Decision) IT-95-16-ES, 16.02.2009; para. 20 *Krnojelac* (President's Decision) IT-97-25-ES, 09.07.2009; para. 9 *Plavšić* (President's Decision) IT-00-39&40/1-ES, 14.09.2009; para. 18 *Radić* (President's Decision) IT-98-30/1-ES, 23.04.2010; para. 21 *Krajišnik* (President's Decision) IT-00-39-ES, 26.07.2010; paras. 22, 25 *Simić* (President's Decision) IT-95-9-ES, 15.02.2011; para. 18 *Rajić* (President's Decision) IT-95-12-ES, 22.08.2011; paras. 29, 32 *Stakić* (President's Decision) IT-97-24-ES, 15.07.2011; para. 22 *Zelenović* (President's Decision) IT-96-23/2-ES, 21.10.2011.
[280] Para. 20 *Rajić* (President's Decision) IT-95-12-ES, 31.01.2011; para. 24 *Bala* (President's Decision) IT-03-66-ES, 15.10.2010.
[281] Para. 20 *Tadić* (President's Decision) IT-94-1-ES, 17.07.2008; para. 15 *Jokić* (President's Decision) IT-02-60-ES, 13.01.2010.
[282] Para. 25 *Bala* (President's Decision) IT-03-66-ES, 15.10.2010; para. 35 *Stakić* (President's Decision) IT-97-24-ES, 15.07.2011.
[283] Para. D.4.2 (49) MDP, 162.
[284] Para. 14 *Delić* (President's Decision) IT-96-21-ES, 24.06.2008.

Acceptance of responsibility for crimes committed and expressions of remorse, both during the trial or post-conviction, are also considered by the ICTY to be strong indicators of rehabilitation.[285] Even nuanced views of responsibility will be accepted as signs of rehabilitation if they are accompanied by sincere expressions of remorse for the suffering of victims.[286] National reports have noted that some prisoners have denied their crimes, their responsibility for the crimes or have had an ambivalent approach to responsibility.[287] Such statements have often been dealt with cautiously as full reports have been missing or provided reports have noted that a lack of meetings, language barriers and cultural misunderstandings hampered the ability to provide accurate or conclusive reports on the prisoner's acknowledgment of responsibility, psychological state of mind and risk of recidivism.[288] Decisions have stated that "a failure to take responsibility ... is not necessarily determinative of rehabilitation but such behaviour is one factor in the overall determination of rehabilitation".[289] This approach was adopted even when the applicant completely denied committing the offences he was convicted of (rehabilitation was a neutral factor because he had behaved well in detention).[290]

Judicial discussions of rehabilitation also include references to the prisoners' ability to reintegrate back into society. Factors such as the on-going support of family, qualifications that will lead to employment, successful efforts to secure accommodation and work and efforts to help others during the conflict have been raised in this connection.[291] Some

---

[285] See para. 7 *Landžo* (President's Order) IT-96-21-ES, 13.04.2006; para. 8 *Plavšić* (President's Decision) IT-00-39&40/1-ES, 14.09.2009; paras. 8, 13 *Banović* (President's Decision) IT-02-65/1-ES, 03.09.2008; para. 11 *Šantić* (President's Decision) IT-95-16-ES, 16.02.2009.

[286] Para. 29 *Simić* (President's Decision) IT-95-9-ES, 15.02.2011; paras. 26–7 *Šljivančanin* (President's Decision) IT-95-13/1-ES, 05.07.2011.

[287] Para. 18 *Radić* (President's Decision) IT-98-30/1-ES, 23.04.2010; para. 30 *Stakić* (President's Decision) IT-97-24-ES, 15.07.2011; para. 19 *Rajić* (President's Decision) IT-95-12-ES, 22.08.2011; paras. 27, 29 *Zelenović* (President's Decision) IT-96-23/2-ES, 21.10.2011.

[288] Para. 20 *Radić* (President's Decision) IT-98-30/1-ES, 23.04.2010; paras. 19, 22, 24 *Bala* (President's Decision) IT-03-66-ES, 15.10.2010; paras. 27, 29 *Zelenović* (President's Decision) IT-96-23/2-ES, 21.10.2011.

[289] Para. 31 *Stakić* (President's Decision) IT-97-24-ES, 15.07.2011.

[290] Para. 21 *Radić* (President's Decision) IT-98-30/1-ES, 23.04.2010.

[291] See paras. 11–12 *Josipović* (Decision) IT-95-16-ES, 30.01.2006; paras. 6, 11 *Vuković* (President's Decision) IT-96-23&23/1-ES, 11.03.2008; paras. 6, 12–13 *Banović* (President's Decision) IT-02-65/1-ES, 03.09.2008; para. 19 *Kordić* (President's Decision) IT-95-14/2-ES, 13.05.2010; paras. 24–5 *Simić* (President's Decision) IT-95-9-ES, 15.02.2011.

references to reintegration, however, seem confused. For instance, participation in a French language class was considered to be a sincere attempt at social reintegration.[292] While this may have improved the prisoner's communications with staff and prisoners during the service of his sentence, the prisoner in question was deported to Serbia. An ability to speak French would not enhance his ability to reintegrate in Serbian communities.

The prisoner's psychological condition and risk of recidivism are also assessed under the rehabilitation criterion.[293] The risk of recidivism is often classified as low due to the fact that the conflict situation no longer exists,[294] although persistent denial of responsibility and internalised racist and violent views may be presented as signs of dangerousness.[295]

In relation to cooperation with the Prosecutor,[296] testimony at other international or national trials, active cooperation and/or a willingness to testify are considered to be positive factors in support of release.[297] Mere availability or willingness to testify is not considered to be cooperation for this purpose. Nor is cooperation with the Prosecutor prior to conviction, as this would have been a factor in sentencing.[298] If, on the other hand, cooperation was not requested by the Prosecutor, this is deemed to be a neutral factor.[299] A lack of or limited cooperation is not viewed negatively given that an accused person is not obliged to assist the Prosecutor in proving its case and that any evidence provided is cooperation which he is entitled to withhold without adverse consequences.[300] Recent jurisprudence in relation to cooperation provided pursuant to plea agreements has stated that this constitutes a factor in

---

[292] Para.13 Banović (President's Decision) IT-02-65/1-ES, 03.09.2008.
[293] Para. 21 Vasiljević (President's Decision) IT-98-32-ES, 12.03.2010; para. 20 Kordić (President's Decision) IT-95-14/2-ES, 13.05.2010; para. 23 Krajišnik (President's Decision) IT-00-39-ES, 26.07.2010; para. 21 Rajić (President's Decision) IT-95-12-ES, 31.01.2011; para. 28 Simić (President's Decision) IT-95-9-ES, 15.02.2011; para. 33 Stakić (President's Decision) IT-97-24-ES, 15.07.2011.
[294] See para. 28 Zelenović (President's Decision) IT-96-23/2-ES, 21.10.2011.
[295] Paras. 19, 21 Bala (President's Decision) IT-03-66-ES, 15.10.2010.
[296] Para. 3(C) ICTY PDER.
[297] See para. 14 Banović (President's Decision) IT-02-65/1-ES, 03.09.2008; para. 13 Šantić (President's Decision) IT-95-16-ES, 16.02.2009; para. 12 Plavšić (President's Decision) IT-00-39&40/1-ES, 14.09.2009; para. D.4.3(51) MDP, 162.
[298] Para. D.4.3(50) MDP, 162.
[299] Para. 10 Josipović (President's Decision) IT-95-16-ES, 30.01.2006; para. 13 Strugar (President's Decision) IT-01-42-ES, 16.01.2009.
[300] Para. 17 Jokić (President's Decision) IT-02-60-ES, 13.01.2010; para. 27 Krajišnik (President's Decision) IT-00-39-ES, 26.07.2010.

favour of early release but, even if such cooperation is substantial and provided in good faith, it has diminished strength.[301] In some cases, the Prosecutor has sought to place submissions before the ICTY President, expressing opposition to the release of an individual.[302] These submissions have not been considered as the Practice Direction only allows the Prosecutor to make submissions on cooperation, unless specifically requested to do otherwise by the President.[303]

The criteria set out in the Rules are non-exhaustive and the President may consider any other relevant information.[304] ICTY Presidents have been willing to consider media material and information provided by third parties in support of a release application, although they may reject such information as irrelevant or failing to demonstrate an individual's rehabilitation.[305] The suffering of the prisoner's family due to their loved one's conviction and imprisonment,[306] the physical and mental health of the prisoner and the adequacy of the care provided have also been considered.[307] Age, by itself, and time spent in isolation due to harassment are not considered to be factors pertinent to rehabilitation assessments.[308]

The ICTR's release criteria exactly mirror those of the ICTY. In contrast to the ICTY's practice, however, the consideration of these criteria has only resulted in two early release decisions at the ICTR. Both decisions stated that, in these particular cases, the gravity of the crimes could be considered even though it had already been considered in sentence determination and the fact that it was high did not *per se* bar consideration for release if it was otherwise appropriate.[309] The lack of a

---

[301] Para. 23 *Rajić* (President's Decision) IT-95-12-ES, 31.01.2011; paras. 30–1 *Zelenović* (President's Decision) IT-96-23/2-ES, 21.10.2011.
[302] See para. 9 *Delić* (President's Decision) IT-96-21-ES, 24.06.2008; para. 9 *Tadić* (President's Decision) IT-94-1-ES, 17.07.2008.
[303] See para. 10 *Delić* (President's Decision) IT-96-21-ES, 24.06.2008; para. 10 *Tadić* (President's Decision) IT-94-1-ES, 17.07.2008.
[304] Para. 8 ICTY PDER.
[305] Para. 22 *Krajišnik* (President's Decision) IT-00-39-ES, 26.07.2010; paras. 23–4 *Bala* (President's Decision) IT-03-66-ES, 15.10.2010.
[306] Para. 21 *Delić* (President's Decision) IT-96-21-ES, 24.06.2008.
[307] See para. 20 *Krnojelac* (President's Decision) IT-97-25-ES, 09.07.2009; para. 11 *Plavšić* (President's Decision) IT-00-39&40/1-ES, 14.09.2009; para. 19 *Radić* (President's Decision) IT-98-30/1-ES, 23.04.2010.
[308] Para. 19 *Radić* (President's Decision) IT-98-30/1-ES, 23.04.2010; para. 22 *Krajišnik* (President's Decision) IT-00-39-ES, 26.07.2010.
[309] Para. 7 *Bagaragaza* (President's Decision) ICTR-05-86-S, 24.10.2011; para. 7 *Rugambarara* (President's Decision) ICTR-00-59, 08.02.2012.

criminal record and ethnic discrimination prior to the genocide, as well as assistance to Tutsi refugees and intervention which saved lives during the genocide, were significant factors in one of the decisions.[310] While the President was willing to take ICTY practice in relation to the treatment of similarly situated persons into account, this was not considered binding or directly applicable for those convicted of genocide.[311] A three-quarters point for eligibility was considered more appropriate for this international crime. It should be noted however, that ICTR interpretation of this criterion does appear to differ slightly from that of the ICTY, as the President was willing to compare the actual situation of the applicants involved, and not just the time served.[312] In relation to rehabilitation, factors previously considered in mitigation, such as surrender, guilty pleas, confessions, remorse and acknowledgment of responsibility, were still considered to be strong positive factors.[313] These factors saved judicial resources and contributed to national reconciliation.[314] Good behaviour was also considered. The *Rugambarara* decision noted that the family situation of an individual can be a positive factor in release decisions. This discussion did appear slightly confused, however, as it used the term rehabilitation to discuss the potential for reintegration post-conviction.[315] Overall, though, the overriding consideration in both cases appears to have been the significant value attached to the voluntary, substantial and long-term cooperation provided by both parties, which at times resulted in isolation in detention.[316]

The procedures for making release decisions are set out in the courts' rules and practice directions. Following notification of eligibility, the Registrar prepares a file for the President with information in relation to the pre-determined criteria. The file contains reports from the enforcing state's authorities on behaviour during incarceration, conditions of imprisonment and the prisoner's mental condition as well as a report from the Office of the Prosecutor on the cooperation of the convicted person and any other information the President considers relevant.[317]

---

[310] Para. 6 *Rugambarara* (President's Decision) ICTR-00-59, 08.02.2012.
[311] Paras. 8–10 *Bagaragaza* (President's Decision) ICTR-05-86-S, 24.10.2011; para. 11 *Rugambarara* (President's Decision) ICTR-00-59, 08.02.2012.
[312] Para. 12 *Rugambarara* (President's Decision) ICTR-00-59, 08.02.2012.
[313] Paras. 5–6, 11–12 *Bagaragaza* (President's Decision) ICTR-05-86-S, 24.10.2011; para. 13 *Rugambarara* (President's Decision) ICTR-00-59, 08.02.2012.
[314] Paras. 8–9 *ibid*.   [315] Para. 14 *ibid*.
[316] Para. 13 *Bagaragaza* (President's Decision) ICTR-05-86-S, 24.10.2011; paras. 10, 13 *Rugambarara* (President's Decision) ICTR-00-59, 08.02.2012.
[317] Para. 3(b)–(d) ICTY PDER.

The Presidents of the UN Tribunals and the SCSL consult with members of the Bureau and the judges of the Sentencing Chamber about the appropriateness of granting release on the basis of this information and the President's views on the prisoner's demonstration of rehabilitation.[318] The prisoner is also involved in the process. Once the Registrar is informed of the prisoner's eligibility for release, he informs the convicted person of such eligibility and advises him of the steps that will be taken.[319] The convicted person is given a copy of the file prepared by the Registrar for the President and is given ten days to examine it before he submits written submissions or an oral submission to the President by video-link or telephone.[320] Although the President is directed to take the views of the other judges on board, he or she is not bound by their views.[321] The President's decision is final and is not subject to appeal.[322] If the President determines that release is not appropriate, the decision should specify the date when the prisoner will next become eligible for consideration for release, unless this is specified by the enforcing state's law.[323]

The SCSL has not issued a practice direction or elaborated on the criteria it will derive from the vague statutory reference to the interests of justice and general principles of law[324] but it is likely they will use the same range of factors used by the UN Tribunals. The RSCSL may adopt more detailed rules or a practice direction to govern release decisions.

3.2.3.2 The ICC
The criteria and the procedure for the reduction of sentences at the ICC differ slightly. The Rome Statute lists criteria to be applied by the Review Panel: the early and continuing willingness of the person to cooperate with the Court in its investigations and prosecutions and the voluntary assistance of the person in enabling the enforcement of the judgments and orders of the Court in other cases, in particular providing assistance in locating assets subject to orders of fine, forfeiture or reparation which may be used for the benefit of victims.[325] This latter factor reflects the Court's new penalty options[326] and powers to order

---

[318] Rule 124 ICTY RPE; para. 6 ICTY PDER; Rule 125 ICTR RPE; Rule 124 SCSL RPE.
[319] Para. 3(a) ICTY PDER.   [320] Paras. 4–5 ICTY PDER.
[321] See para. 8 ICTY PDER; para. D.3(45) MDP, 161; para. 12 *Vuković* (President's Decision) IT-96-23&23/1-ES, 11.03.2008; para. 13 *Plavšić* (President's Decision) IT-00-39&40/1-ES, 14.09.2009.
[322] Para. 10 ICTY PDER.   [323] Para. 9 ICTY PDER.
[324] Art. 23 SCSLSt; Rule 124 SCSL RPE.   [325] Art. 110(4)(a)–(b) ICCSt.
[326] Art. 77(2) ICCSt.

convicted persons to make reparations to, or in respect of, victims.[327] These factors are added to in the rules,[328] to include conduct in detention which shows a genuine dissociation from the crime convicted of, the prospect of resocialisation and successful resettlement, the likelihood that release would give rise to significant social instability, any action taken by the prisoner for the benefit of victims, the impact of the release on victims and their families and the individual circumstances, age or health of the prisoner.[329] These factors make it clear that good conduct alone is not sufficient, and that the prisoner must demonstrate dissociation from crime. The prisoner's actions for the benefit of victims are also important. The criteria therefore not only look at how the prisoner has dealt with the past, but also how the prisoner will cope in the future, in particular, his ability to reintegrate with his own and the victims' community.

The ICC Review Panel may also take the prisoner's age and health into account. The last factor may enable a review prior to the threshold established in Article 110 Rome Statute. Even those imprisoned at Spandau were released when diagnosed with terminal illnesses.[330] The court must have an inherent jurisdiction to consider early applications for release on humanitarian grounds.[331] Overall, these factors reflect the rules and practice of the ICTY, the court's commitment to victims and the "reformative aim"[332] of the International Covenant for Civil and Political Rights.

Unlike the temporary courts' written procedure, the ICC Statute provides for oral hearings. For first-time reviews, three Appeal Chamber judges are appointed to conduct a hearing with the sentenced person, who may be assisted by counsel and interpreters. The Prosecutor, the enforcing state, and to the extent possible, the victims or legal representatives may also be invited to participate or submit observations. In exceptional circumstances, the hearing may be conducted by videoconference or in the enforcing state by a delegated judge.[333] If the judges determine that the sentence should not be reduced, the sentence will be reviewed again by three Appeal Chamber judges in three years (or a shorter interval if this is established at the

---

[327] Art. 75(2) ICCSt.   [328] Art. 110(4)(c) ICCSt.   [329] Rule 223 ICC RPE.
[330] N. J. W. Goda, *Tales from Spandau: Nazi Criminals and the Cold War* (2007), 132, 193.
[331] See E. Gumboh, "The Penalty of Life Imprisonment under International Criminal Law" (2011) 11 *African Human Rights Law Journal* 75–92 at 90.
[332] Van Zyl Smit, "International Imprisonment", 377.   [333] Rule 224(1) ICC RPE.

review).[334] At subsequent reviews, the judges can either invite written representations from the prisoner or his counsel, the Prosecutor, enforcing state authorities and, to the extent possible, victims or their legal representatives, or hold a hearing.[335] The ICC has therefore continued the practice of the UN Tribunals of taking the views of the prisoner into account.[336]

3.2.4 International control over the length of the sentence to be served

Historically, it has been demonstrated that it is essential to ensure international control over release. Although Japan had been barred from reducing sentences, granting clemency or parole without the support of a majority of the governments represented at the IMTFE, all prisoners were unconditionally released six years after the peace agreement; less than ten years after the sentences were imposed.[337] The international nature of the sentences dictates that an enforcing state should not be able to reduce the term of imprisonment to be served or release an international prisoner against the wishes of the sentencing court.[338] To ensure that the modern temporary international criminal courts were in a position to prevent states doing this,[339] their statutes state that only the President of the court can alter the length of the sentence or grant pardon.[340] Though this gives judicial officials the power to make quasi-political decisions,[341] it was considered necessary to prevent abuses by states that would detrimentally impact on the legitimacy of the court and to avoid outside parties bringing pressure to bear on states to grant pardon to international prisoners serving sentences on their territory.[342]

In accordance with the courts' statutory control over release and pardon decisions, enforcing states agree to be bound by the length of

---

[334] Art. 110(5) ICCSt; Rule 224(3) ICC RPE.   [335] Rule 224(3) ICC RPE.
[336] See Art. 110(2) ICCSt; Art. 11(2) ICC–Austria BEA.
[337] Kreß and Sluiter, "Imprisonment", 1763–4; Penrose, "Spandau Revisited", 564–5; Van Zyl Smit, "International Imprisonment", 360.
[338] Paras. 71–3 *Erdemović* (Judgment) IT-96-22, 29.11.1996.
[339] Tolbert, "The International Criminal Tribunal and the Enforcement of Sentences", 662.
[340] Art. 28 ICTYSt; Art. 27 ICTRSt; Art. 23 SCSLSt.
[341] Klip, "Enforcement of Sanctions", 161.
[342] See Tolbert, "The International Criminal Tribunal and the Enforcement of Sentences", 661–2.

the sentence imposed by the international court.[343] Some states qualify this seemingly straightforward stipulation, by adding that this depends on conditions set out in enforcement agreements.[344] Therefore, in spite of the strong statutory premise that international courts should retain control over the length of the sentence, the consensual nature of the enforcement system has resulted in the inclusion of provisions that deviate from this statutory scheme.

The deviating provisions in enforcement agreements are not uniform. Some agreements state that if the national government disagrees with the President's decision relating to release, the state will no longer enforce the sentence and the prisoner will be transferred to serve the sentence elsewhere.[345] Others reserve the right to choose whether or not to continue enforcing the sentence in these circumstances.[346] Some states put the onus on the international court to decide to transfer the prisoner in the event of a disagreement.[347] In relation to the transfer itself, the time the court has to arrange the transfer ranges from immediately,[348] twenty-four hours,[349] sixty days[350] and ninety days.[351] Some agreements are problematic as they only refer to transfer back to the Tribunal, which may not be open at that stage.[352] Others refer to transfer to either the Tribunal or another state.[353] Some agreements place the responsibility for making transfer arrangements on the Tribunal generally,[354] the Registrar,[355] or the national Minister for Justice.[356]

Some states that do not accept the courts' decisions on release will accept determinations in relation to pardon.[357] However, other states also view the question of pardon as being too closely linked to sovereignty

---

[343] Art. 3(1) ICTY BEAs (except Art. 2(1) ICTY–Germany BEAs re Tadić/Kunarac/Galić/Tarčulovski), Art. 3(1) ICTR BEAs; Art. 22(2) SCSLSt; Art. 3(1) SCSL BEAs.
[344] See Art. 3(1) ICTY–France BEA; ICTR–France/Sweden BEAs.
[345] Art. 3(4) ICTY/ICTR–Italy BEAs; Art. 3(5) ICTY–Belgium/Portugal/Spain BEAs.
[346] Art. 3(4) ICTY/ICTR–France BEAs; Art. 3(4) ICTR–Sweden BEA; Art. 4(3) ICTY–Slovakia BEA; Art. 8(2) SCSL–Sweden BEA.
[347] Art. 8(3) ICTY–Denmark/Estonia/Sweden BEAs; Arts. 8(3), 9(2), 9(4) SCSL–Sweden BEA.
[348] Para. 2(4) ICTY–Germany BEA re Galić.   [349] Art. 3(5) ICTY–Belgium BEA.
[350] Art. 10 ICTY–France/Italy/Portugal/Sweden BEAs; Art. 11 ICTY–Slovakia BEA.
[351] Art. 10 ICTY–Spain BEA.
[352] Art. 3(4) ICTY/ICTR–France/Italy BEAs; Art. 3(4)ICTR–Sweden BEA.
[353] Art. 3(5) ICTY–Belgium BEA; Art. 8(3) ICTY–Estonia BEA.
[354] Art. 3(5) ICTY–Belgium BEA.
[355] Art. 3(5) ICTY–Portugal/Spain BEAs; Art. 9(2) ICTY–Slovakia BEA.
[356] Art. 3(4) ICTY/ICTR–Italy BEAs.   [357] Para. 7(2) ICTY–Germany BEA re Galić.

to allow for external control.[358] They simply repeat their position that if there is a disagreement, the prisoner must be transferred.[359] Other states that have retained the choice on how to proceed in relation to disagreements over the appropriateness of release will not continue to enforce sentences if there is a dispute over the appropriateness of pardon.[360]

The reality is that only half of the enforcement agreements entered into by the UN follow the statutory scheme whereby the President makes the decision on early release.[361] At the SCSL, while the British, Finnish and Rwandan agreements follow the statutory scheme,[362] the Swedish agreement deviates from it in respect of release.[363] These deviations may result in the loss of international control over the sentence. There have been cases where national judges have granted early release to ICTY prisoners, albeit subject to an authorising decision from the ICTY President[364] or, conversely, state authorities have notified the ICTY of decisions not to grant release.[365] Reliance on national procedures to determine release eligibility has resulted in one international prisoner requesting the ICTY, the ICRC and the Serbian Embassy to petition for his release with German authorities directly.[366] ICTY judges have expressed concern that some enforcing states have assumed more responsibility than their statutory role to simply notify the international court of a prisoner's eligibility, as the final decision to grant release should rest solely with the President.[367] They have also expressed concern that national regulations on remission eligibility, that enable prisoners to gain significant reductions in the time they must serve, may create inequality among international prisoners.[368]

Procedural incompatibilities between the national and international release systems have resulted in the ICTY relying on the deportation

---

[358] See Van Zyl Smit, "International Imprisonment", 372.
[359] Art. 8(2) ICTY–Spain/Italy BEAs; Art. 8(2) ICTR–Italy BEA.
[360] Art. 8(2) ICTY/ICTR–France BEAs; Art. 9(2) ICTY–Slovakia BEA.
[361] Art. 3(4) ICTY–Finland/Norway/Albania/Ukraine BEAs; Art. 3(6) ICTY–Poland BEA; Art. 8 ICTY–Norway/Austria/Finland/Belgium/Poland/Portugal/UK/Albania BEAs; Art. 8 ICTR–Benin/Mali/Rwanda/Swaziland BEAs.
[362] Art. 8(2) SCSL–UK BEA; Art. 8(3) SCSL–Rwanda BEA; Art. 9(2) SCSL–Finland BEA.
[363] Art. 8 SCSL–Sweden BEA.
[364] Para. 8 *Josipović* (President's Decision) IT-95-16-ES, 30.01.2006.
[365] Para. 2 *Tadić* (President's Decision) IT-94-1-ES, 17.07.2008.
[366] Paras. 3, 5, 11 *Tadić* (President's Decision) IT-94-1-ES, 17.07.2008.
[367] Para. 12 *Josipović* (President's Decision) IT-95-16-ES, 30.01.2006.
[368] See para. 14 *Šantić* (President's Decision) IT-95-16-ES, 16.02.2009; paras. 13–14 *Bala* (President's Decision) IT-03-66-ES, 15.10.2010.

process in one enforcing state to secure release.[369] Excessive reliance on domestic procedures by enforcing states has also caused delays in the release process.[370] In one case, serious delays by Italy to provide the ICTY with information on the prisoner's eligibility for release[371] led to the ICTY President ordering the Registrar to terminate the enforcement of Mr Krnojelac's sentence in Italy[372] and to have him transferred from Italy to his country of domicile, Bosnia-Herzegovina.[373]

The provisions in the ad hoc Tribunals' bilateral agreements that deviate from the Statute and Model Agreement were sanctioned by the UN Office of Legal Affairs.[374] Indeed, the ICTY's Practice Direction on Release allows enforcing states to execute the President's decision on release in accordance with the terms of their bilateral enforcement agreement.[375] This accommodating approach was considered to be a necessary practical solution to overcome conflicts between the domestic law of states willing to cooperate and the Tribunal's Statute as it avoided "states having to engage in lengthy parliamentary or internal discussions reviewing their domestic legislation".[376]

It may be argued that the deviating provisions are unnecessary given that the enforcement agreements all contain an impossibility clause, which allows enforcing states to terminate enforcement if it becomes impossible for practical or legal reasons.[377] Indeed, some deviating provisions explicitly[378] or implicitly[379] refer to impossibility. However, impossibility clauses were intended to be used to deal with unforeseen events such as a change in law.[380] Deviating provisions relate to disagreements over decisions about release rather than a change in the national law governing release. Transfers due to disagreements over the appropriateness of release should be based on provisions relating to release, not impossibility.[381]

---

[369] *Tadić* (President's Decision) IT-94-1-ES, 17.07.2008.
[370] Paras. 10–11 *Banović* (President's Decision) IT-02-65/1-ES, 03.09.2008.
[371] Paras. 3–6 *Krnojelac* (President's Decision) IT-97-25-ES, 09.07.2009.
[372] Art. 9(2) ICTY–Italy BEA.
[373] Para. 24 *Krnojelac* (President's Decision) IT-97-25-ES, 09.07.2009.
[374] Fofana, ICTY, 29.08.2007.   [375] Para. 11 ICTY PDER.
[376] Para. A.1(11) MDP, 153.
[377] See Arts. 10 ICTY/ICTR/SCSL BEAs (except Art. 11 ICTY–Slovakia BEA); Art. 16 ICC–Austria BEA; Art. 15 ICC–UK BEA; Art. 16(1) ICC–Finland/Serbia BEA; Art. 17(1) ICC–Belgium/Denmark BEAs.
[378] Art. 3(5) ICTY–Portugal/Spain BEAs.
[379] Art. 3(4) ICTY–Italy BEA; Art. 3(5) ICTY–Belgium BEA.
[380] Exchange of Notes between Germany and ICTY re Kunarac and Tadić, 17.10.2000.
[381] Letter from the Ambassador of the Federal Republic of Germany to the Registrar of the ICTY re Tarčulovski, 16.06.2011.

It has been argued that it was necessary to deal with the difficult issue of eligibility for release, sentence reduction, remission or pardon under domestic law in a manner that ensured the equal treatment of international prisoners and respected state sovereignty. This, it is claimed, was achieved by including flexible provisions in the bilateral enforcement agreements that enabled the President to address the appropriateness of the measure, leaving the final decision to national authorities, and to transfer the prisoner should it be deemed inappropriate.[382] However, it is apparent from the enforcement agreements and practice that some states view the question of the length of the sentence to be served as an issue of shared competence. These deviations are in sharp contradiction to the statutory direction that international prisoners will only be released if the President so decides and the provisions in the bilateral enforcement agreements that enforcing states will respect the length of the sentence imposed by the court, and fundamentally undermine the basic principle that international courts retain supervisory control over the length of the sentence.

These provisions do not, however, enable enforcing states to release international prisoners unilaterally. Until the prisoner is transferred to the court or another state, the enforcing state remains bound by the duration of the sentence imposed by the court.[383] However, given the temporary nature of the UN Tribunals and the SCSL and their respective detention facilities,[384] the lack of alternate sites for enforcement may be an influential decision in the President's decision to grant release. The prioritisation of national law therefore dilutes the power of the court to control the implementation of the sentence of imprisonment, de-internationalising the sanction. Moreover, it creates variations between the release schemes of different enforcing states. This disparity runs "directly counter to the concept of a uniform enforcement of international sentences"[385] and results in an unpredictable system.

It is possible to have a more predictable system that also accommodates national legal and constitutional variations. As has been

---

[382] Cassese, *International Criminal Law*, 433–4.
[383] See Art. 13(3) ICTY–Austria BEA; Art. 14(1) ICTY–Slovakia BEA; Art. 14(2) ICTY–Denmark BEA; Art. 13 SCSL–Sweden BEA.
[384] The second SCSLSF was closed in 2009. See SCSL Press Release "Special Court Hands over Detention Facility to the Government of Sierra Leone", 16.11.09. The Sierra Leone Prison Service now uses this facility as a prison for women and their children born in custody. See SCSL Ninth Annual Report, 37.
[385] Kreß and Sluiter, "Imprisonment", 1819.

previously stated, enforcing states can make their cooperation conditional on conditions contained in enforcement agreements. Both Ukraine and Poland have stated in their agreements with the ICTY that although they will accept persons sentenced to a term exceeding the maximum permitted under national law, the individual will have to be transferred elsewhere when they reach this stage of their sentence.[386] This stipulation avoids the more rigid approach adopted by other states that excludes consideration of cooperation in respect of persons with these type of sentences.[387] Moreover, it enables the President to take potential incompatibilities between the national and international procedure for release into consideration when designating an enforcing state and thereby ensures that "the authority of the President over sentences pronounced by the Tribunal is preserved".[388]

The ICC's statutory scheme attempts to avoid the situation arising in the first place. When the Rome Statute was being drafted, there were several options in relation to release. One option was to empower the Sentencing Chamber to stipulate that the sentence will be implemented in accordance with the national law of the enforcing state, and consequently, the court's consent would not be required for release decisions made in line with this law.[389] Another option stated that if national law placed a maximum length on sentences that could be served, any reduction of the international sentence to this maximum would require the prior and express consent of the court.[390] However, the option that was adopted retained court control over the length of the sentence. This was considered necessary to prevent national law being used to reduce the sentence imposed on the prisoner by the court.[391] The Rome Statute therefore repeats the foundational premise of the other courts' systems: its sentences are binding on enforcing states, they cannot be revised or reduced by states, and a state cannot release a person before the expiry of the sentence pronounced by the ICC.[392] While states may still insert conditions in their enforcement agreements,[393] the crucial difference is

---

[386] Art. 3(1) ICTY-Ukraine BEA; Art. 3(3) ICTY-Poland BEA.
[387] Art. 2(2) ICTY-Slovakia BEA; Art. 3(2) ICTY-Portugal/Spain BEAs.
[388] Para. A.1(11) MDP, 153.
[389] See Art. 60(4) ILC Draft Statute for an International Criminal Court, 1994.
[390] See Art. 58 Proposals, Vol. II Report of the Preparatory Committee on the Establishment of an International Criminal Court 1996.
[391] Para. 357, Vol. I Report of the Preparatory Committee on the Establishment of an International Criminal Court 1996.
[392] Arts. 105(1), 110(1)–(2) ICCSt.   [393] See Arts. 103(1)(b), 105(1) ICCSt.

that both the statute and the rules state that these conditions cannot deviate from the statutory scheme.[394] The increased detail of the articles in the Rome Statute on enforcement, and their elaboration in the Rules, has aided the negotiation of more consistent bilateral enforcement agreements, as these articles can be pointed to in order to answer state queries about potentially deviating provisions.[395] Indeed, the majority of the ICC's enforcement agreements reflect the statutory position that enforcing states are bound by the duration of the international sentence and that the ICC has the sole authority to make release decisions.[396]

The agreement with Denmark, however, appears to use the terminology and procedures used in the agreements with the temporary international criminal tribunals. Although the bilateral enforcement agreement states that only the ICC has the right to decide on the reduction of the sentence[397] and that sentenced persons will not be released before the expiry of the sentence pronounced by the ICC,[398] it goes on to add that Denmark will notify the Court if the international prisoner becomes eligible for early release or pardon under domestic law.[399] This is strange given that the ICC Statute determines eligibility for consideration for a reduction of sentence and it does not provide for pardon.[400] What is more worrying, is that it continues to state that should Denmark disagree with the Court's view on the appropriateness of early release or pardon, the Court may transfer the prisoner to another state.[401] The agreement further states that enforcement will terminate "upon release following proceedings under Article 12 of this agreement for the pardon of the convicted".[402] Although it has been argued that the modifications to the model enforcement agreement made by State Parties in their enforcement agreements have not been "dramatic",[403] these modifications would appear to be unacceptable. By confusing and conflating the ICC's and the international criminal tribunals' release procedures, the agreement deviates sharply from the ICC statutory system. It is unclear if these deviations are the result of poor drafting or if they represent a conscious attempt to deviate from the ICC statutory

---

[394] Art. 103(1)(b) ICCSt; Rule 200(5) ICC RPE.   [395] Abathi, ICC, 05.07.2012.
[396] See Arts. 4(1), 10 ICC–UK BEA; Arts. 4(1), 11 ICC–Austria BEA; Arts. 4(1), 11(2)–(3) ICC–Serbia/Finland BEAs; Arts. 4(1), 12(2) ICC–Belgium BEA; Arts. 1(3), 6(1)–(2) ICC–Mali BEA.
[397] Art. 12(1) ICC–Denmark BEA.   [398] Art. 12(2) ICC–Denmark BEA.
[399] Art. 12(3) ICC–Denmark BEA.   [400] See Chapter 2, Section 3.2.1.
[401] Art. 12(4)–(5) ICC–Denmark BEA.   [402] Art. 15(1)(d) ICC–Denmark BEA.
[403] Abathi and Koh, "The Emerging Enforcement Practice of the International Criminal Count", 8.

position. This unfortunate article should not be viewed as a precedent for other states to insert similar deviating provisions in their bilateral enforcement agreements. The changes to the ICC model agreement[404] that were implemented after this agreement was concluded hopefully address this problem.

Like the temporary international courts' enforcement system, ICC enforcing states are under a treaty obligation not to release ICC prisoners unilaterally. Even if they disagree about release decisions, or if enforcement becomes impossible, the enforcing state must continue to implement the sentence until the ICC has arranged for the prisoner's transfer to another state.[405]

3.2.5 Release, deportation and relocation

If release or pardon is granted, the Registrar usually arranges for the transfer of the individual to another state[406] at the court's expense.[407] The Registrar may also, where appropriate, inform persons who testified at the individual's trial about the person's release and the location the person will travel to upon release and any other information the President considers to be relevant.[408]

It is important for international courts to ensure that release decisions are transmitted to the institutions enforcing the sentence. One prison housing an international prisoner found out that he had received his release date from the ICTY from conversations in the hallway. Even though the prisoner would be released directly from that prison, the prison did not receive any release papers.[409] This apparent oversight is unacceptable, particularly given the added complication of an asylum procedure in this case. The international courts must ensure that the local institutions holding international prisoners are provided with all relevant release documentation. This is vitally important as in most enforcing states the international release decision is the legal basis for

---

[404] See Chapter 2, Section 1.
[405] See, for example Arts. 4(1), 6(2), 11(2)–(3), 14(1), 16(3) and 22 ICC–Serbia BEA.
[406] See Art. 9(4) SCSL–Rwanda/Sweden BEA; Art. 10(4) SCSL–Finland BEA; para. D.6(62) MDP, 165.
[407] Art. 11 ICTY BEAs (Art. 12 ICTY–Slovakia BEA), Art. 11 ICTR–France/Sweden/Italy BEAs; Art. 11(1) ICTR–Benin BEA; Art. 11(1)(a)(ii) ICTR–Swaziland/Mali/Rwanda BEAs; Art. 11 SCSL–UK BEA; Art. 12(1)(b) SCSL–Finland BEA; Art. 11(1)(a) SCSL–Rwanda/Sweden BEAs; Art. 107(2) ICCSt; Art. 14(3) ICC–UK BEA; Art. 18(2) ICC–Austria BEA.
[408] Para. 12 ICTY PDER.   [409] Mollan, Trondheim Prison, 27.06.2012.

release. In other words, no additional or supplementary national release papers will be granted. The timely transmission of release dates is also important so that the institution actually implementing the sentence knows the exact date release will occur and can put steps in place to prepare the prisoner for release.[410]

The national law that triggers eligibility for release usually refers to conditional release or parole.[411] Indeed, enforcing states' reports may refer to conditional release and transfer to serve the remainder of the sentence in the prisoner's country of origin.[412] The international legal framework, however, does not allow for the grant of conditional release. There are no means to supervise offenders post-release or to react if conditions are breached; "early release ... is, in fact, an unconditional reduction or commutation of sentence".[413] While earlier drafts of the Rome Statute included references to parole, the final statute does not.[414] As the international criminal justice system does not have a parole system, all release is unconditional. The statutes of the courts therefore discuss procedures for the commutation or reduction of sentence rather than early release.[415]

A parole system to monitor former international prisoners would be very expensive to establish and would have to be aligned with national systems. At present, neither the penal institutions of enforcing states nor the courts make any connections with parole officials in the state to which the prisoner will travel upon release.[416] Parole and probation systems in the state to which the prisoner will return have no legal obligation to supervise such persons and released international prisoners would have no legal duty to comply with any instructions they would issue.[417] Unconditional release may be justified in many cases as there will be a low risk of recidivism as the conflict situation has passed. But this may not always be the case. Moreover, the current system does not

---

[410] Wilkinson, UK, 10.10.2012.
[411] See para. 6 *Josipović* (President's Decision) IT-95-16-ES, 30.01.2006; para. 9 *Šantić* (President's Decision) IT-95-16-ES, 16.02.2009.
[412] Para. 13 *Rajić* (President's Decision) IT-95-12-ES, 31.01.2011.
[413] Para. 2 *Bagaragaza* (President's Decision) ICTR-05-86-S, 24.10.2011.
[414] See draft Art. 100 Draft Statute Report of the Preparatory Committee on the Establishment of an International Criminal Court 1998, 155–6.
[415] This is despite the fact that the ICTY Practice Direction includes early release in its title and the term early release is used in Rule 223(c) ICC RPE.
[416] Lönnberg, Sweden, 07.10.2008; Daw and Wilkinson, UK, 24.05.2006.
[417] Wilkinson, UK, 10.10.2012.

monitor the progress of violent or sexual offenders or provide vulnerable ex-prisoners with practical or psychological support.[418]

Irrespective of the arguments for or against post-release supervision, the release of international prisoners is often linked with, or is conditional upon, deportation.[419] The majority of released ICTY prisoners have been deported to their former states of residence within the former Republic of Yugoslavia.[420] Some prisoners ensure deportation to a different state than their former state of citizenship. Tadić, for example, did not wish to remain in Germany on conditional release or be deported to his state of citizenship Bosnia-Herzegovina, so he secured Serbian citizenship to ensure he was deported to Serbia.[421] Concerns have been expressed that deportation decisions may subsequently adversely affect the former ICTY prisoners' rights to enter the European Union.[422]

In exceptional circumstances, such as when an individual is under threat for giving evidence against others, or his family has been targeted due to his conviction,[423] a former international prisoner may be relocated to a different state under a bilateral relocation agreement.[424] This procedure has only been used for a tiny proportion of ICTY prisoners.[425] The ICTR may have to deal with similar situations as the majority of accused and convicted persons have made it clear that they fear retaliation if they are sent to or remain in Rwanda after the completion of their sentence.[426] Previous attempts to secure state cooperation for the relocation of prisoners released directly from the UNDF have proven unsuccessful, creating a post-release duty of care for the ICTR.[427] Although it has not been stated explicitly, this issue appears to be the source of the Malian request for an advisory opinion from the African Court for

---

[418] See para. 7 *Landžo* (President's Order) IT-96-21-ES, 13.04.2006.
[419] See para. 8 *Josipović* (President's Decision) IT-95-16-ES, 30.01.2006; para. 9 *Šantić* (President's Decision) IT-95-16-ES, 16.02.2009; paras. 1, 6, 11–12 *Banović* (President's Decision) IT-02-65/1-ES, 03.09.2008; Art. 9(4) ICTY-UK/Austria BEAs; Art. 9(4) SCSL-UK BEA.
[420] See para. D.6(62) MDP, 165; para. 8 *Josipović* (President's Decision) IT-95-16-ES, 30.01.2006.
[421] Paras. 14–15 *Tadić* (President's Decision) IT-94-1-ES, 17.07.2008.
[422] Para. D.6(63) MDP, 165.
[423] See paras. 8, 15–17, 21 *Delić* (President's Decision) IT-96-21-ES, 24.06.2008.
[424] Para. D.6(62) MDP, 165.   [425] Fofana, ICTY, 29.08.2007.
[426] Diop, ICTR, 27.06.2007.
[427] See paras. 28, 30–31, 37 R. Amoussouga, "The ICTR's Challenges in the Relocation of Acquitted Persons, Released Prisoners and Protected Witnesses", 26–28.11.2008.

Human and Peoples' Rights.[428] To address this issue, the Senegalese Government has agreed to permit ICTR ex-prisoners who cannot return to the country in which they are legal residents for security reasons to remain on its territory until a solution has been found.[429] The ICTR in its agreements with both Senegal[430] and Rwanda has agreed to pay for the expenses relating to the transfer of released persons to states in which they will be lawfully resident, and the Rwandan Government has promised to facilitate the transfer of ICTR prisoners who serve their sentences in Rwanda by providing the necessary documents.[431]

Asylum issues may also affect release decisions. International prisoners serving their sentences in enforcing states may apply for asylum in that state. Until there is a final decision in relation to the individual's application for asylum, it will remain unclear where the person will go to upon release. These decisions, however, may not be finalised until very close to the end of the international prisoner's sentence. For example, six months before his release date, Mr Blagojević's request for asylum had not been decided.[432] This has implications for sentence and release planning. It is incumbent upon enforcing states to ensure that asylum decisions are finalised as quickly as possible in relation to international prisoners to ensure that plans can be made for their release.

The ad hoc Tribunals' lack of clarity on the procedure to follow in relation to release has the potential to create difficulties in relation to immigration status and does not provide solutions for individuals who are stateless or have double nationality.[433] The Rome Statute addresses the issue for the first time. If the enforcing state refuses to grant non-national prisoners permission to remain on its territory, these prisoners may be transferred to a state obliged to receive them or to a state that agrees to take them, taking into account their wishes.[434] This provision should not be interpreted as permitting expulsion where this would be otherwise forbidden under international law.[435] These options are further elaborated on in bilateral enforcement agreements.[436] Most states undertake to provide thirty days' notice of their intention to allow the

---

[428] Application No. 001/2011.   [429] Art. 12 ICTR–Senegal BEA.
[430] Art. 11(1)(b) ICTR–Senegal BEA.   [431] Art. 11(1)(a)(ii), (c) ICTR–Rwanda BEA.
[432] Mollan, Trondheim Prison, 27.06.2012.
[433] Kreß and Sluiter, "Imprisonment", 1816.   [434] Art. 107(1) ICCSt.
[435] See Marchesi, "The Enforcement Sentences of the International Court", 440.
[436] Art. 15(1) ICC–Austria BEA; Art. 14 ICC–UK BEA; Art. 16(1) ICC–Belgium/Denmark BEAs; Art. 15(1) ICC–Finland/Serbia BEAs; Art. 10(2) ICC–Mali BEA.

prisoner to remain or to deport them to another state.[437] The UK promises to bear the cost of repatriation if no other state offers to and will deport prisoners as appropriate and in accordance with international obligations.[438]

3.3 Responsibility for the international prisoner and the international sentence

While the daily supervision of the sentence's implementation is left to the enforcing state, the international courts retain a supervisory role. This supervisory role enables the courts to "exercise control in critical areas, in order to ensure consistency and compliance with international norms regarding conditions of incarceration".[439] In other words, enforcing states make the decisions governing day-to-day imprisonment but the courts may intervene if the legal position of the prisoners is affected. Although this division of responsibility is easily stated, it is not always clear where the responsibility of the enforcing state ends and where the responsibility of the international court begins. Through the acceptance of deviating provisions that are in direct tension with the temporary courts' statutes, a conflict of competencies has been created. The Rome Statute has attempted to define the macro/micro division of responsibility more clearly by ensuring that the provisions of the enforcement agreements do not result in the loss of international control over the length of the sentence to be served. The agreement with Denmark seems to be the only agreement which takes a different approach. The modified model enforcement agreement should address this issue with future cooperating states.

The Rome Statute also refers to the movement of the prisoner from the ICCDC to an enforcing state as 'delivery' rather than transfer.[440] This more accurately reflects the nature of the relationship: the international courts do not completely transfer responsibility for either the sentence or the prisoner to enforcing states but merely delegate the practical aspects of implementation of sentences to cooperating countries. If the

---

[437] Art. 17(2) ICC–Austria/Finland/Serbia BEAs; Art. 9(2) ICC–Belgium BEA; Art. 10(1)(b) ICC–Mali BEA; Art. 18(2) ICC–Denmark BEA.
[438] Arts. 9(2), 14(3) ICC–UK BEA.
[439] Para. 357 Vol. I Report of the Preparatory Committee on the Establishment of an International Criminal Court 1996.
[440] See Art. 3 ICC–UK BEA; Art. 6 ICC–Denmark BEA.

(proposed) actions of an enforcing state adversely impact on fundamental aspects of the sentence, such as the length of the sentence or the welfare of the prisoner, the courts may intervene, terminate the enforcement of the sentence in that state and transfer the prisoner elsewhere to serve their sentence.[441] At the ICC, the procedure can be requested by either the Prosecutor or the international prisoner, or initiated by the ICC Presidency on its own motion.[442]

4. International punishment in national prison systems

So far, this chapter has outlined the regulatory frameworks governing the enforcement of sentences in a decentralised system, the practicalities of implementing international punishment in the system and the consequences of some of the system's characteristics. This analysis, however, has mostly been from the perspective of the international courts. This section focuses on the reality of implementing and serving an international sentence of imprisonment in a national prison.

International prisoners may either be sent to a specifically designated facility in an enforcing state or dispersed among a variety of prisons within a domestic prison system. In the former scenario, international prisoners will serve their sentences in a prison wing that houses international prisoners only. This consolidation model[443] has been relied on by the ICTR and SCSL for the enforcement of sentences in Mali, Benin and Rwanda[444] and is the model opted for in the ICTR agreement concluded with Senegal.[445] In the latter case, however, international prisoners will typically be the only international prisoner serving a sentence in that particular prison. This dispersal model is used to enforce international punishment in developed countries.

While the consolidation model may create inequalities between the treatment of international and national prisoners, the dispersal model of enforcement can potentially create inequalities between international

---

[441] See Tolbert, "The International Criminal Tribunal for the former Yugoslavia and the Enforcement of Sentences", 659, 661.
[442] Art. 104 ICCSt; Rules 209–10 ICC RPE; Art. 13(1)–(2) ICC–Austria/Finland/Serbia BEAs; Art. 14(1)–(2) ICC–Belgium BEA; Art. 9 ICC–Mali BEA; Art. 12 ICC–UK BEA; Art. 14(1)–(2) ICC–Denmark BEA.
[443] See Culp, "Enforcement and Monitoring of Sentences in the Modern War Crimes Process", 10.
[444] See Chapter 2, Section 3.1.   [445] Art. 11(1)(c) ICTR–Senegal BEA.

prisoners and result in their isolation due to restrictive regimes or fears for safety. Both systems fail to make any real attempt to rehabilitate international prisoners or prepare them for their release and reintegration into society.

4.1 Inequality of treatment among international prisoners

The previous section discussed the inequalities that may result from the inclusion of deviating provisions on release in enforcement agreements. Designation decisions may also result in unequal treatment due to the variations in material conditions and regimes in the national prison systems used by the courts.

While international prisoners await transfer to enforcing states in IDFs, they are all subject to the same rules and have access to the same facilities.[446] Upon transfer and dispersal among national prison systems, they become subject to different rules, regimes and conditions. This is an inherent consequence of the structure of the system. The courts try to ensure a degree of uniform treatment by insisting that the enforcing state's prison system accords to international standards.[447] Indeed, the courts have helped to raise or have provided funds to assist some enforcing states reach these standards. International prisoners held in specially designated facilities are held in the same conditions, although these conditions differ from the conditions in which national prisoners are held. International prisoners dispersed among the prison systems of developed countries, on the other hand, are subject to a wide variety of conditions that differ from facility to facility, country to country.

References to international standards cannot ensure consistency as conditions of detention are dependent on both resources and penal policy.[448] It is inevitable that the prison experience will be different in each enforcing state and indeed within the different prisons used within each state. European prisons will often be "better equipped and offer more possibilities"[449] than African prisons. Even within regions, prison systems are not homogenous. Regional standards may result in the closer alignment of national approaches to penal administration, but the actual

---

[446] Reg. 223 ICC ROR.
[447] Paras. 70, 72, 74 *Erdemović* (Judgment) IT-96-22, 29.11.1996.
[448] See para. 1 HRC General Comment 9.
[449] Safferling, *Towards an International Criminal Procedure*, 355.

86   DECENTRALISED NATIONAL ENFORCEMENT

systems in place still differ considerably.[450] European prison systems have different policies and practices in relation to conjugal visits, temporary leave, work outside prison and the provision of facilities for disabled prisoners, nursing mothers and visiting families. Until the President designates a state, international prisoners are unsure which system they will encounter, and transfers may result in movement to very different regimes in a state far away from their families. Their experience in the enforcing state may be markedly different from that of other persons convicted by the same court. This will certainly be the case for courts that send prisoners to different continents to serve their sentences.

4.2   Inequality between international and national prisoners

During their sentence, international prisoners are to be treated as national prisoners in accordance with national law on imprisonment.[451] Indeed, the Rome Statute demands that enforcing states treat international prisoners no more or less favourably than national prisoners convicted of similar offences.[452] Though the number of persons convicted of war crimes and crimes against humanity is likely to be negligible in most enforcing states, the sentiment remains that international prisoners should be treated in the same way as national prisoners. The practice of the UN Tribunals and the SCSL, however, has shown that the custodial experience is not always the same for international and national prisoners. International prisoners will usually have fewer visits from their families. International prisoners housed in special facilities in developing countries generally have access to better conditions than national prisoners. In many ways, these facilities and the funding international court aim to provide a continuation of conditions of the relevant IDF. At a minimum, international prisoners will be housed with some of the same persons they were detained with at the relevant IDF. International prisoners dispersed among the prisons of developed countries, on the other hand, may have reduced opportunities for social

---

[450] J. Sim, V. Ruggiero and M. Ryan, "Punishment in Europe: Perceptions and Commonalities" in V. Ruggiero et al. (eds.), *Western European Penal Systems: A Critical Anatomy* (1995), 5.

[451] Art. 3(2) ICTY BEAs (except Art. 3(3) ICTY-Estonia/Portugal/Spain BEAs; Art. 3(4) ICTY-Poland BEA; Art. 4(1) ICTY-Slovakia BEA); Art. 3(2) ICTR/SCSL BEAs; Art.5 ICC-UK BEA; Art. 6(1) ICC-Austria BEA.

[452] Art. 106(2) ICCSt; Art. 6(1) ICC-Austria BEA.

interaction and they may be subject to high security classifications and regimes.

4.2.1 Social interaction within the prison

International prisoners may find it difficult to interact with staff and other prisoners in enforcing state prisons. An inability to speak the national language of the enforcing state can result in social exclusion and lead to isolation.[453] A lack of competence in the national language may also limit participation in activities, educational and work opportunities, and programmes that address criminal behaviour.[454] Although language classes are normally provided, prisoners are not obliged to attend and may not be good at learning new languages. Translators are not available to assist with day-to-day communications. While the situation normally improves over time, as the international prisoner learns a common language that enables communication, linguistic barriers can make the initial period of imprisonment very traumatic and isolating.

Opportunities for social interaction with other prisoners may be reduced due to the difficulties in forming relationships with people with different ages, backgrounds and who committed very different forms of crime.[455] International prisoners may not wish to associate with 'ordinary' prisoners and national prisoners may not wish to associate with international prisoners due to the nature of the crimes of which they were convicted. The age of international prisoners may also be a factor that affects their levels and quality of association with others.[456]

There is also evidence that some international prisoners are choosing to restrict their interaction with others due to fears for their safety. Some international prisoners have turned down offers to be moved to less restrictive wings,[457] and requested placement in the most restrictive

---

[453] See para. 4 *Vuković* (President's Decision) IT-96-23&23/1-ES, 11.03.2008; para. 6 *Banović* (President's Decision) IT-02-65/1-ES, 03.09.2008; paras. 12, 16 *Krnojelac* (President's Decision) IT-97-25-ES, 09.07.2009; Blagojević, Trondheim Prison, 28.06.2012; Dahl, Trondheim Prison, 28.06.2012.

[454] See para. 11 *Josipović* (President's Decision) IT-95-16-ES, 30.01.2006; F. Dunkel and D. Rossner, "Germany" in D. Van Zyl Smit and F. Dunkel (eds.), *Imprisonment Today and Tomorrow*, 2nd edn (2001), 341; A. K. Johnson, "Foreign Prisoners in European Penitentiary Institutions", 2006, 8–9.

[455] Johansson, Hinsberg Prison, 07.10.2008.

[456] Lönnberg, Hinsberg Prison, 07.10.08. Para. 9 *Plavšić* (President's Decision) IT-00-39&40/1-ES, 14.09.2009.

[457] Knudsen, Skien Prison, 26.06.2012; Jensen, Skien Prison 26.06.2012.

wings in the prison,[458] in order to limit the number of people they have contact with and also the number of hours during which they have contact with them. This can result in international prisoners spending long periods of time in a regime that only permits one hour out of the cell per day. It is therefore important that enforcing states ensure that international prisoners can be placed in safe environments that do not entail severely restrictive regimes. Where international prisoners request placement in wings with restrictive regimes due to safety fears, the rules of the wing should be applied flexibly so as to facilitate access to work and education, and as much association as possible.[459] Moreover, efforts should be made to place the individual in a safe but less restrictive environment as soon as possible.[460] These measures are necessary to prevent the isolation and mental deterioration of individuals.

4.2.2 Social interaction with persons outside the prison

Maintaining social relations with those outside the prison may also be difficult. International prisoners are imprisoned far away from their state of origin and, consequently, they are separated from their family, community and culture. As a result they tend to receive much less frequent visits than national prisoners. International prisoners may receive visits from consular or diplomatic representatives, although in some cases, they may not be from the embassy of their country of origin.[461] Unless the prisoner's family or friends live in the enforcing or nearby state, however, it would seem that international prisoners typically receive annual or biannual visits from a few members of their immediate family for a period of between a few days to a fortnight.[462] Others do not receive any visits.[463] The infrequency or lack of visits is normally attributed to financial constraints.[464] The remote location of a prison may also hinder visits from family members who live abroad.[465] Neither the national

---

[458] Mollan, Trondheim Prison, 27.06.2012.
[459] Mollan, Trondheim Prison, 27.06.2012.   [460] Dahl, Trondheim Prison, 28.06.2012.
[461] Dixon, Usk Prison, 27.09.2012; Tuler, Usk Prison, 27.09.2012; Krajišnik, Usk Prison, 27.09.2012.
[462] Mollan, Trondheim Prison, 27.06.2012; Jensen, Skien Prison 26.06.2012; Krajišnik, Usk Prison, 27.09.2012.
[463] Paras. 4, 6 *Vuković* (President's Decision) IT-96-23&23/1-ES, 11.03.2008.
[464] See para. 11 *Tadić* (President's Decision) IT-94-1-ES, 17.07.2008; para. 6 *Vuković* (President's Decision) IT-96-23&23/1-ES, 11.03.2008; para. 12 *Krnojelac* (President's Decision) IT-97-25-ES, 09.07.2009.
[465] Krajišnik, Usk Prison, 27.09.2012.

prison systems of enforcing states nor the international courts (except the SCSL) provide financial assistance to cover the costs of visits of the families of international prisoners.[466] The current enforcement system, therefore, places a large financial and emotional burden on prisoners' families. They must arrange and pay for flights, visas, health insurance, accommodation, suitable clothing etc. Visits must be organised around work and school commitments.[467] The enforcing state may limit the number of visitors that may come at one time. Security clearance can take time as the enforcing state must protect the prisoner[468] and the process usually takes longer for foreign visitors.[469]

The right to family life is well represented in human rights law and belongs not only to prisoners but also to their families.[470] Without visits, it is very difficult to maintain family relations.[471] International prisoners should be provided with assistance in order to safeguard relationships with family and close friends, especially when serving a long sentence.[472] Enforcing states should ensure that visits and other contacts with the outside world can be arranged flexibly.[473] For example, prisoners could be allowed to save up visits and take them collectively, perhaps in a prison near to airports with international flights to accommodate visits from people coming from abroad.[474] National prisons do not typically provide any financial support to assist with the costs of such visits, although charitable or humanitarian funds may be applied to for support at the local level.[475] Some prisons have apartments for family stays that

---

[466] Friman, Sweden, 22.09.2008; Matinpuro, Finland, 25.06.2008; Koeck, Austria, 13.08.2008.
[467] Bralo, Sweden, 08.10.2008.   [468] Johansson, Sweden, 07.10.2008.
[469] Johnson, "Foreign Prisoners in European Penitentiary Institutions", 19.
[470] Art. 16(3) Universal Declaration of Human Rights (UDHR); Art. 23(1) International Covenant on Civil and Political Rights (ICCPR); Art. 10(1) International Covenant on Economic, Social and Cultural Rights (ICESCR); Art. 18(1)–(2) African Charter on Human and Peoples' Rights (ACHPR); Art. 8 European Convention on Human Rights (ECHR); Art. 9 Convention on the Rights of the Child.
[471] S. Easton and C. Piper, *Sentencing and Punishment: The Quest for Justice* (2005), 365.
[472] See para. 22 Management by Prison Administrations of Life-Sentence and other Long-Term Prisoners COE Rec(2003) 23.
[473] See Recommendation II(a)(6) *Foreign Prisoners* COE Rec(84)12.
[474] See Johnson, "Foreign Prisoners in European Penitentiary Institutions", 12; Knudsen, Skien Prison, 26.06.2012.
[475] The Hinseberg Prison has access to 25,000 Kroners p.a. from the Drotting Sophias skyddsfond (Queen Sophia's Foundation). Lönnberg, Hinseberg Prison, 07.10.2008; Knudsen, Skien Prison, 26.06.2012.

enable prisoners to sleep, cook and play with their families,[476] or they may have links with external agencies that can provide accommodation at reduced rates.[477]

While the internet may provide a cheap way of facilitating communication with family members, it is seldom used for this purpose in the prison environment. Even where it is permissible, prisons may not be willing or able to facilitate it. The Norwegian prison rules, for example, permit the use of the internet to facilitate communication in exceptional circumstances, provided it costs no more than other methods and the prison can control transmissions.[478] Skien prison permits the use of video-conferencing for contact with families,[479] whereas Trondheim prison, which has video-conferencing facilities, does not (the facilities were reserved for court appearances).[480] The use of video-conferencing was also limited in Usk prison (Wales) to parole or probation meetings or court hearings.[481]

Visits contribute to upholding human dignity, recognise the rights of prisoners' families and promote the likelihood of successful reintegration.[482] Given that international imprisonment goes against the principle that prisoners should serve sentences close to their place of residence,[483] international courts should establish funds to provide assistance to indigent families wishing to visit their loved ones. The SCSL's practice is innovative in this regard. The SCSL has continued the practice of providing funds to the families of indigent prisoners to cover the costs of visits.[484] The Office of the Principal Defender in Freetown distributes[485] funds to facilitate a visit to Rwanda from one family member each year and one child every other year.[486]

States have been reluctant to allocate funds to assist families to pay for visits to indigent detained persons housed at the ICCDC, who have the

---

[476] See A. Coyle, *A Human Rights Approach to Prison Management: Handbook for Prison Staff* (2002), 98.
[477] Johnson, "Foreign Prisoners in European Penitentiary Institutions", 12.
[478] Para. 3.27 Regulations to the Execution of Sentences Act (Norway).
[479] Knudsen, Skien Prison, 26.06.2012.   [480] Dahl, Trondheim Prison, 28.06.2012.
[481] Millership, Usk Prison, 27.09.2012.
[482] See para. 33 *CPT Eleventh General Report*; S. Klein et al., "Inmate Family Functioning" (2002) 46(1) *International Journal of Offender Therapy and Comparative Criminology* 95–111 at 99.
[483] Principle 20 UNBOP; Para. 22 Management by Prison Administrations of Life-Sentence and other Long-Term Prisoners COE Rec (2003) 23; Rule 17(1) EPR; para. 11 The Execution of Sentences Act, 2004 (Norway).
[484] See para. 42 SCSL Budget 2005–2006, 39.   [485] Ras, SCSL Sub-Office, 05.07.2012.
[486] SCSL Ninth Annual Report at 38. The RSCSL will continue this practice.

additional supporting principle of the presumption of innocence. States fear that any agreement to provide this funding would create a precedent which would have long-term and substantial financial implications and would create pressure on national governments to pay for visits to not only international prisoners but other foreign national prisoners serving sentences on their territory.[487] Governments are cautious about providing such funds as this may also result in calls to provide funding for visits to national prisoners, particularly if the cost of internal travel is more expensive than an international flight.[488] This form of assistance would also have to be means-tested, which has proven difficult in the international criminal justice context. The nature of the crimes the prisoners have committed may also make fund-raising difficult. The ICC has, however, been able to secure donations for the voluntary fund that was established to pay for visits of families of accused persons housed at the ICCDC.[489] This fund could be extended to help finance visits to indigent convicted persons housed in enforcing states.

Without an international probation or parole system, or a police force, the international courts are typically reluctant to grant international prisoners forms of leave that involve international travel. International prisoners are therefore unlikely to be granted temporary leave or permission to attend family occasions that occur in a country other than the state in which their sentences are being enforced. For example, Mr Krajišnik was denied permission to attend both his mother's and father's funerals in Bosnia-Herzegovina.[490] This lack of involvement in important family events can have a detrimental impact on the prisoner's well-being and important relationships.

International jurisprudence has acknowledged that the inevitable isolation that will result from serving a prison sentence in a state far away from family and in which the prisoner does not speak the language may constitute an additional hardship.[491] Although this may be taken into consideration by judges when determining the length of the sentence

---

[487] See para. 15(b) "External audit, internal audit, programme budget for 2009 and related documents" Vol. 1(II) Official Records of Seventh Session of the Assembly of State Parties, 13; paras. 17, 25, 29, 32(a) Report of the Bureau on Family Visits for Detainees, 29.10.2009; paras. 2, 7 Family Visits for Indigent Detainees, ICC-ASP/8/Res.4, 26.11.2009.
[488] Johnson, "Foreign Prisoners in European Penitentiary Institutions", 19.
[489] See para. 1, Section X, ICC-ASP/9/Res.4, 10.12.2010 at 33 and Chapter 3, Section 2.
[490] Krajišnik, Usk Prison, 27.09.2012.
[491] Para. 75 *Erdemović* (Judgment) IT-96-22-T, 29.11.1996; para. 107 *Mrđa* (Judgment) IT-02-59-S, 31.03.2004.

imposed, this common aspect of international imprisonment cannot constitute a mitigating factor.[492] While the structure of the current enforcement system has the potential to aggravate the sentence imposed through social isolation, the level of isolation experienced will be relative to each prisoner, depending on his personality, linguistic ability, proximity to family and their resources to pay for visits. Although they may not be as effective as visits, international prisoners can also use letters, phone calls and, in some cases, video-conferencing and emails to keep in touch with their families. The potential for aggravating the sentence is heightened, however, when the likelihood that international prisoners will be placed in prisons or units with very high levels of security is considered.

4.2.3 Enhanced security

Upon transfer to enforcing states, international prisoners are assessed and moved to prisons allocated on the basis of their needs and security classification. The combination of their nationality, gravity of crimes for which they were convicted, the length of the sentences imposed and pending deportation orders will typically result in international prisoners being placed in high security prisons.[493] Enforcing states undertake to put all necessary measures in place to ensure the security, safety and protection of internationally sentenced persons.[494] As enforcing states view the protection of international prisoners to be in the "national interest",[495] every effort is made to place them among a stable constellation of prisoners and with trusted staff.[496] To prevent escape, the prisoner causing harm or the prisoner being harmed, some international prisoners may be placed in secure units within high security prisons.[497]

By their nature, these units offer a more restrictive regime and extremely limited association with other prisoners. Moreover, prisoners may spend the majority of their sentence in these conditions. Through their allocation decisions, enforcing states try to balance sentence management and penological objectives with their human rights obligations to

---

[492] Paras. 108–9 *Mrda* (Judgment) IT-02-59-S, 31.03.2004.
[493] Daw and Wilkinson, UK, 24.05.2006; Isaksson, Sweden, 07.10.2008. See Johnson, "Foreign Prisoners in European Penitentiary Institutions", 10–11.
[494] See Art. 19 ICC–Belgium BEA; Art. 19(1) ICC–Austria/Finland/Serbia BEAs; Art. 20(1) ICC–Denmark BEA.
[495] Isaksson, Sweden, 07.10.2008.   [496] Lönnberg, Hinsberg Prison, 07.10.2008.
[497] Daw and Wilkinson, UK, 24.05.2006; Johansson, Hinsberg Prison, 07.10.08; Dixon, Usk Prison, 27.09.12.

protect those convicted of war crimes from attacks from other prisoners.[498] Some international prisoners fear revenge attacks from prisoners from the ethnic group they were convicted of committing crimes against and/or retaliatory attacks from members of their own ethnic group for "betrayal" following cooperation with the Prosecutor or a guilty plea.[499] As was outlined above, some international prisoners have feared and complained about abuse from other prisoners,[500] and requested transfer from more open conditions to closed units for their safety.[501] In some instances, transfers to restricted regimes can result in a win–win situation; the enforcing state is at ease as the prisoner is safe and the prisoner is at ease because he is safe.

Prison allocation and security categorisations decisions are the prerogative of the enforcing state. The international courts may need to consider intervening in cases where such decisions, even if they are made in order to protect an international prisoner, risk violating his fundamental rights. In some cases, the need to ensure the prisoner's safety has resulted in "very harsh and restrictive imprisonment and high seclusion".[502] For instance, when Mr Bralo arrived in Sweden, he was told he would spend two weeks in segregation "for his own security". He joked that they were the "longest two weeks of this life"[503] as he actually spent twenty-three hours a day in his cell during the following five months of solitary confinement.

This situation was replicated in the UK. In an attempt to ensure his safety, Mr Krajišnik was placed in Category A prisons (the highest security level available in the UK) with Special Secure Units.[504] However, threats to his safety from other prisoners necessitated his transfer on two separate occasions. Since his arrival in the UK in 2009, Mr Krajišnik has been transferred from Belmarsh prison (Category A), to Full Sutton prison (Category A) and finally to Usk Prison (Category C). While he was at Full Sutton prison, he spent one day less than one year in isolation due to threats from Muslim prisoners.[505] This meant that he was in his cell twenty three hours a day and he could not associate with any other prisoners during his one hour out of the cell. Mr Krajišnik understood that these measures were necessary and that they were only

---

[498] See *Rodić and 3 Others v. Bosnia and Herzegovina* (22893/05) 27.03.2008.
[499] See para. 75 *Erdemović* (Judgment) IT-96-22/T, 29.11.1996.
[500] Para. 11 *Tadić* (President's Decision) IT-94-1-ES, 17.07.2008.
[501] Para. 7 *Delić* (President's Decision) IT-96-21-ES, 24.06.2008.
[502] Isaksson, Sweden, 07.10.2008.   [503] Bralo, Sweden, 08.10.2008.
[504] Dixon, Usk Prison, 27.09.2012.   [505] Tuler, Usk Prison, 27.09.2012.

put in place to protect him. He also noted that the staff had made every effort to try to make it easier for him.[506] The Full Sutton authorities contacted Usk prison and requested his transfer in order to alleviate the restrictiveness of his imprisonment.[507] Although Usk prison is primarily used for the treatment of sex offenders, it has experience of housing non-sex offending prisoners who are considered to be vulnerable. This facility was considered to be appropriate as "in a sense, the prison is one big segregation unit".[508] The restrictiveness of the regime at Full Sutton perhaps only became apparent to Mr Krajišnik when he was moved to Usk. He stated that when he was transferred, he felt like he was free again.[509] Although there were some complaints about his presence at Usk prison from Muslim prisoners, he mingles freely with all prisoners and has recently been moved to an enhanced wing which has a relaxed regime and is unstaffed after it is locked for the evening.[510] While the prison authorities were only exercising caution to prevent the repetition of an incident similar to the attack on Mr Krstić[511] and, indeed, took all measures to ensure he was placed in a less restrictive regime, it should not have taken one year to organise a transfer to a safe facility.

Further examples of long-term solitary confinement have been reported in the jurisprudence of the international courts. For example, a similar situation occurred in France, whereby Mr Radić was placed in isolation for nine months for his own protection following incidents of harassment.[512] Long-term solitary confinement can violate the fundamental rights of a prisoner. In determining whether solitary confinement amounts to torture, inhuman or degrading treatment or punishment, contemporary human rights institutions look at the period involved, the physical conditions, the potential for sensory and social isolation, the ability of the measure to achieve disciplinary or protective objectives, the decision-making process responsible for the imposition of the measure, and the continuing acceptability of the substantive reasons for its implementation, taking into account the criteria of reasonableness, necessity and legality.[513] Solitary confinement should

---

[506] Krajišnik, Usk Prison, 27.09.2012.   [507] Tuler, Usk Prison, 27.09.2012.
[508] Millership, Usk Prison, 27.09.2012.   [509] Krajišnik, Usk Prison, 27.09.2012.
[510] Millership, Usk Prison, 27.09.2012; Dixon, Usk Prison, 27.09.2012; Tuler, Usk Prison, 27.09.2012.
[511] See Chapter 5, Section 2.2.
[512] Para. 19 *Radić* (President's Decision) IT-98-30/1-ES, 23.04.2010.
[513] See N. Rodley and M. Pollard, *The Treatment of Prisoners under International Law*, 3rd edn (2009), 402–6.

be for the shortest time possible and its use must be proportionate to the requirements of the case, as this form of regime can have very harmful consequences for the prisoner, and may amount to inhuman and degrading treatment.[514]

Enforcing states must ensure that international prisoners are placed in facilities that can protect their safety without the need to completely segregate the individual. The lack of suitable accommodation is not an appropriate excuse for failing to protect persons convicted of war crimes.[515] Sweden signed an agreement with the ICTY on 23 February 1999. Mr Bralo was transferred from the UNDU to Sweden on 1 November 2007. A state with eight years of notice of the likelihood of receiving a prisoner into custody cannot cite capacity problems for the inability to provide anything other than solitary confinement for months on end. The same reasoning is applicable to the UK scenario. Not only does this method of sentence implementation risk violating human rights law, it may also go against sentencing objectives of proportionality by aggravating the sentence imposed.[516]

4.2.4 Progression

The focus on the safety of international prisoners and their likely deportation may mean they are not able to progress through the security classifications of the national prison system and thereby enjoy more relaxed regimes. Placement decisions should be regularly reviewed to ensure the regime matches the risk the prisoner actually presents.[517] Initial allocation and subsequent transfer decisions appear, at times, to be based on the international status of the prisoner and the need to protect them rather than any real or objective risk assessment. A "high risk" status is "not an ontological characteristic of an individual but a dynamic definition which must be continuously reassessed and which the prisoner must be able to challenge".[518] On the other hand, there have been times when it appears that a prisoner's security status has been down-graded to facilitate internal transfers[519] or exceptional forms of

---

[514] Para. 56 CPT Second General Report.
[515] See paras. 64–73 *Rodić and 3 Others v. Bosnia and Herzegovina* (22893/05) 27.03.2008.
[516] See N. Walker, *Why Punish?* (1991), 109.
[517] Para. 32 CPT Eleventh General Report.
[518] D. Van Zyl Smit and S. Snacken, *Principles of European Prison Law and Policy: Penology and Human Rights* (2009), 283.
[519] Tuler, Usk Prison, 27.09.2012.

early release.[520] A cynical view would be that this latter form of progression is merely procedural fast-tracking to facilitate the release and subsequent deportation of international prisoners. Yet some international prisoners have naturally progressed to lower security categories[521] or to more open regimes that enable prisoners to go outside the prison for leisure and/or employment purposes.[522] While penological principles argue for progression, popular sentiment seems opposed to more open conditions for international criminals. When it became public that three ICTY prisoners were serving their sentences in semi-open prisons, domestic public and political criticism resulted in their relocation.[523] Yet, progression to more open conditions can play an important role in rehabilitation and preparation for release, particularly for persons serving long sentences.

4.3 Rehabilitation and preparation for release

International and regional law and standards dictate that prison systems should be managed to ensure that prisoners are reformed and make progress towards release and reintegration into society through, *inter alia*, participation in programmes and activities outlined in individualised sentence plans.[524] Irrespective of where international prisoners will go upon release, penological and human rights standards, and public safety considerations, demand that all prisoners should confront their crimes, recognise their offending behaviour and be aided with their transition back into society. International prisoners serving their sentences in national prisons, however, may not have clear or structured sentence plans, access to offending behaviour programmes or assistance with preparation for release.

4.3.1 Rehabilitation

While efforts are made to accommodate the needs of international prisoners, perhaps to a greater extent than they would be for national

---

[520] See para. 6 *Josipović* (President's Decision) IT-95-16-ES, 30.01.2006; para. D.4.5(54) MDP, 163.
[521] Tuler, Usk Prison, 27.09.2012.
[522] See *Furundžija* (President's Order) IT-95-17/1, 29.07.2004; para. 4 *Vuković* (President's Decision) IT-96-23&23/1-ES, 11.03.2008.
[523] See Nemitz, "Execution of Sanctions", 133.
[524] Para. 208 *James, Wells and Lee* v. *UK* (25119/09, 57715/09 and 57877/09) 18.09.2012.

prisoners,[525] international prisoners are often restricted in what they can do within a domestic prison system due to their nationality and the unique nature of their criminality. This is particularly true in relation to rehabilitation. Linguistic barriers may prevent international prisoners from gaining access to, or participating in, national programmes. International prisoners are serving sentences of imprisonment for the commission of a wide variety of crimes and varying levels of responsibility. Some international prisoners have been convicted for offences which are also criminalised under domestic law. Despite the fact that international crimes are committed in a different context, i.e. during a conflict situation, some domestic programmes may be used to address the underlying offending behaviour and the prisoner's dangerousness. Unfortunately, it seems that international prisoners are being denied access to these programmes on the basis of their nationality and likely deportation. The limited places available on specialist programmes may be reserved for individuals who will be released back into society in the state in which the prison is located.[526] Equally worrying is the fact that international prisoners convicted of crimes that are also criminalised under domestic law may be placed in prisons which do not deal with this type of behaviour. For example, an individual convicted of enslavement, rape and outrages against personal dignity for offences committed against children[527] was placed in a prison that had no programmes to deal with sex offences. It is unclear on what basis this allocation decision was made. Not only will this prisoner serve his sentence without addressing his offending behaviour or undergoing any objective assessment of his risk of re-offending, given the lack of a parole system in the international criminal justice system, he will be released without any conditions or supervision. It is hard to believe that this situation, which would not be tolerated in a national prison system, appears to be deemed acceptable for those would have committed "the most serious crimes of concern to the international community".[528]

While some international prisoners have been convicted for acts that constitute crimes under domestic criminal law, others have been convicted for committing acts or for command responsibility for acts that may not constitute crimes under domestic criminal law. National prison systems do not have programmes to address these international crimes

---

[525] Lavis, Usk Prison, 27.09.2012. [526] Tour of Trondheim Prison, 27.06.2012.
[527] *Kunarac, Kovac and Vukovic* (Judgment) IT-96-23-T&IT-96-23/1-T, 22.02.2001 and (AC Judgment) IT-96-23&IT-96-23/1-A, 12.06.2002.
[528] Preamble ICCSt.

or to deal with the different levels of criminal responsibility that can form the basis of a conviction under international criminal law. Irrespective of whether the act in question constitutes a crime under domestic law, it seems that even on an informal level, prison officers and persons involved in the detention of international prisoners avoid discussing their offending behaviour with them.[529]

The decentralised system therefore results in prisoners being placed in prisons that do not and cannot deal with their crimes, even though, for some prisoners, there may be suitable programmes at other national facilities. For example, Mr Kovač, who committed sex offences, was placed in a Norwegian prison that does not provide programmes which address sex offending, whereas Mr Krajišnik who did not commit sex offences was placed in a Welsh prison for sex offenders due to fears for his safety. Poor allocation decisions and safety concerns have resulted in international prisoners being placed in national prisons that cannot provide or implement effective sentence plans.

The problem is, however, more fundamental than the appropriateness of allocation decisions. The programmes provided by national prison systems are typically unsuited to dealing with the majority of international crimes.[530] Unlike national crimes, international crimes are not normally motivated by personal behavioural traits, financial gain or anger:[531] they are essentially politically and militarily motivated offences. National prisons systems do not design programmes to deal with these forms of crime. The majority of international prisoners require access to bespoke programmes, but there is no room for the development of individualised programmes to deal with international crime within a national prison system.[532] National prison systems cannot be expected to design and implement specialist programmes dealing with international criminality for a handful of international prisoners held in a number of different facilities. The upshot of this, however, is that the vast majority of international prisoners will not have a sentence plan or access to programmes necessary for their rehabilitation or preparation for release. Even though national prison systems have established procedures for dealing with foreign national prisoners, long-term prisoners and dangerous prisoners, they do not have experience of, or the requisite expertise for, dealing with international prisoners.[533] Enforcing institutions can

---

[529] Skien Prison, 26.06.2012; Trondheim Prison, 27–28.06.2012; Usk Prison, 27.09.2012.
[530] Wilkinson, UK, 10.10.2012.   [531] Millership, Usk Prison, 27.09.2012.
[532] Millership, Usk Prison, 27.09.2012.   [533] Wilkinson, UK, 10.10.2012.

often do little more than ensure that international prisoners are kept occupied by education, work or leisure activities.

This situation may have implications for the legality of international imprisonment. A recent ECtHR case illustrated that detention after eligibility for release has passed may become arbitrary, and unlawful, if prisoners cannot access the programmes necessary for them to comply with their sentence plan and to demonstrate that they have worked towards release criteria.[534] While this case dealt with a very specific type of indeterminate sentence, it does highlight the need to ensure that prisoners are placed in prisons where they can undertake programmes that enable them to show that they have addressed their offending behaviour and made efforts towards their reintegration into society. A lack of capacity or resources is not a sufficient excuse for the operation of a penal system that does not empower prisoners to demonstrate that they are ready for release on the basis of criteria established by the detaining authority.[535]

This principle is particularly pertinent for the ICC. While the prisoners of the ICTY and ICTR must demonstrate signs of rehabilitation,[536] ICC prisoners will have to demonstrate evidence of progress towards additional reform factors. The ICC Review Panel must consider a range of factors when making decisions about possible reductions of sentences such as the prisoner's dissociation from crime, prospects for resocialisation and successful resettlement, the impact of release on victims and broader social stability and actions taken for the benefit of victims.[537] In addition to being clear and explicit, release criteria must be realistic and attainable through access to and participation in relevant programmes.[538] If the ICC criteria were to be applied strictly and therefore result in the denial of release on the basis that the prisoner in question had failed to demonstrate that he had taken steps towards attaining these implicit goals for punishment, then the continued legality of detention may become questionable. A penal system that lacks initiatives which enable prisoners to progress and comply with sentence plans or release requirements may result in detention becoming arbitrary and therefore unlawful.[539]

---

[534] Para. 221 *James, Wells and Lee* v. *United Kingdom* (25119/09, 57715/09 and 57877/09) 18.09.2012.
[535] See paras. 31, 38, 103–4, 207, 210, 218, 220 *James, Wells and Lee* v. *United Kingdom* (25119/09, 57715/09 and 57877/09) 18.09.2012.
[536] Rule 125 ICTY RPE; Rule 126 ICTR RPE.   [537] Rule 223 ICC RPE.
[538] See recommendation18 Conditonal Release (Parole), Rec (2003) 22 24.09.2003.
[539] See Art. 9 UDHR; Art. 5(1) ECtHR; Art.9(1) ICCPR; Art.7(3) ACHR; Art. 6 ACHPR.

4.3.2 Preparation for release

Many international prisoners have been released after serving their sentences or being granted early release. The enforcement of international punishment in domestic prisons far from the prisoner's state of origin does not facilitate preparation for release or support with reintegration into society. Not only will many international prisoners spend the majority of their sentences in high security, restrictive regimes with limited access to appropriate rehabilitation programmes and their family and friends, they will seldom qualify for progression or temporary release options designed to assist prisoners approaching the end of their sentence to adjust to freedom and ease transition from prison life to life in the community.

Bilateral enforcement agreements recognise that international prisoners may be eligible for programmes or benefits that take place outside the prison.[540] International prisoners have been entitled to engage in social and leisure activities outside prison. For example, international prisoners have attended religious services in other towns, gone shopping and been for meals in restaurants accompanied by prison guards.[541] Permission has also been granted to an international prisoner to leave prison unaccompanied for short periods of time to visit friends living nearby.[542] In other countries, however, requests for leave to attend events outside the prison have been denied.[543] Like other non-national prisoners, many international prisoners will be less likely to be able to avail of temporary leave measures.[544] Even though permission may be granted for half-day or day trips, experts advocate that prisoners spend longer periods outside prison to avoid institutionalisation.[545] Some international prisoners seem reluctant to avail of opportunities to leave the prison for even short periods of time.[546] Limited social engagement can result in nervousness in every-day scenarios and dependence on others.[547] Reduced social skills and social support caused by long-term imprisonment in a foreign state may make the transition back into

---

[540] See Art. 4(4) ICC–Mali BEA; Art. 6(3) ICC–Denmark/Finland/Serbia BEAs; Art. 8(2) ICC–Belgium BEA.
[541] Para. 6 *Landžo* (President's Order), IT-96-21-ES, 13.04.2006; Johansson, Hinseberg Prison, 07.10.2008; Jensen, Skien Prison 26.06.2012.
[542] Knudsen, Skien Prison, 26.06.2012.   [543] Lavis, Usk Prison, 27.09.2012.
[544] Daw and Wilkinson, UK, 24.05.2006; Johansson, Hinseberg Prison, 07.10.2008; Matinpuro, Finland, 25.06.2008; Chetwynd, CPT, 08.06.2007.
[545] Johnson, "Foreign Prisoners in European Penitentiary Institutions" 13, 19.
[546] Dahl, Trondheim Prison, 28.06.2012.   [547] Jensen, Skien Prison 26.06.2012.

society difficult for some international prisoners. One prisoner recalled how he found it difficult to recognise many people who came to visit him during a short period of temporary leave after nine years in detention. He felt that they all had changed and aged but he had not.[548]

Unlike the process put in place for national prisoners, whereby the prison begins assessing the prisoner's risk, housing and employment needs and making contacts with parole and probation boards, the process for foreign prisoners usually involves little more than making contact with the Government body responsible for deportation.[549] International prisoners may even fall outside the process for foreign prisoners as the paperwork and decision-making process tend to be different. Moreover, the decision in relation to release often comes very close to the actual release date, meaning national prisons can do little in terms of effective resettlement planning.[550] National prisons housing international prisoners are, therefore, often unsure what they are supposed to do with such prisoners to prepare them for release.[551]

The failure of the decentralised enforcement system to prepare international prisoners for transition back to society is extremely significant in the international criminal justice system as it does not have a parole or probation system which can support or supervise ex-international prisoners. Although the majority of international prisoners will be transferred to another state when they have completed their sentence, there is no liaison between the implementing prison or the international court with the probation or parole services in the receiving state. There may also be insufficient preparation for those who may remain in the state, as asylum decisions may not be finalised until a few months prior to release. For example, Mr Blagojević was due to be released on 31 December 2012. However, as of June 2012, it was unclear where he would go upon release, as a request for asylum, filed two years previously, had yet to be decided. The failure to resolve asylum issues puts the releasing prison in a difficult position: how does a prison prepare an individual for release if it is not known which country the person will live in when released? If asylum is not granted, then deportation will have to be arranged. Again, this procedure may not be straightforward as it will not always be clear which country to deport the released individual to.

---

[548] Krajišnik, Usk Prison, 27.09.2012.
[549] Dixon, Usk Prison, 27.09.2012; Millership, Usk Prison, 27.09.2012.
[550] Wilkinson, UK, 10.10.2012.
[551] Mollan, Trondheim Prison, 27.06.2012; Dixon, Usk Prison, 27.09.2012.

Contemporary penological standards advocate that prisoners be prepared for release in good time and that their sentences are managed so as to facilitate their reintegration into society.[552] International prisoners are released unconditionally and transferred to another state without any connections being made with probation or parole services in that country. During their time in prison, they do not have any opportunity to address the crimes for which they were convicted. This may mean that potentially dangerous criminals are released back into society without supervision. The current decentralised system therefore not only fails to prepare international prisoners for release, but it releases them without support or supervision.

5. Conclusion

This chapter has charted the processes involved in the implementation of international punishment in the decentralised national system of enforcement, analysed the procedures involved in its supervision and highlighted some of the problems with its enforcement in domestic prisons. Like the international criminal justice system more generally, the decentralised national system is based on a dual enforcement regime founded on two pillars – a judicial pillar represented by the international courts and an enforcement pillar represented by cooperating states.[553] International criminal courts rely on cooperating states to provide prison cells in which international custodial sanctions can be enforced, subject to their supervision. Given its voluntary nature, however, this system does not always provide the required penal capacity. There are not always a sufficient number of states that are willing or able to implement international sentences of imprisonment. Accordingly, the international courts have had to directly implement international sentences of imprisonment in their own remand centres. This centralised international system of enforcement is described in Chapter 3.

---

[552] Rules 6, 103(2), 103(4)(d), 107(1) EPR.
[553] Abathi and Koh, "The Emerging Enforcement Practice at the International Criminal Court", 1–2.

3

Centralised international enforcement

Decentralised national enforcement is the primary system for the implementation of international sentences of imprisonment. In other words, international courts typically transfer convicted persons to the prison systems of cooperating states to serve their sentences. However, the difficulties encountered in securing state cooperation[1] have led to a situation whereby the international courts have had to enforce their sentences directly. Without international prisons, this direct implementation has taken place in the temporary courts' international detention facilities (IDFs) in The Hague, Arusha and Freetown.[2]

In contrast to national prison systems, which usually fall within the ambit of a Ministry of Justice, IDFs are the responsibility of the administrative section of the court, the Registry.[3] The President/Presidency is responsible for overseeing the Registry's work and therefore plays an oversight role in relation to detention.[4] IDFs are managed by a specialised unit (or personnel) within the Registry[5] and a chief custody officer (CCO). All the IDFs have virtually identical chains of command with the Registrar delegating responsibility for the day-to-day running of the facility to the CCO, who in turn delegates duties to subordinates.[6] Senior managers are recruited specifically for the job. To date, they have brought experience of working in national prison inspectorates, national prison services, international peacekeeping missions and even managing other IDFs.[7] The CCO is responsible for the financial management of the facility, the welfare of detained persons

---

[1] See Chapter 2, Section 1. [2] See Chapter 1, Section 3.
[3] C. De Sampayo Garrido, "Problems and Achievements Seen from the Viewpoint of the Registry" (2004) 2 *Journal of International Criminal Justice* 474–9 at 478.
[4] Rule 19(A) ICTY/ICTR/SCSL RPE; Art. 38(3)(a), 43(2) ICCSt.
[5] ICTY – Office of Legal Aid and Detention, ICTR – Defence Counsel and Detention Management Section, ICC – Detention Section, SCSL – legal officers within the Registry.
[6] Rule 2 ICTY ROD; Rule 3 ICTR ROD; Rule 3 SCSL ROD; Reg. 90(2) ICC ROC.
[7] Tim McFadden came to the UNDU from the UNDF and Terry Jackson came to ICCDC from the SCSLDF.

and the security and order of the unit.[8] The CCO is also the focal point for internal communications with other sections of the court and external communications with other IDFs, courts, the Host State, enforcing states, inspection bodies etc. The CCO is assisted in the discharge of these responsibilities by deputy chief custody officers. The next level, the principal officer or international supervisor, may be recruited from the Host State prison service or hired directly by the court. They are responsible for the day-to-day running of the IDF, the welfare of detained persons and for organising and training custodial staff. The vast majority of custodial staff at all the IDFs are seconded from the prison service of the Host State under a negotiated agreement with the court.[9]

The IDFs were designed to operate as international remand centres to house suspects[10] and accused persons awaiting the finalisation of their trial at an international criminal court. Yet in reality, the UNDU, UNDF and SCSLDF have also been used to house convicted persons. In addition to holding persons found guilty but awaiting the finalisation of their sentences, these international facilities have also implemented the sentences of those convicted of contempt of court[11] and witnesses testifying before the court.[12] The IDFs have also directly implemented the sentences of convicted persons awaiting transfer to enforcing states.[13]

Transfer should occur as soon as possible after the time-limit for appeal has elapsed, the sentence has been finalised[14] or the enforcing state accepts the court's designation decision.[15] Pursuant to the principle that prisoners should only be transferred if they have over six months remaining of their sentence,[16] international prisoners with only short periods left tend to serve the remainder of their sentences at IDFs.[17] The

---

[8] Reg. 187(1) ICC ROR.
[9] See Memorandum of Understanding Concerning the Secondment of Sierra Leone Prison Service Staff to the Special Court for Sierra Leone (SCSL MOU (Secondment)).
[10] Rule 40*bis* ICTY/ICTR RPE; Art. 60(3) ICCSt; Rule 118 ICC RPE.
[11] See para. 42 *Šešelj* (Appeal Judgment) IT-03-67.R77.2-A, 19.05.2010; para. 80 *Petković* (Judgment) IT-03-67-R77.1, 11.09.2008; para. 80 *Margetić* (Judgment) IT-95-14-R77.6, 07.02.2007; *Begaj* (Judgment) IT-03-66-R77, 27.05.2005; *GAA* (Judgment) ICTR-07-90-R77-I, 04.12.2007.
[12] See Rule 90*bis*(A) ICTY/ICTR RPE; Art. 93(7) ICCSt; Rules 192–3 ICC RPE.
[13] See Rule 103(C) ICTY RPE; Reg. 223 ICC ROR.
[14] Rule 103(B) ICTY/ICTR RPE; Rule 103(C) SCSL RPE.
[15] Rules 202, 206(2) ICC RPE.
[16] Art. 11, UN Model Agreement on the Transfer of Foreign Prisoners GARes 40/32, 29.11.1985.
[17] D. Van Zyl Smit, "International Imprisonment" (2005) 54 *International and Comparative Law Quarterly* 357–86 at 367.

ICC has ensured this practice now has a legal basis by including a provision in its Headquarters Agreement with the Dutch Government, which states that convicted prisoners with only six months or less to serve may remain in the ICCDC rather than be transferred to an enforcing state.[18] However many convicted persons have a lot longer left to serve on their sentence, and transfers take an average of nine months.[19] This time lag has been attributed to the lack of cooperating states, or more technical procedural requirements such as the necessity to use an exequatur procedure or to grant a visa for the prisoner.[20] Whatever the reason for the delay, an increasing number of persons are remaining in IDFs after their sentences become finalised.[21] At times, convicted persons can outnumber non-convicted persons. Between 2010 and 2012, for example, there were two convicted persons for every non-convicted person at the ICTR's UNDF.[22] In some cases, convicted persons spend the entirety of their sentence at an IDF.[23] In fact, fourteen out of thirty-six persons sentenced by the ICTY served the entirety of the sentences (ranging from two to ten years) in the UNDU.[24] The SCSL has also recently decided to directly enforce sentences imposed on persons convicted of contempt of court in its new detention facility within the court's perimeter.[25] Despite the lack of an explicit legal or political mandate, IDFs are used as international prisons.

1. Imprisonment at an international detention facility

IDFs have been used to house convicted persons with finalised sentences. Indeed, individuals have served periods of up to seven years in IDFs.[26] While the regulations forbid the discriminatory application of rules,[27]

---

[18] Art. 50(1) ICC HQA.
[19] See para. 2.11 Independent Audit of the Detention Unit at the ICTY, 2006.
[20] Dubuisson, Tjonk, Becerra-Suarez, ICC, 06.06.2007; Siller, ICTY, 07.06.2007; Vicente, ICTY, 16.02.2007.
[21] Para. 2.11 Independent Audit of the Detention Unit at the ICTY, 2006.
[22] Para. 70 ICTR Fifteenth Annual Report; para. 69 ICTR Sixteenth Annual Report.
[23] Para. A.2(13) MDP, 153–4; para. 35 ICTR Fifteenth Annual Report.
[24] Kubura, Kvočka, Prcać, Čerkez, M. Tadić, Blaškić, Zarić, M. Simić, Mucić, Kos, Kolundžija, Gvero, Hadžihasanović, Strugar, Šljivančanin.
[25] See SCSL Ninth Annual Report at 25; SCSL Press Releases, "Eric Koi Senessie Sentenced to Two Years in Prison for Contempt of the Special Court", 05.07.2012; "Four Sentenced for Interference in the Administration of Justice" 11.10.2012.
[26] See Chapter 2, Section 2.
[27] Rule 3 ICTY ROD; Rule 2(b) ICTR/SCSL ROD; Reg. 91(1) ICC ROC.

differentiated regimes can be used for different categories of detained persons.[28] The President of the ICTY, in line with international recommendations, ordered the UNDU to separate convicted and non-convicted persons.[29] However, budgetary and infrastructural constraints made it impossible for this order to be implemented.[30] All detained persons were housed on the same wing at the SCSLDF. Although the ICC rules provide for the separate accommodation of those with finalised sentences,[31] this was not possible when the ICCDC occupied a single wing. This will be possible following the 2012 move to a new floor with two wings. Despite this new space, there remain funding issues: there is no budget line to pay for the additional personnel that would be required to staff a separate wing.[32] The ICTR did move convicted persons to a separate part of the UNDF but they remain subject to the same standards as non-convicted persons.[33] In practice, convicted persons in IDFs remain subject to the same conditions and regime as non-convicted persons.[34] The ICC gives legal effect to this practice, stating in the Regulations of the Registry that rules for non-convicted persons apply *mutatis mutandis* to convicted persons awaiting transfer to enforcing states.[35]

International prisoners serving sentences at an IDF are therefore subject to a regime designed with the presumption of innocence in mind.[36] It was considered unnecessary to devise a new set of regulations to govern what was only supposed to be a short, transitory period of incarceration. While this will be true for ICC prisoners at the ICCDC, other international prisoners have served significant portions of their sentences at IDFs. IDF managers did not wish to separate the different groups for several reasons. From a security perspective, there were fears that creating different regimes would create tensions between detained persons.[37] For instance, at the SCSLDF, cells on one wing had

---

[28] Reg. 91(2) ICC ROC.
[29] See Order to the Registrar to Separate Convicted and Non-Convicted Detainees held at the Detention Unit, IT-06-89-Misc.1, 15.06.2006.
[30] Para. 2.8.5 Independent Audit of the Detention Unit at the ICTY, 2006. Vincent, SCSL/ICTY, 27.04.2007.
[31] Reg. 105(2) ICC ROC.   [32] Craig, ICCDC, 04.07.2012.
[33] O'Donnell, ICTR, 25.06.2007; Mwuangulu, Wastelain, Endeley, ICTR, 25.06.2007.
[34] See D. Abels, *Prisoners of the International Community: The Legal Position of Persons Detained at International Criminal Tribunals* (2012), 83–6.
[35] Reg. 223 ICC ROR.
[36] Para. 2.10 Independent Audit of the Detention Unit at the ICTY, 2006; Preambles of ICTY/ ICTR/SCSL ROD.
[37] O'Donnell, ICTR, 25.06.2007.

toilets but cells on the other wing did not. There was also a sense that separation would have a negative impact on emotional health, as detainees and prisoners provide a support structure for each other.[38] In fact, with such small populations, "a total separation regime could lead to situations of forced isolation, likely to have an adverse effect on the individual's mental situation".[39]

Irrespective of the arguments for or against differentiated regimes, prisoners housed in IDFs are subject to the same regime as non-convicted persons. The UNDU and UNDF regime is governed by Rules of Detention (ROD) drafted by judges. These have been revised and supplemented over the years with practice directions on discipline, communication and complaint procedures. The rules governing detention at the ICCDC are more elaborate and explicit in relation to complaints procedures and oversight mechanisms intended to protect detainees' rights. They are, however, more difficult to navigate as they are contained in two documents: the Regulations of Court and the Regulations of Registry. Amendments to the Regulations of the Registry were recently proposed in order to reflect the realities of operating the ICCDC.[40] The SCSLDF's ROD were drafted by the Registry and are much more concise than the others. Overall, the regulatory frameworks governing the operation of the IDFs are all very similar, being derived from international human rights law, international and regional standards governing detention and Host State penal law. They create regimes that aim to protect the rights of detained persons by ensuring respect for humanity and dignity.[41] They also provide a "roadmap on how to do business and ... the basis of detainee expectations".[42]

All IDFs have a single cell policy.[43] The facilities are constructed or adapted to meet international standards on health, hygiene, climate, light, heat and ventilation.[44] Cells can be adjusted to accommodate the needs of persons with disabilities.[45] The ICC is obliged to provide special accommodation for pre-natal and post-natal care and treatment and

---

[38] Cardinal, Moore, SCSLDF, 20.04.2008; Wright, SCSLDF, 22.04.2008; Ewing, SCSLDF, 23.04.2008; Neil, SCSLDF, 23.04.2008.
[39] Para. A.2(13) MDP, 154.
[40] Seminar on the Amendments to the Regulations of the Registry, 4–6.7.2012.
[41] Preamble ICTY/ICTR/SCSL ROD; Reg. 91(1) ICC ROC.
[42] Cardinal, SCSLDF, 20.04.2008. See also Preamble ICTY ROD.
[43] Rules 17–18 ICTY ROD; Rules 14–15 ICTR ROD; Rules 12, 14 SCSL ROD; Reg. 105(3) ICC ROC.
[44] Rule 19 ICTY ROD; Rule 16 ICTR ROD; Rule 15(A) SCSL ROD; Reg. 193 ICC ROR.
[45] Falke, UNDU/ICCDC, 04.07.2012.

nursing assistance to take care of infants when they are not in the care of their parents.[46] Prisoners have unrestricted access to hygiene facilities and drinking water.[47] The UNDF is the only facility to provide showers in cells. The other IDFs have common shower rooms on the wings. Prisoners are provided with toiletries necessary for washing and shaving.[48] In addition to a toilet and sink, IDF cells normally contain a bed, shelves, desk, chair, window, cupboard, radio and TV. IDF wings have a common living area, laundry facilities and kitchen. At the ICCDC, this common area was smaller than usual due to the need to install a work area for the custodial staff. The initial ICCDC wing lacked not only social space but also cells in which to segregate or isolate detained persons or to cater for females. As the UNDU down-sized, the ICCDC expanded, moving into a newly renovated floor with a twelve-cell and a twenty-cell wing and additional access to cells jointly operated with the UNDU that can be used to house female or segregated detained persons.[49]

International prisoners are entitled to food of sufficient quality and quantity according to dietary standards, taking into account their age, health, religion and, as far as possible, cultural requirements.[50] The UNDU and ICCDC rely on the host prison's catering services to provide one hot meal, two cold meals and snacks per detained person per day.[51] This is considered to be a secure arrangement, as the caterers do not know which section of the prison the food is being sent to.[52] The ICCDC has also contracted with a specialist in African cuisine to provide two hot meals a day at a cost of €60 per day per prisoner for those who request it, although this has created tensions as it appears these meals are being thrown in the bin without being opened.[53] The UNDF has a specifically hired chef,[54] who prepares meals from a menu approved by a nutritionist and the Medical Officer.[55] Due to difficulties faced in out-sourcing

---

[46] Reg. 161(1), (3) ICC ROR.
[47] Rule 20 ICTY ROD; Rule 17 ICTR ROD; Rules 15(B), 18 (B) SCSL ROD; Reg. 199(2) ICC ROR.
[48] Rules 22–3 ICTY ROD; Rules 19–20 ICTR ROD; Rules 15(b), 16 SCSL ROD; Reg. 197 ICC ROR.
[49] Craig, ICCDC, 04.07.2012.
[50] Rule 26 ICTY ROD; Rule 23 ICTR ROD; Rule 18(A) SCSL ROD; Reg. 199(1) ICC ROR.
[51] Rule 26 ICTY ROD.
[52] Jackson, SCSLDF/ICCDC, 19.03.2007; Dubuisson, Tjonk, Becerra-Suarez, ICC, 06.06.2007.
[53] Jouthart, ICCDC, 04.07.2012.
[54] Mwuangulu, Wastelain, Endeley, ICTR, 25.06.2007. [55] Diop, ICTR, 27.06.2007.

quality catering at reasonable costs, the SCSL constructed a kitchen within the perimeter of the SCSLDF, and hired chefs to prepare all the prisoners' meals. Prisoners can purchase food products with their own or earned money[56] and cook for themselves. This not only enables the adjustment of the Host State food to cultural or national preferences, but introduces an important social element to the group that can strengthen bonds between detained persons.[57] Although the ICCDC provides a weekly budget of €10 to enable detained persons to buy additional foodstuffs to make their diets more culturally appropriate,[58] the wealthier detained persons are currently purchasing a vast range of food products for all detained persons on the wing.[59]

International prisoners are entitled to practice their religious, spiritual and moral beliefs.[60] They may access religious books and artefacts and religious leaders may visit and hold services within the IDF.[61] Additional resources may be made available to make religious occasions special.[62] For example, former UNDU detainees remembered a multi-denominational Christmas celebration involving music, poetry and food that had been organised by the detainees and attended by staff and management in 1997.[63]

Each IDF provides indoor and outdoor sports facilities and activities to promote recreation and maintain fitness.[64] Prisoners are permitted a minimum of one hour outside per day, weather depending.[65] At the SCSLDF, this was also dependent on staff, security and resources.[66] The ICCDC regulations do not put any restrictions on this entitlement[67] and detained persons are allowed outside twice a day, for one hour and forty minutes respectively.[68] The ICCDC actively encourages detained persons to spend time outside to ensure they receive sufficient amounts of vitamin D.[69] The UNDU provides an "air cage" for those not permitted to use the outside yard.[70] The ICCDC and UNDU share the same yard with basketball nets, and an indoor sports hall, gym and weights room.

---

[56] Harding, SCSLDF, 21.04.2008.   [57] Falke, ICCDC/UNDU, 04.02.2008.
[58] Tour ICCDC, 06.06.2007.   [59] Jouthart, ICCDC, 04.07.2012.
[60] Rule 4 ICTY ROD; Reg. 102(1) ICC ROC.
[61] Rules 66-8 ICTY ROD; Rules 66-9 ICTR ROD; Rules 48-51 SCSL ROD; Reg. 102(2) ICC ROC; Reg. 153 ICC ROR.
[62] Ewing, SCSLDF, 23.04.2008.   [63] Katava, 13.10.2007; Delalić, 20.08.2008.
[64] Rules 27-8 ICTY ROD; Rule 24-5 ICTR ROD; Rule 54(B) SCSL ROD; Reg. 99(1)(g) ICC ROC; Reg. 165(1) ICC ROR.
[65] Rule 27(A) ICTY ROD; Rule 24 ICTR ROD.   [66] Rule 54(A) SCSL ROD.
[67] Reg. 99(1)(f) ICC ROC; Reg. 165(1) ICC ROR.   [68] ICCDC Tour, 06.06.2007.
[69] Craig, ICCDC, 04.07.2012.   [70] Para. A.6.3(29) MDP, 183.

Prisoners can use the indoor sports facilities every day. The UNDU also provides yoga classes. The second SCSLDF had an exercise yard and a small gym with exercise machines, a table tennis table and volley ball.

Detained persons can purchase reading and writing materials and have access to radio and TV, so long as they are compatible with the interests of the administration of justice and the security and order of the IDF,[71] and where applicable the host prison.[72] The IDF may also provide items for social, educational and recreational activities in common areas.[73] At the SCSLDF, staff and management paid for books and a VCR.[74] All IDFs have a library[75] and IDFs in host prisons may use the library and vocational facilities of the host institution.[76] The provision of cultural comforts can help to boost the morale of detained persons and normalise daily life. The UNDU provides television channels from the former Yugoslav states to reduce feelings of alienation and depression.[77] The ICCDC also tries to provide written and visual media from the prisoners' state of origin.[78]

At the UNDU and ICCDC, detained persons have access to English language, art and computer classes.[79] Classes are not career-orientated but are used to engage detained persons and provide alternative support structures.[80] The ICCDC has recently purchased Linguaphone packs in all the official UN languages to encourage detained persons to develop their language skills.[81] The SCSLDF provided English classes but these were only attended by the two prisoners who did not speak the language. The computers provided for skills development[82] were used mainly for playing games.[83] Some felt that the SCSLDF "regime was badly planned, with detained persons having no education provision for three years".[84]

Work opportunities may be provided in the cell or communal areas,[85] although this may necessitate consultation with the director of the

---

[71] Rule 76 ICTY ROD; Rule 75 ICTR ROD; Reg. 101(1) ICC ROC.
[72] Rules 72-3 ICTY ROD; Rules 72-4 ICTR ROD; Rule 53(A), (C) SCSL ROD; Reg. 99(1)(c) ICC ROC; Regs. 166(8), (10) ICC ROR.
[73] Reg. 99(1)(e) ICC ROC; Reg. 164(1) ROR. [74] Neil, SCSLDF, 23.04.2008.
[75] Rule 53(B) SCSL ROD; Reg. 164(2) ICC ROR.
[76] Rule 73 ICTY ROD; Rule 75 ICTR ROD. [77] Para. A.6.4(30) MDP, 183.
[78] Dubuisson, Tjonk, Becerra-Suarez, ICC, 06.06.2007.
[79] ICCDC Tour, 06.06.2007; UNDU Tour 21.08.2007.
[80] Education Officer, ICCDC, 28.08.2007. [81] Craig, ICCDC, 04.07.2012.
[82] SCSL Third Annual Report 36. [83] Ewing, SCSLDF, 23.04.2008.
[84] Neil, SCSLDF, 23.04.2008; Custodial Staff, SCSLDF, 22-25.04.2008.
[85] Rule 69 ICTY ROD; Rule 70 ICTR ROD; Rule 52(A) SCSL ROD; Reg. 163(1) ICC ROR.

host prison.[86] Unlike international prisoners serving their sentences in enforcing states, international prisoners in IDFs are not required to work.[87] This is due to the fact that there is no differentiated regime for convicted persons. Beyond cleaning, there are few jobs that can be offered in such small facilities.[88] Volunteers receive a small payment which they can use to purchase items from the canteen.[89] Prisoners working at the ICCDC could transfer earnings to the Trust Fund for Victims.[90]

2. Contact with the outside world

Prisoners housed at IDFs are typically from states far away from the Host State of the court. International prisoners, like all prisoners, miss their homes and families, particularly when their children are growing up.[91] Prisoners may phone or write to their families and friends,[92] though communication with certain individuals may be prohibited or restricted if it is considered to affect security or the administration of justice.[93] Prisoners can send and receive mail,[94] though non-legal and non-confidential correspondence will be subject to security inspections.[95] While prisoners may make phone calls,[96] these calls are passively monitored (recorded without simultaneous listening).[97] Calls may be actively monitored if they are considered to pose a security threat, interfere with witnesses or the administration of justice.[98] Indigent detained persons are assisted with the costs of communication.[99] For example, convicted

---

[86] Rule 69 ICTY ROD; Rule 70 ICTR ROD.
[87] Rule 70(A) ICTY ROD; Rule 71 ICTR ROD; Rule 52(B) SCSL ROD; Reg. 99(1)(a) ICC ROC; Reg. 163(2) ICC ROR.
[88] Jackson, SCSLDF/ ICC DC, 19.03.2007.
[89] Rule 70(B) ICTY ROD; Rule 71 ICTR ROD; Rule 52(C) SCSL ROD; Reg. 163(3) ICC ROR.
[90] Reg. 163(3) ICC ROR.
[91] ICCDC Custodial Staff, 22-28.08.2007; Para. 2.7.2 Independent Audit of the Detention Unit at the ICTY, 2006.
[92] Rules 58(A), 61(A) ICTY ROD; Rules 58, 60(i) ICTR ROD; Rules 40(A), 41(A) SCSL ROD; Reg. 99(1)(i) ICC ROC.
[93] Rules 61(E), 64 ICTY ROD; Rule 64 ICTR ROD; Rule 47(A), (E) SCSL ROD; Reg. 101(2) ICC ROC.
[94] Reg. 1 UNDU VCR; Reg. 99(1)(b), (h) ICC ROC.
[95] Regs. 2-4, 6-8 UNDU VCR; Rule 59 ICTY ROD; Rule 59 ICTR ROD; Rule 46 SCSL ROD; Reg. 168 ICC ROR.
[96] Reg. 173(2)-(4) ICC ROR.   [97] Reg. 174 ICC ROR.
[98] Reg. 20 UNDU VCR; Rule 47 SCSL ROD; Reg. 175 ICC ROR.
[99] Regs. 5, 18 UNDU VCR; Rule 58(B) ICTY ROD; Rule 58 ICTR ROD; Rule 40(B) SCSL ROD; Regs. 172(2), 176(2) ICC ROR.

persons at the SCSLDF received 300 minutes of calls per month.[100] The ICCDC previously gave all detained persons 200 free minutes per month and used a staff rate billing system once this limit was exceeded,[101] but free phone calls are no longer permitted for non-indigent detained persons.

IDF prisoners can receive visits. Normal visits take place within the sight and hearing of custodial staff.[102] Visiting hours depend on the demands of the daily schedule of the IDF and the facilities and staff available.[103] In contrast to national systems, IDF visiting hours are generous. For instance, UNDU prisoners are entitled to seven consecutive full days (eight hours) of visits in any thirty day period, including conjugal visits.[104] Access can only be denied to visitors for security reasons forwarded by either the IDF or the host prison (where relevant) and in the interests of the administration of justice.[105] IDFs have experienced difficulties in ascertaining the identity or risk posed by proposed visitors due to the lack of links with intelligence agencies in the relevant countries.[106]

While the regulatory frameworks provide a liberal visiting and communications policy in comparison to national systems, the location of the IDFs can inhibit visits. While some prisoners may receive more frequent visits if their families are located in nearby countries, the distance and cost of travel between IDFs and the states of residence of families can often prevent or reduce the families' ability to visit. Neither of the UN Tribunals has a regular budget line for funding visits from indigent detained persons' families. It seems that the governments of the states of origin of detained persons were providing families with funding to assist with the cost of visits to the UNDU. For example, the Serbian Government provided detainees with a sum of £200 per month during their time at the UNDU and provided families with tickets to visit their loved ones every two months.[107] This funding stopped once individuals were convicted by the Tribunal. This funding was limited by some states to those who surrendered voluntarily to the ICTY and it appears that this

---

[100] Rule 40(B) SCSL ROD; Cardinal, Moore, SCSLDF, 20.04.2008
[101] ICCDC Tour, 06.06.2007.   [102] Reg. 43(A) UNDU VCR; Rule 41(B) SCSL ROD.
[103] Reg. 177 ICC ROR.   [104] Para. A.6.2(28) MDP, 183.
[105] Rule 64(A) ICTY ROD; Rule 64 ICTR ROD; Rule 41(A), (C) SCSL ROD; Regs. 100(1), (3) ICC ROC.
[106] R. Vincent, *An Administrative Practices Manual for Internationally Assisted Criminal Justice Institutions* (2007), 72; Craig, ICCDC, 05.07.2012.
[107] Blagojević, Trondheim Prison, 28.06.2012; Krajišnik, Usk Prison, 27.09.2012.

funding has been stopped completely by the Republika Srpska. The ICTY considered granting funding for family visits to one individual not in receipt of national support as part of legal aid but as he was found to be only partially indigent this was not considered to be necessary.

The families of UNDF detained persons appear to have secured funding for visits in a more creative manner. Defence counsel would call family members as witnesses. Accordingly, their travel costs were covered by the Witness Section. Following testimony, they would request a visit with their loved one, which was usually granted. This method was also extremely useful for visitors who were illegal in their state of residence, as they could benefit from cooperation agreements entered into by the ICTR.

The ICRC has also provided some families with support to cover the costs of visits.[108] But again, this is an ad hoc and exceptional source of finance. As the forms of funding from the Tribunals (the use of legal aid and funds for witness testimony) both relate to detention prior to the finalisation of a sentence, these forms would not be available to convicted persons housed at IDFs.

Since 2006, the ICC has paid for the visits of the families of indigent detained persons housed at the ICCDC. All natural and adopted children are recognised for the purposes of family visits.[109] State Parties became concerned about the level of expenditure on this costly initiative, particularly given that it is not based on an enforceable right and has no regular budget line.[110] The Registry argued for continued funding for several interrelated reasons: the right of detained persons to receive visits, that this was unlikely to happen without financial support due to the distances involved and the indigent status of the detained persons, that detained persons were presumed innocent, that their families had rights to family life, and that, in line with international and regional penal standards, the Registrar was charged with paying specific attention to family visits with a view to maintaining such links.[111] On the other hand, the Committee for Budget and Finance expressed concern about the "substantial and long-term financial implications" of the recognition of a

---

[108] Delalić, 20.08.2008. [109] Sant-Anna, ICC, 06.07.2012.
[110] See para. 15, External Audit, Internal Audit, Programme Budget for 2009 and Related Documents, Vol. 1(II) Report of the Seventh Session of the Assembly of State Parties, ICC-ASP/7/20, 14–24.11.2008, 12.
[111] See Reg. 179(1) ICC ROR; Report of the Court on Family Visits To Indigent Detained Persons, ICC-ASP/7/24.

right to receive financial assistance for visits.[112] Moreover, states were keen to avoid setting any precedent for either the ICC or themselves to fund visits to foreign national or international prisoners housed in their prison systems.[113]

The Committee on Budget and Finance suggested that funds should be raised from voluntary contributions rather than the regular Court budget.[114] This recommendation was rejected by many, including Amnesty International, Human Rights Watch and the International Bar Association, who argued that states were unlikely to view this as a priority cause and that it was inappropriate for the Court to rely on voluntary contributions to fulfil its obligations to uphold the rights of those presumed innocent.[115] In 2009, the Assembly of State Parties (ASP) temporarily extended regular budget funding until a mechanism for the voluntary funding of visits could be established,[116] and reluctantly granted a fixed sum[117] of €40,500[118] for the costs of visits for indigent detainees.[119] In 2010, the ASP transferred responsibility for the funding of family visits for indigent detainees from the ICC budget to a special fund in the Registry financed entirely through voluntary donations from State Parties, other States, NGOs, civil society, individuals

---

[112] See para. 67 Report of the Committee on Budget and Finance on the Work of its 11th Session in Annex II, Vol. 2(B) Report of the Seventh Session of the Assembly of State Parties, ICC-ASP/7/20, 14–24.11.2008.

[113] See para. 15(b) External Audit, Internal Audit, Programme Budget for 2009 and Related Documents, Vol.1 (II) Report of the Seventh Session of the Assembly of State Parties, ICC-ASP/7/20, 14–24.11.2008, 13.

[114] See para. 68 Report of the Committee on Budget and Finance on the Work of its 11th Session, 2008 in Annex II, Vol. 2(B) Report of the Seventh Session of the Assembly of State Parties, ICC-ASP/7/20, 14–24.11.2008, 225–6.

[115] See Amnesty International, "ICC, Concerns at the Seventh Session of the ASP", 2008, 17; International Bar Association, Human Rights Institute Report, The ICC under Scrutiny: Assessing Recent Developments at the ICC 2008, 52, 58; section C(4) Human Rights Watch, Memorandum for the Seventh Session of the ICC, ASP 07.11.2008, 21–2.

[116] See paras. 4–6 Family Visits for Indigent Detainees, ICC-ASP/8/Res.4, 26.11.2009.

[117] See para. 15 External Audit, Internal Audit, Programme Budget for 2009 and Related Documents, Vol. 1(II) Report of the Seventh Session of the Assembly of State Parties ICC-ASP/7/20, 14–24.1.2008, 12.

[118] This sum was reduced from an original €84,600 which would cover one visit per year of the full nuclear family of a detained person (up to seven family members). See para. 58 Proposed Programme Budget for 2009 of ICC, Volume II (A) Report of the Seventh Session of the Assembly of State Parties, ICC-ASP/7/20, 14–24.1.2008, 17.

[119] See para. 106 Report of the Committee on Budget and Finance on the Work of its 11th Session, ICC-ASP/7/20, 14–24.11.2008.

and other entities.[120] Germany contributed an initial €80,000 to the fund.[121] The ICCDC currently finances two visits per year for three persons or three visits per year for two persons from this fund, although in practice it depends on the circumstances of the individual's family; the family may prefer one visit of the entire family annually. If an individual has more than more than one core family, visiting arrangements and funding will be decided on a case-by-case basis.[122] Such funding will not be available to ICC prisoners housed in either the Host State or enforcing states.[123] The only exception may be prisoners with six months or less to serve who remain at the ICCDC,[124] as the same rules apply to convicted persons.

The SCSL provided the families of indigent detained persons with a monthly stipend of 198,000 Leones (just over £30) to assist with the cost of visits from its regular budget.[125] Funding has continued post-conviction to facilitate visits to both the SCSLDF in Freetown and Mpanga Prison in Rwanda.[126]

While IDF prisoners are permitted to receive frequent and often long visits from their families, the costs involved mean that in practice this does not normally occur. More modern forms of technology such as email and video-conferencing have been discussed and in some sense this progression is inevitable. While international authorities are often cautious about this mode of communication due to the potential for abuse and the difficulties in locating a secure site,[127] ICCDC detained witnesses have been permitted to communicate with their families via a video-link to an ICC field office in the DRC.[128]

UNDU, UNDF and ICCDC prisoners are entitled to engage in sexual relations with their partners during non-supervised visits in rooms equipped with a bed.[129] The rooms provided at the UNDU have been criticised as "shabby and downright unpleasant"[130] and it is necessary to cover a window connecting two visiting rooms in the ICCDC with a

---

[120] Para. 1, Section X Independent Oversight Mechanism, ICC-ASP/9/Res.4, 10.12.2010, 33.
[121] Tjonk, ICC, 04.07.2012.   [122] Sant-Anna, ICC, 06.07.2012.
[123] Para. 7 Family visits for Indigent Detainees ICC-ASP/8/Res.4, 26.11.2009.
[124] Art. 50 ICC HQA.   [125] Para. 42 SCSL Budget 2005–6, 39.
[126] See Chapter 2, Section 4.2.2.
[127] O'Donnell, ICTR, 25.06.2007; Vincent, SCSL/ICTY, 27.04.2007; Jackson, SCSLDF/ICCDC, 19.03.2007.
[128] Bremmers, ICCDC, 04.07.2012.   [129] Regs. 183(1), 185(1) ICC ROR.
[130] Para. 2.8.3 Independent Audit of the Detention Unit at the ICTY, 2006.

blanket during private visits.[131] The entitlement to conjugal visits at the UNDU created public interest when *Le Figaro* published an article stating that an accused's counsel had sent him a prostitute for his birthday.[132] Although this was found to be inaccurate, it did create a debate about the appropriateness of allowing such visits.[133] At present, the right to conjugal visits is only offered to pre-existing couples, and is not available for prostitutes. It is not clear if the international courts should respect local law or local custom relating to recognised relationships. In other words, should partners from polygamous relationships, deemed illegal under local law, but acceptable according to the individual's religion, custom or tradition, be permitted conjugal visits? The current policy is to permit persons who the public perceive as being in an established relationship.[134] In any event, the identity of partners must be determined before permission is granted.[135] Visitors must sign a waiver form accepting responsibility for what might happen during unsupervised visits.[136] Although two pregnancies have resulted from conjugal visits at the ICCDC to date, contraception is provided to those who request it.[137] A child-minder can be made available during this intimate time.[138]

3. Medical care

All IDFs provide prisoners with on-site medical care. IDF clinics are staffed by a doctor and nurses who provide basic health-care, testing, a pharmacy and emergency services.[139] Basic dental and optical care is provided by visiting practitioners.[140] In line with the requirement of consent to medical treatment, detained persons have the right to decline medication prescribed by the IDF doctor, although the detained persons

---

[131] ICCDC Tour, 06.06.2007.
[132] J. C. Nemitz, "Execution of Sanctions Imposed by Supranational Criminal Tribunals" in R. Haveman and O. Olusanya (eds.), *Sentencing and Sanctioning in Supranational Criminal Law* (2006), 125–44 at 140.
[133] Ibid.   [134] Sant-Anna, ICC, 06.07.2012.
[135] Reg. 185(2) ICC ROR; Dubuisson, Tjonk, Becerra-Suarez, ICC, 06.06.2007.
[136] McFadden, UNDU, 21.08.2007; ICCDC Tour, 06.06.2007.
[137] Sant-Anna, ICC, 06.07.2012.   [138] ICCDC Tour, 06.06.2007.
[139] Rule 30(A) ICTY ROD; Rule 27 ICTR ROD; Rule 19(A) SCSL ROD; Regs. 103(1), (3)–(4) ICC ROC; Reg. 154 ICC ROR.
[140] O'Donnell, ICTR, 25.06.2007; Harding, SCSLDF, 21.04.2008; Falke, UNDU/ICCDC, 04.02.2008.

must be informed about the detrimental effects of such a refusal.[141] Subject to security requirements, prisoners can request a visit from a doctor or dentist of their choice, at their own expense.[142] The ICC Registrar will decide if it is appropriate to provide support for indigent persons to seek a second opinion.[143] However, treatment or medication recommended by external practitioners can only be administered by the IDF's medical officer, and he may refuse to do so.[144] The ICC further qualifies that the external practitioner must be on a list of experts and registered in The Netherlands before they can perform medical procedures at the ICCDC, unless the situation is life threatening.[145] Moreover, it is explicitly stated that external practitioners are liable for any misconduct and must have insurance.[146]

At times, it can be difficult for IDF doctors to get a complete picture of a prisoner's medical health. Linguistic and cultural barriers can hinder accurate diagnosis. While communication assisted by Google translator or using a common language may be sufficient for the discussion of minor issues, it may be necessary to rely on an interpreter to discuss more serious issues. Language assistance by phone has recently become available at the UNDU and ICCDC.[147] The use of language assistants may not, however, be appropriate in all instances or overcome cultural understandings of medical terms or diseases. In addition, prisoners may refuse to have tests conducted or may fail to disclose certain conditions or diseases due to the perceived social stigma surrounding them.[148]

While Spandau prisoners initially only had access to an operating theatre constructed in the prison's old execution chamber, they were later granted access to external military hospitals.[149] International prisoners who require specialist treatment or surgery not available at the IDF clinics or host prison hospitals may be transferred to external civil hospitals.[150] The ICTR has used the AICC Hospital and the Kilimanjaro Christian Medical Centre, Moshi. The SCSL has an agreement with

---

[141] See *Tolimir* (TC Decision) IT-05-88/2-T, 01.09.2010.
[142] Rule 31(A) ICTY ROD; Rule 28 ICTR ROD; Rule 20(A) SCSL ROD; Reg. 103(4) ICC ROC; Rule 157(1) ICC ROR.
[143] Reg. 157(2) ICC ROR.
[144] Rule 31(C) ICTY ROD; Rule 28 ICTR ROD; Rule 20(B) SCSL ROD; Reg. 157(10) ICC ROR.
[145] Regs. 157(3)–(5), 158 ICC ROR. [146] Reg. 159 ICC ROR.
[147] Falke, UNDU/ICCDC, 04.07.2012.
[148] Harding, SCSLDF, 21.04.2008/24.04.2008.
[149] N. J. W. Goda, *Tales from Spandau: Nazi Criminals and the Cold War* (2007), 67–9.
[150] Rule 32 ICTY ROD; Rule 29 ICTR ROD; Rule 21 SCSL ROD; Reg. 103(5) ICC ROC.

Choithram International Hospital in Freetown.[151] However, due to the limited scope of services provided by this hospital, the SCSL also had to sign an agreement with Senegal to enable the use of a military hospital in Dakar.[152] Treatment at external hospitals is very expensive. In addition to the price of the treatment and medicine,[153] the prisoner must remain in the continuous custody of the court. Patients must therefore be accompanied by both security and custody officers during transit to and from the hospital and during their stay.[154]

Given the older than average age of international detainees and the lack of good medical care in conflict situations, it is not surprising that there have been deaths at the international remand centres. To date, seven people have died from natural causes while in the custody of an IDF.

Two UNDU detainees died of natural causes. Dr Milan Kovačević died in August 1998 from a ruptured aneurysm. His health had been poor due to hypertension and cardiac rhythm disturbances. The doctors appointed by his defence counsel complained about the care and treatment being administered at the UNDU. However, specialist care at the host prison hospital or the nearby civil hospital was available.[155] The ICTY report found no negligence on behalf of the IDF doctor or the custodial staff who administered first aid. While it acknowledged that they had been delays and problems with the treatment, these were not found to be causally related to his death.[156]

Slobodan Milošević died from a heart infarction on 11 March 2006. The ICTY report held that the medical care provided by the UNDU, independent cardiologists and specialists was proper and that Mr Milošević's health problems had been complicated by his self-representation against medical advice, refusal to be tested or hospitalised, failure to take prescribed medication while taking non-prescribed medication which disrupted the effectiveness of prescribed medication, which was smuggled into the UNDU during privileged visits.[157]

---

[151] Art. 3(3) Memorandum of Understanding between The Choithram Charities Trust and the SCSL, 27.03.2006 (SCSL MOU (Choithram)).
[152] SCSL Fourth Annual Report, 11.   [153] See Art. 10 SCSL MOU (Choithram).
[154] Reg. 103(5) ICC ROC; Articles 2, 5(1) SCSL MOU (Choithram).
[155] Paras. 21, 22, 24 Judge Rodrigues, Report on the Findings of the Inquiry into the Circumstances Surrounding the Death of Dr. Milan Kovacevic, 27.08.1998.
[156] Paras. 25–7 Judge Rodrigues, Report on the Findings of the Inquiry into the Circumstances Surrounding the Death of Dr. Milan Kovacevic, 27.08.1998.
[157] Judge Parker, Report to the President on the Death of Slobodan Milošević, May 2006.

Three persons in ICTR custody have died; one before his trial began, one during trial and one post-conviction. Mr Musabyimana died on 24 January 2003 at the Kilimanjaro Christian Medical Centre following a long illness.[158] The ICTR spokesman stated that a commission of inquiry could not be ordered by the President as the detainee did not die at the UNDF.[159] Mr Serugendo died on 22 August 2006 at the Nairobi Hospital in Kenya[160] while serving his sentence, also following a long illness. Mr Nzirorera died on 1 July 2010 during his trial following sudden complications from a long illness.[161]

Two SCSL detainees also died. Mr Sankoh was transferred to Choithram Hospital in Freetown shortly after being taken into custody and died there on 29 July 2003.[162] Independent psychological and psychiatric examinations as to the cause of his catatonic state proved inconclusive.[163] Mr Norman died on 22 February 2007 at the Hôpital Aristide Le Dantec in Dakar, Senegal, while recovering from a hip replacement operation.[164] The autopsy revealed he died "of natural causes from a myocardial infarction".[165] The internal inquiry[166] affirmed the autopsy findings on cause of death and further found that Mr Norman's refusal to accept the SCSLDF doctor's advice to follow a healthier life style contributed to his cardiac problems and that in both Freetown and Senegal proper medical care had been provided.[167]

While the physical health of some detained persons may improve during their time at an IDF, many suffer from post-traumatic stress disorder as a result of their involvement in a conflict.[168] According to a

---

[158] ICTR Press Release, "Bishop Samuel Musabyimana Dies", 24.01.2003.
[159] Hirondelle, "ICTR Detainees want Commission of Enquiry on Musabyimana's Death", 05.02.2003.
[160] See *Serugendo* (Decision) ICTR-2005-84-I, 22.06.2006.
[161] ICTR Press Release, "Accused Joseph Nzirorera Dies", 01.07.2010; para. 68 Sixteenth ICTR Annual Report.
[162] SCSL Press Release, "Registrar Announces Death of Foday Sankoh", 30.07.2003.
[163] SCSL Press Release, "Sankoh Needs Further Evaluation"; 21.03.2003, SCSL First Annual Report, 8.
[164] SCSL Press Release, "Body of Sam Hinga Norman Handed Over to Family", 07.03.2007; "Autopsy Shows Sam Hinga Norman Died of Natural Causes", 28.03.2007. Harding, SCSLDF, 24.04.2008.
[165] SCSL Press Release, "Autopsy Shows Sam Hinga Norman Died of Natural Causes", 28.03.2007.
[166] See SCSL Fourth Annual Report, 11; Rule 22(C) SCSL ROD.
[167] SCSL Press Release, "Inquiry finds Special Court Provided Proper Care to Hinga Norman", 16.07.2007.
[168] Para. A.1.1(9) MDP, 179.

former UNDU CCO, those who had lived on their nerves during the chaos and danger of conflict fell apart when they entered the safe and organised environment of an IDF.[169] Moreover, many are imprisoned at an age when their coping mechanisms are getting weaker. The average age of UNDU occupants is over sixty.[170] Research has demonstrated that elderly prisoners are five times more prone to depression than younger prisoners and elderly persons living in normal society.[171] Mental health problems are exacerbated by detention and the resulting feelings of anger, anxiety, frustration, agitation and stress may manifest themselves as depression and psychosomatic illnesses etc.[172]

Prisoners often turn to each other for social and emotional support. Over the years of detention in IDFs, they can establish good relationships.[173] They have access to psychological and psychiatric assistance. UNDU detained persons have access to a psychiatrist from the same ethnic and linguistic background.[174] SCSLDF prisoners also had access to a psychiatrist. The SCSLDF doctor would have preferred a psychologist, but none in Freetown were willing to work with the prisoners.[175] The UNDF has an officer dedicated to addressing the psycho-social and psychiatric welfare of detained persons, who can recommend counselling, psychotherapy, restorative justice conferences and psychiatric treatment.[176]

The IDFs try to reduce the risk of self-harm or suicide through the provision of services and surveillance. The distribution of medication is controlled and supervised by the IDF doctor.[177] Custodial and medical staff try to establish and maintain relationships with prisoners to enable the observation of changes in moods.[178] The SCSLDF medical team, for example, worked hard to improve their psycho-social skills and to develop relationships of trust with the prisoners.[179] If it is felt that there is a risk that a detained person may harm himself, he can be moved to cells with infra-red video-surveillance, that are free from

---

[169] McFadden, UNDU, 21.08.2007.
[170] Falke, UNDU/ICCDC, 04.07.2012; Para. A.1.1(8) MDP, 179.
[171] Fazel, Hope, O'Donnell and Jaboby cited in D. Van Zyl Smit and S. Snacken, *Principles of European Prison Law and Policy: Penology and Human Rights* (2009), 156.
[172] Harding, SCSLDF, 21.04.2008.   [173] Falke, UNDU/ICCDC, 04.02.2008.
[174] Para. 2.9 Independent Audit of the Detention Unit at the ICTY, 2006.
[175] Harding, SCSLDF, 21.04.2008.   [176] Okitapoy, UNDF, 08.08.2007.
[177] Rule 77(A) ICTY ROD; Rule 79 ICTR ROD; Rule 56(A) SCSL ROD; Reg. 166(5) ICC ROR.
[178] McFadden, UNDU, 21.08.2007.   [179] Harding, SCSLDF, 21.04.2008.

dangerous objects.[180] The ICC regulations also state that the court may order the transfer of mentally ill detainees to a specialised institution for treatment.[181] Yet despite these measures, there have been suicides at IDFs. At the UNDU, Slavko Dokmanović committed suicide on 29 June 1998 and Milan Babić committed suicide on 5 March 2006.

When a prisoner dies, naturally or otherwise, the Registrar must inform the next of kin and arrange an inquest in accordance with the Host State's law.[182] The President may also order an internal inquiry into the circumstances surrounding the death.[183] To comply with human rights standards and to allay suspicions of foul play,[184] it is important that all deaths that are not evidently natural are investigated to the highest standard.

4. Maintaining order

In addition to the well-being of detained persons, security and order are key goals for IDF administration. A notable, though perhaps surprising, feature of IDF life is the harmonious co-existence of detained persons. Although the regulations permit segregation to avoid conflict,[185] IDF detainees were not housed according to their previous affiliations or ethnic backgrounds. Instead, the potential for conflict was reduced by creating wings comprised of "a respectful and varied group of individuals ... taking into account the individual characteristics of each detainee".[186] For example, three formerly warring factions lived together peacefully on one wing at the SCSLDF, which they called "the Village".[187] Like UNDU inmates, they had a new common enemy: the court that detained them.[188] They formed good relationships and were very affectionate with each other's children during visits.[189] Relationships between detained persons at the ICCDC are also good.[190]

---

[180] See Rule 39(A) ICTY ROD; Regs. 155(4), 195(2), 196 ICC ROR.
[181] Reg. 103(6) ICC ROC.
[182] Rule 33(A)-(B) ICTY ROD; Rule 30 ICTR ROD; Rule 22(A)-(B) SCSL ROD; Reg. 162(1)-(3) ICC ROR.
[183] Rule 33(C) ICTY ROD; Rule 30 ICTR ROD; Rule 22(C) SCSL ROD; Reg. 103(7) ICC ROC.
[184] See Goda, *Tales from Spandau*, 266-7.
[185] Rule 44(A) ICTY ROD; Rule 42 ICTR ROD; Rule 28 SCSL ROD; Reg. 202(1)-(2) ICC ROR.
[186] Para. A.7(31) MDP, 183.   [187] Cardinal, Moore, SCSLDF, 20.04.2008
[188] Jackson, SCSLDF/ICCDC, 19.03.2007.   [189] Ewing, SCSLDF, 23.04.2008.
[190] Bremmers, ICCDC, 04.07.2012.

Former UNDU detainees attribute this phenomenon to the unwritten rule that no-one asks about another detainee's business. This arose not only from the desire to keep underlying tensions below the surface but also because people found it very difficult to listen to the confessions of other detained persons. This reciprocal respect for privacy enabled the creation of a calm environment, which was maintained by the sympathy detained persons had for each other's predicament; they were all there for the same reason and all faced similar problems.[191] As the past was not forgiven or forgotten, this harmony may only be a "superficial illusion that is neither deep nor fruitful".[192] As one international prisoner recalled, the situation was more akin to that of "natural enemies in the animal world during a flood – you don't attack each other as you don't want to waste energy".[193] It has also been suggested that this "somewhat remarkable situation" was possible due to the detainees' social skills and an understanding that conflict would result in poorer conditions, and possible isolation.[194] This harmonious co-existence does not mean however that security and order are not issues at IDFs. This section looks at both the regulatory frameworks for their maintenance and the subjective approaches of management and staff to such issues.

4.1 Regulatory frameworks governing the maintenance of order

The regulatory frameworks governing the operations of IDFs contain numerous provisions related to the maintenance of order. These provisions deal with segregation, discipline, the use of isolation, instruments of restraint and force.

Segregation may be used to separate different sexes,[195] witnesses from accused persons, persons in joint cases, and individuals who pose a threat to security, order or the safety and health of others.[196] Individuals can request to be segregated from others.[197] Segregation orders must be reported to the Registrar.[198] At the ICC, the doctor must agree to segregation beyond a week.[199] The Registrar may vary

---

[191] Katava, 06.10.2007. [192] Krajišnik, Usk Prison, 27.09.2012. [193] *Ibid.*
[194] Para. 2.7.2 Independent Audit of the Detention Unit at the ICTY, 2006.
[195] Reg. 105(1) ICC ROC.
[196] See para. 101 ICTR Fifth Annual Report; Rule 44(A) ICTY ROD; Rule 39 ICTR ROD; Rule 26 (a)(iii), (B) SCSL ROD; Reg. 201(1) ICC ROR.
[197] Rule 42(A) ICTY ROD; Rule 40 ICTR ROD; Rule 27 SCSL ROD; Reg. 201(8) ICC ROR.
[198] Rules 43(D), 44(C) ICTY ROD; Rule 41 ICTR ROD; Rule 29 SCSL ROD.
[199] Reg. 201(5) ICC ROR.

the nature, basis or conditions of the segregation.[200] Although segregation is not to be used as punishment following a disciplinary procedure,[201] those subject to the process at the ICC may be temporarily segregated.[202]

Disciplinary regimes may be implemented when detained persons fail to obey instructions, are verbally or physically abusive or possess illegal objects.[203] The ICC recently proposed the increase of the length of time permitted for the conduct of disciplinary hearings and the imposition of a penalty because of the difficulties of doing so within current time frames with only two senior managers and the requirement for transcription and translation of proceedings.[204] The impossibility of meeting current targets means that disciplinary incidents are often dropped.[205]

If the disciplinary charge is upheld, the CCO may confiscate prohibited items, remove privileges for stated time periods, issue a warning, suspend punishment, impose a fine or put the prisoner in isolation.[206] It has also been proposed that the period for the withdrawal of privileges at the ICCDC should be increased.[207] Even if this increased time-frame is granted, it will remain to be seen if the sanctions currently available are adequate to deal with serious breaches of discipline.[208] The ICCDC does not allow the use of isolation as a punishment.[209] The SCSL Rules explicitly prohibit the use of corporal punishment, placement in a dark cell and all cruel and inhuman punishments.[210] The SCSLDF doctor had an input into the punishment imposed and could advise the CCO or Registrar not to impose, or to terminate the imposition of, certain punishments if they affected the health of a prisoner.[211] Prisoners can appeal disciplinary decisions and punishments to the Registrar or President,[212] and may be able to avail of counsel and interpreters to do so.[213]

---

[200] Rule 44(C) ICTY ROD; Rule 42 ICTR ROD; Rule 29 SCSL ROD; Regs. 201(2), 202(3) ICC ROR.
[201] Rule 43(C) ICTY ROD; Rule 39 ICTR ROD; Rule 26(D) SCSL ROD; Reg. 201(3) ICC ROR.
[202] Reg. 209(1) ICC ROR.   [203] Reg. 2 UNDU DPR; Reg. 207 ICC ROR.
[204] Proposed amendments to Regs. 208(2), 214(2), 215(2) ICC ROR.
[205] Craig, ICCDC, 04.07.2012.
[206] Reg. 7 UNDU DPR; Regs. 208, 210, 211, 214 ICC ROR.
[207] Proposed amendment to Reg. 211 ICC ROR.   [208] Craig, ICCDC, 04.07.2012.
[209] Reg. 212(1) ICC ROR.   [210] Rule 25(E) SCSL ROD.   [211] Rule 25(F) SCSL ROD.
[212] Rule 41(v) ICTY ROD; Regs. 3, 9 UNDU DPR; Rules 36(d), 37 ICTR ROD; Reg. 95(2) ICC ROC; Regs. 206, 215(1), 216 ICC ROR.
[213] Rule 25(b)(iv), 25(d) SCSL ROD; Reg. 215(5) ICC ROR.

UNDU, UNDF and SCSLDF prisoners can be placed in isolation pursuant to an order of the Registrar, decided after consultation with the President or following a request from an interested person.[214] The CCO may also make such an order to prevent the infliction of injury to others,[215] to preserve security and good order[216] or as a punishment.[217] Orders made by the CCO must be reported to the Registrar, who must inform the President, who may order release at any time[218] (this role was reserved for the SCSL Registrar).[219] All uses of isolation must be reported to the doctor who must give advice on its implementation and monitor the physical and mental fitness of detained persons[220] and visit detained persons at their request at any time.[221] Extensions beyond a week need confirmation from the medical officer.[222] Detained persons in isolation at the ICCDC must be visited by the CCO and doctor every day.[223] SCSL prisoners in isolation could communicate with and receive visits from Counsel.[224]

Instruments of restraint can only be used for pre-determined reasons, such as to prevent escape, on medical grounds, to prevent injury to self or others or to avoid serious damage to property.[225] The SCSL added to ensure good order and security of the unit,[226] although the SCSL and the ICC forbid the use of restraints as a punishment for disciplinary offences.[227] The ICC also explicitly prohibits the use of chains or irons.[228] Irrespective of the reason for the use of restraints, the CCO must consult with the medical officer and report to the Registrar, who may inform the President.[229] During use, restrained persons must be under constant

---

[214] Rule 45(A)(i) ICTY ROD; Rule 43(a) ICTR ROD.
[215] Rule 45(A)(ii) ICTY ROD; Rule 43(b) ICTR ROD.
[216] Rule 45(A)(ii) ICTY ROD; Rule 43(b) ICTR ROD.
[217] Rule 45(A)(iii) ICTY ROD; Rule 43(C) ICTR ROD; Rule 30(a) SCSL ROD.
[218] Rule 48 ICTY ROD; Rule 46 ICTR ROD; Reg. 213 ICC ROR.
[219] Rule 32(b) SCSL ROD.
[220] Rule 46 ICTY ROD; Rule 44 ICTR ROD; Rules 30(A), 31(A) SCSL ROD; Reg. 212(3) ICC ROR.
[221] Rule 47 ICTY ROD; Rule 45 ICTR ROD; Rule 31(B) SCSL ROD; Reg. 212(8) ICC ROR.
[222] Rule 49 ICTY ROD; Rule 47 ICTR ROD; Rule 34(a) SCSL ROD; Reg. 212(4)-(6) ICC ROR.
[223] Reg. 212(7) ICC ROR.   [224] Rule 30(C) SCSL ROD.
[225] Rule 50 ICTY ROD; Rule 48 ICTR ROD; Rule 33(A) SCSL ROD; Reg. 203(2) ICC ROR.
[226] Rule 33(A)(iv) SCSL ROD.   [227] Rule 33(B) SCSL ROD; Reg. 203(1)-(2) ICC ROR.
[228] Reg. 203(2) ICC ROR.
[229] Rule 50(B) ICTY ROD; Rule 48 ICTR ROD; Rule 33(C) SCSL ROD; Reg. 203(3)-(4) ICC ROR.

supervision[230] and the restraints must be removed at the earliest possible opportunity.[231]

IDF staff are not armed in the normal course of duty, although SCSLDF reception staff and host prison perimeter staff are. Force should be used only as a last resort[232] and be no more than is strictly necessary[233] or, in other words, the minimum required to restrain the detained person and restore order.[234] For instance, SCSL custodial staff have received training in control and restraint techniques that enable them to deal with situations effectively with the least force possible.[235] Justifications for the use of force include preventing escape, responding to active or passive resistance to an order, maintaining order and security in self-defence or the defence of others.[236] All incidents must be reported to the CCO, who must report them to the Registrar.[237]

In situations of serious danger of disturbances at an IDF or host prison, the CCO or Registrar may suspend the rules of detention. The length of the permitted suspension varies among the courts but all suspensions must be reported to the Registrar and President, who must work with the Host State authorities to decide on the best course of action to restore security and order.[238]

4.2 Management and staff approaches to the maintenance of order

The procedures outlined above describe the processes to be followed and the permissible actions that may be taken in particular and exceptional circumstances. They do not provide guidance on how to maintain order on a daily basis. The approach taken ultimately depends on the views of managers and staff, and the IDF culture generally. As senior managers are recruited internationally and have different professional backgrounds and experiences, it is inevitable that their approaches to penal

---

[230] Rule 52 ICTY ROD; Rule 50 ICTR ROD; Rule 33(E) SCSL ROD; Reg. 203(6) ICC ROR.
[231] Rule 51 ICTY ROD; Rule 49 ICTR ROD; Rule 33(D) SCSL ROD; Reg. 203(5) ICC ROR.
[232] Reg. 204(1) ICC ROR.
[233] Rule 53(B) ICTY ROD; Rule 51 ICTR ROD; Rule 34(B) SCSL ROD.
[234] Reg. 204(1) ICC ROR. [235] SCSL Sixth Annual Report 46.
[236] Rule 53(A) ICTY ROD; Rule 51 ICTR ROD; Rule 34(A) SCSL ROD; Reg. 204(2) ICC ROR.
[237] Rule 53(B) ICTY ROD; Rule 51 ICTR ROD; Rule 34(B) SCSL ROD; Reg. 204(3) ICC ROR.
[238] Rule 57 ICTR ROD; Rule 55 ICTR ROD; Rule 37(A), (C) SCSL ROD; Reg. 96 ICC ROC.

management will differ. Even among the more homogenous custodial staff, seconded from the Host State's national prison system, views vary.

Crawley notes that the manner in which officers interact with prisoners is dependent on a range of situational and social factors, such as the type of prison, its category, the type of inmate, the staff's prior work experience and the occupational culture of the prison. She found that some staff preferred to help and support inmates while others preferred to keep a distance "either for reasons of efficiency ... or to express a view that prison is for the punitive degradation of offenders".[239] These different approaches can also be observed in the work of IDF managers and custodial staff.

Those that advocate a security approach are more likely to distrust detained persons and to maintain formal and detached relationships, as they feel this improves control and makes the implementation of difficult decisions easier. Those that advocate a detention/dynamic security approach feel that good social relationships are vital to ensuring both the welfare of detained persons and the security of the facility. This group is more likely to try to improve conditions and the regime and find a variety of ways to interact with detained persons, such as through sport or cooking.[240] At the UNDU, an independent audit found that staff relationships with detained persons were informed by a sense of mutual respectfulness, which translates in practice as creating a distance and leaving each other in peace.[241] At the UNDF, there were concerns that staff and detainees may have become too friendly with each other and that consequently there was a need to keep the role of the staff distinct and separate.[242] At the ICCDC, staff try to engage proactively with detained persons to prevent their deterioration and to create respectful relations while retaining control.[243]

On the one hand, the combination of the different approaches of management and staff may be positive, if they have a synergistic effect. These differing approaches can, however, create tensions among management and staff as some perceive the lack of interaction as a lack of interest in the welfare of the detained persons,[244] whereas high levels of

---

[239] E. Crawley, "Doing Prison Work: the Public and Private Lives of Prison Officers" in Y. Jewkes and H. Johnston (eds.), *Prison Readings: A Critical Introduction to Prisons and Imprisonment* (2006), 214.

[240] Custodial Staff, UNDU, 22–27.08.2007.

[241] Para. 2.6.3 Independent Audit of the Detention Unit at the ICTY, 2006.

[242] O'Donnell, ICTR, 25.06.2007.   [243] Custodial Staff, ICCDC, 22–28.08.2007.

[244] Wright, SCSLDF, 22.04.2008

interaction are viewed by others as unnecessary and as having the potential to undermine security and result in a different regime depending on who is on duty.

For example, the SCSLDF international supervisors who had experience of dealing with conflict-related imprisonment in Ireland felt that compromise was important, and consequently, regulations should be interpreted and applied in light of both welfare and safe custody considerations.[245] They believed that the security-orientation of other international supervisors and managers led to a rigid application of the rules that failed to provide the necessary emotional support for detained persons and created unnecessary tension.[246] The culture adopted by IDF management informs the methods used in daily contact and influences the attitude of staff and therefore affects order. For example, on one occasion a detained person complained that his handcuffs were too tight. Rather than simply readjusting the cuffs, staff reacted in a heavy-handed manner which resulted in the detainee being injured and disciplined.[247] They also felt that security-focused training, such as how to use firearms and riot control techniques, while necessary to react to violent situations, was not sufficient to help staff deal with the reality of "visiting rooms full of screaming women and trembling husbands ... you can't shoot or put hand locks on the wives and yet this is the only form of interaction the staff know".[248] Although having to calm wives down and hide threatened mistresses at visiting times made the SCSLDF seem like a "different planet",[249] this level of accommodation was considered to be justified by many of the staff and management due to the length of remand and sentences imposed.

Rostaing has categorised prison staff who adopt a security focus as "statutory" and those that adopt a detention or dynamic security approach as "missionary". However, she feels that these categorisations are not static and staff can move from a statutory to missionary approach over time as they gain confidence and experience in their interactions with prisoners.[250] This transition was evident in interviews with prison staff and management working at the IDFs. It was notable that it was not only the approaches of the individual managers and staff that changed over time, but the general culture of the IDF too. The IDF regimes have

---

[245] Neil, Wright, Ewing, SCSLDF, 22–23.04.2008. [246] Wright, SCSLDF, 22.04.2008.
[247] Neil, SCSLDF, 23.04.2008. [248] Ibid. [249] Ibid.
[250] See Van Zyl Smit and Snacken, *Principles of European Prison Law and Policy*, 44.

moved from an initial focus on security and order, towards a focus on creating more humane detention regimes.

The initial UNDU regime required segregation which amounted to isolation (detainees were not permitted to speak to each other), an extremely limited regime (detainees were only allowed out of their cell for one hour a day), heavily restricted and actively monitored phone calls, numerous searches and the use of handcuffs, blindfolds and cages in vans for transport to trial.[251] The strict regime was not altogether surprising, given the unprecedented nature of international detention, the elevated gravity of the crimes detainees were accused of and the fact that the whole world was watching. During these early days, detainees felt as though staff perceived them to be "the worst people on the face of the planet"[252] and the regime reflected this perception. Even with a relaxation of the regime, the detainees felt compelled to request further changes, particularly in relation to medical care, exercise, access to media from their own states, visits and food.[253] Over time, the tight hold on every aspect of the regime loosened and a more humane system was introduced. Detainees felt that staff and management came to see that they were "just normal people".[254] A more relaxed regime that allowed detained persons to spend most of their time out of their cells and to have access to a yard with fresh air out of sight of Dutch prisoners was also possible due to a change of building and revisions of the House Rules.

SCSLDF detainees had a similar experience. The first SCSLDF, in Bonthe, Sherbo Island, was initially managed by a former US Marine from the SCSL's Security Section. He viewed the British prison management style as laissez-faire and his strong security focus resulted in a containment rather than detention system.[255] The regime was very strict, with association forbidden and staff had access to batons, leg constraints and manacles.[256] A former Registrar banned the use of weapons and unnecessary restraints and felt these early days of detention provided a clear "lesson that when dealing with custody, one shouldn't mix security and detention regimes".[257] Upon transfer to the new facility in Freetown, the regime was relaxed to allow for more time out of cells and

---

[251] Delalić, 20.08.2008; McFadden, UNDU, 21.08.2007. P. Skoplak, *Uknik*, (2004), 307.
[252] Katava, 13.10.2007.
[253] ICTY Press Release, "Open Letter from the Detainees Regarding their Conditions at the ICTY's Detention Unit", 12.08.1998.
[254] Katava, 13.10.2007.
[255] SCSL First Annual Report, 24; Jackson, SCSLDF/ICCDC, 19.03.2007.
[256] Vincent, SCSL/ICTY, 27.04.2007.   [257] Ibid.

association.[258] With the focus on the provision of a detention regime based on interaction, management rarely had to use disciplinary measures.[259] It is hoped that the new SCSLDF, managed by the SCSL's Security Section does not revert to a containment system.

IDF management appears to have moved from a control model of management that emphasises obedience, monitoring and vigorous rule enforcement to a consensual model that relies on a more relaxed regime and grievance processes and allows staff to deal with inmates in a firm but fair way.[260] The adoption of a caring professional approach to detention not only leads to better relationships between staff and prisoners but creates a more stable environment. The IDFs' experiences are in line with penal research that shows that prisons with better staff–prisoner relationships, interaction and active and liberal regimes experience lower levels of violent conflict.[261]

Penological experts and scholars acknowledge that by treating prisoners fairly and with respect, prisoners are more willing to comply with the regime, creating stability.[262] Respect can be demonstrated during everyday life of a prison. Former UNDU detainees were appreciative of small gestures, such as an extra piece of fruit, as this was viewed as recognition of their humanity when the world appeared to view them as monsters.[263] While former UNDU occupants were unanimous in their animosity towards the court that deprived them of their liberty, and the Prosecutor in particular, they had nothing but praise for the professionalism of the UNDU staff and management.[264] Overall, they felt that they were treated with respect and decency and that their requests were facilitated where possible.[265]

The primary function of an IDF is to act as a remand centre for the international courts. On the one hand, attempts to create a calm environment may relate, not so much to penological objectives, but to the

---

[258] SCSL First Annual Report, 24; Second Annual Report, 32.
[259] Vincent, SCSL/ICTY, 27.04.2007.
[260] See Vincent, *An Administrative Practices Manual*, 71 and the discussion of DiIulio's models in K. McEvoy, *Paramilitary Imprisonment in Northern Ireland* (2001), 180.
[261] See Van Zyl Smit and Snacken, *Principles of European Prison Law and Policy*, 43.
[262] See McEvoy, *Paramilitary Imprisonment in Northern Ireland*, 189.
[263] Skopljak, *Uznik*, 339.
[264] Delalić, 20.08.2008; Kupreškić, 13.10.2007; Bralo Sweden, 08.10.2008. ICTY Press Release, "Open Letter from the Detainees Regarding their Conditions at the ICTY's Detention Unit", 12.08.1998.
[265] Delalić, 20.08.2008; Katava, 13.10.2007; Kupreškić, 13.10.2007; Bralo, 08.10.2008; Krajišnik, 27.09.2012. Skoplak, *Uknik*, 307.

pressure to ensure detention issues do not interfere with the judicial process. On the other hand, IDFs are occupied by persons deprived of their liberty against their will, for very long periods of time, often in a foreign state far from their families and who are presumed innocent. These realities make high security levels inhumane and necessitate compromise. Yet, concern has been expressed that the IDFs are trying to achieve the unachievable: satisfied prisoners. This risks turning the implementation of penal regulations into a policy of appeasement. Some feel that the whims of detained persons are being accommodated due to fears about defence counsel intervention. For instance at the SCSL, prisoners were, at times, verbally and physically abusive to staff. Rather than react as they would in the national system, staff discussed the fact that they were more polite and cautious in their dealings with international prisoners due to the very legalistic nature of the process and that some detained persons had "made a sport out of complaining to lawyers".[266] The readiness of defence counsel to become involved in disciplinary procedures meant they were rarely put into place,[267] leaving an impression that "international detainees have a free hand".[268] The numerous avenues available to legally challenge detention issues means that results have to be achieved through "negotiation and planning with a smile, rather than by using force and power".[269]

The increased power of the detained persons resulted in some custodial staff feeling that they are no longer authority figures in their own right, but that they are simply the "means of both management and detainees".[270] In comparison to national prison systems, some staff felt that there is a degree of reversal of the power dynamic in the staff–prisoner relationship. Further, the inconsistent application of regulations can also create unfairness and unpredictability. While a degree of flexibility is necessary, excessive flexibility can result in discriminatory treatment.[271]

Order should be maintained in the interests of safe custody and to ensure the smooth operation of IDFs.[272] Order should be controlled with fairness and with no more restrictions than are necessary.[273] While this is easily

---

[266] Custodial Staff, ICCDC, 22–28.08.2007.
[267] Custodial Staff, SCSLDF, 22–25.04.2008; Wright, SCSLDF, 22.04.2008.
[268] Van Breda, SCSLDF, 25.04.2008.   [269] Bremmers, ICCDC, 04.07.2012.
[270] Custodial Staff, UNDU, 22–28.08.2007.
[271] Jackson, SCSLDF/ICCDC, 19.03.2007.
[272] Rule 40 ICTY ROD; Rule 35 ICTR ROD; Reg. 95(1) ICC ROC.
[273] Rule 25(A) SCSL ROD.

stated, it is more difficult to strike a balance between the security and detention requirements of IDFs in practice. The CPT recommends that measures of control and containment should be accompanied by "a spirit of communication and care".[274] However, achieving the correct balance of power can be difficult. Without a welfare approach to operations, security becomes the main focus but this fails to take the individual needs of detained persons into account and risks creating an overly restrictive regime. To avoid the creation of repressive regimes, contemporary prison practice seeks to achieve a "tolerable modus vivendi through compromise and accommodation".[275] Yet a focus on creating positive relationships can be viewed as appeasement or "pandering to prisoners".[276] Focusing on the creation of a liberal regime, the protection of rights and the provision of good material conditions, to the exclusion of order and security concerns, can jeopardise the control of IDFs.

5. Oversight

IDFs provide international prisoners with high standards in terms of material conditions, regime, facilities, medical care etc. But like all penal regimes, it is inevitable that prisoners will be dissatisfied with aspects of their treatment. As prisoners are considered to be "part of a customer group with expectations ... entitled to complain if they don't receive expected standards"[277] IDF regulations create complaint mechanisms and oversight systems.

5.1 Complaints

At IDFs, complaints have referred to the use of restraints during transfers, searches, the quality and quantity of food, access to drinking water, activities, purchasing items from the canteen, the cost of calls, the length of time required for security clearance for visitors and the right to conjugal visits.[278] Rather than use formal mechanisms to complain

---

[274] Para. 45 CPT Second General Report.
[275] See Van Zyl Smit and Snacken, *Principles of European Prison Law and Policy*, 40.
[276] Crawley, "Doing Prison Work", 215–16.
[277] Jackson, SCSLDF/ICCDC, 19.03.2007.
[278] Diop, ICTR, 27.06.2007; Custodial Staff, UNDU, 22–27.08.2007; Custodial Staff, ICCDC, 22–28.08.2007; Custodial Staff and National Supervisors, SCSLDF, 22–25.04.2008; Vincent, *An Administrative Practices Manual*, 67.

about standards that are in some cases vastly superior to those of the local population, some detained persons prefer to "agitate internally".[279] Others make public complaints. For example, Mr Norman claimed the Bonthe Island SCSLDF was a "mosquito infested cave which formerly held West African slaves".[280] Although he did not submit a formal complaint, a former Registrar rejected the accusation on the facts.[281] Moreover, he found it amusing considering that, as former Minister for the Interior, Mr Norman had been responsible for this prison.[282]

The group dynamic can influence how the complaints procedure is used and whether or not a culture of complaining is created. Formerly rich and powerful detainees tend to complain a lot as prison provides a reduced quality of life for them. They may also manipulate others to complain as they feel that increased pressure will give credence to their causes.[283] The lack of interest in the trial procedure by asylum-seeking witnesses detained at the ICCDC has been blamed for the creation of a complaints culture there. While some feel that the complaints procedures can be abused and used to make frivolous complaints,[284] many of these so-called "toothpaste" complaints that appear petty on the surface can be important to detained persons and in most cases are issues that can be solved easily.[285] Other complaints prove to be unfounded. For example, ICCDC detained persons complained they were not receiving enough milk when there were eighteen and a half litres in the detained persons' freezers.[286]

The formal procedure for making complaints is virtually identical at all IDFs. The detained person can make a complaint to the CCO, and if he is dissatisfied with the reply, he may send privileged correspondence to the Registrar.[287] If the complainant is unsatisfied with the Registrar's reply, the issue may be referred to the President/Presidency.[288]

Due to the repetitive nature of many complaints and the need to ensure that the IDF management and Registrar retain control over day-to-day detention issues, there is a threshold for the admissibility of complaints to the Presidents of the UN Tribunals. Complaints will only

---

[279] Jackson, SCSLDF/ICCDC, 19.03.2007.
[280] SCSL Press Release, "Detainees Claim to be on Hunger Strike", 27.05.2003.
[281] SCSL Press Release, "Status of Detention of the Accused", 07.04.2003.
[282] Vincent, SCSL/ICTY, 27.04.2007.   [283] O'Donnell, ICTR, 25.06.2007.
[284] Mwuangulu, Wastelain, Endeley, ICTR, 25.06.2007.
[285] O'Donnell, ICTR, 25.06.2007.   [286] Craig, ICCDC, 04.07.2012.
[287] Regs. 1, 3–4 UNDU; Regs. 217, 220 ICC ROR.
[288] Reg. 7 UNDU CPR; Reg. 221 ICC ROR.

be considered if all other stages of the procedure have been exhausted and the act or omission involves an alleged breach of a substantive human right or policy concern that is non-administrative in nature.[289] Currently, there is no such threshold for judicial review of detention issues by the Presidency at the ICC.[290]

It has been argued that the current ICC complaints system is not feasible in the long-term due to its potential to interfere with the efficient and effective management of the ICCDC. Judicial decisions based on solely legal factors may not be implementable in the custodial setting. For example, the President upheld a request by detained witnesses to have a computer installed on the basis that they were entitled to the same rights as other detained persons.[291] The CCO had denied the request on the basis that as they did not have a trial, they did not need access to documents, and as there was very limited space in the wing, the installation of a computer should be postponed until the move to the new floor where there would be more space. The Presidency's decision, made without consultation with the ICCDC management, was difficult to implement given the limited space available.[292] Likewise, an ICTY judicial order that Mr Milošević should be the only person to have a key to access the additional cell in the UNDU that he used as an office was clearly unacceptable from a detention perspective.

Judicial orders made without consultation with IDF management may result in unfeasible orders being handed down by individuals with no detention experience. The constant threat of judicial review at the ICC means that "the chief of detention is never chief of detention".[293] The ICCDC CCO has argued that as the often "mind-numbingly mundane" complaints create an endless stream of paperwork that eats into time that could be used to actually resolve the issue, the majority of day-to-day detention issues should stop at the IDF management level with oversight provided by the Registry.[294] This view was supported by other management levels who felt too much energy was being expended on bureaucratic procedures and complaints involving minor issues.[295]

The SCSL differed from the UN Tribunals and the ICC and omitted the final level of appeal to the President,[296] although the SCSLDF

---

[289] Para. 4 *Ngeze* (Decision) ICTR-1999-52-A, 14.09.2005.
[290] See Reg. 221 ICC ROR and the proposed Reg. 220*bis* ICC ROR.
[291] Reg. 223 ICC ROR.   [292] Craig, ICCDC, 04.07.2012.
[293] Jouthart, ICCDC, 04.07.2012.   [294] Craig, ICCDC, 04.07.2012.
[295] Bremmers, ICCDC, 04.07.2012.   [296] Rule 59 SCSL ROD.

detainees could raise issues in chambers and the SCSL detainee housed at the ICCDC could use both the ICC and SCSL complaints procedures.[297] This dual procedure has been used to try to secure the import of expensive cigars not available through the Scheveningen prison canteen service by Mr Taylor.

It is necessary to establish a threshold for the judicial review of detention-related complaints for two reasons. First, judicial time and resources should not be wasted dealing with frivolous and repetitive complaints. Second, it is essential that there is agreement between the custodial, administrative and judicial officers charged with overseeing detention "where the responsibility lies for the implementation of those rules and any challenges to them".[298] Detention issues should be dealt with by the CCO in the first instance, with a right to appeal to the Registrar if a cause of dissatisfaction with the decision can be demonstrated. Appeals to the Presidency should be reserved for decisions that have potential to violate the detained person's fundamental rights. It has also been suggested that the system could be reformed by only allowing the review of CCO decisions or decisions not resolved by a mediation board.[299]

5.2 Internal oversight

The ICRC has highlighted the importance of having different levels to approach in a complaints procedure. The IDF complaints procedure, for example, involves both administrative and judicial elements of the court structure. In addition to these complaints procedures, there are other internal methods of oversight.

The Registrar, a judge or officials can be appointed to inspect the IDF and report on the administration of the facility, the implementation of the rules of detention and conditions.[300] There are also informal avenues detained persons can use to make requests or complaints. As the Registry section responsible for detention is tasked with ensuring that the IDF conforms to international standards, it liaises with independent inspection bodies, deals with complaints and may become involved in disciplinary

---

[297] Backman, ICCDC, 04.02.2008.
[298] Vincent, *An Administrative Practices Manual*, 67.
[299] Seminar on the Amendments to the Regulations of the Registry, 4–6.7.2012.
[300] Rules 6, 34 ICTY ROD; Rules 6, 32 ICTR ROD; Reg. 94(1) ICC ROC.

procedures.[301] Moreover, the Registrar can delegate responsibility for the IDF to the Deputy Registrar, who can visit the legal officers of the Registry detention section, the CCO and detained persons to discuss conditions or to hear informal complaints.[302] At the UNDF, the Social Welfare officer may also deal with internal complaints about treatment.[303]

The IDF doctor plays an often overlooked but important oversight role. In addition to his regular duty to monitor and maintain the physical and mental health of prisoners,[304] he can inspect the facility and report to the CCO on conditions of imprisonment.[305] His input is required for decisions relating to diet, exercise, punishment, segregation, isolation, the use of restraints etc.[306] Moreover, any detained person against whom force has been used has the right to immediate examination and treatment by the IDF doctor in the absence of non-medical staff and a record of the examination should be made available to varying combinations of the Chief of Detention, Registrar, Prosecutor, Principal Defender and President depending on the court.[307]

As the medical officer comes as part of the product price for renting detention capacity, the IDF doctor is an employee of the host state. Consequently, the international courts cannot directly order him to act. The medical officer therefore holds a uniquely independent position. The current UNDU and ICCDC doctor welcomes this relative autonomy. He feels it is necessary in the complex environment of the IDF as it enables him to make his own decisions based on medical need and recognised ethical norms for practice.[308]

For instance, during a hunger-strike at the UNDU, this position enabled the doctor to avoid complying with an order of the ICTY President to force-feed an individual should he lapse into unconsciousness.[309] Although the

---

[301] Mwuangulu, Wastelain, Endeley, ICTR, 25.06.2007; para. 87 ICTY Eighteenth Annual Report.
[302] O'Donnell, ICTR, 25.06.2007; Mwuangulu, Wastelain, Endeley, ICTR, 25.06.2007.
[303] Okitapoy, UNDF, 08.08.2007.
[304] Rules 34(B), 36 ICTY ROD; Rules 31, 33 ICTR ROD; Rule 19(B) SCSL ROD; Reg. 155(1) ICC ROR.
[305] Rule 19(c), (d), (f) SCSL ROD; Reg. 155(2) ICC ROR.
[306] Rules 29(A), 34(A), 42(B), 43(A), 46, 47, 49, 50(A)(ii), 54 ICTY ROD; Rules 26, 44, 45, 47, 48 ICTR ROD; Rules 30(A), 31, 33(A)-(C), 34(C), 54(C) SCSL ROD; Regs. 165(3)-(4), 201(5), 203(2)-(4), 212(3)-(8) ICC ROR.
[307] Rule 54 ICTY ROD; Rule 52 ICTR ROD; Rule 34(C)-(D) SCSL ROD; Reg. 204(4)-(5) ICC ROR.
[308] Falke, ICCDC/UNDU, 04.02.2008.
[309] See para. 15.1 Šešelj (TC Order) IT-03-67-T, 06.12.2006.

order was intended to revive the detained person and prevent his death, the procedure would have involved using physical force and manacles on an unwilling subject in front of his family.[310] In extreme cases, force-feeding a prisoner may result in a breach of the prisoner's right not to be subjected to torture, inhuman or degrading treatment.[311] It may also result in a breach of the prisoner's right to privacy and physical integrity.[312] As the national expert on hunger-strikes, the UNDU doctor informed the ICTY, UN and ICRC that force-feeding is viewed as unethical by many states and that in physical terms it is impracticable. Under the 1975 Tokyo Declaration,[313] prisoners on hunger-strike should not be force-fed if they have refused such intervention and are capable of forming an unimpaired and rational judgment.[314] Rodley and Pollard feel this may provide "an appropriate general approach to the problem" as it is based on respect for the rule of consent and can be more easily reconciled with the duty to respect the inherent dignity of prisoners.[315] However, this does not address situations where a prisoner has given instructions not to be resuscitated but is unconscious and about to die. The 1991 Malta Declaration[316] does not resolve the problem: "it provides only that the ultimate decision on whether or not to intervene should be left to the medical doctor".[317] Regional standards and human rights courts and bodies prefer the medical management of hunger-strikes, as opposed to a security approach.[318] Van Zyl Smit and Snacken argue that medical principles indicate that a doctor should not force-feed an unconscious prisoner, if that prisoner was capable of making an informed decision and wished to continue with the hunger-strike. Consequently, an institution which follows the direction of a medical doctor in this regard will not fail in its duty to protect the prisoner's life.[319] Conversely, in addition to violating the right to freedom from torture, inhuman or degrading treatment and punishment, force-feeding a prisoner without his consent may result in a violation of the right to health, as well as a violation of the international ethics for health

---

[310] Vincent, SCSL/ICTY 27.04.2007.
[311] See paras. 93–4 *Nevmerhitsky* v. *Ukraine* (54825/00) 05.04.2005.
[312] See paras. 71–72 *Juhnke* v. *Turkey* (52515/99) 13.05.2008.
[313] The World Medical Association Declaration of Tokyo: Guidelines for Physicians Concerning Torture and other Cruel, Inhuman or Degrading Treatment or Punishment in Relation to Detention and Imprisonment, 1975.
[314] Para. 6.
[315] N. Rodley and M. Pollard, *The Treatment of Prisoners under International Law*, 3rd edn (2009), 419.
[316] World Medical Association, Declaration of Malta on Hunger Strikers, 1991.
[317] Van Zyl Smit and Snacken, *Principles of European Prison Law and Policy*, 167.
[318] *Ibid.*, 167–9.   [319] *Ibid.*, 170–1.

professionals.[320] Although the situation never arose, the UNDU doctor felt that his unique employment status meant that he could interpret the order and international standards in a way that gave him room to manoeuvre that he would not have had if he had been a direct employee of the UN or ICTY.[321]

The UNDU has since issued a document, *Voluntary Protest Fasts: Information for Detainees*,[322] which sets out the newly revised policy in relation to hunger-strikes. The Declaration of Malta has been identified as the leading international document to be applied. Accordingly, detained persons are advised that "should you be determined to take your protest to its ultimate end, you will be allowed to die with dignity rather than being resuscitated against your will" and "force-feeding will not be undertaken". The ICC has also adopted a protocol to deal with detained persons on hunger-strike. IDF detainees that lapse into unconsciousness following a hunger-strike must be transferred to a hospital. The IDF protocols would continue to apply however as the IDF medical officer would remain the case manager and therefore have the ultimate say on treatment.[323]

There has also been an on-going debate about the limits of doctor–patient confidentiality when an international court demands the disclosure of medical and psychiatric records without the patient's consent.[324] All medical records of prisoners are strictly confidential,[325] and accordingly, can only be consulted by the doctor, an independent inspecting authority or staff directly involved in a prisoner's treatment without the express written consent of the prisoner[326] (or a representative of the prisoner if he is incapable of giving consent[327]). Beyond this, they may only be disclosed without consent if the health or safety of the prisoner or others is in danger.[328] However, this consent was not deemed necessary at the ICTY when the disclosure was ordered by a judge "in the interest of justice and the good administration of trial".[329] Although this should only happen after consultation with the UNDU medical officer,[330] the doctor claims he was never consulted but simply ordered to provide information he could not give for ethical reasons.[331] Due to

---

[320] Para. 82 Special Procedures Joint Report on the Situation of Detainees at Guantánamo Bay UN Doc E/CN.4/2006/120, 27.02.2006.
[321] Falke, UNDU/ICCDC, 04.02.2008.   [322] UNDU Doc No 090325, 25.03.2009.
[323] Falke, UNDU/ICCDC, 04.07.2012.   [324] See para. C.3(54) MDP, 188.
[325] Reg. 156(1) ICC ROR.   [326] Rule 34 (D)(i) ICTY ROD; Reg. 156(2)–(4) ICC ROR.
[327] Reg. 156(6) ICC ROR.   [328] Reg. 156(3) ICC ROR.
[329] Rule 34 (D)(ii) ICTY ROD.   [330] *Ibid.*   [331] Falke, UNDU/ICCDC, 04.02.2008.

his independent status, the doctor was able to refuse these requests from the ICTY judges for access to information about the health of detained persons in the absence of their consent. When this approach failed, the ICTY tried to obtain the information indirectly by using external independent experts, but the ethical principle of informed consent meant they had to disclose the purpose for which they were seeking the information and therefore to declare that they were not acting in their capacity as medical doctors. This procedure left the doctor feeling that, at the ICTY, the "efficient administration of the trial is seen as more important than the welfare of the detainees".[332] This approach resulted in unnecessary requests for updates on detained persons' health every two weeks for years.[333] The friction with the ICTY judges lessened over time due to an increased awareness that this information cannot simply be demanded without consent.[334] While the ICTY stated that "keeping the Medical Officer free from the judicial process as much as possible, and maintaining the confidentiality of all medical records, helps strengthen the trust relationship"[335] with detained persons, it also stated that it continues to rely on independent medical experts to get the same information under Rule 74*bis* ICTY RPE.[336] The doctor feels that many people within the courts would prefer the doctor to be part of the court structure so that direct orders could be given and clear lines of responsibility established (although it should be noted that this is not considered to be appropriate by IDF managers). Such a move would be counter to regional recommendations that medical staff be independent and aligned to mainstream health-care provision in the community so that medical decisions are governed by medical criteria.[337]

While medical confidentiality is respected and protected by IDF medical and custodial management and staff, grey areas remain. Do international or national rules apply? To what extent do judicial demands for information have to be met? The medical officers at the UNDU and ICCDC are seeking clarification on the correct procedure to follow and have requested the Dutch Ministry of Justice to issue guidelines in relation to immunity from suit or disciplinary action for actions taken in light of international requests.[338] Accordingly, there is on-going

---

[332] Falke, UNDU/ICCDC, 04.02.2008. See also para. A.1.1(8) MDP, 179.
[333] Falke, UNDU/ICCDC, 04.02.2008.
[334] See para. 13 UNDU, Voluntary Protest Fasts, Doc No 090325, 25.03.2009.
[335] Para. A.1.2(11) MDP, 179.   [336] Para. A.4.1(18) MDP, 181.
[337] Paras. 71–72 CPT Third General Report.   [338] Falke, UNDU/ICCDC, 04.07.2012.

work to amend and clarify the UNDU and ICC rules in this regard. The ICC recently proposed amendments to its provisions regulating access to medical files with the aim of ensuring the highest level of confidentiality was respected and that any granted disclosure is for a temporary period to the minimum number of persons necessary.[339]

5.3 External oversight

In addition to the internal oversight mechanisms, the courts have established procedures for the independent oversight of IDFs by individuals and bodies outside the IDF and court structures. Detained persons, subject to security considerations, may communicate confidentially with their lawyers, diplomatic representatives and external independent inspection bodies.[340] Upon the occurrence of particular events or complaints by detained persons, independent inspection bodies may be requested to conduct an ad hoc audit of the facility or investigation.[341] Interested bodies may also be granted access to IDFs. For instance, the SCSLDF was visited by the Human Rights Section of UNAMSIL,[342] the former UN Secretary-General[343] and the Human Rights Committee of the Sierra Leone Parliamentarians.[344] Like national prisoners, international prisoners may submit complaints to the police and national criminal courts of the Host State.

To ensure regular monitoring by an independent expert body, all the international courts to date have appointed the ICRC as the inspection body for their IDFs. A visit may be complete (thorough and detailed inquiry), a follow-up (check on problems noted or particular cases) or ad hoc (specific problems of an individual detainee or the detained population as a whole).[345] The ICRC's unannounced visits must be facilitated by the Registrar and CCO, who must ensure the ICRC has unlimited access to the IDF, all detained persons and documentation therein.[346]

---

[339] Proposed amendment to Reg. 156(1) ICC ROR. Craig, Comments made at The Seminar on the Amendments to the Regulations of the Registry, 4–6.07.2012.
[340] Rules 12, 63, 65 ICTY ROD; Rules 10, 63, 65 ICTR ROD; Regs. 11(A), 30–31 UNDU VCR; Rules 40(B), 41(D), 43, 44(A), (D) SCSL ROD; Regs. 97, 98 ICC ROC; Regs. 169(1), 183(1), 184 ICC ROR.
[341] See Independent Audit of the Detention Unit at the ICTY, 2006 and A. Cassese, Report on the Special Court for Sierra Leone, 12.12.2006.
[342] SCSL Third Annual Report, 36.   [343] SCSL Fourth Annual Report, 50.
[344] SCSL Press Release, "Detainees Claim to be on Hunger Strike", 27.05.2003.
[345] Art. 6(2) ICC–ICRC Agreement.
[346] Reg. 150 ICC ROR; Arts. 2, 4, 6(1), 8, 12(1)–(2) ICC–ICRC Agreement.

Discussions with detained persons must occur out of sight and hearing of custodial staff.[347] The ICRC can also bring a medical officer to inspect detained persons.[348]

After the visit, the ICRC submits a confidential report containing recommendations to the IDF CCO and either the Registrar or Presidency, depending on the court.[349] The recommendations are not binding. The Presidency and/or Registry should however take steps to give effect to ICRC recommendations, though this may require consultation with the Host State and prison.[350] The IDF is usually given a few months in which to implement the recommendations before a follow-up visit. A former Registrar acknowledged the ICRC's contribution to the development of the UNDU regime: "the ICRC came to our rescue ... conditions of detention have greatly improved over the years ... partly due to the ICRC recommendations".[351] Despite the potential contribution of their recommendations to the development of international penal policy and practice, these reports and recommendations are not published.[352] Moreover, there have been criticisms about the professionalism and thoroughness of the ICRC's inspection procedure.[353]

5.4 Oversight of imprisonment at IDFs

IDF regulations create an oversight regime that is both reactive, in that there are formal complaints procedures, and proactive, in that several internal and external bodies are charged with ensuring that detained persons are treated in a rights compliant manner. Conditions of imprisonment and the treatment of international prisoners are therefore subject to formal and informal, internal and external oversight from administrative, medical, legal and judicial officials. Due to their

---

[347] Reg. 13 UNDU CPR; Para. 3 Letter from the ICTY President to the ICRC President, 28.04.1995; Rule 60 SCSL ROD; para. 8 ICCDC Complaints Procedure: Guide for Detained Persons. An amendment to regulation 183 ICC ROR has been proposed to make it explicit that ICRC visits are not supervised.
[348] See SCSL Third Annual Report, 36.
[349] Rule 6(B) ICTY ROD; paras. 12, 13 Letter from the ICTY President to the ICRC President, 28.04.1995; Rule 6 ICTR ROD; Rule 4(A) SCSL ROD; Reg. 94(2)–(3) ICC ROC; Art. 11 ICC–ICRC Agreement.
[350] Rules 6, 36 ICTY ROD; Rules 6, 34 ICTR ROD; Rule 4(B) SCSL ROD; Reg. 94(4)–(5) ICC ROC; Art.11(2) ICC–ICRC Agreement.
[351] De Sampayo Garrido, "Problems and Achievements", 478.
[352] Art. 11(3)–(4) ICC–ICRC Agreement.   [353] Craig, ICCDC, 04.07.2012.

international status, IDFs attract more media and political attention[354] and pressure to conform to international standards. In some ways, they are more open institutions than domestic prisons. They post images of facilities on their websites and accommodate visits from interested parties.

Yet, despite the growing body of international jurisprudence on international penal matters, it is seldom made public. While the ICC is currently considering ways to redact detention-related decisions,[355] there is generally very little public information about this form of prison administration. Given the uniqueness of IDF operations, and in the interests of transparency, the courts should consider publishing annual reports and/or inspection reports of the IDFs. Although the ICRC has a policy of confidentiality,[356] it may be possible to publish certain aspects of its reports. Indeed the ICRC's agreement with the ICTY specifically states that the ICTY "may, after securing the ICRC's agreement, have the report, together with the comments of the Tribunal, made public".[357] Information that would violate the privacy of detained persons or pose a threat to security could be removed. It would also be interesting to see the courts' responses to the reports and recommendations, as is the practice of states responding to CPT reports. Reports may contain positive feedback that would bolster public perceptions about IDFs and dispel suspicions of mistreatment.[358] However, the ICRC stance is that it is not a public relations agency for the international courts and as its primary concern is the welfare of detained persons it does not wish to jeopardise access by publishing reports.[359] While the access issue may be relevant in the ICRC's relations with states, it seems unfounded in its relationships with international courts that requested their services and invited them into their detention facilities to make recommendations on improvements that could be implemented.

The international courts could appoint another independent monitoring body whose report could be published. A Swedish audit of the UNDU instigated following the deaths of Mr Babić and Mr Milosevic, and an audit of the SCSL which included a report on the SCSLDF, have been made available to the public.[360] Although the Host State prison

---

[354] Para. 2.3 Independent Audit of the Detention Unit at the ICTY, 2006.
[355] Sant-Anna, ICC, 06.07.2012.   [356] See Chapter 2, Section 3.1.
[357] Para. 11 ICTY–ICRC Agreement.   [358] Jackson, SCSLDF/ICCDC, 19.03.2007.
[359] See Chapter 2, Section 3.1.
[360] See Independent Audit of the Detention Unit at the ICTY, 2006; Cassese, Report on the Special Court for Sierra Leone, 12.12.2006.

inspectorate can be granted access to the ICCDC, this form of evaluation may not be perceived to be wholly independent given that the Dutch Prison Service provides the facilities, staff and medical care under the Product Price Agreement.[361] Alternatively, the courts could create an independent oversight mechanism that could report on IDF operations as part of its general report on the court. Either body could and should provide a more thorough evaluation of an IDF's operations than the current oversight focus on the detained person's perceptions. While this is a necessary element of oversight to protect against human rights violations, this singular focus fails to evaluate wider systemic issues. More thorough inspections and evaluations could report on medical care, staff training, management structures, infrastructure, costs etc.

The ICC's Assembly of State Parties has created an Independent Oversight Mechanism (IOM) to investigate, inspect and evaluate the work of the court.[362] Its creation demonstrated that there is a degree of consensus that states that fund the ICC should ensure there is adequate oversight of its operations to ward off accusations designed to undermine its credibility.[363] However, the IOM is not fully operational at present; the ASP has only authorised the operationalisation of its investigative function, not its inspection or evaluation functions.[364] Moreover it remains unclear if this IOM's mandate would extend to the evaluation of detention- or enforcement-related issues.

International courts must implement more transparent and thorough inspections of their IDFs. By themselves, unpublished reports that rely almost exclusively on dialogue with detained persons are insufficient to guarantee the systemic development of international detention regimes. While a focus on the outcomes for detained persons is a necessary aspect of detention oversight, a more comprehensive and intensive inspectorate system should be implemented to analyse all aspects of the regime from the buildings, to the management structure, to procedures and processes that are used. The lack of detail on significant aspects of the international detention regime is one of the reasons for the current lack of strategic focus. In addition, the policy not to publish inspection reports adds a

---

[361] Dubuisson, Comments made at The Seminar on the Amendments to the Regulations of the Registry, 4–6.07.2012.
[362] See Art. 112(4) ICCSt; Establishment of an Independent Oversight Mechanism ICC-ASP/8/Res.1, 26.11.2009.
[363] See Human Rights Watch, Memorandum for the Seventh Session of the Assembly of State Parties, 07.11.2008, 22–3.
[364] Para. 1 Independent Oversight Mechanism, ICC-ASP/9/Res.5, 10.12.2010.

shroud of secrecy to the international detention system that is unnecessary. Indeed, all those involved in international detention management want a more detailed inspection and published reports with specific recommendations to aid and direct the progressive development of a principled detention regime.

6. Standards at IDFs

As IDFs are the responsibility of international organisations and courts (UN, ICC, SCSL) they must operate in accordance with international standards governing the deprivation of liberty. In practice, these organisations aim not only to attain these standards, but to create advanced penal systems that will act as an example for the development of national penal systems.[365] IDF regimes tend to be liberal due to the lengthy periods persons spend in detention before the finalisation of their sentence, during which time they must benefit from the presumption of innocence. Moreover, international prisoners are often far from their homes and families. To counteract the aggravating consequences of being housed in an IDF, the international courts have attempted to provide high standards in terms of conditions, facilities and regime.

It may be possible to differentiate the regime in IDFs in developed states from the Host States' prison systems in terms of regime. For instance, the ICCDC permits a longer liberty day[366] than the Dutch prison system. While regime differences are also notable between IDFs in developing countries and local prison systems, the material conditions provided to international prisoners in IDFs in developing countries are often far superior to those available to national prisoners, and indeed the victims of the international prisoners.

For instance, in Sierra Leone, the local high security prison (Pademba Road Prison) located just a few hundred metres away from the SCSLDF, operates under vastly different conditions. Whereas the national prison struggles to provide one meal a day for prisoners and there is no running water,[367] those housed at the SCSLDF received three to four meals a day, with snacks and desserts. Generous portions were provided so that prisoners could bring food for their families during visits and they

---

[365] Jackson, SCSLDF/ICCDC, 19.03.2007; O'Donnell, ICTR, 25.06.2007; Backman, ICCDC, 04.02.2008.
[366] Time not locked in a cell.
[367] Observation, Pademba Road Prison, Freetown, 25.04.2008.

could earn money to purchase extra items.[368] Moreover, the prisoners had access to medical, dental and optical treatment that is not available to ordinary people.[369] This placed SCSL prisoners in a more comfortable position, not only in relation to national prisoners, but also the custodial staff who guarded them and the vast majority of the population, including their victims.[370]

Although all IDFs strive to provide systems that operate in accordance with international standards, there is no homogenous international approach to penal management. Recently, there have been developments that have aligned practices, but the President/Presidency of the respective court still maintains ultimate control over the rights of those held under the custody of the court. This can mean that penal practice depends on the subjective views of an individual or group of individuals, rather than an internationally accepted approach to detention.

Conjugal visits provide a good example. Although the UNDU and ICCDC allow conjugal visits, the UNDF did not until much later on in its operation.[371] While the right to marry was recognised, a former ICTR President did not accept that there was a derivative right to consummate the marriage. An application requesting conjugal visits was refused as there was no such practice in the Tanzanian prison system, there was no uniform practice in other domestic systems and there was no explicit positive right under international law.[372] Moreover, this refusal was not considered to constitute discriminatory treatment as the UNDF operated in different conditions to the UNDU: consequently, persons detained at the UNDF did not have a right to be transferred to the UNDU to facilitate conjugal visits.[373] In spite of these numerous arguments, the UNDF now facilitates conjugal visits as a new President permitted them.

SCSLDF detained persons were not entitled to private visits. Although neither the Registrar nor detention management objected, they did acknowledge that their provision would have created a "logistical nightmare"[374] given the number of wives and mistresses some prisoners had. The ultimate decision lay with the President of the Court, who objected to their facilitation in a confidential motion in 2005.[375] The President

---

[368] Neil, SCSLDF, 23.04.2008; Cardinal, Moore, SCSLDF, 20.04.2008.
[369] Harding, SCSLDF, 21.04.2008.
[370] International and National Supervisors and Custodial staff, SCSLDF, 22–25.04.2008.
[371] O'Donnell, ICTR, 25.06.2007.
[372] See paras. 7–14 *Ngeze* (Decision) ICTR-1999-52-A, 14.09.2005.
[373] See paras. 3, 15–17 *Ngeze* (Decision) ICTR-1999-52-A, 14.09.2005.
[374] Cardinal, Moore, SCSLDF, 20.04.2008. [375] Vincent, SCSL/ICTY, 27.04.2007.

viewed conjugal visits as a discretionary privilege rather than a right. Yet this policy could have been reversed by the new President, particularly in light of the ICTR's policy reversal after a decade. The concentration of decision-making power over penal administration decisions with one judicial official should perhaps be reconsidered to ensure IDF management have the necessary discretion to operate a regime in line with contemporary best practice.

The standard of care provided by the IDFs can also be differentiated in relation to access to medical facilities and treatment. Although a recent audit identified numerous issues that need to be addressed, the ICRC has praised the medical facilities at the UNDU and ICCDC as being state-of-the art.[376] For the majority of international detainees, the medical services available at IDFs are superior to what they could receive in national health systems and certainly their national prison systems. However, for IDFs operating in developing countries, medical issues have the potential simultaneously to create double standards between the inmates and the general population and to violate the rights of the prisoners.

International human rights law recognises a general right to health-care.[377] Because of the dependency imprisonment creates,[378] the institution responsible for depriving the person of their liberty is under a positive obligation to provide modern medical treatment of the same standards afforded to those not in custody.[379] A prisoner's right to health-care cannot be interpreted as requiring the accommodation of a prisoner's every wish: "the practical demands of legitimate detention may impose restrictions".[380] Moreover, a lack of medication or treatment for short periods of time and/ or for less serious illnesses is not sufficiently severe to violate prisoners' rights.[381] However, the failure to provide *timely, appropriate and effective* treatment, where necessary, may amount to inhuman or degrading treatment as it causes both risks to health and anxiety beyond that inherent in the deprivation of liberty.[382] In extreme circumstances, where there is a

---

[376] Falke, ICCDC/UNDU, 04.02.2008.
[377] See Art. 25(1) UDHR; Art. 12(1) ICESCR; Art. 16(1) ACHPR.
[378] See para. 3 HRC General Comment 21.
[379] Principle 1 GA Res 37/194, 18.12.82; Preamble Ethical and Organizational Aspects of Health Care in Prison COE Rec(98)7.
[380] Para. 186 *Mathew* v. *Netherlands* (24919/03) 29.09.2005.
[381] See para. 80 *Rehbock* v. *Slovenia* (29462/95) 28.11.2000.
[382] See paras. 78–91 *Sarban* v. *Moldova* (3456/05) 04.10.2005; paras. 210–20, 231–41 *Popov* v. *Russia* (26853/04) 13.2007.2006; paras. 90–7 *Khudobin* v. *Russia* (59696/00) 26.10.2006; paras. 73–85 *Paladi* v. *Moldova* (39806/05) 10.07.2007; paras. 90–102 *Yakovenko* v. *Ukraine* (15825/06) 25.10.2007.

high degree of indifference and negligence on the part of the detaining authority and medical authorities, a breach of the right to medical treatment can constitute a violation of the right to life.[383]

While ill-health by itself does not necessitate the release of a detained person, appropriate conditions of imprisonment and medical treatment must be provided.[384] A failure to do so creates dependency on others which can humiliate and debase the individual and may constitute degrading treatment.[385] Moreover, if the seriousness of the ailment or disablement and/or the unavailability of appropriate medical treatment results in a finding that continued imprisonment is inappropriate, a failure to release the individual may result in a finding of inhuman or degrading treatment as the continued detention infringes on the dignity of the person and causes physical and psychological suffering.[386] This is not an automatic finding, and factors such as the degree of autonomy of the individual, the availability of appropriate facilities at other sites and the detained person's cooperation are taken into consideration.[387] The CPT has given examples of those unsuited to continued detention, which include those with a short-term fatal prognosis, or a serious disease which cannot be treated properly in prison, those with severe handicaps and persons of advanced age.[388]

General compliance with the obligation to provide medical care will normally be deemed sufficient in cases involving persons charged with serious offences, who had been in positions of responsibility, particularly where release is denied due to fears of recidivism and absconding.[389] Current international jurisprudence demonstrates that terminal illnesses will be taken into account as a significant mitigating factor at sentencing, and that during any time spent at an IDF, all necessary medical treatment should be provided.[390] The ICTY has also noted that significant ill health may result in the transfer of a convicted person from an IDF to an

---

[383] See paras. 88–9 *Tarariyeva v. Russia* (4353/03) 14.12.2006.
[384] See para. 20 *Krnojelac* (President's Decision) IT-97-25-ES, 09.07.2009; para. 11 *Plavšić* (President's Decision) IT-00-39&40/1-ES, 14.09.2009; para. 19 *Radić* (President's Decision) IT-98-30/1-ES, 23.04.2010.
[385] See *Vincent v. France* (6253/03) 24.10.2006.
[386] See *Farbtuhs v. Latvia* (4672/02) 02.12.2004; *Yildiz v. Turkey* (22913/04) 10.11.2005; *Yildirim v. Turkey* (2778/02) 03.05.2007.
[387] *Matencio v. France* (58749/00) 15.01.2004.
[388] Para. 70 CPT Third General Report.
[389] *Sakkopoulos v. Greece* (61828/00) 15.01.2004.
[390] See para. 74 *Serugendo* (Judgment) ICTR-2005-84-I, 12.06.2006; ICTR Press Release, "Prisoner Joseph Serugendo Dies", 22.08.2006.

enforcing state being delayed.[391] International courts must also seriously consider the pressure that could be placed on the court to release convicted persons if suitable medical treatment is not found or available. This is a particularly pertinent issue given that the majority of convicted persons will have been involved in a conflict, lived in a developing or poor state and be a lot older than normal national prisoners.

The medical care provided to prisoners should mirror the positive aspects of medical care in the community, particularly given the higher occurrence of physical and mental illnesses among prison populations.[392] Both the Human Rights Committee and the ECtHR have ruled that inadequate medical treatment can violate a prisoner's rights if it results in inhuman or degrading treatment.[393] International prisoners should, therefore, to the extent possible, have access to medical care that conforms with international human rights standards.

Given the dire state of medical systems in post-conflict and/or developing states, international courts must provide a higher standard of care than is available in the host state. International standards governing imprisonment recognise the right of prisoners to be transferred to hospitals for specialist treatment not available within the prison system.[394] Where international courts cannot rely on the Host State's medical system, they must look to third states for assistance.

The SCSL experienced numerous practical and political obstacles in relation to this issue. Senegal was the only state to sign a medical treatment agreement with the SCSL. Senegal was considered to have one of the best medical care systems in West Africa and therefore able to provide standards superior to those available in Sierra Leone.[395] The Registry faced several major obstacles in its pursuit of further agreements for this purpose. International prisoners are often subject to international travel bans that make it legally impossible for states to accept them for treatment.[396] States may be unwilling to cooperate for political reasons. For example, Ghana reneged on an earlier agreement to accept Mr Sankoh for medical treatment after the SCSL Prosecutor issued an

---

[391] Paras. 12, 15 *Strugar* (President's Decision) IT-01-42-ES, 16.01.2009.
[392] Van Zyl Smit and Snacken, *Principles of European Prison Law and Policy*, 103, 153.
[393] Rodley and Pollard, *The Treatment of Prisoners under International Law*, 407–10.
[394] Rules 22(2) UNSMR; Principle 9 UNBP; Rule 46(1) EPR; Para. 3 Concerning the Ethical and Organizational Aspects of Health Care in Prison COE Rec (98) 7.
[395] Von Hebel, SCSL, 24.04.2007.
[396] See SCSL Press Release, "No Country Found to Take Sankoh for Medical Treatment", 11.06.2003.

arrest warrant for Mr Taylor while he was in Ghana. A former Registrar felt that this act signed Mr Sankoh's death warrant, but that his death played on the international conscience to the extent that the agreement with Senegal could be signed.[397]

International courts must exercise caution in signing and using such agreements, as a state could provide political asylum to transferred prisoners or the transferred prisoner could invoke the law of the state to block their return to the Host State.[398] However, given the difficulties involved in negotiating such agreements and the potential violations of rights that could arise without them, it is incumbent that they be secured "well before the occasion to transfer a detainee may arise".[399] Accordingly, it should be one of the set-up priorities of future international courts with IDFs operating in developing states.

Even with a secured agreement, arranging medical treatment outside of the Host State can be an expensive "logistical nightmare".[400] The transfer must be prompt and humane, and the prisoner should be accompanied by medical personnel in a suitable mode of transport.[401] On top of transport costs, security is required for movements within the Host State, to and from the receiving state and internal and external security for the duration of the detained person's hospitalisation. As the hospital bed becomes an extension of the IDF, it also requires custodial staff. The duty to treat prisoners humanely extends to their detention in hospitals.[402] Security should be ensured by the creation of a mini-custodial unit within the medical institution rather than through the inhumane use of physical restraints.[403]

The medical care provided to prisoners should represent the positive aspects of care provided in the community,[404] which in the case of international prisoners, is the international community. Although the provision of this standard of treatment can cause a degree of controversy in that persons convicted of international crimes have access to a

---

[397] Vincent, SCSL/ICTY, 27.04.2007.   [398] Harding, SCSLDF, 21.04.2008.
[399] SCSL Press Release, "Inquiry finds Special Court Provided Proper Care to Hinga Norman", 16.07.2007.
[400] Cardinal, Moore, SCSLDF, 20.04.2008.
[401] Para. 9 Ethical and Organizational Aspects of Health Care in Prison COE Rec(98) 7, para. 37 CPT Third General Report; paras. 112–17 *Tarariyeva v. Russia* (4353/03) 14.12.2006.
[402] Para. 2 HRC General Comment 21.
[403] Para. 36 CPT Third General Report; paras. 109–11 *Tarariyeva v. Russia* (4353/03) 14.12.2006.
[404] See Van Zyl Smit and Snacken, *Principles of European Prison Law and Policy*, 103, 105, 153.

superior standard of treatment than normal prisoners or indeed the population at large, international courts and IDFs must provide international standards of care.[405] Moreover, the imprisonment of very ill persons and deaths in custody can fuel allegations of mistreatment and create perceptions of a biased and illegitimate court.[406] For instance, a former SCSL Registrar acknowledged that the deaths of 20 per cent of indictees, one during arrest[407] and two of natural causes while under the court's custody[408] did not bode well for the perception of the court.[409] UNDF inmates have accused the ICTR of failing to provide treatment for Mr Musabyimana's physical and psychological problems and called for an independent investigation into his death. The ICTR rejected these accusations and maintained that everything "humanly possible" was done to save the life of the bishop, including taking him to different hospitals in Tanzania and Nairobi at his request and hiring a specialist to help with his psychological problems.[410] Deaths affect not only the public perception of the court but also the mental state of other detained persons[411] and custodial staff.[412] Deaths create rumours and suspicions that leave staff feeling untrusted.[413] Medical staff are also affected; the UNDU doctor was referred to as "Doctor Death" in certain newspapers after Mr Milošević's death.[414] It is important, therefore, that policies are put in place to support those involved and to ensure that investigations are sensitive to the trauma caused.[415]

The prevention of deaths is not solely related to the provision of good medical care. It also involves security and surveillance procedures. For example, the special security arrangements put in place to enable Mr Milošević to represent himself contributed to his death, as they enabled non-prescribed medication to be smuggled into the UNDU.[416]

---

[405] Von Hebel, SCSL, 24.04.2007.
[406] See T. W. Thyness, "Samuel Hinga Norman Dies, 22 February 2007".
[407] See *Bockarie* (Withdrawal of Indictment) SCSL-03-04-PT, 08.12.2003.
[408] See *Sankoh* (Withdrawal of Indictment) SCSL-03-02-PT-054, 08.12.2003; *Norman* (Decision) SCSL-040140T-776, 21.05.2007.
[409] Von Hebel, SCSL, 24.04.2007.
[410] Hirandelle, "ICTR Detainees Want Commission of Enquiry on Musabyimana's Death", 05.02.2003.
[411] ICTY Press Release "Open Letter from the Detainees regarding their Conditions at the ICTY's Detention Unit", 12.08.1998.
[412] Custodial Staff, UNDU, 22–27.08.2007.
[413] Custodial Staff, UNDU, 22–27.08.2007.   [414] Falke, UNDU/ICCDC, 04.07.2012.
[415] Custodial Staff, UNDU, 22–27.08.2007.
[416] Judge Parker, Report to the President on the Death of Slobodan Milošević, May 2006.

When the UNDF experienced problems with counsel smuggling prohibited items into detained persons, the security regulations were altered to allow for more systematic searches of defence counsel and assistants.[417]

Self-harm and suicide are also important concerns. Although inquiries into the circumstances surrounding the suicides at the UNDU found no evidence of criminal conduct or negligence by custodial staff,[418] the suicides were possible due to the availability of dangerous items.[419] Two suicides were committed using items found in the prisoners' cells (a belt, tie and plastic bag). These individuals could also have laces, cutlery and razors in their cells.[420] Under IDF regulations, such items need only be removed from cells if they posed a threat to security, order, health or safety.[421] Both individuals were known to be depressed and were under the highest degree of supervision and 24-hour CCTV surveillance.[422]

As a failure to prevent suicide due to a lack of precautions may result in the violation of a prisoner's right to life,[423] IDFs should consider implementing the procedure in place at the State Court of Bosnia-Herzegovina's Detention Facility, where items that could be used to self-harm are kept in a locker outsider the cell door.[424] IDF custodial staff have also expressed concern that requests to move detained persons to surveillance cells can take a long time to process.[425]

IDFs do not have bare cells and individuals at risk may have to be moved to hospital wings, aggravating feelings of isolation. The ICC's focus is therefore on the mitigation of risk by keeping detained persons as healthy and stimulated as possible.[426] In line with this prevention policy, the ICC recently proposed the adoption of a new provision in its

---

[417] O'Donnell, ICTR, 25.06.2007; para. 185 ICTR Sixth Annual Report.
[418] Judge Parker, Report to the President on the Death of Milan Babic 08.06.2006; ICTY Press Release, "Completion of the Internal Inquiry into the Death of Slavko Dokmanovic", 23.07.1998; Judge Rodrigues, Report on the Finding of the Inquiry into Mr Dokmanovic's Death, 21.07.1998.
[419] Kupreškić, 13.10.2007.
[420] Paras. 3–4 Judge Rodrigues, Report on the Finding of the Inquiry into Mr Dokmanovic's Death, 21.07.1998.
[421] Judge Parker, Report to the President on the Death of Milan Babic, 08.06.2006.
[422] ICTY Press Release, "Completion of the Internal Inquiry into the Death of Slavko Dokmanovic", 23.07.1998.
[423] See paras. 89–102 *Keenan* v. *UK* (27229/95) 03.04.2001.
[424] Tour, BiH State Court Detention Facility, 05.10.2007.
[425] Custodial staff, UNDU, 22–27.08.2007.   [426] Craig, ICCDC, 04.07.2012.

regulations which would establish a self-harm and suicide prevention team and guidelines for creating a humane environment, identifying potential risks, preventing attempts and supporting those at risk.[427] A working group currently meets every three months to discuss general and specific risks and to draw up an appropriate action plan.[428] The group analyses the individual self-harm risk reports that are compiled for each detained person on the basis of staff observations and information provided by the individual's internal and external networks.[429] Suicide kits have also been placed in the ICCDC to provide custodial staff with the equipment they need to react to self-harm and suicide attempts in an effective manner.[430] The ICCDC also has a high staff–detained person ratio, with two guards for each detained person. This increases staff awareness of changes in moods and possibilities for heightened risk.

Yet it can be very difficult to prevent suicide when an individual is determined to end his life. Rudolf Hess, the "most heavily guarded prisoner in the world", committed suicide at the age of 93.[431] Mr Dokmanović died on the third attempt on his life on one evening; the previous two attempts (slitting his wrists and an attempted hanging) had not been visible to guards when they checked on him.[432]

7. Release

Some IDF prisoners will be released when their sentences are finalised, or soon afterwards, as they have already served the term imposed. Other prisoners are not transferred to enforcing states and therefore serve a significant portion of their sentences at IDFs.[433] As the direct enforcement of sentences at IDFs was not foreseen by the UN Tribunals' Statutes or Rules, there was no special procedure to govern the release of prisoners housed in IDFs; the procedure in place required enforcing states to notify the Tribunal of individuals' eligibility for release.[434] To ensure equality of treatment, the ICTY and ICTR Presidents accepted direct

---

[427] See the proposed Reg. 162*bis*(1) ICC ROR.
[428] Falke, UNDU/ICCDC, 04.07.2012.   [429] Craig, ICCDC, 04.07.2012.
[430] Craig, ICCDC, 04.07.2012.   [431] Goda, *Tales from Spandau*, 3, 265.
[432] Paras. 5–6 Judge Rodrigues, Report on the Finding of the Inquiry into Mr Dokmanovic's Death 21.07.1998.
[433] See para. A.2(13) MDP, 153–4; para. 35 ICTR Fifteenth Annual Report.
[434] See Art. 28 ICTYSt.

applications for release and applied the same procedure.[435] The ICTY Practice Direction governing release has been amended to acknowledge that prisoners may directly apply to the President for release and that the same procedure applies to such applications.[436]

Like the decentralised enforcement system, IDFs do not provide prisoners with the means to demonstrate that they have met some of the criteria for release. IDFs do not provide convicted persons with a sentence plan or a regime that takes account of their rehabilitative and reintegration needs. Prisoners have no opportunity to participate in programmes dealing with criminal behaviour or to prepare them for release back into the community. Given the difficulties in maintaining contact with families, such prisoners may have lost one of the most vital post-release support structures.

Having been imprisoned for crimes relating to conflicts, prisoners may not wish to or be able to return to their state of origin or previous state of residence. For those released from the UNDU to date, this did not appear to pose any great difficulties. Problems mostly arose in relation to protected witnesses who had to be relocated and given a new identity under bilateral agreements entered into between the ICTY and cooperating states. The ICTR, on the other hand, has faced and will continue to face difficulties in this area. Prisoners do not wish to return to Rwanda. The ICTR has already failed to find states to accept persons released directly from the UNDF: as they could not remain on Tanzanian soil, the ICTR was responsible for housing these free men.[437] The ICTR is therefore working hard to secure the cooperation of states to which prisoners released from the UNDF (and enforcing states) can be relocated.[438]

For some convicted persons, preparation for release or transfer will involve negotiating the relaxation or lifting of international travel bans.[439] For example, it took the ICC one week to negotiate the suspension of a travel

---

[435] See paras. 2–4 *Tadić* (President's Decision) IT-95-9-T, 03.11.2004; *Zarić* (President's Order) IT-95-9, 21.01.2004; ICTR Press Release, "Elizaphan Ntakirutimana Released After Serving Sentence", 06.12.2006; ICTR Press Release, "Vincent Rutaganira Released After Completing his Sentence" 03.03.2008; paras. 5, 6, 9 *Strugar* (President's Decision) IT-01–42-ES, 16.01.2009; paras. 1, 14 *Šljivančanin* (President's Decision) IT-95-13/1-ES, 05.07.2011.
[436] Para. 2 ICTY PDER.
[437] See paras. 28, 30–1, 37 R. Amoussago, "The ICTR's Challenges in the Relocation of Acquitted Persons, Released Prisoners and Protected Witnesses", 2008.
[438] See Chapter 2, Section 3.2.5.   [439] Ras, SCSL Sub-Office, 05.07.2012.

ban on Callixte Mbarushimana to facilitate his release[440] following the Pre-Trial Chamber decision to decline confirming the charges against him.[441]

8. Centralised national enforcement: the ICC's residual facility

The chapter so far has discussed the reality that international prisoners may serve their sentences in international remand centres. The temporary international criminal courts were put in a position whereby they had to directly enforce some or part of the sentences they imposed in their remand centres as their statutes did not provide for an alternative solution in situations where a suitable enforcing state could not be found. To avoid the direct enforcement of international sentences of imprisonment in the ICCDC, the Rome Statute provides that if no state is designated, the sentence will be served in a prison facility made available by the Host State.[442] This provision does not mean that ICC sentences can be implemented in the ICCDC. Persons convicted by the ICC will instead be transferred to a Dutch prison to serve their sentence in accordance with Dutch prison law.[443] The Dutch prison service will accept a person into custody if they have not been transferred to an enforcing state within six months of the finalisation of the sentence,[444] although the six-month rule will be applied flexibly so that a person that will be transferred to a state in seven months will not have to go to the residual facility in the interim.[445] As yet, no particular wing or facility has been allocated for this purpose by the Dutch Prison Service.

Like the decentralised enforcement system, the implementation of the sentence will remain subject to the ICC's supervision.[446] This form of state cooperation, however, can be differentiated from the decentralised system in several ways. First, the ICC remains liable for the costs incurred during enforcement.[447] Second, the Host State cannot refuse to accept a particular individual.[448] Third, this cooperation is limited to the provision of temporary custodial capacity pending the prisoner's transfer elsewhere, rather than a general commitment to enforce

---

[440] Tjonk, ICCDC, 04.07.2012.
[441] *Mbarushimana* (PTC Decision) ICC-01/04-01/10-465-Red, 16.12.2011.
[442] Art. 103(4) ICCSt.   [443] Art. 49(4) ICC HQA.   [444] Art. 50(1) ICC HQA.
[445] Dubuisson, Tjonk, Becerra-Suarez, ICC, 06.06.2007.
[446] Art. 49(4)–(5) ICC HQA; Art. 103(4) ICCSt.   [447] Art. 103(4) ICCSt.
[448] A. Marchesi, "The Enforcement of Sentences of the International Criminal Court" in F. Lattanzi and W. Schabas (eds), *Essays on the Rome Statute of the International Criminal Court* (1999), 427–45 at 435–6.

sentences. Although a general agreement setting out the practical arrangements may be entered into, each request will require a separate agreement and all decisions will be made on a case-by-case basis.[449]

This form of cooperation is not to be viewed as an alternative to decentralised enforcement: it may only be used by the ICC as a last resort. Moreover, this cooperation is conditional on continuing ICC efforts to find an enforcing state for the prisoner being held in Dutch custody.[450] The Dutch Government is wary of setting a precedent that they will take all convicted persons, and therefore they will only take persons in exceptional circumstances and for very short periods of time while awaiting transfer to an enforcing state.[451] This approach made the negotiation of an agreement difficult as the Dutch Government wanted guarantees from ICC about the operation of the process that the ICC could not give beyond a promise that it would always do its best to secure the cooperation of another state for the enforcement of the particular sentence.[452]

This statutory mechanism does provide the ICC with breathing space and means it will not be forced to exhaust its list of states if they are grossly inappropriate for the implementation of a particular sentence.[453] While it involves a more reluctant and conditional form of cooperation than that usually offered by states under the decentralised system, the Host State's provision of a residual facility is an unprecedented and extremely important infrastructural addition to the ICC's statutory options, which avoids the situation of international sentences of imprisonment being served in remand centres. Although convicted persons at the ICC will be subject to the same regime as detained persons at the ICCDC,[454] this will only be the case for six months after the finalisation of their sentence. After this, they will either be transferred to an enforcing state or the residual facility in the Host State.

9. Conclusion

The reality is that the UN and SCSL have been responsible for the direct implementation of custodial sanctions.[455] In addition to the implementation of sentences of persons awaiting transfer, the SCSL has recently decided

---

[449] Art. 49(6) ICC HQA. Dubuisson, Tjonk, Becerra-Suarez, ICC, 06.06.2007.
[450] Art. 49(1), (3) ICC HQA. [451] Mochochoko, ICC, 30.08.2007.
[452] Blom, Moonen, The Netherlands, 24.08.2007.
[453] C. Kreß and G. Sluiter, "Imprisonment" in A. Cassese *et al.* (eds.), *The Rome Statute of the International Criminal Court* (2002), 1757–821 at 1790.
[454] Reg. 223 ICC ROR. [455] See Rule 2 ICTY ROD; Rule 3 ICTR ROD; Rule 3 SCSL ROD.

to implement sentences imposed on persons convicted of contempt of court in its new detention facility within the court's perimeter.[456] The UNDF, in particular has been operating as a long-term prison facility for some time, often housing more convicted persons than accused persons. Despite the regular occurrence of IDFs enforcing sentences, the role remains unacknowledged for a range of reasons. The direct enforcement of sentences of imprisonment is outside the mandate of the courts[457] and the mandate of their detention facilities.[458] Moreover, both of the UN Tribunals' Host States, Tanzania and The Netherlands, insist that convicted persons spend no longer than six months on their territory. Some feel that the Host States turn a blind eye to the situation owing to fears that if this role is recognised, the pressure would be taken off third states to cooperate in relation to enforcement.[459]

To prevent reliance on IDFs for this purpose, it will be necessary for future courts to ensure they have agreements with an adequate number of cooperative and appropriate enforcing states and that transfer procedures are efficient. In addition, future courts could take the lead from the ICC and ask their Host States to provide a residual facility in the event that a swift transfer cannot be arranged. However, until these safeguards are put in place, international courts will remain responsible for the implementation of international sentences of imprisonment. International courts and their IDFs will therefore have to seriously consider drafting new rules to govern the regime to put in place for convicted persons, and funds to do so. Unlike the current situation, whereby IDFs have no penal policy or practices in place for convicted persons, procedures will be necessary to deal with the realities of prison life and penal management. International imprisonment in IDFs cannot remain a temporal extension of international remand. If international prisoners are to serve part or all of their sentences in IDFs, these facilities must provide a regime for convicted persons that accords with international human rights and penological standards. In other words, the international courts must ensure that, *inter alia*, international prisoners are rehabilitated and adequately prepared for release.

---

[456] See SCSL Ninth Annual Report, 25; SCSL Press Release, "Eric Koi Senessie Sentenced to Two Years in Prison for Contempt of the Special Court", 05.07.2012.
[457] A. Klip, "Enforcement of Sanctions Imposed by the International Criminal Tribunals for Rwanda and the Former Yugoslavia" (1997) 5(2) *European Journal of Crime, Criminal Law and Criminal Justice* 144–64 at 163.
[458] Paras. 2.8.5, 2.11 Independent Audit of the Detention Unit at the ICTY, 2006.
[459] Vincent, SCSL/ICTY, 27.04.2007.

4

Localised national enforcement

International sentences of imprisonment are typically enforced in either national or international facilities located in states unrelated to the conflict in question. In some cases, international punishment may also be enforced in the state in which the crimes were committed. While this was not a possibility for the ICTY, imprisonment in the state in which the crimes were committed was explicitly permitted in the statutes of both the ICTR and SCSL and is implicitly permitted by the Rome Statute. To date, however, these statutory mechanisms have not been used to implement sentences imposed for the commission of international crimes. In order to gain some understanding of the difficulties that would be associated with the localised enforcement of international sentences of imprisonment, the Rule11*bis* mechanism is examined. This chapter sets out the statutory possibilities for localised enforcement and analyses the realities of the local implementation of international punishment by exploring the mechanisms for the transfer of persons under the custody of international courts to local courts for trial.

1. Statutory options for localised national enforcement

When the ICTY was being established, the UN Secretary-General barred the ICTY from enforcing sentences in the states of the Former Republic of Yugoslavia due to the "nature of the crimes in question and the international character of the tribunal".[1] The ICTY Appeal Chamber ruled that as the Secretary-General's Report is considered to have been approved by the UN Security Council as an explanatory document for the ICTY Statute, there is no legal possibility for ICTY sentences to be

---

[1] Para. 121 Report of the Secretary-General pursuant to para. 2 of Security Council Resolution 808, 03.05.1993.

enforced in the former states of Yugoslavia.[2] Offers of unconditional cooperation in relation to enforcement from Croatia and Bosnia-Herzegovina could not therefore be translated into bilateral enforcement agreements.[3] As the ICC Statute's provisions relating to enforcement are silent on the matter, is may be possible to implement sentences in states in which the crimes of the convicted persons took place. The Statutes of both the SCSL and ICTR, on the other hand, contain express statutory provisions which appear to promote the enforcement of international sentences of imprisonment in the state in which the relevant atrocities were committed.

1.1 The SCSL and Sierra Leone

From the very early days of the SCSL's operations, there was a reluctance to enforce SCSL sentences in Sierra Leone. This reluctance initially centred on fears that the presence of high-profile prisoners would have a detrimental impact on local and regional stability.[4] However, after the deaths of two high-profile detainees[5] and the transfer of Mr Taylor to The Hague to stand trial,[6] concerns began to focus on the ability of the Sierra Leone Prison Service to keep international prisoners behind bars. Ex-combatants had escaped or been freed from Pademba Road Prison, the national maximum security facility where SCSL prisoners would most likely have been sent if they remained in Sierra Leone.[7] This prison had to send prisoners outside to fetch water due to the lack of a direct supply.[8] When these facts are considered alongside the reality that national prison staff were outnumbered, overworked and underpaid,[9] the possibilities for bribery and escape were too high to make the

---

[2] Paras. B.1.1(26)–(27) MDP, 156–7; para. 11, Shahabuddeen's Separate Opinion, *Strugar* (Appeal Decision) IT-01-42.Misc.1, 07.06.2007.
[3] See para. 189 ICTY Third Annual Report.
[4] See para. 49 Report of the Secretary-General on the Establishment of a Special Court for Sierra Leone 04.10.2000.
[5] See Chapter 3, Section 3. [6] See SCRes 1688(2006).
[7] Vincent, SCSL/ICTY, 27.04.2007; Custodial Staff, SCSLDF, 21–25.04.2008. See also A. O'Rourke, "The Writ of Habeas Corpus and the SCSL: Addressing an Unforeseen Problem in the Establishment of a Hybrid Court" 44 *Columbia Journal of Transnational Law* (2005) 649–85 at 662.
[8] Observation, Pademba Road Prison, 24.04.2008. See also Awoko, "Prison Watch Raises Concerns over Prison Water Shortages", 05.09.2008.
[9] See Section 1(c) US Department of State's 2007 Report on Sierra Leone 19.05.2008.

national prison system a secure option for the implementation of international punishment.

In addition to security fears, there were also humanitarian considerations relating to conditions and the treatment of prisoners. Sierra Leonean prisons do not meet international standards.[10] Many prisons are severely overcrowded and shortages of food, water, bedding and adequate sanitation frequently cause malnutrition and disease.[11] The Sierra Leone Prison Service openly acknowledged that these problems existed and agreed with the SCSL that it was not appropriate for international prisoners to serve their sentences in Sierra Leone.[12]

Despite the SCSL Statute's explicit preference for the enforcement of SCSL sentences of imprisonment in Sierra Leone,[13] all persons convicted of international crimes by the SCSL were transferred to Rwanda to serve their sentences.[14] Mr Taylor will likely be sent to a European state to serve his sentence should his conviction be upheld on appeal.[15] The SCSL has, however, decided to directly implement sentences of imprisonment imposed on persons convicted of contempt of court in a new detention facility located within the perimeter of the court in Freetown.[16] What will happen if the SCSL closes before these sentences are completed remains unclear.[17]

While punishments imposed for administration of justice offences may be enforced under a centralised international system, punishments imposed for international criminal offences have been enforced under a decentralised system.[18] Therefore, despite the statutory preference for localised enforcement, the SCSL has relied on other enforcement options and cooperating states for the implementation of sentences of imprisonment imposed for international crimes.[19]

---

[10] Von Hebel, SCSL, 24.04.2007; Showers, SLPS, 25.04.2008. Para. 47 Residual Issues Conference Report.
[11] See paras. 35, 39, 42, 49 Report of the UN High Commissioner for Human Rights, Assistance to Sierra Leone in the Field of Human Rights A/HRC/13/28, 12.02.2010.
[12] Showers, SLPS, 25.04.08.   [13] Art. 22 SCSLSt.
[14] See SCSL Press Release, "Special Court Prisoners Transferred to Rwanda to Serve Their Sentences", 31.10.2009.
[15] See Chapter 2, Section 2; BBC, "UK agrees to jail Charles Taylor" 15.06.2006.
[16] See SCSL Ninth Annual Report, 25; SCSL Press Release, "Eric Koi Senessie Sentenced to Two Years in Prison for Contempt of the Special Court", 05.07.2012.
[17] Ras, SCSL Sub-office, 31.08.12.
[18] See SCSL Press Release, "Four Sentenced for Interference in the Administration of Justice", 11.10.12.
[19] See Art. 22(1) SCSLSt; Rule 103(A) SCSL RPE; SCSL Ninth Annual Report, 24.

1.2 The ICTR and Rwanda

The ICTR Statute provides that sentences of imprisonment "shall be served in Rwanda or any of the states ... which have indicated their willingness to accept convicted persons".[20] When the statute was being drafted, the Rwandan national prison system was barely operational and the facilities that remained were overflowing with persons accused of participating in the genocide. This led to many believing that the inclusion of the statutory provision, "imprisonment shall be served in Rwanda",[21] was not intended to be implemented but was simply a form of political appeasement to the Rwandan Government.[22] This was unsuccessful as the inclusion of the latter part of the provision, "or any of the states..." led to the Rwandan Government voting against the UN Security Council Resolution that established the Tribunal: it could not accept that those convicted by the ICTR could be imprisoned outside Rwanda in better conditions.[23] Over the years, the Rwandan Government has continuously objected to the transfer of ICTR convicted persons to other states, as it interprets the ICTR Statute as prioritising enforcement in Rwanda.[24] The belief that the ICTR Statute obliges it to enforce ICTR sentences[25] made the negotiation of a bilateral enforcement agreement with the Tribunal difficult; it took three years to finalise. But, fourteen years after the Tribunal's establishment, an enforcement agreement between the ICTR and Rwanda was finally concluded. Despite the considerable legal, judicial and penal reform measures instituted to make the conclusion of the agreement possible,[26] the ICTR has still not transferred any prisoners to Rwanda to serve their sentences. The Rwandan Government has repeatedly questioned the ICTR's decision to send its convicts to other African countries and has

---

[20] Art. 26 ICTRSt.   [21] Art. 26 ICTRSt.
[22] M. Penrose, "Spandau Revisited: The Question of Detention for International War Crimes" (1999)16 *New York Law School Journal of Human Rights* 553–91 at 567.
[23] See Rwanda's Statement, UNSC 3453rd Meeting, 08.11.1994; C. Kreß and C. Sluiter "Imprisonment" in A. Cassese *et al.* (eds.), *The Rome Statute of the International Criminal Court* (2002), 1757–821 at 1753; W. Schabas, *The UN International Criminal Tribunals: The former Yugoslavia, Rwanda and Sierra Leone* (2006), 29.
[24] Special Representative of Rwandan Government to ICTR, Aloys Mutabingwa cited in Hirandelle, "Two Rwanda Genocide Convicted Transferred to Mali amid Tight Security", 03.12.2008.
[25] Preamble ICTR–Rwanda BEA.
[26] See para. 26 *Hategekimana* (Decision) ICTR-00-55B-R11*bis*, 19.06.2008; ICTR Press Release, "Rwanda signs Agreement on Enforcement of ICTR Sentences", 05.03.2008.

continually sought the transfer of ICTR prisoners to Rwanda to serve their sentences.[27]

Localised enforcement may provide a more visible and meaningful form of punishment than decentralised or centralised imprisonment and create a stronger sense that justice has been achieved.[28] Despite these arguments and the possibility for localised enforcement under the statutes of the ICTR and SCSL, it has not occurred in practice for those convicted of international crimes.

2. Rule 11*bis* transfers

Rule 11*bis*[29] was introduced to free up the time and resources of the temporary UN Tribunals as they moved towards the completion of their mandates.[30] By facilitating the transfer of low-level cases and accused persons to national courts for trial, the rule enabled international prosecutorial strategy to focus on the investigation, indictment and prosecution of the highest level perpetrators in terms of the seniority of the accused and the gravity of the offence.[31] This rule has been used to transfer persons held in ICTY custody in The Hague to Bosnia-Herzegovina and persons held in ICTR custody in Arusha to Rwanda.

Rule 11*bis* does not create a system for the enforcement of international punishment. National courts impose national sentences of imprisonment which are implemented in national prisons. However, international referral jurisprudence and the modalities of this transfer mechanism can provide insights into the realities of serving a sentence for international crimes in the state in which they were committed. This section looks at the operation of the rule in relation to Bosnia-Herzegovina and Rwanda.

---

[27] See J. Munyaneza, "Why Rwanda wants ICTR Convicts", *The New Times*, 05.04.2012.
[28] See L. Moghalu, *Rwanda's Genocide: The Politics of Global Justice* (2005), 206; R. Amoussaga, "The UN–Rwanda Prisoner Agreement: The ICTR Replies", 10.03.2008.
[29] Rule 11*bis* ICTY/ICTR RPE.
[30] See O. Bekou, "Rule 11*bis*: An Examination of the Process of Referrals to National Courts in ICTY Jurisprudence" (2010) 33 *Fordham International Law Journal* 723-91 at 726.
[31] See SCRes 1503(2003); SCRes 1534(2004); Statement by the President of the Security Council on the ICTY, 23.07.02.

2.1 The ICTY, Rule 11bis and Bosnia-Herzegovina

Between September 2005 and June 2007, the ICTY utilised the Rule 11*bis* mechanism to transfer thirteen cases to the states of the former Yugoslavia. The majority of the ICTY referrals (ten of the thirteen) have been to Bosnia-Herzegovina. Only the referrals to Bosnia-Herzegovina[32] involved the transfer of persons in ICTY custody.[33] The penal system in operation in Bosnia-Herzegovina mirrored the ICTY's decentralised enforcement system in many ways.

Persons transferred from the ICTY's UNDU in The Hague were sent to a specifically built, state-level Detention Facility in Sarajevo.[34] Like the ICTY, the State Court does not have a prison in which its sentences can be enforced. Although the State Court remains liable for the costs of imprisonment, it must rely on the prison systems of two Bosnian entities (Federation of Bosnia-Herzegovina and Republika Srpska) to implement the sentences it imposes.[35] Like ICTY prisoners in enforcing states, State Court prisoners serving their sentences in entity prisons remain subject to the jurisdiction of the State Court. While the law dictates that their regime should be dictated by the State Law on the Execution of Criminal Sanctions and State House Rules, entity level prison law often prevails in practice. The Bosnian State Court's experience highlights several difficult aspects of the localised enforcement of custodial sanctions imposed for war crimes. In particular, there have been issues relating to the local prison system's ability to ensure sufficient conditions of imprisonment, as well as safe and secure custody.

---

[32] See Rule 11*bis*(A), (D)(i) ICTY RPE; para. 5 *Mejakic, Gruban, Fustar and Knezevic* (AC Decision) IT-02-65-AR11BIS.1, 07.04.2006. The following cases were transferred from the ICTY to Bosnia-Herzegovina: *Janković* (IT-96-23/2), *Stanković* (IT-96-23/2), *Todović and Rašević* (IT-97-25/1), *Ljubičić* (IT-00-41), *Mejakić, Gruban, Knežević and Fuštar* (IT-02-65), *Trbić* (IT-05-88/1).

[33] The sole case remitted to Serbia involved the transfer of the case of an individual detained in a mental institution there (see paras. 6, 23–24 *Kovačević* (Decision) IT-01-42/2-I, 17.11.2006) and the two cases referred to Croatia involved the referral of the cases of persons who were resident in or were serving a prison sentence in Croatia (see paras. 17–18 *Ademi, Norac* (Decision) IT-04-78-PT, 14.09.2005).

[34] See ICTY Press Release, "OHR-ICTY Working Group on the Development of BiH Capacity for War-Crime Trials Successfully Completed", 21.02.03.

[35] Art. 203, The Law of Bosnia-Herzegovina on the Execution of Criminal Sanctions, Detention and Other Measures, 2005.

2.1.1 Conditions of imprisonment

ICTY referral jurisprudence states that conditions of detention and the treatment of referred persons, both before and after conviction in Bosnia, are matters that touch upon the fairness of the national criminal justice system and therefore investigations into these issues fall squarely within the Referral Bench's mandate.[36] As there is no state-level prison, the State Court had to send convicted persons to entity-level prisons to serve their sentences. This occurred despite the fact that serious doubts had been raised about the suitability of entity-level prisons.[37] Inadequate material conditions and financial resources meant that there was often a "wide gap ... between the legal and regulatory norms and the realities prevailing in the prison system".[38] In spite of extensive reform programmes,[39] conditions in many prisons were bleak,[40] with regimes so restricted and cells so overcrowded that many prisons simply did not conform to regional or international standards.[41]

Yet despite these facts, the ICTY held that the system for post-conviction imprisonment was not inadequate and was not, therefore, a bar to transfer.[42] This decision was influenced by the anticipated opening of a state-level prison that would conform to international standards. Given the repeated extension of the time-frame for its completion, the ICTY Appeals Chamber asked the ICTY Prosecutor to report on any serious issues regarding post-conviction conditions of imprisonment to the Referral Bench.[43] With only a boundary wall in place in 2012, the

---

[36] Para. 34 *Stanković* (Appeal Decision) IT-96-23/2.AR11*bis*.1, 01.09.2005.
[37] Para. B.1.1(23) MDP, 156.
[38] See para. 42 CPT Report to the Government of BiH CPT/Inf (2004)40.
[39] See BiH Justice Sector Reform Strategy, 2008–2012; Graham Mumby-Croft, "Report of Visit to Prison Establishments in Federation BiH and Republic Srpska on behalf of the Council of Europe to Advise on the Conversion of Dormitory Type Accommodation in to Smaller Units" 2002; UK Department for International Development, Examination of the Effectiveness and Efficiency of the Execution of Criminal Sanctions in BiH, 2006, 30–1, 57.
[40] See UK Department for International Development, Examination of the Effectiveness and Efficiency of the Execution of Criminal Sanctions in BiH, 2006, 30; paras. 60–70 CPT Report to the Government of BiH CPT/Inf (2004)40; paras. 59–60 CPT Report to the Government of BiH CPT/Inf (2009)25.
[41] See Joint Programme of Cooperation Between the European Commission and the Council of Europe to assist BiH in fulfilling Post Accession Commitments and Developing and Maintaining Democratic Institutions, 27.10.2004, 3–5; Sections 2.2–2.3 BiH Justice Sector Reform Strategy 2008–12, 26–7.
[42] See para. 58 *Mejakic, Gruban, Fustar, Knezevic* (Appeal Decision) IT-O2-65-*AR11BIS*.1, 07.04.2006.
[43] See para. 43 *Ljubičić* (Appeal Decision) IT-00-41-AR11*bis*.1, 04.07.2006.

concerns raised by defence counsel now appear to have been well-founded. Indeed entity-level politicians are suggesting that the state-level prison project may be abandoned altogether due to soaring costs and a lack of funding.[44]

Given the lack of a state prison, the dire state of conditions in entity-level prisons, the inability to act after the finalisation of the sentence and the questionable independence and expertise of the Prosecutor to make decisions on penal matters, it was important to ensure there was independent oversight of the detention and imprisonment of persons transferred under Rule11*bis*. State-level mechanisms at the time of the transfers lacked independence and an ability to intervene. The state-level Prison Inspectors were Ministry of Justice staff and they were only permitted to examine the implementation of state, not entity-level, law.[45] The Institute of Human Rights Ombudsmen of Bosnia-Herzegovina and its Department for the Protection of the Rights of Detainees/Prisoners did not become operational until several years after the Rule 11*bis* transfers were executed. While state prisoners housed in entity-level prisons could be visited by both the CPT and the ICRC, the ICTY entered into an agreement with the OSCE. The OSCE agreed to assist the ICTY's Prosecutor with monitoring war crime trials transferred to Bosnia-Herzegovina[46] for the duration of its mission in the country.[47] If there were serious concerns, the Referral Chamber, upon request of the Prosecutor, could revoke the referral order and request the transfer of individuals back to the ICTY at any time before the person was found guilty or acquitted by the State Court.[48] Despite the concerns raised about conditions of detention, this mechanism was not relied upon.

2.1.2 Safe custody

The UN Secretary-General's bar on the enforcement of ICTY sentences in the states of the former Yugoslavia was intended to prevent allocation decisions that "would have impermissibly risked the lives of convicted persons".[49] Yet, Rule11*bis* transfers resulted in situations that had the potential to risk the lives of convicted persons sent to

---

[44] N. Trbic and D. Dzidic, "Serbs Threaten to Scupper Bosnia's First State Prison", 21.03.2011.
[45] Bladnjar, BiH, 09.10.2007. [46] Rule 11*bis*(D)(iv) ICTY RPE.
[47] OSCE, Cooperation between the OSCE and the ICTY, PC.DEC/673, 19.05.2005.
[48] Rule 11*bis* (F) ICTY RPE. [49] Para. B.1.1(23) MPD, 156.

entity-level prisons. For example, in 2008, state prisoners housed in Kula Detention Facility in Republika Srpska began a hunger-strike in reaction to an order issued by the State Court's President stating that they must attend a medical clinic in the Federation of Bosnia-Herzegovina.[50] Even though the prisoners refused to be examined by or receive treatment from medical staff at this clinic, the court continued to transport them there for scheduled appointments. The consequent dependency on the very limited medical facilities at Kula Prison put both the medical staff and prisoners in a very difficult position and the on-going stalemate resulted in one prisoner requiring dialysis.[51]

While this was a very specific situation with consequences for medical treatment, there was also a more general concern about the risk of attacks based on the prisoner's ethnicity and criminal convictions. Despite numerous reports from NGOs outlining problems of inter-prisoner violence in Bosnian prisons,[52] the ICTY appears to have ignored the obvious risk that the lack of a state prison would fundamentally affect the ability of the State Court to ensure the safety of Rule 11*bis* transferees. This very issue was raised by accused persons under the ICTY's custody during an attempt to resist referral to Bosnia. In light of reported assaults on prisoners in Zenica Prison, they claimed they would be in personal danger if transferred to Bosnia-Herzegovina.[53] Both the ICTY's Referral Bench and Appeal Chamber rejected these arguments, stating that in the absence of a specific and substantiated threat, the issue was one for the Bosnian authorities to deal with.[54] While this reasoning reflects ICTR decisions where there was no serious risk to the lives of the proposed transferees, the decisions can be differentiated as the ICTR qualified this reasoning by stating that transferees would be housed in a specific wing with a special regime and independent oversight.[55] In contrast, the ICTY did not have the luxury of knowing that transferees would be sent to a secure prison. Rather, there was a high likelihood that they would be placed in violent and severely overcrowded prisons that could not

---

[50] Crnjak, Kula Detention Facility, 08.10.2007.
[51] Clinical doctors and nurses and Custodial staff, Kula Detention Facility, 08.10.2007.
[52] See Amnesty International "Bosnia and Herzegovina 'Better Keep Quiet' Ill-Treatment by the Police and in Prisons", 07.02.2008.
[53] See para. 45 *Ljubičić* (Decision) IT-00-41-PT, 12.04.2006.
[54] See para. 87 *Rašević and Todović* (Decision) IT-97-25/1-PT, 08.07.2005.
[55] See paras. 76–7 *Hategekimana* (Decision) ICTR-00-55B-R11*bis*, 19.06.2008; para. 91 *Kanyarukiga* (Decision) ICTR-2002-78-R11*bis*, 06.06.2008.

guarantee the segregation of vulnerable prisoners.[56] The ICTY's approach also contrasts with that of the ECtHR, where it was not considered necessary to establish a specific threat. The ECtHR held that it was foreseeable that the placement of persons convicted of war crimes among a prison population composed of 90 per cent of the victims' ethnic group would create a serious risk to the prisoners' well-being.[57]

The ICTY also felt that by establishing an internal commission to investigate the matter and by imposing disciplinary sanctions on the perpetrators, the Bosnian authorities had taken appropriate steps in response to the Zenica attacks.[58] However, the prisoners were only provided with separate accommodation ten months after entering the prison, after two domestic reports highlighting the threat to their safety and a hunger-strike to raise awareness of their situation. The ECtHR, in sharp contrast, unanimously held that the Bosnian authorities had failed to protect the prisoners from persecution by fellow inmates. Furthermore, the ECtHR rejected the submission that it was acceptable to place vulnerable prisoners on a normal wing with a serious shortage of staff due to the lack of an alternative secure prison. Structural shortcomings, it held, were not an answer for failing to secure the safety of prisoners when there is a known and serious risk.[59] The constant mental anxiety caused by threat of violence was considered by the ECtHR to have exceeded the unavoidable level inherent in detention, bringing the suffering beyond the threshold of severity necessary to cause a violation of Article 3 ECHR.[60]

While the Bosnian Government has since made capacity available to house vulnerable prisoners,[61] the ECtHR's ruling casts serious doubt on the ICTY's decision not to postpone transfers until the state prison had been completed or a suitable alternative made available. The Tribunal was aware of discrepancies between statements of different Bosnian representatives as to when the state prison would be completed and knew that its funding relied almost exclusively on donations that had

---

[56] See paras. 39–51 CPT Report to the Government of BiH CPT/Inf (2009) 25.
[57] See para. 70 *Rodić and 3 Others* v. *Bosnia and Herzegovina* (22893/05) 27.05.2008.
[58] Paras. 46–48 *Ljubicic* (Decision) IT-00-41-PT, 12.04.2006.
[59] See para. 71 *Rodić and 3 Others* v. *Bosnia and Herzegovina* (22893/05) 27.05.2008.
[60] See para. 73 *Rodić and 3 Others* v. *Bosnia and Herzegovina*, (22893/05) 27.05.08.
[61] Communication from Bosnia and Herzegovina concerning the case of Rodić and 3 others against Bosnia and Herzegovina (Application No. 22893/05) DH – DD (2011) 361, 19.05.2011.

not been secured by the State Ministry of Justice.[62] The original promise that it would be completed by the end of 2006 has proven to be extremely optimistic, given that, since the cornerstone-setting ceremony in November 2006, only the external perimeter wall and its surveillance towers have been erected.

2.1.3 Secure custody

In addition to these health and safety issues, the lack of a state prison in Bosnia-Herzegovina also had serious consequences for the secure custody of referred detainees. The State Court was responsible for designating an entity prison for a person to serve their sentence in, on the basis of criteria set out in state law. The input of the designated entity's Ministry of Justice was limited to the provision of information on the individual's security categorisation under entity-level law.[63] According to state rules, ethnicity was not a consideration to be taken into account when making designation decisions.[64] While this approach was based on the principle of non-discrimination, it created security problems in the case of one particular referred prisoner.

The first person transferred from the ICTY to Bosnia-Herzegovina, and subsequently convicted by the State Court, escaped from an entity prison. Radovan Stanković absconded in a car after arranging a transfer based on a falsified medical certificate. Instead of giving chase, the nine guards that had been accompanying him simply returned to the prison to inform it of the escape.[65] Following the escape, the High Representative for Bosnia-Herzegovina argued that ethnicity should be a pertinent factor in all allocation decisions made in the absence of a secure state prison.[66] The State Court's designation decision was strongly criticised, both nationally and internationally, as it was considered by many to be foreseeable that Mr Stanković would meet sympathetic staff, given that he was placed in a prison in the town he was from.[67] It was argued in

---

[62] See paras. 39–42 *Ljubičić* (Appeal Decision) IT-00-41-AR11bis.1, 04.07.2006.
[63] Articles 13–14 State Rulebook on Criteria for Placement of Convicted Persons, No: 01-02–263/05, 18.06.2005.
[64] See Art. 11 State Rulebook on Criteria for Placement of Convicted Persons, No: 01-02-263/05, 18.06.2005.
[65] See OSCE, Sixth Report in the Case of Convicted Person Radovan Stanković, Transferred to the State Court pursuant to Rule 11*bis*, June 2007, 9–10.
[66] See C. Schwarz-Schilling, "Stankovic Fiasco Highlights Need for State Prison", 01.06.2007.
[67] See OSCE, Sixth Report in the Case of Convicted Person Radovan Stanković, Transferred to the State Court pursuant to Rule 11*bis*, June 2007, 12.

response that the State Court received no warning that it could not rely on the entity's highest security prison to be secure or its staff to be professional.[68]

McEvoy argues that escape challenges both the raison d'être of imprisonment and the power of an institution.[69] Mr Stanković's escape certainly caused considerable embarrassment to the State Court, the State Government, and the Republika Srpska Government and strongly challenged the legitimacy of the ICTY's Rule 11*bis* system. This embarrassment continued throughout the five-year period that he evaded recapture. Despite the fact that the escape was facilitated by the support of prison staff, Mr Stanković was reportedly transferred back to the same prison following his re-arrest due to the lack of a state-level secure facility.[70] This incident provides another clear example of why it is important for international tribunals to postpone transfers until there is a suitable and secure facility available to hold individuals before, during and after their trial.

2.2 The ICTR, Rule 11bis and Rwanda

The ICTR has used the Rule 11*bis* mechanism less frequently and more cautiously than the ICTY. Until 2011, referral orders were only granted to France[71] (a request for the referral to Norway was refused[72] and an order granting referral to The Netherlands was later revoked[73]). While the ICTR was willing to transfer the files of non-indicted suspects, it was more hesitant to transfer the files of indicted suspects to Rwanda. To date, only two individuals have been transferred from the ICTR's custody in Arusha to Rwanda for prosecution under Rule 11*bis*.

The consistent refusals to grant referral orders to transfer persons in ICTR custody to Rwanda were founded on fears in relation to the inadequacy of due process rights for defendants and the possibility that if

---

[68] *Ibid.*
[69] K. McEvoy, *Paramilitary Imprisonment in Northern Ireland: Resistance, Management and Release* (2001), 44.
[70] Amnesty International, "Bosnia and Herzegovina: Stanković Arrest: Victims of War-Time Rape Must Feel Safe to Testify", 23.01.2012.
[71] *Bucyibaruta* (TC Decision) ICTR-2005-85-I, 20.11.2007; *Munyeshyaka* (TC Decision) ICTR-05-87-I, 20.11.2007.
[72] See *Bagaragaza* (Decision) ICTR-05-86-R11*bis*, 19.05.2006; *Bagaragaza* (AC Decision) ICTR-05-86-AR11*bis*, 30.08.2006.
[73] See *Bagaragaza* (Decision) ICTR-05-86-R11*bis*, 13.04.2007; *Bagaragaza* (Decision) ICTR-05-86-R11*bis*, 17.08.2007.

convicted, transferees may face life imprisonment in solitary confinement, violating the right not be subjected to cruel, inhuman or degrading punishment.[74] In response, the Rwandan Government initiated material changes to its domestic law to ensure that it explicitly upholds international standards on imprisonment and due process rights, provides an appropriate penalty structure that does not allow for the imposition of the death penalty or life imprisonment in solitary confinement for referred persons and facilitates external monitoring.[75] These changes, along with the provision of a custom-built remand centre in Kigali (twelve cells) and prison in Mpanga (seventy-three cells), assured the ICTR Referral Chambers that persons transferred pursuant to Rule11*bis* would be housed in accordance with international standards before, during and after their trials.[76] The ICTR agreed to transfer two individuals from Arusha to Rwanda to stand trial, subject to the Tribunal's oversight.

To ensure that the monitoring role was responsive to the accused's concerns, Rule 11*bis* was amended to enable Chambers, in addition to the Prosecutor, to appoint monitors to observe the trial[77] (although Rwandan law has not yet been amended to reflect this change[78]). The ICTR requested that the African Commission on Human and Peoples' Rights (ACmHPR) appoint at least two experienced professionals to conduct full-time monitoring and to submit reports every three months to the President through the Registrar.[79] While the ACmHPR agreed to undertake the task, problems relating to staffing and funding appear to have delayed the finalisation of an agreement.[80] Although

---

[74] See paras. 25, 78(iii) *Hategekimana* (Decision) ICTR-00-55B-R11*bis*, 19.06.2008; paras. 94–6, 104 *Kanyarukiga* (Decision) ICTR-02-78-R11*bis*, 06.06.2008.
[75] See paras. 15, 47–9, 51, 58, 222–4 *Uwinkindi* (Decision) ICTR-2001-75-R11*bis*, 28.06.2011; paras. 68–73, 202, 220 *Munyagishari* (Decision) ICTR-2005-89-R11*bis*, 06.06.2012.
[76] Paras. 15, 52–3, 58–9 *Uwinkindi* (Decision) ICTR-2001-75-R11*bis*, 28.06.2011; paras. 74, 77–80, 85 *Munyagishari* (Decision) ICTR-2005-89-R11*bis*, 06.06.2012.
[77] See Rule11*bis*(D)(iv) ICTR RPE; paras. 200, 205, 208–9 *Uwinkindi* (Decision) ICTR-2001-75-R11*bis*, 28.06.2011; paras. 200, 208 *Munyagishari* (Decision) ICTR-2005-89-R11*bis*, 06.06.2012.
[78] Para. 214 *Uwinkindi* (Decision) ICTR-2001-75-R11*bis*, 28.06.2011; para. 209 *Munyagishari* (Decision) ICTR-2005-89-R11*bis*, 06.06.2012.
[79] Para. 213, Disposition *Uwinkindi* (Decision) ICTR-2001-75-R11*bis*, 28.06.2011.
[80] Para. 207, 210, 219, 221, Disposition *Uwinkindi* (Decision) ICTR-2001-75-R11*bis*, 28.06.2011; ICTR Press Release, "Decisions in Fulgence Kayishema and Jean Uwinkindi Cases Made – Tribunal Refers Case of Kayishema to Rwanda – Tribunal Stays Transfer of Uwinkindi to Rwanda Pending Establishment of Suitable Monitoring Mechanism", 27.02.2012; ICTR Press Release, "Registrar Directed to Immediately Resume Discussions with ACHPR", 10.04.2012.

the ACmHPR remains the Tribunal's "first choice," the ICTR was forced to appoint interim monitors from its legal staff to facilitate transfers and to acknowledge that other organisations may have to be approached if an agreement is not reached or the agreement reached proves to be ineffective in practice.[81] The ICTR President handed down guidelines to direct the internal monitors in their task of ensuring that transferred individuals receive a fair trial in accordance with international standards.[82] The ICTR has acknowledged that reliance on internal officials to monitor the proceedings was not ideal and that the transferred persons' rights would be best safeguarded by an independent body.[83]

In particular, independent monitors have an important role to play in any potential requests for revocation. Unlike extradition, whereby the sending state surrenders control over the subsequent trial, "referral is a *sui generis* mechanism wherein the referring Tribunal retains the power to revoke its decision if fair trial rights are not respected".[84] Monitors are expected to act with a "great degree of diligence" and investigate the circumstances surrounding any application for revocation.[85] Despite this instruction and the explicit acknowledgment that referred persons have direct standing to bring perceived violations of referral conditions to the attention of the ICTR or MICT's President and to request revocation,[86] the likelihood of an order of revocation being granted is limited. The ICTR referral chambers stated that the delay that would be caused to the trial means that revocation is "a remedy of last resort".[87]

---

[81] ICTR Press Release, "Registrar Directed to Immediately Resume Discussions with ACHPR", 10.04.2012; ICTR Press Release, "Appeal's Chamber Dismisses Uwinkindi's Motion for Stay of Transfer to Rwanda", 19.04.2012; paras. 210–12, 218 *Munyagishari* (Decision) ICTR-2005–89-R11*bis*, 06.06.2012.

[82] See paras. 1.1, 2.2 Guidelines on Monitoring Trials Referred to National Jurisdictions under Rule11*bis* by ICTR Staff Monitors, Annex A *Uwinkindi* (President's Order) ICTR-01–75R11*bis*, 29.06.2012.

[83] Paras. 212, 214, Disposition *Munyagishari* (Decision) ICTR-2005-89-R11*bis*, 06.06.2012.

[84] Para. 26 *Munyagishari* (Decision) ICTR-2005-89-R11*bis*, 06.06.2012.

[85] Para. 218 *Uwinkindi* (Decision) ICTR-2001-75-R11*bis*, 28.06.2011; para. 217 *Munyagishari* (Decision) ICTR-2005–89-R11*bis*, 06.06.2012.

[86] Disposition *Uwinkindi* (Decision) ICTR-2001-75-R11*bis*, 28.06.2011; Disposition *Munyagishari* (Decision) ICTR-2005–89-R11*bis*, 06.06.2012.

[87] Para. 217 *Uwinkindi* (Decision) ICTR-2001-75-R11*bis*, 28.06.2011; para. 216 *Munyagishari* (Decision) ICTR-2005–89-R11*bis*, 06.06.2012.

2.3 Rule 11bis *and its operation post-completion*

For a long time, the ICTY's "presumption of referral"[88] to states where the crimes had been committed could be contrasted with the ICTR's presumption of refusal to similar referrals. From the 1 July 2012 (and 1 July 2013 for the ICTY), however, the MICT became responsible for referral decisions and the oversight of cases referred to national jurisdictions by either UN Tribunal or the MICT itself. Although the MICT has been urged to refer cases wherever possible,[89] it is foreseeable that its statutory scheme will only be used to refer MICT indictments for administration of justice offences and to oversee ICTR referrals.[90]

Like the UN Tribunals, the MICT must be satisfied that the accused will receive a fair trial and that the death penalty will not be imposed or carried out.[91] This direction will probably be interpreted in line with ICTR jurisprudence to include a duty to ensure there is an appropriate penalty structure and that transferred persons will be housed in conditions of detention that accord with international standards.

It has been argued that until 2011, the ICTR adopted a broad factual inquiry into the reality on the ground in Rwanda that could be contrasted with the narrow legal inquiry adopted by the ICTY which focused solely on the sufficiency of domestic legal frameworks in light of international standards.[92] The ICTY may have been more willing to transfer persons in its custody to the State Court of Bosnia-Herzegovina due to the Tribunal's and international community's involvement in its establishment and operation.[93] Yet, even within its own referral jurisprudence, the ICTR appeared to submit African countries to a

---

[88] Sarah Williams cited in A. S. Canter, "'For these reasons, the Chamber Denies the Prosecutor's Request for Referral': The False Hope of Rule 11*bis*" (2009) 32 *Fordham International Law Journal* 1614–56 at 1629.

[89] Para. 11 SCRes 1966(2010); Arts. 1(3), (4), 6(1) MICTSt.

[90] See C. Denis, "Critical Overview of the 'Residual Functions' of the Mechanism and its Date of Commencement (including Transitional Arrangements)" (2011) 9(4) *Journal of International Criminal Justice* 819–37 at 828; R. Frolich, "UN Security Council Resolution 1966: International Residual Mechanism for the ICTY and ICTR" (2011) 50(3) *International Legal Materials* 323–39 at 324.

[91] Art. 6(4) MICTSt.

[92] See Bekou, "Rule 11*bis*", 769–70; J. Melman, "The Possibility of Transfer (?): A Comprehensive Approach to the ICTR's Rule 11*bis* to Permit Transfer to Rwandan Domestic Courts" (2010) 79 *Fordham Law Review* 1271–332 at 1275, 1298–300, 1303.

[93] See para. 5 SCRes 1503(2003); Art. 2(1), (3) Law No. 12/04 (01.12.2004) *BiH Official Gazette*; Melman, 'The Possibility of Transfer(?)", 1300–1.

different level of inquiry than European states.[94] Recent decisions, granting referral to Rwanda, however, have stated that the referral chamber is "limited to an assessment of the applicable legal framework".[95] Although referral criteria should be applied consistently across the board, the MICT should bear in mind the lessons that have been learned by the UN Tribunals. Factual inquiries may be necessary to determine whether satisfactory, safe and secure detention conditions can be provided to referred individuals during their trial and any sentence that may be imposed. This may involve ensuring that designated facilities exist and will continue to exist during the trial and punishment of transferred individuals.

The ICTY was unwilling to delay transfers until the completion of the state prison (which has still not occurred) or to interfere with the national enforcement of sentences by directly monitoring post-conviction conditions.[96] The lack of a state prison in Bosnia resulted in the escape of an individual transferred from the ICTY and potential risks to the well-being and safety of state prisoners housed in entity prisons.

The ICTR, unlike the ICTY, was willing to delay Rule 11*bis* transfers until the new and specifically designed wings in Kigali Central Prison for remand prisoners and Mpanga Prison in Nyanza for convicted prisoners had been completed.[97] Even after these facilities had been completed, defence counsel raised concerns about the continuing existence of the custom-built remand centre in Kigali due to proposed works at the Central Prison and the possible relocation of referred detainees to unsuitable premises. The ICTR felt this was unlikely to occur and in any event Rwandan law guaranteed detention in accordance with minimum standards and accordingly, another acceptable facility would be made available should the remand centre have to close.[98]

Unlike the discretionary nature of monitoring under the UN Tribunals' rules,[99] monitoring is mandatory for the MICT.[100] The task of observing cases transferred to national jurisdictions has been

---

[94] See Canter, "'For These Reasons, the Chamber Denies the Prosecutor's Request for Referral'", 1651.
[95] Para. 80 *Munyagishari* (Decision) ICTR-2005-89-R11*bis*, 06.06.2012.
[96] Para. B.1.1(23) *MDP*, 156.
[97] See para. 77 *Hategekimana* (Decision) ICTR-00-55B-R11*bis*, 19.06.2008.
[98] Paras. 54–5 *Uwinkindi* (Decision) ICTR-01-75R11*bis*, 28.06.2011; paras. 34, 37, 39 *Uwinkindi* (Appeal Decision) ICTR-01-75-AR11*bis*, 16.12.2011; paras. 77, 82 *Munyagishari* (Decision) ICTR-2005-89-R11*bis*, 06.06.2012.
[99] Rule 11*bis*(D)(iv) ICTY/ICTR RPE.   [100] Art. 6(5) MICTSt.

outsourced to the OSCE, the ACmHPR and law firms by the UN Tribunals.[101] The MICT can also outsource the monitoring role to international and regional organisations and bodies.[102] It may choose to work with the bodies already used by the UN Tribunals. The MICT should seek to conclude agreements with suitable bodies as soon as possible to avoid the delays caused to ICTR referrals due to a failure to finalise an agreement with the ACmHPR and the consequent reliance on internal officials. In the case that referral conditions are breached and if it is in the interest of justice to do so, the MICT may, acting on its own motion or following a request from the Prosecutor, revoke a referral order and make a formal request for deferral.[103] Like its predecessors, the statutory provision states that this power is only exercisable before an accused person is found guilty or acquitted by the national court.[104] In other words, the international institution has no right to intervene once the national judgment has been pronounced.

Although this principle was also clearly stated in the UN Tribunals' rules, their referral jurisprudence has not always been clear about the scope of its oversight role. The ICTY Appeals Chamber asked the ICTY Prosecutor to report on any serious issues regarding post-conviction conditions of imprisonment to the Referral Bench.[105] ICTR referral jurisprudence typically referred to monitoring the conditions of detention of accused persons during the trial and appellate process rather than the conditions of imprisonment of convicted persons.[106] Indeed, the ICTR guidelines suggest that the monitoring role in relation to detention conditions is limited to the trial period and, even then, only insofar as the detention conditions are relevant to the fair trial rights of the accused person.[107] The Referral Chambers, however, requested that monitoring be undertaken post-conviction or through to the enforcement of any sentence imposed, if necessary.[108] Although the MICT lacks direct authority to revoke a referral order post-conviction, the Rwandan authorities appear to be willing to facilitate international oversight of

---

[101] Para. 36 Residual Mechanism Report.   [102] Art. 6(5) MICTSt.
[103] Art. 6(6) MICTSt.   [104] Art. 6(6) MICTSt.
[105] See para. 43 *Ljubičić* (Appeal Decision) IT-00-41-AR11bis.1, 04.07.2006.
[106] Para. 74 *Munyagishari* (Decision) ICTR-2005-89-R11bis, 06.06.2012.
[107] See paras. 3.8.1, 4.1.2, 6.3, 6.4.7 Guidelines on Monitoring Trials Referred to National Jurisdictions under Rule11bis by ICTR Staff Monitors Annex A; *Uwinkindi* (President's Order) ICTR-01-75R11bis, 29.06.2012.
[108] Para. 213, Disposition *Uwinkindi* (Decision) ICTR-2001-75-R11bis, 28.06.2011; para. 78 *Uwinkindi* (Appeal Decision) ICTR-01-75-AR11bis, 16.12.2011; para. 81 *Munyagishari* (Decision) ICTR-2005-89-R11bis, 06.06.2012.

the enforcement of national sentences imposed post-referral in the same way as it facilitates the oversight of the national implementation of international punishment.[109]

3. Conclusion

Though there are many arguments in favour of the localised enforcement of international sentences of imprisonment relating to the local ownership of punishment and the attainment of penological objectives of rehabilitation and reintegration, there remain many political and practical obstacles that prevent it from being a realistic option. In the initial post-conflict phases, the severe lack of resources and damaged prisons mean that most available domestic facilities are not in line with the requisite standards. Moreover, the ethnic, political or military affiliations of prisoners and their conviction for the commission of international crimes can make it difficult to ensure either safe or secure custody in domestic prisons.

Although the international courts have not relied on statutory systems for the local enforcement of international punishment, the UN Tribunals have been willing to transfer persons in their custody to the states in which the crimes were committed to stand trial under Rule 11*bis*. While some view the Rule11*bis* procedure as a form of complementarity,[110] others feel the procedure is an institutional tool used to bring domestic criminal justice procedure and penalties into line with international standards.[111] The majority of resulting changes, however, only relate to the trial of referred cases and persons. The impact on domestic prison conditions is also limited as international courts are only interested in the standards that apply to referred prisoners in the specifically designated facilities and not the general conditions of imprisonment in a particular country.[112]

---

[109] See para. 76 *Hategekimana* (Decision) ICTR-00-55B-R11*bis* 19.06.2008; paras. 90, 92 *Kanyarukiga* (Decision) ICTR-2002-78-R11*bis*, 06.06.2008; SCSL Ninth Annual Report, 38.

[110] M. M. El Zeidy, "From Primacy to Complementarity and Backwards: (Re)-visiting Rule 11*bis* of the Ad Hoc Tribunals" (2008) 57(2) *International and Comparative Law Quarterly* 403–15 at 404–6.

[111] See M. Drumbl, "Collective Violence and Individual Punishment: The Criminality of Mass Atrocity" (2005) 99(2) *Northwestern University Law Review* 539–610 at 607; M. Drumbl, *Atrocity, Punishment and International Law* (2007), 12; Canter, "'For These Reasons, the Chamber Denies the Prosecutor's Request for Referral'", 1626, 1631.

[112] See para. 84 *Munyagishari* (Decision) ICTR-2005-89-R11*bis*, 06.06.2012.

Despite the improved political, judicial and penal conditions that facilitated Rule11*bis* transfers, neither the ICTY nor the ICTR have transferred international prisoners to Bosnia-Herzegovina or Rwanda for the enforcement of international sentences of imprisonment. The absence of ICTR prisoners in Rwanda is perhaps more notable given the statutory preference for imprisonment in Rwanda, the conclusion of a bilateral agreement between the Tribunal and Rwanda for this purpose and the fact that the Mpanga facility is currently housing eight international prisoners from the SCSL. The Rwandan authorities hope that the recent referral orders to Rwanda will result in the transfer of ICTR convicts to serve their sentences in Rwanda.[113] The different attitudes towards referral and enforcement appear to be based on the fact that referrals under Rule 11*bis* only permit the transfer of low to intermediate ranking accused, whereas transfers pursuant to bilateral enforcement agreements would facilitate the national implementation of international sentences imposed on the most senior international criminals.[114] If conditions in a state in which the crimes occurred were such that it was possible to permit the localised enforcement of international punishment, the Rule11*bis* experience has demonstrated that it is important to ensure that there are secure facilities available that provide safe custody and conditions in line with international standards. Although the SCSL has been willing, with the passage of time, to implement short sentences imposed for administration of justice convictions in its detention facility in Freetown,[115] it is not willing to implement sentences imposed on those also convicted of international crimes in Sierra Leone.[116] Moreover, this decision involves the international enforcement of custodial sanctions rather than the localised national enforcement of international punishment. To date, therefore, no international sentence of imprisonment has been enforced in the national prisons of a country in which the relevant international crimes were committed.

---

[113] J. Munyaneza, "Why Rwanda wants ICTR Convicts", 05.04.2012.
[114] See paras. B.1.1 (23)-(25) *MDP*, 156; para. 27 Shomburg's Dissenting Opinion *Strugar* (AC Decision) IT-01-42.Misc.1, 07.06.2007.
[115] See SCSL Press Release, "Eric Koi Senessie Sentenced to Two Years in Prison for Contempt of the Special Court", 05.07.2012.
[116] See SCSL Press Release, "Four Sentenced for Interference in the Administration of Justice", 11.10.2012.

5

The contemporary international penal system

The international penal system operates using a variety of statutory and non-statutory systems for implementing international custodial sanctions. The previous chapters described and analysed each of these systems and their operations. This chapter adopts a more systemic approach to the analysis of the contemporary international penal system. In particular, it highlights the challenges the system faces in ensuring international control over sanctions implemented by national prison systems, the equal treatment of prisoners, independent and transparent oversight of international punishment and the attainment of penological or justice objectives.

1. The international penal system

International punishment can be enforced in a decentralised, centralised or localised manner. *Decentralised national enforcement* involves the transfer of persons convicted by international courts to facilities in national prison systems to serve their sentences of imprisonment. National implementation is overseen by both the sentencing international court and independent oversight bodies. The experience of the UN Tribunals to date, however, has shown that international oversight cannot prevent variations in the implementation of international sentences of imprisonment in the different enforcing states in relation to conditions, regimes, release procedures etc. The consensual nature of the legal framework governing decentralised enforcement may also lead to a loss of international control over fundamental aspects of the sentence. The decentralised system may aggravate the sentence imposed due to risk of isolation. International prisoners may be isolated within the prison due to a lack of opportunities to participate in work or education programmes or outings, linguistic barriers and/or security-related restrictions to movement and communication. International prisoners may also experience difficulties in maintaining relationships with family and friends due to their location far from their state of origin. The implementation of international sentences of imprisonment in national prison systems makes it difficult to rehabilitate or prepare international prisoners for release.

Centralised international enforcement involves the direct implementation of international sentences of imprisonment by the sentencing international court in their IDFs. These international facilities provide high standards, operate liberal regimes and there is a lower risk of isolation. However, prisoners often remain in a facility far from their homes. Moreover, as IDFs do not have an explicit mandate to enforce sentences of imprisonment, they do not provide a prison regime suitable for long-term prisoners. Like the decentralised system, international prisoners serving their sentences in IDFs are not rehabilitated or prepared for release.

The UN Tribunals and the SCSL have been forced to rely on their IDFs due to a lack of state cooperation. The ICCDC, in contrast, cannot house convicted persons for more than six months. The Rome Statute introduced the new alternative of *centralised national enforcement* in a residual facility provided by the Host State. The Dutch Government provides the penal capacity but the ICC is responsible for the costs associated with implementation and oversight. This alternative hybrid model removes the need to depend on the default position of long-term centralised international enforcement used by the temporary courts. As this statutory option is only to be relied upon as a last resort, however, the ICC will ultimately rely on decentralised national enforcement.

Finally, *localised national enforcement* involves the national implementation of international sentences in the state in which the conflict occurred, with international oversight. While the structure is very similar to the decentralised system, convicted persons are imprisoned in the state in which the international crimes were committed. In most cases, this will be the state of origin of the prisoner. This method is intended to enhance the visibility, and the victims' ownership, of the punishment. Localised enforcement is also supported as it is purported to promote the likelihood of rehabilitation and successful reintegration due to the increased possibilities for maintaining important social relationships. This statutory option available to the ICTR and SCSL, however, has not been relied on to enforce sentences imposed for the commission of international crimes.

The Rule 11*bis* process has demonstrated that the political and economic situation in post-conflict and/or developing states can create difficulties for ensuring the humane, safe and secure custody of international prisoners. The ICTR may be more willing to send convicted persons to Rwanda to serve their sentence now that accused persons have been transferred to Rwanda under Rule 11*bis*.[1]

The SCSL, on the other hand, remains worried about the potentially detrimental impact that the international prisoners' continued presence would have on local and regional stability and the domestic prison system's ability to provide humane conditions or keep the prisoners behind bars.[2] The SCSL statute allows for the enforcement of sentences in Sierra Leone but it does not specify that enforcement should occur within a national prison system. This facilitated the SCSL's decision to use its latest detention facility to directly implement sanctions imposed on those convicted of contempt of court.[3] The utilisation of the SCSLDF as a prison for the enforcement of sentences will ensure that persons convicted by the court will be held in a secure facility operated in accordance with international standards by internationally employed staff and supervisors.[4] This localised international enforcement method will not, however, be used to enforce sentences imposed for international crimes. SCSL prisoners convicted of both international crimes and contempt of court will remain in Rwanda to serve the remainder of their terms of imprisonment[5] and Mr Taylor, despite his expressed preference to be housed in Africa, will be sent to a European prison (if his conviction is upheld on appeal) due to fears that his presence would de-stabilise peace in the region.

Even though international courts can and have relied on other enforcement methods, the international penal system is primarily dependent on states unconnected with the relevant conflict to provide sufficient and suitable penal capacity. While some states have concluded agreements with multiple international courts in relation to enforcement,[6] the number and location of enforcing states does not reflect the number of nations

---

[1] See Chapter 4, Section 2.2.
[2] R. Mulgrew, "Implementing International Sentences of Imprisonment: Challenges Faced by the Special Court for Sierra Leone" (2009) 7(2) *Journal of International Criminal Justice* 373–96 at 375–6.
[3] SCSL Ninth Annual Report, 25; Ras, SCSL Sub-Office, 05.07.2012.
[4] See Mulgrew, "Implementing International Sentences of Imprisonment", 391–2.
[5] See SCSL Press Release, "Four Sentenced for Interference in Administration of Justice", 11.10.2012.
[6] UK [ICTY, SCSL, ICC]; Sweden [ICTY, ICTR, SCSL]; Finland [ICTY, SCSL, ICC]; Austria [ICTY, ICC]; Italy [ICTY, ICTR], France [ICTY, ICTR]; Denmark [ICTY, ICC]; Belgium [ICTY, ICC]; Mali [ICTR, ICC]; Rwanda [ICTR, SCSL]. See Appendix II.

willing to join the "global confederation"[7] to end impunity for international crime. Of the 121 State Parties to the Rome Statute,[8] only eight have concluded bilateral enforcement agreements with the ICC. Therefore, while international crimes may be investigated by the ICC in Africa, Europe, Asia-Pacific, Latin America, the Caribbean, Canada, Australia and New Zealand, convicted persons can only be imprisoned in a handful of Western European countries, Mali or Colombia.

The geographical spread of the ICC's enforcing states is representative of the international penal system as a whole. Eighteen enforcing states of the international penal system are European, four are African and one is South American. Of the twenty-four countries that have concluded agreements with international courts, sixteen have implemented or are currently implementing international sentences of imprisonment.[9] These enforcing states are all located in either Europe or Africa.

It is not surprising that all current enforcing states are situated in Europe and Africa, given that the courts in question deal with conflicts that occurred in these regions. To date, 79 persons have been transferred to states to serve their sentences.[10] When the transfers are analysed, a pattern of placement in the prisoner's region of origin emerges. The ICTY could sign agreements with any state, bar the states of the former Yugoslav Republic.[11] However, a deliberate policy decision was made to aim for enforcement within Europe. Even though non-European states expressed their willingness to enforce ICTY sentences,[12] agreements have only been signed with European states. All ICTY prisoners are currently, therefore, serving sentences in Europe. The ICTR has agreements with states in both Africa and Europe.[13] To date, all African prisoners, bar one, have been transferred to African States (Mali and

---

[7] L. Moreno-Ocampo, "How Prosecution Can Lead to Prevention" (2011) 29 *Law and Inequality* 477–94 at 478.
[8] ICC Press Release, "ICC Hosts Welcome Ceremony Honouring Guatemala as a New State Party" 13.07.2012.
[9] Italy, Finland, Norway, Sweden, Austria, Germany, France, Spain, Denmark, UK, Portugal, Belgium, Estonia, Mali, Benin, Rwanda have enforced or are currently enforcing sentences. Ukraine, Slovakia, Poland, Albania, Serbia, Swaziland and Colombia have not done so to date.
[10] ICTY 47, ICTR 24 and SCSL 8.
[11] Para. 121 Report of the Secretary-General pursuant to para. 2 of Security Council Resolution 808 (1993) 03.05.1993.
[12] Iran and Pakistan. See para. 189 ICTY Sixth Annual Report.
[13] Italy, France, Sweden, Mali, Benin, Swaziland, Rwanda.

Benin)[14] and the only convicted person of European origin, an individual with both Belgian and Italian nationality,[15] was transferred to Italy.[16] The only African ICTR prisoner to serve his sentence in Europe (Sweden) spent three years of pre-trial detention in The Hague.[17] The SCSL has concluded agreements with three European states and one African state.[18] All eight convicted persons housed in Freetown were transferred to Rwanda to serve their sentences.[19]

The policy of regional placement that has developed in international enforcement practice is supported for primarily humanitarian reasons: prisoners should be placed in more culturally and linguistically familiar environments and in locations that are accessible to prisoners' families for visits.[20] In addition to humanitarian concerns, the SCSL wanted sentences to be implemented in Africa in order to respect the wishes of the Sierra Leonean Government.[21] Some argue that more visible punishment enhances the deterrent effect of the sentence. Consistency of conditions[22] and placement in conditions comparable to those available in the prisoners' state of origin also seem to be relevant considerations.[23]

Yet, these arguments exaggerate the homogenous nature of the prison systems, cultures and languages within a region. Conditions vary widely between the domestic prisons systems in a particular region. International prisoners are unlikely to speak the local language of the state they are transferred to, posing linguistic barriers for both staff and prisoners. Moreover, regional placement does not necessarily place a prisoner closer to home or make travel easier for his family.[24]

---

[14] See ICTR Press Release, "Former Prime Minister and Five Other Convicts Sent to Prison in Mali", 11.12.2001; ICTR Press Release, "Nine ICTR Convicts Transferred to Benin", 30.06.2009; ICTR Press Release, "More ICTR Convicts Transferred to Mali and Benin to Serve their Sentences", 03.07.2012.
[15] Para. 13 *Ruggiu* (President's Decision) ICTR-97-32-A26, 13.02.2008.
[16] See ICTR Press Release, "Georges Omar Ruggiu Transferred to Italy", 28.02.2008.
[17] Bagaragaza (ICTR-05-86).   [18] UK, Sweden, Finland, Rwanda.
[19] SCSL Press Release, "Special Court Prisoners Transferred to Rwanda to Serve Their Sentences", 31.10.2009.
[20] See para. A.1(7) MDP, 152; paras. 4(a),(d),(e), 5 ICTY PDD; paras. 3(i), (iv), (v), 4 ICTR PDD; paras. 4(i), (iv)–(vii), 5 SCSL PDD; C. J. M. Safferling, *Towards an International Criminal Procedure* (2001), 355–7.
[21] See para. 50 Report of the Secretary-General on the Establishment of a Special Court for Sierra Leone, 04.10.2000.
[22] Siller, ICTY, 07.06.2007; Vicente, ICTY, 16.02.2007.
[23] See para. 158 ICTR Third Annual Report.
[24] See M. Penrose, "Spandau Revisited: The Question of Detention for International War Crimes" (1999) 16 *New York Law School Journal of Human Rights* 553–91at 568.

Irrespective of the arguments for or against a regional placement policy, designation decisions essentially depend on the availability and suitability of willing states. For example, the ICC is presently detaining one convicted person and four accused persons. Eight bilateral enforcement agreements concluded by the court would therefore seem to provide a sufficient amount of penal capacity. Penal capacity must, however, be suitable, safe and secure. Despite the African origin of all accused and convicted persons at the ICC, it has only concluded one agreement with an African State. Mali, however, may no longer be a suitable enforcement state due to a recent military coup and rebellion. When the enforcement agreement was signed in January 2012, Mali was one of the most stable countries in Africa and it could not have been predicted that the political and security situation would deteriorate so quickly.[25] In just a few months, Mali had gone from being a potential enforcing state for the ICC, to one of the potential situations being considered for investigation at the ICC following a referral by the Malian Government.[26] While the ICTR has continued to transfer international prisoners to Koulikoro Prison in Bamako,[27] these transfers appear risky given the instability of the country. It is also questionable whether international organisations should transfer prisoners to a country that has been accused of holding detained persons in appalling conditions and subjecting them to torture and sexual abuse.[28] International courts should not transfer prisoners to states that are experiencing widespread insurgency or rebellion and they must ensure that feasible evacuation plans and stand-by capacity are put in place to deal with unexpected events in enforcing states post-transfer.

In addition to security and safety concerns, designation decisions must also take broader social and human rights issues into account. Is it acceptable for an international court to transfer African prisoners to European or South American prisons against their will? Although designation decisions are constrained by the fact that states must agree to accept individuals, such transfers would go against international penological goals to place prisoners as close as possible to their homes and militate against rehabilitative and reintegration efforts. Although the

---

[25] Abathi, ICC, 05.07.2012.
[26] ICC Press Release, "ICC Prosecutor Fatou Bensouda on the Malian State referral of the situation in Mali since January 2012", 18.07.2012.
[27] See ICTR Press Release, "More ICTR Convicts Transferred to Mali and Benin to Serve their Sentences", 03.07.2012.
[28] Amnesty International, "Mali: Investigate Enforced Disappearances, Extra-judicial Killings and Torture of Junta Opponents", 31.07.2012.

ICC has recourse to the residual facility provided by the Dutch Government should no state be considered suitable, safe or secure, this is a short-term option only. As it stands, therefore, the international penal system provides access to limited and uncertain capacity located in three continents with vastly differing conditions, regimes and governing law.

2. Humane punishment

International prisoners may be considered extraordinary on account of the crimes they were convicted of. They may also be considered extraordinary due to the unique penal system in which they must serve their sentences. Although the international courts have acknowledged that the international nature of sanctions may make them more onerous,[29] they have failed to acknowledge that the structure of the international penal system and the potentially resulting isolation may aggravate the sanction imposed. Long-term imprisonment can have "a devastating effect on the mental health of even the toughest individuals".[30] International prisoners are often isolated from their family and friends.[31] Those serving their sentences in national prisons may also be further isolated due to linguistic barriers, their security status or fears for their safety. Even if it is unintentional, a regime that results in long-term solitary confinement may constitute inhumane or unusual punishment.[32] It is vital to ensure that those judged against the standards of humanity must be treated according to the same standards. Persons convicted by the same court should be treated the same way to the extent possible. As the international courts (or their residual mechanisms) retain ultimate responsibility for international sanctions and the welfare of international prisoners, they must also ensure that the oversight of international punishment is independent, transparent and effective.

---

[29] Para. 290 *Furundžija* (Judgment) IT-95-17/1-T, 10.12.1998.
[30] R. Vincent, *An Administrative Practices Manual for Internationally Assisted Criminal Justice Institutions* (2007), 68.
[31] Para. 42 Report of the UN High Commissioner for Human Rights, Assistance to Sierra Leone in the Field of Human Rights, 12.02.2010.
[32] Safferling, *Towards an International Criminal Procedure*, 354; N. J. W. Goda, *Tales from Spandau: Nazi Criminals and the Cold War* (2007), 39–41, 46–7.

2.1 Equal treatment

As it was originally envisaged, the international penal system was to be a three-step process, whereby suspects arrested in one state would be transferred to the Host State of the international court to stand trial and then transferred to a third state for the enforcement of custodial sanctions imposed following the finalisation of the sentence. In practice, political and structural constraints have complicated the process. Some international prisoners serve their sentences in special facilities on the territory of cooperating states. Rather than being transferred to enforcing states, other international prisoners may serve their sentences in IDFs or a residual facility provided by the Host State. International prisoners transferred to third states may be extradited to other states to stand trial for separate charges,[33] transferred back to the international court to testify as a witness[34] or if the international court or enforcing state terminates the enforcement agreement.[35] In reality, the international penal system is a multi-directional and multi-dimensional system, comprised of a jumble of jurisdictions and penal pathways. This complicated system does not bode well for the equal treatment of prisoners. The experience of the temporary courts has demonstrated the potential of the current international penal system to create inequalities between international prisoners and between international and national prisoners in enforcing states.[36]

Though, in principle, there should not be any "significant disparities from one State to another as regards the enforcement of penalties pronounced by an international tribunal"[37] the current system of the temporary courts whereby the domestic law of the state governs daily detention and release eligibility, inevitably results in those serving similar sentences doing so in differing conditions. The international courts have also been forced to rely on their IDFs to implement international sentences of imprisonment. This adds another level of disparity of treatment. While different treatment resulting from being housed in different conditions is not a prohibitive ground of discrimination, and is inherent to a certain degree in all penal systems, the degree of variation that results from the international penal system's structure is significant. There are vast differences in the conditions, regimes and opportunities

---

[33] See Art. 4(3) ICC–UK BEA. [34] See Art. 4(2) ICC–UK BEA.
[35] See Arts. 13, 15 ICC–UK BEA.
[36] Mulgrew, "Implementing International Sentences of Imprisonment", 380.
[37] Para. 72 *Erdemović* (Judgment) IT-96-22-T, 29.11.1996.

available in the various national prisons and international facilities that can be used in Africa, Europe and Colombia.[38]

The prioritisation of a regional placement policy may add yet another level of disparity to the system. Placement in a region of origin may involve imprisonment in developing and/or post-conflict states. Prisons in these countries may not conform to international standards. To ensure equality of treatment, international courts are helping to raise funds or undertaking to pay for renovations and daily costs incurred during the enforcement of international sentences in special facilities.[39] Rather than disperse international prisoners throughout a national prison system, they are "consolidated" in designated facilities that house international prisoners only.[40] In the consolidation model, international prisoners are segregated from rather than integrated with national prisoners.[41] The obligation to provide international standards and ensure the equal treatment of international prisoners may create double standards between national and international prisoners. It is "difficult to escape the reality that when compared to most African prisons, international detainees are treated well".[42] Culp notes that some African states were reluctant to enforce international sentences due to fears of a backlash from national prisoners if international prisoners were placed in "country club" facilities.[43] These special facilities often provide international prisoners with living conditions, diets and medical treatment that far exceed those available to their victims and local people.[44] For example, when a video detailing a recent independent inspection of the Mpanga facility in Rwanda used to house SCSL prisoners was broadcasted on Sierra Leonean television networks, it resulted in complaints from the Special Court's Interactive Forum that

---

[38] R. Culp, "Enforcement and Monitoring of Sentences in the Modern War Crimes Process: Equal Treatment before the Law?", 2011, 12; K. Hoffmann, "Some Remarks on the Enforcement of International Sentences in the Light of Galić case at the ICTY" (2011) ZIS 838–42 at 841.

[39] See Chapter 2, Section 3.1 and R. Mulgrew, "The International Movement of Prisoners: Explaining the Evolution of the Inter-State and International Criminal Justice Systems for the Transfer of Sentenced Persons" (2011) 22 *Criminal Law Forum* 103–43 at 135, 139.

[40] See Culp, "Enforcement and Monitoring of Sentences", 10; SCSL Ninth Annual Report, 24.

[41] Culp, "Enforcement and Monitoring of Sentences", 10.

[42] O'Donnell, ICTR, 25.06.2007.

[43] Culp, "Enforcement and Monitoring of Sentences", 12.

[44] D. Chuter, *War Crimes: Confronting Atrocity in the Modern World* (2003), 221–2; Vincent, *An Administrative Practices Manual for Internationally Assisted Criminal Justice Institutions*, 66.

"the conditions of imprisonment were too good, especially given the existence of poverty in Sierra Leone".[45]

Notwithstanding the potential for creating such double standards, it is imperative that international punishment is implemented in facilities that operate in accordance with international standards. The conditions in national prisons and the situation of the local population are the responsibility of the local government. International criminal courts were not created to be development agencies to improve prison standards throughout cooperating states or the national quality of social life more generally. It is difficult, however, to understand how the ICC will operate a regional placement policy while fulfilling its statutory obligation to ensure that international prisoners are in no case treated more or less favourably than prisoners convicted of similar offences in enforcing states.[46] Marchesi argues that this statutory provision should be interpreted to mean that while the treatment of international prisoners must not go below the standards set by international law, such prisoners should not benefit from positive discrimination or privileges.[47] It is not clear how the ICC could ensure that punishment would be implemented in accordance with international standards in Mali or Colombia without special arrangements for international prisoners. The ICTR has not been able to implement international sentences of imprisonment in Mali without positive discrimination and the ICRC recently highlighted the range of systemic problems facing the Colombian prison system, where detainees are held in overcrowded and violent prisons that lack access to medical care, water, adequate sanitary conditions, education and employment opportunities.[48]

Despite the implicit rule that international prisoners can only be sent to states that have prison conditions that conform to international standards,[49] the reality is that the international courts are only really concerned with the standards in facilities that will be used to house international prisoners. It is important, however, that the public

---

[45] SCSL Ninth Annual Report, 24.
[46] See Art. 106(2) ICCSt; Art. 4(2) ICC–Mali BEA.
[47] A. Marchesi, "The Enforcement of Sentences of the International Criminal Court" in F. Lattanzi and W. Schabas (eds.), *Essays on the Rome Statute of the International Criminal Court* (1999) 427–45 at 438–9.
[48] ICRC, "Colombia: People Deprived of their Liberty in State Detention Facilities", 18.04.2012.
[49] W. Schabas, *An Introduction to the International Criminal Court*, 4th edn (2011), 337; A. Cassese, *International Criminal Law* (2008), 433; Art. 106(1) ICCSt.

understands that the higher standards are not provided due to the former status of the prisoners but due to the international legal obligation incumbent on international courts to enforce international punishment in a humane manner.

2.2 Oversight of international punishment

Although states are normally the custodians of internationally convicted persons, the international courts remain the custodians of the sentences being enforced. The temporary courts' experience, however, demonstrated that international courts can lose a degree of control over the length of the sanction that will be served due to the acceptance of the ability of national authorities to determine whether an international prisoner is eligible or suitable for release.[50] This problem arose due to the acceptance of provisions in enforcement agreements that deviated from the statutory system governing release decisions. While it seemed that the Rome Statute and the ICC's rules would prevent this problem arising, the court's agreement with Denmark created the same problems.[51] It is hoped that the amendments to the model agreement will prevent this happening in future agreements entered into by the ICC.

In addition to overseeing the enforcement of international sanctions, the international courts must also ensure that the rights of international prisoners are "effectively and equally protected".[52] International courts must ensure that international prisoners are housed in accordance with international standards in safe and secure conditions.[53] This supervisory role extends beyond the designation phase and is engaged until the prisoner is released. Rather than react to situations that arise, the international penal system has attempted to prevent problems occurring by introducing an oversight system. The independence, transparency and effectiveness of this system could be improved in several respects.

The highest level for internal complaints in relation to international detention or imprisonment lies with the President/Presidency of the sentencing court. These judicial officials also make decisions relating to designation and release that may have a significant impact on the rights of prisoners.[54] The lack of independence of this review mechanism and

---

[50] See Chapter 2, Section 3. [51] See Chapter 2, Section 3.2.3.
[52] Para. 81 Residual Mechanism Report.
[53] See Art. 106(1)–(2) ICCSt; Art. 19(1) ICC–Finland BEA.
[54] Mulgrew, "The International Movement of Prisoners", 116.

the absence of a right to appeal decisions[55] have been criticised for falling short of contemporary human rights standards.[56] The lack of independence of the oversight mechanisms used to oversee international punishment in Spain and Germany has also created problems.[57] The ability of enforcing states to choose their preferred inspecting body has created a situation whereby international prisoners housed in different countries are visited by different inspecting bodies on behalf of the international court. These different bodies have different expertise, and may apply different standards.

These variations may be minor in reality. The real problem lies with the fact that their recommendations are not only non-binding, but they are not published. A lack of public information can feed victims' perceptions of country club prisons and pour fuel on the flames of allegations of ill-treatment. Goda notes that secrecy "added to the mystique of Spandau as a house of horrors rather than a mundane place with increasingly mundane men living terribly mundane lives".[58] Reports from independent inspectorates can provide objective information about the realities of international punishment that can be used to dispel ill-informed criticisms of conditions or malicious allegations of the ill-treatment of detained persons.[59] The strict application of confidentiality principles in the context of the international penal system is unwarranted. International courts contract with inspection bodies to inspect their facilities or to conduct visits in states that have signed international treaties agreeing to their regular presence. The publication of reports would enable public scrutiny of a key aspect of the international criminal justice system's operations and provide incentives for international courts and states to implement suggested recommendations.[60]

Further, the current approach to oversight looks only to ascertaining the views of prisoners on their individual treatment. There is no systemic overview or evaluation. Piecemeal, localised solutions are not sufficient

---

[55] Para. 3 *Rutaganira* (AC Decision) ICTR-95-IC-AR, 24.08.2006.
[56] D. Abels, *Prisoners of the International Community: Legal Position of Persons Detained at International Criminal Tribunals* (2012), 771–2; D. Scalia, "Long-term Sentences in International Criminal Law: Do They Meet the Standards set out by the European Court of Human Rights", (2011) 9(3) *Journal of International Criminal Justice* 669–87 at 676–7.
[57] See Chapter 2, Section 3.1. [58] Goda, *Tales from Spandau*, 274.
[59] Vincent, *An Administrative Practices Manual for Internationally Assisted Criminal Justice Systems*, 67.
[60] Abels, *Prisoners of the International Community*, 772–3.

to ensure that the international penal system is operating in a humane and effective manner. To ensure consistent oversight and the regular evaluation of the international penal system, it is imperative to establish, or contract with, an inspectorate qualified to review all aspects of the operations of the systems used to implement international punishment.

Inspections and systemic appraisals, however, cannot prevent human rights violations from occurring. In 2010, for example, Radislav Krstić was attacked by three men in Wakefield prison and had his throat slashed in revenge for the death of Muslims in Srebrenica. Although the national courts prosecuted the three men responsible and downgraded Mr Krstić's security status so that he could be moved to a different prison within the UK,[61] the prisoner was returned to the UNDU at the ICTY's request.[62] While the remedy of terminating enforcement in one state and transferring a prisoner to another state or an international facility is the remedy of last resort available to international courts, it may not always be possible to rely on it. Moreover, it only ensures the discontinuation of the situation in question and does not provide international prisoners with a remedy for the violation of their rights. Though international prisoners housed in national prisons systems may have access to national and regional courts, international prisoners housed in international facilities will struggle to find a court that has jurisdiction to hear such claims. The international criminal justice system must guarantee remedies for human rights violations that occur as a result of or during the implementation of sentences it imposes. To respect international prisoners' rights to remedial justice, international courts must ensure that international prisoners have access to independent bodies capable of hearing and dealing with complaints.

3. The effectiveness of international punishment

The legal frameworks and jurisprudence of the international courts do not state any goals to be achieved during the implementation of international custodial sanctions. The designation process essentially involves the sentencing court considering whether a proposed enforcing state can effectively enforce the international sentence in modern and secure

---

[61] BBC News, "Three Guilty of Attacking War Criminal Radislav Krstic", 18.02.2011; Culp, "Enforcement and Monitoring of Sentences", 10.
[62] Wilkinson, UK, 10.10.2012.

facilities.[63] The designation process does not consider humanitarian and penological factors that are usually relevant to the transfer of prisoners to other states.[64] The pragmatic focus on securing capacity has resulted in international punishment being implemented in a system that fails to achieve penological or broader justice objectives. At present, the international penal system seems to do no more than provide a "cheap and convenient" custody system in which national prisons act "as babysitters" for international prisoners.[65] This is unfortunate as enforcing states "want to do more than provide a prison cell in which international prisoners can be held until they are to be released".[66]

Irrespective of where international prisoners are housed, the international penal system fails to rehabilitate or prepare international prisoners for release. The jurisprudence of the international courts reveals an under-developed concept of rehabilitation. The notion is often used inter-changeably with good behaviour while in prison. This may be attributable to the fact that neither international nor national facilities have programmes that deal with international criminality.[67] Even international prisoners who committed offences which are criminalised under national law have been placed in national prisons that do not have programmes that address these particular crimes.[68] Moreover, international prisoners may not be able to access programmes relating to the crimes they committed due to the fact that they are foreign and will be deported at the end of their sentence. Poor allocation decisions and the lack of specialist programmes may result in international prisoners serving their entire sentence without addressing their crimes, criminal behaviour or their consequences.

As it currently operates, the international penal system does not provide international prisoners with the means necessary to demonstrate that they have worked towards the implicit goals for international punishment set out in the release criteria of the international courts. This deficiency may have serious implications for the legality of international imprisonment.[69]

Despite this, many international prisoners have been or will soon be released.[70] Good behaviour and a lack of disciplinary events during a

---

[63] Mulgrew, "The International Movement of Prisoners", 107–9.   [64] *Ibid.*, 125.
[65] Millership, Usk Prison, 27.09.2012.   [66] Wilkinson, UK, 10.10.2012.
[67] See Chapter 2, Section 4.3.1 and Chapter 3, Sections 7 and 9.
[68] See Chapter 2, Section 4.3.   [69] See Chapter 2, Section 4.3.1.
[70] For example, thirty-six ICTY convicted persons have been released after serving their sentences, and of the twenty-four currently serving their sentences, many are due for

term of imprisonment should not be so readily accepted by the international courts as proof that prisoners have been rehabilitated or are ready for release.[71] International prisoners may go from almost total confinement to total freedom. The transition back to real life after release may be difficult for those who have spent a long time serving a sentence in another country in restrictive conditions, with little social support or interaction. International criminals who have failed to address their crimes may still pose a threat to society. As release is unconditional and there is no parole system, international prisoners are released back into society without supervision or support.

In practice, the international penal system provides "confinement only ... no thought is given to progression or rehabilitation".[72] A penal system that simply warehouses individuals and does not address their criminality or potential to re-offend is an irresponsible and potentially dangerous system that fails the victims and the offender. This basic and regressive system fails to accord with contemporary standards on imprisonment and may have serious consequences for public safety and social stability. To ensure punishment is principled and progressive, international prisoners must be given feasible sentence plans which prioritise their rehabilitation and preparation for release from the outset of their incarceration.

Moreover, this sentence plan must be feasible: international prisoners must have access to appropriate programmes that address their crimes and enable them to demonstrate that they have worked towards the goals set out in their sentence plan. This is particularly important when release decisions are based on the attainment of pre-determined criteria.[73]

While it is evident that a penal system should aim to achieve penological goals, an international penal system should also contribute to the attainment of broader justice goals. International punishment should be implemented in a manner that contributes to the achievement of the international criminal justice and transitional justice goals of reconciliation and the maintenance of peace. Given the context in which the international penal system was created and operates, it seems futile to deal with the consequences of conflict and international crime without addressing their causes. To contribute to the attainment of

---

release soon. See ICTY Key Figures at www.icty.org/sections/TheCases/KeyFigures (08.08.2012).

[71] See Chapter 2, Section 3.2.3.1.   [72] Jensen, Skien Prison, 26.06.2012.
[73] See Chapter 2, Section 4.3.1. *James, Wells and Lee v. UK* (25119/09, 57715/09 and 57877/09) 18.09.2012.

broader justice objectives, international punishment should be implemented in a system that is accessible, meaningful and culturally relevant to the stakeholders of the justice process. The accommodation of the large range of stakeholders and subjects of the international criminal justice system will require the development of innovative methods, collaborations with external mechanisms or both. This more comprehensive approach to the management of international punishment will also require the adoption of new modalities.

4. The evolution of the international penal system

The majority of the courts in the international criminal justice system are temporary and will soon close. The RSCSL will take over the SCSL's mandate when the case against Mr Taylor has been finalised.[74] From July 2013, the MICT will supervise all sentences imposed by the ICTR and the ICTY.[75] Though agreements concluded with the UN on the enforcement of sentences will remain in force for the MICT,[76] (some explicitly contemplate the change-over to a different supervisory body[77]) it will be necessary to conduct a review to ensure that all agreements actually remain in force.[78] The designation and release procedures established by the MICT's statute, rules and practice directions are virtually identical to the applicable enforcement regime of the ad hoc Tribunals.[79] As persons convicted by the ICTY, ICTR and MICT must all now refer enforcement related issues and release requests to the MICT President,[80] there may be a greater degree of consistency in the treatment of these

---

[74] SCSL Ninth Annual Report, 38.   [75] Art. 25(2) MICTSt; Rule 128 MICT RPE.
[76] Arts. 1, 25 MICTSt. See also para. 4 SCRes 1966(2010).
[77] See Art. 13 ICTR–Senegal BEA.
[78] Para. 75, Assessment and Report of Judge Patrick Robinson, President of the International Tribunal for the Former Yugoslavia, provided to the Security Council pursuant to paragraph 6 of Security Council Resolution 1534(2004), covering the period from 15 May to 15 November 2011S/2011/716, 16.11.2011.
[79] See Arts. 25–6 MICTSt; Rules 127(A), 149–51 MICT RPE. The MICT's Practice Direction adds a new provision which explicitly recognises that the MICT President, in consultation with the Registrar, may withdraw a convicted person and transfer him to a different state to serve the remainder of his sentence if the enforcing state disagrees with or is unable to accept the President's decision not to allow the early release of an ICTR, ICTY or MICT prisoner. See para. 11 Practice Direction on the Procedure for the Determination of Applications for Pardon, Commutation of Sentence and Early Release of Persons Convicted by the ICTR, the ICTY or the Mechanism, MICT/3, 05.07.2012.
[80] See Art. 11(1)–(2) MICTSt.

THE EVOLUTION OF THE INTERNATIONAL PENAL SYSTEM 191

international prisoners. Despite the foreseen need to oversee the punishments imposed by the UN Tribunals until at least 2030,[81] the UNSC has only granted the MICT an initial four-year mandate that may be extended for subsequent two-year periods.[82] It is, therefore, unlikely that this mechanism will remain operational until the end of the sentences it is currently charged with overseeing. Indeed, it is envisaged that enforcement supervision will be handed over to another body,[83] although the modalities of this transfer of functions will only be decided by the UNSC upon the completion of the MICT's operations.[84] Any consistency of approach that may be gained by having a single body to make decisions in relation to enforcement issues risks being lost with the hand-over of responsibility to yet another body.

Perhaps more fundamentally, the MICT's legal framework demonstrates that the enforcement system first adopted by the ICTY has been replicated by each emerging court without question. Drumbl notes that the assumption that the distant and isolated incarceration of convicted persons is an appropriate punishment was so ingrained that there was little to no discussion about the modalities of enforcement at the Rome Conference.[85] Although there have been some developments in the legal frameworks governing enforcement and the introduction of new methods to implement international punishment, these are not sufficient to ensure that international punishment is implemented in a humane and effective manner. The replication of enforcement systems without appraisal or evaluation is resulting in the replication of a basic and regressive penal system.

Even though the international penal system is a relatively young system, it has implemented numerous sentences in full. With the world's permanent international criminal court handing down its first sentence in 2012, it is important to appraise the international penal system and learn lessons from the experiences of the temporary international courts. The time has come to reconceptualise the way in which international punishment is implemented. States and the international courts must step up to the challenge they have created and design and develop a humane and effective enforcement system.

---

[81] Para. 102 Residual Mechanism Report. [82] Preamble, para. 17 SCRes 1966(2010).
[83] Rule 128 MICT RPE. [84] Para. 18 SCRes 1966(2010).
[85] M. Drumbl, "Collective Violence and Individual Punishment: The Criminality of Mass Atrocity" (2005) 99(2) *Northwestern University Law Review* 539–610 at 576.

While it may not be fair to judge the international penal system on the basis of the "availability and efficacy"[86] of programmes provided by national prisons systems, nor is it fair to expect national prison systems to provide specialist programmes for a handful of international prisoners. As international criminal courts are ultimately responsible for international sanctions and prisoners, they should be responsible for devising and implementing international penal strategy. International penal strategy, with tailored policy objectives and modalities, can further standardise the treatment of international prisoners, provide support to enforcing institutions and ensure international punishment is implemented in a principled and progressive manner.

International courts delegate the task of implementing international punishment to cooperating states. The consensual nature of the decentralised system means that international court officials have to spend a great deal of time persuading states to say maybe. In reality, this system has not always produced sufficient or timely cooperation from states, resulting in the international courts having to rely on detention facilities operated or funded by the international courts. The ICC seems to have accepted the need to develop new models for the enforcement of international punishment beyond those established by its statute.

In 2009, the ASP acknowledged and encouraged the option of concluding trilateral agreements that would facilitate one State Party funding the enforcement of sentences of convicted persons on the territory of another State Party or include an international or regional organisation in the enforcement process.[87] This proposal was brought forward and elaborated on during the 2010 Review Conference in Kampala. Norway proposed an amendment[88] to Article 103(1)(a) of the Rome Statute to enable ICC sentences of imprisonment to be implemented in both national prisons and facilities "made available to the State by an international or regional organisation, arrangement or agency".[89] In addition to increasing the pool of potential enforcing states, this amendment aims to increase the number of prisoners that can be accommodated by cooperating states, to decrease the risk of isolation by placing prisoners in more socio-culturally familiar

---

[86] S. Beresford, "Unshackling the Paper Tiger: The Sentencing Practices of the ad hoc International Criminal Tribunals for the Former Yugoslavia and Rwanda" (2001) 1 *International Criminal Law Review* 33–90 at 45.
[87] See para. 16(i) Cooperation, ICC-ASP/8/Res.2, 26.11.2009.
[88] See Art. 121(1) ICCSt.
[89] Norway: Proposal of Amendment C.N.713.2009.TREATIES-4, 29.10.2009.

environments and improving possibilities for family visits, and to mobilise donors.[90] It is unclear from the proposal if the funding body would run the prison or simply provide funding for its operation.[91] What is clear is that, although states differed in relation to the degree of urgency surrounding the issue and the legal method that should be used to incorporate the requested changes to enforcement policy, the majority of states agreed that the issue was important and required further discussion.[92]

The proposal implicitly validates the need to move towards methods of enforcement that enable placement in the prisoners' region of origin, even if this move requires external financial input or the involvement of international bodies to guarantee appropriate material conditions and the secure custody of prisoners. This proposal also recognises that the international penal system cannot continue to operate solely on the basis of the traditional model of reliance on national prison systems to receive international prisoners.

The international penal system is unique in terms of the nature of the criminality it punishes, the prisoners it houses and its structure. The international criminal justice system does not have a Ministry of Justice, a prison system, penological expertise or a parole system. The resulting reliance on penal capacity provided by cooperating states has failed to ensure sufficient capacity or effective or humane punishment. National prison systems are not designed to deal with international criminals. Nor are international remand centres. Some potential enforcing states may not be able to provide adequate, safe or secure conditions, meaning international courts have to raise or spend money upgrading facilities. The current international penal system results in the unequal treatment of persons convicted by the same court, risks isolating international prisoners and fails to rehabilitate them or prepare them for release. It also fails to contribute to the attainment of any of the stated objectives of the international criminal justice system other than punishment. A penal system that involves little more than warehousing international prisoners in a network of facilities is basic and regressive. The current

---

[90] See Norway: Proposal of Amendment C.N.713.2009.TREATIES-4, 29.10.09; paras. 48–9 Report of the Bureau on the Review Conference 15.11.2009; para. 55 Annex II Report of the Working Group of the Review Conference, ICC-ASP/8/20.
[91] See para. 53 Report of the Bureau on the Review Conference, ICC-ASP/8/43 15.11.2009.
[92] See paras. 50–2 Report of the Bureau on the Review Conference 15.11.2009; paras. 55–8 Annex II Report of the Working Group of the Review Conference, ICC-ASP/8/20.

enforcement regime involves the separation of responsibility for the imposition of international punishment from responsibility for implementing it. It is perhaps time to re-connect these two stages of the international criminal justice process and increase central control over international punishment.

The creation of capacity or designated facilities funded by the international community for international prisoners within cooperating states and the direct implementation of international punishment by international courts in international facilities means that the international penal system has the precedence and practice necessary to create its own international prison system. The development of international penal policies and practices and the creation of international penal capacity will enable the international courts to become more self-sufficient in enforcement terms. An international prison system would ensure international control over international custodial sanctions, alleviate the isolation experienced by international prisoners and enhance the equality of treatment of international prisoners. Institutions that uphold human rights and accountability must ensure that their penal processes promote and protect the same ideals. An international prison system would also enable the international courts to implement international punishment in accordance with penal policies and practices designed to achieve international criminal justice objectives.

5. Conclusion

Part II examined the various systems that can be used to enforce international punishment. This chapter adopted a more systemic approach to the analysis of the international penal system and highlighted a number of fundamental problems with its structure and operations. To remedy these problems and ensure the development of an effective and humane penal system, the international courts must take a more active role in the enforcement process. International courts must devise and help to implement specifically tailored international penal policies and practices, either in enforcing states or their own international prisons. The remainder of this book looks at how the international criminal justice system can develop its international penal strategy and structure.

PART III

Strategy: developing and operationalising international penal strategy

6

International penal policy

As the international courts are ultimately responsible for both the welfare of international prisoners and the sentences they are serving, international penal policy should be developed by the international courts. Rather than continue to rely on an uneasy conflation of the penal goals of international and national prison systems, international punishment should be implemented in accordance with a uniform strategy. International penal policy should ensure that sentences are implemented in a principled and progressive manner that facilitates the achievement of penological and broader justice objectives. This chapter discusses the need for international penal policy, proposes resocialisation as the normative foundation for its development and outlines a theoretical framework for the incorporation of a resocialisation-focused policy within the currently retributive justice process.

1. The need for international penal policy

International penal policy should address aspects of international punishment that are not being dealt with at present. At a basic level, international penal policy is needed to ensure that international punishment is implemented in a manner that seeks to prevent the aggravation of the sentences imposed and facilitates the courts' responsibility to provide enforcing states with support.

1.1 Preventing the aggravation of international punishment

If the suffering caused by imprisonment goes beyond what retribution intended, it becomes disproportionate, excessive and solely punitive.[1] Yet international jurisprudence clearly states that international custodial

---

[1] N. Walker, *Why Punish?* (1991), 109; R. Matthews, "The Myth of Punitiveness" (2005) 9(2) *Theoretical Criminology* 175 at 179.

sanctions "must not be aggravated by the conditions of its enforcement".[2] International punishment, as it is currently implemented, risks aggravating the sentence imposed. Prisoners are housed far from their homes, families and social support networks, in culturally unfamiliar surroundings.[3] As a group, they have characteristics which differentiate them from national prison populations. Most international prisoners are older than national prisoners.[4] Consequently, they tend to have fewer coping mechanisms to deal with prison life[5] and suffer from age-related health problems. Yet, national prison systems are largely designed for young men and tend not to cater for the needs of "greying" or infirm inmates.[6] International prisoners that are past retirement age do not have to attend work or education programmes and therefore risk marginalisation and long sentences filled with nothing but boredom.[7]

International prisoners also experience many of the problems faced by other non-national prisoners. Many national prison systems recognise the distinct needs of foreign prisoners and attempt to put positive measures in place to offset the disadvantages of being housed far from home and to equalise their treatment with that of national prisoners.[8] But international prisoners can be distinguished as a specific subcategory of foreign national prisoner. Foreign national prisoners committed crimes in the state in which they are incarcerated, whereas international prisoners committed a crime in one state, were transferred to another to stand trial and transferred to a third state, often without their consent, to serve their terms of imprisonment. The responsibility for mitigating the aggravating effects of imprisonment in a foreign country must therefore be shared by the court that transferred the prisoner. While the international courts may claim that they have no other option due to the structure of the enforcement system, contemporary standards place a duty on authorities to alleviate such suffering.[9]

---

[2] Para. 74 *Erdemović* (Judgment) IT-96-22-T, 29.11.1996. See also Rule 57 UNSMR; Rule 102(2) EPR.
[3] Para. A.1(6) MDP, 178.
[4] In 2008, for example, the average UNDF detainee was fifty-seven and the average UNDU detainee was fifty-five (the youngest was thirty-eight and the eldest seventy-one).
[5] Paras. A.1(6), (8) MDP, 178–9.
[6] See E. Crawley and R. Sparks, "Older Men in Prison: Survival, Coping and Identity" in A. Liebling and S. Maruna (eds.), *The Effects of Imprisonment* (2005), 343–4.
[7] Johansson, Hinseberg Prison, 07.10.2008.
[8] See UN Recommendations on the Treatment of Foreign Prisoners 1985; Foreign Prisoners COE Rec(84)12; Rules 37–8 EPR.
[9] See Rules 57, 60(1) UNSMR; Rules 4, 5, 102(2) EPR.

At present, the international courts are not assisting enforcing states to do so.

1.2 International courts' support role

Until recently, states had no experience of enforcing international sentences of imprisonment. Yet, the international courts do not provide enforcing states with guidance on the manner in which these sentences should be implemented or the goals they should achieve. Although the enforcement agreements suggest that the courts should provide enforcing states with support, the courts have a very low level of engagement with the penal process. Despite the bilateral agreement provisions that state that the international courts and enforcing states should consult with each other on all matters relating to enforcement,[10] there is no ongoing dialogue in practice. Communication is typically ad hoc, and deals with specific issues relating to particular individuals. Yet, it is clear that enforcing states require more support. At a Council of Europe Council on Penological Cooperation meeting, a Committee Member requested that the Council discuss the issue of how to deal with international prisoners in national prison systems.[11] At the local or institutional level, requests have been made for more information and guidance on procedures. More specifically they have requested real support on a range of matters, including the provision of risk and needs assessments conducted prior to the international prisoner's transfer, support for the prisoners during their initial adjustment period, assistance with programmes to deal with their particular crimes and situation and information about and links with relevant bodies for post-release support for such prisoners.[12] A coherent international penal policy would enable the courts to provide enforcing states with advice on how to respond to critical situations and, more generally, how to plan and implement international sentences of imprisonment.

1.2.1 Critical situation reaction

At present, communication between the international courts and enforcing institutions is of a trouble-shooting nature. As problems are only

---

[10] See for example Art. 7(2) ICTR–Senegal BEA; Art. 9(3) ICC–Serbia BEA.
[11] Dr Koeck, COE Council for Penological Cooperation (PC-CP) Second Plenary Meeting, Strasbourg, 28.03.2012.
[12] Mollan, Trondheim Prison, 27.06.2012.

dealt with as they arise, there is often uncertainty at times when rapid decision-making is essential. To ensure clarity and effectiveness, protocols should be devised that outline procedures to follow in critical situations, such as escape, hunger-strike or death, particularly as the division of responsibility between the international court and enforcing state may be unclear in these circumstances.

For instance, prior to the Rome Statute,[13] there was no explicit procedure to follow in the event of the escape of an international prisoner, beyond an obligation to inform the court.[14] Yet, Mr Stanković's escape in Bosnia-Herzegovina highlighted the need to ensure that clear and urgent procedures are in place for the issuance of international arrest warrants and for enforcing state authorities to have in place the documentation required by Interpol to do so.[15] A pre-determined procedure would ensure that these necessary reactive measures can be put in place immediately. The ICC's bilateral enforcement agreements go some way towards achieving this but would benefit from more detail.[16]

The ICTY's UNDU has demonstrated that it is possible to produce a policy document that deals with hunger-strikes.[17] The international penal system should have a similar protocol which outlines which international recommendations should be used to deal with the situation, and which institution holds the balance of power in decisions relating to the treatment of international prisoners in life-threatening situations. It is also important for procedures to be put in place to deal with the death or suicide of an international prisoner. In addition to investigatory and autopsy procedures, there are practical decisions in relation to burial and the repatriation of the body that must be made in accordance with the wishes of the prisoners' family within a relatively short time-frame.

When an ICTY prisoner died in Sweden, there was a great deal of confusion about whether the enforcing state or the ICTY was responsible for arranging and paying for the repatriation of the body, even though this was covered in the enforcement agreement.[18] This case also highlighted the difficulties national authorities may face when trying to locate a prisoner's family if they have protected status.[19] This confusion can be

---

[13] See Art. 111 ICCSt; Rule 225(1)-(4) ICC RPE.   [14] Art. 7(1) ICTY/ ICTR BEAs.
[15] OSCE Sixth Report in the Case of Convicted Person Radovan Stanković Transferred to the State Court pursuant to Rule 11bis 2007, 10–11.
[16] Art. 13 ICC–Belgium BEA; Art. 12 ICC–Finland/Serbia BEAs, Art. 7 ICC–Mali BEA.
[17] See Voluntary Protest Fasts – Information for Detainees.
[18] Isaksson, Sweden, 07.10.2008.   [19] Ibid.

overcome by access to pre-determined protocols. Such protocols, however, will only provide guidance in the event of particular and foreseen situations. They cannot provide national prisons with guidance on how to create or implement a sentence plan for international prisoners.

1.2.2 International sentence planning

Sentence plans should address the rehabilitative and reintegrative needs of prisoners. National prisons are ill-equipped to do so in relation to international prisoners due to their distinct characteristics, the uniqueness of international crime and the structure of the international enforcement system. Unlike many national prisoners, the majority of international prisoners are not "habitual criminals".[20] Many international prisoners were former military, political, religious and community leaders, with a higher than average intellect.[21] After their conviction, international prisoners are placed in the unique position of being classified as international criminals, a newly constructed and serious tier of criminality.[22] Yet during their time in prison, international prisoners tend to have little access to work and rehabilitation programmes. International prisoners may not have the language skills necessary to participate in national programmes and their participation may not be prioritised due to the high likelihood that they will be deported. Moreover, national programmes do not address the specificities of international crime. In addition to the fact that the rehabilitative needs of international prisoners are not catered for, national prison programmes cannot prepare international prisoners for release or re-entry to society.[23] A lack of access to programmes that enable prisoners to work toward sentence plan objectives or criteria for release may jeopardise the legality of continued detention.[24] Prisons should ensure that prisoners have opportunities to gain skills and create social structures that will facilitate their transition from prison to life in society.[25] Resettlement facilitation should relate to the prisoner's linguistic, cultural and social context.[26] As international prisoners are normally foreigners that will be

---

[20] McFadden, UNDU, 21.08.2007; para. A.1(6) MDP, 178.
[21] See para. 2.6.3 Independent Audit of the Detention Unit at the ICTY, 2006; para. A.1(6) MDP, 178.
[22] See M. Penrose, "No Badges, No Bars: A Conspicuous Oversight in the Development of an International Criminal Court" (2003) 38(3) *Texas International Law Journal* 621-42 at 642.
[23] See Chapter 2, Section 4.3 and Chapter 5, Section 3. [24] See Chapter 2, Section 4.3.1
[25] Rule 33(3) EPR. [26] See Foreign Prisoners COE Rec (1984)12.

deported at the end of their sentences, national programmes cannot adequately meet these requirements. Further, international prisoners are less likely to be able to benefit from temporary release, external placements or be moved to lower security prisons towards the end of their sentence.[27] As international prisoners are released unconditionally, they should also have access to post-release support agencies that provide assistance with readjustment and employment.[28] While Van Zyl Smit and Snacken acknowledge that this continuity of care is more difficult to provide for foreign national prisoners, they argue that "all reasonable steps should be taken to establish the necessary links".[29] At present, it seems that neither the international courts nor enforcing states make any contact with agencies in the state to which the prisoner will be deported. Even if contact was made, it is unclear what services could or should be provided. The current enforcement system is in danger of simply warehousing international criminals in foreign prisons until their release date, without any preparation for life in society. This has consequences not only for the prisoner and his family, but also victims, their families and communities, and society more generally.

1.3 International penal policy

The international status of the sanctions and the responsibility of the international courts for the welfare of international prisoners demand that the support and supervisory roles of the international courts are regarded as more than passive responsibilities only activated upon the receipt of a negative report from inspecting bodies, a complaint from an international prisoner or notification from an enforcing state of eligibility for release. The international courts should set out protocols for dealing with foreseeable events and key principles for the implementation of international sentences. In so doing, the courts can fulfil their support obligations to enforcing states, ensure a higher degree of consistency in the treatment for international prisoners, protect the international status of international punishment and achieve both penological and international criminal justice goals.

---

[27] See Chapter 2, Section 4.2.
[28] Rule 107(3)–(5) EPR; paras. 12, 14 Conditional Release (Parole) COE Rec (2003)22.
[29] D. Van Zyl Smit and S. Snacken, *Principles of European Prison Law and Policy: Penology and Human Rights* (2009), 341.

2. A normative foundation for international penal policy

Effective regimes require a principled basis to guide decision-making and the development of practice; "without an account of what we hope to accomplish in punishing offenders we cannot determine what to do with or to them".[30] Yet, the international criminal justice system does not currently have a stated penological goal to govern the implementation of international punishment. As the courts' statutes and regulatory documents do not provide a penal goal, it is necessary to look at the political justifications for the establishment of international criminal courts and the judicial explanations for the imposition of international custodial sanctions to determine what would be an appropriate administrative principle for the implementation of international punishment.

2.1 Justifications for the establishment of international criminal courts

The establishment of the international criminal courts to prosecute and punish international criminals represented the crystallisation of the international vows that international crime would no longer be tolerated.[31] International crime would now be responded to by judicial institutions authorised to impose individual criminal liability and custodial sanctions on those bearing greatest responsibility. These new courts were commissioned to perform anti-impunity and deterrent functions.[32] The international criminal justice process has also been heralded as a means to uphold the rule of international law,[33] to restore and maintain both international[34] and national[35] peace and security and as having the potential to contribute to national reconciliation.[36]

2.2 Justifications for the imposition of international custodial sanctions

The statutes and rules of the international courts are silent as to the purposes of punishment, leaving the development of penal rationales to

---

[30] R. C. Lippke, *Rethinking Imprisonment* (2007), 2.
[31] SCRes 827(1993); SCRes 955(1994); Preamble ICCSt.   [32] See Preamble ICCSt.
[33] See the Spanish and Brazilian Statements, UNSC 3453rd Meeting, 08.11.1994.
[34] See the French, Spanish and Hungarian Statements, UNSC 3175th Meeting, 22.02.1998 and the Pakistani, Russian and French Statements, UNSC 3453rd Meeting, 08.11.1994.
[35] See Art. 1(1) SCSLSt.   [36] SCRes 955(1994).

the discretion of the judiciary. An analysis of international sentencing jurisprudence reveals that deterrence and retribution are the main sentencing objectives of the international criminal justice system.[37]

A general *deterrence* objective seeks "to dissuade for good those who will be tempted in the future to perpetrate such atrocities by showing them that the international community is no longer willing to tolerate serious violations".[38] In other words, "persons who believe themselves to be beyond the reach of international criminal law must be warned that they have to abide by [it] ... or face prosecution".[39] Although no criminal justice system can be expected to deter crime completely, the international criminal justice system seems even less able to do so. The defiant non-cooperation of some states with, and the low number of cases brought before, the international courts, may lead to a perception among potential perpetrators that prosecution is a marginal risk. Although it is extremely difficult to verify the deterrent effect of the threat or imposition of international punishment empirically,[40] it seems that the threat of prosecution does not result in the cessation of atrocities.[41] The Allies' warnings of prosecutions in 1941 did little to prevent the commission of atrocities during the Second World War.[42] The ICTY's work did little to deter atrocities in Srebrenica and Kosovo. Similarly, the operation of the ICTR and ICC has not deterred the commission of international crimes in Darfur or the DRC.[43] The causes and nature of mass atrocities may mean that potential international criminals have a different perpetrator rationality and therefore a different approach to the cost-benefit analysis that controls behaviour.[44] Atrocities may provide a military benefit that outweighs a distant and

---

[37] See para. 2594 *Gotovina et al.* (Judgment)(Vol.2) IT-06-90-T, 15.04.2011; para. 1794 *Perišić* (Judgment) IT-04-81-T, 06.09.2011; para. 13 *Taylor* (Judgment) SCSL-03-01-T, 30.05.2012.

[38] Para. 2 *Kayishema, Ruzindara* (Judgment) ICTR-95-1-T, 21.05.1999.

[39] Para. 34 *Zelenović* (Judgment) IT-96-23/2-S, 04.04.2007.

[40] See M. Drumbl, *Atrocity, Punishment and International Law* (2007), 16; R. Henham, *Punishment and Process in International Criminal Trials*, (2005), 141; D. Gallón, "The ICC and the Challenge of Deterrence" in Shelton (ed.), *International Crimes, Peace and Human Rights: The Role of the ICC* (2000).

[41] M. Damaška, "What is the Point of International Criminal Justice?" (2008) 83 *Chicago-Kent Law Review* 329–65 at 339.

[42] D. Wippman, "Atrocities, Deterrence, and the Limits of International Justice" (1999) 23 *Fordham International Law Journal* 473–88 at 474.

[43] See K. Moghalu, *Rwanda's Genocide: The Politics of Global Justice* (2005), 202–3.

[44] Drumbl, *Atrocity, Punishment and International Law*, 17.

slight risk of prosecution.[45] The threat of prosecution may simply result in increased efforts to conceal evidence and avoid detection.[46]

As a utilitarian objective, general deterrence may result in unfair and repressive sentences.[47] In fragile post-conflict environments, perceptions of harsh treatment may adversely affect state-building exercises.[48] For these reasons, general deterrence has not been accorded "undue prominence"[49] as an international sentence determining factor. As the possibility of an international criminal ever being faced with the opportunity to commit the same offence again is "so remote as to render its consideration in this way unreasonable and unfair",[50] neither has the objective of specific deterrence.[51]

Given the gravity of the crimes within the courts' jurisdictions, **retribution** is often deemed to be the dominant sentencing objective of the international criminal justice system. Even when other rationales for punishment are forwarded, the courts tend to "synthesise and contextualise their discussions of appropriate punishment objectives within a predominantly retributive paradigm".[52] Retribution's expressive function conveys indignation over the heinous nature of the atrocities, stigmatising the act.[53] The international courts' retributive focus prioritises the pursuit of justice over the prevention of crime.[54] Unlike deterrence, retribution does not allow for the imposition of repressive sentences. Just deserts doctrine dictates that a sentence must be proportionate to the culpability of the offender and the gravity of the criminal act,[55] taking into account both mitigating and aggravating factors. By equating the sanction with the crime committed, the principle of proportionality aims to insulate the objective from accusations of being

---

[45] D. Chuter, *War Crimes: Confronting Atrocity in the Modern World* (2003), 272, 274; Wippman, "Atrocities, Deterrence and the Limits of International Justice", 476.
[46] Wippman, "Atrocities, Deterrence and the Limits of International Justice", 480.
[47] Para. 840 *Kunarac, Kovač, Vuković* (Judgment) IT-96-23/1-T, 22.02.2001.
[48] See para. 95 *Fofana, Kondewa* (Judgment) SCSL-04-14-J, 09.10.2007.
[49] See para. 805 *Krajišnik* (Appeal Judgment) IT-00-39-A, 17.03.2009.
[50] Para. 840 *Kunarac, Kovač, Vuković* (Judgment) IT-96-23/1-T, 22.02.2001.
[51] Para. 31 *Zelenović* (Judgment) IT-96-23/2-S, 04.04.2007.
[52] Henham, *Punishment and Process in International Criminal Trials*, 129.
[53] Paras. 64–5 *Erdemović* (Judgment) IT-96-22-T, 29.11.1996.
[54] S. Beresford, "Unshackling the Paper Tiger: The Sentencing Practices of the International Criminal Tribunals for the Former Yugoslavia and Rwanda" (2001) 1 *International Criminal Law Review* 33–90 at 40.
[55] Para. 65 *Erdemović* (Judgment) IT-96-22-T, 29.11.1996.

vengeful.[56] However, it may not be possible to achieve just deserts in the context of international crimes as the punishments imposed are generally the same as those imposed in national courts for single acts of serious crime.[57] Moreover, retributive rhetoric simply demands that the international community "ought to punish as it ought to punish".[58] This circular justification is therefore conceptually lacking as it represents no more than a conflation of a sentence determining factor with the moral justification for establishing the judicial institution in the first place.

Incapacitation has also been cited. However, it does not seem conceivable that it could operate as a sentencing factor given the difficulties associated with proving that first time offenders in the international context have the propensity to commit such acts again[59] and the foreseeable unwillingness of many enforcing states to enforce indeterminate sentences of this nature. Sentencing judgments have also discussed the need to protect society, uphold the rule of law, to create awareness of and trust in international legal order, to end impunity, to assist reconciliation and to restore peace.[60]

Overall, sentencing jurisprudence demonstrates a lack of clarity about the purposes of sentencing[61] and, as a consequence, this subject remains "a relatively undeveloped aspect of international criminal law".[62] It seems as though domestic sentencing objectives have been transplanted without consideration of their appropriateness in the international criminal justice context.[63] Indeed, Henham argues that the vaguely

---

[56] See para. 140 *M. Nikolić* (Judgment) IT-94-2-S, 18.12.2003; para. 1075 *Kordić, Čerkez* (Appeal Judgment) IT-95-14/2-A, 17.12.2004; para. 804 *Krajišnik* (Appeal Judgment) IT-00-39-A, 17.03.2009; para. 15 *Brima, Kamara, Kanu* (Judgment) SCSL-04-16-T, 19.07.2007.
[57] Drumbl, *Atrocity, Punishment and International Law* 15.
[58] N. Lacey, *State Punishment; Political Principles and Community Values* (1988), 17.
[59] Para. 843 *Kunarac, Kovač, Vuković* (Judgment) IT-96-23-T & IT-96-23/1-T, 22.02.2001.
[60] Para. 139 *Dragan Nikolić* (Judgment) IT-94-2-S, 18.12.03; para. 848 *Kupreškić et al.* (Judgment) IT-95-16-T, 14.01.2000; para. 455 *Rutaganda* (Judgment) ICTR-96-3-T, 06.12.1999; para. 762 *Blaškić* (Judgment) IT-95-14-T, 03.03.2000; para. 29 *Fofana, Kondewa* (Judgment) SCSL-04-14-J, 09.10.2007; para. 93 *M. Nikolić* (Judgment) IT-02/60/I-S, 02.12.03; para. 882 *Ntakirutimana* (Judgment) ICTR-96-10&ICTR-96-17-T, 21.2.2003; paras. 753–4 *Kamuhanda* (Judgment) ICTR-99-54-T, 22.01.2004; paras. 12, 16 *Taylor* (Judgment) SCSL-03-01-T, 30.05.2012.
[61] S. D'Ascoli, *Sentencing in International Criminal Law: The UN ad hoc Tribunals and Future Perspectives for the ICC* (2011), 33–4, 38.
[62] R. Cryer et al., *An Introduction to International Criminal Law and Procedure*, 2nd edn., (2010), 496.
[63] Damaška, "What is the Point of International Criminal Justice?", 339; D'Ascoli, *Sentencing in International Criminal Law*, 140; Henham, *Punishment and Process in International Criminal Trials*, 129.

articulated justifications for international punishment are simply *ex post facto* rationalisations designed for international consumption.[64]

Disappointingly, reliance on vague and implicit objectives has continued at the ICC. The Rome Statute is devoid of any reference to a purpose to govern the imposition of international punishment. In its first sentencing judgment, the Chamber simply referred to the Rome Statute's preambular reference to ending impunity by punishing serious crimes of concern to the international community as a whole.[65] This failure to explicitly state the purposes for which international punishment is imposed is not acceptable from the world's only permanent criminal court.

2.3 A justification for the implementation of international custodial sanctions?

To date, the focus has been on the arrest, trial and conviction of international criminals, and not on how to punish them. Despite the many, often lengthy sentences that have been imposed, the international courts have not elaborated on which rationales should govern the implementation of international punishment. International jurisprudence discusses sentences of imprisonment as though they are an end in themselves, considering how objectives might be achieved solely through the imposition of a penal sanction at a particular point in time. It does not discuss what goals should or could be achieved by international punishment. It is necessary to assign a purpose to the implementation of international punishment to demonstrate the goals it is meant to achieve and to establish the benchmark against which it is to be evaluated.[66] International penal strategy requires a normative backbone that can inform the development of international penal policy and practice.

The dominant sentencing objectives of the international criminal courts are not suitable guides for the implementation of international punishment. Deterrence is unsuitable as it may result in unacceptably harsh regimes and disproportionately long sentences. International standards and jurisprudence explicitly state that the conditions of enforcement must not aggravate the sentence imposed.[67] While retribution appears to be the dominant

---

[64] Henham, *Punishment and Process in International Criminal Trials*, 127.
[65] Para. 92 *Lubanga* (Sentence) ICC-01/04-01/06, 10.07.2012.
[66] D'Ascoli, *Sentencing in International Criminal Law*, 32–3.
[67] Rule 57 UNSMR; Rule 102(2) EPR; para. 74 *Erdemović* (Judgment) IT-96-22-T, 29.11.1996.

sentencing objective, retributive rhetoric neglects to consider how international criminal justice objectives might be achieved through or during the implementation of custodial sanctions and fails to provide any insight into how an international sentence of imprisonment should be implemented.

Lippke has argued that retribution is a suitable guide for penal policy. He claims the objective not only limits the duration of the sanction but also the harshness of the punishment imposed. He argues that retributive theory demands that imprisonment should be implemented in a manner that does not erode a prisoner's capacity for morally responsible citizenship.[68] Prisons should therefore offer the least restrictive regimes and reasonably humane conditions.[69] This involves minimum conditions, the fair and consistent enforcement of rules, respect for the prisoner's moral agency and autonomy, and the provision of purposive and constructive activities.[70] In essence, prison regimes should be tailored with the specific goal of ensuring that offenders are capable of re-entering society as productive and law-abiding citizens.[71] Retributive constraints on legal punishment prevent the operation of regimes that impose "a kind of living death on prisoners",[72] as this burden greatly exceeds any potential crime reduction benefits.[73]

Yet it would appear that the international criminal justice system's retributive rhetoric has not resulted in purposive punishment that prepares prisoners for life upon release, but simply creates a punitive regime that warehouses prisoners in foreign facilities. The other objectives cited in international sentencing judgments also fail to provide clues to a suitable penological goal. In fact, they appear to be little more than attempts to align sentencing policy with the justifications for establishing the courts in the first place. International penal policy must be based on an objective that can inform international sentence planning and the development of modalities for its implementation.

3. Rehabilitation

While rehabilitation has been acknowledged as both a national and international purpose for punishment,[74] the international judiciary feel

---

[68] Lippke, *Rethinking Imprisonment*, 13, 111.   [69] *Ibid.*, 104–5.   [70] *Ibid.*, 112–16.
[71] *Ibid.*, 117.   [72] *Ibid.*, 122.   [73] *Ibid.*, 122–3.
[74] Para. 33 *Serugendo* (Judgment) ICTR-2005-84-I, 12.2006.2006; para. 11 *Rugambarara* (Judgment) ICTR-00-59-T, 16.11.2007; para. 15 *Taylor* (Judgment) SCSL-03-01-T, 30.05.2012.

it is less important than others and accordingly, it is not given a predominant role or undue weight.[75] Whether or not rehabilitation has a role to play in international sentencing as a sentence determining or mitigating factor,[76] it should be recognised as an important objective for the enforcement of international punishment. Rehabilitation provides a workable and developed penological goal. This goal provides a similar regime and advocates the same respect for moral agency as Lippke's retributive goal for punishment. Unlike Lippke's interpretation of retribution, however, rehabilitative theory and practice has been developed in domestic prison systems for over half a century, following its adoption as the objective of choice in international and regional human rights law and penal standards. In addition to providing a workable penological goal for the development of international penal policy, rehabilitation also provides a normative and legal link that binds all the constituent elements of the international penal system.

3.1 The normative common denominator of the international penal system

As subsidiary bodies of the UN Security Council, the Tribunals are bound by the UN goals of humanising criminal justice and protecting human rights.[77] The SCSL, though an independent court, was created through an agreement between the UN and the Sierra Leonean Government and therefore also adheres to the principles of its co-founding organisation. The Rome Statute explicitly states that the ICC reaffirms the purposes and principles of the UN Charter.[78] Consequently, all the judicial institutions of the international criminal justice system must respect human rights principles.

While these courts have not ratified any human rights treaties, international jurisprudence refers to the relevance of human rights law and supra-national penal standards for the implementation of international custodial sanctions.[79] The centrality of rights and penal standards have

---

[75] Para. 806 *Delalić et al.* (Appeal Judgment) IT-96-21-A, 20.02.2001; para. 1092 *Brđanin* (Judgment) IT-99-36-T, 01.09.2004; para. 35 *Zelenović* (Judgment) IT-96-23/2-S, 04.04.2007; para. 443 *Bikinki* (Judgment) ICTR-01-72-T, 02.12.2008.
[76] See F. P. King and A. La Rosa, "Penalties under the ICC Statute" in F. Lattanzi and W. Schabas (eds.), *Essays on the Rome Statute of the International Criminal Court* (1999), 311–38 at 332; para. 144 *Bisengimana* (Judgment) ICTR-00-60-T, 13.04.2006.
[77] See Preamble UNBP and Chapter 10, Section 2.1.   [78] See Preamble ICCSt.
[79] See para. 74 *Erdemović* (Judgment) IT-96-22-T, 29.11.1996.

also been acknowledged in the enforcement agreements, which stipulate that contemporary international standards on the treatment of persons deprived of their liberty shall govern the enforcement of international sentences.[80] In particular, the UN soft law in this field (UNSMR, UNBP, UNBOP) is mentioned.[81] The Rome Statute, for the first time, introduces a statutory obligation that directs states to enforce sentences in conditions of imprisonment that are consistent with "widely accepted international treaty standards governing treatment of prisoners".[82] So despite the variations between the penological policies and practices of enforcing institutions, international human rights law and derivative penal standards represent the common denominator for the enforcement of international sentences of imprisonment.

Human rights law is often viewed as an individualistic discourse that protects the "ethical primacy of the individual".[83] However, in relation to prisoners' rights, it is often addressed to prison authorities, discussing how prisons should be managed and the objectives prison regimes should attain. The ICCPR is one of the most widely ratified human rights treaties. Its direction that prisoners must be treated with respect for their dignity has been interpreted to mean that purely retributory penitentiary systems are insufficient.[84] Moreover, Article 10(3) explicitly places a positive duty on states to provide prison regimes that strive for the reformation and social rehabilitation of prisoners.[85] The UN standards, referred to in the enforcement agreements, echo this duty to facilitate the social rehabilitation of offenders.[86] These more detailed rules are used as a guide to interpret this ICCPR direction.[87]

Indeed, the international courts appear to have implicitly adopted rehabilitation as a penological objective. Their rules set out that prisoners must demonstrate their rehabilitation and that this is one of the factors that will be considered by the President or Review Panel of the court when deciding if it is appropriate to grant release.[88]

Consequently, the penological goal of rehabilitation normatively binds the international penal system, both horizontally and vertically. The mode of creation of the courts situates them in an environment of respect for human rights law on the treatment of persons deprived of

---

[80] See Chapter 2, Section 3.1. [81] Ibid. [82] Art. 106(1)–(2) ICCSt.
[83] C.A. Gearty, *Principles of Human Rights Adjudication* (2004), 92.
[84] See para. 10 HRC General Comment 21. [85] Art. 10(3) ICCPR.
[86] See Rules 64–5, 80 UNSMR. [87] See para. 5 HRC General Comment 21.
[88] Rule 125 ICTY RPE; Rule 126 ICTR RPE; Rule 223 ICC RPE.

their liberty. The courts in turn impose a rights-based policy on cooperating states, explicitly mentioning the relevance of international standards in this field. These penal standards form the benchmarks used by the courts in the exercise of their supervisory role over the national implementation of international sentences. As all the states involved in the incarceration of international prisoners have ratified the ICCPR without reservation to Article 10(3)'s reference to the goal of social rehabilitation,[89] their penal systems share an obligation to provide rehabilitative penal systems. Coming full circle, all of the enforcing states of the international penal system were direct or indirect co-founders of the international criminal justice system. All the enforcing states for the UN Tribunals and the SCSL are members of the UN and all ICC enforcing states are party to the Rome Statute. Moreover, the international courts consider whether an international prisoner has demonstrated signs of rehabilitation when deciding whether or not to grant release.

3.2 A theoretical framework for the incorporation of a rehabilitative penal policy within a retributive justice process

Rehabilitation has been identified as the normative basis for international penal policy. Yet retribution remains a valid sentencing objective for the international criminal justice system. In addition to the morally intuitive need to respond to acts that are repugnant to the conscience of mankind,[90] there is a growing consensus that amnesty is not appropriate in relation to international crime.[91] Retributive punishment is "a relevant and important consideration" given the serious nature of the international crimes.[92] It is therefore necessary to design a theoretical

---

[89] Australia, Austria, Belgium, Denmark, Finland, Iceland, Ireland, Netherlands, New Zealand, Norway, Samao, Sweden, Trinidad and Tobago, UK and US have entered reservations to Art. 10(3) ICCPR, but only in relation to the second paragraph of the article that refers to the segregation of juveniles from adults.

[90] See Walker, *Why Punish?* 81; L. Walgrave, "Integrating Criminal Justice and Restorative Justice" in G. Johnstone and D. W. Van Ness (eds.), *Handbook of Restorative Justice* (2007), 568.

[91] The East Timor Community Reconciliation Scheme ruled out amnesties for serious crimes and the SCSL was established, in part, due to the amnesty granted in the Lomé Peace Agreement. See C. Stahn, "Accommodating Individual Criminal Responsibility and National Reconciliation: The UN Truth Commission for East Timor" (2001) 95 *American Journal International Law* 952–66 at 955; W. Schabas, "The Relationship Between Truth Commission and International Courts: The Case of Sierra Leone" (2003) 25 *Human Rights Quarterly* 1035–66 at 1036–8.

[92] Para. 848 *Kupreškić et al.* (Judgment) IT-95-16-T, 14.01.2000.

framework that enables the incorporation of rehabilitative penal policy into a criminal justice process dominated by retributive rhetoric.

The need for prison law and prison systems to be relatively autonomous from criminal law and criminal justice systems has become increasingly recognised in both national law and academic works.[93] Whereas "the sentencing decision is primarily directed towards the past ... the implementation of the prison sentence must ... be oriented towards the future and the prison regime must be organised accordingly".[94] By conceptually distinguishing international sentencing objectives used to justify the imposition of international custodial sanctions from penal objectives for the implementation of international sentences of imprisonment, different justifications can be put forward. By sequentially positioning justifications governing different stages of progress through the international criminal justice system, a retributive rationale for the imposition of international sentences can be retained while paving the way for the introduction of a rehabilitation goal for the implementation of international punishment.

This conceptual division shown in Figure 1 is in fact inherent in the structure of the decentralised and localised enforcement systems:[95] the international courts are responsible for the imposition of sanctions, whereas enforcing states are responsible for their day-to-day implementation. Furthermore, this theoretical framework has received implicit judicial approval. The international courts acknowledge that while rehabilitation may not be a primary sentencing objective for the international criminal justice system,[96] it may for national judiciaries.[97] Moreover, the international courts acknowledge that rehabilitation is a valid goal for the enforcement of sentences of imprisonment in national prison systems.[98] The rules of the courts demand a consideration of a prisoner's demonstration of rehabilitation during the release decision-making

---

[93] See L. Lazarus, "Conceptions of Liberty Deprivation" (2006) 69(5) *Modern Law Review* 738–69 at 742–3; Van Zyl Smit and Snacken, *Principles of European Prison Law and Policy* 76, 79–80.

[94] Van Zyl Smit and Snacken, *Principles of European Prison Law and Policy*, 79.

[95] See C. Kreß and G. Sluiter, "Imprisonment" in A. Cassese *et al.* (eds.), *The Rome Statute of the International Criminal Court: A Commentary*, Vol. II (2002), 1752.

[96] Para. 806 *Delalić et al.* (Appeal Judgment) IT-96-21-A, 20.02.2001.

[97] See para. 28 *Fofana and Kondewa* (Judgment) SCSL-04-14-J, 09.10.2007; para. 17 *Brima, Kamara, Kanu* (Judgment) SCSL-04-16-T, 19.07.2007.

[98] See para. 844 *Kunarac, Kovač, Vuković* (Judgment) IT-96-23-T & IT-96-23/1-T 22.02.2001; para. 66 *Erdemović* (Judgment) IT-96-22-T, 29.11.1996; para. 291 *Furundžija* (Judgment) IT-95-17/1, 10.12.1998.

IMPOSITION (Justification for Sanction)	IMPLEMENTATION (Justification for the Penal Regime)
Retribution	Rehabilitation

Figure 1. A Divisible Concept of Punishment

process.[99] This appears to indicate that rehabilitation is an important and legitimate objective for the execution phase of international punishment.[100]

By separating and distinguishing sentencing objectives from enforcement objectives, the international criminal courts can fulfil their core role of prosecuting those liable for international crimes,[101] while also ensuring that the sentences they impose can be implemented in a manner that contributes towards the rehabilitation and reintegration of offenders.

3.3 Reconceptualising rehabilitation for the international penal system

Solely retributory penal systems may violate international human rights law.[102] A rehabilitative penal policy is therefore necessary to prevent international punishment being solely retributory. Rehabilitation, however, first emerged as a guiding principle for penal policy in international law in the mid 1960s. The concept in the international context is therefore over half a century old and derived from documents addressed to states. It is therefore necessary to explore what rehabilitation means today and how it can be adapted to meet the requirements of the international penal system.

3.3.1 The evolution of rehabilitation

Traditionally, rehabilitation was a utilitarian goal that aimed to reduce crime through the treatment and reform of individuals, so they could contribute to society in future.[103] Yet by the time the 1966 ICCPR entered into force in 1976, empirical research was suggesting that

---

[99] Rule 125 ICTY RPE; Rule 126 ICTR RPE; Rule 223 ICC RPE.
[100] D'Ascoli, *Sentencing in International Criminal Law*, 243, 301-2.
[101] See Moghalu, *Rwanda's Genocide*, 203.
[102] See para. 10 HRC General Comment 21.
[103] S. Easton and C. Piper, *Sentencing and Punishment: The Quest for Justice* (2005), 285.

rehabilitative intervention did not reduce recidivism.[104] Moreover, the notion that a criminal was sick and could be cured was viewed as "ill-conceived romanticism"[105] which diluted notions of individual criminal responsibility and resulted in the imposition of repressive indeterminate sentences that did not reflect the severity of the offence.[106] The "collapsed rehabilitative consensus"[107] resulted in the loss of a normative reference for penal theory.[108] The theoretical gap was quickly filled by the rational and long-standing doctrine of retribution.[109] Despite the new sentencing priorities, it seemed that prisons remained committed to rehabilitation in practice.[110] This commitment has been attributed to the centrality of rights in the modern nation state and the erosion of the empirical foundations for discrediting rehabilitative practices.[111] Over the years, rehabilitative theory began to evolve in answer to the criticisms levied against it. More significantly, the growing strength of human rights law and penal standards facilitated the transformation of the concept from an objective used to justify the imposition of sentences or for determining their length, to a modern model of rehabilitation that provides both a principled basis and valid goal for the administration of penal institutions and practices.[112]

3.3.2 Adapting "rehabilitation" for the international penal system

Rather than use rehabilitation as a sentencing objective, elements of rehabilitative theory and practice can be adapted to form penal objectives for the implementation of international punishment.

---

[104] See M. Vitiello, "Reconsidering Rehabilitation" (1991) 65 *Tulane Law Review* 1011–54 at 1032; N. Morris, *The Future of Imprisonment* (1974), 13; D. Garland, *Punishment and Modern Society: A Study in Social Theory* (1990), 186; G. Hallevy, "Therapeutic Victim–Offender Mediation within the Criminal Justice Process" (2011) 16 *Harvard Negotiation Law Review* 65–94 at 68.
[105] E. L. Rubin, "The Inevitability of Rehabilitation" (2001) 19 *Law and Inequality* 343–77 at 343.
[106] See Easton and Piper, *Sentencing and Punishment*, 14.
[107] Bottoms cited in I. Crow, *The Treatment and Rehabilitation of Offenders* (2001), 30.
[108] Garland, *Punishment and Modern Society*, 6.
[109] See Crow, *The Treatment and Rehabilitation of Offenders*, 33.
[110] See Easton and Piper, *Sentencing and Punishment*, 285.
[111] See Rubin, "The Inevitability of Rehabilitation," 344–52; Vitiello, "Reconsidering Rehabilitation", 1032.
[112] See Crow, *The Treatment and Rehabilitation of Offenders*, 29; E. Rotman "Beyond Punishment" in R. A. Duff and G. Garland (eds.), *A Reader on Punishment* (1994), 300–2.

Rehabilitative theory places a negative duty on authorities to protect the dignity of the offender by preventing deterioration while in prison and a positive obligation to enable prisoners to maintain relationships with the outside world and to provide opportunities for personal development.[113] Rehabilitative programmes should address the internal and external causes of criminal behaviour.[114] In contrast to the formerly coercive and invasive medical style of intervention, the modern model of rehabilitation advocates liberty-centred methods that provide prisoners with opportunities to spend time in prison constructively and to gain the skills and support necessary to make the transition back into society after release.[115]

Penal systems do not exist in a vacuum and their operations should not be based solely on their impact within the walls of the prison.[116] Penological goals should be based on the social objectives of the criminal justice system and penal processes should promote the development of both its subjects and the society it serves.[117] In addition to an individualistic rehabilitation focus, international sentences of imprisonment should also be applied in a manner that achieves the wider goals of the international criminal justice system and meets the expectations of the stakeholders of the international penal process. Therefore, in addition to the penological objectives of reformation and reintegration, international penal policy should seek to contribute to the broader justice objectives of reconciliation and the maintenance of peace in conflict-torn communities. The need to adopt a broader approach to the management of international punishment is evident in the ICC release criteria. The governing rules look beyond the individual prisoner's rehabilitation to focus on attempts taken by the prisoner to repair relations with victims and the effect release will have on victims and social stability.[118] To achieve this broader range of goals, international punishment must focus on not only the reform of the prisoner but also his relationships with others.

---

[113] See paras. 11–12 HRC General Comment 21; Rotman, "Beyond Punishment", 284, 295–7.
[114] Hallevy, "Therapeutic Victim–Offender Mediation within the Criminal Justice Process", 70–1.
[115] See Rules 61, 79–80 UNSMR; Rule 7 EPR; Principle 10 UNBP; paras. 2, 21–3 Management by Prison Administrations of Life-Sentence and other Long-Term Prisoners, COE Rec (2003)23; A. Coyle, *A Human Rights Approach to Prison Management: Handbook for Prison Staff* (2002), 83–4, 93; Crow, *The Treatment and Rehabilitation of Offenders*, 5, 107.
[116] A. Coyle, *Managing Prisons in a Time of Change* (2002), 57.
[117] See Principle 4 UNBP.   [118] See Rule 223(c)–(d) ICC RPE.

In the international context, it is more appropriate to refer to **resocialisation**. Not only is this term favoured by the ICC,[119] but by re-branding rehabilitation as resocialisation, "a unilateral top down institutional perspective of crime control is discarded for a bottom up perspective of justice-seeking at various levels – the individual, the relational, the informal community, the societal structural and the cultural".[120] The broader goal of resocialisation moves away from the traditional, individual-focused rehabilitation model that has a tendency to ignore critical post-release factors.[121] Resocialisation focuses not only on individual entitlement but goes further to introduce inter-relational elements of social exchange and interaction between all the stakeholders of the international penal process.[122] These stakeholders include the prisoner, his family and community, victims, their families and communities, the post-conflict society, the courts and the international community.

4. Conclusion

This chapter outlined the need to devise an international penal policy. The seriousness of the crimes prosecuted before the international criminal courts and the need to ensure the imposition of proportional sentences dictates that retribution must be retained as the dominant factor in international sentence determination. To ensure that international punishment is enforced in a humane and effective manner, however, it is necessary to adopt a resocialisation objective to govern the planning and implementation of international custodial sanctions. With an international penal policy focused on both individual and inter-relational resocialisation, international punishment can move beyond its current warehousing approach to a principled process that aims to facilitate the personal development of prisoners, the penological goals of rehabilitation and reintegration and the international criminal justice goals of reconciliation and the maintenance of peace. In order

---

[119] See Rule 223(b) ICC RPE.
[120] See I. Aersten, "The Intermediate Position of Restorative Justice: The Case of Belgium" in I. Aersten et al. (eds.), *Institutionalising Restorative Justice* (2006), 82.
[121] See S. Klein et al., "Inmate Family Functioning" (2002) 46(1) *International Journal of Offender Therapy and Comparative Criminology* 95–111 at 95.
[122] See G. Bazemore and S. O'Brien, "The Quest for a Restorative Model of Rehabilitation: Theory-for-practice and Practice-for-theory" in L. Walgrave (ed.), *Restorative Justice and the Law* (2002), 46.

to implement a resocialisation policy, it will be necessary to employ new penal practices. The unique nature and structure of the international penal system means that it will not be possible simply to replicate national practices. A novel approach to the modalities of international punishment and international sentence plan implementation must be adopted.

7

International penal practice

International penal policy should not only regulate the prison term of international prisoners but it should also map out the final stages of a comprehensive justice system that meets victims' and other stakeholders' needs. It should create post-conviction opportunities for both individual and inter-relational resocialisation. A resocialisation-focused penal policy, with reformative, re-integrative and reconciliatory objectives, requires a methodological framework that can provide a "broad spectrum of constructive interventions [and] positive human services".[1] Modern standards on the treatment of persons deprived of their liberty advocate the use of restorative and reparative programmes.[2] This chapter advocates the utilisation of restorative justice methodologies to deliver international penal strategy. The adoption and adaptation of restorative justice tools will enable prisons to facilitate forms of social interaction that can contribute towards the attainment of the international penal goals of resocialisation and reintegration and international justice goals of reconciliation and the restoration and maintenance of peace.

1. A restorative approach to resocialisation

Custodial sanctions should be implemented in a manner that reflects societal views about punishment and justice. International criminology, however, is often accused of being so heavily influenced by Western legal liberalism that it fails to represent or include direct victims.[3] Purely retributive punishment may alienate those it is meant to serve as it

---

[1] E. Rotman "Beyond Punishment" in R. A. Duff and D. Garland (eds.), *A Reader on Punishment* (1994), 294.
[2] Rules 103(7), 105(5) EPR.
[3] M. Drumbl, *Atrocity, Punishment and International Law* (2007), 7, 14, 124.

does not relate to the victims' needs or expectations.[4] Moreover, the punishment of a handful of perpetrators cannot provide the emotional or economic support required by victims in a post-conflict situation. Yet, in spite of these arguments, the gravity of international crime makes retributive sanctioning a fundamental necessity. International crimes must be investigated, prosecuted and punished.

While it is important to ensure the end of impunity for heinous crimes, conflict cannot be resolved through trials or custodial punishment alone. Societal healing is an enormously complex task that cannot be approached with one institutional form or method. A comprehensive criminal justice process should involve punishment, the recognition of harm and the restoration of relationships through dialogue and reparation, simultaneously providing justice and the promise of social peace.[5] This combination of objectives points to the use of restorative justice methodologies.

Traditionally, restorative justice was viewed as an alternative to retributive processes in the transitional justice tool-box. While they employ different methodologies, retributive and restorative approaches to justice share the morally intuitive foundation that an imbalance has been caused by the wrong-doing of the offender, who owes something to victims, and both attempt to restore this balance by addressing accountability through censuring reproachable behaviour and appealing to responsibility.[6] They are now viewed by many as complementary conflict resolution tools that represent "the two sides of the coin of rejecting collective blame".[7] For instance, Drumbl advocates restructuring the international criminal justice system to include bottom up and local approaches to procedure and sanctions, alongside procedural diversifi-

---

[4] See L. Van Garsse, "The Meaning of Mediation within the Criminal Justice Context" 2003, 12; D. Garland, *Punishment and Modern Society, A Study in Social Theory* (1990), 78.
[5] See B. Oomen, "Transitional Justice and Its Legitimacy: The Case for a Local Perspective" (2007) 25(1) *Netherlands Quarterly of Human Rights* 141–8 at 144–7.
[6] See H. Zehr, "Journey to Belonging" in E. G. M. Weitekamp and H. Kerner (eds.), *Restorative Justice: Theoretical Foundations* (2002), 29; L. Walgrave, "Integrating Criminal Justice and Restorative Justice" in G. Johnstone and D. W. Van Ness (eds.), *Handbook of Restorative Justice* (2007), 570; M. Findlay and R. Henham, *Transforming International Criminal Justice: Retributive and Restorative Justice in the Trial process* (2005), 279.
[7] N. J. Kritz and J. Finci, "A Truth and Reconciliation Commission in Bosnia and Herzegovina: An Idea Whose Time has Come" (2001) 3 *International Law Forum du Droit International* 50–8 at 53.

cation to include quasi-legal accountability mechanisms.[8] Findlay and Henham have also advanced arguments in favour of incorporating restorative justice elements into the retributive international criminal trial process.[9] They feel that the harmonisation of retributive and restorative approaches to justice, through the inclusion of victim communities in the trial process and the consideration of their views at sentencing, will enhance the moral legitimacy of international punishment. Moreover, they feel that this collaborative justice model is better placed to contribute to the process of maintaining peace and achieving reconciliation in affected post-conflict societies.

Restorative justice principles may not be relevant guides for the imposition of international punishment, but they can operate alongside other penal principles to guide the implementation of international punishment.[10] Instead of restorative justice displacing traditional criminal justice procedures, it can be adopted as a penal modality to complete the process and provide a more comprehensive justice system.[11] Indeed, the adoption of restorative principles and practices post-conviction complements the retributive view that offenders are rational and moral agents whose rehabilitation is only achieved through internal reasoning and moral choice.[12] This approach moves beyond the legal accountability of individuals to address broader justice objectives of peace, reconciliation and social reconstruction.[13]

Restorative justice principles and practices have been increasingly accepted and integrated at various stages throughout the domestic criminal justice process.[14] Indeed, the employment of restorative methods

---

[8] Drumbl, *Atrocity, Punishment and International Law*, 18.
[9] See Findlay and Henham, *Transforming International Criminal Justice*; Henham, *Punishment and Process in International Criminal Trials* (2005).
[10] S. D'Ascoli, *Sentencing in International Criminal Law* (2011), 38; D. Goulding et al., "Restorative Prisons: Towards Radical Prison Reform" (2008) 20(2) *Current Issues in Criminal Justice* 231–42 at 235–7.
[11] R. A. Rossi "Meet Me on Death Row: Post-Sentence Victim-Offender Mediation in Capital Cases" (2008) 9(1) *Pepperdine Dispute Resolution Law Journal* 185–210 at 187–8.
[12] Henham, *Punishment and Process in International Criminal Trials*, 146.
[13] A. Triponel and S. Pearson, "What do You Think should Happen? Public Participation in Transitional Justice" (2010) 22 *Pace International Law Review* 103–44 at 103.
[14] L. Walgrave, "Restorative Justice: An Alternative to Responding to Crime?" in S. G. Shoham et al. (eds.), *International Handbook of Penology and Criminal Justice* (2008), 613–89 at 615; F. D. Hill, "Restorative Justice: Sketching a New Legal Discourse" (2008) 4(2) *International Journal of Punishment and Sentencing* 51–81 at 52; G. Hallevy "Therapeutic Victim–Offender Mediation within the Criminal Justice Process" (2011) 16 *Harvard Negotiation Law Review* 65–94 at 75.

post-conviction is not unprecedented. One of the countries that concluded enforcement agreements with the ICTY and ICC, Belgium, introduced legislation which established restorative action plans in all national prisons for both accused and convicted detainees.[15] Specialist counsellors operate in all national prisons to facilitate the introduction of restorative justice practices.[16] Post-conviction mediation has been advocated even for the most serious crimes in the domestic context, "not to replace punishment, but to work in conjunction with criminal adjudication".[17]

There have been signs of the incorporation of restorative principles and processes into the international criminal justice process. At the temporary international criminal courts, victims could only participate in the trial process if they were called as witnesses.[18] The ICC has strengthened victims' rights by granting them the right to participate in proceedings with legal representation and to make presentations to the court if their personal interests have been affected.[19] The ICC has also strengthened victims' rights to reparations. While the temporary courts' provisions that facilitate restitution to and compensation for victims have not been used to date,[20] the ICC has established a Trust Fund for Victims (TFV) that acts as a depository for both money collected from fines and forfeiture and reparations awarded by the court for the benefit of victims of crime and their families.[21] The ICC's remedial provisions have been praised as enabling the reconciliation of retributive and restorative aims.[22]

Restorative factors have also been considered during sentencing. For example, the international courts have accepted sincere expressions of

---

[15] L. Roberts and T. Peters, "How Restorative Justice is Able to Transcend the Prison Walls: A Discussion of the 'Restorative Detention' Project" in E. Weitehamp and M. Kerner (eds.), *Restorative Justice in Context: International Practice and Directions* (2003), 95–122; Belgian Ministry of Justice, Office of the Director General of Penitentiary Establishments Circular Instruction, Restorative Justice Consultants, CM 1719, 04.10.2000.

[16] Goulding *et al.*, "Restorative Prisons", 234.

[17] Rossi, "Meet Me on Death Row", 186.

[18] See S. Servaes and N. Birtsch, *Engaging with Victims and Perpetrators in Transitional Justice and Peace Building Processes* (2008), 7.

[19] See Art. 68 ICCSt.

[20] Rules 98*ter*(B), 105–6 ICTY RPE; Rules 105–6 ICTR RPE; Rules 104(C), 105 SCSL RPE. See also Rules 129, 130 MICT RPE.

[21] See Arts. 75(2), 79 ICCSt.

[22] T. Antkowiak, "An Emerging Mandate for International Courts: Victim-Centred Remedies and Restorative Justice" (2011) 47 *Stanford Journal of International Law* 279 at 329.

remorse,[23] conduct subsequent to the conflict with respect to promoting peace and reconciliation, and assistance to victims as mitigating factors at the sentencing stage of the process.[24] Guilty pleas may also result in mitigation for similar reasons. They are also considered to be potential mitigating factors as timely guilty pleas ensure the efficient and speedy administration of international criminal justice and save judicial time and resources.[25] Many feel that the prioritisation of administration of justice factors is detrimental to the attainment of other key objectives and principles of international criminal justice.[26] More recently, the international courts have been keen to play down this factor,[27] stating that the administration of justice should not be given "undue weight".[28] It is also argued that the acceptance of guilty pleas in mitigation means that the punishment imposed is no longer proportionate to the gravity of the crime and results in defendants being treated differently depending on the quality of information they are willing and able to provide.[29] Despite these criticisms, negotiated plea agreements have become increasingly accepted as an important part of international criminal procedure.[30] At the ICTY at one stage, nearly one third of all convictions resulted from guilty pleas.[31]

Perhaps more significantly, there have also been indications of the incorporation of restorative justice principles into the legal framework

---

[23] See para. 69 *Nzabirinda* (Judgment) ICTR-2001-77-T, 23.02.2007; paras. 30, 33–4 *Rugambarara* (Judgment) ICTR-00-59-T, 16.11.2007; para. 63 *Serugendo* (Judgment) ICTR-05-84-I, 12.06.2006; paras. 138, 140 *Bisengimana* (Judgment) ICTR-00-60-T, 13.04.2006; paras. 75–6 *Bralo* (AC Judgment) IT-95-17-A, 02.04.2007.

[24] See para. 752 *Orić* (Judgment) IT-03-68-T, 30.06.2006; para. 177 *Vasiljevic* (Ac Judgment) IT-98-32-A, 25.02.2004; paras. 40, 63–5 *Fofana, Kondewa* (Judgment) SCSL-04-14-J, 09.10.2007; paras. 36–7 *Rugambarara* (Judgment) ICTR-00-59-T, 16.11.2007.

[25] Paras. 30, 33, 35 *Rugambarara* (Judgment) ICTR-00-59-T, 16.11.2007; paras. 126, 140 *Bisengimana* (Judgment) ICTR-00-60-T, 13.04.2006; para. 47 *Bralo* (Appeal Judgment) IT-95-17-A, 02.04.2007.

[26] R. Henham and M. Drumbl "Plea Bargaining at the ICTY" (2005) 16 *Criminal Law Forum* 49–87 at 52, 57–8, 77, 85; A. Tieger and M. Shin "Plea Agreements in the ICTY: Purposes, Effects and Propriety" (2005) 3 *Journal of International Criminal Justice* 666–79 at 669.

[27] Para. 32 *Serugendo* (Judgment) ICTR-05-84-I, 12.06.2006.

[28] Para. 45 *Zelenović* (Judgment) IT-96-23/2-S, 04.04.2007.

[29] Henham and Drumbl, "Plea Bargaining at the ICTY", 56; D'Ascoli, *Sentencing in International Criminal Law*, 46–7; Tieger and Shin, "Plea Arguments in the ICTY", 67.

[30] See Rules 62, 62*bis*, 62*ter* ICTY RPE; Rules 62, 62*bis* ICTR RPE; Rules 61, 62 SCSL RPE; Arts. 64(8)(a), 65 ICCSt.

[31] Henham and Drumbl, "Plea Bargaining at the ICTY", 53; Tieger and Shin, "Plea Agreements in the ICTY", 667.

for the enforcement of international custodial sanctions, particularly in relation to release procedures. For instance, the ICTY President can direct the Registrar to inform all those who testified at the trial of a convicted person of his release, the destination the person will travel to upon release and any other information considered relevant.[32] The ICC procedure goes further. The Review Panel must invite, to the extent possible, victims or their legal representatives who participated in proceedings, to participate in hearings for the reduction of sentences or to submit written observations.[33] The release procedure is moving from informing victims about release decisions to inviting them to participate in the decision-making process. Yet both measures are limited to victims that participated in the trial. Therefore, despite the increased efforts to involve victims in international criminal process, the goal of imposing individual criminal liability within the constraints of due process guarantees means that the process remains perpetrator-orientated.[34]

Beyond these limited procedural developments, there are also indications that restorative principles are influencing release decisions. The temporary courts have acknowledged expressions of remorse and acceptance of liability as indicators of a prisoner's demonstration of rehabilitation.[35] More importantly, the ICC has elaborated criteria that appear to create implicit goals for international punishment that are restorative in nature. ICC release decisions will be based, *inter alia*, on a consideration of the prisoner's ability to be successfully reintegrated into the community, whether the prisoner has dissociated from his crime or taken any action for the benefit of victims and the effect the prisoner's release will have on victims, their families and the stability of wider society.[36] It is difficult to see how even the most genuine and enthusiastic prisoner could demonstrate the attainment of these implicit goals for international imprisonment, in order to secure release, without having recourse to restorative methods of communication and an ability to make reparative actions post-conviction. Therefore, not only is a restorative approach compatible with a vision for a resocialisation-based international penal policy, but also it appears to be necessary to ensure that the international punishment complies with contemporary international human rights standards.[37]

---

[32] Para. 12 ICTY PDER.   [33] Rule 224(1) ICC RPE.
[34] Servaes and Birtsch, *Engaging with Victims and Perpetrators*, 7–8.
[35] See Chapter 2, Section 3.2.1.   [36] Rule 223 ICC RPE.
[37] See Chapter 2, Section 4.3.1, Chapter 5, Section 2 and Chapter 6, Section 3.

Despite the developments noted above, the international criminal justice process needs to evolve from a legal process that imposes individual criminal liability and punishment to a justice process that also examines other forms of guilt and collective accountability with a view to encouraging reconciliation and the maintenance of peace. Rather than view retributive and restorative approaches to justice as parallel alternatives, they should be viewed as complementary components of the international criminal justice process. Just as resocialisation can be adopted as a post-conviction objective, restorative methods can be adopted as post-conviction penal policy implementation tools.

2. Restorative justice principles and processes

Restorative justice is concerned with healing the victim, the offender and their relationship with each other, to allow for the reintegration of all parties back into the community. A post-conviction resocialisation policy, guided by restorative principles, would therefore involve the recognition of harm caused to these relationships (and society) by international crime and conflict and efforts to repair that harm through constructive dialogue and reparative actions. This section discusses restorative justice principles and how their translation into international penal practice could contribute to the achievement of reintegrative, reconciliatory and peace restoration and maintenance objectives.

2.1 Recognition of harm

Retributive trials can acknowledge harm caused to victims by classifying acts as international crimes,[38] and imposing punishment on perpetrators. But, a retributive justice process can impose punishment whether or not a convicted person accepts liability: the court recognises the harm but the perpetrator need not. Indeed, some argue that a process in which "confrontation prevails over communication"[39] provides accused persons with incentives to deny responsibility and encourages the adoption of "exculpatory strategies".[40]

---

[38] See A. Mafwenga, "The Contribution of the ICTR to Reconciliation in Rwanda" in D. Shelton (ed.), *International Crimes, Peace and Human Rights: The Role of the ICC* (2000), 16–17.
[39] Walgrave, "Restorative Justice", 647.   [40] Hill, "Restorative Justice", 57.

The censuring and stigmatising message of retributive punishment may not be internalised by offenders due to feelings of innocence, lack of conscience or perceptions that the court is illegitimate.[41] Mr Krajišnik, for example, has spent many years in prison working on documents and seeking support to request a review of his case.[42] He stated that while he accepted the verdict of the ICTY insofar as he had failed to prove his innocence during the nine years of the trial, he is innocent and lives for the day when the judges of the ICTY will say he was not guilty.[43] Even if an accused person admits liability, guilty pleas are not followed up beyond the trial process.[44] Many international prisoners continue to dismiss the criminality of their acts or their guilt throughout their prison sentence. As domestic prison systems are not in a position to provide programmes which deal with international crime,[45] offenders may return home without ever having recognised the criminal nature of their behaviour. In this light, the imposition of retributive punishment, without more, may make victims feel that they are being pressured into a one-sided reconciliation process whereby they are expected to forgive those that have never accepted responsibility or demonstrated remorse.[46]

The length of sentences is not the only reference point for victim expectations; victims need to be listened to and the harm suffered repaired. A restorative approach to resocialisation encourages an active engagement with responsibility, empathy towards victims and efforts to repair the harm caused by the criminal act.[47] Restorative communication encourages offenders to give up a passive stance in relation to responsibility and, in contrast to retributive processes, demands that a

---

[41] See M. Walker, *Why Punish?* (1991), 26–30, 80; P. Roberts, "Restoration and Retribution in International Criminal Justice: An Exploratory Analysis" in A. von Hirsch et al. (eds.), *Restorative Justice and Criminal Justice: Competing or Reconcilable Paradigms* (2003), 126.

[42] Lavis, Usk Prison, 27.09.2012.   [43] Krajišnik, Usk Prison, 27.09.2012.

[44] See D. Saxon, "Exporting Justice: Perceptions of the ICTY Among the Serbians, Croatians and Muslim Communities in the Former Yugoslavia" (2005) 4 *Journal of Human Rights* 559–72 at 561; Henham, *Punishment and Process in International Criminal Trials*, 127.

[45] See K. Hoffmann, "Some Remarks on the Enforcement of International Sentences in the Light of Galić case at the ICTY" (2011) ZIS 838–42 at 842.

[46] See S. Coliver, "The Contribution of the ICTY to Reconciliation in Bosnia and Herzegovina" in D. Shelton (ed.), *International Crimes, Peace and Human Rights: The Role of the ICC* (2000), 19.

[47] See Appendix "Paradigms of Justice, Old and New" in H. Zehr, "Retributive Justice, Restorative Justice" in G. Johnstone (ed.), *A Restorative Justice Reader* (2003), 81–2; Walgrave, "Integrating Criminal Justice and Restorative Justice", 569.

convicted person acknowledges and accepts liability for criminal acts and omissions as a non-negotiable pre-condition for dialogue.[48] In contrast to the retrospective approach to responsibility adopted by retributive justice, restorative justice invokes both retrospective and prospective responsibility.[49]

2.2 Repairing harm

Criminal sanctions symbolise a public acknowledgement of victims' pain. Some victims may feel better seeing offenders suffer.[50] Yet, despite the cliché that serving a sentence "pays a debt to society", time spent passively behind bars does not directly address the harm caused by crime. In contrast to retributive models of accountability that require harm to offenders to balance the harm caused to victims, a restorative approach, based on a norm of reciprocity, dictates that an offender should repair harm and attempt to restore violated trust.[51] Rather than regard externally imposed retributive custodial sanctions as a ceiling for accountability, a restorative approach enables convicted persons to take the initiative to offer to make amends during their time in prison. A restorative approach facilitates post-conviction engagements during which prisoners can recognise victims' suffering and try to repair harm through the exchange of emotions, information, expressions of remorse, apologies, reparations etc.[52]

2.3 Reconciliation

International criminal courts operate either during conflict or its aftermath. By imposing individual rather than collective responsibility, the

---

[48] See Van Garsse, "The Meaning of Mediation within the Criminal Justice Context", 4.
[49] Walgrave, "Restorative Justice", 664–5, 657.
[50] D. Roche, "Retribution and Restorative Justice" in G. Johnstone and D. W. Van Ness (eds.), *Handbook of Restorative Justice* (2007), 82.
[51] G. Bazemore and J. Stinchcomb, "Civic Engagement and Reintegration: Towards a Community-Focused Theory and Practice" (2004) 36 *Columbia Human Rights Law Review* 241–86 at 254.
[52] See G. Bazemore and G. O'Brien, "The Quest for a Restorative Model of Rehabilitation: Theory-for-practice and Practice-for-theory" in L. Walgrave (ed.), *Restorative Justice and the Law* (2002), 54; C. Stahn, "Accommodating Individual Criminal Responsibility and National Reconciliation: The UN Truth Commission for East Timor" (2001) 95 *American Journal of International Law* 952–66 at 954; Van Garsse, "The Meaning of Mediation within the Criminal Justice Context", 1–2.

international criminal justice process aims to stigmatise actors rather than communities. By forcing groups to confront the worst parts of their history and placing liability with individuals, international criminal trials aim to contribute to the process of reconciliation.[53] While guilty pleas have been heralded as contributing towards the process of national reconciliation as they provide information, acknowledge responsibility and encourage other offenders to come forward,[54] the fact that they are often part of negotiated plea agreements that may result in less punishment diminishes their impact in practice.[55] Further, there is little empirical evidence to show that international criminal trials have helped to resolve differences in post-conflict societies.[56] Despite the fact that reconciliation was cited as a primary reason for establishing the ICTR, the UN Security Council did not address how a temporary international tribunal could achieve this goal.[57] Indeed, one Security Council member noted that while international criminal trials may be vehicles for justice, they are not designed to be vehicles for reconciliation.[58] Purely retributive approaches to justice that focus on the past and blame, may not be conducive to reconciliation: "an eye for an eye leaves everyone blind."[59] Punishment by itself, particularly if it is considered to be too harsh or too lenient in terms of length or effect, rarely contributes to reconciliation. The current international trial process, it seems, fails to achieve the reconciliatory aims of the international criminal justice system.[60]

---

[53] See GARes 51/203(1997).
[54] Paras. 30, 33, 35 *Rugambarara* (Judgment) ICTR-00-59-T, 16.11.2007; paras. 6, 32, 34, 52–3, 55, 59, 89 *Serugendo* (Judgment) ICTR-05-84-I, 12.06.2006; paras. 126, 139, 201 *Bisengimana* (Judgment) ICTR-00-60-T, 13.04.2006; paras. 45, 48 *Zelenović* (Judgment) IT-96-23/2-S, 04.04.2007.
[55] J. N. Clark, "Plea Bargaining at the ICTY: Guilty Pleas and Reconciliation" (2009) 20(2) *European Journal of International Law* 415–36 at 416, 422, 429–30.
[56] See T. Delpla, "In the Midst of Injustice: The ICTY from the Perspective of some Victim Associations" in X. Bougarel *et al.* (eds.), *The New Bosnia Mosaic; Identities, Memories and Moral Claims in a Post-War Society* (2007), 215; J. N. Clark, "The Impact Question: The ICTY and the Restoration and Maintenance of Peace" in B. Swart *et al.* (eds), *The Legacy of the International Criminal Tribunal for the Former Yugoslavia* (2011), 55–80 at 57.
[57] See L. A. Barria and S. D. Roper, "How Effective Are International Criminal Tribunals?" (2005) 9(3) *International Journal of Human Rights* 349 at 362.
[58] Czech Republic Statement, UNSC 3453rd Meeting, 08.11.1994.
[59] Gandhi cited in M. Wright, "Restorative Justice: from Punishment to Reconciliation: The Role of Social Workers" (1998) 6 *European Journal of Crime, Criminal Law and Criminal Justice* 267 at 270.
[60] See Findlay and Henham, *Transforming International Criminal Justice*, 278, 285; Walgrave, "Integrating Criminal Justice and Restorative Justice", 567–8.

To have reconciliatory effect, a justice process must be accessible to and inclusive of the relevant society and stakeholders. Restorative methods are concerned with healing cracks in relationships. A restorative approach to penal practice would be inclusive and aim to create, repair, maintain and strengthen inter-personal links with the offender's family, victims, the community and society at large. By taking responsibility for the offence and trying to put things right, an offender can try to put himself back in touch with society and overcome the disconnections caused by his crime and punishment.[61]

Reconciliation requires more than punishment. It is necessary to facilitate "genuine dialogue and conflict analysis of a mutual, interactive nature".[62] Restorative communication enables the discussion of subjective truths after individual liability has been imposed on **and** accepted by offenders. In contrast to the instrumental view of victim participation in the retributive justice process, restorative communication provides an empowering and supportive platform for victims to share their experiences.[63] Victims are no longer constrained by the court's remit, the charges contained in the indictment or the convictions that were handed down. Restorative dialogue can go beyond the temporal and territorial jurisdictional constraints of the trial process and discuss crimes and conflict in a wider moral, social, economic and political context. Events can be discussed in lay terms rather than in the legal language of a courtroom.[64] No longer constrained by the technical limits of the trial, participants can address issues from the past and the present and look forward to the future. Moreover, dialogue is not confined to negativity and may include positive experiences that can assist with reconciliation.

In addition to facilitating a more honest discussion of the causes and consequences of conflict, restorative communication may also enhance the legitimacy of international punishment. International punishment may be considered illegitimate by both offenders and victims. Offenders, and their communities, may reject sanctions imposed by international

---

[61] See Zehr, "Journey to Belonging", 21–2.
[62] Fisher cited in Clark, "The Impact Question", 79.
[63] See Findlay and Henham, *Transforming International Criminal Justice*, 273–5, 291; Kritz and Finci, "A Truth and Reconciliation Commission in Bosnia and Herzegovina", 52–3; Stahn, "Accommodating Individual Criminal Responsibility" 954; Walgrave, "Integrating Criminal Justice and Restorative Justice", 569.
[64] See Saxon, "Exporting Justice", 568; Findlay and Henham, *Transforming International Criminal Justice*, 297; A. Skelton, "Africa" in G. Johnstone and D. Van Ness (eds.), *Handbook of Restorative Justice* (2007), 468.

courts due to perceptions that perpetrators are martyrs or heroes or that the courts are biased.[65] Mr Krajišnik, for example, receives "fan" mail and requests for his photograph to be autographed at Usk Prison.[66]

Victims, and their communities, may reject international punishment due to its poor visibility and their lack of control over the way in which perpetrators are punished.[67] Victims may feel resentful that those most responsible for atrocities are sent to "luxurious prisons"[68] while they are trying to pick up the pieces of their lives. King and Meernik noted that while most interviewees were aware that Biljana Plavšić had access to a sauna while in prison, the vast majority were unaware that she had pleaded guilty.[69]

Retributive sanctions may also be viewed as culturally irrelevant, with a more traditional justice focus on the restoration of social harmony and reconciliation being preferred.[70] The engagement of all sections of a post-conflict society in post-conviction restorative communication projects may lead to an acceptance of the legitimacy of international punishment by underlining the reality of the impact of international imprisonment on convicted persons and by giving the community a sense of ownership in the process. Restorative communication's focus on social interaction can also make positive contributions to reconciliation by moving beyond the dichotomisation of victim and offender that results from retributive processes, towards the depolarisation of post-conflict societies.[71] Bottom-up reconciliation that includes all relevant stakeholders can complement top-down retributive punishment.

---

[65] See J. Cockayne, "Hybrids or Mongrels? Internationalized War Crime Trials as Unsuccessful Degradation Ceremonies" (2005) 4 *Journal of Human Rights* 455–73 at 456; Coliver, "The Contribution of the ICTY to Reconciliation in Bosnia and Herzegovina" 23, 25; Saxon, "Exporting Justice", 562–5.

[66] Lavis, Usk Prison, 27.09.2012.

[67] The Rwandan delegation stated it was "hard to accept that those condemned will be imprisoned outside Rwanda and that those countries be given authority to reach decisions about the detainees; this is for the International Tribunal or at least for the Rwandese people to decide". See UNSC 3453rd Meeting, 08.11.1994, 15.

[68] Oomen, "Transitional Justice and Its Legitimacy", 144.

[69] K. L. King and J. D. Meernik, "Assessing the Impact of the ICTY: Balancing International and Local Interests While Doing Justice" in B. Swart *et al.* (eds.), *The Legacy of the International Criminal Tribunal for the Former Yugoslavia* (2011), 7–54 at 29.

[70] See Rwanda's Statement, UNSC 3453rd Meeting, 08.11.1994; Henham, *Punishment and Process in International Criminal Trials*, 128, 151; Skelton, "Africa", 469–70; Barria and Roper, "How Effective are International Criminal Tribunals?", 363; K. Moghalu, *Rwanda's Genocide: The Politics of Global Justice* (2005), 205.

[71] See Roberts and Peters, "How Restorative Justice is Able to Transcend the Prison Walls", 98.

2.4 Reintegration

Current enforcement systems fail to facilitate the reintegration of international prisoners back into society. This has implications not only for offenders, but for their families and communities, for victims and their communities, and for society at large. The current assumption appears to be that international prisoners will welcome release and be able to adjust to life at home without assistance. Release may be feared by those who have served long sentences abroad. Over the years, they may have lost all meaningful social relations, their businesses and may now be too old to work. Their release may create anxiety for their families who have lived without them for long periods. It may also be traumatic for victims and their families and affect the stability of a fragile post-conflict society. The need to address this glaring gap in the international penal process is now even more critical given that the ICC takes these issues into consideration when deciding whether or not to grant release.[72] The ICC's statutory commitment to relocate prisoners at the end of their sentence[73] must therefore be interpreted to include more than a one way ticket home. This is crucially important in a criminal justice process that does not have a parole or probation system.

The current enforcement systems result in both the physical and moral exclusion of international prisoners from society. Compulsory transfers to enforcing states may be seen as a form of exile. International convictions also act as a stigmatising condemnation of the perpetrator and the acts committed. Through stigmatisation, international punishment aims to reduce the political and economic benefits of international crime. This stigma, however, can hinder the attainment of international penal objectives. An irremovable criminal label may create low self-esteem, isolate individuals from important social support networks and detrimentally impact on prisoners' ability to reintegrate.[74] Even association with the international courts, in the absence of a conviction, can tarnish a person's reputation. Mr Delalić, whose indictment was later withdrawn by the ICTY,[75] counted over 900 negative articles about himself in the media and felt that, despite his innocence, he would always be referred to as "the one from The Hague".[76] Another former UNDU detainee, Mr Kupreškić, who was later acquitted by the

---

[72] See Rule 223 ICC RPE. [73] Art. 107 ICCSt.
[74] See B. Steels, "Forever Guilty: Convict Perceptions of Pre and Post Convention" (2009) 21(2) *Current Issues in Criminal Justice* 242.
[75] See *Delalić et al.* (Judgment) IT-96-21, 16.11.1998. [76] Delalić, 20.08.2008.

Appeals Chamber,[77] said that when the Trial Chamber handed down a ten-year sentence he "died from shame ... and didn't know what to do ... all I could imagine were the headlines saying I was a war criminal".[78] The finalisation of an international sentence does not prevent international prisoners seeking the removal of the war criminal label. Mr Krajišnik admitted that he could not physically look at his sentencing judgment until six months after it had been handed down and pledged to spend the rest of his life working on this case until the ICTY understands that he was not guilty. He stated that he would rather spend time in prison and eventually be found not guilty than to be free and considered guilty.[79]

International punishment, without more, excludes and ostracises convicted persons. In other words, it does not facilitate the resocialisation or reintegration of international prisoners. Yet international standards state that "the treatment of prisoners should emphasise not their exclusion from the community, but their continuing part in it".[80] Unlike a retributive view of punishment that sees stigma as irremovable, a restorative approach views stigma as removable through restorative communication and action.[81]

Braithwaite argues that "tolerance of crime makes things worse; stigmatisation or disrespectful outcasting shame of crime makes things worse still ... disapproval within a continuum of respect for the offender ... terminated by rituals of forgiveness, makes things better".[82] Restorative justice's ideological commitment to inclusion and healing, rather than alienation and division, gives it reintegrative potential by focusing penal practice on repairing or remodelling important relationships.[83] By providing possibilities for society to reconnect, critical

---

[77] See *Kupreškić et al.* (Appeal Judgment) IT-95-16-A, 23.10.2001.
[78] Kupreškić, 13.10.2007.   [79] Krajišnik, Usk Prison, 27.09.2012.
[80] Rule 61 UNSMR.   [81] Goulding *et al.*, "Restorative Prisons", 233.
[82] Cited in Bazemore and O'Brien, "The Quest for a Restorative Model of Rehabilitation", 56.
[83] See Henham, *Punishment and Process in International Criminal Trials*, 212; Van Garsse, "The Meaning of Mediation within the Criminal Justice Context", 12; K. Buntinx "Victim Offender Mediation in Severe Crimes", 2007, 1; R. A. Duff, "Restoration and Retribution" in von Hirsch *et al.* (eds.), *Restorative Justice and Criminal Justice: Competing or Reconcilable Paradigms* (2003), 51; L. Llewellyn, "Truth Commissions and Restorative Justice" in G. Johnstone and D. W. Van Ness (eds.), *Handbook of Restorative Justice* (2007), 355–61; Appendix "Paradigms of Justice, Old and New" in Zehr, "Retributive Justice, Restorative Justice", 81–2; T. Rugge and R. Cormier, "Restorative Justice in Cases of Serious Crime: an Evaluation" in E. Elliot and R. Gordon (eds.), *New Directions in Restorative Justice* (2005), 267.

reintegration factors can be addressed, such as victim and community attitudes to offender re-entry[84] and familial and social support.

By engaging the offender's family, victims and the wider community through restorative communication post-conviction, the enforcing institution can assist the offender to create or re-establish social links and support that can positively affect the prisoner's transition back into life in the community after prison.[85] Participation in a restorative communication process gives parties a form of ownership over the reintegrative process and its outcomes.[86] The social interaction component of restorative dialogue enables the offender to present a more acceptable social identity to those to whom he wishes to return.[87] The offender can take steps towards leaving the crime and the associated stigma behind and form a new ethical identity.[88] Victims can raise fears or concerns about the offender's release and they may come away with an understanding or commitment about what will happen at the end of the sentence. Finally, restorative dialogue constructively engages and empowers the community as both a facilitator (providing informal support) and a participant (that needs to be supported) in the reintegrative process.[89]

2.5 Restoring and maintaining peace

Retributive criminal justice processes that erode impunity may act as a catalyst for reconciliation and societal reconstruction.[90] The threat of indictment can moderate political landscapes, either by removing extremists from public life[91] or through the so-called "born-again" effect

---

[84] Bazemore and Stinchcomb, "Civic Engagement and Reintegration", 247, 253.

[85] G. Bazemore and E. Erbe, "Reintegration and Restorative Justice; Towards a Theory and Practice of Informal Social Control and Support" in G. Maruna and R. Immarigeon (eds.), *After Crime and Punishment* (2004), 28, 40–1; Bazemore and Stinchcomb, "Civic Engagement and Reintegration", 243, 248, 252.

[86] Bazemore and Erbe, "Retributive Justice, Restorative Justice", 31.

[87] See Bazemore and Stinchcomb, "Civic Engagement and Reintegration", 247–57; Bazemore and Erbe, "Reintegration and Restorative Justice", 41, 44.

[88] Walgrave, "Restorative Justice", 641; L. Branham, "The Mess We're In: Five Steps Towards the Transformation of Prison Cultures" (2010) 44 *Indiana Law Review* 703–33 at 719.

[89] See Bazemore and Stinchcomb, "Civic Engagement and Reintegration", 246–7; Oomen, "Transitional Justice and Its Legitimacy", 145. See also s7(2) Truth and Reconciliation Commission Act 2000.

[90] See Rwandan Statement, UNSC 3453rd Meeting, 08.11.1994.

[91] See Moghalu, *Rwanda's Genocide*, 205; King and Meernik, "Assessing the Impact of the ICTY", 46.

whereby politicians lower the tone of their nationalistic rhetoric.[92] But trials alone "will not undo the tragedy".[93]

International criminal courts seek to contribute to the protection of the peace, security and well-being of the world.[94] Although these intangible objectives are difficult to measure, there is little empirical evidence that international criminal trials contribute, or are capable of contributing, to the restoration or maintenance of peace.[95] Social peace requires more than negative peace (the lack of violence).[96] Lasting social order can only be achieved when the cause and effects of the conflict are openly discussed and fragile social relationships restored.[97]

Retributive justice does not deal with the root causes of conflict or indeed all the crimes perpetrated.[98] When the social tissue of a community is devastated, the response cannot be solely judicial. Healing requires facing the past, drawing boundaries around it and incorporating experiences of hurt into a new blueprint for society.[99] The healing process necessitates not only personal soul-searching but a societal analysis of what went wrong. The aim is not simply to reconstruct what had been before but to rebuild based on lessons learnt from experience.[100]

Restorative methods provide an opportunity to discuss and understand the past without shying away from the objective truth. Rather than attempt to harmonise views or avoid controversial issues, restorative communication involves the creation of a climate for conflict resolution between individuals and/or groups. A restorative exploration of the causes and consequences of criminal behaviour in a climate of respect can help overcome societal polarisation.[101]

---

[92] See Coliver, "The Contribution of the ICTY to Reconciliation in Bosnia and Herzegovina", 26–7.
[93] Czech Republic Statement, UNSC 3453rd Meeting, 08.11.1994. See also Roberts, "Restoration and Retribution in International Criminal Justice", 127.
[94] See Preamble ICCSt.
[95] Clark, "The Impact Question", 55–7; Walgrave, "Restorative Justice", 618.
[96] Clark, "The Impact Question", 61.
[97] Ibid., 78; M. Drumbl, "Collective Violence and Individual Punishment: The Criminality of Mass Atrocity" (2005) 99(2) *Northwestern University Law Review* 539–610 at 591.
[98] See Moghalu, *Rwanda's Genocide*, 203.
[99] See Zehr, "Journey to Belonging", 24; G. A. Aneme, "Apology and Trials: The Case of the Red Terror Trials in Ethiopia" (2006) 6(1) *African Human Rights Law Journal* 64 at 81.
[100] See Section 6(1) Truth and Reconciliation Commission Act, 22.02.2000; Llewellyn, "Truth Commissions and Restorative Justice", 357, 363.
[101] See Skelton, "Africa", 470.

In the international context, "bulging prisons"[102] or mass public executions[103] may not be conducive to moving forward.[104] The fate of those responsible for serious crime can impact greatly on long-term stability,[105] yet retributive justice does not value their contribution to solutions to the social problems caused by conflict and crime.[106] Rather than view international criminals solely as part of the problem, a transitional or restorative approach views former warring parties as also being part of the solution. Even if only a small number of international prisoners participate in reconciliatory efforts, this may have a "ripple effect"[107] in post-conflict societies due to the former status of the prisoners and their acknowledgement of culpability.

Restorative communication provides a safe opportunity for all elements of society to identify and address underlying issues or problems that may arise in the future with a view to improving the quality of social life.[108] It is a more suitable approach to penal practice for dealing with crimes related to conflicts as it concentrates on healing relationships and transforming the community through constructive dialogue and negotiated agreements that involve all stakeholders.[109] By re-connecting collectivities and putting responsibility for the future in their hands, society is empowered to move forward. With its anticipated reconciliatory and reintegrative outcomes, a restorative approach to international penal policy implementation can help the international criminal justice system fulfil another goal for creating international criminal courts: the restoration and maintenance of peace. Restorative tools will, however,

---

[102] Findlay and Henham, *Transforming International Criminal Justice*, 292.
[103] See Roberts, "Restoration and Retribution in International Criminal Justice", 124.
[104] D. Wippman, "Atrocities, Deterrence, and the Limits of International Justice" (1999) 23 *Fordham International Law Journal* 473–88 at 82.
[105] See Stahn, "Accommodating Individual Criminal Responsibility and National Reconciliation", 966.
[106] Walgrave, "Restorative Justice", 656.
[107] L. Walker and L. Hayashi, "Pono Kaulike; A Pilot Restorative Justice Program" (2004) *Hawaii Bar Journal* at 10.
[108] See Walgrave, "Integrating Criminal Justice and Restorative Justice", 569; Walker and Hayashi, "Pono Kaulike", 9–10.
[109] See Table 7.1 Models of Treatment of Penal Conflict in J. Faget, "The French Phantoms of Restorative Justice: The Institutionalisation of Penal Mediation" in I. Aersten *et al.* (eds.), *Institutionalising Restorative Justice* (2006), 153; Bazemore and Erbe, "Reintegration and Restorative Justice", 29; Roberts and Peters, "How Restorative Justice is Able to Transcend the Prison Walls", 100; Duff, "Restoration and Retribution", 44; Roberts, "Restoration and Retribution in International Criminal Justice", 115.

need to be adapted to address the uniqueness of international criminality and to be implementable within the international penal system.

3. Utilising restorative tools to implement international penal policy

According to Feeley and Simon, penal policy development depends on not only the emergence of new discourse and objectives for a system, but also the deployment of new techniques.[110] If resocialisation is the primary objective of international penal policy, it is necessary to devise new modalities for the implementation of international sentences of imprisonment. Restorative tools, such as restorative communication and reparative actions, can assist with both the individual and inter-relational aspects of resocialisation and contribute to the achievement of reintegration, reconciliation and peace maintenance goals.

Although there has been national practice of using restorative tools in a non-diversionary, post-conviction manner, it is not possible to simply transplant domestic approaches. Consultation with both potential participants and wider stakeholders in the international penal process is necessary to ensure that the models that are put into action are contextually relevant and culturally appropriate.[111] While local practices may not be replicated, local and traditional values and conflict resolution techniques can be incorporated into the design of conflict-specific models.[112] Given the broad range of interested parties, the consultation and design process may be time-consuming and complex. Yet, this is a crucial part of the process. Unlike more traditional rehabilitation models, the participants, not the professionals, are the core providers of the service.[113] Consequently, the more control participants have over the process, the more effective it will be. The following sections suggest possible post-conviction uses for restorative communication models to

---

[110] See M. Feeley and S. Simon, "The New Penology: Notes on the Emerging Strategy of Corrections and its Implications" (1992) 30(4) *Criminology* 449 at 450.
[111] See Llewellyn, "Truth Commissions and Restorative Justice", 362; Oomen, "Transitional Justice and its Legitimacy", 146–7; Triponel and Pearson, "What Do You Think Should Happen?", 107, 123, 133.
[112] See Zehr, "Evaluation and Restorative Justice Principles" in E. Elliot and R. M. Gordon (eds.), *New Directions in Restorative Justice* (2005), 299; Triponel and Pearson, "What Do You Think Should Happen?", 127.
[113] See Bazemore and Stinchcomb, "Civic Engagement and Reintegration", 245.

assist with both the individual and inter-relational elements of a resocialisation policy.

3.1 Individual resocialisation

Individual resocialisation programmes should address the past, alleviate the hardships of the present and look to the future. This element of resocialisation for international prisoners can include participation in programmes available in enforcing states. However, these are often inaccessible to and unsuitable for international prisoners.[114] Restorative communication models can be tailored to address the unique nature of international crime and experiences of international criminals. These initiatives can prepare international prisoners for release and enhance the chances of successful reintegration back into society. In particular, they can assist with therapeutic and educative aspects of international sentence planning.

3.1.1   Therapeutic models

A therapeutic model could be used, not only to help international prisoners deal with the negative effects of long-term imprisonment in a foreign state, but also to deal with the potential traumatisation and/or victimisation issues that may be present due to their involvement in a conflict. Many international prisoners have been diagnosed with, or are suspected to be suffering from, post-traumatic stress disorder.[115] Perpetrators can suffer traumatisation as a result of their participation in violence but also due to their simultaneous status as victim. "Perpetrator" and "victim" are not mutually exclusive categories. The International criminal justice process focuses on the liability of perpetrators and tends to ignore the extent to which perpetrators may have also been victimised.[116] Many perpetrators also lost loved ones during the conflict.[117] For example, Mr Krajišnik's wife, daughter-in-law and cousin were killed and his father was injured during the conflict.[118]

---

[114] See Chapter 2, Section 4.3.1 and Chapter 5, Section 3.
[115] McFadden, UNDU, 21.08.2007.
[116] Servaes and Birtsch, "Engaging with Victims and Perpetrators in Transitional Justice and Peace Building Processes", 5–7.
[117] See Deronjić's Guilty Plea, 28.01.2004; Bralo's Guilty Plea, 07.10.2005; Rajić's Guilty Plea, 07.04.2006.
[118] Krajišnik, Usk Prison, 27.09.2012.

While it is crucial that the international criminal trial process focuses on the crimes the accused are indicted for, the international penal process can be used to explore perpetrators' "narratives of victimisation".[119] International prisoners may also wish to address their guilt for their crimes. Some convicted persons have testified that they find this hard to live with or that they fear that it will haunt them for the rest of their lives.[120] Trauma, victimisation and guilt can affect international prisoners' ability to re-enter society and therefore should be addressed by international penal policy.

3.1.2 Educative models

Restorative communication models could be used to discuss international crime and to increase international prisoners' awareness about the effects of their actions. Some international prisoners do not believe that the acts they were prosecuted for were wrong as they occurred during a war. At present, this lack of empathy or acceptance of responsibility is simply ignored due to the inability of national prisons or their programmes to really deal with these issues.

One way to address this is to highlight the criminal nature of the acts. This could entail a legal analysis of international crime, international humanitarian law and international human rights law. Another, perhaps more effective, approach is to address the effect of their acts. This more emotive approach would involve creating awareness of the impact of their crimes on victims and the wider community. The impact of international crimes on victims and their families can be conveyed during the international trial process.[121] This could be developed in the prison setting. International prisoners could discuss the causes of the crimes with prison officials, attend presentations by victim representatives or participate in conferences with surrogate victim associations.[122] Participation in such programmes can constitute preparation for more direct forms of communication with actual victims. Indeed, it has been

---

[119] Zehr, "Evaluation and Restorative Justice Principles", 298.
[120] See Babić's Guilty Plea, 27.01.2004; Plavšić's Guilty Plea, 17.12.2002; Jokić's Guilty Plea, 04.12.2003; Mrđa's Guilty Plea, 22.10.2003; Češić's Guilty Plea, 27.11.2003; Deronjić's Guilty Plea, 28.01.2004; Kolundžija's Guilty Plea, 09.10.2001; Simić's Guilty Plea, 22.07.2002; para. 157 *Rutaganira* (Judgment) ICTR-95-IC-T, 14.03.2005.
[121] Tieger and Shin, "Plea Agreements in the ICTY", 675.
[122] See Branham, "The Mess We Are In", 722 and information on the Graterford State Correctional Institution Project, Pennsylvania at Correctional Services Canada "International Perspectives on Restorative Corrections: A Review of the Literature", 2007.

argued that those convicted of serious crime should have to complete programmes that address the causes of offending before meeting victims in order to acquire the psychological tools and sense of responsibility necessary for a process that demands genuine moral engagement.[123] Participation in these sensitisation programmes can help mediators determine a prisoner's ability to empathise and communicate emotions, and ultimately, their suitability for participation in mediation with victims.[124] Proof that the offender has participated in preparatory steps may also alleviate victims' suspicions of opportunism on the part of the offender.[125]

3.2 Inter-relational resocialisation

The inter-relational aspect of resocialisation requires engagement with persons whose relations with the offender are crucial for both the prisoner's reintegration **and** societal reconciliation. Based on the principle of social exchange, restorative communication can accommodate a wider range of participants than traditional "offender-focused treatment and punishment paradigms".[126] The offender's family and community and the offender's victims and their communities should all be included in the international penal process. Their inclusion in international sentence implementation necessitates a movement away from social work models of rehabilitation, in which professionals dominate and direct the process, towards a resocialisation model whereby professionals act as facilitators, encouraging participation and autonomous decision-making among participants.[127] This section looks at two possible modes of inter-relational resocialisation; family mediation and criminal mediation.

3.2.1 Family mediation

Restorative communication principles can be used to design prison-based family mediation services that can help prisoners and their families maintain their relationships, repair harm that resulted from the

---

[123] See Bastiansen and Vercruysse (2002), Van Camp (2002), Katounas and McElrea (2002) in Correctional Services Canada "International Perspectives on Restorative Corrections"; Van Garsse, "The Meaning of Mediation within the Criminal Justice Context", 5.
[124] Roberts and Peters, "How Restorative Justice is Able to Transcend the Prison Walls", 108.
[125] See Buntinx, "Victim Offender Mediation in Severe Crimes", 6.
[126] Bazemore and Erbe, "Reintegration and Restorative Justice", 28.
[127] See I. Aertsen, "Victim Oriented Work with Offenders Post-sentence: A Restorative Justice Perspective" (2003), 6.

prisoners' convictions and imprisonment and prepare for the prisoners' release.

All imprisonment disrupts relationships, results in "social severance"[128] and thereby diminishes the social capital stock of prisoners.[129] International imprisonment is often lengthy and served in a foreign state, making it very difficult for prisoners and their families to maintain relationships.[130] Flights and accommodation are expensive and visits may be difficult to arrange due to work and school commitments and complicated procedures for obtaining visas. In addition to the practical difficulties, many families find the visiting experience emotionally challenging. Prison procedure can result in officials treating family visitors as if they too have broken the law.[131] They are searched, locked in a room and subjected to visual and oral surveillance. This creates an unnatural environment for family interaction. Mills and Codd point out that a combination of a lack of time and privacy during visits can result in the avoidance or concealment of serious family issues, with potentially damaging effects for re-adjustment after release.[132] The visiting experience could be improved through small steps to normalise the process and increase opportunities to live out family rituals, from normal every-day things like eating together to celebrating occasions or religious festivals.[133]

Outside the prison, prisoners' families face an array of challenges as a consequence of their loved one's imprisonment including marital difficulties, financial and housing problems, social stigma and victimisation, loneliness, anxiety and emotional hardship. Prisoners' children may experience psychological harm and develop behavioural problems.[134] International prisoners' families have also experienced problems as a

---

[128] See J. Kleinig, "The Hardness of Hard Treatment" in A. Ashworth and M. Wasik (eds.), *Fundamentals of Sentencing Theory* (1998), 295-6.
[129] See A. Mills and H. Codd, "Prisoners' Families and Offender Management: Mobilizing Social Capital" (2008) 55(1) *Probation Journal* 9-24 at 15; N. G. La Vigne et al. "Examining the Effect of Incarceration and In-Prison Family Contact on Prisoners' Family Relationships" (2005) 21 *Journal of Contemporary Criminal Justice* 314-55 at 316.
[130] See Chapter 2, Section 4.2.2.
[131] A. Coyle, *Managing Prisons in a Time of Change* (2002), 95.
[132] Mills and Codd, "Prisoners' Families and Offender Management", 15.
[133] S. Klein et al., "Inmate Family Functioning" (2002) 46(1) *International Journal of Offender Therapy and Comparative Criminology* 95-111 at 108.
[134] See Mills and Codd, "Prisoners Families and Offender Management", 16; Klein et al., "Inmate Family Functioning", 98.

direct result of their loved one's conviction or imprisonment. Some have been subjected to harassment and attacks in retribution for the crimes their loved ones committed.[135] Others lost their jobs or employment opportunities.[136]

The distress caused to spouses and children is generally considered to be a regrettable but an unavoidable side-effect of legal punishment.[137] While national prisoners' families may have access to local or national support groups, the families of international prisoners do not.[138] They lack visibility as a group, live in various nations and are from communities that were once at war with each other. International penal policy should therefore include measures that enable these families to address the harm caused by their partners' acts and imprisonment. Mediation would also enable prisoners to express their true feelings to their families. International prisoners have stated that they wished to apologise to their families for the position they have been put in, for acts committed or to explain the circumstances that lead to their conviction and imprisonment.[139]

International penal practice should also involve prisoners' families in sentence planning and preparations for release. Family and community ties provide social capital and support which improve the likelihood of successful resocialisation, resettlement and reintegration.[140] Families can help released prisoners find somewhere to live and employment while also providing emotional support, advice and encouragement.[141] Family members may also have questions or fears about their loved one's release or have unrealistic expectations for post-release happiness.[142] To provide opportunities for these important issues to be addressed and to prevent prisoners' families being burdened with the entire responsibility for the prisoner's resettlement, the prisoners' families should be included in discussions with the prisoner and professionals about plans for the prisoner's transition from prison to normal life.[143]

---

[135] See paras. 16–17 *Delić* (President's Decision) IT-96-21-ES, 24.06.2008.
[136] Blagojević, Trondheim Prison, 28.06.2012.
[137] N. Walker, *Why Punish?* (1991), 106–8. [138] Krajišnik, Usk Prison, 27.09.2012.
[139] See Erdemović's Guilty Plea, 20.11.1996; Sikirica's Guilty Plea 08.10.2001; Deronjić's Guilty Plea, 28.01.2004.
[140] See La Vigne et al., "Examining the Effect of Incarceration and In-Prison Family Contact", 316; para. 39 *Rugambarara* (Judgment) ICTR-00-59-T, 16.11.2007.
[141] Mills and Codd, "Prisoners' Families and Offender Management", 11–12.
[142] Klein et al., "Inmate Family Functioning", 98.
[143] See Mills and Codd, "Prisoners' Families and Offender Management", 17.

3.2.2 Criminal mediation

Victim–offender mediation provides victims with a supportive forum to express feelings, tell perpetrators about the impact of their acts or omissions, ask 'why' and request that offenders make attempts to repair harm while giving offenders the opportunity to explain, apologise and try to remedy the situation.[144] While offenders may offer mitigating circumstances to enhance understanding, it is not an opportunity to profess innocence.[145] In contrast to the educative models suggested for individual resocialisation, this model involves dialogue with direct victims. The process is conducted through a mediator and can involve face-to-face meetings or a form of shuttle diplomacy where the mediator acts as a go-between. International convictions that impose liability on individuals for direct participation in international crimes may provide opportunities for victim–offender mediation, but the widespread nature and magnitude of international crime may make such an individualistic form of communication impossible. If an offender is convicted on the basis of command responsibility, he may not have answers for victims in regards to the details of, and motivations for, particular acts or omissions.[146]

Given the unique nature of international crime, the potential number of victims, the broad range of stakeholders in the international penal process, and the variety of domestic prison services being relied on by the international criminal courts, it may be preferable to use a conferencing rather than a mediation model for communication. In so doing, the process can be extended to include not only the victims' and offenders' communities, but support groups and associations, wider society and the international community. Both micro-communities with personal and community relationships with victims or offenders and macro-communities that experience vicarious victimisation (society, government and the international community) need to be assured that what happened was wrong and that steps are being taken to ensure it will not happen again.[147]

A conferencing format enables different combinations of interested parties to discuss facts and perceptions about the causes and consequences of the conflict, as well as how to move forward.

---

[144] See Rugge and Cormier, "Restorative Justice in Cases of Serious Crime", 273–4.
[145] See Duff, "Restoration and Retribution", 50; Rossi, "Meet Me on Death Row", 189.
[146] See Buntinx, "Victim Offender Mediation in Severe Crimes", 5.
[147] Hill, "Restorative Justice", 54, 61.

Dialogue is facilitated by a neutral coordinator. As the process is premised on the recognition that one party has harmed another, the coordinator is not morally neutral. Neutrality refers to the duty to treat all participants equally and with respect[148] and to their institutional independence. For instance, in Belgium, an NGO called Suggnomè organises and conducts mediation sessions in prisons in the Flemish-speaking part of the country. Institutional independence prevents the communication process being viewed as a risk assessment tool or an extension of punishment by offenders or as an offender-orientated process by victims.[149]

The coordinator would be responsible for inviting potential participants, preparing them by explaining the process and ensuring they have realistic expectations, coordinating restoration-orientated activities, facilitating communication and providing support to participants. Fine-tuning preparation procedures will involve a steep learning curve given the lack of any real experience of post-conviction dialogue in relation to this form of crime. As it relates to international crime and mass atrocity, victims must be therapeutically prepared and offenders screened to ensure that "intractably recalcitrant, violent or mentally disturbed individuals"[150] are excluded, reducing the risks of re-victimisation.[151]

The degree of participation will depend on the willingness of identified victims to participate, their progress through the restorative process and the accessibility of the prison.[152] Potential participants may be spread across the globe, given the tendency of communities to disperse and leave countries during conflict situations. They may not all speak the same language. Moreover, many national prisons holding international prisoners may not be willing or able to accommodate the level of

---

[148] Buntinx, "Victim Offender Mediation in Severe Crimes", 2.
[149] See Wright, "Restorative Justice", 272; Buntinx, "Victim Offender Mediation in Severe Crimes", 8; Van Garsse, The Meaning of Mediation within the Criminal Justice Context", 15; L. Van Garsse, "Mediation in a Detention Context: Moralisation or Participation?", 2006, 10–12.
[150] See Correctional Services Canada "International Perspectives on Restorative Corrections". See also Rossi, "Meet Me on Death Row", 205.
[151] See Rugge and Cormier, "Restorative Justice in Cases of Serious Crime", 268.
[152] See D. W. Van Ness, "Prisons and Restorative Justice" in G. Johnstone and D. W. Van Ness (eds.), Handbook of Restorative Justice (2007), 315 for examples of national practice; para. 1 Belgian Ministry of Justice Circular Instruction, Restorative Justice Consultants.

disruption that would be caused by facilitating the attendance of all identifiable victims that are willing and able to participate.

Both models provide possible international penal policy implementation tools. Victim–offender mediation will probably be most effective in cases of specific requests for information or dialogue from a direct victim to the perpetrator of a particular crime. The conferencing model may be more useful for broader discussions of particular events or the conflict more generally.

Although a collective communication model risks losing the interpersonal nature of restorative mediation[153] and may appear to sit uneasily with the individual liability focus of the retributive international criminal justice process, it is more conducive to fulfilling reconciliation and reintegration aims. An inclusive approach is necessary to achieve a "durable solution".[154] Societal healing and transition must take place with the support and participation of all members of that society. A communitarian approach may also be more relevant given the religious and cultural perspectives of participants in relation to responsibility.[155]

Although it is possible to utilise criminal mediation models within a prison setting, the unique nature of international crime and the structure of the international penal system may create obstacles for doing so in the international criminal justice system. It is accepted that "stretching the [restorative justice] paradigm to fit extreme crimes alters its original shape".[156] The unique structure of the international penal system may require further adjustments to traditional approaches to restorative mediation. Rather than focusing on mediation between perpetrators and victims, for example, there may be scope for mediation between perpetrators. In the international criminal justice context, mediation involving only international criminals may have social value as this population consists of former warring parties. This form of mediation between international prisoners would, however, have to be facilitated by the utilisation of modern communication technologies such as video-conferencing. The utilisation of restorative justice tools in the

---

[153] Van Garsse, "The Meaning of Mediation within the Criminal Justice Context".

[154] J. Leinward, "Punishing Horrific Crime: Reconciling International Prosecution with National Sentencing Practices" (2008) 40 *Columbia Human Rights Law Review* 799–852 at 810.

[155] See V. Hancock "'No-self' at trial: How to Reconcile Punishing the Khmer Rouge for Crimes Against Humanity with Cambodian Buddhist Principles" (2008) 26(1) *Wisconsin International Law Journal* 87–129.

[156] Antkowiak, "An Emerging Mandate for International Courts", 286.

international penal system will ultimately require imagination, strict organisation and dedication. If practical obstacles prevent the facilitation of criminal mediation within national cooperating prisons, international prisoners should be permitted to cooperate with or participate in programmes and mechanisms operating in the community.

3.3 Links with external mechanisms

The incorporation of restorative communication models into the international criminal justice process post-conviction may also open the door to the creation of links with external resocialisation, reconciliation and reintegration processes. A communitarian restorative communication model may in fact already be operating in the relevant post-conflict society. To avoid the duplication of resources and effort, and to enhance local ownership over transition, conflict resolution mechanisms and programmes operating in post-conflict communities should be allowed to work with international prisoners. These programmes may also offer opportunities for individual and inter-relational resocialisation.

For example, in 2009, the ICTY Outreach Section worked with a local NGO trying to organise a conference to debate the guilty pleas of ICTY prisoners in order to explore possibilities for reconciliation[157] and met with several groups trying to form a coalition to establish a Regional Commission for Establishing Facts about War Crimes.[158] International prisoners, who wished to, could make significant contributions to both types of schemes. ICTR prisoners could benefit from programmes like the Awareness Raising Programmes for Lessons Learned from the Genocide of 1994 that were conducted in six prisons in Rwanda in 2011[159] and participation in the National Unity and Reconciliation Commission's civic education programmes, conflict mediation and community initiatives.[160]

External programmes may also be better placed to prepare international prisoners for release or reintegration into society. Just as "solutions to the problem of crime have to be sought by inclusion within the

---

[157] ICTY Outreach Activities 2009. [158] *Ibid.*
[159] Para. 59 ICTR Sixteenth Annual Report.
[160] B. Oomen, "Rwanda's Gacaca: Objectives, Merits and their Relation to Supranational Criminal Law" in R. Haveman and O. Olusanya (eds.), *Sentencing and Sanctioning in Supranational Criminal Law* (2006), 161–84 at 168.

community itself ... and not by exclusion from it",[161] the reintegration of international prisoners into post-conflict societies requires inclusive processes. Restorative models enable the discussion of past problems and the design of a transition plan that can serve as a blueprint for international sentence planning and release preparation. Restorative conferences may also facilitate the release planning process. International criminals are well known, as are the details of their crimes. Unless they are given protection as witnesses, it may be difficult for them to reintegrate into society upon release. Victims and society may have concerns about their release, ranging from potential for recidivism, to where the person is going to live and if they will have to see them. Information provision and honest discussion could go a long way to easing these concerns or finding a way to address them.

Without access to programmes in enforcing states or the assistance of an international parole system, international prisoners could benefit from local reintegration mechanisms. For example, in Rwanda, the NURC organised Ingando solitary camps to facilitate the transition of national detainees back into society by providing work and access to workshops on the causes of the genocide and national reconciliation.[162] A Community Reconciliation Process was also established in East Timor. Although this is a diversionary mechanism, it also provides an example of a local transitional justice mechanism used to reintegrate former perpetrators back into society using community-based dialogue.[163]

Rather than exist as an alternative to imprisonment, reconciliation initiatives should be able to penetrate prison walls. This permeability should, however, be two-way. Indictment, prosecution and conviction by an international court should not preclude participation in local, national or regional mechanisms. In other words, international prisoners should be able to contribute to national peace and reconciliation efforts.

The inter-relational aspect of international penal policy's aim to create more harmonious relationships for example could have knock-on effects for wider societal reconciliation. For example, the peaceful co-existence of former warring parties at the IDFs could act as a catalyst for peace in

---

[161] Faulkner cited in A. Rutherford, "Criminal Policy and the Eliminative Ideal" (1997) 31 (5) *Social Policy and Administration* 116–35 at 132.
[162] Oomen, "Rwanda's Gacaca", 179.
[163] Triponel and Pearson, "What Do You Think Should Happen?", 125.

society. The UNDU detainees publicly refuted claims of animosity between the different groups and openly socialised together.[164] In 1997, all of the UNDU detainees came together to create a cultural and entertainment programme to celebrate Christmas.[165] This harmony went beyond the celebration of occasions. One international prisoner described how it was difficult to tell family members about the strong friendships he had formed with other detained persons from previously opposite sides of the conflict, as he sometimes found it hard to believe himself.[166] Conveying this image of tolerance and respect between former warring factions, even from within such a constrained environment, could counter propaganda that these communities cannot co-exist peacefully.

Taking it one step further, those deemed most responsible for atrocities committed during the conflict could be encouraged to discuss issues among themselves. The harmonious living arrangements in the IDFs may be due to an unwritten rule not to ask about or discuss reasons for an individual's detention. Yet discussions could centre on the general causes and consequences of conflict and the way forward rather than an examination of actual crimes. Macro-level harmony and debate could prove to be a very powerful catalyst for micro-level reconciliation or the creation of conditions for peace in a fragile post-conflict society.

Logistical considerations may make it difficult to facilitate face-to-face discussions with international prisoners housed in various enforcing states but other forms of communication could be used. Communitarian models and external collaborations need not require the movement of international prisoners as other modes of communication, such as letter, phone, CD, DVD, email or video-link, can be used to exchange information.

4. Dealing with conflict, crime and transition

Whichever model is used to facilitate post-conviction communication, dialogue can go beyond criminal mediation and embrace wider conflict resolution issues. The utilisation of restorative justice modalities post-conviction may provide a more culturally relevant and responsive

---

[164] ICTY Press Release, "Open Letter from the Detainees Regarding their Conditions at the ICTY's Detention Unit", 12.08.1998.
[165] Katava, 13.10.2007.   [166] Bralo, Sweden 08.10.2008.

approach to dealing with conflict and crime.[167] Restorative justice's origins have been traced to traditional and indigenous practices for addressing criminal justice issues throughout the Americas, Africa, Asia, the Middle East and the Pacific that are still used today.[168] These communication mechanisms are typically less formal and more flexible than legal process and have demonstrated their ability to evolve and adapt in response to different situations.[169] Traditional, indigenous and local approaches to dispute resolution that focus on restoring relationships and reconciliation may have greater "cultural authenticity."[170] Rather than require victims to set aside their identity to conform to legal due process requirements,[171] restorative justice enables people to discuss conflict and crime in a more familiar manner. There is evidence of increasing use of locally initiated traditional mechanisms to deal with conflict, crime and transition.[172] Unlike retributive justice's focus on the past, restorative justice encourages the discussion of the past, present and the future. Restorative justice-orientated communication can be used to discuss the context and causes of conflict and international crime, to create a shared and accepted truth and ultimately to break cycles of violence.

4.1 Context and causes of conflict and crime

Restorative justice modalities provide a form of social intervention that goes beyond normal penal practice to engage with affected parties to address the historical, social, cultural, structural, institutional and ideological causes of conflict and related criminality.[173] For example, Oomen highlights that the 1994 Rwandan genocide involved both state sponsorship and popular participation and came against a history of ethnically motivated murders with a myriad of underlying legal, social, cultural,

---

[167] Henham, *Punishment and Process in International Criminal Trials*, 147.
[168] Hill, "Restorative Justice", 52; Antkowiak, "An Emerging Mandate for International Courts", 285; Oomen, "Rwanda's Gacaca", 168; M. Findlay, "The Challenge for Asian Jurisdictions in the Development of International Criminal Justice" (2010) 32 *Sydney Law Review* 205–19 at 212.
[169] Hill, "Restorative Justice", 52.   [170] Oomen, "Rwanda's Gacaca", 168.
[171] Antkowiak, "An Emerging Mandate for International Courts", 285.
[172] Triponel and Pearson, "What Do You Think Should Happen?", 123.
[173] See R. Henham, "Theorizing the Penality of Sentencing in International Criminal Trials" (2004) 8 *Theoretical Criminology* 429–63 at 445; Henham, *Punishment and Process in International Criminal Trials*, 148; Hill, "Restorative Justice", 51.

economic and political causes.[174] Just as all conflicts are different, so too are the reasons for atrocities and perpetrators' participation in them.[175] The "magnifying glass"[176] approach to criminal conduct adopted by international criminal trials means that the context in which the conflict and crimes occur is only important "insofar as it impinges on questions of innocence or guilt".[177]

Restorative dialogue can facilitate an understanding of what went wrong, outside of the technical and jurisdictional constraints of trial process. Guilty pleas at the ICTY included references to the causes of the conflict and reasons for involvement, including political propaganda,[178] feelings of duty,[179] fear for survival,[180] a lack of choice,[181] grief, and the chaos of war.[182] Some of those convicted of international crimes at the SCSL claimed that they became involved in the conflict to support a just cause or to restore democracy.[183] These motivations can be explored in greater detail in a post-conviction setting.

Restorative communication, unlike the trial process, can also address collective responsibility for the conflict and the temporarily normalised nature of criminal behaviour. International criminal trials exclude consideration of collective responsibility and systemic repression by focusing on individual criminal responsibility for particular acts or omissions.[184] Yet many conflicts are caused by the devaluation of one group by another, which legitimises the exclusion or abuse of that group's members.[185] What was once a criminal act becomes classified

---

[174] Oomen, "Rwanda's Gacaca", 164–5.
[175] See D. Chuter, *War Crimes: Confronting Atrocity in the Modern World* (2003), 274.
[176] M. Damaška, "What is the Point of International Criminal Justice?" (2008) 83 *Chicago-Kent Law Review* 329–65 at 337.
[177] R. A. Wilson, *Writing History in International Criminal Trials* (2011), 8.
[178] See Deronjić's Guilty Plea, 28.01.2004; Rajić's Guilty Plea, 07.04.2006.
[179] Rajić's Guilty Plea, 07.04.2006.
[180] See Plavšić's Guilty Plea, 17.12.2002; Mrđa's Guilty Plea, 22.10.2003.
[181] See Erdemović's Guilty Plea, 20.11.1996; Sikirica's Guilty Plea, 08.10.2001; Mrđa's Guilty Plea, 22.10.2003; Obrenović's Guilty Plea, 30.10.2003.
[182] See Todorović's Guilty Plea, 04.05.2001; Došen's Guilty Plea, 08.10.2001.
[183] See paras. 554–5, 559–60 *Fofana, Kondewa* (Appeal Judgement) SCSL-04-14-A, 28.05.2008.
[184] See Drumbl, *Atrocity, Punishment and International Law*, 29, 35; Drumbl, "Collective Violence and Individual Punishment", 542, 569, 570, 573; R. Teitel, "The Universal and the Particular in International Criminal Justice" (1998) 30 *Columbia Human Rights Law Review* 285–303 at 295–301.
[185] See Drumbl, *Atrocity, Punishment and International Law*, 29, 32; Servaes and Birtsch, *Engaging with Victims and Perpetrators*, 5.

as a heroic deed in this social environment,[186] making it very difficult for individuals to disobey orders or intervene to protect those being persecuted.[187] An acknowledgement of collective responsibility for the conflict and its perpetuation does not diminish the individual responsibility of convicted persons, but it does help to create a more comprehensive account of the conflict.[188]

Post-conviction dialogue may also be valuable as international prisoners who originally deny responsibility, may, with time and a chance to think about the conflict outside of a trial environment, acknowledge the criminal nature of their acts and their responsibility.[189] Some may still reject the legal process due to a sense of betrayal, unfair treatment or a belief that the prosecuting court is illegitimate. But guilt comes in many forms. For instance, in addition to legal criminal guilt, Jaspers argues that there is also moral and metaphysical guilt.[190]

Criminal guilt refers to acts ordered or executed by individuals and it can be aligned with both individual and command responsibility imposed by international courts. Moral guilt refers to acts which are ignored out of fear or due to advantages that may accrue. Guilty pleas at the ICTY and ICTR referred to guilt for keeping silent or giving the impression through presence at the site of atrocities that the acts being committed were approved of.[191] Others accepted command responsibility, even though they did not order the acts in question, due to a moral obligation to accept responsibility for the acts of subordinates.[192] Metaphysical guilt relates to the failure to act to prevent the commission of crimes. ICTY and ICTR guilty pleas have also referred to guilt for the failure to take steps to protect vulnerable persons.[193] In some cases, individuals tried to help but regretted not doing more.[194] These other

---

[186] Para 2.7.2 Independent Audit of the Detention Unit at the ICTY, 2006.
[187] See Todorović's Guilty Plea, 04.05.2001; Sikirica's Guilty Plea, 08.10.2001; Došen's Guilty Plea, 08.10.2001; Mrđa's Guilty Plea, 22.10.2003; Bralo's Guilty Plea, 07.10.2005; paras. 132, 137 *Bisengimana* (Judgment) ICTR-00-60-T, 13.04.2006.
[188] See Drumbl, *Atrocity, Punishment and International Law*, 32.
[189] See para. 71 *Ruggiu* (Judgment) ICTR-97-32-I, 01.06.2000; Bralo's Guilty Plea, 07.10.2005; para. 32 *Rugambarara* (Judgment) ICTR-00-59-T, 16.11.2007.
[190] Drumbl, *Atrocity, Punishment and International Law*, 36.
[191] See Babić's Guilty Plea, 27.01.2004; para. 132 *Bisengimana* (Judgment) ICTR-00-60-T, 13.04.2006.
[192] See Jokić's Guilty Plea 04.12.2003; Rajić's Guilty Plea, 07.04.2006.
[193] See Babić's Guilty Plea, 27.01.2004; para. 156 *Rutaganira* (Judgment) ICTR-95-IC-T, 14.03.2005; para. 132 *Bisengimana* (Judgment) ICTR-00-60-T, 13.04.2006; para. 67 *Nzabirinda* (Judgment) ICTR-2001-77-T, 23.02.2007.
[194] See Došen's Guilty Plea, 08.10.2001; Kolundžija's Guilty Plea, 09.10.2001.

forms of guilt may be felt more profoundly and sincerely by international prisoners[195] and may, in some cases, be more relevant to victims than legal guilt. Legal guilt can only refer to the acts or omissions in the indictment. Restorative communication can be used to discuss responsibility for acts or omissions that may not directly correlate with the indictment. International prisoners may not be willing to accept responsibility for or feel liable for the crimes for which they were convicted. This does not mean they are not willing to discuss other acts or the conflict more generally. Even within the international trial process, apologies that failed to acknowledge personal participation were accepted as mitigating factors if they were sincere, as they were considered to be expressions of empathy for victims that could be viewed as a symbolic guarantee of non-repetition.[196]

4.2 Creating an accepted truth

The ICTY heralded the discovery of the truth as "a cornerstone of the rule of law and a fundamental step on the way of reconciliation: for it is the truth that cleanses the ethnic and religious hatreds and begins the healing process".[197] Yet, as Damaška notes, international courts have a limited capacity to discuss the context and etiology of crime-producing conflicts.[198] International trial process constrains the truth that can be discovered. Legal liberalism prioritises the evidentiary determination of individual criminal responsibility over the need to establish a historical record:[199] "what is proved cannot be more than what is alleged, and what is alleged will often be what prosecutors think can be proved".[200] The temporal, territorial and subject-matter jurisdictions of the courts and their prosecutorial strategies limit the time-frame, crimes and individuals that can be investigated.

Victims' stories only emerge if they are identified and selected as witnesses, and, even then, their version of events will often be curtailed by the remit of the court and the charges on the indictment, delivered by legal professionals and reconstructed during cross-examination.[201]

---

[195] See Deronjić's Guilty Plea, 28.01.2004.
[196] See para. 752 Orić (Judgment) IT-03-68-T, 30.06.2006; paras. 63–5 Fofana, Kondewa (Judgment) SCSL-04-14-J, 09.10.2007.
[197] Para. 21 Erdemović (Judgment) IT-96-22-Tbis, 05.03.1998.
[198] Damaška, "What is the Point of International Criminal Justice?", 332.
[199] Wilson, *Writing History in International Criminal Trials*, 2–6.
[200] Chuter, *War Crimes*, 228.   [201] Findlay, "The Challenge for Asian Jurisdictions", 210.

Procedures that expedite the presentation of evidence and the acceptance of guilty pleas have further reduced the time available to victims to speak in court.[202] Though courts often view these measures as being beneficial for victims as they reduce the risk of re-traumatisation,[203] this may overlook the cathartic value testifying can have.[204] While testifying at trial may have benefits for some witnesses, traditional or restorative dispute resolution mechanisms often provide more inclusive and "comfortable sites for story-telling".[205]

Guilty pleas can contribute to the establishment of the truth as accused persons admit to the charges brought under the indictment, and at times, go beyond this by clarifying issues of investigative doubt and even revealing information about previously unknown events.[206] On the other hand, this truth, limited to what has been agreed with the Prosecutor, prevents the collection and presentation of evidence and may not reflect the full truth.[207] International judges have acknowledged that plea agreements may create "an unfortunate gap in the public and historical record".[208] While the residual value of a plea bargain may be greater than that of an acquittal, the vacation of charges buries allegations, bars the determination of those truths in a judicial forum and hurts and frustrates victims who feel their suffering has become a mere bargaining chip.[209]

International trials cannot and should not be the "final arbiter of historical facts".[210] Some argue that as international courts are not able to produce comprehensive historical records, truth and reconciliation commissions, which are not bound by the same jurisdictional or evidentiary hurdles, are necessary to assume "responsibility for the broader

---

[202] Tieger and Shin, "Plea Agreements in the ICTY", 674–5.
[203] Paras. 32, 52, 55, 57 *Serugendo* (Judgment) ICTR-05-84-I, 12.06.2006; para. 30 *Rugambarara* (Judgment) ICTR-00-59-T, 16.11.2007; para. 126 *Bisengimana* (Judgment) ICTR-00-60-T, 13.04.2006; paras. 45, 49 *Zelenović* (Judgment) IT-96-23/2-S, 04.04.2007.
[204] Henham and Drumbl, "Plea Agreements in the ICTY", 57.
[205] Drumbl, "Collective Violence and Individual Punishment", 594.
[206] Paras. 32, 55–6, 61 *Serugendo* (Judgment) ICTR-05-84-I, 12.06.2006; para. 30 *Rugambarara* (Judgment) ICTR-00-59-T, 16.11.2007; paras. 126, 136 *Bisengimana* (Judgment) ICTR-00-60-T, 13.04.2006; paras. 45, 52 *Bralo* (Appeal Judgment) IT-95-17-A, 02.04.2007; paras. 45, 48 *Zelenović* (Judgment) IT-96-23/2-S, 04.04.2007.
[207] D'Ascoli, *Sentencing in International Criminal Law*, 46–7.
[208] Para. 122 *D. Nikolić* (Judgment) IT-94-2-S, 18.12.03.
[209] Henham and Drumbl, "Plea Bargaining at the ICTY", 82–3; Clark, "Plea Bargaining at the ICTY", 427–8.
[210] Para. 135 *Deronjić* (Judgment) IT-02-61-S, 30.03.04.

historical narrative".[211] TRCs may facilitate "more contextual and open-ended inquiry and garner deeper insights into the origins and causes"[212] of crime-producing conflicts. Trials do, however, produce extensive documentary archives that contain witness statements, photographs and technical reports that can guard against revisionism and are invaluable for creating a historical record.[213] The authoritativeness of international trial findings, judgments and categorisations of acts or events that occurred as international crimes also contributes to the establishment of historical truth.[214] The establishment of legal fact, however, does not establish accepted truth.

International trials have had little "effect on the way in which the conflicts are generally perceived".[215] Despite the vast jurisprudence of the ICTY, for example, denial about international crimes remains prevalent throughout the states of the former Republic of Yugoslavia.[216] The "truth" provided by international courts located far-away is often not accepted by local populations who view the courts as selective or biased.[217] Legal fact and the admissions of responsibility that emerge from international criminal trials can, however, add to a growing body of authoritative information that gradually becomes accepted as the truth.[218]

Restorative or transitional justice mechanisms may provide more accessible truths. International trials are legalistic, complex and often produce "mind-numbingly monotonous" accounts of events.[219] Unlike a trial which is based on logical and forensic truth, restorative communication produces truth based on personal narrative and social dialogue.[220] In contrast to the trial process, which endorses one version of truth over

---

[211] W. Schabas, "Criminology, Accountability and International Justice" in M. Bosworth and C. Hoyle (eds.), *What is Criminology?* (2011), 346–57 at 354.
[212] Wilson, *Writing History in International Criminal Trials*, 10.
[213] Chuter, *War Crimes*, 229; Tieger and Shin, "Plea Agreements in the ICTY", 670; Wilson, *Writing History in International Criminal Trials*, 18; G. K. McDonald, "The International Criminal Tribunals: Crime & Punishment in the International Arena" (2001) 25 *Nova Law Review* 463–84 at 481.
[214] Schabas, "Criminology, Accountability and International Justice", 353.
[215] Chuter, *War Crimes*, 229.   [216] Clark, "Plea Agreements in the ICTY", 425.
[217] Chuter, *War Crimes*, 231; Wippman, "Atrocities, Deterrence, and the Limits of International Justice", 486.
[218] Chuter, *War Crimes*, 232.
[219] Wilson, *Writing History in International Criminal Trials*, 11.
[220] Chuter, *War Crimes*, 245; Drumbl, "Collective Violence and Individual Punishment", 593.

all others,[221] restorative dialogue does not demand that all other truths be subsumed or ignored but instead recognises the value of alternatives and embraces multiplicity.[222] Restorative dialogue facilitates the unpacking of "subjectivities and difference".[223] This is important as conflict resolution mechanisms should avoid the "worship of the victim" or "treating subjective experiences and recollections as though they were always objectively true ... [the] subjective experiences of perpetrators must also be taken into account".[224]

The "indispensable perspective of the perpetrator"[225] not only balances the historical account, but it can provide insights into why the crimes were committed.[226] One international prisoner noted that while "it is important to tell the whole story, it is not always important for the court for the full story to be told".[227] Questions of political, moral and collective responsibility, which cannot be addressed by the international criminal trial process, are often "the questions of most interest".[228] As Tieger and Shin note, "the most haunting questions of all for both victims and historians – why former neighbours destroyed communities that had lived in harmony for decades – can only be answered fully by those who committed the crimes or were present when objectives were determined and orders given".[229] Perpetrators can also provide information about previously unknown incidents and motivations.[230] In the international context, this is significant as international prisoners are often former military, political and community leaders.

International prisoners have acknowledged responsibility for crimes they are charged with during the trial process.[231] Acknowledgments by offenders of the crimes that were committed and their role in them may be more meaningful for victims than a finding of guilt imposed by the international courts and may create openings for dialogue and

---

[221] Wilson, *Writing History in International Criminal Trials*, 8.
[222] Hill, "Restorative Justice", 52.
[223] Drumbl, "Collective Violence and Individual Punishment", 594.
[224] Chuter, *War Crimes*, 245.
[225] Tieger and Shin, "Plea Agreements in the ICTY", 671.
[226] Clark, "Plea Agreements in the ICTY", 424.
[227] Blagojević, Trondheim Prison, 28.06.2012. [228] Chuter, *War Crimes*, 226.
[229] Tieger and Shin, "Plea Agreements in the ICTY", 671.
[230] Chuter, *War Crimes*, 246.
[231] Paras. 55, 58–9 *Serugendo* (Judgment) ICTR-05-84-I, 12.06.2006; para. 140 *Bisengimana* (Judgment) ICTR-00-60-T, 13.04.2006; paras. 45, 47 *Zelenović* (Judgment) IT-96-23/2-S, 04.04.2007.

reconciliation.[232] Such admissions can bring a degree of closure for victims and may gradually create an environment for political acknowledgment of acts and responsibility.[233]

4.3 Breaking cycles of violence

Admissions of responsibility and the discussion of motivations by former leaders may not necessarily provide new information but they can highlight the need to address the past in order to break cycles of violence.[234] The truth about the reality of war can act as a deterrent to future potential perpetrators. Some ICTY guilty pleas contain very vivid and emotional descriptions of the conflict that emphasised how all sides had suffered.[235] Deronjić's statement in particular recalls the true consequences of the conflict in the former Yugoslavia;

> There was nothing it did not touch ... When everything was over and it seemed to last for an eternity, those of us who survived, instead of the paradise that everybody promised, found ourselves in hell ... Today, the town that I am speaking about ... is situated between two graveyards. One contains the bodies of one group, and the other contains the bodies of another group, divided even in death. Both graveyards came to be during and after the war. When you count all of those who are buried in those graveyards, there are twice as many of those than those who today inhabit that town. That is the result of war ... That is the result of mindless political concepts to which we agreed and in which we participated. The town of Srebrenica does not exist anymore. Whom does it belong to today? The Serbs? The Muslims? It is a town of the dead.[236]

It is important to destroy romantic notions of war by reminding future generations about the stark reality of conflict and its long-lasting effects. It is also important to address the potentially cyclical nature of conflict. The ascription of a victim identity to a particular group may result in the denial of responsibility and it may be used to legitimise the abuse of other groups in the future.[237] Past experience has shown that both individuals and groups that suffer persecution may become victimisers

---

[232] Para. 72 *M. Nikolić* (Judgment) IT-02-60/1-S, 02.12.2003.
[233] Paras. 111–2 *Obrenović* (Judgment) IT-02-60/2-S, 10.12.2003; Tieger and Shin, "Plea Agreements in the ICTY", 672–3.
[234] Clark, "Plea Bargaining at the ICTY", 425; Damaška, "What is the Point of International Criminal Justice?", 332.
[235] See Obrenović's Guilty Plea, 30.10.2003.   [236] Deronjić's Guilty Plea, 28.01.2004.
[237] See Servaes and Birtsch, *Engaging with Victims and Perpetrators*, 4, 9.

themselves.[238] Mrs Plavšić highlighted this phenomenon in her guilty plea: "I believe, fear, a blinding fear that led to an obsession, especially for those of us for whom the Second World War was a living memory, that Serbs would never again allow themselves to become victims ... In this obsession of ours to never again become victims, we had allowed ourselves to become victimisers."[239]

If these issues are openly discussed, society can work together to prevent the dissemination of political propaganda that creates fear, glorifies violence and generates an atmosphere in which persecution of others becomes normalised. Given the "high recidivism rate of post-civil-war states relapsing into further violence"[240] it is vitally important that international prisoners are not released without having discussed or been made aware of the impact and effect of their conduct. The handful of individuals punished by the international community can provide insight into the causes and effects of international crimes but as they represent only a tiny segment of those responsible for the initiation and continuation of the related conflict, society as a whole must be involved in efforts to secure reconciliation, reintegration and transition to a peaceful society.

5. Reparative actions

There is increasing recognition of a right to reparations under international and human rights law.[241] Reparative actions can contribute towards reconciliation and the redefinition of the victim–offender relationship.[242] Both victims and the international courts have acknowledged the positive effect of offenders' efforts to atone for their crimes through admissions of guilt, expressions of remorse and reparative actions.[243] The uniqueness of international criminality, the structure of the international penal system and the utilisation of restorative communication models in a post-conviction setting mean that international criminal mediation would focus on the therapeutic and social healing

---

[238] See Drumbl, *Atrocity, Punishment and International Law*, 44; Servaes and Birtsch, *Engaging with Victims and Perpetrators*, 5.
[239] Plavšić's Guilty Plea, 17.12.2002.
[240] King and Meernik, "Assessing the Impact of the ICTY", 46.
[241] Para. 185 *Lubanga* (TCI Decision) ICC-01/04-01/06-2904, 07.08.2012. See also D. Shelton, *Remedies in International Human Rights Law*, 2nd edn (2005).
[242] Para. 193 *Lubanga* (TCI Decision) ICC-01/04-01/06-2904, 07.08.2012.
[243] See para. 72 *Bralo* (AC Judgment) IT-95-17-A, 02.04.2007.

that dialogue can bring rather than the more tangible restitutionary outcomes sought in domestic diversionary practice.[244] This does not, however, rule out the possibility of reparative actions.

Options for reparations will be more limited in an international penal system and "devising an agreement will require some creative thinking".[245] The ICC has stated that reparations need not be confined to restitution, compensation and rehabilitation but may include other forms of reparation with symbolic, preventative and transformative values.[246] International prisoners could offer apologies or agree to provide information, report on progress or promise to do some reparative act for the benefit of victims or their communities.

Apologies may be addressed to direct victims, their families, victim communities and indirect victims, such as those that had to leave the country as refugees during the war.[247] They can be made on a private or public basis.[248] Apologies offered during the trial process have contained admissions of liability, acknowledgments of the innocence of victims, expressions of shame, regret, remorse and guilt and requests for forgiveness.[249] Restorative principles encourage forgiveness without forgetting, but victims need not accept the apology. Restorative dialogue in a post-conviction setting may be more conducive to apology offerings. Accused persons may be wary of apologising before the verdict is given due to a fear of self-incrimination. Apologies may also be more readily accepted at this stage as an apology given during trial may be viewed as a tactical move to secure more lenient treatment rather than a sincere expression of remorse.[250] In the case of serious crime, an apology may be insufficient

---

[244] Rossi, "Meet Me on Death Row", 192–4; Walgrave, "Restorative Justice", 619–22; Hill, "Restorative Justice", 56.
[245] Branham, "The Mess We're In", 721.
[246] Para. 222 *Lubanga* (TCI Decision) ICC-01/04–01/06–2904, 07.08.2012.
[247] Mrđa's Guilty Plea, 22.10.2003; Bralo's Guilty Plea, 07.10.2005; D. Nikolić's Guilty Plea, 06.11.2003; M. Nikolić's Guilty Plea, 29.10.2003; para. 130 *Bisengimana* (Judgment) ICTR-00-60-T, 13.04.2006.
[248] Paras. 241, 269 *Lubanga* (TCI Decision) ICC-01/04–01/06–2904, 07.08.2012.
[249] See Babić's Guilty Plea, 27.01.2004; Banović's Guilty Plea, 03.09.2003; Deronjić's Guilty Plea, 28.01.2004; Došen's Guilty Plea, 08.10.2001; Mrđa's Guilty Plea, 22.10.2003; D. Nikolić's Guilty Plea, 06.11.2003; Todorović's Guilty Plea, 04.05.2001; Sikirica's Guilty Plea, 08.10.2001; para. 32 *Rugambarara* (Judgment) ICTR-00-59-T, 16.11.2007; para. 67 *Nzabirinda* (Judgment) ICTR-2001-77-T, 23.02.2007; para. 157 *Rutaganira* (Judgment) ICTR-95-IC-T, 14.03.2005; para. 40 *Serushago* (Judgment) ICTR-98-39-S, 05.02.1999; para. 14 *Serugendo* (Judgment) ICTR-2005-84-I, 12.06.2006; para. 137 *Bisengimana* (Judgment) ICTR-00-60-T, 13.04.2006.
[250] See Aneme, "Apology and Trials", 81–2.

to demonstrate repentance and may need to be coupled with reparative efforts.[251] Moreover, as expressions of remorse offered during sentencing or release hearings are often viewed cynically, behaviour and actions that demonstrate remorse may be more conducive to promoting reconciliation.[252]

Examples of reparative efforts offered by international offenders include spreading the truth to contribute to reconciliation, the provision of information about the location of the bodies of missing persons, assisting with de-mining operations and donating blood to pay society back for the acts committed.[253] Convicted persons may also offer to pay financial reparations. Reparations may be direct or indirect and include compensation or donations to projects. The UN Tribunals could only forward a finding of criminal liability to national authorities, where victims could then make claims for reparations.[254] This has not occurred to date.

The ICC is the first international court empowered to award reparations, other than restitution, directly to victims. Reparations, considered to be critical components of the Rome Statute,[255] can relate to compensation or the rehabilitation needs of victims and can be ordered directly from a convicted person by the court acting on its own motion or at the request of victims.[256] Such reparations "oblige perpetrators to repair the harm caused to victims and enable the court to ensure that offenders take account for their acts".[257] The fact that ICC reparations are based exclusively on the individual criminal responsibility of the convicted person,[258] and are ordered rather than negotiated,[259] makes them appear more punitive than restorative. The ICC, however, can only order monetary reparations. All non-monetary and symbolic reparations are voluntary.[260] Offenders should be able to volunteer to

---

[251] Duff, "Restoration and Retribution", 51.
[252] Clark, "Plea Bargaining at the ICTY", 433; Tieger, "Remorse and Mitigation in the ICTY" (2003) 16 *Leiden Journal of International Law* 777–86 at 777, 780–2.
[253] See para. 50 *Kambanda* (Judgment) ICTR-97023-S, 04.09.1998; Sikirica's Guilty Plea, 08.10.2001; para. 130 *Bisengimana* (Judgment) ICTR-00-60-T, 13.04.2006; para. 247 D. *Nikolić* (Judgment) IT-94-2-S, 18.12.2003; para. 71 *Bralo* (Appeal Judgment) IT-95-17-A, 02.04.2007. Bralo, Sweden, 08.10.08.
[254] Rule 106 ICTY/ICTR RPE.
[255] Preamble, Reparations, ICC-ASP/10/Res.3, 20.12.2011.   [256] Art. 75 ICCSt.
[257] Para. 179 *Lubanga* (TCI Decision) ICC-01/04-01/06-2904, 07.08.2012.
[258] Para. 2 Reparations, ICC-ASP/10/Res.3, 20.12.2011; Art. 75(2) ICCSt.
[259] Art. 75(2) ICCSt.
[260] Paras. 179, 241, 269 *Lubanga* (TCI Decision) ICC-01/04-01/06-2904, 07.08.2012.

contribute directly to the Trust Fund for Victims, which can then be applied to by victim associations and community reconciliation projects. In addition and in order to align reparation policy with the restorative approach of international penal policy, reparations should also be a possible negotiated outcome of constructive dialogue between offenders and victims.

The availability of options ultimately depends on the imprisoned offender's ability to earn or access finances. Many national prison systems experience difficulties in providing paid work for prisoners. The Belgian model could be adapted to facilitate this form of scheme. In Belgium, offenders can access finances (up to a specified limit) to make reparations to victims from a restoration fund administered by an NGO. The prisoners receive the funds in exchange for community service performed either in prison or in society.[261] In principle, the ICC could facilitate such a process. Under current regulations, the Trust Fund may accept voluntary contributions from individuals and other entities.[262] Moreover, it may grant collective awards and allow for their distribution through external bodies.[263] Under the regulations, the decision on whether or not to accept a voluntary offer from an indicted or convicted person presently lies with the Board of the Trust Fund and not victims or intended recipients.[264] However, the ICC has noted that "due to the voluntary nature of reparations, victims must give informed consent prior to their receipt".[265] The ICC Trust Fund's mandate could be amended to include a third function; it could act as a depository for voluntary reparations generated in compliance with restorative agreements produced during restorative communication initiatives. This twin approach of ordered and negotiated reparations would be more in line with the European Prison Rules.[266]

Just as criminal mediation in the international penal system may require a communitarian model or links with models operating in the community, reparations in the international penal system are likely to be granted on a collective basis and used by community projects. While

---

[261] See A. Verstraete *et al.*, "Introducing Restorative Justice in Belgian Prisons", 6; Roberts and Peters, "How Restorative Justice is Able to Transcend the Prison Walls", 113.
[262] See Arts. 21(a), 23 Regulations for the Trust Fund.
[263] Rules 97–8 ICC RPE; Shelton, *Remedies in International Human Rights Law*, 234, 237.
[264] Art. 30 Regulations for the Trust Fund.
[265] Para. 204 *Lubanga* (TCI Decision) ICC-01/04-01/06-2904, 07.08.2012.
[266] See Rules 103(7), 105(5) EPR.

money collected by the ICC's TFV may be used to compensate victims using pro rata payments,[267] it is unlikely to be possible to compensate all victims financially. International crimes involve large numbers of victims, many of whom will not testify at the court or indeed be identified during trial proceedings. Moreover, international offenders are typically declared to be indigent with the result that the TFV will mostly depend on voluntary contributions from states. For example, in the *Lubanga* reparations hearing it was held that "the convicted person has been declared indigent and no assets or property have been identified that can be used for the purposes of reparations. Lubanga is only able to contribute to non-monetary reparations".[268] Consequently, the ICC, in its guidelines on reparations,[269] stated that reparations granted by the TFV should be applied in a broad and flexible manner to benefit direct and indirect victims, as well as NGOs, charities, statutory bodies, schools, hospitals, colleges, companies etc.[270] It declined invitations to restrict reparation entitlement to victims that participate in the relevant trial, or indeed those who apply for reparations to the court.[271] While the statute and rules permit the concurrent grant of individual and collective reparations, the ICC felt that the latter option would be necessary to ensure that reparations reached unidentified victims.[272] Various forms of reparations have been recognised by the ICC, such as campaigns to prevent future conflict, create awareness of the crimes committed and improve the position of victims, certificates that acknowledge the harm caused to individuals and outreach and promotional programmes that aim to reduce stigmatisation and marginalisation of victims in the community.[273] The ICC justified its preference for communitarian grants in lieu of individual awards due to their greater utility given the limited funds available and the fact that they do not require "costly and resource intensive verification procedures".[274] The community-based approach advocated by the ICC is reflected in the current work of the TFV on large-scale community projects in Uganda and DRC that have directly benefited over 8,000 individuals.[275]

---

[267] Shelton, *Remedies in International Human Rights Law*, 236.
[268] Para. 269 *Lubanga* (TCI Decision) ICC-01/04-01/06-2904, 07.08.2012.
[269] Art. 75(1) ICCSt; Decision establishing the principles and procedure to be applied to reparations, *Lubanga* (TCI Decision) ICC-01/04-01/06-2904, 07.08.12.
[270] Paras. 180, 195, 197 *Lubanga* (TCI Decision) ICC-01/04-01/06-2904, 07.08.2012.
[271] Para. 187 *ibid*.   [272] Paras. 219–20 *ibid*.   [273] Paras. 239–40 *ibid*.
[274] Para. 274 *ibid*.   [275] TFV Programme Progress Report, Summer 2012, 3–4.

Reparations can form part of international penal practice. International prisoners, even those who are indigent, can offer symbolic reparations. They should also be able to offer money they own or earn to individuals, a central fund or particular community projects. Such reparative efforts may result from an international prisoner's own initiative, a request from a victim or victims' group or an agreement following restorative dialogue. Opportunities to participate in restorative communication and offer reparative efforts will enable international prisoners to demonstrate that they have addressed and worked towards some of the criteria for release established by the ICC. In particular, dialogue and reparations can demonstrate the prisoner's ability to reintegrate into the community upon release, facilitate efforts to dissociate from crime and take actions for the benefit of victims and give some indication of the effect the prisoner's release will have on victims, their families and the stability of wider society.[276] Reparative actions can also contribute to the attainment of international justice goals of reconciliation and transition towards a more peaceful society.

6. Ethical issues

The implementation of restorative projects in the penal setting creates some ethical dilemmas. It is of paramount importance to ensure that restorative processes do not become subsumed into the sanction.[277] Asking an offender to meet with or hear the views of large numbers of victims may transform the nature of the process from restorative to punitive.[278] In the prison environment, there is often a very fine line between active encouragement and coercion. For example, there is a risk that the restoratively-orientated early release criteria of the ICC will, in effect, make participation in such programmes a pre-condition for release; undermining the ability of the authorities to ensure that participation is voluntary. There is also a danger that victims will view the offender's participation or offers of reparation as a tactical move to earn

---

[276] Rule 223 ICC RPE.
[277] J. Blad, "Institutionalising Restorative Justice? Transforming Criminal Justice? A Critical View on the Netherlands" in I. Aersten et al. (eds.), *Institutionalising Restorative Justice* (2006), 111–12.
[278] See Duff, "Restoration and Retribution", 54; Roche, "Retributive and Restorative Justice", 83–5; A. Von Hirsch et al., "Specifying Aims and Limits for Restorative Justice: A 'Making Amends' Model?" in A. Von Hirsch et al. (eds.), *Restorative Justice and Criminal Justice: Competing or Reconcilable Paradigms* (2003), 27.

an early ticket home at the expense of their emotional well-being. It is therefore imperative that procedural safeguards are put in place to ensure that participation is voluntary and based on informed consent.

The concept of voluntary participation relates not only to procedural issues but also to the substantive content of the dialogue. The employment of restorative models for communication should not be viewed as an opportunity to coerce prisoners into internalising moral standards or to "educate" insufficiently empathetic offenders.[279] Compulsory attitudinising is demeaning and violates the duty to respect human dignity.[280] Transformative effects should be the result of personal choice and an internal process rather than an external imposition of moral values.

Just as offenders should not be moralised, victims should not be viewed instrumentally and used as moralisation or political tools. They are, and should be treated as, active participants. While it is important to create a safe and respectful atmosphere for dialogue, all emotions should be acknowledged and accepted. Historical and socio-political contexts and organisational mandates may, albeit unintentionally, dictate a particular form of discourse or create expectations for dialogue. For example, Verdoolaege argues that the political momentum to strive for national unity in post-apartheid South Africa resulted in the Truth and Reconciliation Commission's rejection of genuine feelings of anger, hatred and revenge as they did not fit into the pre-planned masternarrative. The micro-narratives of victims were constrained by the reconciliation-orientated "contextualisation cues" of the commissioners which created expectations for forgiveness and compassion and placed subtle but strong pressure on participants to standardise their testimonies.[281] The "intimidating atmosphere of religiosity"[282] made the experience traumatic for some and cast doubt on the genuineness of declarations of reconciliation.

Restorative communication should be facilitated, not manipulated, by the coordinator. Restorative justice, unlike traditional criminal justice

---

[279] See N. Lacey, *State Punishment; Political Principles and Community Values* (1988), 31; Henham, *Punishment and Process in International Criminal Trials*, 146; Van Garsse, "Mediation in a Detention Context", 11–12.

[280] Von Hirsch *et al.*, "Specifying Aims and Limits for Restorative Justice", 32–4; Rotman, "Beyond Punishment", 290, 294.

[281] See A. Verdoolaege, "'Would You be Prepared to Reconcile, Please?', The Discursive Introduction of Reconciliation at the Human Rights Violations Hearings of the TRC", 2003. See also Servaes and Birtsch, *Engaging with Victims and Perpetrators*, 11.

[282] Chuter, *War Crimes*, 247.

processes, "views the expression and exploration of emotions as key to understanding the effects of the crime".[283] All emotions are valid and participants should not be forced to act a certain way simply to align their interaction with higher organisational or political goals. The dialogue should remain personally relevant and real to participants and dictated by their experiences and emotions.

Voluntary participation also encompasses issues relating to the use of the dialogue. National practice dictates that only the participants have the right to decide if and how the content of the dialogue and resulting restorative agreements are published.[284] Assurances of confidentiality may entice parties to discuss conflict situations they may not otherwise be comfortable discussing due to wishes for privacy or fears of self-incrimination. However, the high social relevance of this form of dialogue and the collective format preferable for the international penal system may make it more difficult to protect the privacy of participants and the confidentiality of proceedings.[285] Further, not all participants may wish to keep the outcome of the communication private. The public value of the coming together of the different groups may have been a primary motivating factor for participation in the first place. While the information relayed during such meetings may be confidential and inadmissible as evidence in some countries, the rules are not clear in all jurisdictions.[286] It is crucial, therefore, for all parties to be made aware of the legal consequences of such dialogue and to reach a consensus-based decision at the outset regarding future access to the substance of the dialogue and its usage.

7. A comprehensive justice system

At present, international punishment is an externally imposed form of justice that fails to achieve any stated penological objective[287] or contribute to the attainment of international criminal justice goals. International courts have stated that their mandates go beyond prosecution and punishment to include national reconstruction and

---

[283] Hill, "Restorative Justice", 63.
[284] See Buntinx, "Victim Offender Mediation in Severe Crimes", 3, 9; Van Garsse, "Mediation in a Detention Context", 10–11.
[285] See Van Garsse, "Mediation in a Detention Context", 10–11.
[286] Hallevy, "Therapeutic Victim–Offender Mediation", 75; Rossi, "Meet Me on Death Row", 208.
[287] Drumbl, *Atrocity, Punishment and International Law*, 181.

reconciliation, establishing the truth and restoring and maintaining peace.[288] While some feel that contemporary international criminal justice is limited to the delivery of "a process-based conception of the rule of law",[289] others hope that the system can evolve to also address broader social issues.[290] The ICC has noted that there is "growing recognition in international criminal law that there is a need to go beyond the notion of punitive justice, towards a solution which is more inclusive, encourages participation and recognises the need to provide effective remedies for victims".[291] Victims also view justice as more than punitiveness and imprisonment. They often prefer justice systems that use a variety of sentencing objectives, provide access to a range of effective mechanisms that allow for restoration and reflect culturally familiar approaches to punishment.[292]

These objectives cannot be attained solely through legal process. It is necessary to adopt a range of methodologies throughout the various stages of the international criminal justice process. Restorative justice principles and methodologies can be used to provide access to a broader justice system that ensures greater levels of involvement and satisfaction and addresses the social and personal needs of victims.[293] While some feel that restorative justice is "of limited relevance and application to situations of mass atrocity",[294] this chapter has argued that restorative justice tools may be adapted to provide effective post-conviction tools to attain penological and justice goals. At the punishment stage of the international criminal justice process, restorative justice methods can facilitate the implementation of a resocialisation-focused penal policy with reintegrative, reconciliatory and peace maintenance goals. It has been argued that restorative justice methods should not be used as treatment programmes: if the causes of crime are discussed this is merely a beneficial side effect and influencing offenders should be a secondary

---

[288] Para. 21 *Erdemović* (Judgment) IT-96-22-T*bis*, 05.03.1998; para. 31 *Serugendo* (Judgment) ICTR-05-84-I, 12.06.2006.
[289] Teitel, "The Universal and the Particular in International Criminal Justice", 286.
[290] See Antkowiak, "An Emerging Mandate for International Courts", 287.
[291] Para. 177 *Lubanga* (TCI Decision) ICC-01/04-01/06-2904, 07.08.2012.
[292] See Drumbl, *Atrocity, Punishment and International Law* 43, 125, 127, 148; R. Matthews, "The Myth of Punitiveness" (2005) 9(2) *Theoretical Criminology* 175 at 191.
[293] Findlay, "The Challenge for Asian Jurisdictions", 206; Walgrave, "Restorative Justice", 618.
[294] Schabas, "Criminology, Accountability and International Justice", 351.

objective only.[295] Restorative justice has increasingly, however, been recognised as a source of principles and methodologies that can inform penal policy and practice.

The international criminal justice process should operate in conjunction with other transitional mechanisms: "justice is most effective when it works in consort with other processes of social reconstruction".[296] As conflict resolution institutions share similar objectives, there is no reason why they cannot "coexist in a transitional context".[297] Whether or not it is feasible to introduce mediation or facilitate reparative efforts from within enforcing states, international prisoners should be entitled and encouraged to participate in or contribute to external transitional justice processes. Working with existing mechanisms and programmes will avoid the duplication of effort and result in a more comprehensive and inclusive approach to dealing with conflict, crime and transition.

Rehabilitative and restorative principles and methodologies can operate alongside and within a retributive framework. Different methods are required to achieve different objectives but this does not prevent their simultaneous or sequential operation within the same justice process. For example, the restorative label attributed to the Gacaca courts in Rwanda obscures the fact that the process also has transitional, retributive, reconciliatory and distributive justice objectives and outcomes.[298] Whether various conflict resolution methodologies are adopted contemporaneously or consequentially, the synergistic results of a holistic approach to justice are more likely to contribute to a lasting peace.

8. Conclusion

The adoption of a resocialisation-focused penal policy implemented using restorative practices can complement the current retributive sanctioning model and thereby enable the international penal system to fulfil a broader range of international criminal justice objectives. The incorporation of restorative approaches to justice at the penal stage enables the international criminal justice process to provide a more "social response"[299] to a social problem and to move from a "law to justice"

---

[295] Walgrave, "Restorative Justice", 623–4, 635.
[296] Stover and Weinstein, cited in Clark, "The Impact Question", 61.
[297] Findlay, "The Challenge for Asian Jurisdictions", 209.
[298] Oomen, "Rwanda's Gacaca", 174–5, 184.
[299] Hallevy, "Therapeutic Victim–Offender Mediation", 75.

approach.[300] In sum, it will help to provide a more comprehensive and effective justice system.

Justice demands more than remembrance and punishment; it must also include a vision of cultural change.[301] Part III has outlined a vision for international penal strategy that aims to ensure the delivery of principled and progressive punishment in a humane and effective manner. Implementing this vision in the current international penal system will, however, require a transformation in the thinking and *modus operandi* of enforcing states and international institutions.

---

[300] Drumbl, *Atrocity, Punishment and International Law*, 181.
[301] Antkowiak, "An Emerging Mandate for International Courts", 281.

8

Operationalising international penal strategy

As it stands, the international penal system fails to achieve the penological objectives of resocialisation and reintegration or to contribute to the attainment of broader international criminal justice objectives of reconciliation and the maintenance of peace. International punishment simply punishes. Even the international courts have admitted that it is controversial to assume that imprisonment alone can have a rehabilitative effect.[1] Some have argued that international courts are not concerned with reformation due to the fact that international prisoners are not their citizens[2] and these courts lack links to any particular social environment.[3] It is not acceptable, however, for international courts to recognise the heinous nature of the crimes they prosecute and then place offenders in prisons incapable of dealing with international criminality or to ignore the potential dangerousness of those they release back into society without support or supervision. Courts established to uphold human dignity cannot ignore the potential isolation and inequality caused by their penal system. International forums created to provide a voice to victims should not prevent victims speaking with those most responsible for the conflict and crimes that affected them. Institutions created to promote and protect international peace and security must work to create lasting social peace.

To achieve or contribute to the attainment of these objectives, it is necessary to initiate radical changes to the way international punishment is conceived and implemented. International punishment must consist of more than captivity in a foreign state. To ensure its legitimacy, it is imperative that the international penal system is transformed into an efficient and humane system that delivers principled and progressive

---

[1] Para. 844 *Kunarac, Kovač, Vuković* (Judgment) IT-96-23-T & IT-96-23/1-T, 22.02.2001.
[2] F. Hassan, "The Theoretical Basis of Punishment in International Criminal Law" (1983) 15 *Case Western Reserve Journal of International Law* 39–60 at 51.
[3] S. D'Ascoli, *Sentencing in International Criminal Law* (2011), 37.

punishment. Chapters 6 and 7 advocated the introduction of a resocialisation-orientated international penal policy implemented using restorative justice methods. The incorporation of these principles and methods is not only possible, but necessary in the international criminal justice system due to the need to fulfil the system's objectives and meet stakeholders' expectations. The proposed international penal policy and practice would create an international penal system more in line with contemporary human rights and penal standards. Moreover, these proposed changes would enable the system to contribute towards the attainment of the important goals of reintegration, reconciliation and the maintenance of peaceful relations in post-conflict societies. Although the proposed reforms would provide a more effective and principled penal regime, there are several foreseeable obstacles to the implementation of the advocated international penal strategy. In spite of the international criminal justice system's foreseeable continued reliance on a decentralised system of enforcement, the task of devising, implementing and evaluating international penal strategy must be charged to the international courts themselves.

1. Operationalising international penal policy and practice

Henham and Drumbl have argued that the predominantly retributive approach to international penality will prevail unless guidance on how to operationalise different ideologies for punishment is introduced.[4] Though the international penal strategy proposed in Part III provides suggestions for international penal policy and practice, it must be implemented within a unique penal system. International penal policy objectives will not be attained by simply recommending a focus on the resocialisation of international prisoners.[5] Despite their international human rights obligation to do so, enforcing states are not equipped with the programmes or resources necessary to rehabilitate or prepare international prisoners for release. The proposed penal strategy contains recommendations that go outside the policy objectives, mandates and budgets of most national prison systems. The introduction of restorative practices within traditional penal environments requires cooperation,

---

[4] R. Henham and M. Drumbl, "Plea Bargaining at the ICTY" (2005) 16 *Criminal Law Forum* 49–87 at 71.
[5] See D'Ascoli, *Sentencing in International Criminal Law*, 37.

commitment, training and specialist staff to oversee development and implementation.[6] Specialist staff will also be required to facilitate the implementation of international penal strategy for international prisoners housed in the national prisons of cooperating states.

The responsibility for supervising international punishment is typically tasked to the judiciary of the international criminal courts.[7] The ICC has established an Enforcement Unit to assist the ICC Presidency fulfil its responsibility for overseeing international imprisonment and the enforcement of fines, forfeiture and reparations orders.[8] Although this unit is operational and has contributed to the development of enforcement practice, it remains small and limited in its mandate. To implement the proposed international penal policy, the Enforcement Unit would require a wider mandate and its officials would need the power and finances to be mobile.

International courts should establish a Penal Strategy Support Unit (PSSU) to provide support to enforcing states and to implement the aspects of international penal strategy that fall outside the remit of domestic penal policy and practice. This unit should be staffed by representatives of all bodies and sections that are involved in the enforcement of international punishment. Although the courts' President/Presidency and supporting staff members are tasked with the oversight of enforcement, the Registrar and registry officials are also involved throughout the enforcement process. Registry officials oversee detention prior to transfer, negotiate enforcement agreements, collate the information necessary for designation and release decisions, liaise with inspecting bodies, arrange transfers and the relocation of international prisoners and, in the case of death, the repatriation of bodies.[9] The specialist central unit should also have access to experts in relevant fields and arrange regular meetings with internal and independent monitoring and evaluation bodies.

A PSSU could move beyond the current passive and detached approach to overseeing international punishment, to a proactive engagement with the institutions that implement international sentences of imprisonment. Enforcing states and institutions currently receive no guidance on how to implement such sentences. From the date of the

---

[6] D. Goulding et al., "Restorative Prisons: Towards Radical Prison Reform" (2008) 20 Current Issues in Criminal Justice 231–42 at 234, 238, 240.
[7] See Rule 199 ICC RPE.   [8] Reg. 113(1) ICC ROC.
[9] Paras. 38, 71 Residual Mechanism Report.

transfer of the international prisoner until the date of receipt of the international release order, there is virtually no communication between the sentencing and enforcing institution in relation to international sentence planning. Both enforcing states and enforcing institutions have vocalised their need to receive more information and guidance in relation to the treatment of international prisoners. Given that states and national prisons have no or very little experience in implementing what is an unprecedented form of punishment, it is imperative that the international courts provide some advice and direction.

In addition to the provision of guidance on international penal strategy, the international courts should assist enforcing states with the implementation of the aspects of international policy that fall outside the scope and possibilities of national penal policy and practice. The implementation of international penal policy in a decentralised system therefore requires mobility. Mobility has been recognised as essential for the courts' supervisory role in relation to enforcement: judges and officials may travel to enforcing states to meet with international prisoners.[10] International judicial and administrative officials and independent oversight bodies already have access to enforcing state institutions to fulfil their supervisory role. This access should be extended to enable international officials to fulfil the courts' support role. Permission to operate within the institutions of enforcing states, in respect of international prisoners, will enable international officials to realise the necessary conditions for the implementation of international penal policy. Officials could be despatched, when necessary, to facilitate procedures outlined in the governing legal frameworks such as release hearings and communication between international prisoners and the court, and those established by international penal policy, such as the activation of critical situation reaction protocols or the facilitation of restorative communication.

The new on-site facilitation role, and more frequent communication with all the different parties involved in the international penal system, will enable the PSSU to evaluate the impact and effectiveness of international penal policy. Information can be collected about the functioning and performance of the system. The analysis of this data will facilitate the identification of common problems and best practice that can assist reform and the development of benchmarks for assessment. With on-going evaluation, policy development can move away from localised and

---

[10] See, for example, Rule 211(1)(c) ICC RPE.

piecemeal solutions, towards a more strategic, long-term approach. The increased engagement created by mobility will also enable the international courts to provide stakeholders and interested parties with up-to-date information on what it is trying to achieve and how the system is working, increasing transparency. The PSSU will also be much better placed to provide both international prisoners and their families with crucial information about the prison system to which they will be transferred.

2. Centralised support to centralised control

A centrally devised international penal strategy will elevate the international status of punishment imposed by international courts and international control over it. It will enable the international courts to assist enforcing states in the provision of a principled and progressive form of punishment. The success or otherwise of the operationalisation of international penal strategy will, however, be dependent upon state support and cooperation in terms of financing and access. States must pass the budgetary resolutions to finance the new, non-central activities of a PSSU. Enforcing states must also agree to the presence of international officials in their prisons and their involvement in the implementation of sanctions. Some states may resist the advocated developments due to a lack of political will to finance them or due to perceptions that the centralised facilitation of the implementation of international aspects of penal policy impinges on the sovereignty of enforcing states.

Sovereignty, traditionally viewed as a shield to protect national power and territory, has evolved from a protectionist political concept to one that empowers states to give expression to national values through their foreign policy, external relations and membership of communities of interest.[11] The exercise of sovereign power, therefore, includes the ability to cede authority to an international organisation for tasks typically

---

[11] See A. Slaughter and W. Burke-White, "The Future of International Law is Domestic (or, The European Way of Law)" (2006) 47(2) *Harvard International Law Journal* 327 at 328; R. Jensen, "Globalization and the International Criminal Court: Accountability and a New Conception of State" in I. F. Dekker and W. G. Werner (eds.), *Governance and International Legal Theory* (2004), 166, 168, 173; D. M. Amann, "The ICC and the Sovereign State" in I. F. Dekker and W. G. Werner (eds.), *Governance and International Legal Theory* (2004), 206; D. Sarooshi, *International Organisations and Their Exercise of Sovereign Powers* (2005), 9–11; M. Brus, "Bridging the Gap between State Sovereignty and International Governance: The Authority of Law" in G. Kreijen (ed.), *State, Sovereignty and International Governance* (2002), 6.

considered to be within the ambit of internal powers of the state.[12] States have done so in order to create international criminal courts. As states have ceded authority to the international courts to detain, try and punish individuals, it would be irrational for these states to deny the same courts the authority to enforce sentences in a principled and purposeful manner. Resistance to a more proactive role for the international courts in the implementation of international punishment would also appear irrational as this would not alter the current structure of the enforcement system.

International sentences would continue to be implemented in a decentralised enforcement system premised on consensual cooperation. The division of responsibility between enforcing states and the international courts would remain the same. The only difference would be that international officials could assist enforcing states with the implementation of aspects of international penal policy that go beyond national penal policy and practice. Moreover, this engagement only applies to a miniscule number of prisoners. Centralisation of policy development and implementation facilitation does not diminish the authority of national institutions. States would remain responsible for day-to-day imprisonment, while the international court, through its central policy unit, would be responsible for longer-term strategic decisions in relation to and necessary for the achievement of international penological and justice goals. The centralisation of international penal policy development would not translate into central control but support for states enforcing international sentences of imprisonment. Enforcing states would remain responsible for the tasks most effectively performed by national prison systems and the international courts would take responsibility for the performance of the tasks most effectively performed by international officials.

Political resistance would also appear misplaced given that these policy developments represent a logical progression of the collective desire to create an international criminal justice system. Such a system requires a principled and effective international penal system. Centralised policy development will create expertise on international penal matters and increase the consistency of treatment of international prisoners.

The central development of penal strategy will mean that international punishment is implemented in accordance with international

---

[12] Sarooshi, *International Organisations and Their Exercise of Sovereign Power*, 18–19.

policy in states and institutions assisted by international specialists. However, the reality will remain that international sanctions will be enforced in national prisons and international prisoners will continue to be treated as national prisoners. It is also foreseeable, despite the arguments outlined above, that some enforcing states will be resistant to the developments proposed on principled, political and practical grounds. To facilitate the implementation of international penal policy and further internationalise international punishment, international sentences of imprisonment should be directly implemented by international courts. International punishment must, however, be implemented in facilities that can provide regimes appropriate for convicted persons. With the experience of detaining and imprisoning international criminals in IDFs, and funding designated facilities to hold international prisoners in cooperating states, it is perhaps time the international criminal justice system created an international prison system. Rather than debating reforms that the international penal system can institute through strategy, it is perhaps time to ask how the international penal system can be strengthened structurally. Instead of debating the merits of centralised support, Part IV outlines possibilities for the centralised control of international punishment.

PART IV

Structure: creating an accountable international prison system

9

An international prison system

The contemporary international penal system primarily relies on decentralised enforcement. This means that the system used to implement international punishment typically involves the transfer of international prisoners to foreign states without their consent.[1] A system that involves the forced exile of prisoners to a foreign land, and a subsequent social death, bears the hallmarks of penal transportation. This historic process of shipping "human cargo"[2] abroad also resulted in a "strange lottery"[3] which exposed convicts to unequal punishment.[4] While international punishment does not entail the atrocious conditions of detention, enforced labour[5] or public humiliation associated with penal transportation,[6] the processes remain comparable in their intent and effect: punishment and social exile through removal to a foreign land. Furthermore, the international penal system, like the penal transportation system, focuses not so much on what happens to prisoners once they are transferred, but in ensuring that they will no longer be on the territory of the Host State of the sentencing court.[7] The overly punitive nature of the contemporary system for the enforcement of international sanctions risks aggravating sentences.

---

[1] R. Mulgrew, "The International Movement of Prisoners: Exploring the Evolution of the Inter-State and International Criminal Justice Systems for the Transfer of Sentenced Persons" (2011) 22 *Criminal Law Forum* 103–43 at 110–11.

[2] E. C. Casella, "Prisoner of His Majesty: Postcoloniality and the Archaeology of British Penal Transportation" (2005) 37(3) *World Archaeology* 453–67 at 453.

[3] The House of Commons Select Committee, 1837 cited in A. Rutherford, "Criminal Policy and the Eliminative Ideal" (1997) 31(5) *Social Policy and Administration* 116–35 at 122.

[4] See J. J. Willis, "Transportation versus Imprisonment in Eighteenth and Nineteenth Century Britain: Penal Power, Liberty, and the State" (2005) 39(1) *Law and Society Review* 171–210 at 176.

[5] See Casella, "Prisoner of His Majesty", 454.

[6] E. Gallo, "The Penal System in France: from Correctionalism to Managerialism" in V. Ruggiero et al. (eds.), *Western European Penal Systems: A Critical Anatomy* (1995), 72.

[7] See Hughes cited in Rutherford, "Criminal Policy and the Eliminative Ideal", 123.

Schabas has suggested that the aggravating effect of the current international penal system could be taken into account as a mitigating factor during sentence determination.[8] Ashworth and Player argue that by considering the impact of a penal system on the sentence imposed, and adjusting the sentence accordingly, the judiciary can enhance the proportionality of the sanction, the equality of treatment of prisoners and, ultimately, the legitimacy of the sentence.[9] They also note, however, that the equal treatment of prisoners does not necessarily require homogenous regimes and that it would be nearly impossible to rate conditions in different facilities to enable comparison for sentencing purposes.[10] This task would be even more complicated in the decentralised enforcement system. Moreover, despite the profound impact designation decisions may have on international prisoners, international courts are often constrained by the state cooperation available. In many instances, the courts will not have a choice.[11] In any case, as designation decisions are made after the sentence has been determined, there is no possibility for mitigation in this regard.[12]

Another possible means of enhancing the consistency of treatment of international prisoners is to implement centrally devised international penal policies and derivative practices in the international and national facilities holding international prisoners.[13] However, as Chapter 8 concluded, this poses foreseeable logistical, financial and political obstacles. Irrespective of the nature of the policy governing the implementation of international sentences of imprisonment, the dispersal of prisoners among numerous national prison systems dilutes the international nature of the sanction and the visibility of international punishment.

As the international criminal courts assume responsibility for imposing international criminal justice, they should also assume responsibility for its implementation. Ideally, international courts should be able to cater for and exercise direct control over the prison populations they create. One of the key factors that led to the transition from the use of penal transportation to the use of domestic prisons was the centralisation of control over national

---

[8] W. Schabas, "Sentencing by International Tribunals: A Human Rights Approach" (1997) 7 *Duke Journal of Comparative and International Law* 461–518 at 494–5.
[9] See A. Ashworth and E. Player, "Sentencing, Equal Treatment and the Impact of Sanctions" in A. Ashworth and M. Wasik (eds.), *Fundamentals of Sentencing Theory* (1998), 253–61, 265.
[10] *Ibid.*, 267, 269.   [11] See Chapter 2, Sections 1 and 2 and Chapter 5, Section 1.
[12] See para. B.1.2(30) MDP, 158.   [13] See Chapters 6 and 7.

penal infrastructure and administration.[14] The lack of an international prison has been identified by academic writers as a "major shortcoming"[15] that creates an "institutional lacuna".[16] Rather than being viewed as a radical addition, therefore, the establishment of an international prison system should be seen as part of the logical institutional evolution of the international criminal justice system.[17] Given that imprisonment is the dominant form of punishment in international criminal law, and that international courts have practice of directly implementing international sentences of imprisonment in IDFs, it is perhaps time to seriously consider the creation of an international prison system. This chapter sets out arguments in favour of establishing an international prison system and outlines some of the factors that need to be considered in order to create it and make it operational.

1. Arguments in favour of creating an international prison system

As they have no prisons, international courts currently rely on cooperating states to enforce international sentences of imprisonment. An international prison system would provide current and future international courts with immediate access to permanent custodial capacity in regimes tailor-made to meet the specific requirements of international prisoners and that conform to contemporary standards.[18] This would drastically reduce the time, money and effort spent by the officials negotiating enforcement agreements and securing cooperation in particular cases. Prisoners would no longer face lengthy delays caused by the need to arrange transfers or enable exequatur procedures to be completed. Prisoners can be prepared for the move as IDF staff would have firsthand information about the operation of international facilities. Prisoners could be placed according to risk-related security classifications, removing

---

[14] See Willis, "Transportation versus Imprisonment in Eighteenth and Nineteenth Century Britain", 172, 203.
[15] M. Penrose, "No Badges, No Bars: A Conspicuous Oversight in the Development of an International Criminal Court" (2003) 38(3) *Texas International Law Journal* 621–42 at 636.
[16] C. Kreß and G. Sluiter, "Imprisonment" in A. Cassese *et al.* (eds.), *The Rome Statute of the International Criminal Court* (2002), 1757–821 at 1817.
[17] See Penrose, "No Badges, No Bars", 638, 642.
[18] See M. Penrose, "Spandau Revisited: The Question of Detention for International War Crimes" (1999) 16 *New York Law School Journal of Human Rights* 553–91 at 585–6.

the negative impact of excessive security classifications.[19] As all international prisoners would be subject to the same conditions, regime, treatment and release procedures, a higher degree of equality could be ensured.[20] The potential for isolation could also be reduced through placement with persons who speak the same language, come from the same culture, or who at the very least are in a similar position. Combined, these beneficial outcomes would contribute towards off-setting the aggravation of the sentence caused by forcible transfer to a foreign state. Moreover, the ability to exercise direct control over the enforcement of sentences of imprisonment in international facilities would enable the international courts to assert the international nature of the sanctions they impose[21] and improve the visibility of international punishment. International penal strategy could be directly implemented and the international penal system evaluated on a regular basis to ensure that it provides principled and progressive punishment in an effective and humane manner. An international prison regime could provide programmes specifically designed to resocialise and prepare international prisoners for release.

Like the contemporary IDFs, an international prison could serve multiple purposes. In addition to the enforcement of sentences, they could act as remand centres to facilitate the detention of suspects and accused persons in their region of origin, reducing isolation and enhancing possibilities for family contact. Indeed, the MICT's Rules explicitly facilitate the detention of accused persons in countries other than the Mechanism's Host State and their communication with the Mechanism using video-conferencing technology.[22] International prisons, like IDFs, could also be used to house detained witnesses.[23] The UNDF in Arusha has housed detained witnesses previously in custody in Rwanda and ICTR prisoners who had been serving their sentences in Mali and Benin.[24] It has recently been demonstrated that the detention of testifying witnesses can have significant legal and financial consequences for IDFs. Since May 2011, nearly half of the ICCDC's population has

---

[19] See Chapter 2, Sections 4.2.3 and 4.2.4.
[20] See Kreß and Sluiter, "Imprisonment", 1817; Penrose, "No Badges, No Bars", 640.
[21] See Kreß and Sluiter, "Imprisonment", 1817.
[22] See Rules 67, 69(C)(ii) MICT RPE.
[23] See Rule 90*bis* (A) ICTY/ICTR RPE; Preamble SCSL ROD; Art. 4(2)-(3) ICTR-Rwanda BEA; Art. 4(3) ICC-Austria BEA.
[24] See para. 67 ICTR Sixteenth Annual Report.

consisted of individuals who have not been accused or convicted of committing any crime by the ICC.[25] Four individuals are housed there due to the legal limbo that ensued following the completion of their testimony at the ICC and their submission of asylum applications to the Dutch authorities.[26] The ICC cannot release the prisoners as it is under a duty to return them to custody in the DRC. The Dutch Government does not wish to detain them pending the outcome of the asylum procedure. Their lengthy presence has created financial[27] and staffing problems for the ICCDC and tensions with other detained persons.[28] This situation, particularly if asylum is granted, will create huge difficulties for future ICC reliance on detained witnesses, as the Dutch government is likely to be cautious about allowing such witnesses to be transferred to the ICCDC. An international prison could house witnesses who are already in detention in the region and, to the extent possible having regard to the rights of the defence, facilitate their testimony via video-link.

International prisons could be used by a number of temporary international and internationalised courts. Even if such courts wished to primarily rely on decentralised national enforcement, international prisons could act as residual facilities to provide capacity in situations where it has not been possible for such courts to secure sufficient cooperation with states generally or in a particular case, if an enforcing state declares continued enforcement impossible or if the court orders the termination of enforcement in a particular state when its IDF has closed. In limited cases, where it would serve humanitarian or security purposes, international prisons could also be used to house national prisoners convicted of international crimes.

2. Establishing an international prison system

The international penal system currently relies on capacity provided by the domestic prison systems of cooperating states. In order to create an international prison system, it is necessary to consider the legal basis for its creation and operation, and locations for its facilities. The

---

[25] Until this date, they were housed at the UNDU. The ICCDC has housed a detained witness for the ICTY. Tjonk, ICCDC, 04.07.2012.
[26] See *Katanga, Ngudjolo* (Status Conference) ICC-01-04-01/07-T, 12.05.2011.
[27] Their detention cost the ICCDC €25,000 per month. Tjonk, ICCDC, 04.07.2012.
[28] Craig, ICCDC, 04.07.2012; Tjonk, ICCDC, 04.07.2012; Bremmers, ICCDC, 04.07.2012.

international courts' role in detention and enforcement to date does provide some precedence and practice in this regard.

2.1 Precedence and practice

This chapter has noted the benefits that would result from the enforcement of international punishment in an international prison. While there is no international prison system currently in operation, there have been instances whereby sentences imposed by international tribunals have been implemented in detention and prison facilities operated or funded by international organisations and courts.

Some argue that the IMTN's use of Spandau Prison to implement its sentences provides the proposal to create an international prison with "the authority of history".[29] Others, however, note that this living legacy of a post-war trial is now remembered as "history's most bizarre prison".[30] Although this facility held persons sentenced to terms of imprisonment imposed by an international tribunal, Spandau does not provide a blueprint for a modern international prison. Fishman notes that the regime was, at times, excessively harsh; the rules of detention and the treatment of prisoners failed to conform with contemporary standards and practice; the quadripartite control of operations and subsequent requirement of unanimous decision-making resulted in frequent deadlocks in relation to issues that severely impacted on prisoners; oversight of the regime was highly politicised and the disproportionate cost of operating the prison was imposed on an unwilling Host State.[31] Conditions were austere, food was limited and although there were more guards than prisoners, the strictness of the system varied depending on which country was responsible for the prison on a particular day.[32] Spandau Prison was jointly operated by France, the UK, the US and the USSR on occupied territory which they governed. All executive, operational, legal, medical and day-to-day decisions had to be reached

---

[29] Penrose, "Spandau Revisited", 585.
[30] N. J. W. Goda, *Tales from Spandau: Nazi Criminals and the Cold War* (2007), 3.
[31] See J. Fishman, *Long Knives and Short Memories: The Spandau Prison Story* (1986), 19, 21–3, 25, 27, 82, 87, 89, 121, 128, 135, 187–8, 225–7, 231, 234–5, 240, 244–5, 250, 253–6, 258–9, 261–2, 265–6, 355–6, 358–9, 364–9, 397, 402–3; D. Van Zyl Smit, "International Imprisonment" (2005) 54 *International and Comparative Law Quarterly* 357–86 at 358–9; Kreß and Sluiter, "Imprisonment", 1761–4; Penrose, "Spandau Revisited", 576.
[32] Goda, *Tales from Spandau*, 53, 56–7, 69, 73, 83.

on a unanimous basis, meaning each power had a veto.[33] The prison's four-power administration resulted in it becoming a theatre for playing out Cold War animosities and its retention long after it served any real purpose due to its strategic importance in East–West politics generally and the fate of West Berlin in particular.[34] Far from being an international prison implementing the penal policy of the IMTN, Spandau became a tool in a political battle that had little to do with crimes committed during the Second World War.

Although penal management is not one of the UN's traditional functions, it has become increasingly involved in the establishment, operation and management of facilities holding persons convicted of international crimes.[35] Indeed, UN involvement in international penal administration can be traced back to 1948 when UN staff worked in Spandau Prison.[36] Recently, the UN has directly, or as a co-founding institution, undertaken responsibility to pay for the construction or renovation of facilities, in addition to special operational costs incurred during the enforcement of international sentences of imprisonment by national prisons in cooperating states.[37] This funding means that specifically designated facilities have been used exclusively for the implementation of international punishment of SCSL and ICTR prisoners within the domestic prison systems of Mali, Benin and Rwanda. These facilities operate in accordance with international standards and house only international prisoners. The ICC has also undertaken to raise funds to pay for renovations and implementation costs incurred by national prisons in Mali[38] and it may become responsible for paying for the implementation of sentences at a residual facility provided by the Dutch Government.[39] More significantly, the UN has been directly responsible for implementing international sentences of imprisonment, in whole or in part, in the ICTY and ICTR's IDFs.[40] Indeed, the UNDF has, at times, housed twice as many convicted persons as accused persons.[41] The UN has therefore been responsible for operating a "de facto international prison system"[42] for nearly fifteen years.

---

[33] Ibid. 29–30.   [34] Ibid. 2, 7, 72, 206, 210–13, 220, 275.
[35] See W. Luyt, "Genocide in Rwanda: Detention and Prison Involvement" (2003) 16(4) Acta Criminologica 96–109 at 105.
[36] See para. 2 Spandau Prison Regulations in Fishman, Long Knives and Short Memories, 27.
[37] See Chapter 2, Section 3.1.   [38] Art. 11(4) ICC–Mali BEA.   [39] Art. 103(4) ICCSt.
[40] See Chapter 3.   [41] Para. 69 ICTR Sixteenth Annual Report.
[42] R. Culp, "Enforcement and Monitoring of Sentences in the Modern War Crimes Process: Equal Treatment before the Law?", 2010–2011, 13.

2.2 Legal mandate

Unlike Spandau, an international prison system should be established by an international organisation. The founding institution should be a permanent body, representative of the international community, which has experience in the enforcement of international sentences of imprisonment. Given their experience and mandates, both the UN and ICC are suitable institutions. Rather than having one founding institution, the UN and the ICC could establish an international prison system as a joint venture. According to their bilateral agreement, the two institutions may cooperate on matters of mutual interest and establish common facilities with a view to saving costs, making the most efficient use of specialised personnel, systems and services, and preventing the overlap of operations.[43] The UN and ICC could enter into an agreement to jointly create a network of international prisons to enable the fulfilment of their respective responsibilities, or, alternatively, acknowledge such facilities as the subordinate bodies of the other institution and pledge support for their operations.[44]

Although the statutes and rules of the UN Tribunals, SCSL and ICC refer to the detention of various persons at the seat of the court, they do not formally create IDFs. The regulatory frameworks that govern the operation of the IDFs appear to simply presume the legality of their creation.[45] Host states also appear to implicitly recognise the inherent power of international courts to establish IDFs: the bilateral agreements simply refer to IDFs as another part of the courts' premises.[46] Moreover, the temporary courts have directly enforced sentences of imprisonment at these facilities in spite of the fact that their statutes refer solely to the enforcement of sentences by states.[47] All of the international courts have created, and detained persons in, international facilities without any explicit legal mandate to do so.

International organisations increasingly exercise control over territory and people without explicit mandates to do so. The de facto nature of a regime does not, however, necessarily imply that it is *ultra vires*, just

---

[43] See Preamble, Arts. 3, 8(2)(c), 9 Negotiated Relationship Agreement between the ICC and UN, 04.10.2004 (ICC–UN NRA).
[44] See Arts. 3, 13, 15(2), 21 ICC–UN NRA; Art. 115(b) ICCSt.
[45] UNDU/UNDF/SCSL ROD; Chapter 6 ICC ROC; Chapter 5 ICC ROR.
[46] See Art. XXI(3) ICTY/ICTR HQAs; Art. 23(3) SCSL HQA; Arts. 1(x), 46(2) ICC HQA.
[47] Art. 27 ICTYSt; Art. 26 ICTRSt; Art. 22 SCSLSt.

as the de jure nature of a regime does not mean it is *intra vires*.[48] The enforcement of international punishment appears to be an inherent power of international criminal courts. It seems, therefore, that while there is no statutory basis for the creation of an international prison, there is no statutory bar. Indeed, there seems to be a presumption that international courts have an inherent power to establish and operate international prisons.

2.3 Location

An international prison system should not rely on one facility based in a static location. A single central facility may suffer from the "eggs in one basket syndrome"[49] and become "a powder keg waiting to blow up"[50] or a target for external attacks. While the anticipated ethnic antagonism did not occur at any of the IDFs,[51] an international prison system should have the ability to disperse threatened or dangerous prisoners to other facilities. The term prison does not necessarily have to mean a prison in the traditional domestic sense, but may, like the IDFs, involve smaller units within national prisons. An international prison system should be comprised of a number of facilities located in regions in which the crimes the prisoners are being punished for were committed. In this way, a network of international prisons would continue the trend of internationalising criminal justice and the placement of international prisoners in their region of origin.[52]

Rather than send international prisoners to countries that have "no nexus to or interest in the underlying hostilities",[53] it makes sense to place them in the region their actions affected. For example, the ICC is viewed by some to be a European Court trying African people. Accordingly, "punishment in Africa would allay fears that ...

---

[48] G. Verdirame, *The UN and Human Rights: Who Guards the Guardians* (2011), 230, 232.
[49] R. Vincent, An *Administrative Practices Manual for Internationally Assisted Criminal Justice Institutions* (2007), 70.
[50] R. D. King "The Rise and Rise of Supermax: An American Solution in Search of a Problem?" in Y. Jewkes and H. Johnston (eds.), *Prison Readings: A Critical Introduction to Prisons and Imprisonment* (2006), 87.
[51] See para. 103 ICTY First Annual Report; para. 2.7.2 Independent Audit of the Detention Unit at the ICTY 2006; Vincent, *An Administrative Practices Manual for Internationally Assisted Criminal Justice Institutions*, 72.
[52] See Chapter 5, Section 1.   [53] Penrose, "Spandau Revisited", 572.

proceedings and punishment smack of colonialism".[54] As international punishment is imposed, *inter alia*, in the name of victims, the physical presence of convicted persons close to the conflict-affected area may help to generate feelings of ownership over punishment. This may in turn enhance the legitimacy of the sanction and the credibility of the court. The regionalisation of international penal administration would also contribute towards reducing the socio-cultural isolation experienced by prisoners in enforcing states under the current decentralised system.[55] Regional prisons would enable more culturally appropriate regimes to be put in place and enhance possibilities for achieving important penological objectives. International prisons could provide tailor-made programmes dealing specifically with international crime and regimes designed to help maintain relationships with family and friends, enhancing prospects for successful resocialisation and reintegration.

Contemporary Host States have made it abundantly clear that they do not want international prisoners on their territory, even if they are housed in IDFs.[56] While states may wish to be seen as champions of international criminal justice, they fear that they will be viewed as the Alcatraz of the world. They simply do not want to risk being tainted with any "convict 'stain'"[57] that may result from hosting an international prison or responsibility for dealing with former international prisoners after release. On the other hand, some feel that if a state is willing to accept the financial and political benefits of hosting an international court, they should also be willing to accept the difficulties associated with running it.

An international prison, however, need not be located in the Host State of the relevant court. Indeed, the pursuit of a regional placement policy would dictate against a centralised approach to penal administration. A Host State for an international prison should be in a region that would facilitate the achievement of international penological objectives. The country should be stable and in a position to provide public services, infrastructure and modern medical facilities. Hosting an international prison would bring benefits for the cooperating state. An

---

[54] Mochochoko, ICC, 30.08.2007.
[55] See C. J. M. Safferling, *Towards an International Criminal Procedure* (2001), 354; Schabas, "Sentencing by International Tribunals", 494–5.
[56] See Chapter 3, Section 8 for a discussion of possible centralised national enforcement.
[57] Casella, "Prisoner of His Majesty", 454.

international prison would require construction and maintenance, utilities and custodial, security, medical, transportation, catering and translation staff etc. In return for donating, renting or selling land, providing security and perhaps seconding custodial staff, the Host State would receive an injection of money into the local economy and earn a positive international reputation.

Contemporary requirements would seem to point to Africa as a suitable location for establishing initial facilities. The ICTY appears to have secured a sufficient number of agreements to enable it to fulfil its mandate.[58] The SCSL, ICTR and ICC, on the other hand, have struggled to secure agreements with states in Africa. The SCSL and ICTR have transferred prisoners to facilities in Mali, Benin and Rwanda that they had to raise finances to construct or renovate and that require long-term investment.[59] The ICC is currently investigating or prosecuting cases involving individuals from Uganda, the Democratic Republic of Congo, the Central African Republic, Sudan, Kenya, Libya and Côte d'Ivoire. It is highly likely, therefore, that it will have to secure cooperation with states to enforce sentences imposed on African nationals. Rather than compete with other courts for cooperation or be forced to raise finances to upgrade or maintain national prisons, the ICC should, solely or in collaboration with other courts or international organisations, establish an international prison in Africa to hold African prisoners.

The present situation, however, is liable to change. Indeed, the ICC is currently conducting preliminary examinations into situations in Afghanistan, Georgia, Guinea, Columbia, Honduras, Korea and Nigeria.[60] The ICC may therefore also potentially have to secure penal capacity to implement sentences imposed on individuals originating from East, West and Central Asia, as well as Central and South America. The need to ensure international sentences are enforced in relevant regions and sub-regions was highlighted at the 2010 Review Conference.[61] An international prison system should therefore be flexible and able to respond to the changing characteristics of its population. Given that the ICC is likely to grow and that new temporary international or internationalised tribunals may be

---

[58] See Chapter 2, Section 1.   [59] See Chapter 2, Section 3.1.
[60] See Situations and Cases on the ICC website at www2.icc-cpi.int/Menus/ICC/Situations+and+Cases/.
[61] Preamble and para. 3 Strengthening the Enforcement of Sentences, Resolution RC/Res.3. 08.06.2010.

established in the future, an international prison system should have capacity or facilities located in relevant regions throughout the world.

3. Models for international prisons

While it is obvious that an international prison system requires prisons, the experience of the international courts demonstrates that there are a variety of detention models that can be used in the international context. This section outlines the various models and analyses the pros and cons of independent, hosted and shared facilities.

3.1 An island

An international prison could be constructed or located on an island. This option was proposed for housing those convicted at Nuremberg.[62] The original SCSLDF was located on Sherbo Island, 150 kilometres from Freetown.[63] The facility remained part of the Sierra Leone Prison Service's infrastructure and on Sierra Leonean territory. A prison located on an island which is only accessible by boat and helicopter is naturally more secure than those located in populated areas close to transport facilities.[64] A stand-alone facility also provides unlimited autonomy in decision-making and flexibility in relation to expansion and regime development. On the other hand, an island-based prison would have to be self-sufficient in terms of infrastructure, utilities, communications, food, water, sewage, access by air or boat, accommodation, medical facilities etc.[65] The resulting cost is likely to be hugely disproportionate to the population that it would accommodate and would therefore seem unjustifiable.

3.2 Host State

A more sensible solution, and the one favoured by the international criminal courts to date, involves finding a cooperative Host State. The experience of the contemporary IDFs demonstrates that an international prison based in a Host State could operate from an independent site or

---

[62] Goda, *Tales from Spandau*, 25. [63] SCSL First Annual Report, 24.
[64] Vincent, SCSL/ICTY 27.04.2007; Jackson, SCSLDF/ICCDC, 19.03.2007.
[65] Vincent, SCSL/ICTY 27.04.2007; Jackson, SCSLDF/ICCDC, 19.03.2007.

from a building within a Host State prison, which it may rent in its entirety or share with other international prisons.

3.2.1 An independent site

The second SCSLDF was located within the perimeter of its parent court, the SCSL, in Freetown.[66] Although this land was donated by the national government, there is no reason why an international organisation could not buy land on which to construct a permanent prison. Both the UN and ICC have international legal personality, and accordingly, the capacity to contract and buy immovable property.[67] Outright ownership would ensure control over the site and guarantee freedom to expand and/or develop the regime without the need to consult with the national prison system. The premises' inviolability would only be subject to the Host State's overriding power to enter in the event of a fire or an emergency that required protective action.[68]

Buildings could be custom designed and adapted to meet the requirements of the prison population. For example, the SCSL constructed a catering unit within the SCSLDF's perimeter when other catering options proved too expensive and risky.[69] In contrast, the ICC could not build a stand-alone facility with crèche facilities and cells catering for persons with disabilities due to the need to respect the wishes of the ICCDC's host prison.[70] An international prison on independent ground would also avoid the operation of differing regimes and standards between international and national facilities within the same perimeter. Despite these operational benefits, an independent site would require perimeter security.

Unlike IDFs in host prisons, which contribute to a percentage of such costs under product price agreements, an international facility would be solely responsible for the cost of perimeter security. At Spandau Prison, "fantastically expensive"[71] round-the-clock security was maintained, even when the prison was empty, due to the political nature of the prison and its occupants.[72] Even though the SCSLDF shared its outer perimeter with its parent court, the facility still required two inner layers of security. The presence of a UN military contingent at the prison

---

[66] The third SCSLDF is also located on this site. See SCSL Ninth Annual Report, 25.
[67] Art. I (1)(a)–(b) CPIUN; Art. III ICTY HQA; Art. 4 ICCSt; Art. 2 ICC API.
[68] See Arts. 4(3)–(5), 23(3) SCSL HQA.   [69] Vincent, SCSL/ICTY 27.04.2007.
[70] Dubuisson, Tjonk, Becerra-Suarez, ICC, 06.06.2007.
[71] Fox cited in Fishman, *Long Knives and Short Memories*, 364.
[72] Goda, *Tales from Spandau*, 1, 30, 241–2.

perimeter and SCSLDF custodial staff at the prison entrance resulted in the SCSLDF operating as a "complex within a complex".[73] Even if a Host State undertakes to assist with perimeter security and serious disturbances,[74] it is foreseeable that an independent site would face massive costs in relation to security.

Further, Host States have been reluctant to sell land to international courts. To prevent national soil becoming inviolable international territory, Host States prefer to lend or lease land or rent penal capacity to the international courts. For example, to ensure the Host State's on-going cooperation with its project to construct a court on permanent premises, it was necessary for the ICC to enter into a lease that separated the ownership of the building from the ownership of the land.[75] Unless an international prison is to be situated within the complex of an international organisation or court, practice would suggest that an international prison is more likely to be located within the perimeter of a Host State prison.

3.2.2 Within the perimeter of a Host State prison

Rather than buy land, penal capacity could be rented from a Host State. For example, the ICTY and ICC have negotiated a product price with the Dutch Government for the use of cells within the Scheveningen Penitentiary Complex. While the smallest unit that can be rented is typically a prison wing,[76] the product price denotes the cost of a cell per day and includes sports, education and leisure facilities, custodial and medical staff, medical, dental and optical treatments, security, maintenance, catering, cleaning etc.[77] The price is increased annually in line with inflation or upon review by the Host State. These agreements can, however, take a long time to conclude. Although the first detained person was admitted to the ICCDC in December 2006, the Product Price Agreement between the ICC and the Dutch Ministry of Justice was only finalised in February 2011, six years after negotiations began in December 2005.[78]

Operating from within a host prison brings multiple advantages. The Host State, albeit for a price, provides the international facility with

---

[73] Vincent, *An Administrative Practices Manual for Internationally Assisted Criminal Justice Institutions*, 69.
[74] Art. 6(1) SCSL HQA; Rule 36(A) SCSL ROD.
[75] Para. 4 Permanent Premises ICC-ASP/8/Res.5, 26.11.2009.
[76] McFadden, UNDU, 21.08.2007. [77] See paras. A.3(14)–(15) MDP, 180.
[78] Tjonk, ICCDC, 04.07.2012.

perimeter and reception security, medical facilities and ancillary services such as catering, laundry, teaching, IT systems etc.[79] Not only is the need to conclude service contracts removed but the international prison can rely on an established prison service for support.[80] For example, the host prison authorities would assist the international prison to remove persons posing a threat to security and order or in the event of a disturbance.[81] However, operating from within a host prison can create operational difficulties.

Although an international prison operating from within a host prison would be a legally distinct institution, operating in accordance with its own internal rules and regulations,[82] the experience of the IDFs has demonstrated that control can be lost over some aspects of penal administration and regime development. Autonomy and flexibility are reduced due to the need to pre-arrange many aspects of operations with the host prison.[83] Suggested regime changes may conflict with the schedule, security regulations or employment law of the host prison. In addition, the host prison may be resistant to change, especially if change results in an increase in the cost of providing penal capacity. For example, the UN and the Dutch Prison System argued over the introduction of yoga classes at the UNDU for over a year as it was unclear who would insure the instructor.[84]

Reliance on the host prison's perimeter and reception security also involves the loss of control over security aspects of prison management. As an international prison could only be accessed by passing through the host prison, it would be necessary to create an agreement detailing security and order procedures. There may be instances when the Host State's or host prison's regulations would override the international legal framework. For example, UNDU personnel must observe the rules and instructions of their host prison in respect of security and order, and in the event of a fire, an emergency or an escape.[85] Visitors, and the property they bring into an international prison, would be checked at the international prison's entrance.[86] Being located inside a host prison

---

[79] Para. 99 ICTY First Annual Report. Jackson, SCSLDF/ICCDC, 19.03.2007; Dubuisson, Tjonk, Becerra-Suarez, ICC, 06.06.2007.
[80] Custodial Staff, ICCDC, 22-27.08.2007; Vincent, SCSL/ICTY, 27.04.2007.
[81] See Arts. 9, 14, 15 UNDU ASO; Rule 56 ICTY ROD; Rule 54 ICTR ROD; Rule 36(A) SCSL ROD.
[82] See para. 68 ICTR First Annual Report.   [83] Jackson, SCSLDF/ICCDC, 19.03.2007.
[84] Custodial staff, UNDU, 22-27.08.2007.   [85] See Arts. 16-18 UNDU ASO.
[86] See Art. 13 UNDU ASO.

would add another layer of security, as the host prison authorities would also conduct searches at the national prison entrance.[87] This can create difficulties when the rules differ, as national staff would then be in a position to refuse access to visitors and/or the property they bring.[88] For instance, the ICCDC allows mothers to bring in milk for nursing babies whereas the Dutch prison authorities do not.[89]

3.2.3 A shared facility within the perimeter of a Host State prison

Within a host prison's perimeter, an international prison can operate in a stand-alone building like the former UNDU or UNDF, or from a building shared with other international prisons, like the current UNDU and ICCDC. Further cooperation and compromise are required when several international jurisdictions operate from one building within a host prison.

The ICTY, ICC and Special Tribunal for Lebanon (STL) all currently have access to cells in one building within Scheveningen Prison Complex in The Hague. The UNDU, spread over three floors, has also housed ICTR convicts appealing their cases and ICC-detained witnesses. The ICCDC is contained within one floor and in addition to its own detained persons has housed Mr Taylor for the SCSL. The STL has entered into a standing or floating agreement with the Dutch Government that enables it to reserve penal capacity in this building. This agreement only requires payment for the reserved wing, however, if and when it is required.[90]

The concurrent operation of the independent jurisdictions of the UNDU and ICCDC from one building had created practical difficulties which affect the regime and require time-consuming scheduling to prevent the different groups of detained persons meeting at common facilities, entrances and walkways.[91] The concurrent operation of the two systems also limits the time each IDF has to use shared facilities such as the visiting rooms and the sports hall. The two IDFs share responsibility for staffing their joint reception.[92]

As both IDFs have to operate from within the Dutch host prison, it became necessary to outline procedures that would apply to practical operational issues such as the use of shared spaces, security, contract

---

[87] See Arts. 2–3, 5–6 UNDU ASO.   [88] See Arts. 4, 7–8 UNDU ASO.
[89] ICCDC Tour, 06.06.2007.   [90] McNally, STL, 05.07.2012.
[91] Dubuisson, Tjonk, Becerra-Suarez, ICC, 06.06.2007; Craig, ICCDC, 04.07.2012.
[92] Tjonk, ICCDC, 04.07.2012.

disputes, fire inspections, autopsy, death investigations, evacuation plans and questions of responsibility and liability in a multilateral Detention Cooperation Agreement.[93] The need to deal with and, at times, rely on both the host prison and other international jurisdictions, may make it difficult for entities to maintain their individual identities and independence.

As IDFs have held the detainees, detained witnesses and convicted persons of other courts, there does not appear to be any apparent jurisdictional reasons why persons convicted by one international court could not serve their sentence of imprisonment in an international prison operated by another international court or organisation. Moreover, detained persons in the custody of different IDFs have mixed during social and sporting occasions.[94] To avert the jurisdictional dilemmas faced by the current IDFs operating within a shared building, it would be preferable if international courts sharing the capacity of an international prison could introduce a mandate which treats prisoners from all jurisdictions equally and, subject to security considerations, allows them to mix. There was an attempt to standardise the system used by the detention facilities of the ICC, ICTY and STL while housed in the same building but the working group's suggestions were not acted upon.[95]

3.2.4 The shared responsibility of a Host State and an international organisation

As IDFs are under the control and authority of an international court,[96] their premises are inviolable.[97] Accordingly, the IDF's internal rules and regulations take precedence over the national law of the Host State.[98] An IDF, irrespective of its location, is considered to be international territory. Conversely, everywhere outside the IDF's four walls is within the jurisdiction of the Host State. Yet despite these clear territorial jurisdictional boundaries, the experience of the IDFs has shown that there will be areas of an international prison's operations that will invoke the shared responsibility of the Host State and the relevant international organisation. In other words, there will be times when the responsibility of the

---

[93] Dubuisson, Tjonk, Becerra-Suarez, ICC, 06.06.2007; Blom, Moonen, The Netherlands, 24.08.2007.
[94] Jouthart, ICCDC, 04.07.2012.   [95] Ibid.
[96] Art. VI(1) ICTY/ ICTR HQA; Art. 5(1) SCSL HQA; Art. 8(1) ICC HQA.
[97] See Art. V ICTY/ICTR HQA; Art. 8(1) SCA; Art. 4(1)–(2) SCSL HQA; Art. 6(1) ICC HQA.
[98] Art. VI(2)–(4) ICTY/ICTR HQA; Art. 5(2)–(3) SCSL HQA; Art. 8(7) ICC HQA.

Host State and the international court for an international prisoner will overlap. For instance, while detained persons are being transported from an IDF to court, they remain under the custody of the international court.[99] However, as they are travelling through the Host State's territory, the Host State may insist on providing transport and security.[100] A similar situation arises when a detained person is transferred to a civilian hospital in the Host State for treatment. The court provides detention staff to ensure the continued secure custody of the individual and the Host State provides security staff to ensure their safe custody.[101] These scenarios provide examples of rather obvious instances of jurisdictional overlap. It has proven much more complicated to decide which entity is in a position to dictate procedure in situations where responsibility is shared within the walls of the IDF.

Several incidents at the UNDU provide good examples of this dilemma. Following Mr Babić's suicide in his UNDU cell,[102] it was unclear who was responsible for conducting an investigation into the circumstances of his death. There was no protocol to follow as the event was unprecedented. It becomes even more complicated when international courts issue orders to Host States to act in relation to occupants of international facilities. For example, there was a great deal of uncertainty about how to proceed in relation to an order from an ICTY Trial Chamber to the Dutch Government to force-feed a UNDU detainee on hunger-strike, should he lapse into unconsciousness.[103] The order could not be given directly to the Dutch Medical Officer working at the UNDU as he was not an ICTY employee but a Dutch Government employee.[104] The order was therefore issued to the Dutch Authorities under Article 29 of the ICTY Statute, which states that UN Members States must comply with orders issued by a Trial Chamber of the ICTY. This was problematic as the Dutch Government was bound to comply with the order, but the Dutch Medical Officer felt he could not due to his ethical position and

---

[99] See Rule 3 ICTR ROD: "all detainees shall be subject to the sole jurisdiction of the Tribunal at all times... even though physically absent from the Detention Unit, until final release or transfer to another institution".
[100] See para. 93 ICTR Third Annual Report.
[101] Blom, Moonen, The Netherlands, 24.08.2007.
[102] See Judge Parker, Report to the President on the Death of Milan Babić, 08.06.2006.
[103] Šešelj (Urgent Order to the Dutch Authorities Regarding the Health and Welfare of the Accused) IT-03-67-T, 06.12.2006.
[104] Blom, Moonen, The Netherlands, 24.08.2007; Vincent, SCSL/ICTY, 27.04.2007.

adherence to the Malta Declaration which does not allow force-feeding against the wishes of an individual.[105]

It is clear that it can be difficult to resolve questions about the attribution or division of responsibility for international prisoners housed in a Host State. Many of these situations are unprecedented. The development of policy in this regard has been piecemeal. However, as the operations of the IDFs matured, the international courts and Host States began to elaborate on the provisions of the relevant headquarters agreements. For example, the ICC, ICTY and the Dutch Government have entered into a Detention Cooperation Agreement to pre-determine protocol to be followed for foreseeable events and to establish procedures for detailing with unforeseeable events. While the negotiation of such an agreement may be a time-consuming and difficult exercise, it is a necessity for the operation of an international penal facility on national territory. To avoid foreseeable problems and provide procedures for discussing unforeseeable incidents, international prisons should enter into such liability agreements with Host States, ideally during the "inception phase".[106]

Practical issues may also impact on the division of responsibility. The economic and political situation in a Host State may affect the responsibility of the Host State and the international organisation. For example, Host States undertake to provide public services and utilities at the same rate they are provided to local government agencies and in the case of disruption, at the same level of priority.[107] International prisons operating in states that have been subject to protracted conflicts causing collapsed national infrastructure and severe resource shortages may, however, have to be self-sufficient in terms of the supply of basic utilities.[108]

Further, Host States undertake to provide IDFs with assistance in the event of fire, emergencies, disturbances and attacks.[109] It may be necessary to employ a mixture of Host State and international security personnel to ensure the perimeter security of an international prison, particularly in developing or post-conflict states.[110] Both the SCSL and

---

[105] See Art. 21 World Medical Association, Declaration of Malta on Hunger Strikers, 1991.
[106] Para. C.3(54) MDP, 188.
[107] See Art. XII ICTY/ICTR HQA; Art. 13 SCSL HQA; Art. 9 ICC HQA.
[108] The SCSL, for example, had a generator which provided the SCSLDF with a continuous electricity supply.
[109] See Arts. V(3)–(4), VII ICTY/ICTR HQAs.
[110] Von Hebel, SCSL, 24.04.2007; Vincent, SCSL/ICTY, 27.04.2007.

ICTR rely on a mixture of international and national detention staff, security staff, soldiers and other contracted personnel.[111] International courts should exercise caution in relying on Host State military or police or private security companies in post-conflict countries if there are concerns about their effectiveness and loyalties.[112]

It would be necessary to draw up an evacuation plan for international prisoners and international prison staff for each location. Situations may arise in countries considered to be stable. For instance, the military coup and unrest in Mali in 2012 were unforeseen. Evacuation plans must be practised in advance to ensure they are feasible and ensure alternatives are put into place should they prove not to be. For example, when it became apparent during a practice run of the SCSLDF evacuation plan that it would not be feasible to move prisoners over land in a situation of unrest, a heliport was constructed onsite.[113]

3.3 Choosing a suitable model

An international prison facility's location and design will depend on a number of factors including the estimated number of prisoners, perceived security risks of attacks or escape, the need to build or adapt an existing structure to meet international standards and the resources available.[114] It will be difficult to predict the population of an international prison as numbers may rise or fall depending on the number of situations under investigation, prosecutorial strategy, success in arrest and prosecution and appeals etc. Cost will inevitably, and probably most decisively, impact on the decision regarding which model to use. The founding body will not want to re-create the Spandau situation, where the cost of housing seven persons in a facility built to hold six hundred imposed an intolerable and disproportionate burden on the West Berlin Government.[115] In fact, Spandau has been described as "the most

---

[111] See Art. 16 SCA; Art. 6 SCSL HQA; SCRes 1562(2004); SCSL Press Release, "Mongolian Peacekeepers Takeover Security at Special Court", 08.01.2006; para. 75 ICTR Second Annual Report.

[112] Vincent, *An Administrative Practices Manual for Internationally Assisted Criminal Justice Institutions*, 65.

[113] See SCSL Fourth Annual Report, 50-2. Neil, SCSLDF, 23.04.2008; Ewing, SCSLDF, 23.04.2008.

[114] Vincent, *An Administrative Practices Manual for Internationally Assisted Criminal Justice Institutions*, 66; Goda, *Tales from Spandau*, 24.

[115] See Fishman, *Long Knives and Short Memories*, 250-4; Goda, *Tales from Spandau 2*, 27, 85, 195-6, 248.

unwieldy, inefficient and the most expensive prison" that could be established.[116] The model chosen must be cost-effective and financially sustainable in the long term. The option of an island-based or independent site is probably not justifiable at present due to the huge cost that this would involve to house a relatively minute population. A facility within a host prison appears to be the most cost-effective option.

The choice of a site should also be made with the facility's functionality in mind. The unit must be feasible in terms of its ability to provide work, education, leisure and resocialisation programmes. The international prison's design must provide conditions that meet international minimum standards and enable management to fulfil the custodial mandate of the facility. For example, the ICCDC should be able to cater for persons with disabilities and/or young children.[117] If the site offered by the Host State contains existing infrastructure, this may create difficulties. A pre-determined lay-out and old facilities may not ensure optimal security, operational flexibility or humane conditions.[118] For instance, the second SCSLDF did not have toilets and washing facilities in the cells until 2008, despite the fact that two detained persons suffered from physical handicaps.[119] Like the IDFs, an international prison must have a medical clinic as well as access to external hospitals that provide appropriate levels of care and treatment.[120]

Despite these considerations, the model adopted will depend to a large degree on the sites available. Spandau Prison was only selected as a temporary option after it became clear that a severe shortage of building materials ruled out the construction of a new facility or the renovations necessary to make the proposed anti-aircraft tower, castle or former Gestapo prison habitable.[121] For international courts, this will mean the sites that are offered by the Host State. For example, the ICC was offered an independent site 100 kilometres away from the court and a prison boat in the harbour before the current wing in the host prison was made available to be used as the ICCDC. The Dutch Government eventually opted to renovate an existing wing within the UNDU despite

---

[116] Edgar M. Gerlach cited in Goda, *Tales from Spandau*, 86.
[117] See Regs. 103(2), 104 ICC ROC; Regs. 160–1 ICC ROR.
[118] Cardinal, Moore, SCSLDF, 20.04.2008; Wright, SCSLDF, 22.04.2008.
[119] See paras. 212–16 A. Cassese, *Report on the Special Court for Sierra Leone* (2006), 46–7.
[120] Vincent, *An Administrative Practices Manual for Internationally Assisted Criminal Justice Institutions*, 70. See also Chapter 3, Section 6.
[121] Goda, *Tales from Spandau*, 24–5, 27.

the ICC preference to construct a new independent ICCDC facility within the walls of the host prison.[122] International courts are often in a position whereby they have to make the best of the site made available by the Host State. Therefore, although the founding body may prefer a particular model of detention facility, the decision is likely to be constrained by the options offered by the Host State and influenced by cost, capacity and functionality factors.

4. Operating an international prison system

International prisons must be in a position to enforce often lengthy international sentences of imprisonment in accordance with international standards. It is imperative, therefore, that funding is secured from the outset. To ensure that international prisons can implement international penal strategy effectively, it will also be necessary to recruit and train international management and staff. The section explores possible funding options for an international prison system and makes recommendations in relation to the internationalisation of the system's management and staff based on lessons learned from the operations of IDFs.

4.1 Funding

An international prison system will require funds to build, renovate or rent penal capacity and to pay for its operation at international standards. This will involve a myriad of costs which will depend on the detention model selected, ranging from security, staffing, utilities, policy development and implementation, medical care, communications, food etc. There are several possible funding options.

First, an international prison could be funded directly from the budget of the founding institution. IDFs are funded directly from the budgets of their respective courts. However, there are two instantly foreseeable difficulties with this option; a lack of funds and resistance from contributing states to increase the financial burden on the court. The UN had to provide the UN Tribunals with substantial funding,[123] and the

---

[122] Dubuisson, Tjonk, Becerra-Suarez, ICC, 06.06.2007; Blom, Moonen, The Netherlands, 24.08.2007.
[123] For 2010–11, the UNGA approved a budget of US $286,012,600 for the ICTY (www.icty.org/sid/325) and US $245,295,800 for the ICTR (www.unictr.org/AboutICTR/GeneralInformation/tabid/101/Default.aspx).

increasing high costs of their operations made the UN Security Council push for completion strategies for these temporary courts.[124] The UN may not want sole responsibility for the long-term financial commitment that would be necessary to fund an international prison system. The ICC relies on assessed contributions from member states, funds from the UN and voluntary contributions from other entities.[125] Many promised contributions, however, are not being realised. To receive funds from the general budget, an international prison system would require the support of a two-thirds majority of the ASP.[126] Yet ASP members have been reluctant to implement resolutions creating structural changes[127] and amendments to detention policy[128] that would have significant budgetary impacts. However, the ICC has a statutory obligation to pay for the implementation of international sentences of imprisonment served in a residual facility provided by the Host State.[129] Despite the difficulties faced in raising finances, international courts have promised cooperating states that they will help them find the funds to construct and renovate facilities to hold international prisoners.[130] Although, initially, there was resistance to this form of financial assistance,[131] the UN Security Council has held that international judicial institutions have the lawful power to fund the renovation and refurbishment of prisons facilities in states to bring conditions up to international standards, if those states have concluded agreements with the UN for the purpose of carrying out prison sentences imposed by UN tribunals.[132] Recently, international courts have gone further with their commitments to states, with promises to pay for the maintenance and direct enforcement costs, such as meals, communications and medical care arising from the operations of such facilities.[133] With this level of

---

[124] See W. Schabas, *The UN International Criminal Tribunals: The Former Yugoslavia, Rwanda and Sierra Leone* (2006), 6.
[125] See Arts. 115–16 ICCSt.   [126] See Arts. 112(2)(d), 112(7)(a), 114–115 ICCSt.
[127] See paras. A. 3, C.10, D.1.16 Report of the Bureau on the Establishment of an Independent Oversight Mechanism, 15.04.2009, 1, 2, 4–5.
[128] See Report of the Court on the Financial Aspects of Enforcing the Court's Obligation to Fund Family Visits to Indigent Detained Persons, 06.05.2009.
[129] Art. 103(4) ICCSt.   [130] See Chapter 2, Section 3.1.
[131] See UN Secretary-General's Report, Long-term Financial Obligations of the UN with Regard to the Enforcement of Sentences 26.08.2002; paras. 37–41, Report of the Advisory Committee on Administrative and Budgetary Questions, A/57/593, 07.11.2002; para. 7 Financing of the ICTR, GARes 57/289 (2012).
[132] Statement by the President of the Security Council, S/PRST/2003/18, 27.10.2003.
[133] Art. 11(1)(a)(iii)–(iv) ICTR-Rwanda BEA; Art. 11(1)(c) SCSL–Rwanda BEA.

commitment required to ensure that the enforcement of sentences in national prison systems conforms to international standards, and as this form of expenditure has been sanctioned from the general budget, it may make more sense to contribute to the cost of building and maintaining custom-designed and internationally controlled facilities.

Second, states could continue to support the enforcement of sentences. Instead of providing penal capacity by accepting international prisoners into national custody, cooperating states could make a financial commitment towards the costs of running international prisons. The ICC has already discussed the possibility of concluding this form of enforcement agreement.[134] Whether a state chooses to contribute to the costs of enforcing a particular sentence, to provide a percentage of the annual costs of a facility or to donate a fixed sum annually, it would continue to share the burden of implementing international criminal justice. While there may be more political kudos to be gained within international circles for accepting responsibility to enforce custodial sanctions imposed on renowned war criminals than a state can gain for writing an annual cheque, this re-framed form of enforcement cooperation would reduce the political sensitivity and security risks of accepting high profile international criminals into overcrowded national systems. As the conditions of national prisons are no longer a factor, more states may be willing to cooperate. Costs and the burden may be spread among a larger number of states. A policy of regional placement may also result in more cost-effective enforcement. While some states may prefer to absorb the cost of international cooperation into their national prison service budgets, and although an international prison system may not be able to benefit from the same economies of scale as national prison systems, a regional placement policy may enable facilities to benefit from the cheaper cost of operating in developing countries. The annual cost of housing an international prisoner (excluding staffing costs) at the UNDU in The Hague, for example, is more than seven times more expensive than the cost of doing so at the UNDF in Arusha, Tanzania.[135]

Third, contributions towards the cost of operating an international prison system could be linked to national development aid projects.[136] By simultaneously supporting the international criminal justice system

---

[134] See Chapter 5, Section 4.
[135] US $100,000 and US $14,020 respectively. See para. 173 Residual Mechanism Report.
[136] Friman, Sweden, 22.09.2008.

and penal development in developing or post-conflict countries, cooperating states can kill two birds with one cheque. While the improvement of national prison systems is not a stated goal of the international criminal justice system, it has become an important element of the legacy of the temporary international criminal courts operating in Africa. The UNDF and SCSLDF have actively engaged with the national prison systems of their Host States and others in the region, providing on and off the job training on international standards and modern detention management techniques to both seconded and non-seconded staff.[137] The SCSL has also provided training to staff from the prison service of an enforcing state. To assist the Rwandan prison authorities with the management of the SCSL prisoners housed in Mpanga Prison, the Special Court worked with the Government of Rwanda to provide a two-month training course led by SCSL staff and a former Chief of Detention on international standards of prison management.[138] Regionally placed international prisons could act as a conduit for state, regional or international development aid funds geared toward penal development by providing training to developing prison systems. Such training should, however, be part of a wider approach to systemic change in prison management and operations if it is to be effective.[139]

Fourth, the founding institution could seek voluntary contributions, grants and non-financial forms of assistance from regional or international organisations such as the African Union, the European Union, the Council of Europe, the Organisation of American States, the Association of Southeast Asian Nations etc. Assistance need not come from an intergovernmental body. For example, Utrecht University expressed an interest in taking over the Registry role of the SCSLDF, should the site be maintained as an international prison.[140] The ICC has recently recognised that assistance to support the enforcement of its sentences could be sought from bodies such as the World Bank and the UN Development Programme.[141]

---

[137] See SCSL Press Release, "Prison Officers Recognised by Special Court" 04.02.2008; ICTR Press Release, "ICTR Hands Over Armoured Truck to Tanzania Prison Services", 11.10.2011. Showers, SLPS, 25.04.2008; Cardinal, Moore, SCSLDF, 20.04.2008; O'Donnell, ICTR, 25.06.2007.
[138] SCSL Ninth Annual Report, 24.
[139] Vincent, *An Administrative Practices Manual for Internationally Assisted Criminal Justice Institutions*, 70.
[140] Vincent, SCSL/ICTY, 27.04.2007.
[141] Para. 4 Strengthening the Enforcement of Sentences, Resolution RC/Res.3, 08.06.2010.

Finally, a resolution was adopted at the ICC's Review Conference in 2010 which represented an evolution in the international criminal justice system's approach to enforcement. To facilitate regional placement and to enable more states to volunteer to enforce international punishment in accordance with international standards governing the treatment of prisoners, it was acknowledged that international sentences may be implemented in prisons "made available in the designated State through an international or regional organisation, mechanism or agency".[142] This resolution foresees progression from the traditional approach of reliance on domestic prison systems towards the use of international or internationally funded facilities in cooperating states. This means that states that are willing to cooperate in relation to enforcement, but don't have the means to do so, can access financial assistance, expertise, training or facilities from organisations that do.[143] The wording of this resolution may also be wide enough to encompass the establishment of internationally operated prisons on the territory of designated cooperating states.

This list of funding options is not exhaustive. Moreover, these options are not mutually exclusive. In fact, experience would show that several, if not all, sources would be necessary to ensure the financing of an international prison system. For example, the ICC and/or the UN could provide the construction costs, a Host State could provide the land and security, cooperating states could provide the finances needed for its day-to-day operations and regime development and unforeseen costs could be met by external grants or donations.

4.2 Management

International prisons should replicate the management structure used by the IDFs and maintain their practice of directly recruiting chief custody officers, deputies and supervisors.[144] Managers should come from a range of countries. They should have experience of prison management at a national and international level, as well as during or after a conflict. At present, the majority of senior IDF management positions are held by men.[145] International prisons should try to achieve a greater gender balance in management structures.

---

[142] Para. 2 *ibid.*   [143] Abathi, ICC, 05.07.2012.   [144] See Chapter 3.
[145] All IDF CCO's have been male, and there has only been one female supervisor at the ICCDC and SCSLDF at any given time.

As they are essentially international civil servants, some IDF managers lack prison experience or exposure to national prison systems. It is important to ensure, therefore, that all management personnel recruited by an international prison system are trained in international penal strategy and provided with continuous professional development throughout their careers. Turnover in the senior management of IDFs can be quite high, with the chief custody officer changing every couple of years. This can result in continually changing methods and practices which can affect the regime for both staff and detained persons. In addition to the employment of international policy, international prisons should also adopt a broad, horizontal management structure. To avoid tensions between managers from different backgrounds, international penal policy should also adopt a defined international approach to maintaining security and order.[146]

Managers of remotely located international prisons will have more autonomy in decision-making and regime development than their IDF counterparts. There have been complaints that the decision-making power of IDF managers is diluted by officials whose expertise is far removed from the realities of detention.[147] For example, judges have discussed such trivial issues as the flavour of yoghurts detainees should have.[148] They have also issued orders that were impractical to implement, such as an ICTY order to guarantee medical appointments within twenty-four hours,[149] segregation orders to separate detainees when there was insufficient penal capacity to do so[150] or an ICC order to classify all detainee requests or discussions of issues as formal complaints.[151] Orders have also had significant effects on security and the welfare of detainees. For example, an ICTY order granting facilities to self-representing detainees resulted in un-prescribed medication being brought into the UNDU, which may have been responsible for damage to the physical health, even death of a detained person.[152] As international prisons would

---

[146] See Chapter 3, Section 4.2.
[147] See paras. 2.4, 2.6.1 Independent Audit of the Detention Unit at the ICTY, 2006; Jackson, SCSLDF/ICCDC, 19.03.2007.
[148] Vincent, SCSL/ICTY, 27.04.2007.
[149] Para. 2.4 Independent Audit of the Detention Unit at the ICTY, 2006.
[150] Order to the Registrar to Separate Convicted and Non-Convicted Detainees held in the Detention Unit (President's Order) IT-06-89-Misc.1, 15.06.2006.
[151] Dubuisson, Tjonk, Becerra-Suarez, ICC, 06.06.2007.
[152] See Chapter 3, Sections 3 and 6.

primarily be used to hold persons whose trials have been completed and as they would be remotely located, there may be less judicial and administrative interference in the management of such facilities. The flip-side of this, however, is the need to ensure that independent and effective oversight mechanisms are put in place.

4.3 Custodial staff

The previous section advocated the maintenance of the management structure and recruitment procedures used by the IDFs. It is highly likely that an international prison would operate from within a Host State, and perhaps from within a host prison. IDFs operating within Host State prisons have seconded the overwhelming majority of their custodial staff from the Host State's prison service.[153] Although this may make initial set-up easier, this practice has created several problems.

4.3.1 Selecting suitable staff

Although IDF managers are supposed to have control over, or at the very least, input into the selection of custodial staff,[154] Host State prison services have retained nearly exclusive control over the process in practice. Consequently, IDFs have received staff that had no experience of working directly with detainees. IDFs have received seconded staff from the catering, administrative, transport, reception or perimeter security sections of the national prison service.[155] Such staff do not possess the skill-set necessary to deal with detention-related issues.[156] This lack of control over the selection process has resulted in the secondment of unqualified staff and consequently, the need for IDFs to provide higher levels of training and supervision at the international level. Worryingly, there were also suspicions that some staff sent to the SCSLDF had been selected due to who they knew or who they had bribed.[157]

---

[153] Para. 367 ICTY Eleventh Annual Report; SCSL Third Annual Report, 36; Preamble SCSL MOU (Secondment); Blom, Moonen, The Netherlands, 24.08.2007.
[154] Art. 2(1) SCSL MOU (Secondment); para. A.3(15) MDP, 180.
[155] Custodial Staff, UNDU, 22–27.0.2007; Custodial Staff, ICCDC, 22–28.08.2007; Cardinal, Moore, SCSLDF, 20.04.2008; Wright, SCSLDF, 22.04.2008; Custodial Staff, SCSLDF, 22–25.04.2008.
[156] Vincent, *An Administrative Practices Manual for Internationally Assisted Criminal Justice Institutions*, 70.
[157] Cardinal, Moore, SCSLDF, 20.04.2008; Wright, SCSLDF, 22.04.2008.

4.3.2 National standards and mentality

Another notable consequence of seconding staff from one national prison service is that that national system's standards and mentality prevail. Many seconded staff found it difficult to adjust to, accept and internalise international rules and procedures. Many simply felt that national rules, procedures and systems were better.[158] The transition was particularly difficult as many were still working within the walls of a national prison or still had duties within the national prison service. Reliance on a staff comprised of one nationality makes it difficult to implement an international regime. It would be necessary for an international prison system to train staff coming from domestic prison services on the international regulations and standards.[159]

4.3.3 Neither/nor dilemma

In part, the reluctance to embrace international procedures can be attributed to the "neither/nor" status of seconded staff. Although they wear an IDF uniform, take instructions from international managers and court officials and implement international regulations, IDF prison officers remain the formal employees of their national prison service.[160] They work at an international detention facility, but they are not international court employees.[161] They come as part of the product price agreement entered into with the Host State, and under such agreements, the relevant national ministry remains responsible for their wages, pension, sick pay etc.

They are formally classified as employees of the national prison system, but they are not working as national prison officers. Throughout their secondment to international detention facilities, they are not offered or obliged to take part in training in the national system. As many seconded staff have worked at international detention facilities for long periods of time (since 1994 in some cases), this means that they will no longer have the necessary skills or qualifications to work in domestic prisons.[162]

---

[158] Custodial Staff, ICCDC, 22–28.08.2007.
[159] Vincent, *An Administrative Practices Manual for Internationally Assisted Criminal Justice Institutions*, 69.
[160] See para. A.3(15) MDP, 180; Art. 3 SCSL MOU (Secondment).
[161] See paras. 9, 11–12 Letter of Agreement between ICTY and Ministry of Justice of the Netherlands, 20.10.1997.
[162] Bremmers, ICCDC, 04.07.2012; Jouthart, ICCDC, 04.07.2012.

The uncertainty surrounding the exact organisational status of IDF seconded staff and their perceived neglect by their national employer has impacted on staff morale. IDF staff have noted that their colleagues and managers in the national prison system feel that they are "not real custody officers" but civil servants working in facilities that are "not real prisons".[163] Staff feel that their "neither/nor" status enables the national prison service to avoid dealing with difficult issues by seeking to place responsibility on the international court.[164] The ICCDC and Dutch Prison Service, for instance, could not decide which body was responsible for paying for vaccinations for seconded staff to protect them against tropical diseases that detained persons may have.[165] Seconded staff also feel that their lack of international status is symbolic of the lack of recognition or appreciation of their work by the relevant international court.[166] Their dual status also creates job uncertainty as staff can be rotated or returned to the national system without reason. This uncertainty can be particularly stressful as an IDF down-sizes and the temporary tribunals move towards completion. Rather than feeling like a skilled and valued worker, some seconded staff feel like a commodity hired out for profit.

At the SCSLDF, the "neither/nor" status resulted in quite significant wage discrimination. The seconded staff's wages remained stagnant for over five years,[167] whereas persons hired directly by the court had their wages reviewed every six months. Even those who had been promoted to the role of national supervisor received no pay increase.[168] This discrepancy in wages meant that the local custodial staff could not afford to eat with their international colleagues in the work canteen.[169]

4.3.4 International prison staff

There have been attempts to internationalise the staff at IDFs. The UNDU seconded Danish and Czech custody officers. The ICCDC recently considered directly recruiting international custodial staff. Such a move would require a number of practical decisions to be

---

[163] Bremmers, ICCDC, 04.07.2012.   [164] Principal Officer, UNDU, 22.08.2007.
[165] Dubuisson, Tjonk, Becerra-Suarez, ICC, 06.06.2007.
[166] Custodial Staff, UNDU, 22–27.08.2007; Custodial Staff, ICCDC, 22–28.08.2007.
[167] In addition to their usual salary, seconded custodial staff received an additional monthly stipend of 450,000 Leones (around £75). See Art. 5(1) SCSL MOU (Secondment).
[168] Wright, SCSLDF, 22.04.2008; Ewing, SCSLDF, 23.04.2008.
[169] Custodial Staff, SCSLDF, 22–25.04.2008.

made, such as where to advertise the posts, whether to hire individuals directly or to second them from other prison services and the timeframe that would be required to train recruits on international rules and regulations. Unfortunately, the project was abandoned as the ASP Committee for Budget and Finance rejected the request for additional funds. This rejection was based on the fact that three Dutch custodial officers can be seconded for the same price as directly recruiting two international officers.[170] This purely financial decision is not in the best interests of the detention facility of the world's only permanent court. Unlike the IDFs of the temporary courts which will close in the near future, the ICC will always need a remand centre. The current dual management and status of IDF staff is not conducive to the creation of an international detention or penal system.

If custodial staff are wearing the uniform of an international prison, implementing international penal policy under the instructions of an international manager, they should have international status. An international status would ensure that suitably qualified and experienced staff are selected. Rather than seek the secondment of national employees, the international prison system should directly recruit and train suitably qualified individuals. While this will take time and increase costs in the short-term, this will help to create a properly trained body of international prison officers. The recruitment of staff from a range of cultures and nationalities would make the promotion of an international identity and the implementation of international systems and standards much easier.[171] International wages, permanent posts and better opportunities for promotion would increase solidarity within the international system and lead to specialist expertise in enforcing international punishment.

5. Conclusion

For temporary international courts, decentralised national enforcement will often be the most cost-effective option. However, practice has shown that international punishment implemented in this way risks being inhumane and ineffective. While it may initially cost more to implement international sentences of imprisonment in international facilities, this cost remains relatively small when compared with the cost of

---

[170] Craig, ICCDC, 04.07.2012; Tjonk, ICCDC, 04.07.2012.
[171] See para. A.3(16) MDP, 180.

international trials and the operation of the international courts.[172] The creation of an international prison system would ensure immediate access to penal capacity and regimes that operate in accordance with international standards and facilitate the implementation of international penal policy and practices. The resulting international control over international sanctions and their implementation would ensure the equal treatment of international prisoners to a much greater degree.

IDFs have been operating as de facto prisons and international courts are increasingly becoming involved in the funding of special facilities in cooperating states that house international prisoners. The ICC has encouraged the involvement of non-state entities in the implementation of international punishment. It is now time to recognise the need for the direct implementation of international punishment in internationally controlled facilities. An international criminal justice system must include an international prison system. This institutional evolution will ensure that the international penal system can achieve its penological and broader justice objectives.

Practice to date suggests that the best option is to rent a wing within a domestic prison. A network of international facilities will enable the continuation of the regional placement of international prisoners and the trend of internationalising international criminal justice. Access to a range of facilities will also allow for the creation of a range of security levels and the dispersal of vulnerable or dangerous prisoners where necessary. Rather than maintain staffed facilities at all times, floating agreements could be concluded with cooperating states to reserve penal capacity which would only incur costs if and when it was required.

The proposed direct implementation of international sentences of imprisonment would entail the exercise of power over dependent individuals. International prisons would also operate more autonomously than IDFs. This power brings with it the risk of violating the human rights and freedoms of international prisoners. International prisons must therefore be subject to strict and transparent oversight. Given the difficulties international prisoners would face in bringing criminal, tortious or human rights claims against international organisations, states or indeed individuals, it is also important to clarify the avenues prisoners have to seek redress from the outset.

---

[172] Culp, "Enforcement and Monitoring of Sentences in the Modern War Crimes Process", 13.

10

Guarding the guardians

Chapter 9 advocated the further institutionalisation of the international penal system through the creation of an international prison system. An international prison system would enable international courts directly to enforce the sanctions they impose on persons found guilty of committing international crimes. This direct control would also enable international courts to implement a specifically tailored international penal policy and derivative practices. Control over an international prison system would, however, also bring power over international prisoners. The power to implement custodial sanctions creates power over dependent individuals and, with it, the risk of human rights violations. The creation of an international prison system would, therefore, create responsibility for international prisoners. As international courts are created to end impunity and uphold human dignity, they would have to operate international prisons in a rights compliant manner and provide international prisoners with access to remedial justice if their rights were violated during their incarceration in such facilities. Although it is indisputable that international courts would be responsible for international prisoners held in international prisons, it is not clear how an international prisoner would impose liability on an international organisation, its members or officials for crimes, tortious acts or human rights abuses committed in an international prison. This lack of clarity is not surprising given that international punishment is a relatively new phenomenon, the scenario of an international prison system is hypothetical and international organisation responsibility is a new and developing area of international law. However, the very real potential for human rights abuses in a penal environment makes it imperative to ask; who will guard the guardians?[1]

---

[1] R. Reinisch, "Securing the Accountability of International Organizations" (2001) 7 *Global Governance* 131–49 at 132. See also G. Verdirame, *The UN and Human Rights: Who Guards the Guardians?* (2011).

Due to the unique structure of the international criminal justice system and its institutions, international prisoners would have no right to appeal the decisions of the President/Presidency of the international courts.[2] In addition to the lack of appeal in relation to decisions on internal complaints, the current recommendations of independent oversight bodies are non-binding and their reports are not published.[3] External avenues for redress appear ineffective. Even if liability can be attributed to specific legal entities or persons, there are numerous obstacles hindering the implementation of accountability, including the jurisdictional immunity of international organisations, their organs and officials in domestic systems and the lack of alternative avenues for legal redress at the international level. These gaps in the legal rights and systems for the protection of international prisoners could be detrimental for the legitimacy of the international penal system and the international criminal justice system more generally.

To ensure the legitimacy and effectiveness of international punishment and the international penal system's compliance with contemporary standards on imprisonment, it would be necessary for international courts to engage independent mechanisms to oversee and evaluate the operation of an international prison system and its facilities. To operate in line with human rights standards, it would also be important to ensure that international prisoners have access to an impartial body capable of hearing complaints and awarding effective remedies.

1. Oversight of an international prison system

Effective oversight entails the analysis of the performance of a system and the imposition of a proper model of conduct.[4] An international prison system should be inspected and evaluated by independent and suitably qualified bodies and its operation assessed against benchmarks determined in accordance with international human rights and penological standards governing the treatment of prisoners. In addition to being effective, an international prison system must also be accountable.

---

[2] See Chapter 5, Section 2.2.   [3] *Ibid.*
[4] L. B. De Chazournes, "Changing Roles of International Organizations" (2009) 6 *International Organizations Law Review* 655–66 at 661.

OVERSIGHT OF AN INTERNATIONAL PRISON SYSTEM   309

Accountability requires transparency, regular monitoring and answerability for conduct that falls below expected standards.[5]

International courts are attempting to make their penal systems more transparent by codifying practice and making detention-related jurisprudence public. However, the reports of the regular inspecting bodies remain confidential. An international prison system should publish annual reports that contain external oversight reports and recommendations. Transparency, however, entails more than just access to documents or "informational transparency".[6] To the extent possible, international prisons should be open to the broadest range of external oversight mechanisms.

The collaborative model established by the Optional Protocol to the UN Convention Against Torture[7] could be adapted for an international prison system. The Optional Protocol creates a comprehensive system of prison oversight that provides for concurrent and regular oversight by national and international expert inspectorates[8] and the cooperation of these bodies with other national, regional and international oversight mechanisms and human rights institutions.[9] Many of the current and potential enforcing states of the international penal system have signed, ratified or acceded to this Optional Protocol.[10] In practice, this particular mechanism may not be suitable for an international prison system due to its specific mandate,[11] low rate of ratification,[12] and the need for the UN and/or the ICC to ratify both the UN Convention Against Torture and the Optional Protocol.

A similar model of collaboration between international, regional and national oversight mechanisms should however be established to ensure a comprehensive and synergistic system of support for international prisons and the protection of international prisoners.[13] The ICRC

---

[5] F. Hoffman and F. Mégret, "Fostering Human Rights Accountability: An Ombudsperson for the United Nations?" (2005) 11 *Global Governance* 43–63 at 50.
[6] De Chazournes, "Changing Roles of International Organizations", 659.
[7] Adopted by GARes 57/199 (2002) and entered into force on 22.06.2006.
[8] See Arts. 1, 2(1), 3, 11(1) OPCAT.
[9] See Arts. 11(c), 31 OPCAT; paras. 43, 48, 50, 52–5, 56 (SPT) Second Annual Report.
[10] The Optional Protocol has been ratified or acceded to by Benin, Denmark, Estonia, France, Germany, Mali, The Netherlands, Senegal, Spain, Sweden and the UK and signed by Austria, Belgium, Finland, Italy, Norway, Portugal and Sierra Leone.
[11] Art. 1 OPCAT: "to prevent torture and other cruel, inhuman or degrading treatment or punishment".
[12] OPCAT has been ratified or acceded to by sixty-three states.
[13] See para. 6 SPT Second Annual Report.

could inspect international prisons at regular intervals in the same manner as it inspects current IDFs.[14] Qualified and credible national and regional bodies should also be granted access to inspect international prisons and hear complaints from international prisoners.[15] This reflects practice to a certain extent. International prisoners held in Europe can be visited by both the ICRC and CPT and international prisoners in Africa may, in theory, speak with both the ICRC and the African Rapporteur on Prisons. The conditions of detention in the wing holding SCSL prisoners in Rwanda may be inspected at any time by the ICRC.[16] They are also inspected annually by the SCSL (RSCSL) and additional inspections by delegations composed of national officials, commissions and NGOs have also been facilitated.[17]

The current form of oversight, while necessary, focuses on the human rights concerns of detained persons and does not evaluate operations on a systemic level. It would be crucially important to implement a regular system of evaluation of all operational aspects of an international prison system to ensure it is operating in an effective and humane manner and to make long-term strategic recommendations for its development. An international prison system must operate in line with contemporary standards and in a manner that facilitates the achievement of international penal objectives.

The impact of evaluation or "lessons learned" units to promote institutional change within the UN remains unclear.[18] The ICC has established an Independent Oversight Mechanism. Due to concerns about its operational independence,[19] its office is co-located but not integrated with or subordinated to the ICC's Office of Internal Audit.[20] While it now has the power to investigate internal issues, the ASP has postponed the operationalisation of the IOM's inspection and evaluation functions.[21] It remains unclear if these functions will extend to detention and imprisonment-related aspects of the court's operation.

---

[14] See Chapter 3, Section 5.3.
[15] See M. Penrose, "No Badges, No Bars: A Conspicuous Oversight in the Development of an International Criminal Court" (2003) 38(3) *Texas International Law Journal* 621–42 at 641.
[16] Art. 6(1) SCSL–Rwanda BEA.   [17] SCSL Ninth Annual Report, 24, 38.
[18] Verdirame, *The UN and Human Rights*, 329.
[19] Paras. A. 4, D.2.24–27 Report of the Bureau on the Establishment of an Independent Oversight Mechanism, 1, 6–7.
[20] Para. 5 Annex Establishment of an Independent Oversight Mechanism, ICC-ASP/8/Res.1, 26.11.2009.
[21] Para. 1 Independent Oversight Mechanism, ICC-ASP/9/Res.5, 10.12.2010.

If internal mechanisms are unsuited to the task, the systemic evaluation of the international prison system should be outsourced to a national or international prison inspectorate. This may actually be a preferable option to guarantee that inspectors are independent and have the requisite experience. To ensure consistency, inspections should use international standards as benchmarks, although these may need to be adapted to take the uniqueness and objectives of the international penal system into account. The reports of these inspectorates, like those from oversight bodies, should be published.

The establishment of independent oversight bodies and inspectorates will contribute to the prevention of human rights abuses in an international prison system and assist with the development of its policy, practices and operations. As the recommendations of these bodies are typically non-binding, however, such measures cannot address the question of liability for any abuses that may occur or provide avenues for redress for potential victims.

2. Responsibility for an international prison system

An international prison system would be the responsibility of its founding international organisation, and this responsibility would be regulated by international law. International organisations increasingly exercise direct control over territory and peoples. The exercise of this form of power by international organisations is not necessarily a good thing, nor, indeed, is it always exercised in line with human rights standards.[22] Moreover, as international law continues to operate on the basis of a misplaced presumption that international organisations and states perform different tasks, the exercise of state-like power by international organisations is often not regulated.[23] International prisoners housed in

---

[22] Hoffman and Mégret, "Fostering Human Rights Accountability", 46; Reinisch, "Securing the Accountability of International Organizations", 131; G. Verdirame, *The UN and Human Rights*, 4; G. Verdirame, "UN Accountability for Human Rights Violations in Post-conflict Situations" in N. White and D. Klaasen (eds.), *The UN Human Rights and Post-conflict Situations* (2005), 81–97 at 92, 96.

[23] Reinisch, "Securing the Accountability of International Organizations", 141; R. Wilde, "Accountability and International Actors in Bosnia and Herzegovina, Kosovo and East Timor" (2000) 7 *ILSA Journal of International and Comparative Law* 455–60 at 456–8; R. Wilde, "Enhancing Accountability at the International Level: The Tension between International Organization and Member State Responsibility and the Underlying Issues at State" (2005) 12 *ILSA Journal of International and Comparative Law* 395–415 at 408; Verdirame, *The UN and Human Rights*, 13–4.

international prisons, will therefore find a number of obstacles in the path of redress for criminal, tortious or human rights violations whether they wish to impose liability on international organisations, states, seconded staff or individuals. It is often unclear if conduct and/or responsibility can be attributed to a particular entity. Even if this is established, the grant of, or refusal to waive, immunity often rules out the possibility of access to judicial review.

2.1 The responsibility of international organisations

The growth in the number and power of international organisations led the International Law Commission to produce the 2011 Draft Articles on the Responsibility of International Organisations (DARIO). Although these draft articles do not have the same authority as the ILC's 2001 Draft Articles on Responsibility of States for Internationally Wrongful Acts (DARS),[24] and gaps remain in relation to responsibility under national law and for acts not prohibited by international law,[25] DARIO does codify and progressively develop the law in this field.[26]

International organisations are created by states or other international organisations through agreements or instruments governed by international law.[27] The responsibility of an international organisation at the international legal level is based on the international organisation's possession of international legal personality.[28] If an international prison was created as an independent organisation, its legal personality could be either explicitly vested in it by its founding body or it may be presumed upon the acquisition of "organisationhood" and the performance of acts that can only be explained on the basis of international legal personality.[29] For example, the ICC was explicitly endowed with international legal personality by its member states[30] and the UN's international legal personality was acknowledged by the ICJ in the *Reparation for Injuries Suffered in the Service of the United Nations* case.[31] If an international

---

[24] DARIO Commentary, 2.
[25] See Articles 1(1), (2), 4, 5 DARIO; DARIO Commentary, 4, 6.
[26] DARIO Commentary, 1.   [27] Art. 2(a) DARIO; para. 12 DARIO Commentary, 10.
[28] International Law Association, Accountability of International Organisations, Final Report, 2004, 26 (ILA Final Report); DARIO Commentary, 10.
[29] J. Klabbers, *An Introduction to International Institutional Law* (2002), 55.
[30] See Art. 4 ICCSt; Art. 2 ICC API. The UN has recognised the ICC's ILP. See Art. 2(1) ICC–UN NRA.
[31] *(Advisory Opinion)* [1949] ICJ Reports, 178–9, 182.

prison remained an organ of the ICC, UN or any other international organisation, its acts would be attributable to the respective institution.[32]

As independent legal actors, international organisations can incur responsibility for internationally wrongful acts if their acts or omissions breach their obligations under international law (treaty law, general principles of international law, customary international law and potentially the rules of the organisation), irrespective of the validity of such acts under internal laws and regulations.[33]

Neither the UN nor the ICC are party to any treaties upholding the rights of prisoners. There are, however, numerous bases for imposing human rights obligations on international organisations including their international legal personality, the inherent and inalienable nature of human rights, customary international law, the constitutional effect of their constitutive instruments, the practice of their organs, the delegation of such responsibility to them by member states and their exercise of power over territory and people.[34] Both the UN and the ICC are bound by the principles and purposes of the UN which include upholding and promoting human rights.[35] The UN standards governing imprisonment have been recognised as the standards governing the enforcement of international sentences of imprisonment by international courts and enforcing states. Many fundamental protections for prisoners are also found in the general principles of international law, such as the principles of good faith, equality and non-discrimination or superior rules of law, such as the right to life, medicine and due process of law.[36] Moreover, the prohibition on torture, cruel and inhuman treatment and punishment is considered by many to have attained the status of

---

[32] Art. 6(1) DARIO.
[33] Arts. 3–5 DARIO; DARIO Commentary, 14, 31, 33; C. F. Amerasinghe, *Principles of Institutional Law of International Organisations* (1996), 225, 239; C. Brölman, "A Flat Earth? International Organizations in the System of International Law" (2001) 70 *Nordic Journal of International Law* 319 at 332; ILA Final Report, 22, 27–8.
[34] Verdirame, *The UN and Human Rights*, 56, 60, 73–5, 235; Verdirame, "UN Accountability for Human Rights Violations in Post-conflict Situations", 96; Reinisch, "Securing the Accountability of International Organizations", 135–6; K. Kenny, "UN Accountability for its Human Rights Impact: Implementation through Participation" in N. White and D. Klaasen (eds.), *The UN, Human Rights and Post-conflict Situations* (2005), 438–62 at 441–3; L. Cameron, "Human Rights Accountability of International Civil Administrations to the People Subject to Administration" (2007) 1 *Human Rights and International Legal Discourse* 267–300 at 272.
[35] See Preamble ICCSt; Preamble UN–ICC NRA; Arts. 55–6 UN Charter.
[36] ILA Final Report, 28.

customary international law and is therefore an *erga omnes* obligation binding on all international legal actors.[37] International and regional human rights standards should therefore not be viewed solely as an external benchmark for evaluating the outcomes of international criminal justice processes, but as binding obligations that must be applied and respected by international courts in all aspects of their operations.[38]

An international organisation can also incur responsibility if it aids, assists, directs or controls a state in the commission of an internationally wrongful act, coerces a state or international organisation to do so, or circumvents its international obligations by adopting a decision binding on its members, although such responsibility may also be attributable to the state or international organisation in question.[39] This could apply if an international court or organisation operated an international prison system with or through states or another international organisation.

The responsibility of an international organisation can be invoked by a state or international organisation for the breach of an obligation owed directly to them, to a group to which they belong or the international community as a whole.[40] Non-injured states and international organisations may also invoke the responsibility for an international organisation that violates an obligation owed to the international community (although safeguarding the interests of the international community must be a function of the non-injured international organisation).[41] These provisions mean that all states and several international organisations could invoke the responsibility of an international court or organisation responsible for the operation of an international prison system if the human rights of international prisoners were violated.[42]

Whether a breach is of a continuing nature or consists of a series of acts or omissions, the responsible international organisation must cease the act in question, provide guarantees of non-repetition and provide full reparation for material and moral damage through restitution, compensation and/or satisfaction.[43] To ensure that international organisations can pay reparations, they are directed to actively seek contributions from member states and member states are reminded to ensure that

---

[37] R. Morgan and M. Evans, "Inspecting Prisons: The View from Strasbourg" in R. D. King and M. Maguire (eds.), *Prisons in Context* (1994), 141–59 at 142; ILA Final Report at 18.

[38] See D. Abels, *Prisoners of the International Community: The Legal Position of Persons Detained at International Criminal Tribunals* (2012), 134–54.

[39] Arts. 14–19 DARIO. [40] Art. 43 DARIO. [41] Art. 49(1)–(3) DARIO.

[42] See Verdirame, *The UN and Human Rights*, 142.

[43] Arts. 12(2), 13(1), 30, 31, 34–7 DARIO.

international organisations have sufficient funds to pay such damages.[44] Although DARIO grants the right to invoke responsibility and claim remedies to states and international organisations, this is without prejudice to the rights of individuals and other entities to do so.[45]

While the basic principle that international organisations and their organs are responsible for internationally wrongful acts is easy to state, it is very difficult for either state or non-state actors to seek redress due to the lack of superior courts at the international level[46] and the immunity of international organisations from legal process in states.[47]

Human rights claims are best adjudicated by international human rights organs.[48] Penrose has suggested that the oversight of the operations of international prisons should be linked to regional human rights commissions and courts.[49] While such an initiative would reflect the current regional placement policy of the international courts, some regions do not have these types of review mechanisms. More significantly, these bodies have held that they do not have jurisdiction to review matters relating to the conduct or responsibility of international organisations. The human rights courts' lack of jurisdiction over international organisations "precludes direct review in virtually all cases".[50] The ECtHR has repeatedly refused to adjudicate on human rights complaints brought against international organisations as they are not party to the ECHR.[51] The African Court on Human and Peoples' Rights held recently that despite having legal personality as an international organisation, the African Union cannot be sued before the Court on behalf of, or for obligations attributable to, its member states because it is not party to either the African Charter on Human and Peoples' Rights or the Protocol establishing the African Court on Human and Peoples' Rights.[52]

---

[44] Art. 40(1)–(2) DARIO; paras. 4, 5 DARIO Commentary, 57; paras. 3–4 DARIO Commentary, 65.
[45] Arts. 33(2), 50 DARIO; DARIO Commentary, 59.
[46] D. W. Bowett, *The Law of International Institutions*, 4th edn (1982), 363; Wilde, "Enhancing Accountability at the Investment Level", 409; Verdirame, *The UN and Human Rights*, 343.
[47] See Art. II (2) CPIUN; Art. 48(1) ICCSt; Art. 6(1)–(2) ICC API. Reinisch, "Securing the Accountability of International Organizations", 134, 139; Wilde, "Enhancing Accountability at the International Level", 409.
[48] Reinisch, "Securing the Accountability of International Organizations", 139.
[49] See Penrose, "No Badges, No Bars", 641.
[50] Verdirame, *The UN and Human Rights*, 344.
[51] Reinisch, "Securing the Accountability of International Organizations", 140.
[52] *Femi Falana v. The African Union* (Application No. 001/2011)(Judgment) 26.06.2012.

As the UN and ICC possess the capacity to contract and participate in legal proceedings,[53] they could ratify the treaties that would enable them to have standing at regional human rights courts. Another way to address the current "remedial deficit"[54] would be to extend the mandate of the International Court of Justice (ICJ) to grant international organisations direct standing.[55] While disputes relating to immunity issues between the UN and its member states may be referred to the ICJ for an advisory opinion,[56] international organisations do not have standing before this court.[57] Although the ICC foresees a role for the President of the ICJ in breaking inter-state deadlocks in appointing members to arbitral tribunals,[58] concerns were expressed at the ICC Preparatory Commission that granting standing before the ICJ would lead to conflicting decisions from the ICJ and ICC.[59] However, this is an inevitable outcome of having a higher authority adjudicate on the legality of acts. The International Law Association concluded that the current lack of standing of international organisations before the ICJ is attributable to political rather than juridical reasons and there are no logical policy reasons supporting its continuation.[60] Rather than submit to the contentious jurisdiction of the ICJ, an international organisation could ask for authorisation to request an advisory opinion from the ICJ.[61] Although these opinions are not binding, they are considered to be authoritative and a means of providing legal counsel to the UN.[62] While these options would subject the operations of international prisons to the oversight of a higher judicial authority, they would not provide international prisoners with a form of appeal against decisions or avenues for redress for violations of their rights: international prisoners, as private individuals, would not have standing before the ICJ.

Even if a court at the international or national level had jurisdiction to hear a case involving an international organisation, they are often barred from doing so due to the immunity granted to international

---

[53] Art. I(1)(a), (c) CPIUN; Art. 2 ICC API. [54] ILA Final Report, 21.
[55] See Appendix, ILA Final Report, 51, 52.
[56] Art. VIII(30) CPIUN; Art. 96 UN Charter; Art. 65 ICJSt.
[57] See Art. 93 UN Charter; Art. 34(1), 35 ICJSt.
[58] Art. 32(3) ICC API; Art. 27(2) SCSL HQA.
[59] A. Pellet, "Settlement of Disputes" in A. Cassese et al., *The Rome Statute of the ICC* (2002), 1841–8 at 1842.
[60] Appendix, ILA Final Report, 53.
[61] See Art. 96 ICJSt; Appendix, ILA Final Report, 51, 53.
[62] Klabbers, *An Introduction to International Institutional Law*, 256, 258.

organisations. The immunity granted to international organisations is supposedly limited to acts necessary for the fulfilment of official functions and purposes.[63] Even though it is not granted as an absolute or higher form of immunity than that granted to states, it tends to be interpreted and applied in this way by domestic courts.[64] As international organisations lack territory, there is considered to be a need to ensure that states cannot interfere with the functional independence of the international organisations they host.[65] However, legal actions against states are not considered to endanger their independence and sovereignty.[66] This "shield of absolute immunity" is no longer feasible in light of the evolving operational role of international organisations and the erosion of immunity of states and state leaders under international human rights law and international criminal law.[67] The current restrictive interpretation and application of international organisation immunity leaves victims without adequate means of redress, violating their fundamental rights of access to justice and an effective remedy.[68] The resulting situation, whereby international criminal courts or organisations responsible for an international prison system could evade responsibility for illegal acts, should not be tolerated within an international criminal justice system established to end impunity, uphold the rule of law and provide justice for victims. The immunity granted to international organisations must be applied in a manner that strikes a balance between preserving the functional autonomy of international organisations and ensuring rights are protected and accountability can be imposed.[69] Courts should differentiate between actions that would jeopardise the functional autonomy of international organisations and

---

[63] Art. 48(1) ICCSt; Art. 3 SCSL HQA.
[64] See Art. 57 DARS, GARes 56/83(2001); E. Gaillard and I. Pingel-Lenuzza, "International Organisations and Immunity from Jurisdiction: To Restrict or to Bypass" (2002) 51 *International and Comparative Law Quarterly* 1–15 at 2–3.
[65] See Gaillard and Pingel-Lenuzza, "International Organisations and Immunity from Jurisdiction", 4; para. 63 *Waite and Kennedy* v. *Germany* (26083/94) 18.02.1999; Verdirame, *The UN and Human Rights*, 13.
[66] Gaillard and Pingel-Lenuzza, "International Organisations and Immunity from Jurisdiction", 5.
[67] Verdirame, *The UN and Human Rights*, 358; Cameron, "Human Rights Accountability", 291, 297.
[68] ILA Final Report, 33; Gaillard and Pingel-Lenuzza, "International Organisations and Immunity from Jurisdiction" 5. See also Chapter 4, D. Shelton, *Remedies in International Human Rights Law*, 2nd edn (2005), 104–73.
[69] ILA Final Report, 6; Verdirame, *The UN and Human Rights*, 358.

those which deal specifically with the breach of obligations to and rights of third parties. This dichotomous view of immunity would put the onus on international criminal courts to waive immunity[70] in cases that clearly do not involve the undue interference of states and where not waiving immunity would prevent the proper administration of justice.[71]

In spite of these arguments, the reality remains that an international organisation can insulate itself from legal claims by refusing to waive its immunity.[72] If they do so, they must provide alternative and adequate procedures for settling the dispute.[73] There are no set models for mechanisms for the settlement of disputes between international organisations and other parties.[74] There are no guidelines stating what mandate or powers such a mechanism should have. Moreover, the availability of arbitration relies on the willingness of the responsible international organisation to submit to it. The uncertain and voluntary nature of dispute resolution mechanisms may make them unsuitable for dealing with allegations of human rights abuses in a penal environment.[75] It may be necessary, therefore, for domestic or regional courts to assume jurisdiction over such claims in cases of wrongful refusals to waive immunity or a failure to provide suitable alternative means of dispute resolution.[76]

2.2 The responsibility of states

In light of the foreseeable difficulties associated with imposing liability on the organisation responsible for an international prison, international prisoners may consider relying on states to protect their rights or, alternatively, invoke the responsibility of states. States may exercise diplomatic protection powers to protect or act on behalf of their nationals held in international prisons. Moreover, states may invoke the responsibility of an international prison for failing to uphold the rights of international prisoners in general. If a state is a member of the international organisation responsible for an international prison, it may incur responsibility for failing to ensure that the prison is operated in compliance with human rights standards. States may also incur direct responsibility for complicity in acts that violate the rights of international prisoners.

---

[70] Art. 48(5) ICC St; Art. 6(1) ICC API. [71] ILA Final Report, 41, 46.
[72] Cameron, "Human Rights Accountability", 290. [73] ILA Final Report, 45–6.
[74] Art. 31(b) ICC API; Art. 27(1)(b) SCSL HQA.
[75] Reinisch, "Securing the Accountability of International Organisations", 139.
[76] Verdirame, *The UN and Human Rights*, 356–9.

2.2.1 Responsibility to protect nationals

If the ICJ's mandate was not extended to grant international organisations direct standing, states could indirectly obtain a declaration on the legal validity of the acts of an international organisation through the inter-state dispute procedure before the ICJ.[77] States could also challenge the legality of an international organisation's acts or refusal to waive its or its officials' immunity.[78] As these issues are settled through consultation or negotiation,[79] this option appears to leave the solution in the realm of private diplomatic discussion rather than public judicial reasoning. This is also the case for inter-state disputes relating to the interpretation and application of the jurisdictional immunity of international organisations. States must have first failed to reach a solution after several months of negotiation before an arbitral tribunal can be established.[80] Although such tribunals may issue binding decisions, the structure of the tribunals suggests that such decisions will be a political compromise rather than a legal judgment.[81]

States may therefore consider bringing a case against another state which supplies staff or funds or other forms of assistance to an international prison. While this form of diplomatic protection of citizens by a state is rare,[82] there have been examples. For instance, the Irish Government brought a successful action against the UK Government before the ECtHR, challenging the legality of disorientation and sensory-deprivation techniques employed during interment in Northern Ireland in the early 1970s.[83]

While this form of protection involves the responsibility of a government for the acts of state officials, the right of diplomatic protection is not confined to state–state relations and can be exercised against international organisations.[84] States can invoke the responsibility of an international organisation for breaches of obligations owed to it.[85] This may include obligations owed to its citizens under international human rights law. Non-injured states can also invoke the responsibility of an international organisation if it has breached obligations owed to the international community as a whole.[86] This may enable states, or

---

[77] Art. 34(2)–(3) ICJSt; Appendix, ILA Final Report, 51.   [78] See Arts. 42, 48 DARS.
[79] Art. 32(1) ICC API; Art. 22 SCSL HQA.
[80] Art. 119(2) ICCSt; Art. 32(2) ICC API; Art. 27(3) SCSL HQA.
[81] See Arts. 32(3), 32(5) ICC API; Arts. 27(2), 27(4) SCSL HQA.
[82] ILA Final Report, 37.   [83] See *Ireland* v. *United Kingdom* (5310/71) 18.01.1978.
[84] Verdirame, *The UN and Human Rights*, 337.   [85] Art. 43 DARIO.
[86] Art. 49(2) DARIO.

communities of states, to act in defence of the nationals of other states held in international prisons whose rights have been or risk being violated. In both instances, local remedies must first be exhausted. This term of art restricts the application of the rule to available and effective remedies[87] and, given the lack of effective mechanisms available, it should be relatively easy to satisfy this requirement.[88] The real problem lies in the fact that there are no international bodies to which such claims can be addressed, and consequently, any resolution would remain in the realm of diplomacy.

2.2.2 Lifting the international organisational veil

International organisations are greater than the sum of their parts. In other words, they are not viewed as an aggregate of their member states, but distinct and separate entities.[89] Consequently, international organisations are traditionally viewed as being exclusively responsible for their own acts and their members do not incur legal liability for their acts simply by virtue of their membership.[90] Courts may, however, look behind and lift the organisational veil to impose liability on member states to prevent states hiding behind their creations.[91]

Member states may incur residual or subsidiary responsibility for internationally wrongful acts committed by an international organisation where the international organisation is unwilling or unable to bear responsibility or where victims have exhausted all international avenues for redress and failed.[92] Member states may be held liable, in the place of the international organisation, in order to ensure fairness to victims in cases where the basic principles of international law have been violated or if states are hiding behind the organisational veil.[93] This notion of secondary liability is controversial, as it may be viewed as undermining

---

[87] Art. 45(2) DARIO; DARIO Commentary, 73–4.
[88] Verdirame, *The UN and Human Rights*, 141.
[89] See Brölman, "A Flat Earth?", 320–2; Amerasinghe, *Principles of Institutional Law of International Organisations*, 229.
[90] DARIO Commentary, 64, 96; Wilde "Enhancing Accountability at the International Level", 401–2; J. D'Aspremont, "Abuse of the Legal Personality of International Organizations and the Responsibility of Member States" (2007) 4 *International Organizations Law Review* 91–119 at 92.
[91] Klabbers, *An Introduction to International Institutional Law*, 301, 311; Brölman, "A Flat Earth?", 322.
[92] Klabbers, *An Introduction to International Institutional Law*, 313; Wilde "Enhancing Accountability at the International Level", 401–2.
[93] Klabbers, *An Introduction to International Institutional Law*, 317.

the independence of the international organisation[94] and the equality of states in international law: if a private person or state pursues one member state, could the state argue that all member states are equally responsible?[95] Although there are good policy arguments for imposing liability on member states in the absence of express limitations or exclusions of liability, courts rarely do so.[96] Unlike international treaty law which views states and international organisations as equal, the law on responsibility allows different rules to be applied to states and organisations and ultimately for the relationship between an international organisation and its member states to remain an internal affair.[97]

Despite these arguments, DARIO recognises that subsidiary responsibility may be invoked if the invocation of primary responsibility has not led to reparation, although this form of redress will not permit over-compensation.[98] Member states will also incur subsidiary, joint or severable responsibility for an internationally wrongful act of an international organisation if they explicitly or impliedly accept responsibility for such act or lead an injured party to rely on its responsibility, for example in situations where the international organisation does not have the necessary funds to make reparation.[99]

UN or ICC member states may therefore incur subsidiary responsibility for the acts of an international prison if the relevant founding organisation does not have the ability to pay awarded reparations. This situation should be prevented from arising due to the DARIO direction to both international organisations and member states to ensure that necessary funds are available.[100] The voluntary acceptance by a member state of responsibility for acts attributable to an international prison would not preclude the international responsibility of other states or international organisations.[101]

2.2.3 Direct responsibility

The responsibility of an international organisation does not reduce or preclude the parallel, residual, concurrent or separate responsibility of

---

[94] Wilde, "Enhancing Accountability at the International Level", 404–5; Verdirame, *The UN and Human Rights Law*, 132.
[95] ILA Final Report, 35.   [96] See Brölman, "A Flat Earth?" 333, 335.   [97] Ibid. 337.
[98] Art. 48(2), (3)(a) DARIO.
[99] Art. 62 DARIO; paras. 6, 8, 11, 13 DARIO Commentary, 97–9.
[100] Art. 40(1)–(2) DARIO; paras. 4, 5 DARIO Commentary, 57; paras. 3–4 DARIO Commentary, 65.
[101] Art. 63 DARIO.

states,[102] as to do so would result in the denial of any recourse to justice for victims.[103]

States could incur direct responsibility if they failed to oversee the manner in which an international prison system exercised the powers conferred on it.[104] Although the European Commission on Human Rights refused to sever the liability of the UK for Spandau Prison from that of the other countries jointly responsible for its operation,[105] this is unlikely to be followed today. The ECtHR has held that the conferral of power on an international organisation by states does not remove their responsibility to ensure that the rights granted under the Convention continue to be secured after the conferral.[106] To refuse to recognise state responsibility in this regard would make a mockery of the relevant treaty's intention and the State Parties' undertaking to "guarantee not theoretical or illusory rights, but rights that are practical and effective".[107] This doctrine of equivalent protection creates precedence for the attribution of legal responsibility to a member state of a multi-lateral or international organisation if it fails to ensure the application of human rights law after the transfer of powers and immunities.[108] Although this doctrine facilitates the indirect scrutiny of the acts of international organisations, the responsibility imputed to states is not for the acts of the international organisation, but for the state's failure to exercise due care to ensure that an international organisation of which it is a member does not breach human rights obligations.[109] Although state responsibility in this regard would not preclude the responsibility of an international prison (or its founding organisation) for the act or omission,[110] the

---

[102] ILA Final Report, 18–19, 26, 28; para. 6 DARIO Commentary, 14.
[103] Klabbers, *An Introduction to International Institutional Law*, 311.
[104] Ibid., 302; ILA Final Report, 15; Verdirame, *The UN and Human Rights*, 359–70; D. Sarooshi, *International Organisations and Their Exercise of Sovereign Powers* (2005), 105–6.
[105] *Hess v. United Kingdom* (6231/73) 28.05.1975. The petition was brought against the UK, not only because the UK Government was supportive of proposals to release Hess but as it was the only state that had accepted the ECtHR's jurisdiction to hear individual petitions; France had not and neither the US nor USSR were party to the ECHR. See J. Fishman, *Long Knives and Short Memories: The Spandau Prison Story* (1986), 429.
[106] See paras. 32, 34 *Matthews v. United Kingdom* (24833/94) 18.02.1999; para. 67 *Waite and Kennedy v. Germany* (26083/94) 18.02.1999; ILA Final Report, 18.
[107] See paras. 32, 34 *Matthews v. United Kingdom* (24833/94) 18.02.1999; para. 67 *Waite and Kennedy v. Germany* (26083/94) 18.02.1999.
[108] See DARIO Commentary, 94–5.
[109] Verdirame, *The UN and Human Rights*, 86, 135, 359.
[110] Para. 10 DARIO Commentary, 95.

risk of a state being held liable for failing to oversee compliance with international obligations may be an important tool to ensure that the rights of international prisoners are protected, particularly given the lack of independent institutions that will have jurisdiction to hear direct complaints against an international prison.[111]

States can also incur direct responsibility, not because they are members of an international organisation, but because they were involved in acts or omissions or they supported decisions or practices that amounted to the commission of an internationally wrongful act.[112] This responsibility may be concurrent and joint with that of an international organisation, severable from that of an international organisation or separate responsibility. Despite the fact that many international organisations rely on states to perform or assist in the performance of their functions, there remains a lack of clarity surrounding who is liable for what under such operational relationships, resulting in gaps in the accountability regime.[113] This area of law is particularly pertinent to determining how to attribute the conduct of, and responsibility for, the acts or omissions of national custodial staff seconded to an international prison system.

2.3 Responsibility for seconded staff

To date, international detention facilities have been almost exclusively staffed by guards seconded from the domestic prison services of their Host States. Although they wear an international uniform and work in an international facility, it remains unclear whether they are international or national custodial officers. In addition to the difficulties this causes for the staff and international penal policy implementation,[114] this dual status is also problematic from a responsibility viewpoint. Would the acts of seconded staff be attributable to an international prison or the seconding state?

Seconded staff will be characterised as an organ of an international prison if they are given that status by its internal rules or they are characterised as such under established practice.[115] They will be deemed

---

[111] See Reinisch, "Securing the Accountability of International Organisations", 142–3; Verdirame, *The UN and Human Rights*, 320.
[112] Arts. 58-63 DARIO; Sarooshi, *International Organisations and their Exercise of Sovereign Powers*, 104; Amerasinghe, *Principles of Institutional Law of International Organizations*, 258.
[113] ILA Final Report, 31.   [114] See Chapter 9, Section 4.3.
[115] Art. 2(b), (c) DARIO; paras. 17–18 DARIO Commentary, 11.

to be agents of an international prison if they are tasked with carrying out or help to carry out its functions or if the organisation responsible for the international prison acts through them.[116] If they are fully seconded to an international prison, and act as its organs or agents, their conduct will be attributable to it.[117] It becomes more complicated if the sending state retains some degree of control over the seconded staff.

If an organ or agent placed at the disposal of an international organisation still acts to a certain extent as an organ or agent of a seconding entity, or the seconding entity retains disciplinary and criminal jurisdiction over such individuals, their conduct will only be attributable to the international organisation if it exercises effective control over it.[118] Effective control severs the link with the sending entity and establishes the nexus with the receiving organisation and is determined on the basis of operational rather than ultimate control.[119] The conduct will be attributable to the receiving international organisation even if it exceeds the authority granted to such individuals or contravenes instructions.[120] The attribution of conduct to an international organisation does not preclude its attribution to a state or another international organisation if they have established a joint organ and act through it.[121] An international prison will therefore be responsible for the conduct of seconded staff if it exercises effective control over their conduct, although states and other international organisations may also be responsible for such conduct if they are involved in the conduct or the operation of the facility. Verdirame argues that despite the conceptual clarity introduced by DARIO, a grey area exists in practice as the determination of effective control is essentially a factual enquiry.[122]

If seconded staff wore the uniform of an international prison system, followed international orders and implemented international penal policy over international prisoners held on international territory, it would seem that they would be acting under the effective control of the international organisation responsible for the international prison. As effective

---

[116] Art. 2(d) DARIO; paras. 23, 25, 27 DARIO Commentary, 12; para. 174 *Reparation for Injuries Suffered in the Service of the United Nations (Advisory Opinion)* [1949] ICJ Reports 174 at 178.

[117] Art. 6(1) DARIO; para. 6 DARIO Commentary, 18; para. 1 DARIO Commentary, 20.

[118] Art. 7 DARIO; para. 2 DARIO Commentary, 20.

[119] DARIO Commentary, 20, 23–6; Verdirame, *The UN and Human Rights*, 102, 111; Amerasinghe, *Principles of Institutional Law of International Organisations*, 242; ILA Final Report, 28–30.

[120] Art. 8 DARIO; DARIO Commentary, 26–7.   [121] Para. 4 DARIO Commentary, 15.

[122] Verdirame, *The UN and Human Rights*, 104.

control does not require exclusive control, the conduct of seconded custodial staff could also be attributed to the governing international organisation in cases where the sending state retained some degree of control over the organ or agent.[123] States which second staff to IDFs typically retain responsibility for employment law-related aspects. It is however possible to foresee situations where seconded staff are given orders by the sending entity relating to conduct in an international prison. The determination of effective control may also be affected by the ability of the sending entity to recall seconded staff.[124] Given that seconded custodial staff may be recalled by the host prison, it is not clear whether seconded staff should be classified as an organ or agent of an international prison or the sending state. Seconding states and international organisations often conclude agreements to regulate these issues. As these agreements tend to be limited to the distribution of responsibility rather than the attribution of conduct, however, they are not generally considered to be conclusive on the matter or sufficient to bar claims against either party.[125] A factual enquiry to determine if effective control has been exercised by the international prison may therefore be necessary in each case.

If an international prison exercises effective control over seconded staff, it will be responsible for their conduct and cannot confine the issue to one of individual responsibility or seek to avoid responsibility by terminating the secondment and returning the individual to the sending state.[126] Although the SCSLDF did return seconded staff caught smuggling contraband into detainees, stealing and sleeping on duty[127] these acts constituted a breach of the internal rules and regulations of the IDF rather than a direct violation of prisoners' rights.[128] If the rights of international prisoners are violated, the matter should not be dealt with by internal disciplinary procedures but prosecuted and punished in accordance with the relevant law.[129]

If it is determined that the international organisation did not exercise effective control over the conduct in question, the sending entity and the individual will be responsible for the act in question. It is also possible that responsibility for the act will be jointly attributed to an international prison and the sending state.

---

[123] *Ibid.*, 103.   [124] *Ibid.*, 104.   [125] Para. 3 DARIO Commentary, 20.
[126] See Hoffman and Mégret, "Fostering Human Rights Accountability", 47–8.
[127] Cardinal, Moore, SCSLDF 20.04.2008; Ewing, SCSLDF, 23.04.2008.
[128] Art. 7 SCSL MOU (Secondment).   [129] ILA Final Report, 40.

To avoid this uncertainty, and to avail of the benefits outlined in the previous chapter,[130] international prisons should directly recruit and employ their own custodial staff. The acts of international custodial staff would be directly attributable to an international prison. While this would clarify the issue of attributing conduct and responsibility, it will not solve the difficulties that international prisoners would face in trying to bring a direct claim against officials who violate their rights.

2.4 The responsibility of individuals

The attribution of responsibility to either an international organisation or a state does not preclude the attribution of individual responsibility.[131] Due to the difficulties international prisoners would face in imposing liability upon an international prison, its governing organisation or states involved in operating an international prison, they may wish to instigate proceedings directly against the individuals responsible for the violation of their rights. To do so, the prisoner must overcome the immunity barriers preventing such actions and find a forum that will find such cases admissible.

Persons directly employed by an international organisation are typically granted immunity in respect of any legal process for words spoken or written and all acts performed by them in their official capacity, even after their contract of employment terminates.[132] This rule would apply to directly recruited international custodial staff working at an international prison. It is less clear if this form of immunity would apply to seconded custodial staff. If they are classified as persons recruited locally or persons performing missions for the international prison, they should be accorded this form of immunity.[133] The precise status of seconded staff remains unclear due to the confidential nature of current agreements which outline the exact status and attribution of responsibility for seconded custodial staff. However, legal officers from the ICTY, ICC and the Dutch Government expressed the view that this form of functional immunity should and would be accorded to seconded custodial staff

---

[130] Chapter 9, Section 4.3.4.
[131] Art. 58 DARS; Art. 66 DARIO; para. 11 DARIO Commentary, 74.
[132] Art. V(18)(a) CPIUN; Art. 29(1), (3) ICTRSt; Arts. IV, XV(1) ICTY/ICTR HQA; Art. 13(1) SCA; Arts. 14–15 SCSL HQA; Art. 48(2)–(3) ICCSt; Arts. 15(1), 16(1)(a)–(b) ICC API; Art. 29(3) MICTSt.
[133] Arts. XVI, XVII(1) ICTY/ICTR HQA; Art. 13(1) SCA; Arts. 16(1), 17(1)–(2) SCSL HQA; Art. 17 ICC API; Art. 29(5) MICTSt.

working in IDFs.[134] On the other hand, ICTR officials felt that staff seconded from the Tanzanian prison service could not rely on UN immunity as they were not UN employees.[135]

If they were granted immunity, it would be granted in the interests of the international prison system and not for the individual's personal benefit. In other words, it would relate only to tasks necessary for the independent and proper functioning of an international prison.[136] Individuals enjoying such immunity would have to respect the laws and regulations of states in which they operate[137] and act in a manner consistent with the culture and policy of the international court.[138] Moreover, international prisons would be under a duty to cooperate with the host authorities to facilitate the proper administration of justice, secure the observance of police regulations and prevent the abuse of immunities.[139] In other words, such officials would not be granted absolute impunity but a functional immunity that an international prison would be under a duty to waive where the administration of justice so required.[140]

This form of immunity has been waived to enable the domestic criminal prosecution of international court officials. For instance, a former SCSL Registrar waived the immunity of a former senior investigator accused of sexual offences against a child. The accused was cleared by an internal SCSL investigation and later had the domestic criminal conviction overturned. Many disagreed with the former Registrar's decision to hand the accused person over to national authorities due to the dire prison conditions and lack of due process guarantees in the national system.[141] The former Registrar defended his decision stating that to do otherwise would have seriously undermined the

---

[134] De Witt, ICTY, 07.06.2007; Mochochoko, ICC, 30.08.2007; Blom, Moonen, The Netherlands, 24.08.2007.
[135] O'Donnell, ICTR, 25.06.2007; Diop, ICTR, 27.06.2007.
[136] See Art. V(20) CPIUN; Art. 30(4) ICTYSt; Art. 29(4) ICTRSt; Arts. 15(1), 16(1), 26(1) ICC API; Arts. 16(3), 17(3) SCSL HQA; Art. 29(5) MICTSt; H. Ascensio, "Privileges and Immunities" in A. Cassese *et al.*, *The Rome Statute of the ICC* (2002), 291–2.
[137] See Art. XXI(1) ICTY/ICTR HQA; Art. 23(1) SCSL HQA; Art. 24(2) ICC API.
[138] Vincent, SCSL/ICTY, 27.04.2007.
[139] See Art. V(21) CPIUN; Art. XXI(2) ICTY/ICTR HQA; Art. 23(2) SCSL HQA; Art. 24(1) ICC API.
[140] See Art. V(20) CPIUN; Art. 26(1) ICC API; Arts. 16(3), 17(3) SCSL HQA; ILA Final Report, 42; para. 14 Annex, Establishment of an Independent Oversight Mechanism, ICC-ASP/8/Res.1.
[141] See G. Simpson and M. Daly, "Questions Plague Policeman's Trial", 02.10.2004.

SCSL's duty to promote and uphold the rule of law and would have created a dangerous precedent.[142] Even in the absence of an explicit provision stating there is a duty to waive immunity if so required by the impediments of justice, as there was in the SCSL case, an international organisation may feel political pressure to do so to prevent damage to the organisation's credibility.[143] For instance, while the ICC's IOM will be able to investigate misconduct warranting disciplinary measures, the ICC does not have jurisdiction to deal with criminal offences committed by its staff or officials.[144] Jurisdiction over such acts remains with the national authorities of the state in which the act was committed, the suspect's state of nationality or the victim's state of nationality.[145] The ICC therefore accepts that immunity cannot be invoked to justify unlawful acts, and subsequently, that it is under a duty to inform national authorities of the criminal misconduct of its officials, staff and contractors, waive their immunity and cooperate with national authorities to enable their prosecution.[146] The IOM must, however, take the national system's ability to guarantee a minimum standard of due process into account when deciding whether to waive immunity in a particular case.[147]

An international organisation may, however, refuse to grant a waiver of immunity. Such refusals prevent the judicial review of human rights violations and essentially place international civil servants above the rules and reach of the law.[148] If immunity is not waived, the international organisation should provide access to an appropriate mode of settlement.[149] A failure to provide a reasonable alternative means of redress may enable national courts to exercise jurisdiction over the matter, although there are presently no criteria or bodies to decide on the

---

[142] Vincent, SCSL/ICTY, 27.04.2007.   [143] De Witt, ICTY, 07.06.2007.
[144] Para. 13 Annex, Establishment of an Independent Oversight Mechanism, ICC-ASP/8/Res.1.
[145] Paras. 6(d), 13 Annex, Establishment of an Independent Oversight Mechanism, ICC-ASP/8/Res.1.
[146] Paras. 6(c), 13–14 Annex, Establishment of an Independent Oversight Mechanism, ICC-ASP/8/Res.1; paras. 31–2 Annex, Independent Oversight Mechanism, ICC-ASP/9/Res.5, 10.12.2010.
[147] Para. 14 Annex, Establishment of an Independent Oversight Mechanism, ICC-ASP/8/Res.1.
[148] Cameron, "Human Rights Accountability", 287–90; Wilde "Accountability and International Actors", 459; Hoffman and Mégret, "Fostering Human Rights Accountability", 49.
[149] Art. VIII(29)(b) CPIUN.

reasonableness of mechanisms provided.[150] Moreover, dispute resolution mechanisms provided by international organisations often fail to provide the level of redress required or desired.[151]

Even if the immunity of direct employees or seconded staff of an international prison was waived, international prisoners would still struggle to find a court that could, or would be willing, to find their application admissible. Domestic and regional courts are likely to be reluctant to exercise jurisdiction over acts that occur on international territory, committed by persons with international status, perhaps following international orders, against international prisoners.

3. An accountable international prison system

Even though the 2011 Draft Articles create "a framework for dealing with an international organisation responsible for a breach of an international obligation ... it does not solve the problem of enforcement of the international obligations of international organisations".[152] In spite of the irrationality of immunity being granted to an institution created to end impunity, the current international legal regime would enable an international criminal court or international organisation operating an international prison to protect itself from legal claims in national, regional or international courts. It would also make it difficult to find a forum to impose legal liability on states or individuals involved in the commission of internationally wrongful acts with or on the instructions of an international organisation operating an international prison.

A failure to ensure accountability for human rights violations could potentially be very damaging for the legitimacy of an international prison system.[153] Even if international law facilitates the retention of immunity for international organisations and their officials, this "does not imply exemption from accountability".[154] Accountability demands responsiveness to complaints, acceptance of responsibility for actions and the provision of remedies.[155] Given that an international prison

---

[150] Verdirame, *The UN and Human Rights*, 356; Cameron, "Human Right Accountability", 290.
[151] Cameron, "Human Rights Accountability", 295.
[152] Verdirame, *The UN and Human Rights*, 143.
[153] D'Aspremont, "Abuse of the Legal Personality of International Organisations", 92; De Chazournes, "Changing Rates of International Organisations", 662.
[154] De Chazournes, "Changing Rates of International Organisations", 663.
[155] Hoffman and Mégret, "Fostering Human Rights Accountability", 43, 46.

system would operate within the international criminal justice system, it must be open to scrutiny, deal effectively and fairly with complaints and provide victims of criminal, tortious or human rights violations access to justice and remedies.

The right to a remedy includes both the procedural right of access to justice and the substantive right to a remedy. This right is considered to be part of basic international human rights standards and customary international law.[156] Prisoners held under the authority of the post-Second World War International Military Tribunals were denied recourse to external judicial oversight from their sentencing tribunals,[157] national courts[158] and regional human rights courts.[159] While there is nothing preventing persons under the custody of contemporary international courts bringing a case before national, regional or international courts,[160] international prisoners and representative states face jurisdictional and evidential obstacles at both the domestic and international level when trying to impose liability on international organisations, states, officials and agents. A total lack of remedies amounts to a denial of justice, which gives rise to a separate ground of responsibility on the part of the governing international institution.[161]

An international prison system should therefore ensure the accountability of its regime by ensuring independent oversight and evaluation and providing international prisoners with access to impartial review mechanisms. As touted guardians of accountability and rights, international judicial institutions must enforce sentences in a manner which respects both. International prisons should be inspected and evaluated by human rights bodies and qualified inspectorates, and reports containing their findings and recommendations should be published. Oversight should be provided by a collaborative system of national, regional and international inspections. This variety of feedback would ensure that international prisons were operated in accordance with the highest standards and in line with best practice. Moreover, regular

---

[156] ILA Final Report, 33; Shelton, *Remedies in International Human Rights Law*, 104–73.
[157] M. Penrose, "Spandau Revisited: The Question of Detention for International War Crimes" (1999) 16 *New York Law School Journal of Human Rights* 553–91 at 565–6.
[158] See *Koki Hirota v. General of the Army MacArthur* 338 US 197 (1948).
[159] See *Hess v. United Kingdom* (6231/73) 28.05.1975.
[160] Vicente, ICTY, 16.02.2007; Vincent, SCSL/ICTY, 27.04.2007; O'Donnell, ICTR, 25.06.2007.
[161] ILA Final Report, 33–4, 41.

systemic evaluations would ensure that the system was operated in the most effective manner and in accordance with international standards.

It would be vitally important for an international prison system to ensure that international prisoners had access to independent mechanisms competent to hear complaints, investigate allegations and provide redress and effective remedies.[162] Although international prisons would be linked to, and more than likely be operated by, international courts, these courts do not have jurisdiction to hear these types of claims. The lack of alternative forums and the need to facilitate appeals from the decisions of the President/Presidency of such courts[163] would make it necessary to establish another mechanism to deal with these issues. One possibility would be to establish an independent ombudsperson's office competent to hear complaints from international prisoners, conduct investigations into allegations or more general issues and make recommendations about ways to resolve problems.[164] A permanent ombudsperson's office could contribute to the creation of a culture of accountability and facilitate the development of specialist knowledge.[165] The difficulty with this proposal is that the recommendations of ombudspersons are typically non-binding. The establishment of such an office may not, therefore, add any greater protection than the current system of ICRC inspections, other than the fact that an ombudsperson's recommendations could be made public. Another possible option would be to create a permanent itinerant tribunal empowered to travel to the different international prisons to hear individual complaints about human rights violations, make binding decisions and award remedies where appropriate.[166] Both proposed mechanisms have advantages and disadvantages and, of course, require funding. Ultimately, the most independent and effective model should be adopted.[167] The rights of international prisoners should not be "contingent upon the 'banner' under which power is vested and authority exercised".[168]

---

[162] See Kenny, "UN Accountability for its Human Rights Impact", 440, 455, 458.
[163] See Chapter 5, Section 2.2
[164] Hoffman and Mégret, "Fostering Human Rights Accountability", 53–4, 58.
[165] Ibid., 57.   [166] Cameron, "Human Rights Accountability", 298–300.
[167] See ILA Final Report, 33–4.
[168] Verdirame, "UN accountability for Human Rights Violations in Post-conflict Situations", 96.

4. Conclusion

Chapter 9 advocated moving away from a penal system that disperses international prisoners among the national prison systems of cooperating states, to a system that disperses international prisoners throughout a network of internationally controlled prisons. This regionalised international enforcement system is undoubtedly a long-term vision with political, legal, financial and practical obstacles in its path. However, as the international courts, and not states, bear the primary responsibility for international prisoners and the effectiveness and legitimacy of international punishment, this is a necessary institutional development. This institutional evolution would bring with it responsibility for dependent individuals and a duty to respect the international legal obligation to provide remedies to those whose rights have been violated. Chapter 10 highlighted the difficulties international prisoners held in an international prison system would face in bringing claims against international organisations, states or individuals. Regular oversight and evaluation by a range of qualified and independent international, regional and local bodies would be necessary to ensure the effective and humane operation of an international prison system. Moreover, international prisoners should have access to independent bodies capable of hearing complaints, making decisions about resolutions and awarding remedies where appropriate. This dual approach of prevention and reaction would be necessary to ensure that the international prison system was operated in accordance with contemporary standards and capable of fulfilling penological and justice objectives. An international prison system should also be subject to oversight by the governing international organisation or court, the international community generally and the stakeholders of the international criminal justice system. A transparent, accountable and progressive prison system would be necessary to ensure that the international penal system and the international criminal justice system are perceived to be legitimate.[169]

---

[169] See de Chazournes, "Changing Roles of International Organisations", 664.

PART V

The development of the international penal system

11

The development of the international penal system

The last few decades have witnessed a proliferation of international judicial institutions established to try those accused of international crimes. As a consequence, the international criminal justice system, that was for so long an aspiration, finally became a social reality. Using imprisonment as its sanction of choice, the international criminal justice system finally linked the international condemnation of international crime with its punishment. Since 1997, over 150 sentences of imprisonment have been handed down by international criminal courts. Remarkably, the system used to enforce international punishment, the international penal system, has remained unacknowledged. Under this system, international sentences of imprisonment are implemented in a way that is detached from the international criminal justice process. Without ends discourse (aims for punishment) and means discourse (methods to achieve these goals),[1] it is not surprising that international punishment currently involves little more than warehousing international prisoners in national prison cells. In addition to its lack of goals, discourse and techniques, the current enforcement system also lacks capacity, permanency and specialists. In practice, the system may result in the unequal treatment of persons convicted by the same court, the isolation of international prisoners, the dilution of the international nature of the sanction and a loss of control over the sentence.

In the short-term, the "social distancing"[2] of international criminals may put the system's failure to achieve anything other than retribution out of sight and out of mind. In the long-term, however, the end stage of the international criminal justice process may be critical for the legacy and legitimacy of the international criminal courts. In recognition of the need to develop the international penal system, this book has

---

[1] E. Carrabine, "Discourse, Governmentality and Translation: Towards a Social Theory of Imprisonment" (2000) 4 *Theoretical Criminology* 309–31 at 317.

[2] W. Morrison, "Modernity, Imprisonment and Social Solidarity" in R. Mathews and F. Francis (eds.), *Prisons 2000: An International Perspective on the Current State and Future of Imprisonment* (1996), 105.

recommended the introduction of international penal policies and practices and the establishment of international prisons to facilitate the implementation of international punishment. This final chapter outlines how the processes and outcomes of the international penal system may affect the legitimacy of the international criminal justice system as a whole and how the book's recommendations to institutionalise the system may help to ensure the effectiveness and credibility of international punishment.

1. The legitimacy of the international penal system

Just as the failure to punish may undermine legal order, the converse is true; punishment can affirm the moral basis of the international criminal justice system.[3] The international criminal justice system was established to bring an end to impunity. The moral legitimacy accrued as a result of this inspirational founding aim cannot, however, be assumed automatically to accord legitimacy to all aspects of the system's operations. Legitimacy has both internal and external factors. Internal legitimacy involves objective legality (the compatibility of actions with internal rules and adherence to procedures), whereas external legitimacy involves the additional element of subjective perceptions regarding the morality of processes **and** outcomes.[4] The legitimacy of the international courts will be based not only on the justness of their verdicts and sentences but also the social outcomes of their interventions.[5] International institutions often engage in legitimation processes to justify their existence and operations to the society in which they operate and serve.[6] One method is to try to create links with other legitimate social institutions or practices.[7] International criminal courts attempt to legitimise their penal processes by linking them to contemporary international human rights and penal standards. This link provides access to an "an armoury of rhetorically powerful words".[8] Using this deliberately sanitised,

---

[3] See D. Garland, *Punishment and Modern Society, A Study in Social Theory* (1990), 59–60.
[4] See R. Sparks, "Can Prisons be Legitimate?" in R. D. King and M. Maguire (eds.), *Prisons in Context* (1994), 15.
[5] See J. Cockayne, "Hybrids or Mongrels? Internationalized War Crime Trials as Unsuccessful Degradation Ceremonies" (2005) 4 *Journal of Human Rights* 455–73 at 457.
[6] J. Dowling and J. Pfeffer, "Organizational Legitimacy: Social Values and Organizational Behaviour" (1975) 18(1) *The Pacific Sociological Review* 122–36 at 123, 125.
[7] *Ibid.*, 127.   [8] Sparks, "Can Prisons be Legitimate?", 21.

recognisable and reformist discourse, the international courts can discuss international punishment in a manner that avoids any mention of repression, degradation or isolation and, ultimately, key aspects of its reality.[9] Rhetoric may "fend away the visible features of the problem for the time being",[10] but this façade is not sustainable in the long-term. As the international penal system matures, it is becoming increasingly obvious that, although the facilities used to enforce international punishment generally provide conditions that conform to international standards, it is questionable whether the outcomes of international penal process do.

The lack of attention paid to the legitimacy of international penal outcomes may be attributed to what Barrett and Finnemore term the "irrationality of rationalisation". This phenomenon arises when the rules used to empower an institution become so embedded that actions become impersonal, de-humanising and repressive exercises of power: the means used by the institution become its ends.[11] They argue that the prioritisation of rules may obscure both the overall mission and larger societal goals as it creates a parochial normative environment which erodes connections with the external social environment which it is meant to serve.[12] In other words, the rule-based nature that empowers bureaucratic international organisations also creates the danger that they will become unresponsive to their environments and may act in a way that contradicts institutional aims.[13] The courts of the international criminal justice system are prone to "developing and reproducing their own rationality"[14] without evaluating the real impact of their actions. This should be avoided as a failure to pursue and attain the aims considered important by stakeholders will gradually erode perceptions of the legitimacy of international criminal justice institutions.[15]

---

[9] See P. Pratt, *Punishment and Civilization: Penal Tolerance and Intolerance in Modern Society* (2002), 81, 87, 90, 121–2.

[10] R.D. King and M. Maguire, "Introduction" (1994) 34 *British Journal of Criminology* 1 at 4.

[11] M.N. Barrett and M. Finnemore, "The Politics, Power and Pathologies of International Organizations" (1999) 53(4) *International Organization* 699–732 at 708–9, 720.

[12] *Ibid.*, 718.   [13] *Ibid.*, 699–700, 715.

[14] K. McEvoy, "Letting go of Legalism: Developing a 'Thicker' Version of Transitional Justice" in K. McEvoy and L. McGregor (eds.), *Transitional Justice from Below: Grassroots Activism and the Struggle for Change (Human Rights Law in Perspective)* (2008), 26.

[15] See I. Delpla, "In the Midst of Injustice: The ICTY from the Perspective of some Victim Associations" in X. Bougarel *et al.* (eds.), *The New Bosnia Mosaic; Identities, Memories and Moral Claims in a Post-War Society* (2007), 211–34 at 218–19.

Legitimacy can only be derived from the community that empowers the institution and in whose name the institution acts.[16] International punishment is imposed by international criminal courts, which are empowered by and accordingly serve the international community. On the one hand, the "international community" is an abstract political construct used to develop norms and derivative normative practices.[17] Subsequently, international institutions should "actualise the will of the international community to the extent that their actions reflect and correspond to the community's normative fabric".[18] On the other hand, the "international community" is the aggregation of a number of constituent groups; an umbrella term used to reflect the values and expectations of the stakeholders and subjects of the international criminal justice project. Even if an institution's exercise of power is legal, insofar as it accords with both internal and external rules, it may still be perceived to be illegitimate if it is not considered to be a desirable, proper or appropriate exercise of power by the constituent entities of the social system of values in which it operates.[19] The legitimacy of the processes and outcomes of the international penal system will be judged in light of their humaneness and effectiveness.

The manner in which persons deprived of their liberty are treated is a strong indicator of values of a given society.[20] Indeed, the ICTY has explicitly recognised that it is of paramount importance that international sentences are enforced in a manner that upholds the "principles of humanity and dignity which constitute the inspiration for international standards governing the protection of the rights of convicted persons".[21] Although the conditions in facilities used to implement international sentences of imprisonment generally accord with international human rights and penal standards, the reality of international punishment

---

[16] See Garland, *Punishment and Modern Society*, 265; F. Franck, *Fairness in International Law and Institutions* (1995), 26; M. Findlay and R. Henham, *Transforming International Criminal Justice: Retributive and Restorative Justice in the Trial Process* (2005), 311; R. Henham, *Punishment and Process in International Criminal Trials* (2005), 132.

[17] See N. Tsagourias, "The Will of the International Community as a Normative Source of International Law" in I. F. Dekker and W. G. Werner (eds.), *Governance and International Legal Theory* (2004), 97, 101–3, 107, 113–14.

[18] *Ibid.*, 115.

[19] See B. Oomen, "Transitional Justice and Its Legitimacy: The Case for a Local Perspective" (2007) 25(1) *Netherlands Quarterly of Human Rights* 141–8 at 143.

[20] See Straw in A. Coyle, *A Human Rights Approach to Prison Management: Handbook for Prison Staff* (2002), 3.

[21] Para. 74 *Erdemović* (Judgment) IT-96-22-T, 29.11.1996.

(unequal treatment, isolation, removal to a foreign state without consent, aggravation of sentence) may not.

It is also questionable whether the international penal system effectively achieves penological objectives, the wider goals of the international criminal justice system or meets the expectations of the system's stakeholders. It is doubtful if the current system deters other would-be international criminals, successfully rehabilitates or reintegrates prisoners or contributes to the reconciliation of post-conflict communities. At present, the only tangible outcome of the international penal system is punishment; punishment implemented in a manner which may aggravate the sentence imposed by the international court. But these failings are understandable. It is very difficult to achieve the necessary goals in a penal system which has no clear objectives, policies and practices and no prison cells of its own.

When there is disparity between the social value of an institution's activities and the normative values of the system it serves, there is a threat to legitimacy.[22] Threats to legitimacy result in threats to support for an institution. According to Easton, support for an institution can be categorised as either specific or diffuse. Specific support refers to the level of satisfaction or dissatisfaction members of a system feel in relation to the policies and outputs of authorities.[23] This may change with different events. Diffuse support, on the other hand, is a more stable reservoir of goodwill or commitment towards the system as a whole, which is not generally affected by fluctuations in specific support.[24] Diffuse support therefore results in a commitment or willingness to maintain and defend the structures or norms of a regime, even if, at times, it produces unfavourable outcomes.[25] However, if members feel that power is being exercised illegitimately, or if they are continually disappointed by the outcomes of a system, overall support for the system will decline.[26]

Drumbl notes that while "having the ability to punish is central to the authoritativeness of an institution, it does not follow that the power to punish accords legitimacy to an institution from the perspective of those it governs".[27] If international punishment is not implemented in a

---

[22] Dowling and Pfeffer, "Organisational Legitimacy", 122.
[23] D. Easton "A Re-assessment of the Concept of Political Support" (1975) 5(4) *British Journal of Political Science* 435-57 at 437, 448; V. A. Baird, "Building Institutional Legitimacy: The Role of Procedural Justice" (2001) 54(2) *Political Research Quarterly* 333-54 at 334-5, 339.
[24] Easton, "A Reassessment of the Concept of Political Support", 444.   [25] *Ibid.*, 451.
[26] *Ibid.*, 449, 451.
[27] M. Drumbl, "Collective Violence and Individual Punishment: The Criminality of Mass Atrocity" (2005) 99(2) *Northwestern University Law Review* 539-610 at 603-4.

humane and effective manner, it will be considered an illegitimate use of power and consequently undermine support for the international penal system. When levels of diffuse support are weak and the general perception of a system is negative, it is more difficult to change this view with subsequent positive outcomes of specific policies.[28] So rather than reverse a decline in support, it makes more sense to prevent its occurrence. The shortcomings of the international penal system can no longer be explained away with rhetoric, resource excuses or by blaming the temporary nature of the courts for a lack of development. Instead of attempting to borrow legitimacy by aligning itself with other social institutions, the international penal system should adapt its goals and methods of operation to conform to prevailing notions of legitimacy.[29] The international penal system requires the institutional attributes that will enable it to contribute to a more comprehensive criminal justice system and provide a more principled and progressive form of punishment.

2. The institutionalisation of the international penal system

Despite the evident problems with the current systems for the enforcement of international sentences of imprisonment, they have been replicated by each new international criminal court. While there have been some statutory amendments which strengthen the control of international criminal courts over international sentences and prisoners, they are not enough to solve these systemic problems. Yet, international organisations generally consider themselves to be progressive and strive to be models of best practice.[30] This desire, coupled with the need to ensure the legitimacy of the system, should ignite efforts to re-conceptualise international punishment and the methods for its enforcement so that the international penal system can act as a benchmark to cooperating states and penal systems generally.

A comprehensive penal system should be grounded in principled policy and employ innovative methods that safeguard prisoners' rights, facilitate the achievement of systemic goals and meet stakeholders' expectations. To overcome the detrimental impact and ineffectiveness of the current international penal system, it is necessary to devise and

---

[28] Easton, "A Reassessment of the Concept of Political Support", 444-5.
[29] Dowling and Pfeffer, "Organisational Legitimacy", 127.
[30] See Barrett and Finnemore, "The Politics, Power and Pathologies of International Organisations", 712-13.

adopt tailor-made policy objectives and penal practices and create access to suitable penal capacity. Accordingly, this book recommends the introduction of a resocialisation-focused international penal policy and restorative-based penal practices[31] and the establishment of an accountable international prison system.[32]

Singly or combined, these recommendations represent stages in the institutionalisation of the international penal system and its movement away from reliance on national policies, practices and institutions. If implemented, they would lead to the validation of the system and empower it to act more autonomously.[33] Rather than being viewed as a loose association of national prison services and international detention facilities, the international penal system would become a more readily identifiable element of the international criminal justice system. The international penal system would become a more visible and permanent institution. The institutionalisation of the system would also result in the internationalisation of enforcement. Without international involvement in its implementation, international punishment is delivered through state cooperation with international organisations. This system ignores the fact that states made a conscious decision to create international criminal courts and consequently, an international criminal justice system. It is logical that an international criminal justice system should include and be completed by an international penal system. An international penal system is a foreseeable outcome of the creation of international criminal courts and a necessary development that contributes towards the institutional completion of the international criminal justice system.

The institutionalisation of the international penal system is necessary to ensure that international courts can provide suitable accommodation for existing and future international prisoner populations. As the international criminal justice system has a permanent court, there is likely to be a permanent international prison population. The establishment of the ICC, however, did not make other models of international criminal justice obsolete. Indeed, the potential impunity gaps in the ICC's territorial, subject matter and temporal jurisdiction may have to be filled with the establishment of new temporary and conflict-specific tribunals.[34] For

---

[31] See Part III.   [32] See Part IV.
[33] See Franck, *Fairness in International Law and Institutions*, 34, 36.
[34] See M. Benzing and M. Bergsmo, "Some Tentative Remarks about the Relationship between Internationalised Criminal Jurisdiction and the ICC" in C. P. R Romano *et al.*,

example, in 2007, the UNSC created the temporary Special Tribunal for Lebanon to try those accused of carrying out the attack which killed former Prime Minister Rafiq Hariri and twenty-two others.[35] These trials may result in the imposition of sentences of imprisonment for the remainder of convicted persons' lives[36] that will require supervision long after the Tribunal has closed.[37] The sentences imposed by the ICTR, ICTY and SCSL will also potentially require supervision by another body after their respective residual mechanisms close.[38] An international penal system with the attributes of a permanent institution will be better placed to deal with international punishment issues for not only the ICC, but temporary international criminal courts as well.

A strengthened international penal system will also be more likely to evolve with and to reflect contemporary standards. Institutional models should be positioned at the intersection between idealistic aspirations and the realities of operating in any particular social context.[39] One of the reasons for the slow and piecemeal development of the international penal system is the lack of external and objective data about its operations or its impact. Without relevant and up-to-date "feedback loops"[40] the system risks becoming insular and unresponsive. Views on punishment will change, and the international penal system must be in a position to adapt and thereby continue to reflect the will of the community that empowers it. A lack of information and specialisation will perpetuate the current state of affairs, whereby the system operates solely on the basis of procedural rules rather than responding to and developing in light of the reality of international punishment. The institutionalisation of the international penal system will facilitate its evaluation, development and specialisation. The best way to deflect criticism is to lead the way. The implementation of policies and practices that achieve international penal aims, uphold the international status of international punishment and provide a benchmark for national prison systems will help to protect and strengthen the legitimacy of the international criminal justice system. Legitimacy will also be dependent

(eds.), *Internationalised Criminal Courts: Sierra Leone, East Timor, Kosovo and Cambodia* (2004), 407–415.
[35] See SCRes 1757(2007). [36] See Rule 172(A) STL RPE.
[37] See Arts. 29, 30 STLSt; Rules 175, 195–6 STL RPE. [38] See Chapter 4, Section 2.3.
[39] See J. Faget, "The French Phantoms of Restorative Justice: The Institutionalisation of Penal Mediation" in I. Aersten *et al.* (eds.), *Institutionalising Restorative Justice* (2006), 151–66 at 155–7.
[40] Barrett and Finnemore, "The Politics, Power and Pathologies of International Organizations", 723.

on the accountability of the international penal system and the effectiveness of measures put in place to deal with complaints from international prisoners, wherever they are housed.

3. Towards the development of the international penal system

In many ways, international criminal courts are not created for "what they do but for what they are ... for what they represent symbolically and the values they embody".[41] Penal institutions are also systems of power that have strong symbolic relevance and cultural effects.[42] Penal policy communicates meaning, not only about crime and punishment, but about the cultural identity of the society it serves and the legitimacy of the institution implementing it.[43] International penality is both shaped by and is a cultural symbol of, the international community.[44] Presently, both its processes and outcomes may lead to reduced support for the international penal system. If the international penal system is perceived to be illegitimate, this will affect the legitimacy of the international criminal justice project as a whole.

To date, the focus of the media, states, academics and the international courts has been on earlier stages of the international criminal justice process – arrest, trial, sentencing etc. It is now crucial that international punishment becomes more than an afterthought. It should no longer be accepted at face value without inquiry. International criminal courts must put the same effort into devising a humane and effective international penal system as they put into ensuring that international trial procedure accords with international human rights standards.[45] International prisoners and their custodial sanctions will remain long after the international trial process has finished and, in the case of the temporary courts, even after the international court itself has closed. The international community must therefore ensure that custodial sanctions imposed in its name are implemented in a manner that facilitates

---

[41] *Ibid.*, 703
[42] See Garland, *Punishment and Modern Society*, 199; J. Sim, "The Abolitionist Approach: a British Perspective" in T. Jewkes and H. Johnston (eds.), *Prison Readings: A Critical Introduction to Prisons and Imprisonment* (2006), 101; T. Mathiesen, "The Argument against Building More Prisons" in J. Muncie and R. Sparks (eds.), *Imprisonment: European Perspectives* (1991), 177–84 at 184; R. Morgan, "A Brief History, The Contemporary Scene and Likely Prospects" in M. Maguire *et al.* (eds.), *The Oxford Handbook of Criminology*, 3rd edn (2002), 1121.
[43] See Garland, *Punishment and Modern Society*, 252, 276.   [44] *Ibid.*, 196, 198.
[45] N. J. W. Goda, *Tales from Spandau: Nazi Criminals and the Cold War* (2007), 4, 18, 277.

the achievement of the interests and goals of all the constituent groups that form the international community. For this reason, this book has advocated that international crimes should be punished by and within the international criminal justice system in an effective, humane and accountable manner.

Although the international penal system constitutes a specific and end stage of the international criminal justice process, the manner in which international punishment is perceived and implemented is important for the legitimacy of the international criminal justice system as a whole. To protect support for international criminal justice institutions and processes, it is necessary to understand the social reality of international punishment and address the deficiencies of the contemporary systems for its enforcement. This book has explored and critiqued the systems used to enforce international punishment. While the book did not deal with all issues pertaining to international punishment, it provided a comprehensive overview of the realities of implementing international sentences of imprisonment, an in-depth analysis of the problems inherent in the contemporary international penal system and made innovative recommendations for its strategic and structural development. It is hoped that this book will contribute to knowledge in this field, spark debate on the topic and, ultimately, assist with the development of the international penal system.

Appendix I

Empirical research

This book is based on extensive empirical research that was conducted over several years in several countries. To ensure that the research could be conducted in a morally responsible manner that would avoid or minimise harm to participants and ensure that participation was voluntary,[1] the selected methods and interview protocols were approved by the University of Nottingham's School of Law Research Ethics Committee.[2] This Appendix sets out the details of research undertaken, giving the dates of interviews and the roles of the individuals interviewed.

Date	Institution/Section	Subject/Position	Method *(I) Interpreter
International Criminal Courts and International Detention Facilities			
1. International Criminal Tribunal for the former Yugoslavia			
16.02.2007	Registry Office of Legal Aid and Detention	Alejandra Vicente Associate Legal Officer	Interview
27.04.2007	Registrar's Office	Robin Vincent[3] Former Deputy Registrar	Interview
07.06.2007	Registry Advisory Section on Legal and Policy Matters	Augustus de Witt Gerold Siller	Interview Interview
21.08.2007	UNDU	Tim McFadden Commanding Officer	Interview Tour

[1] See ESRC Research Ethics Framework.
[2] See para 4.6 *University of Nottingham Code of Research Conduct*. [3] See SCSL.

Date	Institution/Section	Subject/Position	Method *(I) Interpreter
22–27.08.2007	UNDU	7 Custodial Staff 1 Principal Officer	Interview
29.08.2007	Registry Victims and Witness Unit/ Registry Advisory Section	Sabrina Fofana Associate Legal Officer	Interview
04.02.2008	UNDU	Paul Falke[4] Doctor	Interview
10.07.2008	President's Office	Agnes Hurwitz Deputy Chef de Cabinet	Interview

2. International Criminal Tribunal for Rwanda

Date	Institution/Section	Subject/Position	Method *(I) Interpreter
25.06.2007	Registry	Everard O'Donnell Deputy Registrar	Interview
	Registry Defence Council and Detention Management Section	Dunstain Mwanglu Director Isaac Endeley Legal Officer Laurent Wastelain Legal Assistant	Interview
26.06.2007	President's Office	Susan Lamb Chef de Cabinet	Interview
	UNDF	Saidou Guindo Commanding Officer	Meeting Single cell viewing
27.06.2007	UNDF	Saidou Guindo Commanding Officer	Second Meeting
	Registry Court Management Services	Matar Diop Deputy Director	Interview
08.08.2007	UNDF	Michel Okitapoy Social Welfare Officer	Email

---

[4] See ICC.

Date	Institution/Section	Subject/Position	Method *(I) Interpreter
3. International Criminal Court			
15.02.2007	Presidency	Hirad Abathi Legal Officer	Interview
19.03.2007	ICCDC	Terry Jackson[5] Former Chief Custody Officer	Interview
06.06.2007	Registry Division of Court Services	Marc Dubuisson Director	Group Interview ICCDC Tour
	Registry Detention Section	Bibiana Becerra-Suarez, Associate Legal Officer	
	ICCDC	Harry Tjonk Acting Chief Custody Officer	
22–28.08.2007	ICCDC	8 Custodial Staff 1 Education Officer	Interview
30.08.2007	Registry Legal Advisory Section	Phakiso Mochochoko Senior Legal Officer	Interview
04.02.2008	ICCDC	Andres Backman Chief Custody Officer	Interview
		Paul Falke[6] Doctor	Interview
04.07.2012	ICCDC	Patrick Craig Chief Custody Officer	Interview
		Harry Tjonk Deputy Chief Custody Office	Second Interview
		Jack Bremmers Principal Officer	Interview
		Dick Jouthart Custody Officer	
		Paul Falke Doctor	Second Interview

[5] See SCSL.   [6] See ICTY.

Date	Institution/Section	Subject/Position	Method *(I) Interpreter
05.07.2012	Presidency	Hirad Abathi Legal Officer	Second Interview
06.07.2012	Detention Section	Dahirou St-Anna Legal Officer	Interview

4. Special Court for Sierra Leone

Date	Institution/Section	Subject/Position	Method *(I) Interpreter
10.03.2007	SCSLDF	Terry Jackson Former Commanding Officer	Interview
27.04.2007	Registrar's Office	Robin Vincent Former Registrar	Interview
20.04.2008	SCSLDF	Ray Cardinal Chief Custody Officer Alex Moore Deputy Chief Custody Officer	Group Interview
21.04.2008	SCSLDF Clinic	Doctor Harding	Interview
22–25.04.2008	SCSLDF	Paul Wright, Billie Neil, Koos van Breda and Raymond Ewing International Supervisors	Interview
		Irene Sessay, Arnold and George Coker National Supervisors 5 Custodial Staff	Interview
23.04.2007	Registry	Shaki Sanusi Legal Advisor to the Registrar	Interview
23.04.2007	Office of the Principal Defender	Vincent Nmehielle Principal Defender	Group Interview
		Elizabeth Ibanda-Nahamya Deputy Principal Defender	
	Victim and Witness Section	Saleem Vahidy Chief of Section	Interview

Date	Institution/Section	Subject/Position	Method *(I) Interpreter
24.04.2007	Registrar's Office	Herman von Hebel Registrar	Interview
05.07.2012	SCSL Sub-Office, The Hague	Alex Ras Head of Detention	Interview
31.08.2012	SCSL Sub-Office, The Hague	Alex Ras Head of Detention	Email

5. State Court of Bosnia-Herzegovina

Date	Institution/Section	Subject/Position	Method *(I) Interpreter
03.10.2007	State Ministry of Justice	Mustafa Bisić Assistant Minister for the Execution of Criminal Sanctions	Interview (I)
05.10.2007	State Court Detention Facility	Husein Hajdarević Deputy Commander	Interview (I) Tour
08.10.2007	Kula Detention Facility Republika Srpska	Vukašin Crnjak Deputy Director	Interview (I) Tour
		Clinic Doctor and Nurses	Interview (I)
09.10.2007	State Ministry of Justice	Mustafa Bisić Assistant Minister for the Execution of Criminal Sanctions	Second Interview (I)
		Rade Bladnjar State Inspector of Prisons	Interview (I)

States

1. Host States

a. The Netherlands

Date	Institution/Section	Subject/Position	Method *(I) Interpreter
24.08.2007	Prison Service	Cor Blom ICTY and ICC Liaison Officer	Group Interview
	Ministry of Foreign Affairs	André Moonen Senior Legal Advisor	

b. Sierra Leone

Date	Institution/Section	Subject/Position	Method *(I) Interpreter
23.04.2008	British Council's Justice Sector Development Programme	Momo Turay	Interview

Date	Institution/Section	Subject/Position	Method *(I) Interpreter
25.04.2008	Sierra Leone Prison Service Pademba Road Prison, Freetown	Moses Showers Acting Director	Interview Tour Informal discussions with staff and prisoners
c. Bosnia-Herzegovina			
06.10.2007	Council of Europe's Penal Reform Project	Several staff and consultants	Informal discussions
2. States of Enforcement			
a. United Kingdom			
24.05.2006	Home Office	Bob Daw Graham Wilkinson	Interview
27.09.2012	Usk Prison, Wales	Steve Dixon Equality Officer	Interview
		Andy Millership Offender Supervisor	Interview
		Deb Tuler Principal Officer	Interview
		Natalie Lavis Head of Residence and Security	Interview
10.10.2012	Ministry of Justice	Graham Wilkinson	Second (Telephone) Interview
b. Austria			
05.02.2008	Office of the Austrian Permanent Representative to the EU	Gregor Schusterschitz Legal Counsellor	Interview
13.08.2008	Federal Ministry of Justice	Dr Irene Köeck Director/Senior Public Prosecutor	Email

APPENDIX I: EMPIRICAL RESEARCH 351

Date	Institution/Section	Subject/Position	Method *(I) Interpreter
c. Finland			
02.06.2008	Ministry of Justice, International Affairs Section	Juhani Korhonen Legal Advisor	Telephone Interview
25.06.2008	Criminal Sanctions Agency	Raili Matinpuro Senior Officer	Email
01.07.2008	Ministry of Foreign Affairs, Unit for Public International Law	Sari Mäkelä Legal Counsellor	Telephone Interview
d. Sweden			
22.09.2008	Ministry of Justice	Hakan Friman	Telephone Interview
07.10.2008	Prison Service	Christer Isaksson Chief of Security	Interview
	Hinseberg Prison	Britt-Marie Johansson Governor	Interview Tour
		Karl Anders Lönnberg Deputy Governor	Interview
08.10.2008	Undisclosed Prison	Coordinator	Interview Tour
e. Norway			
26.06.2012	Skien Prison	Karl Gustav Knudsen Prison Director	Interview
		Kjell Arne Jensen Prison Officer	Interview
27–28.06.2012	Trondheim Prison	Egil Gabrielsen Prison Director	Interview Tour
		Stine Mollan Legal Advisor	Interview
		Arne Dahl Wing Manager	Interview
		Lise Johanne Henriksen Nurse	Interview

Date	Institution/Section	Subject/Position	Method *(I) Interpreter
29.06.2012	Ministry of Justice	Kjersti Lehmann Anne-Li Ferguson	Group Interview

Inspection Bodies

1. Council of Europe Committee for the Prevention of Torture

08.06.2007	Secretariat	Hugh Chetwynd Head of Division	Telephone Interview

2. International Committee of the Red Cross

13.03.2008	–	Confidential	Telephone Interview

Restorative Justice Programmes in Belgian Prisons

05.02.2008	Suggnomè	Leo Van Garsse	Interview
05.02.2008	Secondary Prison, Leuven	Geert van Aerschot Restorative Justice Consultant	Interview

Detained Persons

Date	Status	Name	Method
06.10.2007	Former UNDU detainee Indictment Withdrawn	Marinko Katava	Interview (I)
08.10.2007	Kula Detention Facility Prisoner, Republika Srpska Convicted of war crimes	Momir Glisić	Interview (I)
13.10.2007	Former UNDU detainee Indictment Withdrawn	Marinko Katava	Second Interview (I)
	Former UNDU detainee Acquitted by Appeal Chamber	Zoran Kupreškić	Interview (I)

APPENDIX I: EMPIRICAL RESEARCH 353

Date	Institution/Section	Subject/Position	Method *(I) Interpreter
20.08.2008	Former UNDU detainee Acquittal confirmed by Appeal Chamber	Zejnil Delalić	Written Correspondence (I)
08.10.2008	ICTY Prisoner Serving 20 year sentence in Sweden	Miroslav Bralo	Interview (I)
28.06.2012	ICTY Prisoner Serving 15 year sentence in Trondheim Prison, Norway	Vidoje Blagojević	Interview (I)
27.09.2012	ICTY Prisoner Serving 20 year sentence in Usk Prison, Wales	Momčilo Krajišnik	Interview (I)
Others			
27.03.2008	ICC Expert	Duncan McLaughlin	Telephone Interview
05.07.2012	Chief of Detention, Special Tribunal for Lebanon	Aidan McNally	Meeting

Appendix II

Enforcing states

State	Court
A. EUROPE	
Italy	ICTY
	ICTR
Finland	ICTY
	SCSL
	ICC
Norway	ICTY
Sweden	ICTY
	ICTR
	SCSL
Austria	ICTY
	ICC
Germany	ICTY
France	ICTY
	ICTR
Spain	ICTY
Denmark	ICTY
	ICC
United Kingdom	ICTY
	SCSL
	ICC
Belgium	ICTY
	ICC
Ukraine	ICTY
Portugal	ICTY
Estonia	ICTY
Slovakia	ICTY
Poland	ICTY
Albania	ICTY
Serbia	ICC

State	Court
B. AFRICA	
Swaziland	ICTR
Mali	ICTR
	ICC
Benin	ICTR
Rwanda	ICTR
	SCSL
C. SOUTH AMERICA	
Colombia	ICC

BIBLIOGRAPHY

A

Abathi, H. and S. A. Koh, "The Emerging Enforcement Practice of the International Criminal Court" (2012) 45 *Cornell International Law Journal* 1–23.

Abels, D., *Prisoners of the International Community: The Legal Position of Persons Detained at International Criminal Tribunals* (The Hague: TMC Asser Press, 2012).

Acquaviva, G., "Was a Residual Mechanism for International Criminal Tribunals Really Necessary" (2011) 9(4) *Journal of International Criminal Justice* 789–96.

Aersten, I., "The Intermediate Position of Restorative Justice: the Case of Belgium" in I. Aersten, T. Daems and L. Roberts (eds.), *Institutionalising Restorative Justice* (Cullompton: Willan Publishing, 2006), 69–92.

Amann, D. M., "The ICC and the Sovereign State" in I. F. Dekker and W. G. Werner (eds.), *Governance and International Legal Theory* (Leiden: Martinus Nijhoff Publishers, 2004), 185–214.

Amerasinghe, C. F., *Principles of Institutional Law of International Organisations* (Cambridge University Press, 1996).

Aneme, G. A., "Apology and Trials: the Case of the Red Terror Trials in Ethiopia" (2006) 6(1) *African Human Rights Law Journal* 64–84.

Antkowiak, T., "An Emerging Mandate for International Courts: Victim-Centred Remedies and Restorative Justice" (2011) 47 *Stanford Journal of International Law* 279–332.

Ascensio, H., "Privileges and Immunities" in A. Cassese, P. Gaeta and J. Jones (eds.), *The Rome Statute of the International Criminal Court: A Commentary* (Oxford University Press, 2002), 289–96.

Ashworth, A. and E. Player, "Sentencing, Equal Treatment and the Impact of Sanctions" in A. Ashworth and M. Wasik (eds.), *Fundamentals of Sentencing Theory: Essays in Honour of Andrew von Hirsch* (Oxford University Press, 1998), 251–72.

B

Babbie, E., *The Practice of Social Research*, 9th edn., (Belmont, CA: Wadsworth Publishing Co., 2001).

Baird, V. A., "Building Institutional Legitimacy: The Role of Procedural Justice" (2001) 54(2) *Political Research Quarterly* 333–54.

Barrett, M. N. and M. Finnemore, "The Politics, Power and Pathologies of International Organizations" (1999) 53(4) *International Organization* 699–732.
Barria, L. A. and S. D. Roper, "How Effective Are International Criminal Tribunals?" (2005) 9(3) *International Journal of Human Rights* 349–68.
Bazemore, G. and E. Erbe, "Reintegration and Restorative Justice: Towards a Theory and Practice of Informal Social Control and Support" in S. Maruna and R. Immarigeon (eds.), *After Crime and Punishment: Pathways to Ex-Offender Reintegration* (Cullompton: Willan Publishing, 2004), 27–56.
Bazemore, G. and S. O'Brien, "The Quest for a Restorative Model of Rehabilitation: Theory-for-practice and Practice-for-theory" in L. Walgrave (ed.), *Restorative Justice and the Law* (Cullompton: Willan Publishing, 2002), 31–67.
Bazemore, G. and J. Stinchcomb, "Civic Engagement and Reintegration: Towards a Community-Focused Theory and Practice" (2004) 36 *Columbia Human Rights Law Review* 241–86.
Bekou, O., "Rule 11*bis*: An Examination of the Process of Referrals to National Courts in ICTY Jurisprudence" (2010) 33 *Fordham International Law Journal* 723–91.
Benzing, M. and M. Bergsmo, "Some Tentative Remarks about the Relationship between Internationalised Criminal Jurisdiction and the ICC" in C. P. R. Romana, A. Nollkaemper and J. K. Kleffner (eds.), *Internationalized Criminal Courts: Sierra Leone, East Timor, Kosovo and Cambodia* (Oxford University Press, 2004), 407–15.
Beresford, S., "Unshackling the Paper Tiger: the Sentencing Practices of the ad hoc International Criminal Tribunals for the Former Yugoslavia and Rwanda" (2001) 1 *International Criminal Law Review* 33–90.
Blad, J., "Institutionalising Restorative Justice? Transforming Criminal Justice? A Critical View on the Netherlands" in I. Aersten, T. Daems and L. Roberts (eds.), *Institutionalising Restorative Justice* (Cullompton: Willan Publishing, 2006), 93–119.
Boeije, H., *Analysis in Qualitative Research* (London: Sage Publications, 2010).
Bowett, D. W., *The Law of International Institutions*, 4th edn, (London: Sweet & Maxwell Publications, 1982).
Branham, L., "The Mess We're In: Five Steps Towards the Transformation of Prison Cultures" (2010) 44 *Indiana Law Review* 703–33.
Brölman, C., "A Flat Earth? International Organizations in the System of International Law" (2001) 70(3) *Nordic Journal of International Law* 319–40.
Brus, M., "Bridging the Gap between State Sovereignty and International Governance: The Authority of Law" in G. Kreijen (ed.), *State, Sovereignty and International Governance* (Oxford University Press, 2002), 3–26.

C

Cameron, L., "Human Rights Accountability of International Civil Administrations to the People Subject to Administration" (2007) 1 *Human Rights and International Legal Discourse* 267-300.

Canter, A. S., " 'For these Reasons, the Chamber Denies the Prosecutor's Request for Referral': The False Hope of Rule 11*bis*" (2009) 32 *Fordham International Law Journal* 1614-56.

Carrabine, E., "Discourse, Governmentality and Translation: Towards a Social Theory of Imprisonment" (2000) 4 *Theoretical Criminology* 309-31.

Casella, E. C., "Prisoner of His Majesty: Postcoloniality and the Archaeology of British Penal Transportation" (2005) 37(3) *World Archaeology* 453-67.

Cassese, A., *International Criminal Law*, 2nd edn., (Oxford University Press, 2008).

Chimiba, T. B., "Establishing an Enforcement Regime" in R. S. Lee (ed.), *The International Criminal Court: The Making of the Rome Statute* (The Hague: Kluwer Law International, 1999), 345-56.

Chuter, D., *War Crimes: Confronting Atrocity in the Modern World* (Boulder, CO: Lynne Reiner Publishers, 2003).

Clark, J. N., "Plea Bargaining at the ICTY: Guilty Pleas and Reconciliation" (2009) 20(2) *European Journal of International Law* 415-36.

"The Impact Question: The ICTY and the Restoration and Maintenance of Peace" in B. Swart, A. Zahar and G. Sluiter (eds.), *The Legacy of the International Criminal Tribunal for the former Yugoslavia* (Oxford University Press, 2011) 55-80.

Cockayne, J., "Hybrids or Mongrels? Internationalized War Crime Trials as Unsuccessful Degradation Ceremonies" (2005) 4 *Journal of Human Rights* 455-73.

Coliver, S., "The Contribution of the ICTY to Reconciliation in Bosnia and Herzegovina" in D. Shelton (ed.), *International Crimes, Peace and Human Rights: The Role of the ICC* (Ardsley, NY: Transnational, 2000), 19-31.

Coyle, A., *A Human Rights Approach to Prison Management: Handbook for Prison Staff* (London: International Centre for Prison Studies, 2002).

Managing Prisons in a Time of Change (London: International Centre for Prison Studies, 2002).

Crawley, E., "Doing Prison Work: the Public and Private Lives of Prison Officers" in Y. Jewkes and H. Johnston (eds.), *Prison Readings: A Critical Introduction to Prisons and Imprisonment* (Cullompton: Willan Publishing, 2006), 209-22.

Crawley, E. and R. Sparks, "Older Men in Prison: Survival, Coping and Identity" in A. Liebling and S. Maruna (eds.), *The Effects of Imprisonment* (Cullompton: Willan Publishing, 2005), 343-65.

Crow, I., *The Treatment and Rehabilitation of Offenders* (London: Sage Publications, 2001).

Cryer, R. "Post-conflict Accountability: A Matter of Judgment, Practice or Principle" in N. White and D. Klaasen (eds.), *The UN, Human Rights and Post-conflict Situations* (Manchester University Press, 2005), 267–89.

Cryer, R., H. Friman, D. Robinson and E. Wilmshurst, *An Introduction to International Criminal Law and Procedure*, 2nd edn, (Cambridge University Press, 2010).

D

D'Ascoli, S., *Sentencing in International Criminal Law: The UN ad hoc Tribunals and Future Perspectives for the ICC* (Oxford: Hart Publishing, 2011).

D'Aspremont, J., "Abuse of the Legal Personality of International Organizations and the Responsibility of Member States" (2007) 4 *International Organizations Law Review* 91–119.

Damaška, M., "What is the Point of International Criminal Justice?" (2008) 83 *Chicago-Kent Law Review* 329–65.

De Chazournes, L. B., "Changing Roles of International Organizations: Global Administrative Law and the Interplay of Legitimacies" (2009) 6 *International Organizations Law Review* 655–66.

De Sampayo Garrido, C., "Problems and Achievements Seen from the Viewpoint of the Registry" (2004) 2 *Journal of International Criminal Justice* 474–9.

Delpla, I., "In the Midst of Injustice: The ICTY from the Perspective of some Victim Associations" in X. Bougarel, H. Helms and G. Duijzings (eds.), *The New Bosnia Mosaic; Identities, Memories and Moral Claims in a Post-War Society* (Aldershot: Ashgate Publishing, 2007), 211–34.

Denis, C., "Critical Overview of the 'Residual Functions' of the Mechanism and its Date of Commencement (including Transitional Arrangements)" (2011) 9(4) *Journal of International Criminal Justice* 819–37

Dowling, J. and J. Pfeffer, "Organizational Legitimacy: Social Values and Organizational Behavior" (1975) 18(1) *The Pacific Sociological Review* 122–36.

Drumbl, M., *Atrocity, Punishment and International Law* (Cambridge University Press, 2007).

"Collective Violence and Individual Punishment: The Criminality of Mass Atrocity" (2005) 99(2) *Northwestern University Law Review* 539–610.

E

Easton, D., "A Re-assessment of the Concept of Political Support" (1975) 5(4) *British Journal of Political Science* 435–57.

Easton, S. and C. Piper, *Sentencing and Punishment: The Quest for Justice* (Oxford University Press, 2005).

El Zeidy, M. M. "From Primacy to Complementarity and Backwards: (Re)-visiting Rule 11*bis* of the Ad Hoc Tribunals" (2008) 57(2) *International and Comparative Law Quarterly* 403–15.

F

Faget, J., "The French Phantoms of Restorative Justice: The Institutionalisation of Penal Mediation" in I. Aersten, T. Daems and L. Roberts (eds.), *Institutionalising Restorative Justice* (Cullompton: Willan Publishing, 2006), 151–66.

Feeley, M. and J. Simon, "The New Penology: Notes on the Emerging Strategy of Corrections and its Implications" (1992) 30(4) *Criminology* 449–74.

Findlay, M., "The Challenge for Asian Jurisdictions in the Development of International Criminal Justice" (2010) 32 *Sydney Law Review* 205–19.

Findlay, M. and R. Henham, *Transforming International Criminal Justice: Retributive and Restorative Justice in the Trial Process* (Cullompton: Willan Publishing, 2005).

Fishman, J., *Long Knives and Short Memories: The Spandau Prison Story* (New York: Richardson & Steirman, 1986).

Franck, T., *Fairness in International Law and Institutions* (Oxford: Clarendon Press, 1995).

Frolich, R., "UN Security Council Resolution 1966: International Residual Mechanism for the ICTY and ICTR" (2011) 50(3) *International Legal Materials* 323–39.

G

Gaillard, E. and I. Pingel-Lenuzza, "International Organisations and Immunity from Jurisdiction: To Restrict or to Bypass" (2002) 51 *International and Comparative Law Quarterly* 1–15.

Gallo, E., "The Penal System in France: from Correctionalism to Managerialism" in V. Ruggiero, M. Ryan and J. Sim (eds.), *Western European Penal Systems: A Critical Anatomy* (London: Sage Publications, 1995), 71–92.

Gallón, G., "The ICC and the Challenge of Deterrence" in D. Shelton (ed.), *International Crimes, Peace and Human Rights: The Role of the ICC* (Ardsley, NY: Transnational, 2000), 93–104.

Garland, D., *Punishment and Modern Society, A Study in Social Theory* (Oxford: Clarendon Press, 1990).

Gearty, C. A., *Principles of Human Rights Adjudication* (Oxford University Press, 2004).

Goda, N. J. W. *Tales from Spandau: Nazi Criminals and the Cold War* (Cambridge University Press, 2007).

Goulding, D., G. Hall and B. Steels, "Restorative Prisons: Towards Radical Prison Reform" (2008) 20(2) *Current Issues in Criminal Justice* 231–42.

Grosselfinger, N., "The United Nations Detention Unit" in P. J. Van Krieken and D. McKay (eds.), *The Hague: Legal Capital of the World* (The Hague: TMC Asser Press, 2005), 317–22.

Gumboh, E., "The Penalty of Life Imprisonment under International Criminal Law" (2011) 11 *African Human Rights Law Journal* 75–92.

H

Hallevy, G., "Therapeutic Victim-Offender Mediation within the Criminal Justice Process" (2011) 16 *Harvard Negotiation Law Review* 65–94.

Hancock, V., "'No-self' at trial: How to Reconcile Punishing the Khmer Rouge for Crimes Against Humanity with Cambodian Buddhist Principles" (2008) 26 (1) *Wisconsin International Law Journal* 87–129.

Hassan, F., "The Theoretical Basis of Punishment in International Criminal Law" (1983) 15 *Case Western Reserve Journal of International Law* 39–60.

Haveman, R., "Supranational Expectations of a Punitive Nature" in R. Haveman and O. Olusanya (eds.), *Sentencing and Sanctioning in Supranational Criminal Law* (Antwerp, Oxford: Intersentia, 2006) 145–60.

Henham, R., *Punishment and Process in International Criminal Trials* (Aldershot: Ashgate Publishing, 2005).
  "Theorizing the Penalty of Sentencing in International Criminal Trials" (2004) 8 *Theoretical Criminology* 429–63.

Henham, R. and Drumbl, M., "Plea Bargaining at the ICTY" (2005) 16 *Criminal Law Forum* 49–87.

Hill, F. D., "Restorative Justice: Sketching a New Legal Discourse" (2008) 4(2) *International Journal of Punishment and Sentencing* 51–81.

Hoffman, F. and F. Mégret, "Fostering Human Rights Accountability: An Ombudsperson for the United Nations?" (2005) 11 *Global Governance* 43–63.

Hoffmann, K., "Some Remarks on the Enforcement of International Sentences in the Light of Galić case at the ICTY" (2011) *ZIS* 838–42.

I

ICRC "Action by the ICRC in the Event of Violations of IHL or of Other Fundamental Rules protecting Persons in Situations of Violence" (2005) 87(858) *International Review of the Red Cross* 395–8.

J

Jacobs, J. B., *Stateville: The Penitentiary in Mass Society* (University of Chicago Press, 1977).

Jensen, R., "Globalization and the International Criminal Court: Accountability and a New Conception of State" in I. F. Dekker and W. G. Werner (eds.), *Governance and International Legal Theory* (Leiden: Martinus Nijhoff Publishers, 2004), 159–84.

K

Kenny, K., "UN Accountability for its Human Rights Impact: Implementation through Participation" in N. White and D. Klaasen (eds.), *The UN, Human Rights and Post-Conflict Situations* (Manchester University Press, 2005), 438–62.

King, F. P., and A. La Rosa, "Penalties under the ICC Statute" in F. Lattanzi and W. Schabas (eds.), *Essays on the Rome Statute of the International Criminal Court*, Vol. I (Ripa Fagnano Alto: Editrice il Sirente, 1999), 311–38.

King, K. L. and J. D. Meernik, "Assessing the Impact of the ICTY: Balancing International and Local Interests While Doing Justice" in B. Swart, A. Zahar and G. Sluiter (eds.), *The Legacy of the International Criminal Tribunal for the Former Yugoslavia* (Oxford University Press, 2011), 7–54.

King, R. D. "Doing Research in Prisons" in R. D. King and E. Wincup (eds.), *Doing Research on Crime and Justice* (Oxford University Press, 2000), 285–312.

"The Rise and Rise of Supermax: an American Solution in Search of a Problem?" in Y. Jewkes and H. Johnston (eds.), *Prison Readings: A Critical Introduction to Prisons and Imprisonment* (Cullompton: Willan Publishing, 2006), 84–93.

King, R. D., and M. Maguire, "Introduction" (1994) 34 *British Journal of Criminology Special Issue – Contexts of Imprisonment: An International Perspective* 1–13.

Klabbers, J., *An Introduction to International Institutional Law* (Cambridge University Press, 2002).

Klein, S., G. Bartholomew and J. Hibbert, "Inmate Family Functioning" (2002) 46 (1) *International Journal of Offender Therapy and Comparative Criminology* 95–111.

Kleinig, J., "The Hardness of Hard Treatment" in A. Ashworth and M. Wasik (eds.), *Fundamentals of Sentencing Theory: Essays in Honour of Andrew von Hirsch* (Oxford University Press, 1998), 273–98.

Klip, A., "Enforcement of Sanctions Imposed by the International Criminal Tribunals for Rwanda and the Former Yugoslavia" (1997) 5(2) *European Journal of Crime, Criminal Law and Criminal Justice* 144–64.

Köchler, H., *Global Justice or Global Revenge? International Criminal Justice at the Crossroads* (New York: Springer-Verlag, 2003).

Kreß, C. and G. Sluiter, "Imprisonment" in A. Cassese, P. Gaeta and J. Jones (eds.), *The Rome Statute of the International Criminal Court: A Commentary*, Vol. II (Oxford University Press, 2002), 1757–821.

Kritz, N. J. and J. Finci, "A Truth and Reconciliation Commission in Bosnia and Herzegovina: An Idea Whose Time has Come" (2001) 3 *International Law Forum du Droit International* 50–8.

L

La Vigne, N. G., R. L. Naser, L. E. Brooks and J. L. Castro, "Examining the Effect of Incarceration and In-Prison Family Contact and Prisoners' Family Relationships" (2005) 21(4) *Journal of Contemporary Criminal Justice* 314–35.

Lacey, N., *State Punishment: Political Principles and Community Values* (London: Routledge, 1988).

Lazarus, L., "Conceptions of Liberty Deprivation" (2006) 69(5) *Modern Law Review* 738-69.
Lee, R. S. (ed.), *The International Criminal Court: Elements of Crimes and Rules of Procedure and Evidence* (Ardsley: Transnational Publishers, 2001).
Leinward, J., "Punishing Horrific Crime: Reconciling International Prosecution with National Sentencing Practices" (2008) 40 *Columbia Human Rights Law Review* 799-852.
Liebling, A., *Prisons and Their Moral Performance: A Study of Values, Quality, and Prison Life* (Oxford University Press, 2004).
  "Whose Side Are We On? Theory, Practice and Allegiance in Prison Research" (2001) 41 *British Journal of Criminology* 472-84.
Linton, S., "Cambodia, East Timor and Sierra Leone: Experiments in International Justice" 12 *Criminal Law Forum* (2001), 185-246.
Lippke, R. L. *Rethinking Imprisonment* (Oxford University Press, 2007).
Llewellyn "Truth Commissions and Restorative Justice" in G. Johnstone and D. W., Van Ness (eds.), *Handbook of Restorative Justice* (Cullompton: Willan Publishing, 2007) 355-61.
Luyt, W., "Genocide in Rwanda: Detention and Prison Involvement" (2003) 16(4) *Acta Criminologica* 96-111.

M

Mafwenga, A., "The Contribution of the ICTR to Reconciliation in Rwanda" in D. Shelton (ed.), *International Crimes, Peace and Human Rights: The Role of the ICC* (Ardsley, NY: Transnational, 2000), 11-17.
Maogoto, J., *War Crimes and Realpolitik: International Justice from World War I to the 21st Century* (Boulder, CO: Lynne Reiner Publisher, 2004).
Marchesi, A., "The Enforcement of Sentences of the International Criminal Court" in F. Lattanzi and W. Schabas (eds.), *Essays on the Rome Statute of the International Criminal Court*, Vol. I (Ripa Fagnano Alto: Editrice il Sirente, 1999), 427-45.
Mathiesen, T., "The Argument against Building more Prisons" in J. Muncie and R. Sparks (eds.), *Imprisonment: European Perspectives* (Hemel Hempstead: Harvester Wheatsheaf, 1991), 177-84.
Matthews, R., "The Myth of Punitiveness" 2005 9(2) *Theoretical Criminology* 175-201.
McDonald, G. K., "The International Criminal Tribunals: Crime & Punishment in the International Arena" (2001) 25 *Nova Law Review* 463-84.
McEvoy, K., "Letting Go of Legalism: Developing a 'Thicker' Version of Transitional Justice" in K. McEvoy and L. McGregor (eds.), *Transitional Justice from Below: Grassroots Activism and the Struggle for Change (Human Rights Law in Perspective)* (Oxford: Hart Publishing, 2008) 15-46.
  Paramilitary Imprisonment in Northern Ireland: Resistance, Management and Release (Oxford University Press, 2001).

Melman, J., "The Possibility of Transfer (?): A Comprehensive Approach to the ICTR's Rule 11*bis* to Permit Transfer to Rwandan Domestic Courts" (2010) 79 *Fordham Law Review* 1271–332.

Mills, A. and H. Codd, "Prisoners' Families and Offender Management: Mobilizing Social Capital" (2008) 55(1) *Probation Journal* 9–24.

Moghalu, K., *Rwanda's Genocide: The Politics of Global Justice* (London: Palgrave MacMillan, 2005).

Moreno-Ocampo, L., "How Prosecution Can Lead to Prevention" (2011) 29 *Law and Inequality* 477–94.

Morgan, R. "A Brief History, The Contemporary Scene and Likely Prospects" in M. Maguire, R. Morgan and R. Reiner (eds.), *The Oxford Handbook of Criminology*, 3rd edn (Oxford University Press, 2002).

Morgan, R. and M. Evans, "Inspecting Prisons: The View from Strasbourg" in R. D. King and M. Maguire (eds.), *Prisons in Context* (Oxford: Clarendon Press, 1994), 141–59.

Morris, N., *The Future of Imprisonment* (University of Chicago Press, 1974).

Morrison, W., "Modernity, Imprisonment and Social Solidarity" in R. Mathews and P. Francis (eds.), *Prisons 2000: An International Perspective on the Current State and Future of Imprisonment* (Basingstoke: MacMillan Publishers, 1996), 94–120.

Mulgrew, R., "Implementing International Sentences of Imprisonment: Challenges Faced by the Special Court for Sierra Leone" (2009) 7(2) *Journal of International Criminal Justice* 373–96.

"The International Movement of Prisoners: Exploring the Evolution of the Inter-State and International Criminal Justice Systems for the Transfer of Sentenced Persons" (2011) 22 *Criminal Law Forum* 103–43.

Murdoch, J., "The Work of the Council of Europe's Torture Committee" (1994) 5 (1) *European Journal of International Law* 220–48.

Murray, R., "The African Commission's Approach to Prisons" in J. Sarkin (ed.), *Human Rights in African Prisons* (Pretoria: HRSC Press, 2008), 204–23.

N

Neale, K., "The European Prison Rules: Contextual, Philosophical and Practical Aspects" in J. Munice and R. Sparks (eds.), *Imprisonment: European Perspectives* (Hemel Hempstead: Harvester Wheatshead, 1991), 203–18.

Nemitz, J. C., "Execution of Sanctions Imposed by Supranational Criminal Tribunals" in R. Haveman and O. Olusanya (eds.), *Sentencing and Sanctioning in Supranational Criminal Law* (Antwerp, Oxford: Intersentia, 2006), 125–44.

O

O'Rourke, A., "The Writ of Habeas Corpus and the SCSL: Addressing an Unforeseen Problem in the Establishment of a Hybrid Court" (2005) 44 *Columbia Journal of Transnational Law* 649–85.

Ohlin, J. D., "Proportional Sentences at the ICTY" in B. Swart, A. Zahar and G. Sluiter (eds.), *The Legacy of the International Criminal Tribunal for the Former Yugoslavia* (Oxford University Press, 2011), 322–34.

Oomen, B., "Rwanda's Gacaca: Objectives, Merits and their Relation to Supranational Criminal Law" in R. Haveman and O. Olusanya (eds.), *Sentencing and Sanctioning in Supranational Criminal Law* (Antwerp, Oxford: Intersentia, 2006), 161–84.

"Transitional Justice and Its Legitimacy: The Case for a Local Perspective" (2007) 25(1) *Netherlands Quarterly of Human Rights* 141–8.

Oosterveld, V., "The International Criminal Court and the Closure of the Time-Limited International and Hybrid Criminal Tribunals" (2010) 8(1) *Loyola University Chicago International Law Review* 13–31.

P

Pellet, A., "Settlement of Disputes" in A. Cassese, P. Gaeta and J. Jones (eds.), *The Rome Statute of the International Criminal Court: A Commentary* (Oxford University Press, 2002), 1841–8.

Penrose, M., "Lest We Fail: The Importance of Enforcement in International Criminal Law" (2000) 15 *American University International Law Review* 321–94.

"No Badges, No Bars: A Conspicuous Oversight in the Development of an International Criminal Court" (2003) 38(3) *Texas International Law Journal* 621–42.

"Spandau Revisited: The Question of Detention for International War Crimes" (1999) 16 *New York Law School Journal of Human Rights* 553–91.

Pratt, P., *Punishment and Civilization: Penal Tolerance and Intolerance in Modern Society* (London: Sage Publications, 2002).

R

Reinisch, R., "Securing the Accountability of International Organizations" (2001) 7 *Global Governance* 131–49.

Roberts, L. and T. Peters, "How Restorative Justice is able to Transcend the Prison Walls: A Discussion of the 'Restorative Detention' Project" in E. Weitekamp and H. Kerner (eds.), *Restorative Justice in Context: International Practice and Directions* (Cullompton: Willan Publishing, 2003), 95–122.

Roberts, P., "Restoration and Retribution in International Criminal Justice: An Exploratory Analysis" in A. von Hirsch, J. Roberts, A. E. Bottonis, K. Roach and M. Schiff (eds.), *Restorative Justice and Criminal Justice: Competing or Reconcilable Paradigms* (Oxford: Hart Publishing, 2003), 115–34.

Roche, D., "Retribution and Restorative Justice" in G. Johnstone and D. W. Van Ness (eds.), *Handbook of Restorative Justice* (Cullompton: Willan Publishing, 2007), 75–90.

Rodley, N. and M. Pollard, *The Treatment of Prisoners under International Law*, 3rd edn (Oxford University Press, 2009).

Rossi, R. A., "Meet Me on Death Row: Post-Sentence Victim-Offender Mediation in Capital Cases" (2008) 9(1) *Pepperdine Dispute Resolution Law Journal* 185–210.

Rotman, E., "Beyond Punishment" in R. A. Duff and D. Garland (eds.), *A Reader on Punishment* (Oxford University Press, 1994), 281–305.

Rubin, E. L., "The Inevitability of Rehabilitation" (2001) 19 *Law and Inequality* 343–77.

Rugge, T. and R. Cormier, "Restorative Justice in Cases of Serious Crime: an Evaluation" in E. Elliott and R. Gorden (eds.), *New Directions in Restorative Justice* (Cullompton: Willam Publishing, 2005).

Rutherford, A., "Criminal Policy and the Eliminative Ideal" (1997) 31(5) *Social Policy and Administration* 116–35.

S

Safferling, C. J. M., *Towards an International Criminal Procedure* (Oxford University Press, 2001).

Sarooshi, D., *International Organisations and Their Exercise of Sovereign Powers* (Oxford University Press, 2005).

Saxon, D., "Exporting Justice: Perceptions of the ICTY among the Serbians, Croatians and Muslim Communities in the Former Yugoslavia" (2005) 4 (4) *Journal of Human Rights* 559–72.

Scalia, D., "Long-term Sentences in International Criminal Law: Do They Meet the Standards Set Out by the European Court of Human Rights" (2011) 9(3) *Journal of International Criminal Justice* 669–87.

Schabas, W., *An Introduction to the International Criminal Court*, 4th edn (Cambridge University Press, 2011).

  "Criminology, Accountability and International Justice" in M. Bosworth and C. Hoyle (eds.), *What is Criminology?* (Oxford University Press, 2011) 346–57.

  "Sentencing by International Tribunals: A Human Rights Approach" (1997) 7 *Duke Journal of Comparative and International Law* 461–518.

  The Abolition of the Death Penalty in International Law, 3rd edn (Oxford University Press, 2002).

  "The Relationship between Truth Commission and International Courts: The Case of Sierra Leone" (2003) 25 *Human Rights Quarterly* 1035–66.

  The UN International Criminal Tribunals; The Former Yugoslavia, Rwanda and Sierra Leone (Cambridge University Press, 2006).

  "War Crimes, Crimes against Humanity and the Death Penalty" (1996) 60 *Albany Law Review* 733–70.

Schvey, A. A., "Striving for Accountability in the Former Yugoslavia" in J. E. Stromseth (ed.), *Accountability for Atrocities: National and International Responses* (Ardsley, NY: Transnational, 2003), 39–86.

Seale, C., *The Quality of Qualitative Research* (London: Sage Publications, 1999).
Shelton, D., *Remedies in International Human Rights Law*, 2nd edn (Oxford University Press, 2005).
Shraga, D., "The Second Generation UN-Based Tribunals: A Diversity of Mixed Jurisdictions" in C. P. R. Romano, A. Nollkaemper and J. K. Kleffner (eds.), *Internationalised Criminal Courts: Sierra Leone, East Timor, Kosovo, and Cambodia* (Oxford University Press, 2004).
Sim, J., "The Abolitionist Approach: A British Perspective" in Y. Jewkes and H. Johnston (eds.), *Prison Readings: A Critical Introduction to Prisons and Imprisonment* (Cullompton: Willan Publishing, 2006), 98–104.
Sim, J., V. Ruggiero and M. Ryan, "Punishment in Europe: Perceptions and Commonalities" in V. Ruggiero, M. Ryan and J. Sim (eds.), *Western European Penal Systems: A Critical Anatomy* (London: Sage Publications, 1995), 1–23.
Skelton, A., "Africa" in G. Johnstone and D. Van Ness (eds.), *Handbook of Restorative Justice* (Cullompton: Willan Publishing, 2007).
Skoplak, P., *Uknik* (Vitez, 2004).
Slaughter, A. and W. Burke-White, "The Future of International Law is Domestic (or, The European Way of Law)" (2006) 47(2) *Harvard International Law Journal* 327–52.
Sparks, R. "Can Prisons be Legitimate?" in R. D. King and M. Maguire (eds.), *Prisons in Context* (Oxford: Clarendon Press, 1994), 14–28.
Stahn, C., "Accommodating Individual Criminal Responsibility and National Reconciliation: The UN Truth Commission for East Timor" (2001) 95 *American Journal of International Law* 952–66.
Steels, B., "Forever Guilty: Convict Perceptions of Pre- and Post-Conviction" (2009) 21(2) *Current Issues in Criminal Justice* 242.

T

Tieger, A., "Remorse and Mitigation in the ICTY" (2003) 16 *Leiden Journal of International Law* 777–86.
Tieger, A. and M. Shin, "Plea Agreements in the ICTY: Purposes, Effects and Propriety" (2005) 3 *Journal of International Criminal Justice* 666–79.
Teitel, R., "The Universal and the Particular in International Criminal Justice" (1998) 30 *Columbia Human Rights Law Review* 285–303.
Tolbert, D., "The International Criminal Tribunal for the Former Yugoslavia and the Enforcement of Sentences" (1998) 11 *Leiden Journal of International Law* 655–69.
Tolbert, D. and A. Rydberg, "Enforcement of Sentences" in R. May, D. Tolbert, J. Hocking, K. Roberts, Bing Bing Jia, D. Mundis and G. Oosthuizen (eds.), *Essays on ICTY Procedure and Evidence in Honour of Gabrielle Kirk McDonald* (The Hague: Kluwer Law International, 2001), 533–43.

Triponel, A. and S. Pearson, "What do You Think Should Happen? Public Participation in Transitional Justice" (2010) 22 *Pace International Law Review* 103–44.

Tsagourias, N., "The Will of the International Community as a Normative Source of International Law" in I. F. Dekker and W. G. Werner (eds.), *Governance and International Legal Theory* (Leiden: Martinus Nijhoff, 2004) 97–121.

V

Van Ness, D. W., "Prisons and Restorative Justice" in G. Johnstone and D. W. Van Ness (eds.), *Handbook of Restorative Justice* (Cullompton: Willan Publishing, 2007), 312–24.

Van Zyl Smit, D., "International Imprisonment" (2005) 54(2) *International Comparative Law Quarterly* 357–86.

  Taking Life Imprisonment Seriously: In National and International Law (London: Kluwer Law International, 2002).

Van Zyl Smit, D. and F. Dunkel (eds.), *Imprisonment Today and Tomorrow: International Perspectives on Prisoners' Rights and Prison Conditions*, 2nd edn (Deventer: Kluwer Law International, 2001).

Van Zyl Smit, D. and S. Snacken, *Principles of European Prison Law and Policy: Penology and Human Rights* (Oxford University Press, 2009).

Verdirame, G., *The UN and Human Rights: Who Guards the Guardians?* (Cambridge University Press, 2011).

  "UN Accountability for Human Rights Violations in Post-conflict Situations" in N. White and D. Klaasen (eds.), *The UN, Human Rights and Post-Conflict Situations* (Manchester University Press, 2005), 81–97.

Viljoen, F., "The Special Rapporteur on Prisons and Conditions of Detention in Africa: Achievements and Possibilities" (2005) 27(1) *Human Rights Quarterly* 125–71.

Vincent, R., *An Administrative Practices Manual for Internationally Assisted Criminal Justice Institutions* (New York: International Centre for Transitional Justice, 2007).

Vitiello, M., "Reconsidering Rehabilitation" (1991) 65 *Tulane Law Review* 1011–54.

Von Hirsch, A., A. Ashworth and C. Shearing, "Specifying Aims and Limits for Restorative Justice: A 'Making Amends' Model?" in A. von Hirsch, J. Roberts, A. E. Bottoms, K. Roach and M. Schiff (eds.), *Restorative Justice and Criminal Justice: Competing or Reconcilable Paradigms* (Oxford: Hart Publishing, 2003), 21–41.

W

Walgrave, L., "Integrating Criminal Justice and Restorative Justice" in G. Johnstone and D. W. Van Ness (eds.), *Handbook of Restorative Justice* (Cullompton: Willan Publishing, 2007), 559–79.

"Restorative Justice: An Alternative to Responding to Crime?" in S. G. Shoham, O. Beck and M. Kett (eds.), *International Handbook of Penology and Criminal Justice* (Boca Ratou, FL: CRC Press, 2008) 613–89.

Walker, L. and L. Hayashi, "Pono Kaulike: A Pilot Restorative Justice Program" (2004) (May) *Hawaii Bar Journal* 4–15.

Walker, N., *Why Punish?* (Oxford University Press, 1991).

Wilde, R., "Accountability and International Actors in Bosnia and Herzegovina, Kosovo and East Timor" (2000) 7 *ILSA Journal of International and Comparative Law* 455–60.

"Enhancing Accountability at the International Level: The Tension between International Organizations and Member State Responsibility and the Underlying Issues at Stake" (2005) 12 *ILSA Journal of International and Comparative Law* 395–415.

Willis, J. J., "Transportation versus Imprisonment in Eighteenth and Nineteenth Century Britain: Penal Power, Liberty, and the State" (2005) 39(1) *Law and Society Review* 171–210.

Wilson, R. A., *Writing History in International Criminal Trials* (Cambridge University Press, 2011).

Wippman, D., "Atrocities, Deterrence, and the Limits of International Justice" (1999) 23 *Fordham International Law Journal* 473–88.

Wright, M., "Restorative Justice: from Punishment to Reconciliation: The Role of Social Workers" (1998) 6(1) *European Journal of Crime, Criminal Law and Criminal Justice* 267–81.

Z

Zehr, H., "Evaluation and Restorative Justice Principles" in E. Elliot and R. M. Gordon (eds.), *New Directions in Restorative Justice: Issues, Practice, Evaluation* (Cullompton: Willan Publishing, 2005), 296–303.

"Journey to Belonging" in E. G. M. Weitekamp and H. Kerner (eds.), *Restorative Justice: Theoretical Foundations* (Cullompton: Willan Publishing, 2002), 21–31.

"Retributive Justice, Restorative Justice" in G. Johnstone (ed.), *A Restorative Justice Reader* (Cullompton: Willan Publishing, 2003), 69–82.

TABLE OF CASES

International Military Tribunal for Nuremberg
IMTN, *Judgment and Sentence* (1947) 41 AJIL 172

International Court of Justice
Reparation for Injuries Suffered in the Service of the United Nations (Advisory Opinion) [1949] ICJ Reports 174.

International Criminal Tribunal for the Former Yugoslavia

Trial Chamber Orders

Kordić and Čerkez Order on Prosecutor's Motion for Leave to Withdraw the Indictment against Ivan Santić, IT-95-14/2, 19.12.1997.
Šešelj Urgent Order to the Dutch Authorities Regarding the Health and Welfare of the Accused, IT-03-67-T, 06.12.2006.

Trial Chamber Decisions

Kupreškić et al. Decision on the Motion by the Prosecutor to Withdraw the Indictment against Marinko Katava, IT-95-16, 19.12.1997.
Tolimir Decision on Urgent Registry Submission pursuant to Rule 33(b) concerning the Order regarding the Nightly Monitoring of the Accused, IT-05–88/2-T, 01.09.2010.

Referral Bench

Ademi and Norac Decision for Referral to the Authorities of the Republic of Croatia pursuant to Rule 11*bis*, IT-04-78-PT, 14.09.2005.
Kovačevič Decision on Referral of Case Pursuant to Rule 11*bis*, IT-01-42/2-I, 17.11.2006.
Ljubičić Decision to Refer the Case to Bosnia-Herzegovina pursuant to Rule 11*bis*, IT-00-41-PT, 12.04.2006.

Rašević and Todović, Decision on Referral of Case Under Rule 11bis, IT-97-25/1-PT, 08.07.2005.

Trial Chamber Judgments

Begaj IT-03-66-R77, 27.05.2005.
Blaškić IT-95-14-T, 03.03.2000.
Brđanin IT-99-36-T, 01.09.2004.
Delalić et al. IT-96-21, 16.11.1998.
Deronjić IT-02-61-5, 30.03.2004.
Erdemović IT-96-22-T, 29.11.1996.
Erdemović IT-96-22-Tbis, 05.03.1998.
Furundžija IT-95-17/1-T, 10.12.1998.
Gotovina et al. (Vol.2) IT-06-90-T, 15.04.2011.
Krnjoleac IT-97-25-T, 15.03.2002.
Kunarac, Kovač, Vuković IT-96-23-T, IT-96-23/1-T, 22.02.2001.
Kupreškić et al. IT-95-16-T, 14.01.2000.
Margetić IT-95-14-R77.6, 07.02.2007.
Mrđa IT-02-59-S, 31.03.2004.
Nikolić, Dragan IT-94-2-S, 18.12.2003.
Nikolić, M. IT-94-2-S, 18.12.2003.
Obrenović IT-02-60/2-S, 10.12.2003.
Orić IT-03-68-T, 30.06.2006.
Perišić IT-04-81-T, 06.09.2011.
Petković IT-03-67-R77.1, 11.09.2008.
Zelenović IT-96-23/2-S, 04.04.2007.

Appeal Chamber Decisions

Ljubičić Decision on Appeal against Decision on Referral under Rule11bis, IT-00-41-AR11bis.1, 04.07.2006.
Mejakić, Gruban, Fuštar and Knežević Decision on Joint Defence Appeal against Decision on Referral Under Rule 11bis, IT-O2-65-AR11BIS.1, 07.04.2006.
Stanković Decision on Rule 11bis Referral, IT-96-23/2.AR11bis.1, 01.09.2005.
Strugar Decision on Strugar's Request to Reopen Appeal Proceedings, IT-01-42.Misc.1, 07.06.2007.

Appeal Chamber Judgments

Bralo IT-95-17, 02.04.2007.
Delalić, Mucić, Delić and Land žo (Čelibići) IT-96-21-A, 20.02.2001.
Deronjić IT-02-61-A, 20.07.2005.
Kordić and Čerkez IT-95-14/2-A, 17.12.2004.
Krajišnik IT-00-39-A, 17.03.2009.
Kunarac, Kovač and Vuković IT-96-23 & IT-96-23/1-A, 12.06.2002.
Kupreškić et al. IT-95-16-A, 23.10.2001.
Šešelj IT-03-67.R77.2-A, 19.05.2010.
Stakić IT-97-24-A, 22.03.2006.
Vasiljević IT-98-32-A, 25.02.2004.

President's Decisions

Bala Decision on Application of Haradin Bala for sentence remission, IT-03-66-ES, 15.10.2010.
Banović Decision of the President on Commutation of Sentence, IT-02-65/1-ES, 03.09.2008.
Delić Decision on Hazim Delić's Motion for Commutation of Sentence, IT-96-21-ES, 24.06.2008 (Public Redacted, 15.07.2008).
Jokić Decision of the President on the Early Release of Vidoje Blagojević, IT-02-06-ES, 13.01.2010.
Josipović Decision of the President on the Application for Pardon or Commutation of Sentence of Drago Josipović, IT-95-16-ES, 30.01.2006.
Kordić Decision of President on Application for Pardon or Commutation of Sentence of Dario Kordić, IT-95-14/2-ES, 13.05.2010.
Krajišnik Decision of President on Early Release of Momcilo Krajišnik, IT-00-39-ES, 26.07.2010.
Krnojelac Decision of the President on the Application for Pardon or Commutation of Sentence of Milorad Krnojelac, IT-97-25-ES, 09.07.2009.
Martinović Decision of the President on the Application for Pardon or Commutation of Sentence of Uinto Martinović, IT-98-34-ES, 22.10.2010.
Plavšić Decision of the President on the Application for Pardon or Commutation of Sentence of Mrs. Biljana Plavšić, IT-00-39&40/1-ES, 14.09.2009.
Radić Decision of President on Application for Pardon or Commutation of Sentence of Mlađo Radić, IT-98-30/1-ES, 23.04.2010.
Rajić Decision of President on Early Release of Ivicia Rajić, IT-95-12-ES, 31.01.2011.

Rajić Decision of President on Early Release of Ivicia Rajić, IT-95-12-ES, 22.08.2011.

Šantić Decision of the President on the Application for Pardon or Commutation of Sentence of Vladimir Šantić, IT-95-16-ES, 16.02.2009.

Simić Decision of President on Early Release of Blagoje Simić, IT-95-9-ES, 15.02.2011.

Šljivančanin Decision of President on Early Release of Veselin Šljivančanin, IT-95-13/1-ES, 05.07.2011.

Stakić Decision of President on Early Release of Milomir Stakić, IT-97-24-ES, 15.07.2011.

Strugar Decision of the President on the Application for Pardon or Commutation of Sentence of Pavle Strugar, IT-01-42-ES, 16.01.2009.

Tadić Decision of the President on the Application for Pardon or Commutation of Sentence of Duško Tadić, IT-94-1-ES, 17.07.2008.

Tadić Decision of the President on the Application for Pardon or Commutation of Sentence of Miroslav Tadić, IT-95-9, 03.11.2004.

Vasiljević Public Redacted Version of President on the Application for Pardon or Commutation of Sentence of Mitar Vasiljević, IT-98-32-ES, 12.03.2010.

Vuković Decision of the President on Commutation of Sentence, IT-96-23&23/1-ES, 11.03.2008.

Zelenović Decision of President on the Application for Pardon or Commutation of Sentence of Dragan Zelenović, IT-96-23/2-ES, 10.06.2010.

Zelenović Decision of President on Early Release of Dragan Zelenović, IT-96-23/2-ES, 21.10.2011.

Žigić Decision of President on Early Release of Zoran Žigić, IT-98-30/1-ES, 08.11.2010.

President's Orders

Furundzija Order of the President on the Application for the Early Release of Anto Furundzija, IT-95–17/1, 29.07.2004.

Landžo Order of the President on Commutation of Sentence, IT-96-21-ES, 13.04.2006 (Public Redacted, 15.07.2008).

Order to the Registrar to Separate Convicted and Non-Convicted Detainees held at the Detention Unit, IT-06-89-Misc.1, 15.06.2006.

Zarić Order of the President on the Application for the Early Release of Simo Zarić, IT-95-9, 21.01.2004.

International Criminal Tribunal for Rwanda

Trial Chamber Judgments

Bikinki ICTR-01-72-T, 02.12.2008.
Bisengimana ICTR-00-60-T, 13.04.2006.
GAA ICTR-07-90-R77-I, 04.12.2007.
Kambanda ICTR-97-23-S, 04.09.1998.
Kamuhanda ICTR-99-54-T, 22.01.2004.
Kayishema and Ruzindara ICTR-95-1-T, 21.05.1999.
Mrđa IT-02-59-S, 31.03.2004.
Ntakirutimana ICTR-96-10 & ICTR-96-17-T, 21.2.2003.
Nzabirinda ICTR-01-77-T, 23.02.2007.
Rugambarara ICTR-00-59-T, 16.11.2007.
Ruggiu ICTR-97-32-I, 01.06.2000.
Rutaganda ICTR-96-3-T, 06.12.1999.
Rutaganira ICTR-95-IC-T, 14.03.2005.
Serugendo ICTR-05-84-I, 12.06.2006.
Serushago ICTR-98-39-S, 05.02.1999.

Trial Chamber Decisions

Serugendo Decision on Motion for the Partial Enforcement of Sentence, ICTR-2005-84-I, 22.06.2006.

Decision of Trial Chambers Designated Pursuant to Rule 11bis

Bagaragaza Decision on the Prosecutor's motion for Referral to the Kingdom of Norway, ICTR-05-86-R11*bis*, 19.05.2006.
Bagaragaza Decision on the Prosecutor's motion for the Referral of the Indictment to the Kingdom of the Netherlands, ICTR-05-86-R11*bis*, 13.04.2007
Bagaragaza Decision on the Prosecutor's Extremely Urgent Motion for Revocation of the Referral to the Kingdom of the Netherlands, ICTR-05-86-R11*bis*, 17.08.2007.
Bucyibaruta Decision on Prosecutor's Request for Referral of Laurent Bucyibaruta's Indictment to France, ICTR-2005-85-I, 20.11.2007.
Hategekimana Decision on Prosecutor's Request for the Referral of the Case of Ildephonse Hategekimana to Rwanda, ICTR-00-55B-R11*bis*, 19.06.2008.

Kanyarukiga Decision on Prosecutor's Request for Referral to the Republic of Rwanda, ICTR-2002-78-R11*bis*, 06.06.2008.
Munyagishari Decision on Prosecutor's Request for Referral to the Republic of Rwanda, ICTR-2005-89-R11*bis*, 06.06.2012.
Munyeshyaka Decision on the Prosecutor's Request for Referral of Wenceslas Munyeshyaka's Indictment to France, ICTR-05-87-I, 20.11.2007.
Uwinkindi Decision on Prosecutor's Request for Referral to the Republic of Rwanda, ICTR-2001-75-R11*bis*, 28.06.2011.

Appeal Chamber's Decisions

Bagaragaza Decision on Rule11*bis* Appeal, ICTR-05-86-AR11*bis*, 30.08.2006.
Rutaganira Decision on Appeal of Decision of the President on Early Release, ICTR-95-IC-AR, 24.08.2006.
Uwinkindi Decision on Uwinkindi's Appeal against the Referral of his Case to Rwanda and Related Motions, ICTR-01-75-AR11*bis*, 16.12.2011.

President's Decisions

Bagaragaza Decision on the Early Release of Michel Bagaragaza, ICTR-05-86-S, 24.10.2011.
Ngeze Decision on Hassan Ngeze's Application for Review of the Registrar's Decision of 12 January 2005, ICTR-1999-52-A, 14.09.2005.
Rugambarara Decision on the Early Release of Juvénal Rugambarara, ICTR-00-59, 08.02.2012.
Ruggiu Decision on the Application for Early Release of Georges Ruggiu, ICTR-97-32-S, 12.05.2005.
Ruggiu Decision on the Enforcement of Sentence, ICTR-97-32-A26, 13.02.2008.
Rutaganira Decision on Request for Early Release, ICTR-95-IC-T, 02.06.2006.

President's Orders

Uwinkindi Order on the ICTR Monitoring Arrangements and Annex A *Guidelines on Monitoring Trials Referred to National Jurisdictions under Rule11bis by ICTR Staff Monitors*, ICTR-01-75R11*bis*, 29.06.2012.

Special Court for Sierra Leone

Trial Chamber Judgments

Brima, Kamara and Kanu SCSL-04-16-T, 19.07.2007.
Fofana and Kondewa SCSL-04-14-J, 09.10.2007.
Taylor SCSL-03-01-T, 30.05.2012.

Trial Chamber Decisions

Bockavic Withdrawal of Indictment, SCSL-03-04-PT, 08.12.2003.
Norman Decision on the Registrar's Submission of Evidence of Death of Accused Samuel Hinga Norman and Consequential Issues, SCSL-040140T-776, 21.05.2007.
Sankoh Withdrawal of Indictment, SCSL-03-02-PT-054, 08.12.2003.

Appeal Chamber Judgments

Brima, Kamara and Kanu SCSL-04-16-A, 22.02.2008.
Fofana and Kondewa SCSL-04-14-A, 28.05.2008.

International Criminal Court

Situation in the DRC in the Case of the Prosecutor v. Thomas Lubanga Dyilo Decision establishing the principles and procedures to be applied to reparations, TCI, ICC-01/04-01/06-2904, 07.08.2012.
Situation in the DRC in the Case of the Prosecutor v. Thomas Lubanga Dyilo Decision on Sentence Pursuant to Article 76 of the Statute, TCI, ICC-01/04-01/06, 10.07.2012.
Situation in the DRC in the Case of the Prosecutor v. Callixte Mbarushimana Decision on the confirmation of charges PTCI, ICC-01/04-01/10-465-Red, 16.12.2011.
Situation in the DRC in the Case of the Prosecutor v. Germain Katanga and Mathieu Ngudjolo Chui, Status Conference TCII, ICC-01-04-01/07-T-258, 12.05.2011.

European Commission of Human Rights

Hess v. United Kingdom Decision on the Admissibility of Application (6231/73) 28.05.1975.
Kotalla v. Netherlands No. 7994/77, 06.05.1978, DR 14.

European Court of Human Rights

Ciorap v. *Moldova* [2007] ECHR (12066/02) 19.06.2007.
Farbtuhs v. *Latvia* [2004] ECHR (4672/02) 02.12.2004.
Ireland v. *United Kingdom* (1979–80) 2 EHRR 25 (5310/71) 18.01.1978.
I.T. v. *Romania* (40155/02) 24.11.2005.
James, Wells and Lee v. *United Kingdom* (25119/09, 57715/09 and 57877/09), 18.09.2012.
Juhnke v. *Turkey* (52515/99) ECHR 13.05.2008.
Keenan v. *United Kingdom* (27229/95) ECHR 2001-III, 03.04.2001.
Khudobin v. *Russia* (59696/00) (2006) ECHR 898, 26.10.2006.
Martinelli v. *Italy* (22682/02) ECHR 2002-III, 16.06.2005.
Matencio v. *France* (58749/00) 15.01.2004.
Mathew v. *Netherlands* (24919/03) (2006) 43 EHRR 23, 29.09.2005.
Matthews v. *United Kingdom* [GC](24833/94) (1999) 28 EHRR 361, 18.02.1999.
Nevmerzhitsky v. *Ukraine* (54825/00) (2006) 43 EHRR 32, 05.04.2005.
Paladi v. *Moldova* [2007] ECHR (39806/05) 10.07.2007.
Popov v. *Russia* (26853/04) 13.07.2006.
Rehbock v. *Slovenia* (29462/95) 28.11.2000.
Rodić and 3 Others v. *Bosnia-Herzegovina* (22893/05) 27.05.2008.
Sakkopoulos v. *Greece* (61828/00) 15.01.2004.
Sarban v. *Moldova* (3456/05) 04.10.2005.
Tarariyeva v. *Russia* (4353/03) 14.12.2006.
Vincent v. *France* (6253/03) 24.10.2006.
Waite and Kennedy v. *Germany* (26083/94) 18.02.1999.
Yakovenko v. *Ukraine* (15825/06) 25.10.2007.
Yildirim v. *Turkey* (2778/02) 03.05.2007.
Yildiz v. *Turkey* (22913/04) 10.11.2005.

African Court of Human and Peoples' Rights

Femi Falana v. *The African Union* (Application No. 001/2011) 26.06.2012.

USA

Koki Hirota v. *General of the Army MacArthur*, 338 US 197 (1948).

OFFICIAL DOCUMENTS, TREATIES, RESOLUTIONS AND REPORTS

International Criminal Tribunal for the former Yugoslavia

Practice Direction on the Procedure for the Determination of Applications for Pardon, Commutation of Sentence and Early Release of Persons Convicted by the International Tribunal, IT/146/Rev.3, 16.09.2010.

Practice Direction on the Procedure for the International Tribunal's Designation of the State in which a Convicted Person is to Serve his/her Sentence of Imprisonment, Rev.1, 01.09.2009.

Regulations to Govern the Supervision of Visits to and Communications with the Detainees, IT/98/REV.3.

Regulations for the Establishment of a Complaints Procedure for Detainees, IT/96, 04.1995.

Regulations for the Establishment of a Disciplinary Procedure for Detainees, IT/97, 04.1995.

Rules of Procedure and Evidence, IT/32/Rev. 44, 10.12.2009.

Rules Governing the Detention of Persons awaiting Trial or Appeal before the Tribunal or otherwise Detained on the Authority of the Tribunal, Rev.9, 21.07.2005.

Statute, adopted by SCRes. 827, 25.05.1993 and amended by Resolutions 1166(1998), 1329(2000), 1411(2002), 1431(2002), 1481(2003), 1597 (2005), 1660(2006), 1837(2008), 1877(2009).

Voluntary Protest Fasts – Information for Detainees, UNDU Policy Doc. No. 090325.

Bilateral agreements

Agreement between the Government of the Italian Republic and the UN on the Enforcement of Sentences of the ICTY, 06.02.1997.

Agreement between the Government of Norway and the UN on the Enforcement of Sentences of the ICTY, 24.04.1998.

Agreement between the Government of the Republic of Estonia and the UN on the Enforcement of Sentences of the ICTY, 11.02.2008.

Agreement between the Government of the Republic of Poland and the UN on the Enforcement of Sentences of the ICTY, 18.09.2008.

Agreement between the ICTY and the Federal Government of Germany re Dragoljub Kunarac, 14.11.2002.

Agreement between the ICTY and the Federal Government of Germany re Duško Tadić, 17.10.2000.

Agreement between the ICTY and the Federal Government of Germany re Johan Tarčulovski, 16.06.2011.

Agreement between the ICTY and the Federal Government of Germany re Stanislav Galić, 16.12.2008.

Agreement between the ICTY and the Government of Finland on the Enforcement of Sentences of the International Tribunal, 07.05.1997.

Agreement between the ICTY and the Ministry of Justice of the Kingdom of the Netherlands on Matters relating to Security and Order of the Leased Premises within the Penitentiary Complex, 14.07.1994.

Agreement between the Slovak Republic and the UN on the Enforcement of Sentences imposed by the ICTY, 17.04.2008.

Agreement between the UN and the Federal Government of Austria on the Enforcement of Sentences of the ICTY, 23.07.1998.

Agreement between the UN and the Government of the French Republic on the Enforcement of Sentences of the ICTY, 25.02.2000.

Agreement between the UN and the Government of the Kingdom of Belgium on the Enforcement of Sentences handed down by the ICTY, 02.05.2007.

Agreement between the UN and the Government of Sweden on the Enforcement of Sentences of the ICTY, 23.03.1999.

Agreement between the UN and the Government of the United Kingdom of Great Britain and Northern Ireland on the Enforcement of Sentences of the ICTY, 11.03.2004.

Agreements between the UN and the Kingdom of Denmark on the Enforcement of Sentences of the ICTY, 04.06.2002.

Agreement between the UN and the Kingdom of the Netherlands concerning the Headquarters of the ICTY, Letter from the Secretary-general addressed to the President of the Security Council, 14.07.1994.

Agreement between the UN and the Kingdom of Spain on the Enforcement of Sentences of the ICTY, 28.03.2000.

Agreement between the UN and the Portuguese Republic on the Enforcement of Sentences of the ICTY, 19.12.2007.

Agreement between the UN and the Republic of Albania on the Enforcement of Sentences of the ICTY, 19.09.2008.
Agreement between the UN and Ukraine on the Enforcement of Sentences of the ICTY, 17.08.2007.
Appointment of Inspecting Authority for the Detention Unit, Exchange of Letters between the President of the ICTY and the President of the ICRC, 28.04.1995.
Letter of Agreement between the ICTY and the Ministry of Justice of the Netherlands regarding the Loan of Prison Staff to the International Criminal Tribunal, UN Treaty Series, Vol. 2023, I-34917, 20.10.97.
Letter from the Registrar of the ICTY to the President of the CPT and the Secretary General of the Council of Europe, Appendix Five, 11th General Report of the CPT, CPT/Inf (2001)16, 07.11.2000.

Annual reports

First Annual Report, A/49/342, 29.08.1994.
Third Annual Report, A/51/292, 16.08.1996.
Sixth Annual Report, A/54/187, 25.08.1999.
Eleventh Annual Report, A/59/215, 16.08.2004.
Eighteenth Annual Report, A/66/210, 31.07.2011.

Other reports

Assessment and Report of Judge Patrick Robinson, President of the International Tribunal for the Former Yugoslavia, provided to the Security Council pursuant to Paragraph 6 of Security Council Resolution 1534(2004), Covering the Period from 15 May to 15 November 2011, S/2011/716, 16.11.2011.
ICTY Manual on Developed Practices (Turin: UNICRCI, 2009).
Independent Audit of the Detention Unit at the ICTY, 2006.
Joint Paper of the International Criminal tribunals for the former Yugoslavia and Rwanda *The Legacies and Residual Functions of the Ad Hoc Tribunals*, 30.03.2007.
Judge Parker, Report to the President on the Death of Milan Babić, 08.06.2006.
Judge Parker, Report to the President on the Death of Slobodan Milošević, May 2006.

Judge Rodrigues, Report on the Findings of the Inquiry into the Circumstances Surrounding the Death of Dr. Milan Kovačević, 27.08.1998.
Judge Rodrigues, Report on the Finding of the Inquiry into Mr Dokmanovic's Death, 21.07.1998.

Guilty plea statements

Predrag Banović, 03.09.2003 at www.icty.org/sid/209.
Milan Babić, 27.01.2004 at www.icty.org/sid/208.
Miroslav Bralo, 07.10.2005 at www.icty.org/sid/227.
Ranko Češić, 27.11.2003 at www.icty.org/sid/210.
Miroslav Deronjić, 28.01.2004 at www.icty.org/sid/239.
Damir Došen, 08.10.2001 at www.icty.org/sid/205.
Dražen Erdemović, 20.11.1996 at www.icty.org/sid/212.
Miodrag Jokić, 04.12.2003 at www.icty.org/sid/213.
Dragan Kolundžija, 09.10.2001 at www.icty.org/sid/214.
Darko Mrđa, 22.10.2003 at www.icty.org/sid/216.
Dragan Nikolić, 06.11.2003 at www.icty.org/sid/217.
Momir Nikolić, 29.10.2003 at www.icty.org/sid/218.
Dragan Obrenović, 30.10.2003 at www.icty.org/sid/219.
Biljana Plavšić, 17.12.2002 at www.icty.org/sid/221.
Ivica Rajić, 07.04.2006 at www.icty.org/sid/222.
Duško Sikirica, 08.10.2001 at www.icty.org/sid/223.
Milan Simić, 22.07.2002 at www.icty.org/sid/224.
Stevan Todorović, 04.05.2001 at www.icty.org/sid/225.

Press releases

"Completion of the Internal Inquiry into the Death of Slavko Dokmanovic", CC/PIU/334-E, 23.07.1998.
"OHR-ICTY Working Group on the Development of BiH Capacity for War-Crime Trials Successfully Completed", OHR/P.I.S./731e, 21.02.2003.
"Open Letter from the Detainees regarding their Conditions at the ICTY's Detention Unit", CC/PIU/339-E, 12.08.1998.
"*Stevan Todorovic* Case: President of the Tribunal Grants Request for Commutation of Sentence", JP/MOW/984e, 29.06.2005.

ICTY website

Capacity Building at www.icty.org/sections/Outreach/CapacityBuilding.
ICTY Outreach Activities 2009 at www.icty.org/sid/10596.
The Cost of Justice at www.icty.org/sid/325.

International Criminal Tribunal for Rwanda

Practice Procedure for the Designation of the State in which a Convicted Person is to serve his/her sentence of imprisonment, 23.09.2008.

Rules Governing the Detention of Persons Awaiting Trial or Appeal Before the Tribunal or Otherwise Detained on the Authority of the Tribunal, 05.06.1998.

Rules of Procedure and Evidence, adopted 29.06.1995, last revision, 01.10.2009.

Statute, adopted by SCRes 955(1994), amended by Resolutions 1165 (1998), 1329(2000), 1411(2002), 1431(2002), 1503(2003), 1512 (2003), 1534(2004), 1684(2006) and 1717(2006).

Bilateral agreements

Accord entre le Gouvernment de la Republique Française et l'organisation des Nations Unies concernant l'exécution des peines prononcées par la Tribunal Pénal International pour le Rwanda, 14.03.2003.

Agreement between the Government of the Republic of Benin and the UN on the Enforcement of Sentences of the ICTR, 26.08.1999.

Agreement between the Government of the Republic of Mali and the UN on the Enforcement of Sentences of the ICTR, 12.02.1999.

Agreement between the Government of the Republic of Rwanda and the UN on the Enforcement of Sentences of the ICTR, 04.03.2008.

Agreement between the Government of the Republic of Senegal and the UN on the Enforcement of Sentences Pronounced by the ICTR, 22.11.2010.

Agreement between the Italian Republic and the UN on the Enforcement of Sentences of the ICTR, 17.03.2004.

Agreement between the Kingdom of Swaziland and the UN on the Enforcement of Sentences of the ICTR, 30.08.2000.

Agreement between the UN and the Government of Sweden on the Enforcement of Sentences of the ICTR, 21.04.2004.

Agreement between the UN and the United Republic of Tanzania concerning the Headquarters of the International Tribunal for Rwanda, 31.08.1995, Annex to ICTR First Annual Report, A/51/399, 24.09.1996.

Annual reports

First Annual Report, A/51/399, 24.09.1996.
Second Annual Report, A/52/582, 13.11.1997.
Third Annual Report, A/53/429, 23.09.1998.
Fourth Annual Report, A/54/315, 07.09.1999.
Fifth Annual Report, A/55/435, 02.10.2000.
Sixth Annual Report, A/56/351, 14.09.2001.
Fifteenth Annual Report, A/65/188, 30.07.2010.
Sixteenth Annual Report, A/66/209, 29.07.2011.

Other reports

Report of the Proceedings of the Colloquium of Prosecutors of the International Criminal Tribunals on The Challenges of International Criminal Justice, 25–27.11.2004, at www.unictr.org/Portals/0/English%5CNews%5Cevents%5CNov2004%5Cfinal_report.pdf.

Press releases

"Accused Joseph Nzirorera Dies", ICTR/INFO-9-2-646.EN, 01.07.2010.
"Appeal's Chamber Dismisses Uwinkindi's Motion for Stay of Transfer to Rwanda", ICTR/INFO-9-2-710.EN, 19.04.2012.
"Bishop Samuel Musabyimana Dies", ICTR/INFO-9-2-330.EN, 24.01.2003.
"Decisions in Fulgence Kayishema and Jean Uwinkindi Cases Made – Tribunal Refers Case of Kayishema to Rwanda – Tribunal Stays Transfer of Uwinkindi to Rwanda Pending Establishment of Suitable Monitoring Mechanism", ICTR/INFO-9-2-702.EN, 27.02.2012.
"Elizaphan Ntakirutimana Released After Serving Sentence", ICTR/INFO-9-2-502.EN, 06.12.2006.
"Former Prime Minister and Five Other Convicts Sent to Prison in Mali", ICTR/INFO-9-2-296.EN, 11.12.2001.
"Georges Omar Ruggiu Transferred to Italy", ICTR/INFO-9-2-555.EN, 29.02.2008.

"ICTR Hands Over Armoured Truck to Tanzania Prison Services", ICTR/INFO-9-2-691.EN, 11.10.2011.

"More ICTR Convicts Transferred to Mali and Benin to Serve their Sentences", ICTR/INFO-9-2-726.EN, 03.07.2012.

"Nine ICTR Convicts Transferred to Benin", ICTR/INFO-9-2-601.EN, 30.06.2009.

"Prisoner Joseph Serugendo Dies", ICTR/INFO-9-2-488.EN, 22.08.2006.

"Registrar Directed to Immediately Resume Discussions with ACHPR", ICTR/INFO-9-2-709.EN, 10.04.2012.

"Rwanda signs Agreement on Enforcement of ICTR Sentences", ICTR/INFO-9-2-557.EN, 05.03.2008.

"Vincent Rutaganira Released After Completing his Sentence", ICTR/INFO-9-2-556.EN, 03.03.2008.

ICTR website

Amoussouga, R., "The ICTR's Challenges in the Relocation of Acquitted Persons, Released Prisoners and Protected Witnesses", Presented at the Forum between Offices of the Prosecutors of UN Ad Hoc Criminal Tribunals and National Prosecuting Authorities, Arusha, Tanzania, 26–28.11.08, at www.unictr.org/News/tabid/192/P/70/Default.aspx.

Status of Detainees at www.unictr.org/cases/tabid/202/Default.aspx.

Special Court for Sierra Leone

Agreement between the UN and the Goverment of Sierra Leone on the Establishment of a Special Court for Sierra Leone, 16.01.2002, with annex, Statute of the Special Court for Sierra Leone.

Practice Direction for Designation for State for Enforcement of Sentence, 10.07.2009.

Rules Governing the Detention of Persons Awaiting Trial or Appeal before the SCSL or Otherwise Detained under the Authority of the SCSL, adopted 07.03.2003, last amended 14.05.2005.

Rules of Procedure and Evidence, adopted 16.01.2002, last amended on 31.05.2012.

Bilateral Agreements

Agreement between the SCSL and the Government of Finland on the Enforcement of Sentences of the SCSL, 29.06.2009.

Agreement between the SCSL and the Government of Sweden on the Enforcement of Sentences of the SCSL, 15.10.2004.

Agreement between the SCSL and the Government of the United Kingdom of Great Britain and Northern Ireland on the Enforcement of Sentences of the SCSL, 09.07.2007.

Amended Agreement between the SCSL and the Government of the Republic of Rwanda on the Enforcement of Sentences of the SCSL, 18.03.2009.

Headquarters Agreement Between the Republic of Sierra Leone and the Special Court for Sierra Leone, 21.10.2003.

Memorandum of Understanding concerning the Secondment of Sierra Leone Prison Service Staff to the Special Court for Sierra Leone.

Memorandum of Understanding between The Choithram Charities Trust and the SCSL, 27.03.2006.

Annual Reports

First Annual Report, 2002–3.
Third Annual Report, 2005–6.
Fourth Annual Report, 2006–7.
Fifth Annual Report, 2007–8.
Sixth Annual Report, 2009–10.
Ninth Annual Report, 2011–12.

Other reports

Cassese, A., Report on the Special Court for Sierra Leone, 12.12.2006, at www.sc-sl.org/LinkClick.aspx?fileticket=VTDHyrHasLc=&tabid=176.

Comprehensive Report of the SCSL Residual Issues Expert Group Meeting, Freetown, 20–21.02.2008.

SCSL Budget 2005–6, at www.law.case.edu/grotian-moment-blog/documents/20071012_Budget_of_the_SCSL_2005–2006.pdf.

SCSL Completion Strategy, June 2009, at www.sc-sl.org/LinkClick.aspx?fileticket=yiUyKldb3OY%3D&tabid=53.

Registry press releases

"Autopsy Shows Sam Hinga Norman Died of Natural Causes", 28.03.2007.

"Body of Sam Hinga Norman Handed Over to Family", 07.03.2007.
"Charles Taylor Convicted on All II Courts", 26.04.2012.
"Charles Taylor Sentenced to 50 Years in Prison", 30.05.2012.
"Detainees Claim to be on Hunger Strike", 27.05.2003.
"Eric Koi Senessie Sentenced to Two Years in Prison for Contempt of the Special Court", 05.07.2012.
"Four Sentenced for Interference in the Administration of Justice", 11.10.2012.
"Inquiry finds Special Court Provided Proper Care to Hinga Norman", 16.07.2007.
"Mongolian Peacekeepers Take Over Security at Special Court", 08.01.2006.
"No Country Found to Take Sankoh for Medical Treatment", 11.06.2003.
"Prison Officers Recognised by Special Court", 04.02.2008.
"Registrar Announces Death of Foday Sankoh", 30.07.2003.
"Sankoh Needs Further Evaluation", 21.03.2003.
"Special Court Concludes Enforcement Agreement with Rwanda", 20.03.2009.
"Special Court Hands over Detention Facility to the Government of Sierra Leone", 16.11.2009.
"Special Court Prisoners Transferred to Rwanda to Serve Their Sentences", 31.10.2009.
"Status of Detention of the Accused", 07.04.2003.

International Criminal Court

ICC Detention Centre, Complaints Procedure: Guide for Detained Persons.
Regulations of the Court, ICC-BD/01.01.04, 26.05.2004.
Regulations of the Registry, ICC-BD/03-01-06- Rev.1, 25.09.2006.
Regulations of the Trust Fund for Victims, ICC-ASP/4/Res.3, 03.12.2005.
Rome Statute, A/CONF.183.9, 17.07.1998.
Rules of Procedure and Evidence, ICC-ASP/1/3, 09.09.2002.

Bilateral agreements

Accord entre la Cour penale internationale et le Gouvernement de la Republique du Mali concernant l'execution des peines prononcees par la Cour, ICC/PRES/11-01-12, 13.01.2012.

Agreement between the Government of the United Kingdom of Great Britain and Northern Ireland and the International Criminal Court on the Enforcement of Sentences Imposed by the International Criminal Court, ICC-PRES/04-01-07, 08.11.2007.

Agreement between the International Criminal Court and the Federal Government of Austria on the Enforcement of Sentences of the International Criminal Court, ICC-PRES/01-01-05, 27.10.2005.

Agreement between the International Criminal Court and the Government of the Republic of Finland on the Enforcement of Sentences of the International Criminal Court, ICC-PRES/07-01-11, 24.04.2011.

Agreement between the International Criminal Court and the Kingdom of Belgium on the Enforcement of Sentences of the International Criminal Court, ICC-PRES/06-01-10, 01.06.2010.

Agreement between the International Criminal Court and the International Committee of the Red Cross on Visits to Persons Deprived of Liberty Pursuant to the Jurisdiction of the ICC, ICC-PRES/02-01-06, 29.03.2006.

Agreement between the Kingdom of Denmark and the International Criminal Court on the Enforcement of Sentences of the International Criminal Court, ICC-PRES/12-02-12, 05.07.2012.

Agreement between the Republic of Serbia and the International Criminal Court on the Enforcement of Sentences of the International Criminal Court, ICC-PRES/09-03-11, 28.05.2011.

Agreement on the Privileges and Immunities of the International Criminal Court, ICC-ASP/1/3, 2002.

Headquarters Agreement between the International Criminal Court and the Host State, ICC-BD/04-01-08, 07.06.2007.

Negotiated Relationship Agreement between the International Criminal Court and the United Nations, ICC-ASP/3/Res.1, 04.10.2004.

Assembly of State Parties reports

Corrigendum to the Proposed Programme Budget for 2010 for the ICC, ICC-ASP/8/10/Corr.1, 07.10.2009.

Report of the Bureau on the Establishment of an Independent Oversight Mechanism, ICC-ASP/8/2, 15.04.2009.

Report of the Bureau on Family Visits for Detainees, ICC-ASP/8/42, 29.10.2009.

Report of the Bureau on the Review Conference, ICC-ASP/8/43, 15.11.2009.
Report of the Court on the Financial Aspects of Enforcing the Court's Obligation to Fund Family Visits to Indigent Detained Persons, ICC-ASP/8/9, 06.05.2009.
Report of the Seventh Session of the Assembly of State Parties, ICC-ASP/7/20, 14–24.11.2008.
Report of the Working Group of the Review Conference, ICC-ASP/8/20.

Assembly of State Parties resolutions

Cooperation, ICC-ASP/8/Res.2, 26.11.2009.
Cooperation, ICC-ASP/10/Res.2, 20.11.2011.
Establishment of an Independent Oversight Mechanism, ICC-ASP/8/Res.1, 26.11.2009.
Family visits for Indigent Detainees, ICC-ASP/8/Res.4, 26.11.2009.
Independent Oversight Mechanism, ICC-ASP/9/Res.5, 10.12.2010.
Permanent Premises, ICC-ASP/8/Res.5, 26.11.2009.
Programme Budget for 2011, the Working Capital Fund for 2011, Scale of Assessments for the Apportionment of Expenses of the ICC, Financing Appropriations for 2011 and the Contingency Fund, ICC-ASP/9/Res.4, 10.12.2010.
Reparations, ICC-ASP/10/Res.3, 20.12.2011.

Miscellaneous

Norway: Proposal of Amendment, CN713.2009.TREATIES-4, 29.10.2009.
Review Conference Resolution, Strengthening the Enforcement of Sentences, Resolution RC/Res.3, 08.06.2010.
Trust Fund for Victims, Programme Progress Report, Summer 2012.

Press releases

"ICC Hosts Welcome Ceremony Honouring Guatemala as a New State Party", ICC-CPI-20120713-PR826, 13.07.2012.
"ICC Prosecutor Fatou Bensouda on the Malian State Referral of the Situation in Mali since January 2012", ICC-OTP-20120718-PR829, 18.07.2012.

Mechanism for the International Criminal Tribunals

Practice Direction on the Procedure for Designation of the State in which a Convicted Person is to Serve his or her Sentence of Imprisonment, MICT/2, 05.07.2012.

Practice Direction on the Procedure for the Determination of Applications for Pardon, Commutation of Sentence and Early Release of Persons Convicted by the ICTR, the ICTY or the Mechanism, MICT/3, 05.07.2012.

Rules of Procedure and Evidence, MICT/1, 08.06.2012.

Statute of the International Residual Mechanism for Criminal Tribunals, Annex 1, S/RES/1966 (2010), 22.12.2010.

Transitional Arrangements, Annex 2, S/RES/1966 (2010), 22.12.2010.

Special Tribunal for Lebanon

Rules of Procedure and Evidence, STL/BD/2009/01/Rev.4, adopted 20.03.2009, last amended 08.02.2012.

Statute of the Special Tribunal for Lebanon, Agreement between the United Nations and the Lebanese Republic on the establishment of a Special Tribunal for Lebanon, Annex S/RES/1757 (2007), 30.05.2007.

United Nations

Multilateral conventions

Convention on the Privileges and Immunities of the United Nations, GARes 22(I)A, adopted 13.02.1946, entered into force 17.09.1946.

Convention on the Rights of the Child, GARes 44/25, adopted 20.11.1989, entered into force 02.09.1990.

International Covenant on Civil and Political Rights, GARes 2200A (XXI), adopted 16.12.1966, entered into force 23.03.1976.

International Covenant of Economic and Social Rights, GARes 2200A (XXI), adopted 16.12.1966, entered into force 03.01.1976.

Optional Protocol to the Convention Against Torture, GARes 57/199, adopted 18.02.2002, entered into force 22.06.2006.

Statute of the International Court of Justice, Annex United Nations Charter, 26.06.1945.

Security Council Resolutions

SCRes 827(1993) Tribunal (Former Yugoslavia) 25.05.1993.
SCRes 955(1994) on the Establishment of an International Tribunal and adoption of the Statute of the Tribunal, 08.11.1994.
SCRes 1315(2000) on the situation in Sierra Leone, 14.08.2000.
SCRes 1411(2002) ICTY and ICTR, 17.05.2002.
SCRes 1503(2003) ICTY and ICTR, 23.08.2003.
SCRes 1534(2004) ICTY and ICTR, 26.03.2004.
SCRes 1562(2004) The Situation in Sierra Leone, 17.09.2004.
SCRes 1688(2006) The Situation in Sierra Leone, 16.06.2006.
SCRes. 1757 (2007) The Situation in the Middle East, 30.05.2007.
SCRes 1966(2010) ICTY and ICTR, 22.12.2010.

Security Council (other)

Letter from the President of the ICTR to the President of the Security Council, S/2009/587, 12.11.2009.
Letter from the President of the ICTY to the President of the Security Council, S/2009/589, 13.11.2009.
Provisional Record of the Security Council's 3175th Meeting, S/PV. 3175, 22.02.1993.
Provisional Records of the Security Council's 3453rd Meeting, S/PV.3453, 08.11.1994.
Statement by the President of the Security Council on the ICTR, S/PRST/2003/18, 27.10.2003.
Statement by the President of the Security Council on the ICTY, S/PRST/2002/21, 23.07.2002.

General Assembly Resolutions

Affirmation of the Principles of International Law Recognised by the Charter of the Nurnberg Tribunal, GARes 95(I), 11.12.1946.
Basic Principles for the Treatment of Prisoners, GARes 45/111, 14.12.1990.
Body of Principles for the Protection of All Persons Detained Under Any Form of Detention or Imprisonment, GARes 43/173, 09.12.1988.
Establishment of an International Criminal Court, GARes 49/53, 09.12.1994.

Establishment of an International Criminal Court, GARes 50/46, 11.12.1995.
Financing of the ICTR, GARes 57/289, 12.02.2003.
International Residual Mechanism for Criminal Tribunals, GARes 66/240, 16.02.2012.
Khmer Rouge Trials, GARes 57/228B, 13.05.2005.
Model Agreement on the Transfer of Foreign Prisoners and Recommendations on the Treatment of Foreign Prisoners, GARes 40/32, 29.11.1985.
Principles of Medical Ethics, GARes 37/194, 18.12.1982.
The Situation in Bosnia-Herzegovina, GARes 51/203, 17.12.1996
Universal Declaration of Human Rights, GARes 217A (III), UN DocA/810 at 71 (1948), 10.12.1948.

General Assembly (other)

Report of the Advisory Committee on Administrative and Budgetary Questions, A/57/593, 07.11.2008.

International Law Commission

Draft Statute for an International Criminal Court, 1994 UNGA 49th Session, Supp No 10, A/49/10.
Responsibility of States for Internationally Wrongful Acts, 2001, Annex, GARes 56/83, 12.12.2001, corrected by A/56/49(Vol. I)/Corr.4.
Draft Articles on the Responsibility of International Organizations, with Commentaries, 2011, UNGA 66th Session, Supp No 10, A/66/10.

Preparatory Committee on the Establishment of an International Criminal Court

Report of the Preparatory Committee on the Establishment of an International Criminal Court, GA, 51st Session, Supp No 22, A/51/22, 1996.
Report of the Preparatory Committee on the Establishment of an International Criminal Court, A/Conf. 183/2/Add.1, 14.04.1998.

Other

Official Records of the UN Diplomatic Conference of Plenipotentiaries on the Establishment of an International Criminal Court, Rome, 15.6.1998–17.7.1998, Vol. II, Summary Records of the Plenary Meetings and of the Meetings of the Committee of the Whole, A/CONF.183/13 (Vol.II).

Secretary-General Reports

Report of the Secretary-General on the Establishment of a Special Court for Sierra Leone, S/2000/915, 04.10.2000.

Report of the Secretary-General on the Long-term Financial Obligations of the UN with regard to the Enforcement of Sentences, A/57/347, 26.08.2002.

Report of the Secretary-General pursuant to Para. 2 of Security Council Resolution 808(1993) S/25704, 03.05.1993.

Report of the Secretary-General on the Administrative and Budgetary Aspects of the Options for Possible Locations for the Archives of the ICTY and ICTR and the Seat of the Residual Mechanism(s) for the Tribunals, S/2009/258, 21.05.2009.

Secretary-General (other)

President Kabbah's letter to the UN Secretary-General, UN Doc S/2000/786, 12.06.2000.

Ecosoc

Special Procedures Joint Report on the Situation of Detainees at Guantánamo Bay, UN Doc E/CN.4/2006/120, 27.02.2006.

UN Standard Minimum Rules for the Treatment of Prisoners, ECOSOC Resolutions 663 C (XXIV) 31.07.1957 and 2067 (LXII) 13.05.1977.

Human Rights Committee

General Comment 9 on Article 10 ICCPR (16th Session, 30.07.1982) UN Doc HRI/GEN/1/Rev.1 at 9, 1994.

General Comment 21 on Article 10 ICCPR (44th Session, 10.04.1992) UN Doc HRI/GEN/1/Rev.1 at 33, 1994.

Other

Report of the UN High Commissioner for Human Rights, Assistance to Sierra Leone in the Field of Human Rights, A/HRC/13/28, 12.02.2010.

Second Annual Report of the Subcommittee on Prevention of Torture and other Cruel, Inhuman or Degrading Treatment or Punishment, CAT/C/42/2, 07.04.2009.

UNTAET Regulation 2000/15, On the Establishment of Panels with Exclusive Jurisdiction over Serious Criminal Offences, 06.06.2000.

Council of Europe

Conventions

Convention for the Protection of Human Rights and Fundamental Freedoms, CETS No 005, 04.11.1950.

Committee of Ministers Recommendations and Reports

Communication from Bosnia and Herzegovina concerning the case of *Rodić and 3 others against Bosnia and Herzegovina* (Application No. 22893/05) DH – DD(2011) 361, 19.05.2011.

Concerning the Ethical and Organizational Aspects of Health Care in Prison, Rec (1998)7, 08.04.1998.

Conditional Release (Parole), Rec (2003)22, 24.09.2003.

European Prison Rules, Rec (2006)2, 11.01.2006.

Foreign Prisoners, Rec (1984)12, 21.06.1984.

Management by Prison Administrations of Life-Sentence and other Long-Term Prisoners, Rec (2003)23, 09.10.2003.

Committee for the Prevention of Torture Reports

Second General Report, CPT/Inf (92)3.

Third General Report, CPT/Inf (93)12.

Eleventh General Report, CPT/Inf (2001)16.

2004 Report to the Government of Bosnia-Herzegovina, CPT/Inf (2004)40.

2007 Report to the Government of Bosnia-Herzegovina, CPT/Inf (2009)25.

World Medical Association

Declaration of Tokyo: Guidelines for Physicians Concerning Torture and other Cruel, Inhuman or Degrading Treatment or Punishment in Relation to Detention and Imprisonment, May 2006.

Declaration of Malta on Hunger Strikers, adopted Malta, November 1991, revised at 44th WMA Assembly, Marbella, September 1992 and Pilanesburg, SA, October 2006.

International and Regional Treaties

African Charter on Human and Peoples Rights, OAU Doc CAB/LEG/67/3/ rev.5, 21 ILM 58 (1982), 27.06.1981.

League of Nations Convention for the Creation of an International Criminal Court, Doc C.546(I) 1937.

London Agreement for the Prosecution and Punishment of Major War Criminals of the European Axis and Establishing the Charter of the International Military Tribunal, (1951) 82 UNTS 279, 08.08.1945.

Treaty of Sèvres, 10.08.1920.

Treaty of Versailles, 28.06.1919.

National Legislation and Regulations

Belgium

Belgian Ministry of Justice, Office of the Director General of Penitentiary Establishments Circular Instruction, Restorative Justice Consultants, CM 1719, 04.10.2000.

Bosnia-Herzegovina

Agreement Between the High Representative for Bosnia-Herzegovina and Bosnia-Herzegovina on the Establishment of the Registry for Section I for War Crimes and Section II for Organized Crime, Economic Crime and Corruption of the Criminal and Appellate Divisions of the Court of Bosnia-Herzegovina and the Special Department for War Crimes, Organized Crime, Economic Crime and Corruption of the Prosecutor's Office of Bosnia, Law No. 12/04 (Official Gazette 01.12.2004).

Constitution of Bosnia-Herzegovina, at www.ccbh.ba/eng/p_stream.php?kat=518.

Law of the Human Rights Ombudsman of Bosnia-Herzegovina (Official Gazette 22.01.2004)
State Rulebook on Criteria for Placement of Convicted Persons, No 01-02-263/05, 18.06.2005.
The Law of Bosnia-Herzegovina on the Execution of Criminal Sanctions, Detention and Other Measures, Law No. 13/05 (Official Gazette, 2005).

Cambodia

Law on the Establishment of Extraordinary Chambers in the Courts of Cambodia for the Prosecution of Crimes Committed during the Period of Democratic Kampuchea, NS/RKM/1004/006, 27.10.2004.

Croatia

Law on the Application of the Statute of the International Criminal Court and on the Prosecution of Criminal Acts against International Law on War and Humanitarian Law No. 175/2003 *Narodne novine* (Official Gazette of the Republic of Croatia), 04.11.2003.

Serbia

Law on Organisation and Jurisdiction of Government Authorities in Prosecuting Perpetrators of War Crimes, Law No. 67/2003 *Sluzbeni glasnik Republike Srbije* (Official Gazette of the Republic of Serbia), 01.07.2003.

Sierra Leone

Truth and Reconciliation Commission Act, 10.02.2000.

NGO Reports and Papers

Amnesty International

"Bosnia and Herzegovina 'Better Keep Quiet' Ill-Treatment by the Police and in Prisons", EUR/63/001/2008, 07.02.2008, at www.amnesty.org/en/library/info/EUR63/001/2008/en.

"Bosnia and Herzegovina: Stanković Arrest: Victims of War-Time Rape Must Feel Safe to Testify", EUR 63/001/2012, 23.01.2012, at www.amnesty.org/en/library/asset/EUR63/001/2012/en/53336d7d-bc21-48e7-8dfa-ce2f06a47a58/eur630012012en.html.

"Mali: Investigate enforced disappearances, extra-judicial killings and torture of Junta Opponents", 31.07.2012, at www.amnesty.org/en/news/mali-investigate-disappearances-killings-and-torture-junta-opponents-2012-07-31.

"ICC, Concerns at the Seventh Session of the ASP", October 2008, at www.amnesty.org/en/library/info/IOR40/022/2008/en.

International Bar Association

Human Rights Institute Report, The ICC under scrutiny: Assessing Recent Developments at the ICC, November 2008, at www.ibanet.org/Human_Rights_Institute/ICC_Outreach_Monitoring/ICC_IBA_Publications.aspx.

Human Rights Watch

Memorandum for the Seventh Session of the ASP, 07.11.2008, at www.hrw.org/en/node/76652/section/4.

Suggnomè

Aertsen I., "Victim Oriented Work with Offenders Post-sentence: A Restorative Justice Perspective", CEP Workshop, Prague 15–16.5.2003.

Buntinx, K., "Victim Offender Mediation in Severe Crimes", Paper presented at Meeting of the Probation Service and Facing Forward, 30.05.2007.

Van Garsse, L. "Mediation in a Detention Context: Moralisation or participation?", Suggnomè, February 2006.

"The Meaning of Mediation within the Criminal Justice Context: A Few Reflections Based upon Experience", May 2003.

Media and Press Releases

Amoussaga, R. "The UN–Rwanda Prisoner Agreement: The ICTR Replies", *Jurist*, 10.03.2008, at www.jurist.law.pitt.edu/forumy/2008/03/un-rwanda-prisoner-agreement-ictr.php.

Awoko, "Prison Watch Raises Concerns over Prison Water Shortages" 05.09.2008, at www.awoko.org/index.php?mact=News, cntnt01,detail,0&cntnt01articleid=2674&cntnt01returnid=419.
Baxter, J., "War Criminals Stretch Mali's Hospitality", BBC News, 21.03.2002, at www.bbc.co.uk/news/2/hi/africa/1886161.stm.
BBC News, "UK agrees to jail Charles Taylor", 15.06.2006, at www. bbc. co.uk/news/2/hi/africa/5082664.stm.
BBC News, "Three Guilty of Attacking War Criminal Radislav Krstic", 18.02.2011, at www.bbc.co.uk/news/uk-england-bradford-west-yorkshire-12509858.
Hirondelle, "ICTR Detainees Want Commission of Enquiry on Musabyimana's Death", 05.02.2003, at www.hirondellenews.org/ictr-rwanda/373-trials-ended/musabyimana-samuel/19211-en-en-ictr-detainees-want-commission-of-enquiry-on-musabyimanas-death 82628262.
Hirondelle, "Two Rwanda Genocide Convicted Transferred to Mali amid Tight Security", 03.12.2008, at www.hirondellenews.com/ictr-rwanda/ 404-ictr-institutional-news/22605-en-en-031208-maliconvicts-two-rwanda-genocide-convicts-transferred-to-mali-amid-tight-security 1165611656.
Munyaneza, J., "Why Rwanda Wants ICTR Convicts" *The New Times* 05.04.2012, at www.newtimes.co.rw/news/index.php?i=14953&a=52146.
Simpson, G. and M. Daly, "Questions Plague Policeman's Trial", *The Age*, 02.10.2004, at www.theage.com.au/articles/2004/10/01/ 1096527934866.html?from=storylhs#.
Schwarz-Schilling, C., "Stankovic Fiasco Highlights Need for State Prison" 01.06.2007, Office of the High Commissioner Press Release OHR/EUSR/1/6/2007, at www.ohr.int/ohr-dept/presso/pressa/ default.asp?content_id=39888.
Swedish Ministry of Justice "Request for Pardoning Mrs. Biljana Plasvic has been Rejected" 24.06.2007, at www.regeringen.se/sb/d/586/a/81120.
Trbic, N. and D. Dzidic, "Serbs Threaten to Scupper Bosnia's First State Prison", *Balkan Insight*, 21.03.2011, at www.balkaninsight.com/en/ article/serbs-threaten-to-scupper-bosnia-s-first-state-prison.

Web sources

Correctional Services Canada

International Perspectives on Restorative Corrections: A Review of the Literature, 2007, at www.csc-scc.gc.ca/text/rj/litrvw-eng.shtml.

Council of Europe

Mumby-Croft, G., Report of Visit to Prison Establishments in Federation BiH and Republic Srpska on behalf of the Council of Europe to Advise on the Conversion of Dormitory Type Accommodation in to Smaller Units, 2002, at www.coe.ba/pdf/report_of_visit_Graham_eng.pdf.

Joint Programme of Cooperation Between the European Commission and the Council of Europe to assist BiH in fulfilling Post Accession Commitments and Developing and Maintaining Democratic Institutions, 27.10.2004, at www.jp.coe.int/Upload/17_BiHDetailed Description_E.pdf.

Economic and Social Research Council

Research Ethics Framework, at www.esrc.ac.uk/about-esrc/information/research-ethics.aspx.

International Committee of the Red Cross

Stillhart, D., "Confidentiality: Key to the ICRC's Work but Not Unconditional", 20.09.2010, at www.icrc.org/Web/Eng/siteeng0.nsf/html/confidentiality-interview-010608.

"Colombia: People Deprived of their Liberty in State Detention Facilities", 18.04.2012, at www.icrc.org/eng/resources/documents/feature/2012/colombia-report-2011-detention.htm.

International Law Association

International Law Association, Berlin Conference (2004) Accountability of International Organisations, Final Report, at www.ila-hq.org/en/committees/index.cfm/cid/9.

John Jay College of Criminal Justice

Culp, R., "Enforcement and Monitoring of Sentences in the Modern War Crimes Process: Equal Treatment before the Law?" Lecture, Human Rights Seminar Series 2010–11, 07.04.2011, at www.jjay.cuny.edu/Culp_MonitoringTribunalPunishment_rev_9Apr11_1_.pdf.

OFFICIAL DOCUMENTS, TREATIES, RESOLUTIONS, REPORTS 399

Ministry of Justice, Bosnia-Herzegovina

Bosnia-Herzegovina Justice Sector Reform Strategy, 2008–12, at www.mpr.gov.ba/userfiles/file/Projekti/24__SRSP_u_BiH_-_EJ.pdf.

Organisation for Security and Cooperation in Europe

Permanent Council Decision No 673, Cooperation between the OSCE and the ICTY, PC. DEC/673, 19.05.2005.

Sixth Report in the Case of Convicted Person Radovan Stanković, Transferred to the State Court pursuant to Rule 11*bis*, June 2007, at www.oscebih.org/documents/14067-eng.pdf.

Swedish Prison and Probation Service

Johnson, A. K., "Foreign Prisoners in European Penitentiary Institutions", National Report Sweden 2006, at www.kriminalvarden.se/upload/Informationsmaterial/Forein%20prisoners%20in%20Sweden.pdf.

UC Berkeley War Crime Studies Centre

Thyness, T. W., "Samuel Hinga Norman Dies, 22 February 2007", Weekly Report of the Sierra Leone Trial Monitoring Program, at www.wcsc.berkeley.edu/2007/02/special-report-samuel-hinga-norman-dies-22-february-2007/.

University of Nottingham

Code of Research Conduct, at www.nottingham.ac.uk/ris/html/research-strategy-and-policy/research-governance.php.

US Department of State

2007 Report on Sierra Leone, 19.05.2008, at www.state.gov/g/drl/rls/hrrpt/2007/100503.htm.

Miscellaneous

Charter of the International Military Tribunal for the Far East, 03.05.1946.

European Parliament Resolution on the Special Court for Sierra Leone, B6-0244/2009, 22.04.2009.

Servaes, S. and N. Birtsch, *Engaging with Victims and Perpetrators in Transitional Justice and Peace Building Processes* (Bonn, Germany: FriEnt/KOFF Workshop Report, 12–13.02.2008).

Special Proclamation, General MacArthur, Supreme Commander of the Allied Powers for the Pacific Theatre, "Establishment of an International Military Tribunal for the Far East", 19.01.1946.

UK Department for International Development, "Examination of the Effectiveness and Efficiency of the Execution of Criminal Sanctions in Bosnia-Herzegovina", 2006.

Verdoolaege, A., "'Would you be Prepared to Reconcile, Please?', the Discursive Introduction of Reconciliation at the Human Rights Violations Hearings of the TRC". Ghent University, Belgium, March 2003.

Verstraete, A., H. Verhoeven and I. Vandeurzen, "Introducing Restorative Justice in Belgian Prisons", Paper Presented at the Tenth International Symposium on Victimology, Montreal, 2000.

INDEX

accountability, 7, 307–32. *See also* oversight
  appeals, international prisoners' lack of access to, 308
  DARIO (2011) and, 312, 315, 321, 324, 329
  importance of, 329–31
  of individuals, 326–9
  of international organisations, 312–18
  models of, 308–11
  ombudspersons, 331
  Optional Protocol to the UN Convention Against Torture and, 309
  parties held responsible, 311–29
  problems associated with, 185–7
  proposed international prison system's need for, 307–8
  remedy, right to, 330
  of seconded staff, 323–6
  of states, 318–23
Africa
  European and African prisons compared, 51, 85
  proposal to locate international prisons in, 285
  welfare of prisoners in, 47–51
African Charter on Human and Peoples' Rights (ACHPR), 47, 315
African Commission on Human and Peoples' Rights (ACmHPR), 168
African Court for Human and People's Rights (ACtHPR), 81, 315
African Union, 315
age of prisoner
  disproportionate punishment, avoidance of, 198
  as early release criterion, 71, 146
  mental health and, 120
amnesty, 211
apologies, as form of reparations, 256
Arusha Declaration on Good Prison Practice (1999), 47
Ashworth, A., 276
Austria, 44, 57
Awareness Raising Programmes for Lessons Learned from the Genocide of, 244

Babić, Milan, 121, 141, 292
Bagaragaza, Michel, 60
Barrett, M. N., 337
Belgium
  criminal or victim–offender mediation in, 242
  decentralised national enforcement in, 57
  reparations in criminal justice system, 258
  restorative justice in, 221
Benin
  decentralised national enforcement in, 43, 47, 48, 84, 178
  funding of prison facilities in, 281, 285
Blagojević, Vidoje, 82, 101
Bosnia-Herzegovina. *See also* International Criminal Tribunal for the former Yugoslavia
  Rule 11*bis* transfers to, 161–7, 170–2
  sentences of ICTY not enforceable in, 156–7

Bosnia-Herzegovina (cont.)
  suicide prevention procedures in state court's detention facility, 150
Braithwaite, John, 231
Bralo, Miroslav, 93, 95

capital punishment, 12–15, 168, 170
centralised control of international penal strategy, proposal for, 270–2
centralised international enforcement, 6, 103–55. *See also* international detention facilities; *specific courts*
  complaints, 131–4
  defined, 20, 103
  differentiated regimes for convicted prisoners, 105, 111
  management of, 103–4
  medical care, 115, 116–21, 145–50
  oversight in, 131–43
  problems associated with, 176
  regulations and conditions, 6, 103–55
  release of prisoners, 151–3
  security and order, 121–31
  social interaction with persons outside prison, 111–16
  staff attitudes and management styles, 125–31
  standards governing, 143–51
centralised national enforcement (residual ICC detention facility provided by Netherlands), 21, 55, 153–4, 176
Codd, H., 239
Columbia, 36, 184
Committee for the Prevention of Torture (CPT), Council of Europe, 51–4, 131, 141, 146, 310
commutation of sentence, eligibility for, 56–62
complaints
  at IDFs, 131–4
  Presidency of sentencing court as highest internal level for, 185

conditional release or parole, 80–1
conditions of imprisonment
  in centralised international enforcement, 6, 103–55
  decentralised national enforcement, welfare of prisoners in, 45–55
  Rule 11*bis* transfers to Bosnia-Herzegovina, 162–3
confidentiality
  doctor–patient confidentiality, 137–9
  evaluative reports treated as confidential, 309
  restorative justice and, 262
conflict and restorative justice, 246–55
conjugal visits, 144–5
consolidation model of decentralised national enforcement, 84–5
cooperating non-member states, imprisonment in. *See* decentralised national enforcement
cooperation with the Prosecutor, 67, 69, 70
Council of Europe
  Council on Penological Cooperation, 199
  CPT, 51–4, 131, 141, 146, 310
courts, international criminal, 17–19. *See also specific courts*
Crawley, E., 126
creation of international prison system, 7, 275–306
  accountability, need for, 307–8
  advantages of, 21–9, 277
  choosing a suitable model and site, 294–6
  detained suspects, accused persons, and witnesses, 278
  equal treatment, 275–6
  funding, 281, 285, 296–300
  Host States of courts and prisons, 276, 284–5
  independent sites, 286–94
  islands, 286
  as joint venture of ICC and UN, 282
  legal mandate for, 282–3

location(s) of, 283–6
management, 300–2
multiple facilities, need for, 283
operationalisation of penal strategy via, 271
within perimeter of Host State prison, 288–90
precedents for, 280–1
shared facility within perimeter of Host State prison, 290–1
shared responsibility of Host State and international court/organisation, 291–4, 304
staff. *See* staff
criminal courts, international, 17–19. *See also specific courts*
criminal mediation, 241–4
critical situation protocols, 199–201
Croatia, ICTY sentences not enforceable in, 156–7. *See also* International Criminal Tribunal for the former Yugoslavia
Culp, R., 183
cultural significance of restorative justice, 229, 247
cultural symbolism of international criminal justice, 343
custodial staff. *See* staff
cycles of violence, breaking, 254–5

Damaška, M., 250
death of prisoner in custody, 46, 118–19, 121, 141, 144–50, 157, 199–201. *See also* suicide
death penalty, 12–15, 168, 170
decentralised national enforcement, 6, 33–102. *See also* length of imprisonment in decentralised national enforcement, and *under specific courts*
available enforcing states, 177–9, 354
centralised control of international penal strategy, proposal for, 270–2
defined, 20, 33

designation of and transfer to enforcing states, 39–45
dispersal and consolidation models, 84–5
division of responsibilities between states and international courts, 45
domestic penal policy and practices, international prisoners treated in accordance with, 22
equal treatment, 23, 85–96, 275–6
guidance and support for enforcing states, 199
international bodies' control over, 185
mobility of enforcement officials and, 269
model enforcement agreements, 36
obtaining state cooperation, 33–9
operationalisation of international penal policy within, 267–70
preparation for release, 96, 100–2
problems associated with, 22–3, 175–6
regional placement of prisoners, 178–80, 183
rehabilitation, 96–9
release, deportation, and relocation of prisoners, 79–83
security classifications, 92–6
social interaction between prisoners, 87–8
social interaction with persons outside prison, 88–92
suitability of enforcing states, 180–1
termination and transfer to another state, 187, 190
trilateral enforcement agreement proposals, 192
welfare of prisoners, 45–55
Delalić, Zejnil, 230
Denmark, 62, 78, 185
deportation of prisoners after release, 79–83, 152
Deronjić, Miroslav, 254
designation of enforcing states, 39–45

deterrence as international penal objective, 204–5, 207
development aid projects, international prison facilities as, 298
disciplinary regimes in centralised international enforcement, 123–4
dispersion model of decentralised national enforcement, 84–5
doctors. *See* medical care
Dokmanović, Slavko, 121, 151
Draft Articles on the Responsibility of International Organisations (DARIO, 2011), ILC, 312, 315, 321, 324, 329
Drumbl, M., 22, 191, 219, 267, 339

early release. *See* length of imprisonment in decentralised national enforcement
East Timor Community Reconciliation Scheme, 211, 245
educative models of resocialisation, 237–8
enforcement systems, 6. *See also* centralised international enforcement; decentralised national enforcement; localised national enforcement
enforcing states. *See* decentralised national enforcement; localised national enforcement
equal treatment, 23, 85–96, 182–5, 275–6
escape from prison, 166–7, 199–201
ethical dilemmas in restorative justice, 260–2
European Commission on Human Rights, 322
European Convention on Human Rights (ECHR), 46, 165, 315
European Court of Human Rights (ECtHR), 46, 59–82, 99, 165, 315, 322
European Prison Rules, 46, 258
European Union Parliament, 48
evolution of international penal system, 190–4

extension of term of imprisonment for non-payment of fines, 16
external oversight of IDFs, 139–40

families of prisoners
  conjugal visits, 144–5
  disproportionate punishment, policy of avoidance of, 198
  family mediation, 238–40
  maintaining order and, 127
  notification of death of prisoner, 121
  social interaction with prisoners, 88–92, 111–16
  visits and funding for visits, 88–92, 111–16, 127, 144–5
Findlay, M., 220
fines, 16–17
Finland, 38, 74
Finnemore, M., 337
Fishman, J., 280
force-feeding, 135–7
forfeitures, 16–17
former Yugoslavia. *See* International Criminal Tribunal for the former Yugoslavia
France, 57, 94, 127
funding of prison facilities, 49, 281, 285, 296–300

Germany, 36, 52, 58, 186
Ghana, 147
Goda, N. J. W., 186
good behaviour, 65, 69, 71, 188
gravity of the offence, 64, 68
guilt, recognition and acceptance of, 221, 224–6, 249–50
guilty pleas, 222, 227, 251

Hariri, Rafiq, 342
health issues. *See* medical care
Henham, R., 220, 267
Hess, Rudolf, 151, 322
historical truth, establishing, 250–4
Host State
  imprisonment in (centralised national enforcement), 21, 55, 153–4, 176

INDEX 405

in proposed international prison
    system, 276, 284–5
human rights. *See also* accountability
    disproportionate punishment,
        policy of avoidance of, 197–9
    operational problems in ensuring,
        185–7
    promotion of international
        punishment by advocates of, 24
    rehabilitation as normative goal in
        line with international
        standards, 209–11
    remedy, right to, 330
    suitability of enforcing states in
        decentralised national
        enforcement, 180–1
Human Rights Committee, 147
humane punishment, ensuring, 181–7,
    202
hunger strikes, 135–7, 164, 199–201

ICC Detention Centre (ICCDC). *See
    under* International Criminal
    Court
immunity
    of international organisations,
        316–18
    of persons directly employed by
        international organisations,
        326–9
imprisonment, 11–16, 17
incapacitation as international penal
    objective, 206
Independent Oversight Mechanism
    (IOM), ICC, 142, 310, 328
individuals, international penal
    system aimed at punishment
    of, 21, 226
inspection reports, 309, 311
institutionalisation of international
    penal system, 340–3
inter-relational resocialisation, 238–44
internal oversight of IDFs, 134–9
International Committee of the Red
    Cross (ICRC), 51–3, 136,
    139–40, 141, 184, 309
International Court of Justice (ICJ),
    312, 316, 319

International Covenant on Civil and
    Political Rights (ICCPR), 210,
    213
International Criminal Court (ICC), 18
    accountability of, 312–18
    centralised international
        enforcement at ICCDC
        accountability, 132–42
        detention of witnesses, 278
        length of sentence left to serve
            and, 104
        location and facilities, 287, 288,
            290, 295, 299
        maintenance of order, 121
        medical care, 117–21
        regulations and conditions,
            106–11
        release of prisoners, 152
        social interaction with persons
            outside prison, 112–16
        staff at, 304, 326
        standards, 143–51
    centralised national enforcement at
        residual detention facility, 55,
        153–4, 176
    decentralised national enforcement
        agreements with enforcing states,
            178, 180, 185
        designation of and transfer to
            cooperating states, 41
        equal treatment, 86–91
        length of imprisonment, 60–84
        obtaining state cooperation,
            35–9
        rehabilitation of prisoners, 99
    Enforcement Unit, 268
    evolution of, 191–4
    first sentence of imprisonment
        (2012), 1, 5, 191
    funding and costs, 281, 297, 298,
        299, 300
    human rights principles as
        normative foundation for, 209,
        210, 211
    imprisonment of persons convicted
        by, 19–21
    international legal personality of,
        287, 312, 316

406 INDEX

International Criminal Court (ICC) (cont.)
  IOM, 142, 310, 328
  localised national enforcement permitted by Rome Statute, 156
  location and ownership of court premises, 288
  member state responsibility for actions of, 321
  penalties, 13–17
  prison facilities, struggle to obtain, 285
  purpose or goal of international punishment, failure to state, 207
  reparations, 256–60
  on resocialisation, 216
  Rome Statute establishing, 13
  temporary courts, continuing need for, 341
  TFV, 221, 258–9
  UN, proposed creation of international prison system as joint venture with, 282
  victims' rights and, 221, 223
  welfare of prisoners, 46–55
international criminal justice system, 17–19. *See also specific courts*
International Criminal Tribunal for Rwanda (ICTR), 13, 18
  centralised international enforcement at UNDF
    accountability, 135
    detention of witnesses, 278
    direct implementation of custodial sanctions, responsibility for, 155
    location and facilities, 290, 291
    maintenance of order, 124, 126
    medical care, 117–20
    number of prisoners, 105
    regulations and conditions, 106–8
    release of prisoners, 151–2
    social interaction with persons outside prison, 113–15
    staff, 294, 327
    standards, 144–50
  context and causes of crime and conflict, addressing, 249
  decentralised national enforcement
    designation of and transfer to cooperating states, 41, 42
    dispersal model, 84
    equal treatment, 86, 184
    length of imprisonment, 59–82
    national prison system improvement and, 299
    number of prisoners in, 45
    obtaining state cooperation, 35–7
    regional placement of prisoners, 178
    rehabilitation of prisoners, 99
    suitability of enforcing states, 180
    welfare of prisoners, 48–53
  external restorative justice programmes and, 244
  funding and costs, 281, 296, 298
  human rights principles as normative foundation for, 209, 211
  imprisonment of persons convicted by, 19–21
  localised national enforcement in Rwanda, 156, 159–60, 167–9, 176–7
  MICT responsibilities, 1, 18, 190
  penalties, 13
  prison facilities, struggle to obtain, 285
  reconciliation as reason for establishing, 227
  reparations, 257
  Rule 11*bis* transfers to Rwanda, 167–9, 170–2
  SCSL and, 19
  sentences imposed continuing after closure of court, 342
International Criminal Tribunal for the former Yugoslavia (ICTY), 12, 18
  centralised international enforcement at UNDU
    accountability, 133–41

harmonious coexistence of formerly warring factions at, 245
hunger strike policy, 200
location and facilities, 288, 289, 290-1
maintenance of order, 121-9
medical care, 117-21
number of prisoners, 105
regulations and conditions, 106-10
release of prisoners, 151-2
shared responsibility of Host State and court for, 292-3
social interaction with persons outside prison, 112-16
staff, 304, 326
standards, 144-50
context and causes of crime and conflict, addressing, 248, 249
cycles of violence, breaking, 254-5
decentralised national enforcement
designation of and transfer to cooperating state, 35-8, 41, 43, 44
equal treatment, 86, 91-6
length of imprisonment, 56-81
obtaining state cooperation, 35-8
preparation of prisoners for release, 101
regional placement of prisoners, 178
rehabilitation of prisoners, 98, 99
welfare of prisoners, 51-3
empirical research on persons detained by, 4, 345
external restorative justice programmes and, 244
funding and costs, 24, 281, 296
guilty pleas, percentage of convictions from, 222
human rights principles as normative foundation for, 209, 211
imprisonment of persons convicted by, 19-21
later courts replicating enforcement system of, 191
legitimacy, concern with, 338

localised national enforcement not allowed for, 156-7
MICT responsibilities, 1, 18, 190
penalties, 12
prison facilities, struggle to obtain, 285
reparations, 257
Rule 11*bis* transfers to Bosnia-Herzegovina, 161-7, 170-2
SCSL and, 19
sentences imposed continuing after closure of court, 342
on truth, 250
witness notification by, 223
international detention facilities (IDFs), 20. *See also* centralised international enforcement
continuation of conditions of, 86
differentiated regimes, 105, 111
funding, 296-300
harmonious coexistence of formerly warring factions at, 121, 245
jurisdiction over, 291
legal mandate to establish, 282
management, 300-2
medical care in, 115, 116-21, 145-50
purpose of, 104, 129
single cell policy, 107
staff, 302-5, 325, 326
transferring prisoners from, 43, 44, 104-5
International Law Commission (ILC)
Code of Crimes Against the Peace and Security of Mankind, 13
Draft Articles on the Responsibility of International Organisations (DARIO, 2011), 312, 315, 321, 324, 329
on standing of international organisation before ICJ, 316
International Military Tribunal for Far East (IMTFE), 12, 33, 39, 63, 72, 330
International Military Tribunal for Nurnberg (IMTN) and Spandau Prison

International Military Tribunal for Nurnberg (IMTN) and Spandau Prison (cont.)
  accountability issues, 322, 330
  centralised international enforcement issues, 117, 151
  creation of international prison system and, 280–1, 286, 287, 294–6
  decentralised national enforcement issues, 33, 39, 63, 71
  operation of contemporary system and, 186
  penalties, 12
  reconceptualisation of international penal system and, 21
international organisations
  accountability of, 312–18
  immunity of, 316–18
  persons directly employed by, 326–9
  state responsibility for actions of, 320–1
international penal system, 1–7, 11–29, 335–44. See also purposes and goals of international penal system
  cultural symbolism of, 343
  empirical research on, 3–6, 345
  enforcement systems, 6 See also centralised international enforcement; decentralised national enforcement; localised national enforcement
  establishment of international criminal courts, justifications for, 203
  evolution of, 190–4
  first modern international sentence of imprisonment (1997), 1
  imposition of sanctions, justifications for, 203–8
  individuals, aimed at punishment of, 21, 226
  institutionalisation of, 340–3
  international criminal courts, 17–19. See also specific courts
  legitimacy of, 26, 228, 336–40, 343
  number of sentences handed down in, 335
  operation of, 6, 175–94. See also operation of contemporary international penal system
  paucity of information regarding, 1–3
  penalties, 11–17
  prisons in contemporary system, 19–21. See also creation of international prison system
  reforming, 266–7, 311–29, 343–4
  strategy for, 6. See also operationalisation of international penal strategy; policy; restorative justice
  structural issues, 7. See also accountability; creation of international prison system
international standards. See standards
Ireland, 127, 319
isolation. See segregation or isolation of international prisoners
Italy, 59, 179

Jackson, Robert, 24
Japan and IMTFE, 12, 33, 39, 63, 72, 330
Jaspers, K., 249
judicial review of IDF prisoner complaints, 131–4

Kampala Declaration on Prison Conditions in Africa (1996), 47
King, K. L., 25, 229
Klip, A., 51, 61
Kovač, Radomir, 98
Kovačević, Milan, 118
Krajišnik, Momčilo, 91, 93, 98, 225, 229, 236
Krnojelac, Milorad, 75
Krstić, Radislav, 187
Kula Detention Facility, Republika Srpska, hunger strike in, 164
Kupreškić, Zoran, 230

INDEX

language barriers for international prisoners, 87, 97, 110, 117, 181, 201
Lebanon, Special Tribunal for (STL), 290, 291, 342
legitimacy of international punishment, 26, 228, 336–40, 343
length of imprisonment in decentralised national enforcement, 56–84
  age and health of prisoner, 71
  conditional release or parole, 80–1
  cooperation with the Prosecutor, 67, 69, 70
  eligibility for commutation or pardon, 56–62
  good behaviour, 65, 69, 71
  gravity of the offence, 64, 68
  international control over, 72–9, 83–4
  procedure and criteria for determining early release, 63–72
  rehabilitation, 65–7, 71
  release, deportation and relocation of prisoners, 79–83
  responsibility for, 83–4
  role of enforcing states in early release decisions, 62–3
Liebling, A., 3
life imprisonment, 14–16, 168
Lippke, R. L., 208, 209
localised national enforcement, 6, 156–74. *See also* Rule 11*bis* transfers
  defined, 21, 156
  ICTY, not allowed for, 156–7
  problems associated with, 176–7
  Rome Statute of ICC permitting, 156
  in Rwanda for ICTR, 156, 159–60, 167–9, 176–7
  in Sierra Leone for SCSL, 156, 157–8, 176–7
Lomé Peace Agreement, 211

Mali
  decentralised national enforcement in, 36, 43, 47, 48, 50, 81, 84, 178, 180, 184

  funding of prison facilities in, 281, 285
Malta Declaration (1991), 136, 137
management
  of IDFs, 103–4
  in proposed international prison system, 300–2
Marchesi, A., 184
Mbarushimana, Callixte, 153
McEvoy, K., 167
Mechanism for the International Criminal Tribunals (MICT)
  on detention of accused persons, 278
  legal framework replicating ICTY enforcement system, 191
  lifetime of, 191
  responsibilities of, 1, 5, 18, 190
  Rule 11*bis* transfers and, 169–72
medical care
  accountability of IDFs and, 135–9
  age and health of prisoner as early release factor, 71, 146
  death of prisoner in custody, 46, 118–19, 121, 141, 144–50, 157, 199–201
  doctor–patient confidentiality, 137–9
  in IDFs, 115, 116–21, 145–50
  mental health issues, 119–21, 181
  PTSD, prisoners suffering from, 119, 236
  Rule 11*bis* transfers to Bosnia-Herzegovina, 164
  standard of care, 145–50
  suicide, 120, 150–1, 200, 292
Meernik, J. D., 25, 229
mental health issues, 119–21, 181
Mills, A., 239
Milošević, Slobodan, 118, 133, 141, 149
monitoring. *See* accountability
Mpanga prison, Rwanda, 49, 50, 55, 115, 116–21, 168, 183, 299
Musabyimana, Samuel, 119, 149

National Unity and Reconciliation Commission (NURC), Rwanda, 244, 245
nationals, state responsibility to protect, 319–20

The Netherlands
  accountability of ICCDC and, 142
  decentralised national enforcement in, 167
  ICC Headquarters Agreement with, 104
  on immunity of seconded staff at IDFs, 326
  location of ICC and ICCDC facilities in, 288, 290–1
  medical doctors for ICCDC required to be registered in, 117
  Mpanga prison, Rwanda, funded by, 49
  residual facility provided by, 55, 153–4, 176
  shared responsibility of Host State and court for international prison facilities, 292–3
  six-month limit on presence of convicted persons in, 155
Norman, Sam Hinga, 119, 132
Norway, 90, 98, 167, 192
Nurnberg Tribunal. *See* International Military Tribunal for Nurnberg (IMTN) and Spandau Prison
Nzirorera, Joseph, 119

ombudspersons, 331
Oomen, B., 247
operation of contemporary international penal system, 6, 175–94
  accountability, 185–7
  enforcement systems. *See* centralised international enforcement; decentralised national enforcement; localised national enforcement
  equal treatment, 182–5, 275–6
  evolution of system, 190–4
  goals and effectiveness, 187–90
  humane punishment, ensuring, 181–7, 202
  problems associated with, 175–81
operationalisation of international penal strategy, 6, 266–72
  centralisation of control, 270–2
  policy and practice, 267–70
  reform aims, 266–7
Optional Protocol to the UN Convention Against Torture, 309
Ouagadougou Declaration and Plan of Action on accelerating prison reform in Africa (2002), 47
oversight, 307–32. *See also* accountability
  in centralised international enforcement, 131–43
  external oversight of IDFs, 139–40
  by independent qualified bodies, 308, 309, 311
  internal oversight of IDFs, 134–9
  problems associated with, 185–7
  systematic evaluation of performance, 308–11
  transparency through publication of inspection reports, 309, 311
  welfare of prisoners, monitoring, 51–5

pardon, eligibility for, 56–62
parole or conditional release, 80–1
peace, restoring and maintaining, 221, 232–5
Penal Strategy Support Unit (PSSU), proposal for, 268–70
penal system, international. *See* international penal system
penalties, 11–17
permanent international criminal court. *See* International Criminal Court
physicians. *See* medical care
Plavšić, Biljana, 229, 255
Player, E., 276
Poland, 41, 77
policy, 6, 197–217
  critical situations protocols, 199–201
  disproportionate punishment, avoidance of, 197–9
  establishment of international criminal courts, justifications for, 203
  imposition of sanctions, justifications for, 203–8

need for, 197
normative foundations for, 203–8
operationalising, 267–70
proactive role of international courts, importance of, 202
provision of guidance and support to enforcing states, 199
rehabilitation as, 208–16
sentence planning, 201–2
Pollard, M., 136
post-traumatic stress disorder (PTSD), 119, 236
prisons
  in contemporary system, 19–21
  creation of international system of. *See* creation of international prison system
  international facilities. *See* centralised international enforcement; international detention facilities
  national. *See* centralised national enforcement; decentralised national enforcement; localised national enforcement
privilege. *See* confidentiality; immunity
progression through security classifications, 95
purposes and goals of international penal system
  deterrence, 204–5, 207
  effectiveness of system and, 21–9, 187–90
  IDFs, 104, 129
  incapacitation, 206
  lack of stated goal or penological purpose, 21–9, 203–8, 266
  reconciliation as stated purpose of ICTR, 227
  rehabilitation, 209–11. *See also* rehabilitation
  retribution, 205–6, 207–8, 209, 211
  sentence planning, 96, 201–2
  separation of goals of imposition and implementation of sentence, 212–13

Radić, Mlađo, 94
reconciliation, 221, 226–9
Red Cross, International Committee of the (ICRC), 51–3, 136, 139–40, 141, 184, 309
reform of international penal system, 266–7, 311–29, 343–4
regional placement of international prisoners, 178–80, 183, 283
rehabilitation
  as criterion for early release, 65–7, 71
  evolution of, 213–14
  failure of current system to address, 188–9
  as normative goal in line with international standards, 209–11
  as policy, 208–16
  prison efforts at, 96–9
  reconceptualising, 213–16
  as resocialisation, 216
  retribution and, 208, 209
  sentence planning and, 96, 201–2
  theoretical framework for, 211–13
reintegration efforts, 96, 100–2, 188–9, 201–2, 230–2
release of prisoners
  age and health issues, 71, 146
  from centralised international enforcement, 151–3
  conditional release or parole, 80–1
  deportation and relocation of prisoners after release, 79–83, 152
  early release. *See* length of imprisonment in decentralised national enforcement
  family mediation, 238–40
  reintegration efforts associated with, 96, 100–2, 188–9, 201–2, 230–2
  restorative principles and, 223
  witness notification of, 79, 223
religious freedom of international prisoners, 109

relocation of prisoners after release, 79–83, 152
remand centres of international criminal courts. *See* centralised international enforcement; international detention facilities and *under specific courts*
remedy, right to, 330
reparations, 221, 226, 255–60
Republika Srpska, 164, 167
Residual Special Court for Sierra Leone (RSCSL), 19, 190, 310
resocialisation
    criminal or victim–offender mediation, 241–4
    educative models for, 237–8
    external resocialisation processes, links to, 244–6
    family mediation, 238–40
    individual resocialisation programmes, 236–8
    inter-relational, 238–44
    rehabilitation as, 216
    restorative approach to, 218–24
    therapeutic models for, 236–7
restitution, 16–17
restorative justice, 6, 218–65
    acceptance and use of, 220–3
    comprehensive criminal justice system, as part of, 262–4
    confidentiality issues, 262
    context and causes of crime and conflict, addressing, 247–50
    cultural relevance of, 229, 247
    cycles of violence, breaking, 254–5
    emotions, expression of, 261
    ethical dilemmas, 260–2
    external resocialisation processes, links to, 244–6
    peace, restoring and maintaining, 221, 232–5
    principles and processes, 224–35
    recognition and acceptance of guilt and harm done, 221, 224–6, 249–50
    reconciliation, 221, 226–9
    reintegration efforts, 230–2
    reparations, 221, 226, 255–60
    resocialisation, restorative approach to, 218–24. *See also* resocialisation
    retribution and, 218, 219, 225, 227, 229, 233
    tools of, 235–46
    truth, discerning, 250–4
    victims' rights and, 219, 221, 223, 228–9, 250
    voluntary participation principle, 260–2
    in wider conflict resolution issues, 246–55
restraints, use of, 124
retribution
    as international penal objective, 205–6, 207–8, 209, 211
    restorative justice and, 218, 219, 225, 227, 229, 233
Robben Island Guidelines (2000), 47
Rodley, N., 136
Rome Statute establishing ICC, 13. *See also* International Criminal Court
Rostaing, Corinne, 127
Rugambarara, Juvénal, 60
Rule 11*bis* transfers, 160–73
    from ICTR to Rwanda, 167–9, 170–2
    from ICTY to Bosnia-Herzegovina, 161–7, 170–2
    post-completion operation of, 170–3
    problems associated with, 176
Rwanda. *See also* International Criminal Tribunal for Rwanda
    context and causes of 1994 genocide in, 247
    decentralised national enforcement in, 41, 49–50, 55, 74, 82, 84, 158
    funding of prison facilities in, 281, 285
    ICRC inspections of SCSL prisoners, 310

localised national enforcement of
ICTR sentences in, 156, 159–60,
167–9, 176–7
Mpanga prison, 49, 50, 55, 115,
116–21, 168, 183, 299
restorative justice programmes in,
244, 245
Rule 11*bis* transfers to, 167–9,
170–2

safe custody. *See* security and order
Sankoh, Foday, 147
Schabas, W., 276
SCSL Detention Facility (SCSLDF). *See
under* Special Court for Sierra
Leone
security and order
in centralised international
enforcement, 121–31
in decentralised national
enforcement, 92–6, 180–1
emergencies, 293–4
escapes, 166–7
Rule 11*bis* transfers to
Bosnia-Herzegovina,
163–7
suitability of enforcing states and,
180–1
segregation or isolation of
international prisoners
in centralised international
enforcement, 122, 124
in decentralised national
enforcement
progression through security
classifications, 95
security issues, 92–6
social interaction between
prisoners, 87–8
social interaction with persons
outside prison, 88–92
as humane treatment issue,
181
Rule 11*bis* transfers, 164
Senegal, 49, 82, 84, 118, 147
sentence planning
in decentralised national
enforcement, 96, 98–9

failure of current system to allow for,
189, 201
as policy, 201–2
rehabilitation and reintegration
goals of, 96, 201–2
Serbia. *See* International Criminal
Tribunal for the former
Yugoslavia
Serugendo, Joseph, 119
Shin, M., 253
Sierra Leone. *See also* Special Court for
Sierra Leone
international prisoner conditions in
Rwanda, monitoring, 55, 183
localised national enforcement of
SCSL sentences in, 156,
157–8, 176–7
single cell policy at IDFs, 107
Snacken, S., 136, 202
social interaction
disproportionate punishment,
policy of avoidance of, 198
with persons outside prison, 88–92,
111–16, 144–5
between prisoners, 87–8, 120
solitary confinement. *See* segregation
or isolation of international
prisoners
South African Truth and
Reconciliation Commission, 261
sovereignty issues, 270
Spain, 52, 58, 186
Spandau Prison. *See* International
Military Tribunal for Nurnberg
(IMTN) and Spandau Prison
Special Court for Sierra Leone (SCSL),
18–19
centralised international
enforcement at SCSLDF
accountability, 132–41
direct implementation of
custodial sanctions,
responsibility for, 154
evacuation plan, 294
harmonious coexistence of formerly
warring factions at, 121
location and facilities, 286, 287,
295, 298

Special Court for Sierra Leone (SCSL) (cont.)
   maintenance of order, 121–30
   medical care, 117–20
   national prison systems and, 299
   regulations and conditions, 106–10
   social interaction with persons outside prison, 112–15
   staff, 30, 294, 302, 325
   standards, 143–9
   use of, 105
   Utrecht University and, 299
  context and causes of crime and conflict, addressing, 248
  decentralised national enforcement
   designation of and transfer to cooperating states, 41, 42, 43
   dispersal model, 84
   equal treatment, 86–90
   length of imprisonment, 59–76
   number of prisoners, 45
   obtaining state cooperation, 35–8
   regional placement of prisoners, 179
  first conviction of head of state by, 1
  funding, 281
  human rights principles as normative foundation for, 209, 211
  ICRC inspections, 310
  ICTR and ICTY rules and agreements used by, 19
  on immunity of staff of international organisations, 327
  imprisonment of persons convicted by, 19–21
  localised national enforcement in Sierra Leone, 156, 157–8, 176–7
  Lomé Peace Agreement amnesties and, 211
  prison facilities, struggle to obtain, 285
  RSCSL, 19, 190, 310
  sentences imposed continuing after closure of court, 342

Special Tribunal for Lebanon (STL), 290, 291, 342
staff, 302–5
  in centralised international enforcement, 125–31
  internationalisation of, 304–5
  neither/nor status problem, 303–4
  reliance on mixture of international and national personnel, 294
  seconded staff, responsibility for, 323–6
  selection of, 302
  specialised trained staff, need for, 268
  standards and mentality, 303
Standard Minimum Rules for the Treatment of Prisoners (UNSMR, 1957), 45
standards
  humane punishment, 184
  for IDFs, 143–51
  rehabilitation as normative goal in line with, 209–11
  staff, 303
  UN standards for detention and treatment of prisoners, 45, 46, 47
Stanković, Radovan, 166–7, 200
states
  accountability of, 318–23
  conflict state, imprisonment in. See localised national enforcement
  cooperating non-member states, imprisonment in. See decentralised national enforcement
  Host States of courts and prisons in proposed international prison system, 276, 284–5
  imprisonment in court's Host State (centralised national enforcement), 21, 55, 153–4, 176
  international organisations, responsibility for actions of, 320–1
  nationals, responsibility to protect, 319–20

INDEX 415

seconded staff, responsibility for, 323–6
strategy, 6. *See also* operationalisation of international penal strategy; policy; restorative justice
structural issues, 7. *See also* accountability; creation of international prison system
Suggnomè (Belgian NGO), 242
suicide, 120, 150–1, 200, 292
Swaziland, 48
Sweden
  audit of UNDU by, 141
  decentralised national enforcement in, 61, 74, 93, 95, 179, 200
Switzerland, 38
systems of enforcement, 6. *See also* centralised international enforcement; decentralised national enforcement; localised national enforcement

Tadić, Duško, 81
Tanzania, 155
Taylor, Charles, 19, 42, 134, 148, 157, 158, 190
temporary international courts, 12, 18, 341. *See also specific temporary courts*
temporary internationalised courts, 14, 18–19, 341. *See also* Special Court for Sierra Leone
termination of enforcement in one state and transfer to another, 187, 190
therapeutic models of resocialisation, 236–7
Tieger, A., 253
Tokyo Declaration (1975), 136
transfer of prisoners. *See also* Rule 11*bis* transfers
  to enforcing states, 39–45, 104–5
  termination of enforcement in one state and transfer to another, 187, 190
translation and translators, 87, 117
transparency through publication of inspection reports, 309, 311

trilateral enforcement agreement proposals, 192
Trust Fund for Victims (TFV), ICC, 221, 258–9
Truth and Reconciliation Commissions (TRCs), 244, 245, 252, 261
truth, discerning, 250–4

Ukraine, 77
UN Basic Principles for the Treatment of Prisoners (UNBP, 1990), 45
UN Body of Principles for the Protection of all Persons under any Form of Detention or Imprisonment (UNBOP, 1988), 45
UN Convention Against Torture, Optional Protocol to, 309
UN Detention Facility (UNDF), ICTR. *See under* International Criminal Tribunal for Rwanda
UN Detention Unit (UNDU), ICTY. *See under* International Criminal Tribunal for the former Yugoslavia
UN Special Rapporteur on Prisons and Conditions of Detention (SRP), 52
UN Standard Minimum Rules for the Treatment of Prisoners (UNSMR, 1957), 45
UN Tribunals. *See* International Criminal Tribunal for Rwanda; International Criminal Tribunal for the former Yugoslavia
United Kingdom
  decentralised national enforcement in, 38, 42, 44, 46, 51, 57, 61, 74, 83, 93, 95, 98
  Irish suit on behalf of nationals against, 319
  Spandau Prison, liability for, 322
United Nations
  accountability of, 312–18
  cooperation of states, obtaining, 35, 36, 37
  funding by, 26, 281

United Nations (cont.)
  ICC, proposed creation of international prison system as joint venture with, 282
  international legal personality of, 287, 312, 316
  member state responsibility for actions of, 321
  penal facilities, involvement with, 281
  on penalties, 12–14
  standards for detention and treatment of prisoners, 45, 46, 47

Van Zyl Smit, D., 64, 136, 202
Verdoolaege, A., 261
victims
  criminal or victim–offender mediation, 241–4
  ICC Trust Fund for, 221, 258–9
  instrumental use of, 228, 261
  rights of, 219, 221, 223, 228–9, 250. *See also* restorative justice
violence war and restorative justice, 246–55
visitors and visiting rights, 88–92, 111–16, 127, 144–5

war, violence and restorative justice, 246–55
witnesses
  detention of, 278
  notification of prisoner release, 79, 223

Yugoslavia, former. *See* International Criminal Tribunal for the former Yugoslavia

Zenica Prison, Bosnia-Herzegovina, attacks on prisoners in, 164–5